# MARGINS OF RELIGION

Studies in Continental Thought

*John Sallis, editor*

Consulting Editors

Robert Bernasconi

Rudolph Bernet

John D. Caputo

David Carr

Edward S. Casey

Hubert Dreyfus

Don Ihde

David Farrell Krell

Lenore Langsdorf

Alphonso Lingis

William L. McBride

J. N. Mohanty

Mary Rawlinson

Tom Rockmore

Calvin O. Schrag

†Reiner Schürmann

Charles E. Scott

Thomas Sheehan

Robert Sokolowski

Bruce W. Wilshire

David Wood

# MARGINS OF RELIGION

## Between Kierkegaard and Derrida

John Llewelyn

Indiana University Press

*Bloomington & Indianapolis*

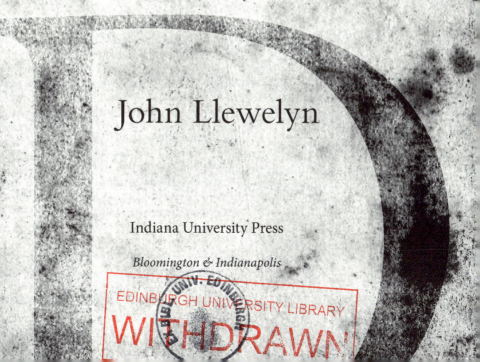

This book is a publication of

Indiana University Press
601 North Morton Street
Bloomington, IN 47404-3797 USA

http://iupress.indiana.edu

Telephone orders: 800-842-6796
Fax orders: 812-855-7931
Orders by e-mail: iuporder@indiana.edu

The paper used in this publication meets
the minimum requirements of American
National Standard for Information Sciences—Permanence of Paper for Printed
Library Materials, ANSI Z39.48-1984.

Manufactured in the United States of
America

Library of Congress
Cataloging-in-Publication Data

Llewelyn, John.
  Margins of religion : between
Kierkegaard and Derrida / John Llewelyn.
    p. cm. — (Studies in Continental
thought)
  Includes bibliographical references (p.    )
and index.
  ISBN 978-0-253-35259-0 (cloth : alk.
paper) — ISBN 978-0-253-22033-2 (pbk. :
alk. paper) 1. Kierkegaard, Søren, 1813–
1855. 2. Derrida, Jacques. 3. Religion—
Philosophy. I. Title.
  B4378.R44L54 2009
  210.92'2—dc22

                                2008023843

1 2 3 4 5 14 13 12 11 10 09

*In boundless gratitude
to Jacques Derrida,
John Austin,
and others*

But it is Kierkegaard to whom I have been most faithful . . .

> — Jacques Derrida, "I have a taste for the secret"

The imadgination is the chief religious faculty.

> — Karen Armstrong, *A History of God,* neither of whom
> is responsible for the unorthographic quirk

Quirk [Of obscure origin and history]
The earliest trace of the word appears in
Salesbury's Welsh Dict. (1547)

> — *Oxford English Dictionary*

A quirkie bodie, capable o' making Law no Law at a'

> — John Galt, *The Entail*

Quirk: not positively illegal. . . .

> — *Chamber's Scots Dialect Dictionary*

We cannot clean up the term "God" and we cannot make it whole, but . . .

> — Martin Buber, quoted in Hans Küng, *Does God Exist?*

Where is my dwelling place? Where I can never stand.
Where is my final goal, toward which I should ascend?
It is beyond all place. What should my quest then be?
I must, transcending God, into a desert flee.

> — Angelus Silesius, *The Cherubinic Wanderer*

These questions can be posed only after the death of a friend. . . .

> — Jacques Derrida, *Memoires for Paul de Man*

# CONTENTS

**Part Two**

# ACKNOWLEDGMENTS

A version of chapter 1 appeared in Elsebet Jegstrup, ed., *The New Kierkegaard* (Bloomington: Indiana University Press, 2004), of chapter 2 in John Sallis, ed., *Research in Phenomenology,* vol. 33 (Leiden, Neth.: Brill, 2003), of chapter 3, in Danish, in Per Krogh Hansen and Roy Sellars, eds., *Kritik og Kulturanalyse 99* 33, no. 1 (Holte, Denmark: Medusa, 2005), of parts of chapters 5 and 6 in Bettina Bergo and Jill Stauffer, eds., *Nietzsche and Levinas: "After the Death of a Certain God"* (New York: Columbia University Press, 2008) and, in Welsh, in John Daniel and W. L. Gealy, eds., *Efrydiau Athronyddol,* vol. 68 (Cardiff: University of Wales Press, 2005), of chapter 10, in German, in Thomas Bedorf and Andreas Cremonini, eds., *Verfehlte Begegnungen: Levinas und Sartre als philosophische Zeitgenossen* (Munich: Wilhelm Fink, 2005), of chapter 13 in John Sallis, ed., *Research in Phenomenology,* vol. 36 (Leiden, Neth.: Brill, 2006). A version of *"Le pas du repas,"* included in note 22 of chapter 13, appeared in Marie-Louise Mallet and Ginette Michaud, eds., *Jacques Derrida* (Paris: L'Herne, 2004). I thank the respective editors and publishers for granting permission to adapt those items in this book.

For inspecting drafts of parts or the whole of this book I am grateful to Paul Davies, Robert Bernasconi, Adriaan Perperzak, John Sallis, Merold Westphal, and David Wood. For reassurance regarding two chapters of it I am grateful to Robin Durie. For detailed comments on other chapters and for forcing me to distinguish quirks from mistakes I am grateful to Basil O'Neill. He, the late Timothy Sprigge, and Douglas and Elizabeth Templeton were participants in informal symposia that were for me food for thought while this work was in progress. Conversations with my friends and colleagues Alexander Beveridge,

Colin Brydon, Fiona Hughes, Percy Jack, Chris Jupp, and Steven Winspur, as well as correspondence with my friend and former colleague in Australia Erle Robinson, helped me remove from my work in progress at least some of its avoidable obscurities of expression. To another friend, Charlie Bigger, I am incalculably grateful not only for the education I have received from his writings but also for the double generosity of dedicating one of them to me without objecting to my looking that gift horse in the mouth in one of my chapters. I am indebted to the staff of the computing service of the University of Edinburgh and of the University and New College libraries, to Dee Mortensen, Laura Mac-Leod, June Silay, Chandra Mevis, and my other friends at Indiana University Press, to copyeditor Carol Kennedy, and to an anonymous reader, the wisdom of whose suggestions I recognize even where I do not follow them. For helping me find a way through computerological aporia I am grateful to my brother Howard and my nephews Simon and Steven. For helping me understand why I could not find a way through certain theological aporia I am grateful to my brother David and to my late lovely cousin Irene. I thank my *caredig* wife Margaret for teaching me the meaning of that Welsh word and of the Hebrew word *hineni,* meanings that I have tried to spell out in the following pages.

# MARGINS OF RELIGION

# PROLOGUE

The quickest way to get an idea of what goes on in this book is to scan its list of contents and its epigraphs. The first of those epigraphs is Derrida's remark "But it is Kierkegaard to whom I have been most faithful . . ." The book seeks to discover the nature of that fidelity via reflections on faith in the field of religion but also on what, in imitation of Derrida's title *Margins of Philosophy,* my title calls margins of religion. The "between" of the subtitle is that of Kierkegaard and Derrida, as it were, synchronically face to face. That preposition also works diachronically. Part 1 focuses on Kierkegaard, but there are interventions throughout from Derrida. Part 2 treats of Nietzsche, Deleuze and Guattari, Heidegger, Sartre, and Levinas, with a view to showing how through their writings some of the topics raised in part 1 are transmuted and transmitted to Derrida, whose writings are focused on in part 3. A main topic in the interim chapters is negation considered with a view to bringing out how the simplicity of the antithetical oppositions between the negative and the positive in classical and dialectical logic and between apophatic and cataphatic theology is complicated by a certain quasi-transcendental affirmation that is presupposed by those oppositions. The topic of the sharpness or otherwise of the traditional distinction is already introduced during the examination in chapter 1 of the debate between Kant and Hegel on the logic of borderlines. That debate widens throughout the rest of the book, culminating in chapters that hover over the threshold of ontology and what Derrida christens [sic] hauntology.

The book is oriented by the citation of texts. How could it be otherwise with one that aims to be faithful to Derrida in the way he declares he has been faithful to Kierkegaard? But how, with a book that aims in some way to be faithful to Derrida and Kierkegaard, could it not be affected by pathos? In the first chapter in particular the reader will find much more textual analysis than pathos. Potential readers for whose taste this chapter may be too dry (Derrida would say SEC) may prefer to skip to chapter 2 or to part 2. Before following either of these routes they might skim through the epilogue, which is in part retrospective. One reader of a draft of the book found it rewarding to read the first three chapters, then the last chapter, then resume part 1. Readers who reach part 3 will find the desert dryness watered by tears. More of these were to come after Jack Caputo used that word (and its homonym) in the title of a distinguished book he devoted to the work of Derrida.

The last in my list of epigraphs, Derrida's comment "These questions can be posed only after the death of a friend," presides especially over part 3, from the beginning of the biographical and thanatographical chapter 13 to the last paragraphs of the epilogue. Pursuing clues given by Caputo and Hent de Vries, chapters 13 and 14 comprise a single continuing argument aimed at exposing an oversight on my part that seemed to place two friends of mine in conflict with each other.

Chapters 15 to 17 experiment with what Derrida writes about "religion in general" to help find room for a notion of the religious that need not depend, unless only contingently and historically (but what does saying this mean?) upon instituted religions. I dare to think that this notion of the religious between the quasi-transcendental and the historical, by investing priority (but what does saying this mean?) in troth over propositional truth and in singularity over universal law, saves the religious from the up-to-a-point justified condemnations (for instance those of Richard Dawkins) to which the religions are exposed. I say "saves." This book is another book about the varieties of religious experience, but without being, as William James's Gifford Lectures are, a book about the variety of religions. It is a book about a variety of salvations. And it is one that is prejudiced, I confess, in favor of that variety of salvation implicit in the remark "There is another world, but it is (in) this one," attributed to Paul Éluard and Rilke. I find this remark acknowledged by neither. Whatever the source and whatever its author (if it has one) intended (see chapter 15, note 22), I interpret this sentence in the spirit of Nietzsche and of a remark that I do find in the writings of Rilke: "What insanity to side-track us toward a Beyond, when we are here surrounded by tasks and expectations and futures! What treachery to purloin the images of actual delight so as to sell them behind our backs to Heaven! O it is high time the impoverished earth collected all those loans we have raised on its splendour, in order to furnish something 'beyond the future' with them, etc." Belief in that fabulous thither side has been all too conducive of late and of old to the commission of crimes in the here and the now. Paradoxically, that belief is fostered, as Derrida, Kierkegaard, and not a few theologians and philosophers throughout the ages have maintained, by a naively this-worldly conception of time incapable of crediting time's out-of-jointness, incapable of imagining eternity as other than continuation, other than the chronology of one generation succeeding another, other than secular periodization.

I question the assumption that the secular and the religiousness of religions constitute an exhaustive dichotomy. To help me make out my case for doing this I draw on what Derrida writes about the unexpectation of the futurality of a certain democracy. I draw also on Wordsworth's (not Kant's) idea of the sublime to hint at an aesthethical [*sic*] archi-sublimity that fits the idea of the oncomingness of democracy about which Derrida wonders whether it might embrace the nonhuman (the nonhuman beings that were much on my mind when I wrote *The Middle Voice of Ecological Conscience* and *Seeing Through God*). Democracy thus outlined and freed from the reputations Nietzsche and Francis Fukuyama impose on it is the wide and political extreme of the religious imadgination [*sic*]. What I say toward the end of the book about imadgination goes back to what in the first chapter I discover Kierkegaard saying about madness. Co-opting as another of my epigraphs Karen Armstrong's words "The imagination is the chief religious faculty," I amplify in this book what I said in *The HypoCritical Imagination,* having profited in the interim from reading Fiona Hughes's *Kant's Aesthetic Epistemology: Form and World* (2007) and Brian Elliot's *Phenomenology and Imagination in Husserl and Heidegger* (2005), both of which I found *génial* and congenial.

The sharp end of democracy, where a democracy impinges on its citizens, is our experiences of birth, and copulation, and death (the death of a friend, say), at once the most bodily and at the same time most spiritual events we undergo or witness. I argue that they and other connected rudimentary occasions or practices or dispositions can be religious in the way Kierkegaard and Derrida explain through the "experience" of the necessarily secret and almost silent moment of address. These singular *Grenzmomente*—unless they are *Schrankenmomente,* as distinguished in the first chapter—are minimally predicative (said) and maximally addressive (to say). One key to my carnate account of, in Durkheim's phrase, "the elementary forms of religious life" (as distinguished from religions) is a sentence in the marriage service in the Anglican Book of Common Prayer: "With my body I thee worship." Although that is a sentence that is uttered within the context of a rite of a particular church, I use it as a clue to a sense of the religious that asks to be saved from being either confined to organized religions or deemed to be a delusion by a secularism captive to an uncircumspect idea of itself. I am grateful to an anonymous reader of a draft of this book for suggesting that other keys I might use in it are offered by

Feuerbach, for instance the remark in the "Concluding Application" of his *The Essence of Christianity* to the effect that what I call the archi-sublime is already announced in the materially real water and wine and bread, whatever may be said about their ritually consecrated varieties. In the chapter entitled "Eucharistics" I employ this remark to enable me to distinguish an interpretation of it I endorse from one I do not, one where I prefer to be guided by Derrida. Feuerbach preaches a humanism. While declining to preach secularism, theism, or atheism, I decline also humanism, including Levinas's humanism of the other human being. In their mindfulness of God or human beings all these -isms are overly unmindful of the world.

Gratitude, which I distinguish from saying Thanks, is a vital ingredient in the sense of the religious pondered in the following chapters. In them I argue that gratitude can attach itself to most of the bodily and even digestive events that I would include in my unconcluding list of possibly religious occasions (the list "birth, and copulation, and death" that T. S. Eliot has his Sweeney draw up is very much too short), events like being overcome beside a cradle by tears of joy or of grief beside a grave, gut-reactions that are not necessarily *Gott*-reactions and not necessarily manifestations of this or that structured religion, but religious responses testifying to a conviction that, to express it in words I steal from an archbishop of Canterbury, the world is more than it is. This world is more and other than it is, but not on account of another world than this.

# PART ONE

ONE

# On the Borderline of Madness

## Absolute Wisdom

The citation with which Hegel's *Philosophy of Mind* concludes licenses the reader of that book to read it through the lens of Aristotle's teaching in *Metaphysics* 1072b that philosophy is thinking as such and thinking in the fullest sense, where

> thinking as such deals with that which is best in itself, and that which is thinking in the fullest sense with that which is best in the fullest sense. And thinking thinks on itself because it shares the nature of the object of thought; for it becomes an object of thought in coming into contact with and thinking its objects, so that thought and object of thought are the same. For that which is *capable* of receiving the object of thought, i.e. the essence, is thought. But it is *active* when it *possesses* this object.[1]

There is much talk here of the object of thought. In a phrase that owes something to Parmenides, Aristotle tells us that, where thought of the best and of the fullest is concerned, thought and the object of thought are the same, *tauton nous kai noēton*. If he had left it at that, the thought in question would be noetically-noematically representative. However, he also tells us that this thought is active and that its highest and fullest object is God. But if, at least for this loftiest and deepest thought, thought and the object of thought are the same, the object of thought must be active, that is to say living. So the objecthood that belongs to what Aristotle refers to as the object of thought, *noētos,* would be that of what Hegel calls an *Objekt,* an objective, as contrasted with that of a *Gegenstand,* something standing over against the thinking. The so-called object, that is to say the objective, could then be *noēsis,* thinking, as when at 1074b of the *Metaphysics* Aristotle says that thinking of the most excellent of things is thinking of thinking, *noēsis noēseōs,* and as when in §237 of the *Logic* of the *Encyclopaedia* Hegel explicitly borrows this expression from Aristotle to characterize the Absolute Idea. Saying that the logic that treats of that Idea in the *Encyclopaedia* and in the *Science of Logic* is concrete is another way of saying that it is a thinking *of* itself, not a thinking *about* itself or about anything else. Hegel observes that if we wish to speak of matter and form in this context we must say that the matter is pure thought and therefore absolute form itself.[2] As the realm of pure thought logic is "the realm of truth as it is without veil." Hegel's notion of truth here is to be contrasted with Heidegger's notion of truth as un-concealing accompanied by concealing. After all, what Hegel is talking about is God's truth. The absolute truth that is the content or matter of absolute thought is "the exposition (*Darstellung*) of God as he is in his eternal essence before the creation of nature and a finite mind."[3] So Hegel is able to write that the *Logic* of the *Encyclopaedia,* the latter's first part, is applied in the other two parts under the titles *The Philosophy of Nature* and *The Philosophy of Mind.* On the other hand this "lesser" *Logic* and the "greater" *Science of Logic* look back to the *Phenomenology of Spirit,* of which Hegel says that it is "the first part of the System of Philosophy."[4] The Absolute Idea expounded in those systems of logic presupposes the pure science of Absolute Wisdom or Absolute Knowing in which this latter work culminates. But in the *Phenomenology* this science has already been deduced. It is a result deduced through a series of mediative negations of negations in which competition is converted into cooperation and, starting with the simplest opposition of immediate consciousness of an object, representational consciousness is superseded, *aufgehoben.*

The principle of formal logic that a double negative yields a positive is enough to remind us that in dialectical logic *Aufhebung* is a transition in which what is lost is at the same time saved. But how saved? Whereas innocent consciousness takes immediate sensory consciousness of an object to be the richest experience we can have, Hegel tells us that the mature human being has learned that "philosophical knowledge is the richest in material and organization, and therefore, as it came before us in the shape of a result, it presupposed the existence of the concrete formations of consciousness such as individual and social morality, art and religion."[5] Consider individual morality. To what extent is the concreteness here attributed to it saved? If by concreteness is meant the becoming one and the same of this form of consciousness and its object, that is a way of saying that in its original form it is lost. Is it well lost? Take religion. Is the loss of its pictorial representations when it gives way to philosophical knowledge a loss that experience no less mature than philosophy would prefer to endure in some non-philosophical way, a way in which separateness is saved? The question may be put in terms of Hegel's summary definitions of Logic as the Idea in and for itself, of the Philosophy of Nature as the science of the Idea in its otherness, and, thirdly, of the Philosophy of Mind as the science of the Idea come back out of that otherness.[6] Might it be important to save an otherness that is not the otherness of the Idea, an otherness that does not come back out of its otherness? The question would be whether to consciousness and its representational apprehension there might be an alternative that, while still leaving consciousness behind, hence without being what Hegel calls "unhappy consciousness,"[7] not only opens out on to the fully rounded totality of circles of philosophy as the love of wisdom, but welcomes an alterity that pierces that circle of circles from an outside that is other than the outside thought of in Hegel's philosophy of nature, morality, art, and religion, other even than the outside from which, for an Aristotle other than the one we have spoken of so far in this chapter, active reason, *nous,* comes in from outside like a god. Let us ask this question first in relation to Kierkegaard's critique of Hegel's concepts of morality, religion, and God, making our way into this critique via what these authors say about insanity, which should be a good guide to what they think about reason.

## The Higher Madness

One of Kierkegaard's most common ways of issuing a warning against commonness is to say that it would drive you mad. Yet saying that someone is mad is one of his most common ways of distinguishing someone's uncommonness. Precisely the borderline between commonness and uncommonness might provoke one to say that "a borderline is precisely a torment for passion."[8]

Under the heading "Literary Quicksilver" Kierkegaard declares that what he is to say under it may be described as "A Venture in the Higher Madness with *Lucida Intervalla.*"[9] He then cites as an epigraph a couplet from Oehlenschlæger's *Dina:*

> I will not sing along in harmony
> But grate as a strange dissonance.

Strange dissonance indeed, strange absurdity, because the very first paragraph of the text that begins after this quotation states that it will be difficult to distinguish the venture in the higher madness from the intervals of lucidity. They will be found to stand alongside each other peacefully, he says. Apparently, then, there will be a harmony, albeit a strange one, as though the two were on the point of suddenly coalescing into a unity, communicating with each other like two drops of quicksilver, like mercury, which gets its name from or gives its name to the god of communication between heaven and earth. The so-called higher madness is evidently a deep madness, deeper, 17,000 fathoms deeper, than the level at which one opposes peace of mind and mental derangement. That this is so, that here the higher is in one sense—though, as we shall discover, not in another sense—the lower, is suggested by entries in Kierkegaard's *Journals and Papers* dating from some time in 1839 stating that the higher madness is "the most concrete of all categories, the fullest, since it is closest to life and does not have its truth in a beyond, the supraterrestrial, but in a subterranean below, and thus, if it were a hypothesis, the most grandiose empirical proof of its truth could be made."[10] We are then told that it is by way of this category that the transition is made from abstract madness to concrete madness. On the one hand it may be expressed in the formula "the unity of madness (*Galskabs*) in the duality of all creation (*Alskabs*)," borrowed from the work by the poet Jens Baggesen ominously entitled "The Abracadabra of the Untimeliness of the Ass," *Asenutidens Abracadabra*. On the other hand, this category of the higher madness may be expressed speculatively (and speculative idealism is what is here being mocked) in the formula "the unity of all creation in the duality of madness." These formulae are written in entries of the *Journals and Papers* that relate to the book attributed to Nicolaus Notabene entitled *Prefaces,* which consists of eight prefaces followed by a very brief postscript. Is this an allusion to the prefatory and introductory parts of the works of Hegel in which comments are made about the anomalous status of prefaces and their relation to the texts that follow them? That this is an allusion to the speculative system is confirmed by the *Writing Sampler,* attributed to A. B. C. D. E. F. Godhaab, which is printed after *Prefaces* in the same volume of *Kierkegaard's Writings* and contains only a preface to eight more prefaces followed by a postscript that repeats (backwards) almost verbatim the first sentence of the first preface: "Finally, please read the following preface, because it contains things of the utmost importance." This is a Joycean riverrun repetition (forward) to the broken circularity of another speculation on the Speculative system, Derrida's guying and gaying of Hegel in generative and degenerative chiasmus with Genet in *Glas*.[11]

But what of the chiasmus of the two formulae cited above? We can only speculate as to how that might work. Perhaps the creation is both unity and duality because it is the whole of what is created and implies a creator. This duality of the creator and the created is at the same time a multiplicity insofar as, to speak with Leibniz, the goodness of the creator implies the greatest possible variety and difference in his creation. To speak with Kierkegaard, all creation implies multiplicity, that is, whatever you wish, "*Quodlibet* or the loonier the better."

The duality of the higher madness is implied in its being a "pathos-filled transition—a dialectical transition,"[12] from abstract madness to concrete madness, these being not disconnected insanities, but species falling under a genus that is the unity of higher madness.[13]

It so happens that the entry in which these distinctions are made is followed immediately in the English edition of the *Journals and Papers* by one dating from three years later in which reference is made to the *Meditations* of Descartes. This is a happy accident. For madness is at stake in these *Meditations*. Furthermore, it is around the treatment of madness in them that turns the debate between Derrida and Foucault concerning the history of madness in the Age of Reason and the question whether madness is deeply embedded in reason and philosophy. Derrida acknowledges Kierkegaard as another contributor to this debate when he takes as an epigraph for his discussion of Foucault the assertion of Johannes Climacus in *Philosophical Fragments* that "the moment of decision is *folly*," "*Afgjørelsens Øieblik er en Daarskab.*"[14] What Kierkegaard contributes to this discussion of reason and philosophy and history cannot be appraised independently of his response to Hegel, as the terms reason, philosophy, and history announce. Before reminding ourselves where Hegel stands on some of these questions let us quickly take note of some of the distinctions made by the philosopher to whom Hegel in his turn is responding, "the honest Kant" who anticipates Kierkegaard by denying reason in order to make room for faith and of whom Kierkegaard says that he declares the relationship to God to be a mental derangement.[15]

## The Limits of Reason

Hegel is discontented with the way Kant draws a line between understanding (*Verstand*) and reason (*Vernunft*). Because Kierkegaard is ultimately concerned with what he contrasts with both reason (Danish *Fornuft*) and understanding, no serious misunderstanding may result from translating his word "*Forstanden*" by "reason," as in the Swenson version of the paragraphs of the *Philosophical Fragments,* which is changed, however, in the Hong and Hong translation to "understanding."[16] At issue with Kierkegaard is the question of philosophical translation from understanding or reason to religion regarded as exceeding both, as madness or folly or foolishness, where the second and third of these are the translations of "*Daarskab*" given respectively by Swenson and the Hongs. But Hegel's difference with Kant turns on the prior question whether, like drops of quicksilver—or indeed "two drops of water" (*Critique of Pure Reason* B319)—

understanding flows into reason or whether they remain discrete. It turns also therefore on this discretion, on how a *discrimen,* a borderline, is to be conceived, on what it is to be on a border or at a limit or frontier. And here this philosophical question of translatability across a line brings us up against a question of textual translation that cannot be as easily passed over as may be the question of textual translation raised above in connection with Kierkegaard.

At B322 of the *Critique of Pure Reason* Kant writes, in Kemp Smith's translation, "as regards things in general unlimited reality was viewed [by former logicians] as the matter of all possibility, and its limitation (negation [*Negation*]) as being the form by which one thing is distinguished from others according to transcendental concepts."[17] Kemp Smith's words "unlimited reality" translate *"unbegrenzte Realität,"* and his word "limitation" translates *"Einschränkung."* Although in B322 Kant is speaking of pre-Critical logicians, and it is arguable therefore that an ambiguity is tolerable in this context, he himself does not use one and the same root word. To do so would be to blur a distinction made at B789, at B795, and in §57 of the *Prolegomena* between what following Kemp Smith's translation of the *Critique* would have to be called a bound, a *Schranke,* and what following that translation would have to be called a limit, a *Grenze.* In P. G. Lucas's translation of the *Prolegomena* the terms are reversed.[18] Provided they are employed consistently, it does not matter much which pairing we prefer. I follow Lucas's because, as we shall soon see, it enables us to maintain a continuity of usage from Kant to Hegel. Postponing the question whether this enables us to maintain a continuity of usage from them both to Kierkegaard, and postponing a question raised by Kant's repetition of the word or particle *"gleich,"* let us consider the distinction made in §57 of the *Prolegomena.*

> Boundaries (*Grenzen*)—in extended beings—always presuppose a space which is come across outside a certain determined place and encloses it; limits (*Schranken*) do not need any such thing (*dergleichen*), rather are they mere negations (*Verneinungen*) which affect a magnitude in so far as it does not have absolute completeness. But our reason sees as it were (*gleichsam*) around it a space for knowledge of things in themselves, although it (*ob sie gleich*) can never have determined concepts (*bestimmte Begriffe*) of them and is limited merely to appearance.

Thus, as Kant goes on to explain in the sentence immediately following this paragraph, "As long as knowledge by reason is homogeneous (*gleichartig*)," as in mathematics and the natural sciences, we have mere *Schranken,* limits, with the ever-open possibility of knowledge being extended beyond a particular point it has reached. But, he observes in the sentence immediately preceding the paragraph just cited, "although (*obgleich*) it cannot be refuted" or grounded in intuition, the idea of a being that somewhere serves as a *Grenze,* a bound, to this infinite or indefinite extendibility of mathematical and physical knowledge is demanded by reason. However, he goes on to say a few paragraphs after the one just cited, this demand of reason can lead only, "as it were (*gleichsam*) to the contact of filled space (phenomenal experience) with empty space (the noumenal, the unknowable)." The "as it were" signals that the connection between filled and empty space is being invoked only as an analogy to illustrate the difference between the sheer negativity of a limit, a *Schranke,* and the positivity of a boundary, a *Grenze.* A surface is the boundary of a three-dimensional physical volume, but it is still spatial; a line is the boundary of a surface, but it is still spatial; a point is the boundary of a line, but it is still spatial. Here what is beyond each boundary is homogeneous (*gleichartig*) with the boundary. It is therefore a better analogy for Hegel's account of reason than it is for Kant's. For although Kant says that a boundary belongs to both sides of what it bounds, on one side are the concepts that have a constitutive use only over indefinitely extendible experience of the spatio-temporal, whereas on the other side are the ideas of reason whose legitimate use is not constitutive but regulative. For Hegel reason is constitutive on both sides of a given bound. That is to say, what Kant calls a boundary, a *Grenze,* and contrasts with a limit, a *Schranke,* is assimilated to a limit by Hegel. Hence, according to Hegel, understanding and reason have between them a limit, not a boundary, which they have according to Kant's definitions. If Kant goes as far as to say that a boundary participates in what lies on both sides of it, the line between a boundary and a limit becomes unstable according to Hegel. It is more like a colon than a period. It is to be compared not with a wall but with a passageway (a *pas*-sageway, to the topic of which we shall pass in chapter 13 below), however narrow or aporetic. That is what the etymological derivation of the word "limit" from Latin "*limes,*" meaning either limit or passage, would lead us to think.

To say with Hegel that there is a limit between understanding and reason is to say that they are not utterly heterogeneous. Reason, Hegel argues, is the truth of what Kant calls understanding. Understanding finds that it is not opposed to reason, but is an immature form of it. In the supplement to §386 of the *Philosophy of Mind* Hegel writes:

> We make ourselves finite by receiving an Other into our consciousness; but in the very fact of our knowing this Other we have transcended this limit (*Schranke*). Only he who does not know is limited (*beschränkt*); whereas he who knows the limit knows it not as a limit of his knowing, but as something known, as something belonging (*Gehörenden*) to his knowledge; only the unknown would be a limit of his knowledge, whereas the known limit on the contrary is not; therefore to know one's limit means to know of one's unlimitedness (*Unbeschränktheit*). But when we pronounce mind to be unlimited, truly infinite (*unendlich*), this does not mean that mind is free from any limit whatsoever; on the contrary, we must recognize that mind must determine itself (*sich bestimmen*) and so make itself finite, limit (*beschränken*) itself. But

the abstract understanding (*Verstand*) is wrong in treating this finitude as
something inflexible, in holding the difference between the limit and the infinitude to be absolutely fixed (*fest*), and accordingly maintaining that mind is
*either* limited *or* unlimited. Finitude, truly comprehended, is as we have said,
contained in infinitude, the limit in the unlimited. Mind is therefore *both*
infinite *and* finite, and *neither* merely the one *nor* the other; in making itself
finite it remains infinite, for it reduces-raises (*aufhebt*) the finitude within it
to what is merely ideal, merely appearing (*nur Erscheinendes*).

It reduces-raises it to what is a merely appearing moment, one could say, in
order to give notice of the violent reinterpretation which that term will undergo
when with Kierkegaard it becomes the *Øieblik* that resists the reduction of the
either-or to the both-and. For Kierkegaard the Critical Kantian case for resisting the both-and is not violent enough. It relies on the distinction between the
constitutive and the regulative uses of reason, from which it follows that Kant's
notion of the mathematical borderline (*Grenze*) can be used only as a sensuous
and therefore not unmisleading picture (*Sinnbild*) in his attempt, as he puts it at
the beginning of §59 of the *Prolegomena*, to fix the limits (*Schranken*) of reason
in respect of its appropriate use. The proper use is non-constitutive, regulative, practical, analogical, symbolic: thinking or faith rather than theoretical
knowledge. Therefore reference to a highest being would tell us nothing about
the being. It would tell us only something about the relationship of that being to
the world of which we have phenomenal knowledge, so that we regard the latter
as if it related to a highest being in the way that a clock relates to its maker.

Hegel's response to this is that Kant the philosopher is obliged to admit that
he knows the appropriate use of reason unrestricted by the forms of sensibility
and understanding to be regulative: "[H]e who knows the limit knows it not
as a limit of his knowing, but as something known, as something belonging
to his knowledge." So the content of Kant's claim is in conflict with his making it. He has failed to take account of his own use of speculative reason as a
philosopher.

Here, then, the question of the limits of reason is one with the question
of the limits of philosophy. And the question of frontiers within philosophical
reason, whether they be borders or limits, flows into the question whether the
apparent others of philosophical reason are ultimately other than it. Either-or
or both-and or either-or and both-and? *Aut-aut* or *vel*?

Of the many others that might be suggested as candidates for being the
other of philosophical reason let us now consider one, madness, bearing in
mind Kierkegaard's references to lunacy, insanity, and folly or foolishness cited
in the first section of our discussion. We shall find it necessary to be more precise about some of these expressions if certain misconceptions of Kierkegaard's
maniology are to be avoided. We return to this question in due course via a

remark made in the section of *Anthropology from a Pragmatic Point of View* in which Kant classifies the different kinds of what he refers to generally as *Verrückung,* or, as I shall provisionally and usually say, madness.

## Madness

Madness, Kant notes, is a *Versetzung,* a distancing and displacement, that is to say a change of place: a *kinēsis,* to use the term Kierkegaard transports to the psychological sphere from Aristotle's *Physics.* Note too that the provisional translation of "*Verrückung*" and "*Verrücktheit*" by "madness" is supported by the fact that the term "mad" comes from "*mutare,*" to change, to alter. It is thus more informative than the privative term "insanity" and less questionably theory-laden than the term "lunacy." "Folly," it may be remarked in anticipation, straddles mental deficiency in the form of foolishness or stupidity, and mental illness. It may be a deficiency of theoretical or practical knowledge or it may be a non-cognitive deficiency of mind. The latter kind of deficiency may be such as to leave room only for causal explanation. The former kind of deficiency may take on a moral tinge, as when it is asked in the Koran, "who turns away from the religion of Abraham except they who debase their souls with folly [befool themselves, *safeha*]?" (Sûrah II, 130). In the *Philosophy of Mind,* also under the heading Anthropology, Hegel gives his own classification of the different varieties of madness, uses the terms "*Verrückung*" or "*Verrücktheit*" for the genus, and underlines the notion of distancing conveyed by it when he writes that in madness the mind is split within itself, is *mit sich selber entzweiten,* schizzed (§402, *Zusatz;* see also below, chapter 8).

Hegel prescribes a talking cure for this splitting. We must humor the patient, appeal to his or her reason and prudence. In general patients may deserve considerate treatment (*rücksichtvolle Behandlung*) because their rational and moral nature is not entirely destroyed. If someone believes he is Mahomet, tell him he will not be confined provided he promises not to abuse his freedom by being a nuisance to others. Or appeal to the insane person's practical reason. For instance, if he believes he has fragile glass feet, get him to think he is being attacked by robbers. That way he'll very soon find how useful his feet are for running away. Hegel, like Kant, observes that madness may have either a psychological or a physical cause. Where the cause is physical the cure may be physical too, as when someone is cured by falling on his head. But generally the most effective treatment is the talking cure, in which an appeal is made to the patient's reason. Presumably that is what Hegel would prescribe for the madman of Descartes's first Meditation, who believes he has a head made of earthenware or glass.

Does this mean that Hegel's philosophy does not exclude madness from reason or from the full-blossoming of reason known as philosophy? Or does it point rather to the apparently opposite conclusion that Hegel does exclude madness from reason and philosophy by refusing to face the full blossoming of madness? Answers to these questions can be approached by reflection on the difference between Derrida's and Foucault's readings of the first Meditation.[19]

Why does Descartes put aside the hypothesis or pseudo-hypothesis that he, Descartes the philosopher, might be as mad as the madman who thinks his head and feet are made of glass? Descartes does this, Derrida says, because he believes that it is not the philosopher but the man in the street or the field who cannot contemplate the possibility that he himself might be mad. Descartes himself reserves the hypothesis that he might be mad only until the hypothesis of the evil genius makes it relevant to bring it back into play in order to show that, although the evil genius could be instrumental in making me in particular think that I am sane when I am in fact insane, the possibility of that deception (like the possibility of the hypothesis that I am always dreaming) is included within the possibility of a general deception contrived by the evil genius. The scope of the systematic deception contrived by the evil genius is wider because it brings into doubt not only beliefs based apparently on sensory experience and the imagination, but also beliefs based apparently on the intellect, for instance the propositions of arithmetic. This increase in scope of the range of beliefs is matched by an increase in force of the thought that whether my feelings or thoughts are all placed in me by a deceiving trickster, I am feeling or thinking, and that while doing so I can be quite certain that I exist. What I still cannot be certain of is that I can count on the truths of arithmetic and rules of inference when I am not thinking about them, when they are written down for the benefit of others and for myself at some later moment. In order that they may be able, in Hegel's phrase, to stand the test of time, to sustain the possibility of rigorous science, they need the support of a valid argument from my existence to the existence of a non-deceiving God. It is only at this stage, Derrida says, that Descartes turns his back on madness as manifested in the hypothesis that I am always dreaming and in the even madder hypothesis that I am always being systematically deceived by an evil genius. However mad I am, while I think that I think, I exist. So Descartes does not need to discount madness. Philosophy as such cannot discount it. So Hegel's philosophy of philosophy cannot. It cannot exclude it even by the talking cure, by appealing to the madman's reason. For reason has its own moment of madness. Before moving to the question of the nature of this moment we must return to the two questions posed above about Hegel in order to ask what answer we should expect Foucault to give to them on the basis of his reading of the first Meditation of Descartes. Would he say that Hegel's philosophy includes madness in reason and in the full blossoming of reason known as philosophy, what we found Aristotle calling thinking in its fullest sense, or would he say that Hegel excludes madness from reason and philosophy by refusing to face the full blossoming of madness?

There is some evidence for concluding that Foucault would emulate Hegel by drawing both of these seemingly opposite conclusions. For, on the one hand, he seems to express a Romantic Rousseauistic nostalgia for a pure *esprit sauvage* of madness reminiscent of Lévi-Strauss's invocation of alternative concrete logics to account for the behaviour of Bororo and other so-called primitive tribes.[20] On the other hand, Foucault refers precisely to the discussion in Hegel's *Phenomenology of Mind/Spirit* of Rousseauistic sentimentalism in order to applaud Hegel for returning madness to the fold of philosophy, from which, Foucault argues, it had been expelled by Descartes. Where Derrida takes Descartes to be saying that it is the vulgar who would find the hypothesis of madness untenable and for that reason drops it, but only temporarily, from consideration, Foucault maintains that in the first Meditation it is Descartes the philosopher himself who refuses to allow that the madman can think. Neither skepticism nor its refutation can be grounded on the thought that the insane take themselves to have heads made of pottery or glass, for once I entertain that thought I shall inevitably discover myself supposing that I myself might be mad. Does not Descartes write, "I should not be any the less insane were I to follow examples so extravagant"? Following examples so extravagant would mean that I could not think, whether to argue for skepticism or for its refutation—or indeed to be able to know that I was following these examples. That is why, according to Foucault, Descartes turns his back on this self-refuting hypothesis in order to consider the hypothesis that I might always be dreaming. So, in contrast with Montaigne, Descartes does in philosophy what was done by the political and social powers-that-be in the seventeenth century, namely, exile the insane in asylums from which, as far as philosophy is concerned, they await liberation by Hegel. The passage in the *Phenomenology* of which Foucault must be thinking in telling this story is one that has a similar content and dialectical pattern to that of many other passages in the *Phenomenology* and *Encyclopaedia,* for example the paragraph cited above from the *Philosophy of Mind.* Like this paragraph from the *Philosophy of Mind,* the passage in the *Phenomenology* makes explicit reference to madness, but there are more unexplicit allusions to forms of madness in the *Phenomenology* and the *Encyclopaedia* than readers usually acknowledge. It is arguable that madness is a key to the reading of these works.[21]

It is also arguable that madness is a key to the reading of the works of Kierkegaard and his pseudonymous and anonymous authors, provided we allow for a displacement of madness, a displacement of displacement, a derangement of derangement, as we move from Hegel to Kierkegaard. This movement from one movement to another, from one *kinēsis* to another, from one moment to another (from *Augenblick* to *Øieblik*), can be traced only if we take time to read Hegel very closely.

The context of Hegel's explicit references to madness in the *Phenomenology* is a treatment of the figure of consciousness that purports to see the law of the heart as the only way to the welfare of humankind. Hegel's treatment has reached the stage of declaring his diagnosis when, under the heading "The Law of the Heart and the Frenzy (*Wahnsinn*) of Self-Conceit," he writes:

> The heart-throb for the welfare of humanity therefore passes into the ravings of an insane self-conceit (*das Toben des verrückten Eigendünkels*), into the fury (*Wut*) of consciousness to preserve itself from destruction; and it does this by expelling from itself the perversion (*Verkehrtheit*) which it is itself, and by striving to look on it and expressing it as something else. It therefore speaks of the universal order as a perversion of the law of the heart and of its happiness, a perversion invented by fanatical priests, gluttonous despots and their minions, who compensate themselves for their own degradation by degrading and oppressing others, a perversion which has led to the nameless misery of deluded humanity. In this its derangement (*Verrücktheit*), consciousness declares its individuality (*Individualität*) to be the source of this derangement and perversion, but one that is alien (*fremde*) and accidental (*zufällige*). It is the heart, however, or the singularity (*Einzelheit*) of consciousness, that would be immediately universal, that is itself the source of this derangement, and the outcome of its action is merely that *its* consciousness becomes aware of this contradiction. For the True is for it the law of the heart—something merely *intended* (*Gemeintes*) which, unlike the established order, has *not stood the test of time,* but rather, when tested, is overthrown. This its law ought to have reality; the law, then, is for it *qua* reality, *qua* valid ordinance, its own name and essential nature; but reality, that very law *qua valid ordinance,* is on the contrary immediately for it something which is not valid. Similarly, its *own* reality, the heart *itself* as singularity of consciousness, is for it its essence; but its purpose is to establish that particular singularity as a *being* (*seiend*). Thus it is rather itself as *not* singular that is immediately for it its essence, or its purpose has the form of a law, hence the form of a universality, which it is for its own consciousness. This its Concept becomes by its own action its object; thus the heart learns rather that its self is not real, and that its reality is an unreality. It is therefore not an accidental and alien individuality, but just this heart, which in all its aspects is, in its own self, perverted and perverting.[22]

Thus the heart learns that it has to take the step of becoming a head. One wonders whether that step might have to be made on feet of which at least one is made of glass, and whether the head itself or at least one of its eyes may be glass too. For is it not possible that the figure of madness outlined in this part of the *Phenomenology* is a metaphor for the moments of destruction, going under, breakdown, sacrifice, and metaphorization that the mind is called to endure patiently in some or all of the other crises of alienation and recuperation or cure of the *Phenomenology,* so that the *Phenomenology of Mind* would be a phenomenology of going out of one's mind or of the mind's going out of itself along with a therapy for this? That would be in a very old tradition, a tradition as old as Plato, as old as philosophy itself, the tradition to which Derrida maintains that Descartes belongs, notwithstanding Foucault's attempt to exile Descartes from it, to commit him to an asylum as though he were mad—which would be one way, against Foucault's own intentions, of bringing Descartes back into the philosophical fold, if we may assume that not only the phenomenology of mind but philosophy itself is a philosophy of psychosis, a psychopathology.

Precisely that is what philosophy is according to the moral that Derrida draws from his meditation on Descartes's first Meditation and from what Foucault writes about that Meditation and about the history of madness (for despite their different readings of that Meditation Derrida concludes that "Michel Foucault teaches us to think that there are crises of reason in strange complicity with what the world calls crises of madness").[23] "Philosophy," Derrida writes, "is perhaps the reassurance given against the anguish of being mad at the point of greatest proximity to madness. This silent and specific moment could be called *pathetic*,"[24] a "first passion."[25] On the other hand, Derrida refers to "Danger as the movement of reason menaced by its own security,"[26] and maintains that it is *pathos* that secures *logos*—reason and philosophy—from this danger. Is this then a reaffirmation of the law of the heart which Hegel says is mad, *verrückt,* because it claims self-contradictorily both that it is immediacy and that it is an objective (*seiend*) reality? Derrida seeks to avoid such a reaffirmation by affirming that the moment of *pathos* in question is silent. But does not this formulation of the difficulty only underline the difficulty raised by Hegel for the proponent of the law of the heart? It is the difficulty that Foucault himself raises for his project of an archaeology—a *logos*—of the silence of madness. Is the only way out of this difficulty, Derrida asks, "to follow the madman down the road of his exile"? Or could one

> perhaps say that the resolution of this difficulty is *practical* rather than *formulated.* By necessity. I mean that the silence of madness is not *said,* cannot be said in the *logos* of this [Foucault's] book, but is indirectly, metaphorically, made present by its *pathos*—taking this word in its best sense. A new and radical praise of folly whose intentions cannot be admitted because the *praise* (*éloge*) of silence always takes place *within logos,* the language of objectification.[27]

The language of objectification is the stumbling-block the defenders of the law of the heart place in their own path when they maintain that the immediacy of feeling is an objective reality. It is to be heard already in the gloss Hegel puts on the term "individuality" used of the one who experiences the allegedly immediate feeling. For this term gets its sense, like all linguistic sense, from the universality to which it is opposed. The individual is posed or posited, and thereby deposed and deposited, in the same dimension of reality as the universal to which it is opposed. So is a new Erasmus who seeks to write a *Praise of Folly* bound to discover that he has written instead a *Praise of Sanity*? If Hegel's psychopathology seems to entail this, so too already does Kant's if it insists that "[t]he one universal characteristic of madness (*Verrücktheit*) is loss of *common sense* (*sensus communis*) and substitution of *logical private sense* (*Eigensinn*) (*sensus privatus*)."[28] It becomes clear at once from the example of madness Kant gives—the case of someone seeing or hearing something no one else sees or hears—that the privacy he intends is a privacy that is only contingently private and that in principle can and should be made public. As with Hegel, no matter how resistant may be the madman's stubbornness (*Eigensinn*), his claims must be put to the test of time, that is to say to the test of corroboration. As with Hegel, the sense of this private sense is still logical and the logic is the logic of representation. The privacy and silence of the *pathos* to which Derrida alludes would be on the borderline of that logic, a disturbing nonsense on the threshold (*limen*) of sense which endangers that sense and causes *logos* to tremble. We can expect to learn more on the alternative geometry of that line and what it is to be on it when from what he says about the *pathos* and silence of madness in connection with Foucault and the *cogito* of Descartes Derrida turns to the fear and trembling of Johannes de silentio and that author's author.

## Imprudence

That author's author writes in an entry in his journals and papers: "They say that experience (*Erfaring*) makes a man wise. This is very unreasonable talk. If there were nothing higher than experience, experience would drive a man mad (*gal*)."[29] That craziness would be a lower madness in comparison with what we may call, borrowing the phrase from the second section of this chapter, the higher madness. The higher madness would be that madness of which Kierkegaard speaks in connection with the Apostle Paul.

> It is easy enough to defend the use of prudence in achieving something by appealing to Paul, who, after all, also used prudence. Well, let's take that. A life which has qualitatively and totally secured its own heterogeneity as madness (something, in fact, achieved by acting in total opposition to prudence), such a life can use prudence without any danger. But it is dangerous for a person not so distinguished to act prudentially, for then prudence makes capital of him *in toto*. Such a person has not secured for himself any heterogeneity (which, relative to Paul, is achieved only by acting decisively against reason at some time). Religious people do not think this. Religious persons undistinguished in this way religiously defend acting prudentially by appealing to Paul, without noticing or wanting to notice that the "total madness" ("*totale Galskab*")

of Paul's life, that is, its dissimilarity with prudence, adequately safeguarded him, while their crumb of religiosity drowns in the total prudence (*totale Klogskab*) of the world and the secular mentality.[30]

Applying to this Derrida's reference to "Danger as the movement of reason menaced by its own security," one could say that Paul is protected from the menace of the security of his prudence by the danger of the heterogeneity he has secured through his madness. The theoretical counterpart to practical total prudence would be ancient Greek contemplation or modern Germano-Greek absolute knowing, the *sagesse* or *savoir absolu* of which the author of *Glas* (*Glasskab*?) is no great friend.[31] Paul took it for his first mission to preach to those for whom the basis of his teaching is described as an offense or a stumbling-block. As Johannes Climacus, the pseudonymous author of the *Philosophical Fragments*, observes in a footnote, the Greek expression for this is *skandalizesthai,* in the middle voice. On the one side the offense is a suffering. "Christianity is really all too joyous, and therefore really to stick to Christianity a man must be brought to madness (*Afsindighed*) by suffering."[32] We say, "He is offended." But the passive voice of this expression is crossed by the active voice of the equally apt expression "He takes offense." (Even more dramatic is the equivocity of the Welsh "*digio*" which means both to offend and to take offense. Such Abelian oppositions, as I shall call them, will be treated below in chapter 11.) This equivocity is manifested also in the words "passion" and "*pathos*." A passion may be regarded either as passive or active. It is this equivocity that gives rise to what Climacus calls an acoustic illusion. This is the illusion that the offense has its source in the understanding, and not in the paradox. (Compare Hegel's objection to philosophers who cannot see their way to granting that contradiction may be objectively real. And compare Derrida's interpretation of that other melancholy Dane's statement that the time is out of joint.)[33] The activity indicated by the fact that we say of someone that he takes offense leads us to mistake the understanding, perhaps the understanding and reason of the philosopher, for the origin of the activity, whereas the initiative is with the paradox itself. In a paragraph of complex and convoluted etymological resonances that prefigures such paragraphs in Heidegger and reveals the comedian within the passionately serious Dane, the words "moment" ("*Øieblik*") and "wonder" ("*Under*") are pronounced, words that Heidegger will adopt. But when Heidegger adopts the second of these words it translates Greek "*thaumazein*." That that is the wonder in which philosophy begins is what we are told by the Greeks. That is the moment that Socrates can know, if only what he knows at that moment is that he knows nothing. And when he begins to teach that we know nothing Socrates is opening the way for another beginning, a beginning in the moment of decision which remains foolishness to the Greeks, for instance those Corinthians to whom Paul directed his message after it had become a stumbling-block for the Jews.

The Jews were offended, but their memory of the story of Abraham and Isaac on the chosen land of Mount Moriah meant that the story of the incarnation and sacrifice of Christ would not be foolishness to them, not *mōria* (1 Corinthians 1:23), meaning (as in its derivative "moron") the kind of dementia that is less a mental derangement than a lack of understanding or of reason. The latter is a typically Greek category, notwithstanding the Platonic acknowledgment that the love in the love of wisdom, in philosophy, is a god-inspired *mania*. For, whatever may be said about this *mania* under the name *furor* when the degrees of madness described in the *Phaedrus* are harnessed via Plotinus to Christianity by, for example, Ficino, knowledge of the universal continues to be the end that Platonism and Neoplatonism seek. What Plato calls *mania* stands to *thaumazein* as what Paul calls *mōria* stands to intellectual *stupor,* the stupidity that is a moment of the moment of wonder, an *Øieblik* of the *Øieblik* of *Under.* The Jews have already learned that there are things that surpass understanding. They have had to accept that the categories of knowledge have been shaken by the category of paradox. But for them the paradox of the incarnation is a paradox too far, a paradox that affronts not just their understanding, but their religious faith, with the exception of the one among them named Jesus and renamed Christ and the other among them named Saul and renamed Paul, the one whose shortness of stature is not an occasion for puffing himself up unless put under pressure by the Corinthians. The folly he tries but fails to avoid—compare verse 6 and verse 11 of 2 Corinthians 12—is *aphrōn,* the mindless excess of self-glorification. For although he takes second place to no one in apostolic authority, he cannot forget the thorn in his flesh and the infirmities, reproaches, necessities, persecutions, and distresses he is called to suffer for Christ's sake.

This description matches that which Kierkegaard gives of himself, except that he never pretends that he is an apostle and often questions whether he dare call himself a Christian. Only by adopting a position he calls "armed neutrality,"[34] denying that he is a Christian and that he has had a revelation, can he deceive another into an awareness of the truth of Christianity. Let us not be deceived about deception. It is required by the indirect communication that is the only kind of communication that Socrates found was appropriate for him and that Kierkegaard finds necessary to his aesthetic and poetic mode of addressing the person who is confused over the difference between the religious and the aesthetic.[35] Kierkegaard humors this person, rather as Hegel humors the madman.

Nor will Kierkegaard and many of his pseudonymous writers go so far as to claim for themselves the title of religious genius. The religious genius has in common with the apostle that he is put under pressure and that he is mad. Of genius generally, Kierkegaard writes, citing Seneca, *De tranquillitate,* 17, 10:

*Nullum unquam exstitit magnum ingenium sine aliqua dementia.* The explanation is very simple. In order truly to be a great genius a man must be the exception. But in order that there shall be seriousness (*Alvor*) in being the exception, he must himself be unfree, forced into it. Herein lies the significance of his *dementia.* There is a fixed point at which he suffers; he cannot ever run with the crowd. This is his anguish. His *dementia* perhaps has nothing at all to do with his real genius, but it is the pain by which he is tormented into isolation—and he must be in isolation if he is to be great, and no man is able freely to hold himself in isolation; he must be constrained if he is to be serious.[36]

The great genius is driven out of his mind because he is driven out of society. He must be driven out of society if he is to be driven out of his mind. This is because the mutation that madness implies also implies muteness; it prohibits at least direct communication. It is true that one way of maintaining an inner secrecy is constantly to indulge in talk. Kierkegaard cites Talleyrand's remark to this effect.[37] He refers to Talleyrand also, however, as an instance of a man of genius who might have become a great religious genius if he had not devoted himself to a career in the public world. Perhaps his clubfoot was a divine sign of this, comparable with Paul's shortness of stature and the thorn in his flesh—comparable too with what Kierkegaard called the thorn in his own flesh and with the spindly legs which protruded so far below his trousers that they provoked taunts from the burghers of Copenhagen. The spindly legs are but the outward physical sign of the inward spiritual splinter.

A genius equipped with all possible capacities, with power to dominate all existence and to make men obey him, discovers in his consciousness one little sticking point, one bit of madness (*Galskab*). He becomes so indignant over it that he decides to kill himself, for to him this one little point is not an externality (for example, being lame, one eyed, ugly, etc.; such would not concern him) but has an element of spirit and thus would seem capable of being removed in freedom—therefore it goads him.[38]

When in the entry in the *Journals and Papers* reproduced before this last one Kierkegaard writes of the great genius, it is the religious genius that he means. That this is so is made clear when he writes elsewhere of the sentence cited from Seneca that it is "the secular expression for the religious thesis: one whom God blesses religiously he *eo ipso* execrates in a secular way. So it must be: the first has its basis in the boundaries (*Grændse*) of existence (*Tilværelse*) and the second in the doubleness (*Duplicitet*) of existence (*Tilværelsens*)."[39] Here, while anticipating the need to come back to ask in precisely what sense the religious is opposed to the secular, we come back to the notion of boundary (*Grenze*), Kant's definition of which was compared with Hegel's definition of limit (*Schranke*) in the third section of this chapter. We discovered there that

Hegel questions Kant's treatment of the line between understanding and reason as a barrier. When we come to the line between, on the one hand, understanding and reason and, on the other hand, what Kierkegaard means by religion, religion is no longer what it remained at its furthest development for both Kant and Hegel, within the boundaries of reason alone, where Passion is the history of the suffering of reason. With Kierkegaard the passion of religion must remain the suffering of the existing singular individual. Not any suffering whatsoever. Not the pain of toothache or of disappointed desire for worldly good fortune. The passion of religion, specifically of *imitatio Christi,* is the suffering of the doubleness of existence.[40] That doubleness or duplicity is described when, in a note mentioning that he has introduced the new pseudonym Anti-Climacus, he writes that "this is precisely the intimation of a halt; that is, the dialectical way of making a halt: you point to something higher which critically forces you back within your boundaries (*Grændse*)."[41] The intimation of a halt is not the arrival at a halt. The dialectical way of making a halt is what Kierkegaard sometimes means when he uses the word "interesting" as a border category (*Grændsekategori*) or *confinium.* The word "*confinium*" is one that he frequently uses because, like the "inter" of "interesting," its first syllable indicates a duplicity. So that the dialectical way of making a halt is always the *dia-,* the *via,* the through and thoroughfare of a turning point on life's way, ultimately the life of a singular individual, therefore in a concrete historical situation, *in discrimine rerum.*[42] This brings us to another turning point in our discussion, a return to Derrida's analysis of Foucault's *History of Madness,* a supplementary either-or on the Kierkegaardian confines of the scriptural and post-scriptural.

## Passion

Derrida argues that a history of madness calls for a history of history, and a history of history and of madness cannot assume that what historicity is goes without saying. An account of historicity is called for, a *logos* of it, a philosophy of it. We have seen that Derrida argues too that such an account reveals that from the beginning philosophy is not simply contaminated by madness, but is quasi-conditioned by it. That is to say, the meaninglessness of madness is what makes philosophy and meaning and language possible, though at the same time it makes them impossible if philosophy and language are conceived as a systematic totality of pure sense, pure science, and pure reason. However, if this is so, it requires to be asked, as Foucault does not, whether the "classical," Cartesian moment at which Foucault maintains madness is excluded is at best an example in the sense of a sample, rather than an example in the sense of an exemplar and paradigm.

Kierkegaard is alive to the difference between objective historiography and existential historicity. The latter is for him the transfiguration of the temporal by the eternal. It is therefore neither pure factuality nor pure eternity. Its history is not to be understood retroactively as, say, "pagans before Christianity."[43] Although and because he stresses this difference, a question similar to the one Derrida puts to Foucault must be put to Kierkegaard. He writes that "the possibility of offence is the dialectically decisive factor, is the 'borderline' ('*Grænse*') between paganism, Judaism-Christianity,"[44] where, always punctilious on matters of punctuation,[45] instead of using a conjunctive "and" Kierkegaard prefers to use a comma ("paganism, Judaism-Christianity") to stand for the decisive factor (*komma* comes from *koptō,* to cut). An implication of his not being primarily concerned with the chronological sequence of "pagans before Christianity" is that he does not limit paganism to what precedes Judaism-Christianity historiographically, say the *Weltanschauung* of the ancient Greeks, of which he sees Socrates to be one of the earliest critics. Rife in his contemporary Denmark was what he calls Christian paganism. Perhaps that is why in the sentence just reproduced he writes "borderline" in quotation marks. This may be in order to mark a less decisive cut that could be marked by "and," where Judaism-Christianity could be mentioned in the same breath as paganism or Mohammedanism or Hinduism or Buddhism and so on. Alternatively, the relation between any one of these and Judaism-Christianity might be marked, as in the cited sentence, by a decisive comma, or by a hyphen (grammatically intermediate in force between the comma and the "and"?) such as marks the discontinuity in the continuity of Judaism-Christianity. We do not have to question Kierkegaard's right to opt his own options. Nor do we have to deny that in saying this we are speaking, as he would say, aesthetically. But he himself and his pseudonymous authors demand that an account of the stages of life's way be given that is dialectical in the sense of reflective but not dialectical in the sense of the System of Hegel. Now Heidegger's thinking of the epochs of being is another way of challenging Hegel. It may be said, as Levinas says, that this is still too close to Hegel for comfort, too close to provide comfort, because it springs from *thaumazein* understood as wonder at the being of there being anything at all (*thauma-sein?*). We might instead, taking as point of departure what Heidegger writes about *Ereignis,* explore with Derrida the chance that both systematic philosophy or metaphysics and the thinking of being have always been on the borderline of madness or of what Levinas goes as far as to call psychotic obsession, possession and persecution by the human or other other—an astonishing eventuality Kierkegaard touches on when in *The Book on Adler* he writes that religion is not something one has, but something one is had by, a circumstance to which we shall return in our last chapter.[46] But religion is something one may be had by in the sense that it may be that by which one is taken in. This possibility is necessary for religion. Religion is necessarily on the borderline of madness. It is always exposed to the chance that its God or its god can be explained away either in the language of rational justification, for instance the rationality of Hegel which talks the madman out of his madness, or in the language of causal explanation, or in both of these languages, as is the case with a feature of sentences reproduced in the third section of this chapter from §57 of Kant's *Prolegomena,* to which we promised to come back.

In the compass of a few sentences Kant has recourse again and again to the word "*gleich.*" It is as though the sound of the word is dictating its use, as though he has lost control of his senses. Do we have here then a phenomenon for which only a causal explanation can be given? Not if his sentences make sense. And they do make sense, even though a purely causal theory ("echolalia"?) may have to be invoked to explain why Kant expresses this sense precisely in this seemingly obsessive way. As Kant's own philosophical theory maintains, accounts in terms of reasons and accounts in terms of causal explanations are not incompatible. But both types of account are objective. Therefore to give either kind of account of what Kierkegaard calls his inward subjective passion is to miss the point, what one of his titles calls "the point of view of my work as an author." He may well agree with Kant that the relationship to God is a kind of mental derangement (*Sindssvaghed*),[47] but the subjectivity of this derangement places it as far beyond the range of all rational or causal accounting as the singular according to Aristotle is beyond scientific knowledge. Subjective passion is unaccountable, being ultimately the condition of accountability. The madness of subjective passion is the madness of the idiot in the etymological sense of the term *idios,* the singular and solitary individual Kierkegaard calls *den Enkelte,* hence for him first of all the author who signs himself S. K. or SK or SAK.[48]

There is both an enormous risk and an enormous security about this subjective passion. It is the passion of choosing myself absolutely. The ab-solution performed is ab-solution with a hyphen, that is to say, it is separation. It is the unbinding of myself in my binding myself to myself. What I unbind myself from is this and that, what Eckhart and Angelus Silesius call things. These things are things of the world. Moreover, these things include what we call God, insofar as God is regarded as a thing, albeit a highest thing. In the archaic script of Silesius's *Der Cherubinischer Wandersmann* God's name is written *GOtt.* There is a God or a god that must go. This is that God that exists—or does not. And the risk of the non-existence of this God is the chance of SK's eternal salvation. Not a duration in time but an endurance in eternity, Kierkegaard's eternal salvation is not contingent upon the contingent or necessary existence of God. "By itself, to have a genuine concern for one's eternal salvation (as Christianity requires), this alone is an enormous weight compared to the manner of living that leaves the eternal an open question."[49] That question ceases to be open when I choose the absolute. "And what is the absolute? It is I myself in my eternal validity."[50] This validity is not undermined by the non-existence of God. My idiocy saves me from the madness by which I might be said to be gripped if I persisted in believing I heard a voice (as Abraham believed he heard God's voice bidding him take Isaac into the land of Moriah and then, on Moriah, the voice of an angel of the Lord bidding him not to lay his hand on the lad) when there was no one there to speak (as "there was no voice, nor any that answered" when on Carmel at Elijah's behest the people called upon Baal [1 Kings 18:26, 29]).[51] My choice of my eternal validity is self-validating. This does not mean that its validity is independent of how I comport myself toward others. The faith in which the choice of myself is made is what saves ethical works from the pure universality of Kantian *Moralität* and the mere public custom of Hegelian *Sittlichkeit*.

In this way Kierkegaard's choice of himself does what in Levinas's teaching on the ethical is performed by my being elected by the other. In Levinas's writings the other may be the human other or God, yet the metaphysical or empirical existence of the other as God is as beside the point for Levinas as it is for Kierkegaard. What Levinas calls psychosis, like what we have called the idiocy of the Kierkegaardian subject, is immune from exposure to the sort of madness we might diagnose in the case of someone who persists in believing that he is being addressed when there is no one there to address him. Now the doctrines that Kierkegaard and Levinas propose are not doctrines that hold only for themselves. As Derrida asks rhetorically, when Levinas writes in reference to the system of Hegel "It is not I who do not accept the system, as Kierkegaard thought, it is the other," "Can one not wager that Kierkegaard would have been deaf to the distinction?"[52] That is to say, Kierkegaard does not deny that there are other subjects capable of passionate subjectivity like himself. Kierkegaard is speaking of subjectivity in general. He knows, to quote Derrida again, that "[t]he name of a philosophical subject, when he says *I,* is always, in a certain way, a pseudonym." Derrida again: "The other is not myself—and whoever has ever maintained that it is?—but it is *an* Ego, as Levinas must suppose in order to maintain his own discourse."

Nevertheless, there remains a difference between Levinas's and Kierkegaard's conceptions of the Ego. What Levinas calls the psychism of the ego, mine or another's, is its being addressed by another. The self owes itself to its being addressed, even accused and persecuted by another, and primarily by another human being, where it is only through the other human being that one can make sense of the word "God." It is by the other that the self's egoity becomes ethical, and this holds too for the other. The psychism of the other is psychotic, being chosen and possessed by yet another. With Kierkegaard, however, the self chooses itself. It remains egological, if not egoistic. With Kierkegaard selfhood is affect or passion. With Levinas it is the affect of affect, the passion of passion before the face of another. In the first place this face is the face of another human being. The other is my center of gravity. Kierkegaard's stress on subjectivity and inwardness makes it difficult to see how for him the center of gravity could be other than oneself. Where he does say things suggesting that my choice of myself is also my being chosen, as when he writes "I can say that I choose the absolute which chooses me,"[53] the absolute that chooses me may be God, but it is not the other human being. Where for Levinas the move to God is made through the other human being, the human being comes after and through God for Kierkegaard. Now although I may be wrong in supposing that the call of this human being is more urgent than the call of that one, there is no room for mistake as to whether another human being calls. My ethical responsibility is unconditional. Not so according to the doctrine of Kierkegaard, not if by the ethical we mean not purely universal morality or public custom, but the religiously ethical that is moved by passionate choice of the self. For if the choice of the self is a response to the voice of God we are back with the risk that I am imagining that voice, imadgining it [sic], one might say. I am on a borderline not only of the madness from which, according to Hegel and Kant, I may be turned by reasoning. I am on the borderline not just of the psychosis which, according to Levinas's humanism of the other human being, is both passion and the rationality of rationality, rationality par excellence, his ultra-passive version of the ultra-active intellect that according to Aristotle and Alexander of Aphrodisias comes into the mind and the world as if from outside as if it were a God. I am on the borderline not simply of the idiocy of excommunication implied by Kierkegaard's notion of the singular individual, the borderline of the *dementia* that "perhaps . . . is the pain by which he is tormented into isolation." All three of these madnesses are in their different ways conditions of ethicality. But ethicality is under threat once I find myself on the borderline of the madness of fancying I hear someone who is not there. This is not a reassertion of the thought that for ethics to grow up it must pass through the test of being suspended. After the test of which Abraham's decision to sacrifice his son is a paradigm, ethics is given back transfigured. There is a transfiguration of ethicality too when its universality is interrupted by the singularity of one's being faced by another human being. In this humanistic transfiguration of the ethical there is a transfiguration also of the metaphysical. The metaphysical becomes the ethical. But the metaphysical retains its traditional sense when it posits God as a being, albeit highest being, believed in on the basis of experience. To cite again Kierkegaard's words, "They say that experience makes a man wise. This is very unreasonable talk. If there were nothing higher than experience, experience would drive a man mad."[54] If to base belief in God on belief of the objectively historical facts of Christianity is to court a lower madness, the higher madness is to choose to believe in God in a way that is independent of the objectively historical facts because in the passionately subjective choice of oneself made in this choice to believe in God the historical is the contemporary. The choice is a choice against objectivity for subjectivity, against the crowd for isolation, for passion, for suffering: "really to stick to Christianity a man must be brought to madness (*Afsindighed*) by suffering."[55] And this brings us back finally to the peaceful coexistence of madness and lucidity referred to in the second section of this chapter on the borderline of madness. We have treated of madness at some length. We have spoken only indirectly of the *lucida inter-valla*. Where lies the borderline between madness and lucidity?

A man is already brought to suffering as soon as he is brought to isolation, for isolation is contrary to the urge toward direct communication that is natural to the human being. Direct communication is the propounding of propositions, the declaration of beliefs and opinions, *doxa*. But "really to stick to Christianity" is to be struck by the paradox of the God-man, to be offended by it. Christianity is not a belief, a teaching. A teaching or a doctrine is such as a Greek may find foolish, a contradiction in terms, even a madness, but only a lower because abstract madness. The madness of Christianity begins to become concrete when the Jew, for instance Peter, is scandalized by the thought of God become man; as we have already observed, according to Kierkegaard "the possibility of offence is the dialectically decisive factor, is the 'borderline' ('*Grændsen*') between paganism, Judaism-Christianity."[56] To this scandalous offense to reason the Christian responds with belief that is not the overcoming of intellectual and therefore abstract doubt, but a passage through a suffering of the paradox.[57] Why a suffering of the paradox? Why does the paradox of the God-man bring pain? Because this paradox is not an abstract formal contradiction, but the suffering willingly accepted when God becomes abased as a suffering servant, and because Christianity is concrete this-worldly *imitatio Christi*. That is what it means for Christ to be one's contemporary. It means that the Christian is patient in the passion which in his human way, and "confirming at every moment the chasmic abyss between the single individual and the God-man over which faith and faith alone reaches,"[58] he shares with the passion of the God-man.

And the passion is a passing. It is a passing through madness. The higher madness is a transition. To what is it a transition? Not to the lucidity in which one recognizes that what seemed to be madness was not madness at all. That would be a return to the lucidity of the purely universal and to the possibility of communicating it directly. That would be a return to Hegel and to Greece. The transition of the higher madness is rather a transition to grace. It is a transition to the space in which direct communication is bent through ninety degrees by irony and humor. Kierkegaard tells of Lucretius, "a Roman poet who was mad but had his more lucid moments and devoted these very moments to his poem

*De rerum natura.*"⁵⁹ Lucretius was a heathen. This may explain why he could not do what the poet of Christianity can do, write "both in and out of season," both in his intervals of madness and in his intervals of lucidity, so that "it will be hard to distinguish the one from the other." It will be hard to distinguish the one from the other because the intervals of lucidity are intervals in madness and the intervals of madness are intervals in lucidity, as the movement of a blink or a wink (*Øieblik*) is a moment both of darkness and of light. Lucidity here is the lucidity *of* madness, madness's lucidity. Madness here is the madness *of* lucidity, lucidity's madness. Here the borderline of madness is neither simply a *Grenze* nor simply a *Schranke,* neither as defined by Kant nor as defined by Hegel in the passages reproduced in the third section of this chapter. For although in the transition across this line lucidity is not left behind, any more than spatiality is left behind by the line that is the border of a square, the lucidity to which one moves is not like that to which reasoning would bring the madman according to the cure prescribed by Hegel. If the lucidity to which humoring brings the madman is still a madness it is only what in the immediately preceding section of this chapter we decided to call a lower madness. When the transition is made not by humoring but by humor, *logos* is crossed with *pathos.* The *Logos is* the Passion, the Word is existed as suffering, is lived as death on the Cross. The line of the borderline of madness that is crossed in becoming a Christian is never finally crossed. The Cross remains an eternal crossing. This eternal crossing of the Cross that saves is eternal salvation. The suffering without end, without point, without *telos* and without pause, period, or stop (*Standsning*), is the eternal rest.⁶⁰ The line between eternal suffering and eternal salvation is invisible. This is why a reader of Kierkegaard can write of a *pathos* of "feeling *absolutely* safe. I mean the state of mind in which one is inclined to say 'I am safe, nothing can injure me whatever happens.'"⁶¹

Wittgenstein, the reader of Kierkegaard just alluded to, writes also that some things one is inclined to say must be consigned to the secrecy of silence. And those servants of the secrecy of silence who bear the name Søren Kierkegaard or pseudonyms like Johannes de silentio would affirm with their countersignatures that the higher madness is in danger of being reduced to the lower if whatever is written on the borderline of madness is said directly, without a sense of irony and humor.

# TWO

## Stay!

### Inward Peace

In the chapter of the *Critique of Practical Reason* entitled "Of the Motives of Pure Practical Reason," Kant speaks of a certain inward peace. This *innere Beruhigung,* he says, adds nothing to our pleasure or happiness. It is a consolation (*Trost*) for a sacrifice of such happiness as we might have acquired for ourselves or "for a loved and well-deserving friend" by disregarding duty, for example by telling "an otherwise inoffensive lie."[1] The inward peace is "the effect of a respect for something quite different from life, something in comparision and contrast with which life with all its enjoyment has no value. He still lives only because it is his duty, not because he finds the least relish (*Geschmack*) in life." Before picking up this matter of inward peace, three points must be made by way of clarification and anticipation.

1. Among our duties, according to Kant, is that of coming to the assistance of others when they are in distress and of contributing positively to their welfare, that is, their happiness, whether they be friends or not.[2] Kant distinguishes perfect from imperfect duties. Setting aside morally neutral deeds, and understanding by nature a system that is under law in the sense that the system is at least purely formally consistent, free from con-

tradiction, to fail to perform a morally motivated perfect duty is to fail to perform a deed out of respect for a maxim, for example "Never lie," that could become a universal law of nature, whereas it is inconceivable that the opposite of the maxim, for example "Lie for the sake of protecting yourself or a friend from discomfort," could become a universal law of nature.[3] This opposite maxim subverts the very concept of communication, just as, Kant maintains, does the closely related maxim "Break a promise when you find it too inconvenient to keep it."

On the other hand, to fail to perform a morally motivated imperfect duty is to fail to perform a deed out of respect for a maxim that could become a universal law of nature but could not without contradiction be willed to become such a law. The contradiction in this case is not conceptual but derivative from the fact that my happiness is put at risk if, for example, I neglect to cultivate my own natural potentialities or I behave in a way that diminishes the good will toward me of others by being indifferent to their well-being. The fulfilment of an imperfect duty such as the duty of benevolence *could* mean failure to perform a perfect duty, for instance the perfect duty to tell the truth or to keep a promise, as in the kind of case described by Kant and referred to above in the first paragraph. The fulfilment of an imperfect duty *would* mean the failure to perform another imperfect duty. This fact will play an important part in Derrida's thinking.

2. A third perfect duty beyond truth telling and promise keeping is touched on in Kant's statement that one who acts not out of love of life but out of regard for duty lives only because it is his duty, not because he relishes the pleasure of life. The duty in question is the duty not to take one's own life when misfortune after misfortune have led one to despair of life. Now although, as noted above, Kant distinguishes between contributing positively to someone's welfare and coming to the assistance of someone in distress, one's distress is not counted as something whose removal by suicide would be consistent with self-love. But the inconsistency turns entirely on Kant's conception of self-love as a feeling whose very nature it is to drive one to promote life. By this definition indeed I cannot consistently destroy myself out of love of myself. But the definition postulates a teleology for which Kant offers no arguments here. He does so elsewhere, however, and readers of Kant must not forget that when he refers to consistency and contradiction these notions have a teleological force already in the *Fundamental Principles of the Metaphysic of Morals*. Nonetheless, the contradiction he sees in suicide turns also on his understanding of self-love as synonymous with love of life or love of one's own life. Might

not self-love be understood simply as self-love? Of course I cannot love myself if I have destroyed myself. But I can destroy myself because I love myself. I can even destroy myself out of self-respect. Perhaps, however, the self-respect here would have to be understood otherwise than as defined by Kant in terms of universal law. Perhaps it would have to be understood in terms of singularity, my own or another's or both. This thought too will play an important part in the thinking of Derrida, as well as in the thinking of Kierkegaard and Levinas.

3. Acting from duty is "quite different from life," we are told.[4] Does this mean that the phrase "ethical life" is a contradiction in terms? Yes and no. Yes, if the phrase is taken to describe a quality intrinsic to natural life itself. No, if it describes a relation that natural life may have to what is deemed quite different from it, a life controlled by respect for the law requiring that one act only on a maxim that could become a universal law or that one can at the same time will to become a universal law[5] This states a necessary condition for moral behavior, according to Kant. It does not exclude the engagement of one's sensible nature in the action, for instance one's affection for the friend. It requires minimally that we refrain from acting out of affection if we think that our maxim either could not become a universal law or could not be consistently willed to become a universal law. To act only on such an universalizable maxim would be a case of refraining from doing something else whose maxim would not be universalizable. So there is a negative force to the Kantian law. It is a necessary condition of moral behavior. Whether or not it is also a sufficient condition is not a question that will be considered here. Any attempt to decide whether it is or is not a sufficient condition of moral behavior should not be made without recalling that the contradictoriness at issue is not purely that of abstract formal logic, but one that has to be interpreted in the concrete context of the particular purposes human beings express in maxims that are in turn expressed through their behavior, and in the context of the teleologicality postulated for humanity in Kant's system viewed as a whole. One thing that must be said here about this purposiveness is that Kant's view of teleologicality will not permit us an understanding of life in which the pleasures and happiness for which life is the desire become so ennobled that the moral law becomes subordinate or instrumental to them. Life and the life of ethics may call to be construed in a third way, however, as neither basely nor elevatedly hedonic or eudaemonic, nor as ethical simply because externally related to the moral law, but, for example, as what Paul has in mind and in heart when he writes to the Romans of "the newness of life"

(Romans 6:4). We shall discover another example, one that interferes with exemplarity. In the meantime we must stay a while longer with the thought that for Kant the highest nobility of which human beings are capable is dignity defined by respect for the moral law, the dignity of what he calls personality.

Kant struggles to explain what he means by personality. Having equated personality with freedom, with independence from the mechanism of nature and with being subject to pure practical laws given by reason, he goes on immediately to write of the person (*Person*) as belonging to the sensible world. He would have done better to write here of the human being (*Mensch*) as belonging to that world and to the intelligible world. For, he observes, we justly attribute personality not only to human beings but also to the divine will. Furthermore, "This respect-arousing idea of personality which sets before our eyes the sublimity of our nature (in its [higher] vocation), while at the same time it shows us the want of accord of our conduct with it, and thereby strikes down self-conceit, is even natural to and easily observed by the most common human reason."[6] Sublime (*erhaben*), of noble (*edel*) descent, holy (*heilig*), and inviolate (*unverletzt*), this idea is yet open to the most common human reason. It is openness itself. It is most easily observed, quite familiar to us all from our refraining from deeds that would lead us to be ashamed of ourselves when we look into ourselves secretly (*insgeheim*). When one thus refrains from such deeds as would lead one to despise oneself (*sich verachten*) privily, there is nothing to be kept to oneself. Everything may be revealed in the light of the sun, indeed is so revealed because the source of our behavior has been the sun itself, that is to say, reason. If there remains anything at all that we could call inward, it is the above-mentioned inward peace. But if this inward peace ensues upon our refraining from deeds that would cause inward war, that is, the conflict with ourselves manifested by a troubled conscience, and if that inward war is something to which the most common human reason is open, then so too must be that inward peace. There is no requirement to keep silent about it.

## Secrecy

Now this pacific aspect of ethical life, understanding ethical life in the relational sense explained earlier, seems to vanish when one turns to the ethical as described by Levinas and to what for the time being we had better call the "ethical" as described by the writers we should in strictness call "Kierkegaard" and "Derrida." Scare-quotes (fear and trembling-quotes?) are in place with the first of these names because the writing from among the works attributed to

Kierkegaard that we are about to cite is attributed by him to one Johannes de silentio (or, louder and in the typography of the text, Silentio or, still louder, SILENTIO). We shall be citing also Derrida's treatment of that work in *The Gift of Death,* where it is often difficult to distinguish what is there offered as a reading of that work from what, if anything, is offered as an endorsement and from what, if anything, may be offered as Derrida's own "position." If Derrida has a "position" it is the proposition that we are inclined to be too confident that we understand what it is to take up a position. Even so, any quotation marks that may seem required for his or Kierkegaard's names will be inserted silently in the present chapter from here on. The reason for wanting to put quotation marks around the word "ethical" or the word "ethics" when we wish to refer to what Kierkegaard means by them is that he himself and his pseudonymous authors usually use these words of, for example, what Kant and Hegel call *Moralität* and what Hegel calls *Sittlichkeit* or *Sitten,* in opposition to what Kierkegaard calls religion or religiousness. But we are going to be referring again also to Levinas, and for him the ethical already has what he is willing to call a religious dimension, as it has too for Derrida. Derrida brings out how Kierkegaard's own construal of Abraham's offer of his only promised son Isaac as sacrifice requires indeed a *con-*strual of ethics and religion at one moment—or in one and the same instant, as Derrida sometimes prefers to say in order to keep a connection with the idea of a tribunal which the French "*instant*" conveys. Similarly, we read in one of Levinas's short pieces on Kierkegaard that, instead of limiting the ethical to the general, Kierkegaard should have perceived that singularity is a moment of the ethical in that I am uniquely responsible for the other human being to whom I respond. This is my secret, Levinas adds, and its secrecy is neither, on the one hand, the secrecy of the Kantian good or bad moral conscience that can be made public in the general terms of linguistic communication, nor, on the other hand, the secrecy of the meeting between God and the human individual anxious for the salvation of his soul, the human individual named Søren Kierkegaard, for example, who is not, however, only an example. The secrecy of the uniquely responsible self is neither the pseudo-secrecy of general ethics nor that of the inwardness of religion as opposed to ethics. It is a secrecy of an ethics in which the priority attributed to the free will of the ego in Kantian ethics and to passionate subjectivity in Kierkegaardian religion gets shifted to the other human being. This priority of the other human being over me is not a hierarchical dependency like that of master and slave, no matter in which direction the order of dependency be taken to hold. The relation is not one of power. Although it is one of service, service is not slavery. And in this service I not only answer *to* the other human being, but answer *for* him or her. And the *to whom* and the *for whom* coincide.[7] This is to be understood literally. The vulnerability of other human beings is clamant. It claims my assistance. And, although I may fail to do anything in response to that call, I have already responded prior to hearing it. Unspoken although that minimal response may be, I find myself to have already addressed the other who addresses, notwithstanding that my having addressed the other is, paradoxically, my having responded. What Heidegger calls *Befindlichkeit*, understood by him as an existential way of being with reference primarily to one's finding oneself with a past of which one has to take charge, gets interpreted by Levinas as finding myself (*mich befinden*) already bound by ethical responsibility simply because I am what Aristotle calls an animal endowed with language. Here, however, the finding is less like the finding of evidence than the finding pronounced by a judge or jury in a court of law, but it is also unlike this. And here language is not just the linguistic system, the *langue* over which I exercise some mastery. Nor is it the act of speech, *parole,* in which that competence is exercised. It is what both of these presuppose yet without being able to pose anything, even in the form of a question. It is the pluperfect a priori posteriority of my having found myself to be already a respondent, one who says "Here I am," "*Hineni.*" This is why Levinas writes that language is already justice.[8] Here "language" translates not *langue,* but *langage* and discourse, which imply address. But his reference to justice implies that more than one single other is involved in this pre-original drama. Less obviously perhaps, this is an implication of the assertion that in responding to the other I am responsible for the other, an assertion invoked above to exclude the inference that I am subordinated to the other as a slave to a master or (allowing for the complexity of this relationship insisted upon by Hegel) as a master to a slave. That inference is excluded because, if we may express the call of the other to me as the command "Thou shalt not kill," I am responsible for that command in the sense that I command the other to address that command to other others, not only to me. As Levinas says, from the face of the other I am looked at by the other other too.

This is where ethics comes upon a difficulty at least as great as the difficulty of Christianity which Kierkegaard emphasizes and indeed welcomes, the difficulty that the story of Abraham and Isaac is intended to bring out. What Levinas proposes is that the difficulty Kierkegaard locates specifically in Judeo-Christianity is mislocated. The difficulty already intrudes in an ethics that is an ethics not of the first person singular, but of the other human being. It already intrudes there because the humanism of the ethics of the other human being is a humanism of the ethics of the other other. Whether in some sense the otherness of the other other is nevertheless haunted by the specter of God is a question to which Derrida's reading of Kierkegaard's account of the events on Mount Moriah will compel us to return. Let us stay for a while longer with Levinas's account of those events and its difference from Kierkegaard's.

Kierkegaard puts "God above the ethical order!" Levinas writes, adding an exclamation mark to indicate his astonishment.[9] He expresses astonishment too at the fact that Abraham was willing to obey God's call to him to sacrifice Isaac. Still, the key to the story is that Abraham kept himself "at a sufficient distance from this obedience to hear the second call," the call from the angel of the Lord commanding Abraham to stay his hand. That distance marks that Abraham was still hearing the voice of ethics even in the very instant that he heard the voice of God commanding "a teleological suspension of the ethical." The distance is that of the secrecy of ethics, the separateness that prevents all fusion, including even the mystical mingling with God that is prevented, we are told, by the reading of the Torah, not least of the account given in it of what happens after Abraham has said "*Hineni*" to the Almighty. That is a secret which is put at a distance, set apart, *secretus*—from "*se-cerno*," where "*cerno*" has the same root as "*krinō*," to decide, pick out, elect. There is a distancing already in Abraham's being elected by God and in one human being's being singled out by the appeal of another human being. There is a second distancing in that my responsibility cannot justly be limited to one other, and this plurality reflects and is reflected in the generality of language and in the generality of Kantian or Hegelian ethics, where secrecy is not absolute but temporary. A third distancing is that of this second distancing thanks to the first, that is to say, as Levinas says, the distancing of what is conceived, propounded, and said by the inconceivable, unproponible, face-to-face saying of "Here I am."

The ethical as understood by Levinas requires all three of these distancings. Kantian and Hegelian ethics limp because they are supported only by universality and generality. Kierkegaard lets the Kantian and Hegelian schemes dictate what is to be understood by ethics. Given that Kierkegaard shares this conception of an ethics founded on the principle of universal justice, it is all the more surprising to Levinas that he makes no mention of Abraham's intercession on behalf of the just citizens of Sodom and Gomorrah. At the risk of provoking the wrath of the Lord, Abraham, who declares himself to be "but dust and ashes" (Genesis 18:27), as though imagining himself "a burnt offering in the stead of his son" and in the stead of the ram (Genesis 22:13), pleads again and again that none of the citizens should be slain if that means that death is inflicted too on the righteous, whether there be fifty of them, forty-five, thirty, twenty, or ten—or indeed one single one, or six million. Here is confirmation of Abraham's unwillingness to let the demands of ethical justice be overridden by God's will. It is as though nothing more shocking could be conceived by Abraham than a course of events fitting Wilfred Owen's description of what took place on Moriah or elsewhere.

> So Abram rose, and clave the wood, and went,
> And took the fire with him, and a knife,

> And as they sojourned both of them together,
> Isaac the first-born spake and said, My Father,
> Behold the preparations, fire and iron,
> But where the lamb, for this burnt-offering?
> Then Abram bound the youth with belts and straps,
> And builded parapets and trenches there,
> And stretchèd forth the knife to slay his son.
> When lo! an Angel called him out of heaven,
> Saying, Lay not thy hand upon the lad,
> Neither do anything to him, thy son.
> Behold! Caught in a thicket by its horns,
> A Ram. Offer the Ram of Pride instead.
>
> But the old man would not so, but slew his son,
> And half the seed of Europe, one by one.[10]

We say that nothing more shocking could be conceived. But we have also said that what can be conceived belongs to that part of ethics ordered by law and the universalizability of maxims. And we have said that there belongs to ethics another part, though the words "belongs" and "part" are not quite at home in this context, any more than are "at home" and "context." For what in ethics exceeds universality and conceptuality also exceeds context, disrupts belonging, renders the home unhomely and interrupts the opposition of wholes and parts, imparting a fresh force to participation, *methexis*. It is precisely the moment of not being at home. It is, Kierkegaard, Levinas, and Derrida would agree, the moment of the absolute secrecy of the secret that is not a secret one keeps to oneself but that could, if one wished, be divulged. It is rather the moment of the secret that cannot be communicated even to oneself, *methexis* being a kind of communication, a communication of kind, kinship, commonality. Absolute secrecy is absolute in the sense of unbound, absolved, *ab-solutus,* yet with an un-boundedness that binds me as singular self to the singular other. This disconnection in my proximity to the neighbor is a separateness in the sense of *se-paratus,* the preparedness of the self to assist the neighbor, though a preparedness that is never sufficient and yet is over-prepared if it is not taken by surprise. This separateness is also the dis-creteness of the secret to which reference has already been made, and so the discreteness of *krinō,* which, we have said, is decision or election, and which, we can now add, is also critique.

For Kant, critique, as in the title and text of his three Critiques, is determination of the scope and limits of the powers of the mind, specifically the powers of pure reason, pure practical reason, and aesthetic and teleological judgment. Kierkegaard, Levinas, and Derrida are much concerned with critique in this sense. They are concerned because they suspect that beneath the powers of the mind mapped by that critique is an impower that one might therefore call hypocritical and hypoCritical. One could just as well call it hypercritical and hyperCritical, for this im-possibility or un-possibility before possibility is as much above as it is below the critical. The way the below and the above are construed as simple opposites is to be reconstrued. That oppositional structure is destructured here. It deconstrues itself, as too does the simple opposition of inside and outside when this is applied to the relation between the critical and the hypo-hypercritical. These distinctions tremble. And this is the trembling that is exemplified in the moment of tremendous decision that faces Abraham. Tremendous. That is to say, causing one to tremble. And monstrous. These are the epithets employed by Derrida. Yet, he goes on to ask rhetorically, employing words that echo Kant's comment on the sublimity that is yet natural to the commonest reason, is not this *mysterium tremendum* the commonest thing?[11] "Abraham is a murderer. However, is it not true that the spectacle of this murder, which seems intolerable in the denseness and rhythm of its theatricality, is at the same time the most common event in the world?"[12] Is Abraham a murderer? He does not kill his son. But in *The Gift of Death* the events recounted in the Hebrew Bible are being examined through the lens of what Christians call the Old Testament. Derrida's scrutiny is guided if not led by the questions—some of them leading questions, some of them rhetorical questions, perhaps therefore ironical questions—that are raised in the essay that is its point of departure, the essay whose title puts the question "Is Technological Civilization in Decline, and If So Why?" published in a collection of essays by Jan Patočka entitled *Heretical Essays on the Philosophy of History*.[13] The essay is an essay in the philosophy of history, specifically the history of religiousness, combined with a genealogy of responsibility from orgiastic religions through Platonism and Neoplatonism to Christianity. It treats therefore principally of Europe, the Europe that is named in the final line of Wilfred Owen's interpretation of Abraham's trial, the trial to which Kierkegaard appeals in support of his "hard" interpretation of Christianity. Now further support for such an interpretation is provided by Christ's hard saying on another mount—unless it too was Mount Moriah (we are not told): "Ye have heard that it was said by them of old time, Thou shalt not commit adultery. But I say unto you, That whosoever looketh on a woman to lust after her hath committed adultery with her already in his heart" (Matthew 5:27, 28). Applied to the story of what took place on Mount Moriah in the old time it follows that Abraham was indeed a murderer, a murderer at least in his heart. And, with its secret Pascalian and here paschal reasons that reason cannot know, it is the heart that matters for Christianity, it would seem, and for the exposition of it offered by Kierkegaard.

This is where we find ourselves at the crux. At a crossroad between a Christian ethics based on love of the neighbor and an ethics based on justice, how many roads intersect? Assuming that it is not a contradiction in terms to speak of a Christian ethics, as it would be in Kierkegaard's strict terms, is it because love is its ground that ethics is so hard, or is an ethics grounded in justice equally difficult? Are we between a rock (Peter) and a hard place?

Kantian ethics is not one based on love if love is understood as some kind of passion rather than as the principle of what Kant means by practical love, which would appear to mean little more than the nearly or totally tautological precept that one should cash one's moral principles in practice. Remember Kant's assertion that when one does this one experiences inward peace. This remark could lead us to wonder whether Kant's ethics, "rigorist" though it may be, admits no space for the aporetic hardness of ethical or ethico-religious decision stressed by Kierkegaard, Levinas, and Derrida. We have still not quite got hold of the nature of this difficulty. However, assuming that it will not escape more rapidly between our fingers the tighter we grasp it, our understanding of it may be increased if we ask whether even Kantian ethics is as pacific as it may at first seem. Let it not be forgotten that the categorical imperativity of the categorical imperative itself is an expression of the painful conflict between the rational will to act morally and the natural desire to do what brings us pleasure. Might there nevertheless be ground in Kantian ethics for suffering not just because of this war between sensible and rational motivation, but also where rational motivation alone is taken into account? Consider again what Kant calls imperfect duties. These are duties where the maxim does not cover the time, place, extent and target of a good deed, such duties as Derrida lists when he writes, first:

> By preferring my work, simply by giving it my attention, by preferring my activity as a citizen or as a professorial and professional philosopher, writing and speaking here in a public language, French in my case, I am perhaps fulfilling my duty. But I am sacrificing and betraying at every moment all my other obligations: my obligations to the others whom I know or don't know, the billions of my fellows, my fellows who are dying of starvation and sickness (not to mention the animals that are even more other others than my fellows).[14]

Then, inversely, two pages later:

> How would you ever justify the fact that you sacrifice all the cats in the world to the cat that you feed at home every morning for years, whereas other cats die of hunger at every instant? Not to mention other people?[15]

Apart from the need to make minor adjustments like that of substituting "German" for "French" and a more material adjustment to accommodate Kant's view that our duties to animals and our duties to other human beings are not on a par, could Kant endorse what Derrida says here? Kant would agree that indeed you cannot justify what in each of these passages is called the sacrifice of one obligation to another. His reason for agreeing would be that there is room for neither justice nor injustice where the decision is as to the time, place, extent, and target of the deed that fulfils an imperfect obligation. Our being bound not to perform an imperfectly obligatory deed to some persons is, given human finitude, entailed by our being bound to perform a particular imperfectly obligatory deed to one person. Kant could say that our non-performance is covered by the non-coverage that distinguishes an imperfect from a perfect obligation. But would "covered" here mean excused? That would imply fault. Where would this fault lie? Would it be a fault of the agent? If not, there is nothing for which he or she may be excused. If there is fault it would seem to be a fault in the nature of things, a non-moral lack of good or bad luck arising from human finitude—for instance our not having enough money to contribute to all the charities whose requests for support arrive in our mail boxes every week. This seems less like an ethical shortcoming than an ontical one, or like an ontological or logical or perhaps theological fact, so that if anyone is to blame it is God, because he made the world and he made it out of joint, quirky.

It should not be overlooked that if a shortcoming of some sort, whether it be ethical or factical, is entailed by this open-texturedness of imperfect obligations, the shortcoming remains even when the way we meet such obligations is co-determined by special obligations we may be under on account, say, of our belonging to a certain family or team or nation. Such belonging introduces the possibility of our being under perfect obligations to a group, but it does not necessarily decide for us which members of the group are to be the targets of imperfectly obligatory deeds, not to mention the possibility that, unless Kant's rigorous doctrine of perfect obligations is valid, we may justly decide not to perform a particular perfect obligation in order to perform an imperfect one. Perfect obligations do not necessarily "trump" imperfect ones. For good or ill, where an imperfect obligation competes with a perfect one answers to ethical questions are not foreordained in the way that a rule of a game may decide for me what move I should make. A fortiori, the question remains open whether we can justify ethically a decision to address our imperfectly obligatory actions in this direction rather than that. Do those whom our decision excludes from receiving the benefit of our good will have a ground for complaint? Do we have a derivative obligation to make reparation to these excluded parties? Suppose we grant that the treasurer of Oxfam were justified in thinking it would not be fair for you to exclude that charity from a long list of charities to which you subscribe. There will be good causes of which you are in no position to know and of which you could not reasonably be expected to have heard, not to mention those that do not yet exist. There is no principle according to which your not subscribing to them is unjust. And if ethical justifications are ones that appeal to principles, as Kant and Kierkegaard believe they do, no ethical justification for your preferences here is available. So if the thought of those whose good is sacrificed by our preferences prevents our experiencing the inward peace of which Kant writes in the *Critique of Practical Reason* and if that thought brings inward anguish instead, this anguish cannot be an experience of ethical conscience if the ethical is understood in the strict way in which it is understood by Kierkegaard and Kant.

This hyper-ethical anguish is certainly non-rational if rationality is defined as the (doubly genitive) invocation of law. But is this anguish irrational? I may be my brother's keeper, and my sister's and my son's, not to mention my dog's or my cat's, but to suppose that I am everybody's keeper, Hecuba's included, is to suppose that I am God. So why do I fret? Why do we all, or at least many of us some of the time? As Derrida asks rhetorically, is this not the most common thing? Yet he also says that the structure of this ordinary circumstance is no different from that of the "extraordinary," "monstrous," and "tremendous" predicament of Abraham. The adjectives here are Derrida's. The noun is not. It must be replaced if we are to remain faithful to a reference he makes to Gabriel Marcel's distinction between a problem and a mystery.[16] "A mystery is a problem which encroaches upon its own data and invades them, and so is transcended *qua* problem."[17] A problem has a solution, even if the solution is tragic in the way of Greek tragedy as read by Kierkegaard in accordance with his understanding of ethics. The structure of tragedy, like the structure of ethics thus understood, is defined by principles. The hierarchical ordering of these would allow for a resolution of an apparent conflict by appeal to a higher principle and a wider view, in the manner, for example, of Hegelian dialectic and of Christianity interpreted along Hegelian or similar lines. A mystery allows for no such solution. In case the word "predicament" just used conveys the idea of a problem, the situation in which Abraham and Isaac find themselves should be described as a mystery in the sense Marcel gives to this word, as a difficulty in the sense Levinas gives to the word "difficult" in the title of his book *Difficult Freedom,* or as an aporia, as in the title of Derrida's book *Aporias,* an aporia such as will be the cause of some personal anguish to me when I move from chapter 13 to chapter 14.

Of the aporia confronting Abraham on Moriah Derrida writes that it possesses "the very structure of what occurs every day."[18] The word "structure" will lead his reader to expect that a destructuring or deconstruction is imminent. What is de-con-structed now is the simple opposition of the ethical and, if you wish, the religious. This is not necessarily the simple opposition of the ethical and God, though Derrida does not wish to close off that option. On two occasions in the course of *The Gift of Death* the phrase "absolute other" is used in apposition to the phrase "God, if you wish," "*Dieu, si l'on veut.*" The opposition between the ethical and God or their respective specters must be kept on stage in this drama since it is the opposition opted for in Kierkegaard's version of the story of what happened on Moriah that is de-con-structed in Derrida's text. It is the opposition whose terms are untied from each other, (de-) and re-tied (con-) to each other otherwise. That is the opposition whose terms turn out not to be terms; they suffer de-termination. This last word is one we have two good reasons to use: it is, to use nomenclature that will be explained further in chapter 11, in Abelian opposition to the word "determination" that is the usual translation for Hegel's "*Bestimmung.*" So it reminds us that Hegel or Hegelianism remains the ultimate addressee of our chapters. Also, it offers an opportunity to rest the quirky quasi-term "deconstruction" from which Derrida longs to get away but to which he finds himself bound by the historical circumstance that it has caught on and come back to haunt him.

Hence the word "God" and with it the word "religion" will no longer mean what they used to mean in the old time, or at least not what they have often been taken to mean. How far away from what they have been taken to mean are they taken already by Kierkegaard? They have been taken some distance from a certain Christian application of the story of the event on Moriah as a "parallel" and anticipation of the story of the event to take place on Golgotha. In what Christians call the Old Testament, Abraham passes a test set by God, and the Heavenly Father gives the son back to the father on earth. In the New Testament God as Christ willingly sacrifices Himself in order that God's children shall be saved. The children's sins are freely forgiven, without their having to pass a test. The children are saved by God's loving grace. However, a sacrificial test would appear to be mentioned in Luke 14:26, verses cited by Kierkegaard,[19] where Jesus is reported as saying: "If any man come to me, and hate not his father, and mother, and wife, and children, and brethren, and sisters, yea, and his own life also, he cannot be my disciple." Some commentators regard this preconditioning hate as "typical Semitic hyperbole"[20] and hurry on to Matthew 10:37, where, instead of saying that we must hate our kin, Jesus says that we must not love them more than we love him. Kierkegaard says that the reference in Luke to hate is a reference to the distinction between human hate and love, and that that is not relevant to Abraham's trial. If we say that as he stretched forth the knife Abraham hated his son, we are speaking the language of ethics. What we say can have nothing to do with absolute duty. Absolute duty demands that as he stretches forth his knife Abraham must love Isaac. Only if his love for his son Isaac is contrasted with Abraham's love for his own Father, Abba, can the deed he is commanded to perform by that Father (and commanded out of that Father's love for him?) be a sacrifice. But Kierkegaard's reading of the preconditioning hate as told in Luke is not a mere softening. The hyperbole, whether Semitic or not, is not so softened that the verses of Luke 14:26 cannot serve as another parallel to the outrageous story narrated in Genesis 22. It continues to exemplify the *paradoxicality* of the life that the knight of faith lives in fear and trembling as against the *tragicality* of the ethical life that would be lived by someone who was required to hate his son by the institutional Church. For Kierkegaard tragicality is a soluble or insoluble problem arising in the general ethics of relativity. Paradoxicality is a necessarily insoluble mystery arising in the absolute religiousness of singularity; as Derrida puts it, one can be forgiven only for what is unforgivable. This is why as Abraham stretches out his hand to sacrifice his son he must love both him and the God who commands the slaughter, and he must be prepared to obey that command without the least thought that God's love for him will provide a ram or scapegoat instead. Once he has hope of being let off the hook the room for forgiving him has contracted. Imagine the unimaginable possibility of the husband of Margaret Hassan forgiving the terrorists who shot her through the head in front of a video camera, notwithstanding her having spent thirty years of her life trying to alleviate the misery of the people of Iraq. As soon as her husband begins to believe there were exonerating circumstances, what happened begins to make sense. It is no longer mad. It is no longer impossible. But it is only the impossible that we can forgive. As Derrida would have said, "Whether he says 'I forgive' or 'I do not forgive,' in either case I am not sure of understanding. I am even sure of not understanding, and in any case I have nothing to say. This zone of experience remains inaccessible, and I must respect its secret."[21]

## Loves

Having spoken so far chiefly of law and justice, we find ourselves now speaking of love. This is not simply because directing our attention on Kierkegaard means directing our attention on the problem or mystery of the hyphenation of Judeo-Christianity, as though that hyphen marked a transition from the topic of law to the topic of love in the history of religiousness and responsibility which Patočka traces from orgiastic religions through Platonism and Neoplatonism to Christianity. It would be unjust to suppose that a transition from law to love is marked by this hyphen—unless this stroke is not a hyphen but a dash, the thought-stroke (*tankestreg*) of which Kierkegaard has delicate things to say in his *Journals and Papers*.[22] One of the laws pre-eminent in this history is the one that prescribes that we love our neighbor as ourselves. And this law is laid down out of love. So with this law the simple opposition between law and love has already been broken down—dashed. Furthermore, this law is proclaimed to the left of the hyphen or dash, that is to say, in the pages of the Hebrew Bible. As we shall find need to re-emphasize again in this book, it would be naive to interpret this stroke as a sign of a clean break between love understood Hebraically as *ahavah* and love understood Christo-Greekly as *agapē*, the love whose bias toward brotherhood gets countervailed in the hints in Derrida's writings of a democracy to come.[23] The Septuagint uses "*agapē*" in preference to "*erōs*" and "*philia*" to translate "*ahavah*." Although the noun "*agapē*" was rare in pre-biblical Greek it sometimes has the sense of erotic religious ecstasy and may have been one of the names of Isis. Against Anders Nygren, who writes that "in Eros and Agape we have two conceptions which have originally nothing to do with one another,"[24] Kenneth Dover refers to an ancient Greek ceramic bearing the image of a half-naked woman and the word "*agapē*."[25] Because erotic love interpreted in this religious sense by Neo-platonism is deemed by Pseudo-Dionysius to be more divine than any sense that he could hear in the word "*agapē*," the word that is preferred in his works is "*erōs*." This erotic sense of love-divine-all-loves-excelling is not one of those carried by the Hebrew word "*ahavah*." This most frequently implies jealous partiality, a connotation of which "*chesed*" is not always free, whether in contexts where it is used of human love for God or of God's love for humankind. By contrast "*agapē*" is much less restricted in this respect, despite the favor it shows to fraternity. "The cosmopolitan Greek loves all the world; the patriotic Israelite his neighbour; the impulse working centrifugally in the one and centripetally in the other."[26] Given the view about the limitations of generality taken in the works of Kierkegaard and more than one Pseudo-Kierkegaard, it is to be expected that he and they would make the most of the new force that the Hebrew word gives to the Greek, leading to an emphasis upon the special relation between God and the singular individual called to the responsibility to which the jealous God had called Israel and Abraham. This is what leads Kierkegaard to emphasize the difficulty of being a knight of Christian faith. The knight of faith has to shoulder a responsibility he cannot share with his neighbor. To appeal to a fellow human being for help is to have recourse to the general terms of language, which, as we have heard Levinas say, is already justice. But if justice is in the realm of the relative responsibilities of ethical or political law, the absolute responsibility to the singular other, Abraham's other other ("God, if you wish"), is betrayed. The knight of faith can be faithful to his absolute and, let us say, religious responsibility only if he betrays his relative ethico-legal-political responsibility. No wonder that the knight of faith's night is without sleep, *søvnløs,* as Kierkegaard writes or silent Johannes in his stead. Kierkegaard is far from silent on the question whether he himself is a knight of faith. He is as scathing toward anyone who might think this as he is to anyone who might mistake him for an apostle. Compare "I am not meet to be called an apostle" (1 Corinthians 15:9). Nevertheless, to all intents and purposes, that is to say, as Kierkegaard says, "teleologically," the plight of the knight of faith Abraham is that of those only on the slopes of the mountain or below in the plain. We too do or should suffer that sleeplessness, the *insomnia* of which Levinas writes. To revert to Derrida's words, the decision Abraham has to make on the top of the mountain is at once monstrous and banal.[27]

Banal? How, for those at the foot of the mountain who do not wish to accept the invitation left open by Derrida's phrase "God, if you wish," can the story of Abraham be banal? How can it even possess the same structure as what is banal? These are not two ways of putting the same question. The difference between them reflects the distinction just made between "be" and "should." Being banal means that we do commonly experience the sleeplessness of which Kierkegaard and Levinas write, whereas the story of Abraham having the same structure as the banal might not be enough to imply that we commonly experience sleeplessness. We may be too complacent or self-centered to do so. These again are not two ways of saying the same thing. We can be complacent without being self-centered. And there are at least two ways of being self-centered. When reading Kierkegaard one can all too easily get the impression that although he is far from complacent, his seriousness is focused relentlessly on his self. The term "narcissism" comes to mind again. One of the contributions Levinas and Derrida make to our reading of Kierkegaard is to bring out that there is more than one kind of "what is so calmly called narcissism."[28] "*Il n'y a pas le narcissisme*," says Derrida.[29] Why not? Because "what is called non-narcissism is generally a narcissism that is more welcoming, hospitable and open to the experience of the other as other."[30] It was noted in the previous chapter that Kierkegaard likes to use the word "*confinium*" for a border category like "interesting" because, as with the "inter" of "interesting," its first syllable indicates a duplicity or multiplicity. Derrida uses the same word in an apocalyptic footnote in pages of *Le toucher* treating of what Levinas has to say of the tangency of the caress. Without wishing to put words into Levinas's mouth, he says, "I admit to being tempted by the inadmissible temptation to go as far as to say not only that the caress touches or borders on (*confine*) the messianic, but that it is the only experience capable, possible, significant for the surfacing (*affleurement*) of the messianic. The messianic can only be caressed."[31] The messianic touches on without touching the always ever more future never-to-be-possessed outcome of love parsed as erotic femininity. As, perhaps, the femininity of Sarah or Hagar vis-à-vis Abraham, which might lead to the fulfillment of the promise of sons, namely Ishmael, Isaac, and their descendents. This thought of other others beyond the face to face with the other is certainly close to the surface in the section of *Totality and Infinity* that is concerned with fecundity and filiation beyond the death of the father. But in the first chapter of that section it is to a Greek myth that reference is made to illustrate the ambiguity of love. It also illustrates a narcissism, a narcissism which, notwithstanding the opening out of the future and "the welcome of the other, hospitality—Desire and language (*langage*)," goes both further than and not so far as language, as though there were a silence and secrecy of both transcendence and immanence. Derrida cites Levinas's words here at length, among them the statement that

> [l]ove as a relation with the Other can be reduced to this fundamental immanence, be divested of all transcendence, seek but a connatural being, a sister soul, present itself as incest. The myth Aristophanes recounts in Plato's *Symposium*, in which love reunites the two halves of one being, interprets the adventure as a return to self. This desire—a movement ceaselessly cast forth (*relancé*), an interminable movement toward a future never future enough—is broken and satisfied as the most egoist and cruellest of needs.[32]

Dissymmetrical though the relation to the other may be, however separated and secret(ed) the other may be in her or his proximity, no matter what priority I accord to the other's death over my own, if I love the other there remains an element of appropriation in that love, of incorporation which is a moment of mourning even when the loved one is still alive. Even when the loved one is before my eyes. This is a description of a gravity without grace on the edge of the grave, *la pesanteur sans la grâce*, Derrida says, to be distinguished from the prescription and self-addressed me-mor-andum delivered by Simone Weil when in *La pesanteur et la grâce* she enjoins us and herself "[n]ever to think of a thing or being we love but have not actually before our eyes without reflecting that perhaps this thing has been destroyed, or this person is dead."[33] As though the heaviness of the being with child experienced by a mother (for instance the several mothers to be mentioned later in this book) anticipated the near unbearableness of the mortality of the child to which she is hostess. Love and the hospitality it implies are testamentary. But just as the mortality of the other can find itself embraced by my mortality, as though it were interior to my *Sein zum Tode,* so hospitality is hospitality to oneself even when it is hospitality to the other. This shows itself in what is called by Levinas love's ambiguity and by Jean-Luc Marion love's aporia, citing (from the same page of *Totality and Infinity* as that from which Derrida cites) Levinas's statement that "by an essential aspect love, which as transcendence goes unto the Other, throws us back this side of immanence itself: it designates a movement by which a being seeks that to which it was bound before even having taken the initiative of the search and despite the exteriority in which it finds it."[34] Is this aporia, ambiguity, or *equivocation,* as Levinas says in italics, a tension between the call to transcendence and a recall to immanence, or is it rather a tension between the call to transcendence and what is "this side of" immanence? Perhaps a "fundamental (*foncière*) immanence" is this side of a non-fundamental immanence. Perhaps it is fundamental not only in the sense of basic, but in the sense of base, in the sense of that low condition of nameless because prelinguistic impersonality for which Levinas contrives a pseudo-nominalization of the phrase "*il y a*," the there-is or, we could say, ilyaity. Ilyaity always threatens to become confused with illeity, the pseudonym, formed from the pronoun "*ille*," that Levinas invents for a certain masculinely marked structure of being ethico-religiously possessed and obsessed, to which a person may transcend from the neuterly marked impersonality of the there-is via a femininely marked moment of erotic love which is not possessive but which intimates a not-yet, a future, an *avenir*, a to-come and to-be-welcomed: a messianicity, as Derrida dares to say, but a messianicity without messianism and Messiah because it is without expectation; because it comes—yet never comes, because it keeps on coming—as an absolute surprise.[35]

So it does not come as a surprise to learn that the equivocity of transcendence and immanence is an equivocity of welcome and hospitality.[36] It is marked by the idiosyncrasy of the French word "*hôte*," which means guest or host or both. Abraham is God's guest, welcomed into the land (*eretz*) which is God's (Leviticus 25:23). God is Abraham's host. God is also his *hostis*, his enemy, whether or not this relationship has an etymological backing.[37] And, whether with etymological backing or not, Levinas would say that Abraham as guest, *hôte*, is hostage of God, no less than Isaac is hostage of Abraham. Since there is an etymological connection between "hostage," that is to say "sacrificial victim," and "*hostie*," that is to say the bread taken into one's mouth in the Mass, could we say that ethical responsibility requires me to take that bread out of my mouth and give it to another? Levinas might not wish to say this, but he is the one who writes of the duty to give to the other the bread from one's own mouth, and the paragraph in which he does this begins "*Sous les espèces de la corporéité*," which is the language of the species of the Eucharist, the hyphenated bread-body and wine-blood.[38]

Quite generally, but at the same time singularly and singly, whether it be to my neighbor or to an absolute stranger that I extend hospitality, the guest is my persecutor. He or she charges me with not being as welcoming as I could be. And as I could *not* be. For the other speaks not only on behalf of himself but on behalf too of the other other, the second and the third and the nth other, who is left out in the cold precisely by my having invited the first other in. It is not only prescribed that we love the neighbor or the stranger or the enemy. In loving the neighbor we *do* love an enemy. An ethical aporia is here being described. Being described here too is the aporia that in loving that enemy we love ourselves as enemy. For, as Heidegger puts it, the call of conscience comes as though from yonder beyond us, but, transcendently immanent, it comes at the same time from within.[39] The call is the call of the other secretly in me. Too close for comfort. Here is a narcissism rather different from what conventionally goes under that name, a narcissism where autonomy does not exclude ethico-religious heteronomy.[40] If that is what we ordinarily call the voice of conscience, it is banal in every sense of the word, that is to say, it is the ban, the interdict, the anathema, or the curse that one addresses to oneself every day. As though, in the senses not only Levinas gives to the words, the holy (*saint*), the separate (*kadosh*), were not entirely separate from its not quite so pure partner, the sacred (*sacré*)? As though, "Oh cursed spight," the one were haunted by the other? As though in order to be fair one may have to dirty one's hands?

## God, If You Wish

What could it mean to say of a heteronomy that it is ethico-religious? Once again everything turns on the connection-disconnection marked by a hyphen or dash—*between* the ethical and the religious, but also *in* the ethical and the religious. The connectedness of being reciprocally together in proximity with others under laws defining an ethical system in which, as in any linguistic system, a signifier stands for a signified meaning or referent, is made to tremble by the separation of the singular human being dissymmetrically offering itself as a stand-in for another singular human being. Human? Or divine? Not to mention animal. In the story of the very old man, the young man, God, and the ram as told by Wilfred Owen, the animal is spared (though not the horses that hauled the guns through the mud of Passchendaele, the valley of the shadow of passion and passover). In the story of Abraham and Ishmael or Isaac and the other others as told in the Koran, the son is not kept in ignorance of what is being planned for him. There is what sounds like an *exchange* of words between the father and the son. The father said "O my son! I see in a vision that I offer thee in sacrifice: Now see what is thy view!" (The son) said: "O my father! Do as thou art commanded: Thou wilt find me, if God so wills, one practising patience and constancy!" (XXXVII, 102). But the next verse says that they "both submitted their wills (to God)." If there is an exchange between the father and the son, there is no exchange between them and God. God has the first word in the vision or dream, and he has the last word in that everything depends on whether Allâh is willing. So a non-exchange is secreted away in the exchange between father and son. This non-exchange remains to haunt the exchange of the ram for the son, which stands for the exchange of a reward in return for Abraham's willingness to submit his will to God's. Despite the fact that in the story as told in Genesis the son is not privy to the threat to his life, whereas in the account in the Koran he is, in both accounts it is Abraham's willingness to submit that is singled out as that for which the saving is exchanged in return. The priviness here is a publicness that retains the privacy of the unspeakable. The threat to the son here is at the same time a promise insofar as the son wills that God's will be done (so that the Koranic version of Abraham's offer of his son is in this respect more like what took place on Golgotha than the version of it given in the Hebrew Bible). The threat to the son is a threat ethically, but a promise religiously. It is not a promise ethically as ethics is understood by Kant, for in Kantian ethics that would be to commit one to a perfect obligation. It is, however, both a threat and a promise if, despite Kierkegaard's critical separation of the ethical from the religious, the religious is the separateness of one single person from another that disturbs the balanced economy of the law, the separateness that for Levinas and for Hebrew means the holy, the *kadosh*.

This holiness is what gives life to what Kant and Kierkegaard call ethics. But is that life to be understood in the way Christianity, say, reads the story of Abraham and Isaac, as doubly the life that must be lost for the sake of an upper-case Son and Father in order that the life of a lower-case son and father shall be saved (Matthew 10:39)? In *Being and Time* Heidegger describes ontological structures that are made concrete in ontic ethics and religion, including Judeo-Christian religion as he finds it described in Kierkegaard. Derrida and Levinas decipher in Kierkegaard's description of that religion clues to a destructuring of that ontology that is not limited to one or other of the manifold moralities or religions, whether theistic or not, past, present, or to come. Kierkegaard introduces us, Levinas says, reflexively, to "a new modality of truth" that is "truly the translation of an epoch that has lost confidence in the historic authenticity of the Scriptures without losing the possibility of hearing through them a voice that comes from yonder (*de là-bas*)."[41] If this new modality of Kierkegaard's is not, as Levinas writes, "a pure invention of philosophy," the word "*illéité*" that Levinas invents is not a pure invention of philosophy either. This is because philosophy is foreign to itself in a way that allows illeity to be no more cut off from philosophy, from Greece, than religion is cut off from the ethical. "Illeity" is a word that could have come from Latin, the next philosophical and legal language to come on the Western scene. The word "*illeitas*" will not be found in Lewis and Short or any other Latin dictionary, but it is rumored there, as already indicated, in "*ille*," he, and "*illic*," yonder. Call it the remote third-personality of God, if you wish, but it allows you to wish otherwise. As does the verse that follows immediately on the one cited a while ago from Matthew 10. There Christ is said to say, "He that receiveth you receiveth me . . ." True, he goes on to say "and he that receiveth me receiveth him that sent me." We can take that to be a reference to God, but according to the readings of Kierkegaard that have been the texts of this chapter, and hearing this time with Derrida a fresh rumor coming from the same dead language, he, *ille-illic,* that sent me could be read, not necessarily as God, but as, if you wish, the wholly hostipi-table other.

# THREE

# Philosophical Fragments

## Savings

The subtitle of the French paperback edition of Derrida's *Glas* reads: "*ce qui reste du savoir absolu,*" that is to say, "what is left *over from* or *of* absolute wisdom." What *Smuler,* what fragments, crumbs, scraps, scrapings, shavings, undigested little bits, what *petits carrés* are saved? And the digestive system itself, what Climacus calls "the hungry monster of the world-historical process,"[1] can that be saved?

This chapter is concerned with the saving of the system, the saving of the self, the saving of the other, the saving of God and the saving of the world. Nothing less. These savings are not all independent of each other. For some of them admit more than one answer to the question "Saving from what?" Sometimes the answer will be suffering. Sometimes the answer will be sin or the combination of suffering and sin called damnation and hellfire. Sometimes the answer will be, almost tautologously, loss or perdition. For this reason, and because the "of" in the case of at least some of these savings records a double genitive, it is not clear whether we are concerned here with five sorts of saving or more or less than five. Here counting—even if counting only to three, as, in memory of the trinitarian dialectic, Kierkegaard counts in the *Concluding Unscientific Postscript,* borrowing Hegel's German, *eins, zwei, drei*—is very,

very, very difficult. It calls for an alternative system of arithmetic or/and an alternative arithmetic of system, perhaps for system and quantification to be left behind without remainder, in what Kierkegaard calls a qualitative leap, the leap he hopes will secure what concerns him most passionately, individually, and existentially, Søren's eternal salvation.

Let us begin, however, with the salvation and saving spelled with upper case SA, as SAving, the SAving of *Savoir Absolu* or *SAgesse* as this is announced in the first of the three fragments quoted in the unbook *Glas* from the *Postscript* to the unbook *Philosophical Fragments or a Fragment of Philosophy,* which is also a fragmentation of philosophy, again in both senses, subjective and objective, of the "of."[2] If we are to conduct our investigation with scholarly responsibility we should take care to keep quotations in quotation marks. In the case of quotations in *Glas* from the writings attributed to Kierkegaard we have to be especially careful to remember that these writings are also attributed to one (or two) Johannes Climacus, though on the title page one (or more) S. Kierkegaard acknowledges responsibility for having the books published. When to or from this layering we add or subtract the fact that the quotations are quoted in another polynymous text, it becomes still more difficult to know how many embeddings of quotation marks are called for, how many levels of reading. Like the reflection these writers request us to perform, is the reading we are called on to do here double? Or must it be multiple? And would the multiplication be one that is marked by the sign of the cross of Judeo-Christian Golgotha, by the dialectical cross of qualitative opposites which, like crossed bayonets, prevents all access to an inner sanctum,[3] or would the multiplication be one that is marked by the asymmetrical crux of the Greek letter χ, a multiplication that is not one, not quite, because its time and its number, its *ruthmos* and its *arithmos,* are or is neither simply one nor simply more than one? Here it is not the case that, as the rhyme reassuringly says, one is one and all alone and evermore shall be so. As S. Kierkegaard, "S. Kierkegaard," or some of his pseudonymous authors would say, I cannot pretend to help you here. I can only decide for myself. And after reading Derrida, it is not certain what could be meant by deciding here today, and whether it would mean the same as deciding there and then in the context of a certain uncertain Søren/Johannes Climacus or that other terrifying John, Johannes de silentio, not to mention the John who wrote "When they were filled, he said unto his disciples, Gather up the fragments that remain that nothing be lost" (John 6:12)—*ta perisseusanta klasmata,* the broken pieces distributed among many recipients like what logicians call token-reflexives or occasional expressions or shifters, like "this," and "my" in the statements "This is my blood," the blood of which a sip makes one one with the Christian community, and "This is my body," the body of which each piece is a whole but broken body to consume which is to be consummated, summed up, made whole, healthy and safe. But what sort of safety is at stake here? With what sort of certainty can one stake something or someone on the cross? Apparently with an unsortal sort of certainty, one that is out of sorts, absurd, *ineptus,* as Tertullian says, that is to say, out of place, out of joint, as another Dane, a prince of Denmark, cited by Derrida in *Specters of Marx,* would say.[4] Something more than this may be said in the light of what is said at p. 66a [78a] of *Glas* concerning the "something more" that takes place, namely the copulation and division (*Ur-teil*) of a judgment (*Urteil*) which reclassifies and reglassifies, identifying one species with another, when the hospitality of the shared meal to which the Arab invites his guest gives way to the eating of the host by the Christian guest. In both cases the sign and its signifier (*signifiant, SA*) are gulped down. However, in the case of the eating of the host there takes place also something more or something less than the "something more" that is judgment: something or some unthing that is *hupo-ousios,* sub-substantial, sub-transubstantial, hypocritical, where the hypocrisy is de-cission before decision, undercutting before cutting (*krinein*), the hypocrisy on which depends the utmost sincerity of any speech act (SA).[5]

But we are talking too soon of decision. The tempo of our discussion is out of joint. One is being too precipitate, as Derrida often remarks of those in whose margins he is writing, of what he is writing there, or of what he is saying in an interview when he is tempted to try to save time by talking even more quickly because he hears the cassette tape accelerating to its end.

## No Time to Waste

(Note, parenthetically, *ergo* "at the risk of cutting the connection between things,"[6] that the topic of the tempo of reading which Derrida's remark about the need to take more time raises for us is also raised by the ghostwriter Kierkegaard when he declares in the "Letter to the Reader" in *Stages on Life's Way,* "I say this without hesitation, and I also have sufficient time for it, for an observer has time in abundance,"[7] and when in the *Postscript* he writes:

> Viewed pathetically, a single second has infinite value; viewed comically, ten thousand years are but a trifle, like yesterday when it is gone. And yet, the time in which the existing individual lives consists of such parts. If one were to say simply and directly that ten thousand years are but a trifle, many a fool would give his assent, and find it wisdom; but he forgets the other, that a second has infinite value. When it is asserted that a second has infinite value, one or another will possibly hesitate to yield his assent, and find it easier to understand that ten thousand years have an infinite value. And yet, the one is quite as hard to understand as the other; provided merely we take time to

understand what there is to be understood; or else are in another manner so infinitely seized by the thought that there is no time to waste, not a second, that a second really acquires infinite value.[8]

Compare:

> By means of "Everything will be made clear at the end . . . ,"[9] and inter-
> mittently by means of the category, "This is not the proper place to discuss
> this question," the very cornerstone of the System [as Derrida would say,
> its *pierre d'attente,* which calls our attention also to a waiting Peter and the
> rock upon which the Christian church supports its weight], often used as
> ludicrously as if one were to cite under the heading of misprints a single ex-
> ample, and then add, "There are indeed other misprints in the book, but this
> is not the proper place to deal with them,"—by means of these two phrases
> the reader is constantly defrauded, one of them cheating him definitely, the
> other intermediately.[10]

Here we are dealing less with the time of reading than with the time of writing, whether the writing of the numbered paragraphs of the philosophical
system or the writing of a play or novel. In *Stages on Life's Way* Frater Taci-
turnus writes in his Letter of "the limitless speed of the ethical."[11] In *Fear and
Trembling* Johannes de silentio says that ethics does not have "such a swift
conception of time" as aesthetics.[12] Despite appearances, these statements are
not at odds with each other. There is a limit to the time ethics can postpone a
decision: "[I]f I . . . think only of the ethical, I demand with ethical sanction to
see the good triumph with boundless speed, to see evil punished with boundless speed." So that time is essential for ethics and maybe ethics is the essence
of time, with the consequence that although poetry and philosophy as aesthetic
objectified system can be in a hurry to reach a happy ending, "to abbreviate
the ethical is to make a fool of it."[13] The statement that on the other hand the
aesthetic has a swift conception of time means that it is so little concerned with
time that for the purposes of the plot it does not matter whether events leading to the dénouement—say a marriage or a broken engagement—filled many
years or only minutes or only a second. Which reminds us that a religious hymn
is not without its aesthetic moment, for instance the hymn which in its first
verse *asserts* that God *is* our eternal home, in its last verse *asks* God *to be* our
eternal home, and in an intermediate verse woven with Psalm 90:41 and 2 Peter
3:8 sings the conceit that "[a] thousand ages in Thy sight are like an evening
gone."[14] Here there is a hybridizing of temporality and ethico-religious eternity
of which the *nunc stans* of aesthetic eternity is the offspring. Compare the beginning of Genesis, where, it is said, the tenses are syncretically past, present,
and future.[15] And perhaps this can be said of the tenses of any or many verbs
that are sung. So that the hymn neither asserts that God is our eternal home
nor asks whether He is. Hence it would have to be a joke if to the words in the

first verse someone rejoined "No He isn't," or to the words in the last verse "He will" or "He won't," or to the words in the intermediate verse "They aren't." This is why it may be said here, anticipating a topic to be raised later in this chapter and developed toward the end of this book, some songs that are not hymns, not songs of praise belonging to an instituted religious cult, may nevertheless be essentially religious. This happens because the song performs or invites the hearer to perform a suspension of belief and disbelief in what is said, thereby enlarging the room left for belief as a trust between the singer and the hearer who is addressed. Although it may be only in the imagination that someone is addressed by the song, the singer takes the real or imagined listener into his or her confidence. And although the words and the tune to which the song is sung are usually borrowed ones, to sing is still to wear one's heart on one's sleeve. The singer therefore not only takes the hearer or hearers into his or her confidence; singing also demands confidence, courage, heart, on the part of the singer. An illustration of this is the ritual in which someone may hold the arm or the hand of the singer of the Irish *sean-nos,* the "old song." The helping hand inspires confidence. It is as though the other person were singing along. This becoming religious of the aesthetic happens especially, we shall learn, when instead of an aesthesis of the beautiful what is experienced is an aesthesis of the sublime, the *Erhaben.*)

## *Aufhebung*

As we were saying a second or ten thousand ages ago, we are talking too soon of decision; we are too close to what in the "Fragment of Life" published by Victor Eremita is called the modernization of the Delphic injunction "Know thyself." Let us therefore take a step back (unless this is a step forward or/ and a marking time) from knowledge and epistemology to decision, diacritology and hypocritology. In one of the fragments of Kierkegaard cited in *Glas* Climacus complains about the way Hegel construes *"Aufhebung,"* the word the latter uses to denote the movement that he promises will culminate in the climactic orgasm of absolute knowing. This sexual discourse of intercourse between Concept and hoped-for or feared conception is, of course, as old as philosophy if not older. Given a new lease of life by Hegel, it is modernly modified when in *Either/Or,* following the letter-cum-treatise on the aesthetic validity of marriage, the author of the treatise-cum-letter on the balance of the aesthetical and the ethical in the construction of personality remarks: "If I desired to be clever I might say at this point that the individual knew himself in the way Adam 'knew' Eve in the Old Testament sense of the word. By the individual's intercourse with himself he impregnates himself and brings himself to birth."[16]

What? Adam, man, brings himself to birth in knowing Eve? This ancient theory of genetics is as confusing as any of our modern and postmodern technologies of reproduction and cloning. For, remember, before Adam knew Eve, Eve was on Adam's side, so that his knowledge was a self-affecting knowing of himself/herself. But the main point of this clever allusion to Hebrew etymology is once more that to know oneself is not to have only contemplative knowledge, but to choose oneself, to decide. So that if I in my turn desired to be clever I might say that the individual must *trancher,* in every sense of the word, including that of copulation, which, *Glas* reminds us Hegel reminds us,[17] is an "operation consisting of filling in the gap [between the individual and the genus], of uniting one to the other by carrying out the *Ur-teil* in its most pronounced way." Now this operation and this way may consist in filling the gap between theory and practice. This raises the question whether absolute wisdom is both theoretical and practical or what makes the distinction between these possible, a possibility that could raise the question whether the Kierkegaardian or Climacian reading of Hegel is too precipitate. Is Climacus too quick in drawing his knife? The decision whether he is may depend on the distinctions between two senses of the word "individual" ("*Individ*" or "*Individuum*") and between a Hegelian sense of that word, a Kierkegaardian sense of it, and a Kierkegaardian sense of "*den Enkelte,*" the singular, the *Einzel,* of which Hegel writes as early as 1803 that, along with contingency or accidentality (*Zufälligkeit*), it is *aufgehoben* in or/and from philosophy[18]

Or is it Hegel who is being too quick with the cleaver? According to Climacus Hegel is too clever by half when, instead of recognizing that priority must be given to what he, Hegel, would regard as a Judeo-Kantian cutting, Hegel gives priority to mediation, to translation translated as "*Aufhebung,*" the word that Climacus suspects Hegel abuses. Momentarily as keen a supporter of clear and distinct ideas as the most rigorous Cartesian, and questioning whether "*Ophævelse,*" the apparent Danish equivalent, allows the liberties Hegel takes with his word, Climacus accuses Hegel of talking with his mouth full of mashed potato or "the yellow corn mush" of porridge[19] or perhaps *Rødgrød med Fløde,* the Danish dessert that is as patriotically colored as it is shibbolethically difficult to name, for you are no more able to articulate a speech act (SA) with your mouth full of it than you are with your mouth full of white bread or red wine.[20] Would this mess(e) of pottage be what *Glas* terms, de-terminatedly, the transcendental vomit of Hegel's system, what could be neither simply outside it, uttered, nor simply in, "what could be received, formed, terminated in none of the categories intrinsic to the system"?[21] Hegel, our Dane says, is guilty of sleight of hand when he attributes opposite senses to "*Aufhebung,*" thereby demonstrating that speculative knowledge knows nothing of decisiveness (*Afgørelse*). To get quite clear about this, he says, we only have to do a close reading of the Latin words and of how we employ the words the dictionary gives as their translations. Hegel tells us that as the movement of dialectical mediation "*Aufhebung*" has the force both of "*tollere*," to remove, and "*conservare*," to save. Climacus takes this saving to mean that what is saved is preserved unaltered, nothing whatsoever being done to it. But, notwithstanding his rage for pinning everything down with semantic precision (*nøiatigt*), Climacus is not precise and comprehensive enough. On the one hand, he does not look closely enough at his Latin dictionary. He does not make it clear that although "*tollere*" can mean remove, it can also mean raise up, elevate. This is the third of the senses Hegel sometimes mentions, the sense at work and play in the supposedly Ciceronian pun *tollendum est Octavium,* Octavian must be removed/promoted.[22] On the other hand, Climacus does not look closely enough at political practice when, turning his attention now to "*conservare*," he writes: "If the government abrogates or abolishes (*ophæver*) a political organization it gets rid of it; if anyone keeps or preserves something for me, it is implied that he makes no change in it at all (*slet ingen*)." Has Climacus never heard of reform bills or reorganization? And is it not precisely in the spheres of government and political organization that one gets the "diplomatic turns of phrase" to which, he complains, speculative philosophy has recourse?

Having suppressed the third meaning Hegel hears in the word "*Aufhebung*," the meaning that is perhaps uppermost both in this word and in "*ophæver*," namely, raising up, it is all too easy for Climacus to wonder whether speculative philosophy may be using this word in the sense merely of lowering down or reduction (*nedsætte*). That, he says, would mean the end of the progression toward the end known as absolute wisdom and the beginning of a regression to relativity. It would mean the beginning of a regression to a double relativity: the relativity of relative knowledge and the relativity of knowledge as such. For even if the senses of elevating and saving are saved in speculative philosophy's notion of *Aufhebung,* and even if speculative philosophy is thereby enabled to sustain its project toward absolute wisdom, we know that for Climacus absolute wisdom is relative to absolute choice. This is because at each floor of the system it is an impersonated and in every sense synthesized voice that announces from beyond the ceiling of the dialectical elevator: "Going up." The saving of absolute wisdom is the perdition of the individual person, not least the individual person whose authorship of "the entire series of seventeen volumes"[23] is announced by the signature "G. W. F. Hegel." But, as the author of *Glas* and an unentire series of already more than seventeen volumes repeats, when soon after the beginning of the *Phenomenology of Spirit* Hegel invites the friend of the certainty of sense to write down such words as "Here I am" ("*Hineni*"!), Hegel knows that he is planting a time bomb that is destined to explode in the face not only of this friend of the certainty of self but also of the individual who soon after the end of the *Phenomenology of Spirit* may fancy he can secure the copyright of the work by apposing under it his personal name, "G. W. F. Hegel"—or, come to that, which could come to the same, the name of Magister Adler, which means the same as the name "Hegel" as pronounced by the French synonymously with "*aigle*," which is synonymous with *aile,* wing, which is synonymous with flight, *vol,* which is synonymous with theft.[24] For Kierkegaard wrote a book pointing out that the Master of Arts Adler, who was a follower of Hegel, had written a book in the preface of which he claimed he had received a revelation—an Apocalypse Then, not an Apocalypse Now—in which the Savior spoke certain words that Adler was commanded to write down. But in this book of revelation Adler tried not to reveal that it perpetrated literary larceny, if that is possible, copyings from, among others, the authors of the concluding unscientific PS to that Hegelian science of the experience of the stages on the way of the life of consciousness. These last-named and unnamed authors too know that copyright is less copytight than one might think it is made by the law. That is why one of those authors writes that "theft in the world of the mind is not only not permissible [against Adler who says that it is], but actually impossible, and therefore that it is a necessity that the thief comes to grief."[25] That is why these authors are multiple, according to a law of multiplication that is crossed with a law of division, with the result that oneness is twoness, unity is duality, and sameness is difference.

> The unity, of which it is usual to say that difference cannot issue from it, is in fact itself one of the two moments; it is the abstraction of the simplicity or unitary nature over against difference. But in saying that the unity is an abstraction, that is, is only one of the opposed moments, it is already implied that it is the dividing of itself; for if the unity is *negative,* is *opposed* to something (*ein Entgegengesetztes*), then it is *eo ipso* posited (*gesetzt*) as that which has an antithesis within it. For the different moments of *division* (*Entzweiung*) and of *becoming self-identical* (*Sichselbstgleichwerden*) are therefore likewise only this *movement of self-negating-elevating-saving* (*Sich-Aufhebens*).[26]

So one might almost say that this movement from thesis, *Setzung,* and antithesis (*Entgegensetzung*), to synthesis, is an *Ent-zweiung,* a movement in which a certain duality is removed according to a principle of uncertainty so destabilizingly unprincipial that, except for the fact that it is spatio-temporally schematized, we might have expected to find it enunciated in the *Logic of Science,* the science treating of how things stand before God and before the creation of nature and finite mentality in space and time; except, again, that the operation of this principle of uncertainty is supposed to climax in certainty. This certainty is the certainty of knowledge, what's more. Or what's less, Climacus would say. For, according to him, prior to any uncertainty or certainty of knowledge, is a certainty of decision or choice, namely, the individual's choice of himself, the individual self that is lost when the generality of the upper-case Self's knowledge of Itself is saved.

The concluding sentence of Kierkegaard's paragraph on the elevation, *Aufhebung,* to absolute *Savoir* is cut off sharply by *Glas* just before mention is made of the Savior. The Absolute Savior is left hanging and the dripping of the holy blood is marked only by an ellipsis, three *points de suspension.* It may be as well for Climacus that it is. Maybe the question of the Savior is, as the Shakespearean exergue of *Philosophical Fragments* puts it, "well hanged." But let us rescue that sentence from being passed over in silence, even if it touches on what Johannes Climacus and Johannes de silentio agree we must be silent about. Climacus makes fun of Hegel's triple and penultimately trinitarian *points de suspension* and (in Hegel's German again) of the *eins, zwei, drei* of the numbered paragraphs throughout the three volumes of the *Encyclopaedia* all the way up to five hundred and seventy-seven. He writes in the last of the sentences cited in *Glas* from the paragraph on *Aufhebung* and recited at the beginning of the next-but-one paragraph of the *Postcript:* "Whether speculative philosophy is right or not is another question." He drops that question, for it is another other question that interests Climacus here: the question of the drops of blood, and of the symmetrical cross on which is raised a body whose sacred head is nystagmatic, nods, inclines to one side, like the sanctuary of many Christian churches, and like the lower case Greek letter χ: "[H]ere the only question that is raised is how the speculative explanation of Christianity is related to the Christianity which it purports to explain." His answer to this question springs from his repetition of the Tertullian paradox he adverts to in the *Philosophical Fragments,* the paradox of the *quia absurdum.*

Tertullian does not use the words "*credo quia absurdum*" usually attributed to him. What he says in *de carne Christi* (chapter 5) is "The Son of God died: it is immediately credible, because it is out of order [impertinent, shocking, absurd, out of joint]. He was buried and rose again: it is certain because it is impossible"; *et mortuus est dei filius: prorsus credibile est, quia ineptum est. et sepultus resurrexit: certum est, quia impossibile.*[27] Tertullian and Climacus know full well what a queer "*quia*" this is. It is a "because" that gives a reason that reason necessarily fails to comprehend, a ground that surpasses all understanding, a ground that is an *Abgrund,* an underground on which understanding stands or falls. Now Climacus asserts more than once that Hegel never explains mediation. This assertion may seem unfair in view of the analysis of the meanings of "*Aufhebung*" Hegel gives in the Remark commented upon by Climacus himself, by ourselves, and by *Glas.* However, we may agree at least that Hegel does not make clear the transition from the series of dialectical transitions to the *telos* of absolute knowing, that is to say, he does not explain how the transition from time to eternity could take place, or take time, while taking time away; he does not enable us to comprehend how the Janus-faced adverb of time "*noch*" ("*encore*," "*endnu*"), meaning both "yet" and "still," functions and, at the edge of the abyss between time and eternity, dysfunctions.[28] This shortcoming, this lapse into secrecy which, between you and me—no, not between you and me, because any secret here is not one that can be shared—could be "the secret of Hegel"[29] that saves him from himself. It is what lies behind Climacus's bantering references to the fact that we have to take on faith Hegel's promise that the subordinate dialectical cycles are in due course embraced in a fully rounded whole. And this is perhaps why Climacus asserts that Hegel never explains mediation to us. Hegel cannot explain to us how mediation works. This is because Hegel cannot explain us or himself in our existing individuality. If we are to understand the speculative system we must understand that it proceeds under its own power. We, as existing individuals, not least the Professor himself, are left behind in the march toward absolute wisdom; we are part of *ce qui reste du savoir absolu:* the singular self is lost in order that the General Self may be saved. So, Climacus contends, the very terms of the speculative system stand in the way of its being consistently propounded by Hegel or any other finite being, even if it be said, to our surprise, that "existence (*Tilværelse*) is a system—for God."[30] This is because, despite its claims to make sense of Christianity, its own terms cannot make sense of Christ. It fails to see that no terms can. The only way of making sense of Christ is to see that Christ is a nonsense.

Or, rather, to choose to see this. This choosing is a choosing to choose. That is to say, it is not a choosing between different finite possibilities or probabilities, but a choice of what is not possibility or probability: a choice of im- or un-possibility and of the un-probable. It is not then a choice between a good and a bad, or between a good and an evil. Beyond good and beyond evil, it is a choice for the hyphenation of either-evil-or-good of religio-ethical space beyond the choice for the hyphenated either-true-or-false of logical space which Aristotle draws to our attention.[31] The choice that Kierkegaard draws to our attention is a free choice for choice, a free choice for freedom. Which is difficult to understand. But then, Climacus is in the business of making Christianity more difficult, more difficult than it is according to the gospel of Hegel. The "into thy hands I commend my spirit" of the Cross is as difficult to understand as Abraham's readiness to sacrifice his son. More difficult. It is the most difficult difficulty there can be, "the absolute difficulty," as Climacus says, the absolute difficulty of religious address without which we have aestheticism.[32] The Christian sacrifice took place. So there is no mediation of what Christians call the Old Testament into the New. There is a radical paradigm switch, a switch to the only paradigm that is permitted to faith. Hence instead of a step-by-step movement, *pas* after negative *pas,* toward a hoped-for *telos* that rebounds back toward the beginning, binding the progression into a seamless whole, instead of such an integrating resaltation (*Resultat*), what is demanded is a prior saltation, a leap which is not a quantum leap, but that qualitative leap which is a leap from quantity and calculation to the incalculable. This is a leap from despair about the relative improbabilities of fortune, which are matters of external contingency, to a chance more uncertain than the uncertainty that was feared by Einstein and even by the proposer of the uncertainty principle and of the eponymous freak known as Schrödinger's cat that is indecidably neither dead nor alive. This qualitative assault is a leap from objectivity to an inward, eternal, but still passionate, that is to say suffering, happiness, for "is it not also true here that those whom God blesses he curses in the same breath," be they Abraham or Mary?[33] In this projection from objectivity to subjectivity, from objective to subjective spirit, what is saved, *saltem,* in this *salto* is the singular subjectivity of the signatory whose choice is not a choice for wisdom, *sophia,* out of, in the sense of from, wisdom. The signatory Søren Kierkegaard's choice is a choice out of wisdom in another sense, an opposite sense, of "out." It is an opting out of wisdom in favor of madness: an opting for what is folly to the Greeks and a stumbling-block to the Jews.[34] Søren-Climacus-silentio is sailing on deep waters here—17,000 or even 34,000 fathoms deep, deeper than the Red Sea, well beyond the shallows where a fellow human being might wade out to save him, so far beyond the shallows that he could not be rescued even by a fellow human being with faith so strong that he could walk on the water (Matthew 14:28–29). Philosophy can be saved from itself or for itself only by a choice of religion, and Kierkegaard and some of his pseudonymous authors do make such a choice. As it happens, it is the same choice as is made by Hegel. But Hegel gives reasons for his choice. SK is bound not to give reasons, more tightly bound than Isaac, as tightly bound as the man who was not only bound by the bonds with which the soldiers led him away, but bound by his own free will in order that God's will be done and that the Scriptures be fulfilled, even the scripture that tells of the suffering servant in what some Christians regard as the mediatory scripture of Isaiah. This is a paradox in the sense that it beggars belief understood as the assent to information, the *pistis* of a *doxa*. What's more, and/or again what's less, it exceeds knowledge. Knowledge is denied to make room for faith, for *Tro* as troth, the trust one may have in a person, the trust one must have in someone one loves.

SK chooses Christ. But he thereby chooses himself. Only this choice, he tells us, can bring what he calls his eternal salvation. This can be accomplished, we are told, by a decision which is doubly foolish. It is folly to the pagan Greeks—yet Socrates, although he does not jump, is in the gymnasium practicing his runups, so that he would be only one step behind the scribe of whom Jesus says discretely in Mark 12:33, "Thou art not far from the kingdom of God." But if SK's decision is folly to pagans, it is folly to most Christians too.

Christo-Kierkegaardian salvation is crazy. Its soteriology is a *sottise*. But it is also the graveyard and Golgotha in which other religions are interred or scattered on the wind blowing from the East across the deserts to the West. Hegel sketches a religeography in which the source of Mohammedanism is specified in relation to the source of Judaism and Christianity to the South-East of it, *südöstlich davon,*[35] as though it were a marginal appendage. Hegel goes on to argue that Islam can achieve completion only if it is taken over by Christendom, as the mosque in Cordova was incorporated into a Roman Catholic cathedral, rounding off the story told in *Glas* of the mosque in Algeria that the colonists would have transformed into a synagogue. See *Glas* 240bi [268bi]. See also in *Glas,* however, places that refer to the holocaust that engages history that engages chimney-corners where, we have been assured by one of Kierkegaard's readers, the gods are also present,[36]—but also where millions of singular human beings go up in smoke.[37] (In Danish the word "*Glas*" is used of the chimney of a paraffin lamp.) Essentially the same history of religious colonization is told in the ventriloquial voice (*glas*) of Søren de silentio-Climacus et al. Although when the German story is turned into a Danish one a movement from apparent singularity peaks not in absolute concrete generality but in the Capital Moment of absolute singularity, the implication this revised version has for religion is that the other religions are cases of Religiousness A, religious movements in general as distinct from the incomparable Religiousness B of paradoxical Christianity.

## Choice

So far our discussion of the savings of Kierkegaard's fragments in *Glas* has been concerned with the saving of the dialectic of absolute wisdom and, but more fleetingly, with Kierkegaard's preoccupation with his eternal salvation through the divine-human Saver. As a preface to some questions about saving the divine Saver or God or at least the word "God," and as an *envoi* to a saving we have saved for the last in this chapter, the saving of the world, let us swiftly remind ourselves of the stages through which SK's soteriological dialectic of absolute singularity runs.

Like the Hegelian dialectic, the Kierkegaardian dialectic is a dialectic of passion. His passion or Passion, however, is not the suffering of the Idea. It is the suffering of the existing human individual passionately concerned to secure his own eternal salvation through the suffering of the human-divine individual on the Cross. The lid was lifted a little from the engine of this dialectic of suffering when we were told that without the absolute difficulty of religious address (*Tale*) we have aestheticism. That is to say, without religious address even the ethical stage or sphere intermediate between the aesthetic and the religious stages is ethico-aesthetic. This holds whether ethics be understood as Kantian *Moralität* or as Hegelian *Sittlichkeit*. Also aesthetic is the whole of the so-called science of philosophy as expounded in Hegelian categories which, despite the room they make for the ethical understood as *Sitten*, do not make room for the ethical enthused by religious passion. The categories of the Hegelian method are connected together as a continuum of mediations. The earlier categories of the Kierkegaardian stages on life's way also merge into each other, the border between the aesthetic and the ethical being marked by irony, that between the ethical and the religious by humor.[38] There is a discontinuity between the ethical stage and the sphere of Religiousness B, but once the leap to the latter is made, the aesthetic and the ethical are given back, though transfigured. Thanks to the decision to choose God and thereby oneself, a higher immediacy of transcendence supersedes the immediacy of immanence which characterizes the aesthetic way of life.

So we discover that if one first saves oneself, that is to say, if one loses oneself by allowing oneself to be saved by God, hence by allowing God to be saved, not getting rid of him, one also saves the world. Although the aesthetic and what we could call ethicality A are preconditions of reaching Religiousness B, only through having achieved my own eternal salvation is it possible for me to enter into the fully ethical relationship of what we could call ethicality B with my fellow human beings and a proper involvement with the non-human.

Consideration of these four or so sorts of savings would require close consideration (if we had time) of at least the following four overlapping questions:

1. Would ethicality B, a fully ethical relationship with one's fellow human beings, be identical with Religiousness B, or would they constitute together what we might call Religiousness C, the topic, it might be said,[39] that is treated in *Practice in Christianity, Works of Love* and *Self-Examination: Judge for Yourself!*?

2. Is a fully ethical relationship with other human beings the only way of making sense of the word "God," as is maintained in some of his writings by Emmanuel Levinas?

3. Can there be respect for non-human and human beings only in respect of God?

4. What, if anything, remains today of respect for non-human beings other than God?

Responses, if not answers, to some of these questions lie at the heart of the chiasmus where Derrida's and Kierkegaard's paths cross. Listen first to Kierkegaard confiding in his papers that "Judaism is godliness which is at home in this world; Christianity is alienation from this world. In Judaism the reward of godliness is blessing; Christianity is hate toward this world."[40] We have heard it said that although the world is alienated by Christianity, it is given back, but it is given back transfigured. What sort of transfiguration does it undergo? Two years later Kierkegaard observes: "Abraham draws his knife—then he gets Isaac back again; it was not carried out in earnest; the highest earnestness was 'the test' (*Prøvelsen*), but then once again it became the enjoyment of this life."[41] Kierkegaard stresses that the key difference between Judaism and Christianity is that the loss of the things of this world is for Judaism only a threat, staged make-believe—the category of the "test" being, he says, a "childish" one—while in Christianity the things of the world are lost really in earnest. However, there is no difference, according to Kierkegaard, between the way he and Christianity and Judaism regard the things of this earth. These things are regarded as there to be enjoyed. Which is all well and good. But, spurred by Paul's injunction to "work out your own salvation with fear and trembling" (Philippians 2:12), a text Kierkegaard and his authors often repeat, Kierkegaard seems to have been so concerned about seeking his own eternal salvation that he had no time to consider whether he and we might have some responsibility to regard the things of the world for their own sakes, not just as things to be sacrificed for our own enjoyment and service.

Listen now to Derrida touching first on the question of religious colonialism in general, not just Christian or Jewish, but also such as is explicit in the Koran when it asks rhetorically "And who turns away from the religion of Abraham but such as debase their souls with folly?" then proceeds to assure us that because "God hath chosen the faith for you; then die not except in the faith of Islam" (II, 130, 132). Might the human and the non-human things in this world be saved if the world is unbound from the bindings of a particular positive historical religion and we say with Derrida: "God is the name of the possibility I have of keeping a secret that is visible from the interior but not from the exterior," the name of "the absolute 'me' or 'self,' . . . that structure of invisible interiority that is called, in Kierkegaard's sense, subjectivity"?[42] But, in Kierkegaard's sense, subjectivity is choosing or decision, a double choice, choosing myself and in so doing being chosen by God, which is an aspect of what he calls double reflection, for instance in one of the three Kierkegaardian fragments from the *Postscript* inserted in *Glas*.[43] In the second part of *Either/ Or* the anonymous author called B writes:

> I can say that I choose the absolute which chooses me, that I posit the absolute which posits me; for if I do not remember that this second expression is equally absolute, my category of choice is false, for the category is precisely the identity of both propositions. That which I choose I do not posit, for in case

this were not [already] posited, I could not choose it, and yet if I do not posit it by the fact that I chose it, then I did not choose it. It exists, for in case it were not in existence I could not choose it; it does not exist, for it only comes into being by the fact that I choose it, otherwise my choice would be an illusion.

But what is it I choose? Is it this thing or that? No, for I choose absolutely, and the absoluteness of my choice is expressed precisely by the fact that I have not chosen to choose this or that. I choose the absolute. And what is the absolute? It is I myself in my eternal validity.[44]

The Jew, and specifically Abraham, the author B continues, did not choose himself or God absolutely. What matters is not the what, but the how. "Even the Jew who chose God did not choose absolutely, for he chose, indeed, the absolute, but did not choose it absolutely, and thereby it ceased to be the absolute and became a finite thing." Earlier in the piece from which these words are reproduced Echo had been mentioned, that Echo who, like SK, existed between loquacity and silence, and who, unlike SK, in her own way ended by making the stones speak. "Echo," B had remarked, "is heard only in emptiness." On a later page the emptiness is the emptiness of the death that must be endured, an echo, yet with sharply unHegelian overtones, of Hegel's remarks on the absolute master and his bondsman. The emptiness of death is the emptiness of the sacrifice of things we enjoy in this world, those things of which Eckhart too had said we must rid ourselves. SK: "The fact of the matter is that Christianity is really all too joyous, and therefore really to stick to Christianity a man must be brought to madness by suffering. Most men, therefore, will be able to get a real impression of Christianity only in the moment of their death, because death actually takes away from them what must be surrendered in order to get an impression of Christianity."[45] That is to say, adapting Sophocles, none can be called unhappy until the day he carries his unhappiness down to the grave.

To return to the sentences describing the dialectic of choosing and positing: following the example of Kierkegaard's subversion of the essentially communicational and recognitive story Hegel tells about the risk of death, these sentences too must be heard as a deflationary, deconceptualizing parody of the epistemological dialectic of the Hegelian science of logic whose kind of reflectiveness is not that of what Kierkegaard calls double reflection. In the paragraph following immediately after the largest of the three Kierkegaardian tranches cited in *Glas,* the author of the *Concluding Unscientific Postscript* invites us to marvel at the peculiarity that, unlike knowledge generally, where what is known is not altered by our knowing it, speculative knowledge is itself what is known, and comes into existence only at the same time as it is known. Except for the fact that Kierkegaard's dialectic is one of absolute choice or decision, not speculative knowing, its intricacy repeats that of the dialectic of speculation and anticipates the dialectic of locution in which John Austin discovers that one cannot simply oppose the constative to the performative. With the simultaneity of decision and position and with the strained simultaneity of my choosing God and God's choosing me, the crux of temporality and eternity that Kierkegaard would not attempt to explain, we are also within hearing distance of the thought that one has faith only by grace.

In these Kierkegaardian duplicities Derrida hears the twofold call of which he writes that "what I call God exists (*il y a ce que j'appelle Dieu*), there is (*il y a*) what I call God in me, it happens that (*il y a que*) I call myself God—a phrase which it is difficult to distinguish from 'God calls me,' for it is on that condition that I can call myself or that I am called in secret." Still glossing Kierkegaard or at any rate glassing what Johannes de silentio writes about the quasi-Quixotic Knight of Faith astride his jennet or *genet*,[46] brandishing his sword, Derrida writes, "the history of God and the name of God as the history of secrecy" would be "a history that is at the same time secret without any secrets." The only secret would be that there is no secret. One story being told in this history of God now is that the blade must be brought down on a God of yesterday if either He or She or It is to be saved for today. Indeed one can already hear it being said of that story that "[t]hat's the truth of what we have always said, heard, tried to make heard. The misunderstanding is that you hear us better than you think or pretend to think. In any case, no misunderstanding on our part, from now on, it's enough to keep talking, not to interrupt. . . . It's enough not to interrupt the colloquium, even when it is already late."[47]

Before the knife is brought down on this chapter concerning the fragments cut from Kierkegaard by *Glas,* it must be asked what happens precisely to cutting in Derrida's rereading of Kierkegaard. For that reading returns us to another economy, another saving, one in which the name of God is saved by God's sacrifice. Sacrificed with that God, it would seem, is everything that Kierkegaard denotes by decision, choice, and leap of faith. For this decision is *selten,* seldom, *exaiphnēs,* sudden, so sudden, momentous, and rare that one after another of Kierkegaard's pseudonymous authors and Kierkegaard *in propria persona* deny their capacity to achieve the status of cavaliers of faith. Yet religious faith, according to Derrida, is homely, familiar, and banal. Is it credible that there is an identity of opposites here? Thus if faith is not unfamiliar, the reason may be that it is no different from familiar behavior, from works, works of love, practice, what some would call practice in Christianity—or Religiousness C, which would be the same as what we have dubbed ethicality B if, as Levinas almost incessantly insists, the ethicality of love for one's neighbor is already holy, "*kadosh,*" without its having to be transfigured by a qualitative bound and binding to a religious stage above it. Everything turns at least for the Christian here on *how* close the likeness is when we are told that the commandment to love one's neighbor is like unto (*homoia*) the commandment to love God (Matthew 22:39), and on *how* much is much (*hoson*) when it is said that "[i]nasmuch as ye have done it unto the least of these my brethren, ye have done it unto me" (Matthew 25:40), and on whether there is more to loving God than is implied in the statement that "ye are my disciples, if ye have love one to another" (John 13:35).[48] For Levinas the vital moment in the story of what happened and did not happen on Mount Moriah is not what Kierkegaard calls the teleological suspension of the ethical. The vital moment is when Abraham turns his attention to the suspension of that suspension, the moment of his return to the ethical in response to the accusing look in Isaac's eyes.[49] The ethical, prior to any leap of faith, is already a *religio* the ligature of which is consistent with atheism, the belief that there is no God, and with a-theism, the absence of belief that there is or that there is not a God. But how can the separation denoted by the word *kadosh* be reconciled with the homeliness of religious faith, with a religious economy?

Relevant to this question are those pages in the works of Heidegger (the thinker to whom we have just heard it said that it is enough not to interrupt the colloquium) in which he would persuade us that familiarity, for example the familiarity of the hearth and the cookhouse, may be haunted by unfamiliarity, *Unheimlichkeit*. It is not, however, sufficient to recall those pages if the *Unheimlichkeit* and *Geheimnis* evoked in them are the inwardness of a secret which is kept close but which could in principle be let out of the bag. The economy of secrecy of which Derrida writes is not that of propriety or of property, that is to say of apt phenomenal or noumenal representation.[50] It is to *another* economy that Derrida alludes, the inadequate, inept, *ineptus*, precondition of the economy of representation, position, and opposition, an economy of the other where the colloquium *is* interrupted, as also is the *com*-municative colloquy that goes on in a colloquium. Further, notwithstanding the equation the Kierkegaardian *personae* make of decision with the will, let us not forget that, according to these authors themselves, namely SK and his co-signatories, my will and God's will inhabit each other somehow in the economic *chōra* between my electing God and God's electing me. We are familiar with the idea that a decision is a cut, and that a decision for God, in both senses of the preposition, would be a very Big Deal, an extraordinarily unfamiliar partition. But the fragment "de-" of the words "decision" and "decisiveness" can function like "dis-," like the "*Af-*" of Kierkegaard's Danish equivalent "*Afgørelse,*" which, at least according to the Dahlerup dictionary, can indeed have the economic and commercial sense of payment and settlement of a debt, but where the first syllable is the ablative "*ab,*" the ablative absolute that ablates (*abhebt*) -cision, cuts off cutting (*ent-scheidet*) so that although we may meet this or that relative debt in particular, an absolute indebtedness remains, a remainder (*reste*) of restlessness. No rest, no settling down, but a gnawing residual unsettled-ness. As Kierkegaard or his pseudonymous authors maintain, for the knight of faith repentance is the one thing to be repeated without end. This is because, as Levinas and Derrida repeat in their wake, we are never entitled to claim that we are released from *Schuld,* guilt, debt. From this absolute indebtedness and guilt not even a Savior can save us. And this is because, somewhat like the word *"Aufhebung"* according to what Hegel writes in the passage commented upon by Climacus in one of the fragments from him repeated in *Glas,* "deci-sion" too is a word with opposite senses. However, the separateness in proxim-ity of these senses is marked not by the logician's so-called non-exclusive *vel,* nor by Kierkegaard's exclusive *aut . . . aut.* The relation of these senses one to the other is even more "fundamental" than the indeterminate relationality in general we are wont to express nowadays by the phrase "in terms of." The rela-tion of relation marked by the de-terminate word "de-cision" is interminable and anarchic, a chiasmic crossing where there takes place a dis-connecting connection that is paralogical, such that in terms of the logic of *vel* and *aut . . . aut* it would be deemed to be quite mad, astonishing, amazing, as we are wont to say nowadays, confirming, appearances to the contrary, that banality is not exclusive of the madness of choice, of decision that gets one into ever deeper debt because choice for someone or something is choice against someone or something else. De-cision would be like what in his piece "At this very moment in this work here I am"[51] Derrida calls *sériature,* seriasure, sererasure, from *sero,* to bind, but with echoes of the homonymous *sero,* which means to sow or disseminate, and which has as a root the Indo-European *SA-.* Note, however, that *"raturer"* and "erasure" mean to obliterate or uproot. Note too, neverthe-less, that the hope of a rerooting and rerouting is made by every scattering of seed, by every seminar or work of writing, including *this* work, in a later chapter of which sererasure will return.

## Religion

*"Sériature"* or *"sérirature"* or "serirooture" would indicate faithfully the paral-ogical connection and disconnection between the Kierkegaardian corpus and what fragments remain of or over from it in the corpus of Derrida. On the one hand, Kierkegaard's paradox of the folly or foolishness of religious faith is tied to the paradox that religious faith is consistent or "consistent" with the faith of atheism according to Derrida. In this, as already noted, he is in agreement with Levinas, although, as also noted, there remains over from Levinas the problem as to how the faith of confessional and institutional religion connects or does not connect with the *religio* of ethical allegiance. On the other hand,

as construed by Derrida, the faith of religion, by which I take him to mean the faith of the religion that is the binding ligament of the ethical, is consistent with paganism. This construal or deconstrual is facilitated by Derrida's sometimes allowing the word "religion" to lean on inverted commas, raising the question whether the word thus guarded is an echo of the unguarded word or vice-versa.[52] Leaving this question open and before closing this chapter by posing a few other questions, here are three summary and provisional suggestions as to how the "positions" occupied by Derrida, Kierkegaard, and Levinas relate to each other.

> *Eins.*  In saying that the faith of religion or "religion" is consistent with paganism of some kind (see *Drei* below), Derrida is closer than Levinas to Kierkegaard insofar as we identify pagans with the chronologico-historical pre-Christian Athenians, including Socrates. On *that* definition of paganism, because Kierkegaard is a friend of Socrates he would be a friend of paganism. However, Kierkegaard is a friend of Socrates because he sees him as a John the Baptist *avant la lettre*. He sees Socrates as this because he sees him as a critic of the Athenian paganism of his time who in his life and death exemplifies the ethical priority precisely of criticism and of the singular existing individual. If the reference to John the Baptist be dropped and singularity be spelled out otherwise than it is by Kierkegaard, the latter's admiration of Socrates could be shared by Levinas. Kierkegaard's admiration of Socrates means that Kierkegaard is an enemy of the paganism of Socrates's contemporaries. That is an enmity Levinas shares with Kierkegaard, but not, unless I am mistaken, with Derrida. In saying, as I take Derrida to say, that religion or "religion" is consistent with some form of what could plausibly be called paganism (see again *Drei* below), Derrida's path diverges from that of both Kierkegaard and Levinas.

> *Zwei.*  Derrida's economy of religious faith, like that of Kierkegaard and Levinas, saves the holy, the *saint*, in the sense of the *kadosh*, the separate.

> *Drei.*  Unlike Levinas's economy, the secrecy of Derrida's economy allows room also for the sacred, the *sacré*. Perhaps we are primed to discover this when we hear Derrida saying *"il y a du secret,"* *"il y a ce que j'appelle Dieu,"* for in these sentences one could fancy one heard also that for which *"il y a"* stands for Levinas, namely the anonymous rustling of a certain pagan sacredness that causes him fear and trembling. Paganism would continue to horrify Levinas were it

to be understood not as entailing polytheism, but (see *Eins* above) as entailing no more than a simple respect for the *pagus,* the heath, our natural surrounding universe and all that therein is. Paganism thus understood as panpaganism or catholic heathenism, as what might perhaps be called a new international and interplanetary democracy, does not run the risk Levinas fears of becoming the regional and racial economy of blood and earth that, he rightly or wrongly believes, lurks in the later thinking of Heidegger.

Without being any more friendly than Levinas is to such an exclusive and parochial telluric economy as may or may not be germane to that later Heideggerian thinking, Derrida's economy of religion within the bounds of the ethical is more generous than either Levinas's or Kierkegaard's to the non-human things of this world. This is because Derrida takes more seriously than Kierkegaard himself does the latter's assertion that he cannot pretend to help us here, that he can only decide for himself. Kierkegaard communicates, albeit indirectly, that no decision is religiously valid unless it is ultimately a decision for Christ. Is this not, albeit without specific reference to Christ, what (in the essay carrying the title "Cogito and the History of Madness" and, as an exergue, the statement from Kierkegaard that the moment of decision is madness or folly) Derrida finds Foucault doing in the account he gives of what the latter too calls decision?[53] Is this not to mistake for an example in the sense of exemplar what is an example only in the sense of a sample? But can this be described as Kierkegaard's mistake? Is it not exactly Kierkegaard's decisive "take"? What else is it to decide for himself for Religiousness B against Religiousness A? Is that decision not made in order to escape the generality of Religiousness A? And, by the way, would not that generality be analogous to the ethical indifferentism Levinas might see implied in what we have called panpaganism and catholic heathenism? Having been saved by recourse to this from one danger that Levinas sees in Heidegger, namely the thinking and worship of the regional site, would we have exposed ourselves and the world in general to the other danger Levinas sees threatened by Heidegger, the danger threatened by what Levinas calls the "there is," the "*il y a*"?

Analogously, how can religion or "religion" as reconstrued by Derrida escape being the religion or "religion" only of Religiousness A, that is to say, religiousness without decision? It can escape this only by running the risk threatened by the *il y a*—the risk Levinas too affirms it is necessary to run—because only by running that risk can religion or "religion" as reconstrued by Derrida avoid being either the religion only of the Jew or the religion only of the Christian or the religion of the Genetic Mother of Christ[54] (see below chapter 14) or the religion only of the Mohammedan instead of the crossed-out religion or "religion" of which positively religious monotheisms, polytheisms, and atheisms are instances or quasi-instances and effects. Religion or "religion" as reconstrued by Derrida can escape Religiousness A only if an example can be an exemplar and a sample at one and the very same time, only if there is an undoing of the simple opposition of the paradigm and the instantial case, of the archetype and the ectype, because the moment of typology in which takes place the decisive deed of signing and the decisive signing of a deed is at the same time a moment of pseudonymity whose secrecy cannot be kept unless the security of saving is lost.

## Unsafety First

What is the upshot of all this? as Hippias asks Socrates in the words Kierkegaard nails as an exergue above his *Concluding Unscientific Postscript:* "But I must ask you, Socrates, what do you suppose is the upshot of all this? As I said a little while ago, it is the scrapings and shavings of argument, cut up into little bits."[55] As is asked in the words that re-edit each other in the "first" and "last" lines of *Glas,* "what, after all, of the remain(s) today, for us, here, now," at this very moment in this work, is left over either from or of the fragments of Kierkegaard applied to the sinister column in *Glas*? What can be saved from these scrapings and shavings of argument, cut up into little bits like the mosaic of Genet's Rembrandt and Derrida's talmudesque (not to say Talmudic or Mosaic) tablets? However matters may stand with the how, which for Kierkegaard matters far more than the what, the answer must be that ultimately no what can be saved, that our question cannot therefore be a proper question and that our answer cannot therefore be a proper answer. So let us say in scare-quotes either that the "answer" (*"svar"*?) or that the unconstative answear (*sværgen*?) or that the passionately responsible response (*ansvarlig reaktion*?) must be a threefold solicitation of threefold *Aufhebung*.

> *Eins.* What is saved is unsafety. Unsafety first of the "what" of classification and of concepts, including the concept of classification, and so of questions of the form "what is—?". Such questions—for example the question "what is beauty?" "what is the essence, *eidos,* of the beautiful or fine, to *kalon*?" posed and deposed in the perhaps pseudo-Platonic dialogue *Hippias Major*—are the questions with which Plato's perhaps pseudonymous Socrates simultaneously inaugurates philosophy and immediately almost brings it to an end by demonstrating how much more difficult such questions are than his interlocutors would like to believe. (And what is the sublime? More anon.)

*Zwei.* Kierkegaard is in the business of showing how much more difficult the decision for Christ is than philosophy and its questions are shown to be by his perhaps pseudonymous pagan Socrates, and how much more difficult, because absurd, that decision is than Christians would like to believe.

*Drei.* When the fragments of Kierkegaard are shaken up with those of Hegel and Genet et al. in the kaleidoscope of *Glas,* the difficulty of philosophy emphasized by Socrates and the absurdity of the Scriptures emphasized by Kierkegaard turn out to be effects of a hypo-absurd archi-scriptural indecidability which, prior to *glas* as speech, prior to *glas* as class and as religious or other sect, prior to straight answerable questions, calls into question any security that may be implied by the Kierkegaardian or Christian notion of eternal salvation.

# FOUR

# Standstill

## Absolutes

In the tradition of Hegelian absolute idealism from which a Kierkegaardian tradition seeks to wean itself, the idea of the absolute retains the sense of completeness, perfection, and infiniteness that the original Latin term "*absolutus*" conveys. In some of the writings through which the most recent phase of this weaning is being attempted there continues to be talk of absoluteness, and not only in order to characterize the Hegelian position from which the authors of these writings seek to break away. In the thinking of that position the idea of the absolute is still applied to the idea of God, as it is in pre-Hegelian traditions, but it gets articulated in a variety of ways by Hegel, for example as the identity of subject and object, the identity of the one and the many, the identity of identity and difference. In many of the texts in which strategies have been adopted for effecting this break, writers have demonstrated how painfully aware they are that if the Hegelian position is simply opposed, any attempt to break with it will be playing along with the logic of negation by which that position is defined. Hence their strategy includes redefinition. But for redefinition to be persuasive it must be shown to be to some degree a requirement of the accepted meanings of the terms that undergo redefinition. It must be shown to be a requirement that was not explicitly recognized as a requirement. It must be shown that there is a blind spot in the tradition as previously defined. These are the tasks undertaken in Kierkegaard's endeavors to save himself from Hegel and in the endeavors of others to do likewise. In their pursuit of this end they find that the term "absolute" serves to pick out not only the ideas of termination, perfection, and completeness which it has for Hegel. Through a simultaneous shift of emphasis in a reconception of the ideas of identity and difference absoluteness would now be the difference of identity and of difference, where both of these genitives are doubly "subjective" and "objective," and where this way of trying to formulate the difference between the old and the new indicates how careful one must be not to construe naively this pairing of the old and the new. This explains the quotation marks used here, where they function both as scare-quotes and as marks that the terms are being mentioned, but not in a manner in which mention excludes use.

Risking what may be another too neat formula, one could say that whereas in the Hegelian context the absolute is infinite in a positive sense, in some post-Kierkegaardian writings, among them those that have been invoked and those that will be invoked in chapters of this book, the absolute is infinite in, let us not say simply a negative sense, but in the sense of the un-finished. This does not exclude altogether what it is difficult to avoid calling a positive or "positive" sense, but in calling it this it must not be understood as positive in the sense of what is posited or propounded, *gesetzt*. For the infinite in the writings of, say, Levinas and Derrida, has less to do with only propounded fact or truth than with an ethical and/or religious requirement or responsibility. The writings of Heidegger that speak of truth are aimed at bringing out how ontic factuality and truth are secondary to being and truth in senses presupposed by the senses that being and truth have after thinking has become compartmentalized into theory of knowledge, philosophy of science, epistemology, ethics, aesthetics, and so on. And in those writings what is emphasized is the priority of the finite over the infinite. The finite as the unfinished in Heidegger undergoes a rapprochement with the infinite as the unfinished in the writing of Levinas and Derrida.

The present chapter considers whether this rapprochement is anticipated in the writings of Kierkegaard, particularly his journals and papers, and particularly in his contribution to the question whether salvation is an earned achievement or a gift, whether the way to it is grace or good works. Kierkegaard's clarifications of these and related religious doctrines put them in an order of which he helps his readers keep track by, in a manner reminiscent of Luther, repeatedly invoking the notion of an eschatological timetable through his employment of expressions such as "first," "next," "then," "following," and so on. He employs the term "dialectic" of the passage from one moment to a second via a third, as though to show that the dialectic of Christianity is other than the *eins-zwei-drei* dialectic of Hegel's enlargement of Christianity. Where in the conceptual dialectic of the Hegelian philosophical system the absolute is an identity of subjectivity and objectivity, in the existential dialectic of Christianity as Kierkegaard interprets it, the absolute is a subjectivity that is never absorbed into an objectivity. Here absoluteness has the force "absolvedness" has in a religious context, that of being freed, forgiven and saved. Our question is whether that salvation is to be understood as a state of completion. Is salvation to be understood as security? Evidently this question is one that, in a Christian or non-Christian and sometimes confessedly and even confessionally secular form, motivates much post-Kierkegaardian reflection. This should not surprise us, given that such a boost to this reflection was given by Heidegger, who proclaims that he is adapting cues given him in one segment of the Kierkegaardian corpus. Among other writers to whom the direction of Heidegger's thinking owes something is Martin Luther. Luther has a hand in what is written on the pages signed by Kierkegaard or some of his pseudonymous authors. In general the explicit references made to Luther there express admiration and agreement. But one of the doctrines Kierkegaard admires most in Luther's writings occasions one of his most profound disagreements with him. This is none other than the above-mentioned doctrine that salvation is by faith alone.

## Faith Works

Luther is right to insist, says Kierkegaard, that salvation is not earned by conduct according to or out of respect for the law as prescribed on Sinai. He is right to stress that the performance of good works is a training exercise, an *Øvelses-Gjerninger,*[1] such as is intended by the title of the book by him and Anti-Climacus, *Indøvelse i Christendom. Indøvelse* is a gymnastic drill or dressage. In using this word Kierkegaard is thinking of unquestioning obedience such as is drilled into a horse. Pascal refers to this as a process of becoming an animal, *s'embêtir,* and recommends it as a way of becoming a Christian. This comparison would give support to the decision to translate Kierkegaard's title as *Practice in Christianity* or *Training in Christianity.* But the Danish title refers to Christendom, *Christendom,* not to Christianity. Kierkegaard commonly uses the term Christendom pejoratively—and then sometimes in quotation marks—to denote the established institution. Although there are what he describes as essential and genuine Christians in Christendom, the book in question is as much about what leads out of or away from genuine Christianity as about what prepares a way into it. His title has an ambiguity similar to that of Heidegger's title *Einführung in die Metaphysik.* Heidegger's book is not an introduction to metaphysics. Rather is it a book concerning induction into metaphysics, and concerning metaphysics in both an old and a new sense of the term. Heidegger hopes that his readers will hear in "induction" or "introduction" the echo of "seduction" ("*Verführung*"). This is why philosophy and what he calls thinking have to be done slowly. Perhaps Kierkegaard hopes his readers will see why a certain slowness is called for in the approach either into Christianity or into Christendom, whether or not the latter be understood pejoratively; for, after all, if getting into a bad habit is a sort of seduction, so too is getting out.

These ambiguities open up the possibility that in endorsing Luther's statement that works are training exercises Kierkegaard takes Luther to be speaking of the malpractice of Christendom, ungenuine Christianity's bad habits. For Luther is charged with inculcating those bad habits. The justice of this charge becomes manifest when Luther's doctrine that faith alone saves is put in the context of the Reformer's own life. For instance, Kierkegaard observes— quite aware that his observation must be put in the context of his, Søren's, own life—Luther got married, and failed to underline that he was thereby reducing Christianity or, more exactly, New Testament Christianity, the Christianity that distances itself from the view he finds expressed in the Hebrew Bible that a man lives in sin when he lives without wife and child.[2] Luther rejects both this Old Testament doctrine and the Roman Catholic doctrine that marriage is a sacrament. Kierkegaard's appraisal of Luther is in agreement with the judgment expressed in those paragraphs of *The World as Will and Representation* in which Schopenhauer contends that Luther "reduces" the claims of Christianity.[3] He does this, Kierkegaard maintains, by bringing about certain "alterations," for instance alterations in the Christian notions of virginity and martyrdom. Luther maintains that except for those like Jeremiah and Paul and Christ who are "specially called," chastity is possible only within marriage sanctified by God. Against this Schopenhauer asks, What about communities like those of the Shakers, who practice celibacy? Kierkegaard himself anticipates the riposte that the natural consequence of Shaker celibacy is that their communities have almost died out.

> The error in Catholicism is not that the priest is unmarried—no, the error is that a qualitative distinction has been introduced between laity and clergy which is directly opposed to the New Testament and is a concession of weakness in the direction of numbers. No, the error is that the priest is unmarried—a Christian ought to be unmarried.
>
> "But if this is going to be stressed, you won't get any Christians."—what difference does it make!
>
> "If, on the other hand, you make marriage into Christianity, you will get millions of Christians"—again, what difference does it make![4]

Where with paganism and Judaism offspring are a substitute for metaphysical immortality, with essential Christianity numbers don't count. And if Kierkegaard's response to Luther's reduction of Christianity seems to reduce itself to absurdity, that might only go to confirm his assertions elsewhere that essential Christianity is essentially absurd. However, he has a little more to say about the vanishing of Christianity from this world. This world is a sinful world from which Christianity has always already vanished. But Christendom has every chance of persisting, and therewith persists the chance of genuine Christians. This biological chance is kept open by a distinction that replaces the distinction between laity and clergy, namely the distinction between those who, like Paul, have had a direct concrete relation with God, and those who have not. The latter will go forth and multiply. So when Kierkegaard complains that Luther should have scrupulously made it clear that his marriage was an exception, he could be meaning that marriage, anyone's marriage, is an exception to what is demanded of the apostle. There is a second sense in which Luther's marriage might be seen as an exception. It may be seen as an exception when compared with marriages motivated by the sexual drive. For although Luther—who had once said, "They'll never force a wife on me!"— went on to become a paterfamilias, his wife was originally one of twelve persecuted nuns. He married her in order to give her protection after failing to find anyone else who would. Luther himself was a monk, hence his marriage was an exception in a third sense. It was an exception to the rule laid down by Rome. In the light of this it is understandable why Kierkegaard says also that Luther's marriage was a corrective, notwithstanding the Reformer's failure to emphasize this.

If virginity is one of the conditions that make Christianity a religion of the spirit,[5] another is martyrdom. Although martyrdom cannot be required except of the apostle, it is of the essence of Christianity. Here again Luther redefines Christianity, watering it down so that it becomes comfortable, *gemütlich*. Kierkegaard himself uses the German word. The first syllable of this word signifies collectivity and the second syllable signifies mood, mind, or feeling. So together they signify the shared mood, mindedness, and feeling of sympathy. Luther toppled the pope only to set "the public" upon his throne.[6] He taught that one wins by numbers, whereas the victory of Christianity turns on the incalculable. And incalculable is the harm Luther has done by not becoming a martyr.[7]

Kierkegaard's criticism extends even to what he most admired in Luther, his reaffirmation of the Pauline and Augustinian teaching on the place of grace. In the Preface of 1545, which is also a postface in that 1545 was the last year of his life, Luther mentions several phrases in which use is made of a genitive "of" that means datively *to* or ablatively *by* or *with* or *from*. First, there is the phrase "the righteousness of God" (Romans 1:17, 3:5, 10:3) which was the vehicle of a breakthrough.

> Though I lived as a monk without reproach, I felt that I was a sinner before God with an extremely disturbed conscience. I could not believe that he was placated by my satisfaction. I did not love, indeed, I hated the righteous God who punishes sinners, and secretly. At last, by the mercy of God, meditating day and night, I turned to the context of the following words: "In it [the Gospel] the righteousness of God is revealed, as it is written, 'He who through faith is righteous shall live.'" There I began to understand the righteousness of God is that by which the righteous live through a gift of God, namely by faith. And this is the meaning: The righteousness of God which is revealed by the gospel, is a passive righteousness with which the merciful God justifies us by faith, as it is written, "He who through faith is righteous shall live." Here I felt that I was altogether born again and had entered paradise itself through open gates. There a totally other face of the entire Scripture showed itself to me. So then I ran through the Scriptures from memory. I found analogies in other phrases as: the work of God (*opus Dei*), that is, what God does in us; the power of God (*virtus Dei*), with which he makes us strong; the wisdom of God (*sapientia Dei*), with which he makes us wise; the strength of God (*fortitudo Dei*), the salvation of God (*salus Dei*), the glory of God (*gloria Dei*).[8]

An ocean of theology in a drop of grammar. The change of aspect these genitives undergo would be described by Luther through one of them as "a gift of God." It could be described too as a *metanoia,* an expression that had itself undergone a change of aspect for Luther earlier in his career. He had been accustomed to translating this word as "penitence," associating it with the sacrament of "doing penance," in the sense of *poenitentiam agere,* the Vulgate translation of the Greek word. In a letter of 1518 to his superior and mentor Johann von Staupitz he records that the confession and absolution which this practice called for never freed him from torment.[9] Liberation from this came only when it struck him that *metanoia* is literally re-pentance or re-pensation, a re-thinking or after-thought in which one comes to one's right mind. His word is *re-sipiscentia.* It is a *re-pendere,* a weighing again. It is a "journey of the mind" as symbolized in the exodus from Egypt, in the very name given to Abraham when he is called a Hebrew, that is to say, a wayfarer. "The title of the psalm in which the singer is called *idithun,* that is 'one who leads over,' has the same force."[10]

> I saw that *metanoia* can be derived not only from "afterwards" and "mind" but also "change" or "across" and "mind" (admittedly, this may be forced), so that *metanoia* means change of mind and affection, and this seems to suggest, not only the change of affection, but also the mode of the change, namely the grace of God.

"Wonderful, wonderful!" Kierkegaard would say. But, he would quickly add, Luther's journey to this change of mind and heart takes a short cut to grace. That this is so is hinted at in the attitude he takes up with regard to the torment from which his rethinking comes as a release. But a certain torment is inseparable from grace. Luther takes the name of grace in vain. He abstracts it from the suffering of strife that is still necessary, the works that are still called for even though they are not works that earn merit. Although "It is faith which works that one does truly good works,"[11] it is not enough to see grace as a recourse against the despair that ensues from a task which is so superhumanly heavy that we waste our time even trying to begin it. He short-weights Christianity when he infers that because striving in this life wins us no merit for salvation, there is no need for strife. When Luther simply substitutes grace for meritorious works because "otherwise we must despair" he is taking one's suffering in the world as a criterion of what Christianity demands. He is speaking as a patient rather than a physician. At best he is seeing Christ only as the Comforter. "[It] is odd for a person designated to be God's man to the degree he was to end up in ordinary comfortable association with adoring admirers and followers. . . . The *Table Talks* are an example: a man of God sitting in placid comfort, ringed by admiring adorers who believe that if he simply breaks wind it is a revelation or the result of inspiration."[12] The demand made upon Christians to imitate (*efterfølge*) Christ degenerates into the desire to ape (*efterabe*) each other. The reformer becomes a politician, that is to say, the existing individual is sacrificed to the mass in which millions add up to one.

> "100,000 millions, each of whom is just like the others," = one.
> Only when someone comes along who is different from these millions or this one, only then are there two.
> In the world of number unity counts; in the world of the spirit there is no counting at all, or there differentiation counts, and consequently there is no counting.[13]

Hence Kierkegaard's distinction between two concepts of saving. A person can be saved as a Christian individual from the crowd, from the nation, from the whole world, *tout le monde*. This is the salvation with which true Christianity begins (a salvation which, we shall find in chapter 7, has something in common, namely its not being common, with Nietzsche's recipe for a salvation from Christianity as interpreted by him). Alternatively, a person can be saved from individuality with everyone else. "Nowadays we have: all of us are saved, the cat and the dog, too, perhaps—and this is the same teaching which in the New Testament is Christianity!" Reflecting on these two kinds of salvation, Kierkegaard arrives at a standstill.

## Midlife Pause

In what he calls his standstill Kierkegaard still stands by the aristocratic alternative. But he finds himself stopped in his tracks. Is what stops him his own human sympathy, leading him to prefer being saved with others to salvation without them? Only if this "with" can be parsed in a way consistent with the truth that we are deceiving ourselves if we suppose that humans can educate each other into Christianity and that Christian communion is a direct communication with one another based on what makes the other my sister or brother and therefore my ilk and *mon semblable*. That is to mistake the temporality of this world for eternity. "Alas," Kierkegaard adds, "I write this in sadness. Myself unhappy, I loved men and the crowd with melancholy sympathy." But it is not this sympathy that gives him pause, as he goes on to make plain. "Their brutishness to me forced me (that I might endure it) more and more to involve myself with God. The result is that undoubtedly I have come to know what Christianity is, but it pains me, this truth."[14] The truth that pains him is not the truth that knowing what Christianity is means knowing that it is not an expression of human sympathy, whether melancholy or glad. The truth in question is not as simple as that. It has to do not with a tension between what Christianity requires and his own natural sympathy. The latter, though not to be taken as an expression of Christianity, is yet perfectly consistent with Christianity. So he is able to say, "I dare to rejoice upon seeing the joy of others, and I dare *Christianly* to sanction it."[15] *Aber, aber,* but, but, as he writes again in the language of Hegel, what he describes as "the interpretation I have put on my life," "To be loved by a woman, to live in a happy marriage, enjoying life—this is denied me"; "I who have long considered myself chosen for suffering," an Israel chosen by Christ, knowing "that dying to the world, to be loved by God, means to suffer . . . I cannot have the sad joy of rejoicing in their happiness, the sad joy of being loved by them."—"Therefore this difficulty has brought me up short." The difficulty for him stems from the very fact that human sympathy is logically consistent with Christianity. It is a difficulty *for him*. He does not say that it is a difficulty for others, as though they too should deny themselves the joys of life. That would be to deny after all that human sympathy is logically consistent with Christianity, and to deny this would be to be unKantian insofar as it would be affirming that it is unChristian to acknowledge imperfect obligations to promote the earthly happiness of others. However, Kierkegaard is indeed being unKantian. Not teaching unKantianism, but exposing Kant's failure to understand Christianity notwithstanding the importance of his denial of knowledge in order to make room for belief. Kant's conception of Christian belief remains too doctrinal and propositionally didactic. Christian belief, Christian faith, is not universalizable. It is in its essential moment not only not universalizable; it cannot, without betraying itself, be stated even in a proposition that makes no claim to universalizability, for, to vary slightly what Aquinas and Descartes say about God, Christian faith spills over the brim of any concept and therefore of any proposition. It does this because it is absurd. It is absurd because the essential moment of Christian faith is a moment of contradiction. Not a formal logical contradiction, for that would be a contradiction for everyone; nor a contradiction such as is the stuff of tragedy as tragedy is understood by Kierkegaard, for, whether or not such tragedial contradictions can be resolved, they arise within the field of general ethics as this is understood by Kierkegaard. The contradiction is between the sympathy natural to a human being and an existing singular individual's choice of Christ. This contradiction is one of the dilemmas that bring Kierkegaard to a standstill.

There is another dilemma that brings him to a halt, another *aporia* or *angustia*.[16] It is linked to the complex just described, but it adds to it a further fold, a fold over and above such shame as Gabriel Fauré suffered at the thought that his deafness might seem to put him in the company of Beethoven. This time Kierkegaard's anguish is provoked by the question whether he could pray for the love of God if that meant praying for his own suffering. This disturbs him not on account of the suffering, but because to pray for his own suffering might be "*too high*," too lofty, presumptuous, as though he thought he could reach the level of an apostle—a status even Paul says it is not meet for him to claim for himself (1 Corinthians 15:9; but see also 1 Corinthians 9:1–2 and Galatians 1:1). The anguish arises out of the tension between the need to suffer, because to love God is to suffer, and the risk that God's anger may be aroused by my presumption in praying for suffering. The dilemma is this:

EITHER: I risk God's wrath by praying for the suffering implied by God's love. "[N]othing, nothing fills me with such boundless anxiety as the thought of coming too close to God without being called."[17] But this anxiety is in danger of being a "trick on the part of my heart," "letting it seem as if I remained on the outside personally"[18] in poetic, that is to say uncommitted, communication, so escaping the humiliation of revealing the imperfection in my striving. I adopt humility in order to get out of suffering and, as a bonus, I am honored for adopting that humility. It is all right not to aspire to the extraordinary gifts of the apostle in the face of suffering, but to be so "humble" as not to aspire to being exposed to suffering at all would be "outright hypocrisy."

OR: I pray for happiness and good fortune. But this is *too low*, mere *Christendom* in the pejorative sense.[19] I thereby forfeit God's love.

Kierkegaard finds himself chosen to choose the first alternative in this second dilemma. But it remains unclear to him, he says, how he is to pray (as for very different reasons this will remain unclear for one of the participants in an exchange that will be reported in chapter 13). "That is why for some time now my praying has been different, actually a calm leaving of everything to God."[20] This leaves him having to face the risk entailed by the truth that "God is spirit and cannot express his love except by requiring you to suffer; if you are not willing to suffer, you will then be free from God's love."[21] Where rescue waxes, there dwells danger too. Outside the *Gelassenheit* of his newly found way of praying, the only "relief" availed in these circumstances is that afforded by the thought that the anguish is part of the suffering without which there is no *Christianity*. This holds too for the first difficulty. With regard to that difficulty, however, Kierkegaard writes a year before his death of "a sympathetic relief"[22] in a manner that demonstrates his willingness to allow that not every suffering is to be welcomed as a mark or criterion of God's love. The relief is a release from the particular suffering caused by the thought that "the interpretation I have put on my life" makes the standards according to which that life is to be lived so rigorously exacting that others seem to be excluded from Christian salvation. That offends his human sympathy.

The way through this particular anguish is the supplementary interpretation which recognizes that although Christianity promises salvation for all, "with respect to the conditions of salvation every single individual must relate to God as a single individual." This leaves in place the "contradiction" mentioned above between universality and singularity, which is not a plain logical contradiction but a contradiction between the realm of logic and the singular individual's act of faith. Kierkegaard would call this a passionate act. Pascal would say that it is an act whose logic is that of the heart. It is an expression of pathos, the pathos to name which recourse is had to the two-way genitivity of the love of God. Here the love of God dovetails with the love of humankind. This is why the relief provided by Kierkegaard's supplementary interpretation is called sympathetic. As such it is further evidence that if Kierkegaard's preoccupation with his own salvation comes across as a kind of narcissism, its narcissism is not egotism. Although it is in a manner of speaking self-centered—and the self-centeredness has to do indeed with a manner of speaking, a mode of communication—this so-called narcissism manages to escape egotism. And it does this without entrapment in the other extreme, where the singularity of the existing individual gets swallowed up in the oneness of humanity conceived as a crowd, whether as us, as them, or as Heidegger will say, as *das Man,* the oneness of the impersonal "one." Yet Kierkegaard's interpretation of Christianity opens a way of understanding how the love of God leads to the love of the neighbor. What it does not show is whether the way leads in the reverse direction too.

## *Eppur Si Muove*

God shows you his love for you by forsaking you. Becoming a Christian means being "cursed by mankind, hated, tormented in every way, and finally abandoned by God."[23] This is a hard saying. It is in line with Kierkegaard's asseverations that the suffering entailed by becoming a Christian must be hard (as hard, we shall see in chapter 6, as the hard morality Nietzsche distinguishes from the morality of the herd). This hard saying is, however, not in line with his interpretation of Christianity if it is interpreted as a statement of objective fact. It is not in line with this because it is not in line with Kierkegaard's interpretation of religious language as originally subjective in his sense of inward. God's having abandoned Christ and the Christian does not mean that God is not in some sense still there. His having abandoned me is his having brought me to despair. And despair is the worst sort of sin. It is not only sin from weakness: "a person sins out of despair over having been weak or over being weak enough to sin."[24] The depth of sin is the depth of despair. This depth is the height of God's majesty. The height of this majesty, however, must not be so elevated that human beings think it safe to carry on a secular life as though God did not exist or to pursue a religious life lived without taking any risk. God's majesty does not lift him outside "the actualities of this world."[25] Still, as against the all too worldly pagan god's love, the God of love, who is spirit, is better at hiding his love.[26] He secretes it in the loved one's unhappiness and bad fortune. But this bad fortune is also his good fortune, his *Lykke*. For it is only if God punishes the profoundest sin of the loved one by ignoring him so that he thinks all is lost that a person can experience the need for Atonement. This is not a deal in which God promises a gift in return for something. It is a grace. This sequence makes psychological sense independently of the story of the Cross, even if it remains psychologically difficult "to see one thing in its opposite *simultaneously*," in this case to see that "It is in sin that one gets a first sense of blessedness."[27] But can "sin," a term of religion, be translated into the language of secular psychology? And must at least an ungodly religious sense of "sin" and/or of sin be retained if we are to understand what Kierkegaard is saying here? If such a sense has to be kept, then, assuming that the secular and the religious are exhaustive alternatives (an assumption that will be questioned and complicated below), any good psychological sense that his statement makes will have a non-secular dimension.

As for the psychological, so for the moral and for moral psychology. We may choose to restrict the moral to the secular domain. That restriction, Kierkegaard would seem to say, is what explains the protestations of Job's friends. They can make sense of Job's sufferings only by interpreting sin as criminal guilt, and by supposing that those sufferings are punishment for a wrong Job has done. (Here is a key to understanding what Levinas and Derrida mean by responsibility.) "This is essentially human selfishness, which desires to avoid the earnest and disturbing impression of suffering, of what can happen in this life—therefore in order to protect ourselves against this we explain suffering as guilt: It is his own fault. O, human cruelty."[28]

Similarly, the "earnest and disturbing" impression of love is avoided when we assume that one must love someone for the happiness he or she brings instead of for nothing: "the greatest possible striving is for nothing, signifies nothing."[29] Love for someone because he or she makes you happy is not love that springs from within oneself. It is a love contingent on something that is outside the self and for this very reason may be love of self, essentially narcissistic human self-ishness again. Striving is an expression of the greatest possible love only when it is a love for one who makes you unhappy.[30] Such love is love of God. In the Christian context at least this means imitation of Christ. Imitation of Christ means experiencing another's pain in a way that one does not experience a pain that is only one's own. A severe headache wraps me up in myself. The pain suf-fered in the imitation of Christ takes one out of one's self. But cannot the love of one human being for another be that selfless? Aside from the doctrine that Christ is a human being, would not such selfless love for another human being make morality or ethicality religious, without making it dependent on love of God? Is one necessarily *Keeping Religion out of Morality,* as is declared by the subtitle of the fine book Richard Holloway entitles *Godless Morality*?[31] Is not atheism religious? Are not untheistic versions of Buddhism? And are they not capable of being forms of morality or ethics?

Kierkegaard himself frequently yokes the ethical with the religious in the hyphenated phrase "ethical-religious." If the second of these linked adjectives denotes Religiousness A, which is theistic, his phrase "ethical-religious" can-not apply to the godless religious ethicality that would seem to be excluded by the conjunction of the title and subtitle of Richard Holloway's book if we take the word *"Religion"* there to mean religiousness, not instituted religions. Nor, a fortiori, could this space for a godless religious morality be occupied by Religiousness B, which is the religiousness intended on some of the occasions when Kierkegaard hyphenates the ethical and the religious. One such occasion is that on which in *The Sickness unto Death* aesthetic spiritlessness is contrasted with spiritfulness and spiritlessness as defined by the categories of the *ethisk-religieuse.*[32] Another such occasion is that point of the *Concluding Unscientific Postscript* where we read that the ethical and the religious are in constant com-munication with each other, such communication as is demonstrated most terrifyingly by the so-called suspension and renewal of the ethical by the reli-gious on Moriah.[33] But the godless religious morality that the title and subtitle of Richard Holloway's book taken together seem not to allow does not do away with God. It only does without him—or her or it. The question of the possibility of such a godless religious morality is still open.

Still open too is the question that brings Kierkegaard to the halt which makes room for prayer as a calm leaving everything to God—an anticipation of Nietzsche's *amor fati,* of Heidegger's finding himself able to let metaphysics be and of Derrida's demonstration that the mourning (*deuil*) of metaphysics is not getting rid of it, *en faire son deuil,* but imagining its survival in unimaginable ways. That calm leaving of everything to God is also a calm coming back to the subjectivity of inwardness. Therefore the place at which Kierkegaard comes to a standstill is far removed from that at which Luther proclaims, "Here I stand." Without daring to place himself near the apostle, Kierkegaard would not want the position at which he is brought to a halt to be likened to that at which Luther exclaimed "I can no other. God help me. Amen." For where "'The apostle' expresses Christianity in God's interest . . . Luther expresses Christianity in man's interest."[34] Kierkegaard's standstill is not a full stop. It punctuates his life in the manner of a colon: it introduces an advance. No more than the wonder-struck aporia with which Aristotle and Plato say philosophy begins is the aporia with which religion and theology begin a point of rest. Kierkegaard's aporia is a point of restlessness: "[N]o Christian can remain in security and at rest. If one is to become a Christian, there must be restlessness, and if one has become a Christian, restlessness continues."[35] The calm with which Kierkegaard waits for a response to his prayer is the calm of a waiting that is a holding back *pour mieux sauter,* a preparation for the qualitative leap. This holds too for the halt when he writes: "A man doubts that the sin he commits out of weakness can be forgiven. All is lost, he thinks, and thus he sins. Therefore it takes the Atonement to bring him to a halt."[36] The Atonement is the grace referred to in Luther's statement that "[h]aving been justified by grace, we then do good work."[37] By Kierkegaard's lofty standards Luther may have made too little of strife in his life, but he did make enough of it in his doctrines.

This criticism of Luther does not prevent Kierkegaard writing that works are jest (*Spøg*) in comparison with the earnestness (*Alvor*) of grace. He means not that works are in themselves a jest, but that in comparison with grace they are not a way of or a way to salvation. How can works in themselves be a jest if they are works of love, if they take the form of striving to love one's neighbor as oneself? Striving is restlessness made more restless by the knowledge that one will continually fall short.

So the standstill at some critical point during one's life is not stasis unless this word is taken in the sense not of rest, but in the other sense that its Greek root allows, discord. Kierkegaard's standstill is coming up against the absolute which is the inwardness of subjectivity. It is to this that he is referring when, with veiled allusion to the break with Regine, the repercussions of which persisted until the end of his life, he writes: "[V]ery early in life I was 'halted' ('*Standset*') myself by being set outside the universally human in unspeakable sufferings and thrust solely upon the relationship to God."[38] *Eppur si muove.* This standstill *nel mezzo del cammin* still moves. But what about the end of his life, and what about its beginning?

## Salvation

What about beginning as such? The question of beginning, Kierkegaard maintains, is ill-posed by Hegelians,

> as if the question were merely whether we should *begin* with being or becoming. No, the question about becoming, about movement, comes again at every point; if we do not begin by presupposing *kinēsis,* we do not move from the spot with *seyn;* if, however, we assume motion, then we can bring it to a halt at every point, because getting away from the initial spot already involved *kinēsis.*[39]

But what about the end? Is the end of the Christian life becoming a Christian or is it eternal salvation? Is it just possible that these ends are one and the same? Could the Christian life be salvation? If so, despite his endorsements of the statements of Paul and Luther that we must die to this world, Kierkegaard could be our guide to a godless but religious morality that would be a living to this world in a sense lying between, on the one hand, dying to this world as understood by Paul, Luther, and himself, and, on the other hand, a religiousness that is still in the image of God. It will not pass unnoticed by any of Kierkegaard's readers that, like many another thinker, he speaks indiscriminately of eternal salvation and eternal happiness. Any risk of thereby turning salvation into the best of all possible temporal worlds is excluded by the epithet "eternal." But just as the greatest possible happiness in time gets spoken of as a future state, so does eternal salvation. It gets connected with notions of a resurrection to an immortality or after-life. It gets spoken of in this way by Kierkegaard when the end of life as a *telos* gets identified with the end of a life as its close, as in the statement "When in the hour of death it grows dark for a true Christian, it is because the sunlight of eternal happiness shines too brightly in his eyes." (Wonderful, wonderful!) Another temptation to which Christendom succumbs is that of picturing salvation as Paradise regained, a return to the Garden of Eden regarded as a state or a State, the Kingdom of Heaven. "A desperate sinner wakes up in hell and cries out, 'What time is it?' The devil answers, 'Eternity.'"[40] Note well that the devil can be forgiven insofar as if heaven is eternal so too is

hell. One talks of eternal bliss or salvation, but one also talks of eternal damnation. Clearly, in Kierkegaard's joke about the sinner and the Devil the noun
"Eternity" is to be taken in a restricted sense. Eternity is timeless in a way in
which hell is not. One reason why hell is hellish is that time hangs on one's
hands there so heavily. But Eternity too is not exclusive of time. "The relationship between time and eternity is such as is found in the Hebrew word '*ad*,'
which first means *transitus* and then eternity, except that the eternal must not
be understood merely as a denominator of *transitus* but also as a continuous
state of fulfilment."[41] In other words, "Eternity does not abolish temporality
but fulfils it."[42] It does this by being brought into the world so that the world
that has been got rid of is given back renewed. Not, however, as an appendix
or postscript. That would be to confuse essential Christianity with the official
Christianity of Christendom, which "has gained these millions of Christians
by teaching that to love God is to love oneself, that in order really to enjoy this
life one must have the cooperation of God," and that "the expectation of an
eternal salvation is the primary factor in adding flavour to the joys and blessings of this life."[43] True Christianity does not see the highest good, salvation, as
a teleological tag-end. Rather is it "a matter of drawing God into actualities of
this world, where he certainly is, after all."[44] This remark comes as a comment
on that paradigm of soteriology, the shipwreck, in this case the shipwreck that
befell Paul on his voyage to Rome (Acts 27). Drawing God into the actualities
(*Virkelighed*) of this world takes the form here of first distinguishing eternal
salvation from temporal salvation but then reading eternal salvation in terms of
Paul's concern for the temporal salvation of his fellow travelers. Paul does not
say "It is all over now, etc. I will think only of my soul's salvation." One way by
which Paul draws God into the actualities is by making a prayer of intercession
for the temporal salvation of his shipboard companions. That is a beautiful illustration of the way that the temporal and the eternal cross each other—thanks
to the Cross, Kierkegaard would say, *grâce à la grâce*. Kierkegaard says of himself that although in a sense he has lived in a world of his own, he has stood "in
the middle of actuality on a scale unknown to anyone else here at home," adding
with the protection not only of parentheses but also of quotation marks (how
much more "secret" can one get?), "I have more or less reached 'actuality.'"[45]
Actuality is contrasted with possibility. When I understand something as possibility only it is a matter for abstract imagination, contemplating something
in "tranquillity."[46] It is as possibility not as actuality that Christianity is viewed
by "Christendom." Since we have been speaking of a voyage, let us say that the
difference between possibility and actuality is the difference between looking
at a marine chart on dry land and actually putting out to sea. Again, it is the
difference between considering what it would be like to swim and leaping in at
the deep end, knowing that one may sink: "actuality is placed very close to me,

all too close; it has, as it were, swallowed me, and the question now is whether I can rescue myself from it."[47] Kierkegaard's answer to this question is that he cannot, that only God can rescue him.

Tranquillity (*Ro*) is not to be confused with the so-called quiet calm of the halt in which Kierkegaard decides to leave everything to God (*stille Overladen*).[48] The latter anticipates the authentic letting-be (*Seinlassen*) of *Being and Time,* which it would be less misleading to refer to as letting-being-be, for it is not a passive quietism, not inactivity, any more than Kierkegaard's "quiet leaving to God" excludes striving. What Kierkegaard calls tranquillity anticipates Heidegger's "tranquillizing" (*Beruhigung*) that leads to the suppression of authentic concern under an inauthentic busyness.[49] "What human nature constantly seeks, however, is—tranquillity—*nil beatum nisi quietum*—tranquillity, tranquillity in order to be occupied with this finite life, to enjoy life here and now."[50]

And here and now is the point at which Kierkegaard demonstrates his reluctance to acknowledge that the enjoyment of life here and now is not the only alternative to a life expressing the love of God. It is said that God is love. This is not to say that love is God or love of God in either sense of the genitive. And the love of the world that is contrasted with this love can be other than love of the world for the enjoyment we get out of it. In *For Self-Examination: Judge for Yourself* we are told "that what we extol under the name of love is self-love, and that the whole of Christianity becomes confused for us when we do not pay attention to this."[51] A journal entry dated 1841, so preceding the date of publication of *Works of Love* by six years, runs: "and we sometimes hear, frequently enough, those wild cries of grief: If this or that desire is not fulfilled, then what is life, what is the very bliss of heaven, how could it compensate me for the loss of the only thing I desired in the world—but we must not *love the world* in this way."[52] The italics are Kierkegaard's. Instead of stressing those three italicized words, let us stress the three words that follow. That is, let us distinguish from love of the world that is love of oneself, love of the world that is unself-centered *agapē*. A journal entry of the same year runs: "No matter what variations there may be of the Narcissus legend, they all agree that in the end he saw himself in a river, became enamoured of himself, and thus in a horrible manner became a sacrifice to unhappy love."[53] The love of Narcissus is *erōs,* and that is the love with which *Either/Or* and *Works of Love* are heavily concerned. One of the concerns of these writings is to show how forms of love and friendship that appear to be selfless are forms of self-love and narcissism, either love of self directly or love of self through one's self reflected in the alter-ego. The only love that is not self-love is love of the neighbor as the love of humankind as the love of all creatures of God.

Is there no love of the world that is neither love of oneself nor love of God nor love of what is regarded as created by God? Further, could love be love of what is regarded as created by God only if the relevant notion of love is the one that is historically dependent on Christianity? The relevant notion could be historically dependent on Christianity without the notion having to be a Christian one. Although the work of Emmanuel Levinas may be read as an attempt to show that the first of these two questions can be answered in the affirmative, it is, to say the least, improbable that in his work could be discovered an affirmative answer to the second. But in Levinas's work love of the world is defined as love of humankind in the sense of the French phrase *tout le monde*. More work has to be done if love of the world is to be understood as love of *all* of the world, that is to say of the non-human world as well, and of that not solely for the benefits and enjoyment derived from it by humans. Still more work is called for if this love of the world and all that is in it is the love for which we adopt the Greek term *agapē* in order to mark that it includes respect, that is to say, in order to mark that this love is ethical. It remains to be shown in what way that ethical love would be religious yet not necessarily religious through invocation of God. These tasks will be faced in the following chapter and further on in this book. The religious but godless morality outlined there will turn out to be one in which a certain uncertainty, restlessness, and insecurity are unavoidable, for a reason we can give before bringing the present chapter to an end.

The present chapter has underlined the irreducible restlessness that characterizes the godful religion of Kierkegaard. Kierkegaard's Christianity is from before the beginning kinetic. Its apparent midlife standstills are still moments of unresting strife. This holds too for the end of Christian life. The Kierkegaardian and, as he sees it, Christian notion of salvation remains a state of unremaining. It is a state of statelessness. It is as though the promised land were never reached; as though Israel, the Christian Knight of Faith, and Søren Kierkegaard were, in the words of one of the latter's close readers—one who receives those words from and returns them to their author—always underway, *immer unterwegs, altid undervejs*. Kierkegaard is underway to that reader's reading of death not as primarily a datable event, but as the condition of all datability, the *es gibt* that is the dativeness in absolute ablativeness of death as mortality and mortality as a being-toward. Not toward immortality conceived as a state, but, for Kierkegaard and Heidegger—though not, or not so immediately, for Levinas—toward oneself. On this interpretation salvation becomes a kind of becoming. For Heidegger it becomes becoming authentic. For Kierkegaard it becomes becoming eternal understood as becoming a Christian, eternity being adverbial to one's existing (in) the spatiality and temporality of the here and now. Eternal salvation is a mode of the singular individual's existing, the how of his living first hell on earth through his living heaven on earth. "Mercy, grace, infinite grace, now consists in enduring hell on earth through becoming a Christian, and then being eternally saved."[54] His being eternally saved is his living enthusiastically, inspired by God. And, since God is love, being inspired by God means being inspired by love, where love is understood as concern for the beloved, whether the beloved be another or oneself. Understood as *agapē,* love is concern for the other, a restlessness on the beloved's behalf. Being saved is being rescued from concern for one's own security and being turned toward concern for the insecurity of the other. That is to say, if ethics is given back in religion, saved by it, religion or at any rate religiousness is saved by ethics.

# FIVE

## Works of Love

### The Lily and the Dove

To speak of the Kierkegaardian and Christian notion of eternal salvation, as is done at the ends of chapters 3 and 4, is to speak carelessly. For there is more than one Christian notion of salvation. Most notably, aside from the question of what is to be understood by salvation, there is the notion of salvation achieved through works and there is the notion of salvation achieved by grace. Kierkegaard's frequent approving references to Paul and Luther leave no room for doubt that he sees salvation as a gift. Furthermore, the rhetoric of his references to salvation conveys a strong impression that he or his pseudonymous author is primarily speaking of his own salvation, and that that has some kind of primacy. That is the impression that will have been suggested by the references to eternal salvation and eternal happiness cited from the pseudonymous and non-pseudonymous writings of Kierkegaard in this book so far. Incidentally, it is also the impression the reading of Kierkegaard left on Levinas. The philosopher of the you, you, you sees Kierkegaard as the philosopher of the me, me, me, or rather, the I, I, I. In fairness to both authors, however, it should be acknowledged that just as Levinas's you, you, you, do not refer to one and the same you, so Kierkegaard's I, I, I indicate not only Kierkegaard or the bearers of his pseudonyms. If there are passages in his or his pseudonymous authors' works that sound stridently narcissistic, care must be taken to distinguish what kind of narcissism this is, and to observe that where Kierkegaard seems to be going on about the importance of *his* eternal salvation, a plural and distributive narcissism would result if his concentration upon his own eternal salvation entailed indirectly, with an indirection to be explained below, the importance for each other singular self of her or his own eternal salvation. The multiplication of narcissisms only makes narcissism more—to use Kierkegaard's word—"offensive."

Care must be taken also to avoid the assumption that narcissism of every kind would be avoided if priority over grace were given to works. For even though, against Paul, Luther, and Kierkegaard, the way to salvation were deemed to be not grace but works, it could still be my salvation that concerns me ultimately. In chapter 3, however, the question was raised as to how a narcissistic reading of Religiousness B can be squared with the attention to community and works given in, for example, *Works of Love*. How again can such attention be reconciled even with what is written in the section of *Upbuilding Discourses in Various Spirits* entitled "What we learn from the lilies in the field and from the birds of the air."

Having cited at length Matthew 6, Kierkegaard invites us to "consider how by properly looking at the lilies in the field and at the birds of the air the worried person learns: to be contented with being a human being."[1] "Consider the lilies in the field." Kierkegaard's word is *betragte*. This is equivalent to the word *betrachte* that Heidegger uses when he says that "I myself don't ever really consider the landscape."[2] This does not mean that Heidegger cannot accept Kierkegaard's invitation. For Heidegger's "really consider" (*betrachte eigentlich*) is the sightseer's ocular viewing that would hope to capture the landscape in the way that it is trapped through the viewfinder in the camera's box. No more than Heidegger does Kierkegaard wish to lead the landscape into captivity. When Heidegger read Kierkegaard's meditation on Matthew he would have had no difficulty accepting the Dane's invitation "let us (*Lad os*) consider" and to "properly look" (*ret at see til*). Indeed, the "let" of the latter's invitation is not far removed from the letting of Heidegger's *Gelassenheit*. And the lily is an emblem of both. The lilies do not work. They toil not, neither do they spin. They do not spin, so in this they are unlike the woman of whom Kierkegaard now writes and unlike the woman of whom Heidegger writes in his reflections on van Gogh's painting of the shoes of a peasant whom Heidegger assumes is a woman. The woman to whom Kierkegaard refers here is like the lily that is adorned, that receives its adornment as a gift rather than having to work for it. The woman is like the lily too in that, although she spins, she stays at home. The peasant woman whom Heidegger imagines to have been the wearer of the boots in the painting by van Gogh does not stay at home. She has been out all day toiling in the field. "From the dark opening of the shoes the toilsome tread of the worker stares forth."[3]

Her shoes are "pervaded by uncomplaining anxiety as to the certainty of bread."
She is no wallflower. She is no adorned lily like the woman Kierkegaard compares to a lily which, like the rose of Angelus Silesius, does not ask why, or the
rose of Gertrude Stein which "is a rose is a rose." Yet on Kierkegaard's gloss of
Matthew even the worried peasant woman can learn from the lily what it is to
be a human being. She can learn from as insignificant a thing as the lily what
in a note signed "S. K." prefaced to his reflection on Matthew 6 is called "the
significance of appropriation." This last word translates "*Tilegnelsen*." This is
rendered by "*Zueignung*" in the translation of Kierkegaard that Heidegger read.
Now the Danish "*egne*" and the German "*eigen*" do indeed have the meaning
of properness, property, possession, owning, and suitability. The compounds
in which they occur in the texts of Kierkegaard and Heidegger may therefore
be taken to mean self-possession. But the prefixes turn this self-possession outward, giving the compounds the sense of dedication. In Kierkegaard's prefatory
note to the discourse on the lilies of the field the word *Tilegnelsens* (with a final
genitive *s*) is stressed. So too is another word used earlier in the same sentence,
the word *Myndighed*, meaning authority. The sentence runs:

> Although this little book is without the *authority* of the teacher, a *superfluous-
> ness, insignificant* like the lily and the bird—oh, would that it were so!—yet by
> finding the only thing it seeks, a good place, it hopes to find the *significance
> of appropriation* for that single individual, whom I with joy and gratitude
> call *my* reader.
>
> S. K.

The significance of appropriation is contrasted with the insignificance of the
book. The insignificance of the book is likened to the insignificance of the lily
and the bird in Matthew's parable, except that, in an exclamation amounting
almost to a prayer, the author of the book expresses the suspicion that its insignificance may not have the power to teach possessed by the lily and the bird,
who, in what is explicitly called a prayer following the preface, are described as
divinely appointed teachers. This prayer also describes them as counselors to
the worried. The worried turn out to be human beings imprisoned in comparing their possessions with those of others, and in comparing what they own
today with what they will need tomorrow if they are to survive. They need to
learn the lesson taught by the lilies that do not spin—"Once upon a time there
was a lily"—and by the bird—"Once upon a time there was a wood-dove." In the
manner of Hans Christian Andersen—suggesting that the so-called upbuilding or edifying Discourses might with more accuracy be called Tales—we are
told the story of a certain wild wood-dove that began to take thought for the
morrow. It decided its future would be secured if it joined the tame doves fed
by the farmer. But the farmer did not welcome this strange bird. When in the
evening he came to close the dovecot he put the visitor in a box and freed it

from its worries for the morrow by killing it the very next day. "Alas, the worried wood-dove had not only trapped itself in worry but had also trapped itself in the dovecot—unto death"—*til Døden—zum Tod.*

The moral of this tale is that to be a human being in possession of its humanity—Heidegger will say *Da-sein*—is to be a being that does not make comparisons of one day with another or of the properties and property it possesses with those possessed by another. "Is he not simultaneously and scandalously contradicting himself, he who clutches his worries about making a living at the same time that he is keeping them away by means of his treasure, and in his worry about making a living cares for it and increases it!" Although it is pleasing to God when people work in order to eat, it is not pleasing to God if they judge that they are independent providers. True independence is dependence on God. It is this dependence that is indicated by the *Til* of *Tilegnelsen,* introducing into the notion of owning a notion of dedication and owing.

## A Daffodil

Dedication is a giving. It could be the giving of oneself to God. If such self-giving underlies the apparent narcissism of Kierkegaard's going on and on about his eternal salvation or eternal happiness, is not this repetition—which, Kierkegaard insists in *Repetition,* is the willing of one thing (which corresponds to the Good in Levinas's adaptation of Plato)—the narcissism only of the daffodil, the narcissism, that is to say, of the *narcissus pseudo-narcissus*? Still a narcissism, but a pseudo-narcissism, a pseudonymous narcissism? Still a narcissism because the giving of himself to God seems at the same time to be a giving of himself back to himself?

As Levinas will do after him, Kierkegaard sees erotic love as a dyadic intimacy, "the very peak of self-esteem, the *I* intoxicated in the *other I.*"[4] "The more securely one *I* and another *I* join to become one *I,* the more this united *I* selfishly cuts itself off from everyone else." Yet something very like this is said of the becoming one spiritual flesh with God when Kierkegaard poses the rhetorical question: "With whom does a person have his most intimate relationship, with whom can one have the most intimate relationship?—is it not with God?"[5] But here the word "intimacy," which is also Levinas's word, is emphasized, which is again Levinas's word. When *erōs* is hyperbolized as *agapē* this intoxication is superseded by sobriety, which is another word of which both Kierkegaard and Levinas (not to mention again Paul) are very fond. This happens when the fidelity of faith in God intervenes in the confidentiality of one person with another. If two people are to confide completely in each other each must first separately confide in a third, "even if in each individual's confidentiality with God there remains the inexpressible that is precisely the sign that the relationship with God is the most intimate, the most confidential."

This "inexpressible" is precisely what creates the impression that despite the donation to God that concern with eternal happiness demands, Kierkegaard's concern with eternal happiness is turned inward toward himself. Does he not say again and again that the eternal demands inwardness? The eternal is touched on when in the paragraph of *Totality and Infinity* preceding what is called its "Conclusions"—as though it were Levinas's "Concluding Unscientific Postscript"—Levinas distinguishes the eternal from the perpetual and remarks that the framework of his book is exceeded by the problem whether the eternal is a new structure of time or an extreme watchfulness of messianic consciousness. The remark admits of being heard as an echo of the allusions made early in the book and elsewhere to Descartes's statement that the infinity of God cannot be contained in any human thought or idea. This exteriority to any idea is a key to what Levinas means by the ethical. Interpreted Christianly it corresponds to what Kierkegaard and, following him, Wittgenstein, call the inexpressible, what cannot be represented, what, as they and Levinas say, cannot be said. A person can be inward only with regard to what Levinas calls exteriority in the subtitle of *Totality and Infinity,* which describes that book as an essay on exteriority. What Kierkegaard calls externality, for instance throughout *Works of Love,* corresponds to what near the end of his book Levinas calls the perpetual. The external is the realm of the contingent, the realm of happiness in the sense of good fortune. And good fortune is contrasted with grace as that is understood by Kierkegaard in the wake of Luther, Augustine, and Paul. It follows that when Kierkegaard speaks of his eternal happiness, happiness is not the happiness of good fortune, the happiness of the dove whose fortune is to be well-provided for by the farmer's store of grain. On the contrary, eternal happiness is suffering. It is being mocked and deemed to be mad as was Christ on the Cross. For Kierkegaard as for Luther, a theology of glory is superseded by a theology of the Cross. Or glory is defined by them in terms of suffering, as it is defined by Levinas in terms, ones that will be taken up by Derrida, of my responsibility to another who makes me hostage and persecutes me.

Hence the importance of distinguishing two senses of anxiety and two senses of care. This is what Heidegger does when he distinguishes *Sorge* from *Besorgnis.* Kierkegaard's word for the latter is *Bekymring,* worry. This is the indecent worry for the morrow from which the lilies of the field are free. But, it must be asked, is not worry decent when it is worry over the well-being of others, even if their being well means their being free from physical and psychological distress? Some of Levinas's allusions to "materialism" and his qualified approval of Marx suggest that he would give an affirmative answer to this question. The other's needs to which we are called to respond according to him include the need for daily bread understood quite literally in contrast with what according to one doctrinal interpretation is symbolized by, for example, the bread of the Christian Mass! It is this bread, this dough—also in the slang sense of the latter word—that I am required to give to the widow, the orphan, and the stranger. And if I am required to sacrifice my life for other human beings, it may be in order that they may not have to lose theirs here on the earth beneath their feet, whatever the Christian might go on to say about losing life conceived in purely human terms to find a new life in the kingdom or queendom of God.

How does Kierkegaard comprehend this relation between the secular and the sacrosanct? If his perpetual harping upon his quest for eternal salvation only appears to nod its head, like the daffodil, downward and inward toward SK, is it an illusion too that it opens itself, like St. Peter's bell, the daffodil, only in the direction of God?[6] That this is an illusion follows from what we read in *Works of Love*. We are told that this is not a book about love, but one about works of love, and that means, we are told also, that it is about human works. Yet what Kierkegaard seems to mean by a human work of love is a deed that in a certain way assists one's neighbor to love God. In a certain way. In the Lutheran interpretation of Paul endorsed by Kierkegaard, human beings can achieve righteousness, *justitia,* understood not forensically but as a right relation to God, only by God's promising not to count their sins against them. This does not mean that one ceases to be a sinner. *Simul justus et peccator.* One is still a sinner even when made just, that is to say properly adjusted with regard to God, in an appropriate relation in the sense of *Tilegnelsen* and *Zueignung.* The dedication or donation that was seen to be implicit in these words refers here to the response the human being makes to God's promise. That response is the human being's act of faith. It might be said that the promise is accepted as such and that there is, as John Austin would say, "uptake" of it only if the promisee has faith. In the Lutheran and Kierkegaardian context at least, this is indeed an achievement, a decision and an act, but it is an act for which the agent can claim no merit. Her credo earns her no credit. Otherwise the rightwiseness of the human being's relation to God would not be a condition of salvation by faith alone, *sola fide.* It would be something of which one might boast. Theologians divide on the question whether the human being must already be endowed naturally with a predisposition to faith, one that could be strengthened by practice. This Christian Aristotelianism may be traced in Augustine and early Luther, as too, on some readings, in the doctrines of prevenient or of cooperative grace. But, if Luther's famous Preface of 1545 can be relied upon, these doctrines are eliminated from his mature theology in favor of the teaching that salvation is sheer gift without the least tinge of bargain. Salvation is not a return for merit achieved by keeping the Law, nor even for the complete surrender of oneself to God. But must not a remnant of willing survive such surrender? Otherwise surrender is replaced by rape and eternal grace reverts to its pagan parallel, luck or good fortune in the temporal world in which human beings are distinguished from one another by the color of their skin, by their sex, class, wealth, power, and so on. Therefore one surrenders oneself, but one does not surrender one's self. Indeed one gains one's self, where by this is meant the self of the command-ment to love one's neighbor as oneself. This self is the same from one person to another. Whether or not the commandment commands us to love our own selves or only to love others as we do as a matter of fact love ourselves without needing to be commanded to do so depends on which self we take to be referred to. If we take it to be the selfish self that is referred to, religion is on the edge of becoming the sanctification of instinct. And once religion is conceived in this manner we are primed to suspect Kierkegaard of edified narcissism. That he is pseudo-narcissistic becomes plain once we discover how strongly he stresses in *Works of Love* and elsewhere that Christian *agapē* is commanded. And the love that is commanded is both love of one's neighbor and love of God. In both cases, if indeed they are not the same (a question to which we shall return), love includes fidelity, the faith with which one responds to the beloved. Love is a passion, but because it is a passion in regard to a human being *in se,* it brings with it a sense of justice, where justice is not defined in terms of the differences among others or indeed between them and me, but in the light of that in which human beings are incomparable.

Here we have hit upon a matter over which Kierkegaard and Levinas (and perhaps also Derrida) do not agree, despite the many points of agreement we are finding. As children of God, Kierkegaard writes, human beings are equal, and that equality holds not only among one's neighbors, but also between one's neighbors and oneself. So what we think of as the Enlightenment idea of the equality of humankind is explicitly or implicitly a Christian idea according to him. Speaking of equality as equality of certain rights, Levinas acknowledges that such equality holds among my neighbors, but that any rights I may have are mine thanks to my neighbors or, as he sometimes puts it, *grâce à Dieu.* And when it comes to absolute responsibility, that is to say the responsibility neces-sary for the ethicality of the relative responsibilities that are often said to be coordinate with rights, I am more responsible than my neighbor. How deep this difference between Kierkegaard and Levinas is will depend on whether we con-sider that there is ultimately a difference between Kierkegaard's doctrine that God is, as he says, the middle term between me and my neighbor, and Levinas's statement to the effect that it is only through my relation to my neighbor (see however the next section below) that meaning can be given to the word "God"; as though for Kierkegaard what in chapter 3 we considered calling ethicality A becomes what we considered calling ethicality B only when the ethical is narthexed by what he himself calls Religiousness B. For Levinas the entry to religion is a humanism, a humanism of the other person.

Is Levinas's statement that it is only via my relation to my neighbor that meaning can be given to the word "God" tantamount to his statement that the He of what he calls Illeity (He-ity)—a neonym or neopronym, be it noted, that can rhyme with the paleonym Deity—is encountered only through the You who accuses me and in so doing confers upon me my selfhood? On this point, which may be a point of disagreement with Kierkegaard, there yet remains at least this much agreement between Kierkegaard and Levinas that in what the former may prefer to call religiousness and what the latter may prefer to call the ethical there is an accusation and accosting of the self that amounts to persecution. This is a note we have already heard in Levinas. It is heard also when Kierkegaard, still echoing Paul and Luther, insists that the Christian will be stoned and deemed mad by the Gentile. Christianity is folly to the Greek. Now the Jew Emmanuel Levinas insists that he is speaking Greek, for he wants to communicate with philosophers, that is to say, as he and Heidegger understand it, the tradition of occidental rationality deriving from Athens. Levinas speaks Greek. In this he is like Paul, with the difference that Christianity remains a stumbling-block for the first of these two Jews. This is one difficulty that did not have to be faced by a third Jew, the one called Jesus Christ. However, Christ was locked into Aramaic. His isolation could not be palliated by his having Greek in which to communicate with his persecutors. Did that make Christ's Christianity more difficult or less difficult? Perhaps both. For at least on Kierkegaard's account of Christianity—which is already a threat to Christianity to the degree that it is an account, a *logos,* albeit a *logos* of the *Logos*—Christianity is not permitted to have any palliative. However, unless he is speaking with his tongue in his cheek, Kierkegaard lowers his guard when he dares to say:

> even if he was exposed to the derision of the lower class or the mockery of the distinguished or both, that one in the hour of death will dare to say consolingly to his soul, "I have done my part; whether I have achieved anything, I do not know, whether I have benefited anyone, I do not know; but that I have existed for them, that I do know, and I know it because of their derision. And this is my consolation, that I will not take with me to the grave the secret that in order to have a good and undisturbed and comfortable life I denied kinship with other human beings, with the lowly, in order to live in stately seclusion with the distinguished, in order to live in hidden obscurity."[7]

The derision of my hearers is itself a consolation because it lets me know that I have existed for them. What I know is that others have been made aware by my example, by my taking Christ as my example, by my *imitatio Christi.* In the title of Kierkegaard's *Practice of Christianity* the "of" marks a double genitive, and the first word, we have noted, translates *Indøvelse,* which is drill or training, as in the title of another published English version of the book, and as in the statement that to learn what it means to be a Christian one must "practice resorting to grace" in fear and trembling.[8] Now to imitate Christ is to perform works of love, and that means to try to meet my neighbors' material needs. But, if only for the reason Kant gives when he alleges that we cannot be sure what others need or enjoy, I cannot know whether I have in fact brought them benefit. My work can still be a work of love, however, insofar as it is performed in response to the command "Thou *shalt* love thy neighbor." Levinas interprets that command as a command to command that love of others. This is prophecy. Kierkegaard too gives high priority to spreading the word. No more than Levinas does he think that this can be done in the indicative mood. There is no point in affirming doctrinal propositions if your addressee deems you to be mad. Ultimately his or her hearing of the gospel is a gift accepted in faith, and one person cannot have faith for another. Here is hidden the secret that creates the impression of "bad" narcissism when we read some of Kierkegaard's pages. Over against the secrecy of "the secret that in order to have a good and undisturbed and comfortable life I denied kinship with other human beings" is the secrecy that requires me to leave you to discover the secret of the gospel for yourself. Only in this way can love build up. And it is only love that upbuilds.[9]

What Kierkegaard calls upbuilding (*Opbyggelse*) is an expression in the region of religion of what Heidegger's fundamental ontology calls *Rücksicht*, considerate regard. This is a kind of letting-be, for it is a way of assisting others to be themselves by not jumping in and doing for them what they wish to do. To build up is to erect from the ground, and the ground is love. Only God can implant the love in another. If I am to build up the other I must presuppose that there is love in his or her heart.[10] Love is absolutely presupposed. It is not anything I can implant. Hence,

> knowledge and communication of knowledge can indeed also be upbuilding, but if they are, that is because love is present. To commend oneself hardly seems upbuilding, and yet this too, can be upbuilding. Does not Paul at times do it? But he does it in love and therefore, as he himself says, "for upbuilding" [*hyper tēs humōn*, 2 Corinthians 12:19].[11]

So there is both secrecy here and communication. The secret is one to which only the singular individual has access, yet it is one to which many singular individuals can be privy. The communication of it can be only indirect, only, as Kierkegaard writes, through the mediation of God. The daffodil, *narcissus pseudo-narcissus,* is crossed with the heliotrope.

## Coram Mundo

Kierkegaard turns first toward the face of God, *coram Deo*. Levinas turns first toward the face of the other human being, *coram homine*, and, if God is visible at all, it is only his "back parts" that are seen. However, the neatness of this contrast is disturbed once it is recalled that while Kierkegaard appeals to mediation, meaning by that not Hegelian dialectical mediation but the mediation of God or Christ, it is not to be expected that mediation in either of these senses will be acceptable to Levinas. The neatness of the formulation is quite destroyed once an attempt is made to take into account the difference between what Heidegger calls Kierkegaard's theoretical writings, the ones on which the previous chapters concerned with Kierkegaard in this book have chiefly drawn, and the "edifying" or "upbuilding" ones which we have drawn on predominantly in this chapter and which Heidegger finds more philosophically instructive than the theoretical ones, exception made for *The Concept of Anxiety*.[12] Complexity is worse complicated when an attempt is made also to take account of the difference between what Levinas calls his confessional and his philosophical writings. These attempts exceed the framework of this book. This does not mean that a work's frame cannot be exceeded in a book, given a sufficiently complex exegesis of "in" and "book," as the reader of this book is beginning to learn from the exegeses of Levinas and Kierkegaard in the writings of Derrida.

Anticipating what in the next chapter we shall find Nietzsche saying about "attempters," let me therefore attempt to tempt the reader to undertake the experiment of varying in imagination the trope of the heliotrope that has just been invoked. With avowed oversimplification, we have said that for Kierkegaard the sun stands for God. With still further simplification we have said that for Levinas the sun is the face of the other human being. In both cases allowance must be made for the fact that the sun to which in our image the flower turns its face is not the sun as seen but the sun as the source of light, which is not seen, because it bedazzles. Even this metaphor of light, the light of Greece, of enlightenment and of the Enlightenment, will have to concede some place for hearing, as we have discovered it does in the thinking of Heidegger and Levinas when (reversing Pyramus's "I see a voice" in *A Midsummer Night's Dream*) the latter writes that the eyes of the other are the voice of conscience commanding "Thou shalt not kill" and the former traces conscience in consciousness; he traces *syn-eidēsis* understood as knowledge one has with oneself in *syn-eidēsis* understood as knowledge one has with another. The difference between these two translations corresponds to the distinction Kierkegaard draws between what can be communicated directly and what can be communicated only indirectly. This indirectness is connected by him with conscience in the section of *Works of Love* whose title proclaims "Love Is a Matter of Conscience." He is referring to what he calls Christian love. As was noted above, Kierkegaard writes of God as the middle between me and my neighbor, and as was also suggested earlier, that may be one of the points of difference between him and Levinas, who says that it is only through the neighbor that meaning can be given to the word

"God." It should now be added, however, that the difference is diminished if this "through" denotes only the order of learning and teaching. For this would leave open the possibility that "neighbor" and "God" have meaning only in terms of each other. If this is said, however, it must also be said that what is at issue here is more than a conceptual implication. With Heidegger and Kierkegaard conceptuality is to be grounded in—or disgrounded by—existentiality. Because existentiality is ec-sistential in a manner that implies forward intentionality, Levinas would prefer to speak of "exteriority," which invokes what he refers to provisionally as "reversed intentionality."

Another possible source of confusion regarding Kierkegaard's talk of middles and mediation is his phrase "the middle term 'neighbour.'" However, in the paragraph in which he uses this phrase in *Works of Love* he is not speaking only of the relation between "neighbor" and "God."[13] He is speaking of the relation between both of these and the relation of a human being to the beloved or a friend. He is distinguishing "erotic" love (*Elskov*) from *agapē* (*Kjerlighed*). That is, the secrecy and obliqueness of communication demanded by the latter is to be distinguished from the intimacy of the former, in which the lover and the beloved may whisper sweet nothings to each other that no one else, and perhaps not even they themselves, could comprehend.

For Paul (1 Corinthians 10:29) and Kierkegaard conscience is freedom; and, again, just as for Paul conscience is a matter of the heart, the inward self, "the secrets of the heart" (1 Corinthians 14:25, Romans 2:28), so for Kierkegaard "Only then, when it is a matter of conscience, is love out of a pure heart and out of a sincere faith."[14] And "a pure heart is first and last a *bound heart*."[15] Could we take the risk of calling this boundedness religious? Could we allow our hearts to be seduced by the thought of religion without gods or the God to which Kierkegaard repeatedly comes back? He or Kierkegaard-Haufniensis comes back to this thought again when in *The Concept of Anxiety*, after conducting what he calls throughout most of the book a psychological study of anxiety, at the end of the final chapter, entitled "Anxiety as Saving through Faith," he tells his reader this:

> The true autodidact is precisely in the same degree theodidact . . . or to use an expression less reminiscent of the intellectual, he is *autourgos tis tēs philosophias* [one who practices philosophy on his own] and in the same degree *theourgos* [one who tends the things of God]. Therefore he who in relation to guilt is educated by anxiety will rest only in the Atonement.
> Here this deliberation ends, where it began. As soon as psychology has finished with anxiety, it is to be delivered to dogmatics.[16]

A further step back beyond both psychology and dogmatics is made by Heidegger. If Kierkegaard delivers psychology to dogmatics, Heidegger delivers them both to the phenomenological ontology of being and time. By phenomenological ontology one is delivered from Kierkegaardian anxiety concerning deliverance through faith. For phenomenological reduction suspends questions of empirical and metaphysical existence. It therefore subtracts the question of the existence of God insofar as that question is posed in what might be called the supernatural attitude, where this is understood on analogy with the attitude the natural sciences take up regarding their objects or subjects, with the difference that the object or subject of the supernatural attitude taken up by theology is an unobservable object or objective or subject called God. However, the dogmatics of the science of God and the dogmatics of the science of the natural world are each various. Thus, as the objects over which the natural sciences range may include structures and relations and forces irreducible to entities corresponding to names or terms, so too for more than one theology God would be not a being, but a relation called Love. And if it be said that entities and relations are the object or subject of the natural or theological sciences, where what is meant is that they are the topics of these sciences, might not their topic be being? As Heidegger maintains, when Aristotle says that being is the topic of the science of science called metaphysics, perhaps he fails to see the difference between, on the one hand, being construed as a being and, on the other hand, being construed as being as such. And maybe what he calls theology falls short in a similar way. But there has been no dearth of theologians ready to claim that they do grasp what Heidegger calls the ontological difference and that what they call God is what Heidegger calls being as such.[17] Suppose their claim is accepted. For these theologians God-cum-being concerns them as a topic of religious worship and love. Being so regarded is not the concern of fundamental ontology, or at least not its primary concern. Once being as such becomes the focus of religious devotion the ontology that treats of it is regional, not fundamental. The love that God is said to be according to the Christian is but one concrete manifestation of what Heidegger calls care (*Sorge*—the "care" of Kierkegaard's Kjer*lighed*), notwithstanding that his construal of this most embracing of his existentials was guided by his reading of, among others, Paul, Augustine, Luther, and Kierkegaard. So that the last of these will be allowed by Heidegger to say that God is the middle term between me and my neighbor only if he, Kierkegaard, allows that between me, my neighbor, and our god is the middle unterm, the between (*Zwischen*) par excellence, Being.[18]

# PART TWO

SIX

# Between Appearance
# and Reality

### Kierkegaard and Nietzsche

At the end of the last chapter the names of Kierkegaard and Luther were mentioned in one and the same breath. Like Kierkegaard, Nietzsche has a Lutheran background. We have seen how critical Kierkegaard is of Luther. Nietzsche is far more critical of Luther and of that for which Luther stands. He is critical not merely of Christendom, as is Kierkegaard. He hates Christianity. But for Jesus he demonstrates love. In a letter sent from Nice in 1888 to the Danish philosopher Georg Brandes, who had published a book on Kierkegaard and recommended his works to Nietzsche, Nietzsche writes that on his next visit to Germany he hopes to concern himself with what he calls Kierkegaard's psychological problem. What he means by this is not clear. One can only speculate that what draws Nietzsche to Kierkegaard is that they are both professional sufferers. Indeed, at the time of writing that letter to Brandes Nietzsche was about to experience his own psychological problem, the insanity that until then had been the Dionysian leaven of his philosophical imadgination but that a year later was to deprive this lover of words, this philologist, of even slightly misspelled ones. Until then he experienced episodes of rationality, though not all of them are recognized as such: for example the occasion on which, when confronted in a street in Turin by the spectacle of a drayman mercilessly thrashing his horse, he rushed forward and put his arms around the animal's neck. He is not an admirer of universal human compassion. Indeed, he is a candidate for being described as one who wished to "live in stately seclusion with the distinguished," this epithet being a description that, as was noted in the final section of our last chapter, Kierkegaard wished not to use of himself. But Nietzsche is quick to sympathize with a fellow animal.

Among his last words are those with which he took to signing his letters: "*Der Gekreuzigte*," The Crucified One. Kierkegaard would have considered it blasphemous to call himself that. But at the height of his powers Nietzsche saw himself as a Redeemer, albeit a Redeemer who saves one from Christ. Yet the road to redemption on which he eventually sets out is a way of love, albeit love defined as "the spiritualization of sensuality," and "a great triumph over Christianity."[1] Before that he explores the chances of finding salvation through art, in the category of what Kierkegaard calls the aesthetic, the category in which, Kierkegaard would say, there is least chance of finding salvation.

## Redemption through Art

The first edition of Nietzsche's first book, published in 1872, is entitled *The Birth of Tragedy Out of the Spirit of Music*. The spirit of music to which this title refers is what in the second edition of 1878 he explicitly identifies with the spirit of the music of Wagner, to whom the preface of the book is dedicated, and whose idea of a work embracing all the arts (a *Gesamtwerk*) he considers to be a revival of the ideal of ancient Greek tragedy. Before embarking on an account of man as an artist Nietzsche refers to man as himself a work of art created by the cooperation of two principles of nature he compares to the relation between the sexes, which is sometimes conflictual and sometimes conciliatory. One of these is the principle of ecstasy, orgy, and intoxication, named after the god Dionysus. The other, named after the god Apollo, is the principle of individuation and the imposition of quiet form such as is exercised in fantasy and the dream. The Apollonian principle is a principle of sanity, the Dionysian principle is a principle of madness: a principle of absence of principle. But if the Dionysian destroys boundaries and the Apollonian establishes boundaries, what about the relation between the Dionysian and the Apollonian? Is that relation destructive or constructive? Or is it somehow both?

In the works of art created by man the Dionysian principle is most powerfully expressed in the dithyrambic choral hymn of Greek tragedy, which engenders a feeling of oneness among human beings and between human beings and nature. So Nietzsche states that the predominant characteristic of Dionysian music is harmony. This is a statement to which we shall return in the next chapter. The main characteristic of Apollonian music is rhythm. This recognition that music can be Apollonian may seem puzzling in the light of Nietzsche's assertion that Dionysian art is musical whereas Apollonian art is plastic, as represented typically in ancient Greece by sculpture and architecture. Is this slipshod thinking on Nietzsche's part, and is another example of this his reference to "the chisel-blows of the Dionysian world-artist"? Instead of evidence of carelessness, this may be evidence that Nietzsche is taking great care not to suppose that every opposition is antithetical. So his readers must take great care not to suppose that Nietzsche's title *The Anti-Christ* marks a simple opposition between Christ and, say, Dionysus.[2] Maybe he is less interested in polar oppositions than in an interference between the items contrasted. That this is so will become abundantly clear from his later writings. But already with reference to *The Birth of Tragedy* it may be salutary to recall Goethe's (and maybe Pythagoras's?) conceit that architecture is frozen music. Already in this first book Nietzsche himself makes a deceptive ambiguity between seeing and hearing essential to the deception by which the art of Greek and Wagnerian tragedy saves us from the primal suffering that would overcome us did not the Apollonian imaging of the world, for example in the story of the lives and deaths of Tristan and Isolde, make contemplatable the suffering expressed in the music. "Through that glorious Apollonian deception it seems as though the realm of sound has assumed the form of a visible world. . . . The Apollonian lifts man out of his orgiastic self-destruction, and deceives him about the universality of the Dionysian event, deluding him into the idea that he can see only a single image of the world—Tristan and Isolde, for example—and that he will *see* it better and more profoundly *through music*."[3]

In the myths of the tragedies of Aeschylus above all, the image becomes a symbol expressing Dionysian wisdom. In later tragedians and Attic Comedy, the Apollonian begins to become severed from the Dionysian, and wisdom (*Weisheit*) is gradually supplanted by science in the broad sense of the quest for knowledge (*Wissenschaft*) until after Aristophanes, *muthos* gets overtaken by critical Socratic *logos* and a concern for things political and public, *res publica,* the republic. This concern is taken to its extreme in Rome and the Augustan Enlightenment, where justice is secularized through being uprooted from the metaphysico-religious justice of the myth as voiced in the tragedies of Aeschylus. Nietzsche subscribes to Schopenhauer's distinction between phenomenal appearance and reality where the latter is will to life that leads unavoidably to pain and injustice. Pain and injustice are real. He cannot bring himself to believe that they are capable of being shown to be unreal by the contemplative practices of Buddhism. The only way to live with them he can see at this time is to appeal to an art in which there is a rebirth of tragedy such as that in which Wagner's *Tristan* and *Ring* do for the modern age what Aeschylus did in the tragic age of the Greeks. Through the harmony of Dionysian music integrated with Apollonian myth Aeschylus creates an illusion of universal harmony. But it is no more than an illusion. As Nietzsche says, borrowing the expression from Shakespeare's Marcellus and relaying it to Derrida, reality remains "rotten." Its temporality is "out of joint."

When Nietzsche attended part of the first performances of Wagner's music at Bayreuth in 1876 he was appalled to discover that the audience was more interested in the food, the drink, and the chit-chat and in being seen than they were in seeing what was happening on the stage and in hearing the music. This raised doubts in him about the viability of what he calls his metaphysics of art. But metaphysics itself was abandoned once he came to have doubts about the tenability of Schopenhauer's post-Kantian belief in a substantial reality antithetically opposed to appearance. In the conversation he has with himself in the "Attempt at Self-Criticism" added in the edition of *The Birth of Tragedy* published in 1886, he judges the book to be badly written, clumsy, sentimental, so sugary as to be well-nigh effeminate—and Romantic. He condemns it for being as Romantic as by this time he finds the work of the person with whom he imagined himself to be having a conversation in the book itself, his erstwhile friend Richard Wagner. Why Romantic? Because behind the Schopenhauerian pessimism of the book lurks an optimistic longing for an other-worldly metaphysical consolation before "*the* old God." This old God is the God of Christianity. Despite the honor the book seems to pay to ancient Greece, the book now appears to him anti-Hellenic. It is anti-Hellenic because it is pro-Helenic, Helen being she for whom Goethe's Faust yearned, she whom Nietzsche now sees as a metaphor for the metaphysical, for what is beyond the physical, beyond the natural. At least from the time of the first of his *Untimely Meditations* published in 1873 Nietzsche is engaged in an endeavor to forge a non-metaphysical, or what he will call a physiological, idiom that negotiates a path between Darwin and the old God of Christendom whom Darwin had killed. He will eventually discover a principle of selection that is an alternative to Darwinian natural selection, yet that is natural in the sense of a "second nature": not the supernatural second nature of which Paul speaks, but a second nature incorporating a culture that, instead of distinguishing humanity from animality, distinguishes certain select human beings from the rest of humanity. This alternative to both Christendom and Darwindom will show more respect for Jesus than had been shown in *The Life of Jesus,* whose author, David Strauss, is the topic of the essay published first in 1873 and later included in Nietzsche's *Untimely Meditations.* Strauss, failing to recognize that his "scientific faith" is a contradiction in terms, is in too great a hurry to preach Darwinian scientism as the new faith replacing the old faith of Christianity. Not that Nietzsche sees himself as a defender of that old faith. The Pauline and Lutheran Christianity preached by Nietzsche's father is founded on the proposition that redemption turns solely on faith in the Resurrection. Nietzsche will say toward the end of his writing career that with this "impudent doctrine of personal immortality" regarded by Paul as a reward, "the entire concept of 'blessedness,' the whole and sole reality of the Evangel, is juggled away—for the benefit of a state *after* death!"[4] Love is another name for the whole and sole reality practiced by "the noblest human being,"[5] named by some people Jesus, but by others Christ, the Savior, or the Redeemer. It is worth bearing in mind that Dionysus is called the Redeemer (in Greek *lusios,* in German *Erlöser*) and that he was born (at least twice) of a divine father and an earthly mother. Moreover, it will be to a certain non-Christian conception of love that Nietzsche will return when, like Plato calling upon Socrates, he finally calls upon Zarathustra, the "soothlaugher" who pronounces laughter holy, to teach an art that will redeem this world now that the art of aesthetic illusion taught in *The Birth of Tragedy* has proved to be itself an illusion.

## Herd Morality and Hard Morality

One tenet of the teaching presented in that first book was not abandoned. In that book Nietzsche rejects Aristotle's celebrated claim that tragedy purges the emotions by pity and terror. He hears in this claim an introduction of moral concerns into the field of aesthetics. His own "metaphysics of art" had tried to steer clear of any confusion with what Kant calls a metaphysics of morals.

"Stupidity" is a term of abuse much favored by Nietzsche. Among moral philosophers, he observes, stupidity takes the form of a failure to see beyond the morality prevailing in their own time, place, class, or church; it supposes that from one of these limited bases can be reached the foundation of morality itself. But the point of departure from which these philosophers proceed is no more than an unquestioned faith. There is need therefore for a natural history of morals that studies, compares, and arranges the moralities of other times, places, classes, and the like. Here, drawing especially upon French authors of the eighteenth century, Nietzsche the "physiologist" is seeking a scientific method that will not be led astray by the cozy optimism displayed by his German and British contemporaries. At the same time it will discover a way of approaching history that does not, like many of those contemporaries who are subjected to scrutiny in the 1874 essay "On the Utility and Disadvantage of History for Life," republished in *Untimely Meditations,* conceive historiography as the amassing of information about the past to such a point that it suffocates any thought of the future. Balanced between the seductions of the quick utilitarian fix on the one hand and of the collection of undigested knowledge on the other, Nietzsche's natural historical method will prepare the way for a typology of morals. He prefers not to describe either the preparatory historical work or the typology as a science of morality. That would be too pretentious. If there be science here, it is a "joyful science," a *gaya scienza,* the *gai saber* of the poet-knights of Provence. That was an art. Therefore the program announced in *Beyond Good and Evil* (1886) continues the program proposed in *The Birth of Tragedy* insofar as the later work looks at science in the perspective of the artist. The arrangement of material undertaken at the preparatory stage is not described even as classification. It is described as an assemblage of "a vast domain of delicate feelings and value-distinctions which live, grow, beget and perish" and as an attempt to detect in them recurring patterns, "living crystallizations."[6] It is already clear that the language of the later of these two books is still the language of birth used in the title of the earlier one and already the language of genealogy used in the title of *The Genealogy of Morals,* to be published a year after *Beyond Good and Evil.* The language of life is employed again when Nietzsche writes that what is required is a vivisection of the stupid faith of traditional moral philosophy with a view to exposing the subtle nuances that it overlooks.

The new philosophers will be doctors subtle enough to discern the subtleties of motivation concealed behind what previous philosophers, for instance "old Kant," have failed to perceive. The new philosophers are the philosophers of the future whom, with a parodic allusion to a biblical Baptist, Nietzsche baptizes "attempters," *Versucher.* This is the name with which he had baptized himself in the title of the critical postscript he annexed to *The Birth of Tragedy.* He acknowledges that in using this word he is succumbing to a temptation, a *Versuchung,* and that he is attempting to employ a term that is in some respects right but in other respects wrong.[7] (The prefix *ver* often conveys the sense that something is amiss.) These new philosophers will discover that the various classical theories of morality are sign languages, interpretation of which will reveal that what has moved their propounders to produce them is the desire to justify, flatter, abase, elevate, avenge, or forget themselves. The fulfillment of these desires is in all cases sought by the imposition of a constraint, the tyranny of arbitrary laws. Not even the so-called categorical imperative of Kant is categorical. Its necessity is shown to be hypothetical once natural-historical interpretation construes it as "Thou shalt obey someone and for a long time: *otherwise* thou shalt perish and lose all respect for thyself."[8] That is to say, obeying the imperative is a condition of self-respect.

Would not the Kantian philosopher reply that self-respect matters to a person because it matters to any rational and therefore any fully human being as such, to a person as a rational being? The object of respect is not the singular person but the rationality incorporated in him or her, and the highest expression of this rationality with regard to practice is the moral law that presents itself as an imperative to an incarnate being, therefore as a constraint upon the exercise of bodily appetites and of more complex desires inculcated by culture. However, it is precisely this appeal to generality that Nietzsche questions. He questions it for the same reason that he questions the utilitarian account of morality against which the Kantian account is directed. Where the Kantian doctrine is framed in terms of universality, the utilitarian doctrine is framed in terms of maximality, the greatest and best happiness of the greatest number. The criterion central to both is commonality. According to Nietzsche it is precisely this criterion that limits both of these doctrines. It limits them to the sphere of what he variously denominates slave moralities, moralities of the herd, and moralities of the demotic majority.

Democracy embraces the principle of equal rights enshrined in the idea that, as the utilitarian puts it, everyone is to count as one and no one is to count for more than one. As the Kantian puts it, this principle of equal rights is definitive of moral respect. Nietzsche asks his readers to entertain what he acknowledges to be the dangerous thought that moral respect will be conceived otherwise as soon as one allows for the possibility of a morality of the master. In allowing for that one would be allowing for a conception of responsibility different from that of responsibility to one's neighbor, where by neighbor is meant any human being as human. Moral responsibility conceived in this latter fashion is, in the words of one of Nietzsche's titles, all too human. The universality of that responsibility is universal only insofar as we look no further than the foreground. It is a short-sighted responsibility. The respect and responsibility shown to each other by members of the common herd—animal, all too animal—lack vision, in every sense of the word.

The vision that is lacking from the morality of the neighbor, hence from the morality of Judeo-Christianity, is the vision that grows out of "the pathos of distance" felt by members of the aristocracy. From this sociopolitical pathos of the ruling class arises the "more mysterious pathos" pertaining to the *psuchē* that hankers after an elevation in which the all too human and too humanitarian becomes "man" ("*Mensch*"). The quotation marks in which Nietzsche writes this word signal "a self-overcoming of man." It is vital not to underestimate the significance of Nietzsche's assertion that this self-overcoming is continual. The self-overcoming envisaged is not achieved in one step. It is a progression that never comes to a halt. It is an increase in height, rarity, and intensity, as in the ascent of the mountains referred to in the Epode "From High Mountains" appended to the nine chapters of *Beyond Good and Evil*, and as in the ascent of the mountains among which Zarathustra dwelled for ten years until he decided that, like the setting sun, he must go down, become again a man among other human beings, if only for a while.

What does Nietzsche mean when he says that this increase in height, rarity, and intensity is a self-overcoming of man? As will be made clearer in the final stages of the next chapter, to overcome (*überwinden*) is to learn to live with and even love what is overcome. It could be said that it is to learn to love oneself, though not quite in the way that the Bible would have loving oneself be seen as a guide to the way in which one should love one's neighbor. When a man overcomes himself in Nietzsche's sense he gets over his all too human humanity. This is something like, but not entirely like, getting over an illness in putting it behind one. The overman (*Übermensch*) does not leave his humanity behind. However, in saying Yes to his humanity, in a manner to be explained further below, he does leave behind its all too humanness. Therewith the morality of this "highest man" and the morality of the great artist, the contemplative and the statesmen whom Nietzsche refers to collectively as "the higher man," leave behind the Kantian moral law that is held to be valid for everyone. The duties of this superior morality are not duties for everyone.[9] They are duties for superiors in a sense yet to be articulated.

In what way is this increase an increase in distance within the soul itself? Nietzsche writes that to speak in his sense of the self-overcoming of man is "to take a moral formula in a supra-moral sense." Self-overcoming of man taken as a moral formula would be a man's subjection of his passions to the control of a moral principle, perhaps with a view to achieving the ascetic ideal of ridding oneself of those passions. To move from thinking of self-overcoming in this way to thinking of it in a supra-moral way does not mean that morality is being left behind. What is being left behind is morality as morality is all too commonly and all too humanly conceived. For a similar and inseparable question is posed by Nietzsche's use of the term "man" or man (his use of the term with or without quotation marks). Does he mean that man is being left behind or that a new notion of man is envisaged? How are we supposed to understand the prefix when he speaks of the "supra-moral" and the "supra-human"? We are to understand it as the sign of a revaluation of the idea of humanity and as a warning that the nature of humanity remains undecided.

The irony is that the re-vision of humanity in which human beings become, in Nietzsche's words, "more complete" is made possible by their becoming, as he also says, "more complete beasts." For history teaches that the noble class was first the barbarian. Nietzsche, erstwhile professor of philology at the University of Basle, knows that the term "barbarian" means one who speaks as or like a foreigner. His natural-historic genealogy of morals is also philological, a genealogy of language. This point about barbarism therefore has far-reaching implications for our understanding of Nietzsche's teaching. It offers the opportunity to observe that he is not a linguistic determinist if by that is meant someone who maintains that our moral or philosophical thinking is prisoner to linguistic deep structures fixed in advance that are or reflect innate Platonic or Platonesque ideas. What he says about the place of the barbarian suffices to demonstrate his rejection of linguistic determinism thus understood. On the other hand, he also rejects the genetic empiricist atomism of Locke's doctrine of the origin of ideas. Without subscribing to a theory of innate ideas, Nietzsche produces what he considers to be evidence that our philosophical ideas are systematically related and are a function, albeit not a prisoner, of the family of languages to which belongs the one we happen to speak. He remarks that the importance given to the grammatical subject in Indo-Germanic and Arabic in contrast to Ural-Altaic languages may have not a little to do with the importance given to the speaking subject by those whose mother tongue belongs to the former family. He remarks also, however, that the philosophy of the Vedanta teaches that the notion of a metaphysical subject or soul is an illusion,[10] and that the possibility that this notion is illusory is conceded by Kant. Yet the languages in which the Vedanta and the works of Kant are composed belong to the Indo-Germanic group. Here is further evidence that Nietzsche is not a strict linguistic determinist. That he is not is what we are led to expect by the pivotal role played by change in the forces of words in the story he tells of the genealogy of morals in order to point beyond the antithesis of good and evil and, more generally, beyond the faith in antithetical thinking which he declares to be fundamental to metaphysics[11] and which tempts philosophers to oppose antithetically a world of appearance and a world behind the appearances.

## Truth and Free Will

Nietzsche's way of pointing beyond metaphysics to a meta-metaphysics in which a too simple received understanding of "meta-" undergoes a complication anticipates what has since been called deconstruction. Proponents of deconstruction will have come across in Nietzsche's writings reasons for doubting that transcendence, going beyond, crossing from one side to its apparent opposite, is a simple step across a threshold between an outside and an inside. Take, for example, the following comment by Nietzsche on the traditional antithesis of reality and appearance: "The true world—we have abolished. What world has remained? The apparent one perhaps? But no! With the true world we have also abolished the apparent one." These words come from the section of the *Twilight of the Idols* entitled "How the 'true world' finally became a fable."[12] Once more, recourse is had to quotation marks to mark a shift in meaning. The so-called "true world" is the alleged world in itself posited outside all perspectives in which it appears for us. If we can only bring ourselves to accept that to conceive a world is inevitably to conceive it from a perspective, we shall see that what until then we opposed to that reality in itself by naming it appearance is the only real world for which there is room. We now see both that the so-called world in itself was a fable in the sense of a mere fancy and that the world with which we can come to grips is a fable in the sense that it is one we have fabricated. We begin to learn this once we grasp that the very worldhood of the world is constituted in part by the language we speak. The objective is a realm within what is neither subjective nor objective in the old senses of these terms. We do not lose objectivity, but reinterpret it. Nor do we lose truth. We find idle the idea of an absolute truth. It gets superseded by an idea of truth that is understood to imply relations to a plurality of people and their different standpoints, without this implying that "everything is relative" in the sense relativity had when it was opposed to the idea of the absolute subscribed to by the old species of metaphysical philosopher. The hindsighted double adjustment illustrated by these semantic shifts takes place also in the characterization of them as a transcendence beyond the metaphysical, for in them one idea of transcendence is transcended by another.

An analogous shift of view is brought about when with the dismantling of the idea of a human or divine free will alleged to be *causa sui* the antithetically opposed idea of determinism is dismantled too.[13] With the "deconstruction" of this antithetical opposition room is made for Nietzsche to argue that in real life the opposition is one between strong and weak will. This is of great importance for what, now rejecting Schopenhauer's hypostatization of will as the reality behind our representation of the world, Nietzsche calls will to power, where power is analyzed as relations of quanta of force.

Would modern proponents of such deconstruction have been regarded by Nietzsche as members of what he considered to be a new species of philosopher?[14] Of philosophers and their concepts he writes: "Their thinking is in fact not so much a discovering as a recognizing, a remembering, a return and homecoming to a far-off, primordial total household of the soul out of which those concepts once emerged—philosophizing is to that extent a species of atavism of the first rank."[15] Atavism is the reversion to a remote ancestor. And atavism specifically of the first rank would presumably be the atavism of the new species of philosopher. New though they may be, these philosophers are respecters of tradition. Consider the way Heidegger reaches back beyond what he calls the age of the world-picture, the age that represents the world as representation, to the kind of poetic thinking of the pre-Socratics, in the interest not of scholarly antiquarianism, but in order to gesture toward another way of thinking the to-come. Nietzsche's genealogy of morals sometimes follows a similar procedure. It is a procedure of translation (which translates into French as *traduction*): it discovers/invents new meanings for certain key words. It is a practice of betrayal or traducement (which translates into French again as *traduction*): it reveals meanings and forces that are apt to conceal themselves. It is also a theory of tradition: for although revealing the meanings and forces of words is one of the tasks Nietzsche ascribes to those he calls the new philosophers, he is not keen to join in a movement of modernization, any more than was Heidegger, who learns much from the Nietzschean conception of tradition, even though in his course of lectures on Nietzsche he maintains that Nietzsche is not radical enough and remains too tied to philosophical tradition. However that may be, Nietzsche distances himself from men of "modern ideas" who believe in "progress" toward some future humanitarian, socialist, Christian, or Christian-Socialist utopia in which exploitation has become a thing of the past. But his traditionalism is one that penetrates beyond the traditional metaphysics of antithetical opposition. It passes beyond the polar oppositions of future and past, as will be seen when we come to consider his doctrine of eternal return. It questions a traditional conception according to which pain excludes joy. And it leapfrogs over the antithetical opposition of good and evil manifested in traditional moralities to the tradition typified by Leonardo and Machiavelli in Renaissance Italy, and to men such as Frederick II of Prussia, Caesar in ancient Rome, and Alcibiades in ancient Greece, whose command over others is made possible only by command over themselves. Nietzsche's respect for such figures from bygone ages is prospective, as is his respect for the forces of certain words in the languages his heroes spoke. The past that he respects is not one from which a blueprint for the future can be deduced. For what the new philosopher and Zarathustra look forward to is an ever increasing intensity of will to power. That *Wille zur Macht* can be expressed only in self-making and the making (*Machenschaft*) of worldhood, in creating (*Schaffen*). Now there would be no authentic creating if what is created were foreseeable. Over the creation of the world to come there will hang for ever the dangerous "perhaps" affirmed by the new species of philosopher. It is not surprising that Nietzsche has to admit that he cannot see any sign that such philosophers are on the way.[16] The title-page of *Human All Too Human* (1878) advises that this is "A Book for Free Spirits," but already the second section of its preface informs us that outside the author's imagination there are not and never were any such free spirits.

Atavism is also the recurrence of a disease after the intermission of some generations. The word itself is a reversion to a remote ancestor, namely the Latin "*atavus*," which denotes one's great-grandfather's grandfather. The vocabulary in which Nietzsche couches his genealogy of morals is thoroughly geneticist and hygienicist, so that morals are construed as states of good or bad health. Hence Nietzsche's description of his philosophical genealogy as the physiology of an organism. He also says, notoriously, that he does his philosophy with a hammer. The subtitle of the *Twilight of the Idols* leads us to expect that the book will tell us "How one philosophizes with a hammer." This may lead us to expect that his philosophizing will be the wielding of a hammer in order to smash something to the ground. This expectation must allow for the fact that, rather as what Heidegger calls the *Destruktion* of a philosophical system or text is not destruction in that sense, so too when Nietzsche's hammer is brought to bear against idols, reminding us (as Nietzsche does explicitly) of Francis Bacon's attack against what he called the idols of the tribe and of the theatre, and so on, Nietzsche uses his hammer to tap with delicacy upon idols in order to test whether they are hollow or, as we say, unsound. He applies the tool diagnostically as a physician might to sound out the condition of a bone or a bodily organ or as a railwayman might employ a light hammer to check whether the sound produced in striking the wheel of rolling stock suggests that that wheel is cracked. Nietzsche states that his own program is to examine eternal idols, not only the idols of the age to which Bacon attended. The idols to which Nietzsche approaches his fine ear are eternal because they are atavistic in the sense that they are comparable with diseases that may always recur. But his ear, he gives us to understand, is the ear behind the ear. This is the ear that is attuned to hearing what a speaker leaves unspoken. In tandem with the characterization of himself as a physiologist is his description of himself as an "old psychologist." By now it will have begun to emerge how indebted to this old psychologist are the new psychologist Freud and revisers of Freudian psychoanalysis such as Jacques Lacan, Félix Guattari, and Gilles Deleuze. By now too we are prepared for the thought that when he calls himself both a psychologist and a physiologist Nietzsche is not opposing these titles. He has no objection to distinguishing the mind from the body, but that distinction is not one of antithetically polarized opposites.

Nietzsche's psycho-physiology, where both the *psuchē* and the *phusis* studied by it connote *life*, does not aim at a wholesale demolition of the morality he likens to a state of bad health. That morality, the slave morality in which the good is opposed antithetically to the evil (*böse*) rather than to the bad (*schlecht*), is not to be once and for all outgrown. A twilight comes around again, as do night and midday. And a twilight of the idols is a twilight not only in the sense that the idols go down. Twilight, which may be that of the evening or of the dawn, is also the time of the going down of the psycho-physiologist, like Zarathustra descending from the mountain to dwell again among the people, and like Plato's philosopher returning to the cave, except that Zarathustra's message calls into question the message of Plato's philosopher. This cyclic pattern is reflected in Nietzsche's conception of health not as simply a state achieved after illness, but as having a strong constitution, the power to overcome illnesses that are always liable to recur. When Nietzsche writes of power, as in the expression "will to power," he is thinking of power as disposition, with stress on counterfactuality and subjunctivity. Like Kierkegaard, this "old philologist" loved the subjunctive mood more passionately than the indicative. The subjunctive, which is the mood of imagination, and not only of the imagination at work in art, lends its ear to what is other than factuality, to what overcomes and redeems us from resentment over the spilt milk of the relentless "it was," in the way we must now attempt to understand.

# SEVEN

## Love of Fate

### Compassion

As suggested by the fact that "malady," the word of French origin for illness, echoes the French word for evil, "*mal*," a society and an individual may enjoy either mixed physical and psychological health or mixed moral health. A person's morals may be in some respects the morals of the herd and in other respects the morals of the hard, the morals of the master. This duality is not a parallelism. It is a duality of duplicity in the sense of a concealed interference between the noble (the *agathoi*, who in Homer are the courageous), and the ignoble, mean, or base (the *kakoi*). This is an interference in which a stronger force and a weaker force of will give rise to a change of force understood as semantic value, for example of the terms "pity" and "equality." It was observed in the last chapter that equality of rights among all human beings is a principle of herd morality. A master morality suspends the universality of this principle. But it adapts it from the morality of the herd to relationships among the noble. Similarly with regard to pity. A prime mover of herd morality is what, following Schopenhauer, Nietzsche names "*Mitleid.*" If in certain contexts this is translated as "pity" it carries a dyslogistic force in that it implies condescension. Acknowledgment of this takes us some way to understanding why for Nietzsche *Mitleid* as *Mitleid* for those that suffer is ignoble. What Nietzsche refers to as "*your* pity," meaning pity on the part of the ignoble for each other, remains ignoble according to him even if instead of translating his word by "pity" we translate it more literally by "compassion" or "sympathy." It is important not to miss a nuance in our employment of these terms. I may have more than one motive for reporting to the highways department a hole in a pavement. I could be thinking that I myself may pass that way again at night and fall into it. No one can be sure, however, that I am not thinking of the danger the hole poses to others, who may be complete strangers to me. Now I do not pity anyone until they have had the accident or have suffered in some other way. But my getting in touch with the authorities may well presuppose that I experience sympathy or compassion with my fellow human being—or their dogs. Whichever of these words we use to translate Nietzsche's term "*Mitleid,*" they lose any unfavorable resonance they have for him only when, "pity *against* pity," pity as "*our* pity" is restricted to relationships among members of the moral aristocracy who are not preoccupied with seeking the maximization of happiness and the minimization of suffering.[1] That preoccupation is what Nietzsche scorns, and, despite the difference of "climate" that prevails in his world as compared with Kierkegaard's, both of these offspring of Lutheran fathers agree that "there are higher problems than the problems of pleasure and pain and pity."[2] It may reasonably be objected that a narrowing of the range over which a term is applied does not entail a change in its force. When rights formerly limited to men are claimed for women, is it not rights in the same sense of the word that are intended? However, Nietzsche is describing not a synchronic cross-section of usage, but the diachronic genealogy that is the background of a foreground state. Over time the point and the conscious or unconscious purposes with which given terms are required to cope can transform at least their emotive force, as new wine may in due course affect the color and texture of the old bottle into which it is poured. This redistribution of semantic and emotive load is an effect achieved with comparative ease by having recourse to quotation marks. Or the doubling can be marked by taking advantage of the fact that a language is already double thanks to its being a historical outcome of two other tongues, as modern English is a product of Anglo-Saxon and Norman French. But other doublings assist this process, for instance the doubling reflected in the distinction between "compassion" and "pity" within that sphere of English that derives from French. And this duplicity multiplies into a triplicity insofar as "pity" is cognate with "piety." Where a multiplicity of this kind is not provided for by a given language, a term can be coined. This has the disadvantage of appearing to change the subject, and to forfeit the opportunity to re-employ and exploit the powers of the original term. The best of both old and new worlds and words is enjoyed if the neologism proposed is one in which the paleologism resonates, as when Nietzsche complains that what Schopenhauer calls "*Mitleid*" would have been better called "*Ein-leid*" or "*Einleidigkeit.*" For instance, if someone feels hate toward himself, my having one and the same feeling would mean that I hate him too,[3] *ein-leiden* being either suffering-into (empathy) or suffering one and the same feeling. Schopenhauer is thinking of the case where my feeling and the other person's feeling are both feelings of hatred with regard to that person. But Nietzsche wants to leave open the possibility of my feeling *Mitleid* with the person who feels self-hate without this meaning that I too feel hate toward him or myself. As indicated above, it is also necessary to distinguish between *Mitleid* as compassion or sympathy and *Mitleid* as pity.

Under the heading "What is noble?" Nietzsche writes that compassion is all very well among social equals. It is not only good manners. It is a defining condition of society. However, it becomes life-denying when it is extended ever more widely to the point where differences are not recognized. Life wanes when differences are dissolved. Where compassion may be sentimental weakness that assimilates and deadens, life is enhanced by the strength that appropriates, suppresses, or overpowers, for life is the will to the increasing intensity of power. This language of hardness, used by parties to the old morality of the herd to describe what will have vanished from the ideal society of the future where there is no exploitation, describes qualities that are the very essence of life. Life (for instance, the life of words discussed in the previous paragraph) is exploitation. The principle of life is not primarily the principle of self-preservation proclaimed in Proposition VI of Part III of Spinoza's *Ethics:* "Every thing, in so far as it is in itself, endeavours to persevere in its own being." This principle is only an indirect consequence of the will to power. Moreover, its claim to universality exposes it to Nietzsche's objection to any morality that claims to hold for all human beings.

Is Nietzsche not riding roughshod over the distinction between right and might? Is he not confusing what one ought to do with what one can do? On the answers to these questions depends whether we can accept his counting the morality of the master as a morality at all or, in keeping with another manner of speaking he sometimes adopts, as a supra- or meta-morality. Another option is to distinguish the morality of the master from the morality of the slave by characterizing the former as "moralin-frei," a phrase used in the second section of the first book of *The Antichrist* that has suggested to at least one commentator the pharmaceutical analogy with "aspirin." (Nietzsche's *Ein-leid* is moralin-frei.) In the preface to *The Dawn of Day* (or *Daybreak*) Nietzsche goes as far as to describe the transition from moralin morality to moralin-free morality as a *Selbstaufhebung* of morality, daring his reader to compare this transition with Hegelian *Aufhebung,* which is both a destruction and a saving reconstrual.

Nietzsche's linguistic and more than linguistic revaluations are at the same time revaluations of value. The latter are entirely consistent with and inseparable from the former. The notion of value gets dislodged from the conceptions of morality and *mores* in which it has been traditionally at home and finds itself reanimated with the meaning of strength. This is a reanimation because it is a reconnection with the idea of the valuable as the *validus,* the strong and the powerful. *Valeo* means "I am able" not only in the sense of the auxiliary verb "I can," but in the sense of being able-bodied or mentally competent. This revives a concept of value that keeps company with a concept of virtue that goes back via the Italian moralin-free *virtù* to the Latin *virtus* as used in a maxim Nietzsche cites in the preface to the *Twilight of the Idols,* though tantalizingly concealing its source, as he says, from scholarly curiosity (my scholarly curiosity locates its source in the third century BC poet A. Furius Antias): *Increscunt animi, virescit volnere virtus.* "The spirits increase, force blossoms through a wound." Perhaps something less than scholarly curiosity makes it permissible to point out that the third Latin word means "grows green," and to risk associating the maxim with Dylan Thomas's Dionysiac words "The force that through the green fuse drives the flower drives my green age," which Nietzsche might well have used to express part of what he meant by will to power. More than scholarly curiosity requires us to risk noting that manliness, virility, is invoked by the third and the last words of the maxim. They raise the vexed question of Nietzsche's philosophical attitude to women.

## Woman, the Artist, and the Jew

One commentator considers that Nietzsche's judgments concerning women are made by the all too human rather than the human Nietzsche and that they are therefore philosophically irrelevant. In the interval since that commentator's judgment was made public, first in 1950, then in the decisive year 1968, philosophy itself has undergone a revolution and revaluation, so that only out of a now questionable prejudice about philosophy could one write that "Nietzsche's prejudices about women need not greatly concern the philosopher."[4] A history of philosophy must therefore record that Nietzsche's morality for aristocrats is a morality of the master, the masculinely gendered *Herr,* and that the morality befitting woman according to him is the morality of the slave or the herd. In the masculinely entitled *Ecce Homo* he writes that what he wants from music is that it be "individual, frolicsome, tender, a sweet small woman full of beastliness and charm." He says this in the course of a discussion focused on the music of Wagner. One cannot help wondering whether the prototype of this *petite* woman full of beastliness and charm might be Cosima Wagner (*née* Liszt). She was the recipient of the declaration "Ariadne, I love you," signed "Dionysus" by Nietzsche toward the last decade of his life, when he was, in every sense of the adverb, madly in love with her. The fact that he could divulge this love only through the veil of mythological circumlocution is emblematic of a role cast for woman in Nietzsche's philosophy extending through but further than his depiction of woman as a representative of the morality of the ignoble. The weakness of the "weaker sex" is its peculiar strength. During the same late period in which Nietzsche-Dionysus wrote that message to Cosima-Ariadne, explaining "Why the weak conquer," he wrote:

> Finally: woman! One half of humankind is weak, typically sick, changeable, inconstant—woman needs strength in order to cleave to it; she needs a religion of weakness that exalts being weak, loving, and being humble as divine: or better, she makes the strong weak—she rules when she succeeds in overcoming the strong. Woman has always conspired with the types of decadence, the priests, against the "powerful," the "strong," the men—.[5]

What if through this pronouncement upon that one-half of humankind called woman could be heard a diagnosis of "the men" that whispers that there are two corresponding halves in the man? And perhaps also in the woman, as Nietzsche could be inviting us to consider when, in writing that she *rules,* he underlines the masculine verb *"herrscht."* As well as being a professor of philology Nietzsche was, we have said, a philologist in the literal sense of the word, and he requests his readers to be lovers of words too. He requests this explicitly in the closing section of the preface added to the first edition of *The Dawn of Day:* "Philology . . . teaches how to read *well:* i.e. slowly, deeply, looking backwards and ahead, between the lines, with an open mind, with sensitive fingers and eyes." It is not credible therefore that, having stressed the masculine verb *"herrscht,"* he does not wish his reader to look back to the word translated by "exalted" earlier in the same sentence. Nietzsche's word is *"verherrlicht."* This does indeed mean to exalt or glorify or celebrate, but if we are to learn to read Nietzsche as well as he bids us read, and to write of him slowly, we must at least ask whether, since he is about to stress the same word later in the sentence, he means us to pick up on the middle syllable of *"verherrlicht,"* but with enough subtlety to wonder whether its implicit allusion to masculinity is qualified by the prefix *"ver,"* which, as already noted, can convey the notion that something is not as it would normally be expected to be. An ambiguity of gender would seem to be implied by Nietzsche's statements that woman is a name for decadence, and that "almost every man is decadent for half of his life," whether or not this be interpreted as a symptom of his bisexuality.[6] If woman is a name for decadence, "life is a woman," for "the most magical power of life" is that it is "covered by a veil interwoven with gold, a veil of beautiful possibilities, sparkling with promise, resistance, bashfulness, mockery, pity, and seduction."[7] Perhaps this would be the truth of "the opposite sex" to be inferred from Nietzsche's practice of half-revealing behind metaphysical oppositions differences of value as painters talk of value, differences of intensity of tone, differences of will to power. Nietzsche himself asks in the very first sentence of the preface of *Beyond Good and Evil,* What if truth were a woman? Then Nietzsche, the author who hid from scholars' eyes the name of the Latin author whose name a scholar divulged earlier in this chapter, would be entitled to say "I am a woman." *Ecce homo, ecce femina.*

Thinly veiled by Nietzsche's words is the remark of Heraclitus, who was known as Heraclitus the Obscure, that *phusis,* that is to say being or nature or life, loves to hide herself. Implicated in Nietzsche's words too is Heraclitus's saying "kingship is in the hands of a child" or, as that saying may be translated to bring out a particular religious resonance, "a little child shall lead them." Nietzsche relates an anecdote about a child, a girl-child, it should be noted: "'Is it true that God is present everywhere?' a little girl asked her mother; 'I think that's indecent'—a hint for philosophers! One should have more respect for the bashfulness with which nature has hidden behind riddles and iridescent uncertainties. Perhaps truth is a woman who has reasons for not letting us see her reasons?" A hint philosophers might take from this is that pantheism is no more desirable than is the idea of a God not as *being* that loves to hide itself but as *a* being or *the* being par excellence that transcends the world. Could it be that even the Lord, *der Herr,* is a woman? This would not mean that God is not at the same time a man. Perhaps, in order to accommodate both genders and the possibility of a neuter but not neutral third, we should settle for using of God the impersonal "It" or "it," as I have read that Tyndale does somewhere, though I have not discovered where.[8] Of course, this pronoun would have to be parsed according to the syntax of the creative and self-creating will to power as surface theatrical effect, not according to the grammar that encouraged Schopenhauer to posit the will as the substantive metaphysical first cause or motive substituted for the God whose existence he denied.

Wittgenstein—another philosopher who had a love-hate relationship with Schopenhauer and another prophet of a new species of philosophy or what he calls the heir to philosophy—warns against the temptation to try to penetrate to a deep beginning beyond the beginning. But if cause, motive, ego, and God are surface phenomena, if will postulated as a deep inner thing-in-itself is a will-o'-the-wisp,[9] and if there is no hinterland, how can Nietzsche maintain the possibility of the concealment he names woman? He can do this because what is deeply concealed is that there is no depth. The apparently deep is a trick of the light, an appearance of appearance, as the Greeks knew so well. "Oh those Greeks! They knew how to live. What is required for that is to stop courageously at the surface, the fold, tones, words, in the whole Olympus of appearance. Those Greeks were superficial—*out of profundity.*"[10]

The Greeks' concern for appearances, tones, words, and form and for folds of the skin is a concern that makes the Greeks artists. These are concerns artists share with woman. Small wonder that under the same heading, "Why the weak conquer," and immediately under the paragraph beginning "Finally: woman!" just analyzed, Nietzsche adds another (though still not the final) "Finally," in which his topic is the artist. The portrait Nietzsche paints in this paragraph of *The Will to Power* is no more flattering than his depiction of woman. In our reading of the earlier paragraph woman as opposed to man becomes woman as a side of man—a rib. Whether that reading makes his account of woman more acceptable or less, one parallel to it should be considered in the context of the paragraph on the artist. As in the earlier case the reading must be such as to allow Nietzsche to say "I am a woman," so in the second case the reading must be such as to allow him to say "I am an artist" (as in one of his voices Kierkegaard says of himself that he is a poet, which is a way of saying that his commitment falls short of the apostle's). It must also be kept in mind in the case both of the woman and of the artist that Nietzsche's paragraphs belong still to that particular style of dialectical history he calls genealogy. So we find that the paragraph now in question is not on the Greek artist but particularly on "the modern artist, painter, musician, above all novelist, who describes his mode of life with the very inappropriate word 'naturalism.'" Only months before his own last step into certifiable madness Nietzsche writes that this artist is "restrained from *crime* by weakness of will and social timidity, and not yet ripe for the *madhouse,* but reaching out inquisitively toward both spheres with his antennae."[11] A month or so later madness is mentioned again, but this time, harking back to the treatment of madness in Plato's *Phaedrus* and *Symposium,* one of his best-loved texts, it is a noble madness that is referred to, the madness of "the beautiful exception" endowed with strong feelings.[12] What this brings out is that in Nietzsche's notion of genealogy the idea of a scale of values ranging between increasing strength and increasing weakness is married, however uncomfortably, with the idea of revaluation, in which the concept of the good (*gut*) that the weak apply to themselves as a reaction to their judgment of the noble as evil (*böse*) conflicts with the concept of the good that the strong apply to themselves and contrast with the concept of bad (*schlecht*) that they apply to the weak. This marriage is uncomfortable because the values of the slave are both partly constituted by their opposition to those of the aristocrat and threatened with being deconstituted by them. On the other hand, the free power of the noble morality is exposed to the menace of being overpowered by the devious power of the lowly. Thinking of Hegel again, but in order to resist the temptation to suppose that the German term has the same meaning for him as it does for Nietzsche, one could call this an *Abbau* or deconstruction of the antithesis between master and slave.

Below the modern artist in Nietzsche's scale of lowliness are products of the French Revolution: the underprivileged masses with their *ressentiment* against the aristocracy and with their assumption of universal equal rights. After these come the anti-revolutionary, anti-socialist, anti-militarist capitalists who hope to conceal their mediocrity from themselves and others by giving it the nicer name of liberalism. Among the most conservative of these conservatives is the Jew. In addition to being anti-revolutionary, anti-socialist, and anti-militarist, the underprivileged are anti-Semitic. They resent not only the Jew's money. They despise him too, as they also despise other "late races" like the French and Chinese, on account of what they call their *esprit,* using the French word, or "*Geist,*" putting this German word for spirit or mind within quotation marks. This is in line with Nietzsche's view that since its recent founding as a nation, Germany, once regarded as the land of philosophers, ranks the power of the mind or spirit below political power, while it is the power of culture or civilization that is prized more and more in France.[13] This is not a promising basis from which to develop a case for perceiving Nietzsche as a father of Nazism. Moreover, without forgetting his disposition to question antithetical oppositions, it can be said that Nietzsche is anti-anti-Semitic. He is this for a reason that is structurally analogous to his reason for being against the kind of feminism of "the ladies who, instead of feeling their abnormal thirst for scholarship as a distinction, want to disrupt the status of woman in general."[14] These ladies want to disrupt the rule, failing to grasp that in so doing they undermine the value of the exception. Likewise, if the new philosopher is to be an exception, he must protect the rule, he must "keep the mediocre in good heart."[15] The heart may be that of the woman in her status as pregnant with the artist, pregnancy and artistic creativity being the cultivation of form, therefore Greek, as was noted earlier, or, as may now be added, French. Not, however, Jewish. For despite the analogy just drawn between the woman and the Jew in the course of explaining the structure of Nietzschean genealogy, the woman, the Greek, and the French are coupled with the Jew and the Roman in their opposed but complementary functions. "In all modesty"—that is to say, manifesting a virtue he associates with woman, and thereby adding a further complication, a further *pli,* a further fold, to the already manifold analysis—Nietzsche wonders whether the German shares company with the Jew and the Roman, whose genius is to beget, rather than with those, namely the woman, the Greek, and the French, whose genius it is to give birth: "two kinds of genius" that "seek one another, as man and woman do; but they also misunderstand one another—as man and woman do."[16]

These misunderstandings are inevitable. For a Schopenhauer they would be ground for pessimism. For Nietzsche they are occasions for joy. He accepts them as chances of increasingly intense creativity, therefore self-creativity, therefore will to power, that are at the same time that creativity's and that will to power's chances. The chances have their genesis in them, but a genesis that is not to be confused with a beginning. Understanding as a state of stasis at which one believes one has either begun or arrived at the truth would be the death of the will to power.

## The Mobile Army of Metaphors

The changeability of woman is Nietzsche's metaphor for the unceasing mobility of the will to power. Biological conception is a metaphor for the concept. With Nietzsche metaphor is the life of the concept. Metaphorization as such is restlessness. The concept understood classically and classificatorily is rest. It is the residue that remains after a metaphor has passed by and before another has been invented. It is what leads us to overlook the ambiguity of the Latin word *invenire,* to forget that in discovery there is a moment—that is to say a momentum and movement—of making. It is what leads us to believe that what one discovers is an immobile truth. Instead, truth is

> a mobile army of metaphors, metonyms and anthropomorphisms—in short, a sum of human relations, which have been enhanced, transposed, and embellished poetically and rhetorically, and which after long use seem firm, canonical, and obligatory to a people: truths are illusions about which one has forgotten that this is what they are; metaphors which are worn out and without sensuous power.[17]

These words were written in Nietzsche's essay "On Truth and Lying in an Extra-Moral Sense," published in 1873. They have since been cited so often that they themselves are in danger of becoming worn out. Although written that early, they can be read as paving the way for the idea of eternal recurrence that Nietzsche says came to him on an August day in 1881 at the huge rock near Surlei in the Engadine. This rock has the shape of a pyramid, that is to say of a monument associated with death and eternal life. The idea that came to him there is one he would already have come across in reading Schopenhauer, Heraclitus, and Pythagoras. But now this idea of eternal recurrence takes on for him for the first time the significance of "the highest formula of affirmation that is at all attainable."[18] One can begin to explain the significance this idea takes on for him by stating that he, as artist-philosopher, glimpses a new reason why he should accept the worn metaphor referred to in his "On Truth and Lying in an

Extra-Moral Sense." According to that essay, worn-out metaphors are accepted as the truth because of their usefulness as abbreviations. The truth or the concept is a universal that has been cut off from the presumed singularity of the nerve stimulus with which a word originates. According to the account given in the essay, a concept is formed by a process of metaphorism, beginning with the translation of a nerve stimulus into an image, followed by the transformation of the image into a sound. This might be followed by the translation of the sound into a written mark—though Nietzsche here makes no explicit reference to this third stage, possibly because he regards the image as already a kind of inscription. Along either the oral or inscriptive tracks would be generated an open-ended series of metaphors, metonyms, and anthropomorphisms liable to poetical or rhetorical embellishment. When Nietzsche refers to the first and second stages of this process as "first metaphor" and "second metaphor" he is warning that that very description is itself metaphorical. This means that he is calling into question the simplicity of the antithesis between the metaphorical and the literal. He is disturbing the notion of the literal truth understood as words that adequately represent or imitate a state of affairs. Those persons whom he calls the creators of language find this idea of the truth-in-itself and the thing-in-itself quite incomprehensible. The only notion of truth that is comprehensible to them and to Nietzsche is the one for which truth conceived according to the standard of the absolutist notion he finds incomprehensible is a useful illusion or a lie. Or, better, a lying, since what is meant is not a particular deception such as would be condemned as evil by the standards of the morality of the masses, but a deception endemic to language, deception in an extra-moral sense. This is the deception that leads us to give credence to an idea of an absolute Truth of things supposedly viewed from nowhere or everywhere, from the point of view of an ubiquitous God, whereas truthfulness acknowledges that there are truths only in particular perspectives. This holds for the truth of the proposition that says this.

Reference has just been made to the creators of language. And references have been made in earlier paragraphs to creativity. Those paragraphs show how important creativity is in Nietzsche's characterization of the overman. At least three notions of creativity must be distinguished. There is the idea of God the Creator, who is cause of himself and the world. This Creator is the transcendent God in himself whom Nietzsche and his Zarathustra pronounce dead. In a note not published by him he pronounces incoherent this theological notion of a Creator and the cognate idea of a beginning of the world,[19] so he cannot think that this Creator God was ever alive. Given that he regards himself as an artist-philosopher, it can be expected that when he writes of creativity it will often be artistic creativity that he has in mind. That creativity will include the poetic enhancement of language mentioned in the essay "On Truth and Lying."

This is a creativity that would be liable to get out of hand, to become drunkenly and dithyrambically Dionysiac insofar as the Dionysiac is opposed to the Apollonian, and the Apollonian is the principle of order and form associated by Nietzsche, as noted above, with woman and the Greek. The cult of Dionysus was especially popular in Asia Minor, and especially among women. In early representations the god was made to appear effeminate. This confirms Nietzsche's suspicion of antithetical oppositions and prepares us to find that in his later writings the Dionysian is no more sharply opposed to the Apollonian than the womanly is to the manly in Nietzsche's philosophically figurative conception of this duality.

However, in another note not published by Nietzsche himself a certain idea of eternal novelty is scorned. This idea occurs, he explains, to those who wish to break away from a theological or quasi-theological concept of a goal of the world, but are so habituated to this concept that even in preaching the aimlessness of the world they cannot prevent themselves thinking that this aimlessness is intended. Whether God be considered to be outside his creation or as pantheistically identified or panentheistically associated with it, the world is deemed to control itself in such a way as to avoid a goal. According to this piece of self-deception the world is, one could say, twisting Kant's phrase "purposefulness without purpose," a purposed purposelessness. But this, Nietzsche reckons, "is still the old religious way of thinking and desiring, a kind of longing to believe that *in some way* the world is after all the old beloved infinite, boundlessly creative God—that in some way 'the old God still lives'—that longing of Spinoza which was expressed in the words '*deus sive natura*' (he even felt '*natura sive deus*')."[20] This is not a criticism of religious ways of thinking and desiring. It is a criticism of the ways of thinking and desiring of certain old religions, theistic and specifically monotheistic ones.[21] Now might there be a risk that features of these last might return to haunt the artistic and linguistic creativity in which one metaphor succeeds another and another succeeds that, and so on indefinitely, perhaps eternally, attracted by the hope of a final state in which desire is fulfilled? It is to this risk that a third notion of creativity responds, the notion of creativity intrinsic to Nietzsche's teaching of eternal return. This teaching is advanced both as a practical one and as a theoretical one. In both of these forms it is an alternative to the theological conception of creation. In both forms it is also an interpretative supplement to the artistic conception of creation: it prevents this from lapsing back into the theological conception of creation and the conception commonly associated with it of "another place," Platonic or Christian or Islamic, for example, in which seeking has been succeeded by finding, incompleteness has been supplanted by completion, and, as the name of the last-mentioned of these religions promises, one is finally made safe (*salama*).

Paradoxically, despite the emphasis artistic creativity puts upon difference, the teaching of eternal return makes much of sameness, if "same" is an allowable translation here of Nietzsche's word *"gleich,"* which can also mean equal or like—and which, it will be recalled from our first chapter, was also the word that threatened to make an eternal return with Kant. There is a conservatism in the doctrine of the eternal return of the same, as the very name of this doctrine suggests. It is a doctrine of saving in both the economic and the soteriological senses of the word. This is what makes it, as Nietzsche says, the most abyssal or unfathomable (*abgründlichste*) idea. For this doctrine, introduced in *The Gay Science* and further articulated in *Thus Spoke Zarathustra* and *The Will to Power,* challenges us to utter a tremendous, unbounded, and joyful Yes "to all things," to say Amen therefore to what is painful and what is as mean as the all too human morality of the slave. This affirmation is Dionysian in a sense that perhaps picks up the careless or very careful remark made in his first book, regarding which surprise was expressed in the second section of the immediately preceding chapter of our own, that what is proper to Dionysian music is harmony. Whether we consider that remark to be careless or careful may depend on whether we are careful enough to ask whether Nietzsche's word "harmony" is to be understood in contrast with "disharmony" or with "rhythm," the feature he connects with the Apollonian. In any case, it is worth repeating that the Dionysian is no longer opposed to the Apollonian, because to the proliferating differences of images, metaphors, and perspectives is added the sameness constituted by the eternal repetition the overman not only accepts, but rejoices in and loves.

## *Amor Fati*

This love is *amor fati,* that is to say, literally, love of the said (*fatum,* from *"fari,"* to speak). The fated or said in the past tense includes the "it was." In some places Nietzsche writes that what one says Yes to is one's own personal past. The harshness of the thought of eternal return would be that in willing or wanting the eternal return of the past it is the return of one's own pain that is welcomed, not a repetition of Darfur, Rwanda, and Auschwitz. But the conception of the self that is left over from Nietzsche's critique of the ideas of the soul and substantial self does not allow him to separate sharply the self from the world. In some way, whatever happens in the world makes a difference to me, and what I do and suffer has repercussions in what we call the external world. Therefore, as Nietzsche implies in the section of *Ecce Homo* in which *Thus Spoke Zarathustra* is reviewed, it seems that it is to the eternal repetition of all suffering that the doctrine of eternal return bids us assent. Or bids some of us assent, namely those of us who are not still adherents of the moralities fixated on the abolition or reduction of pain. The rest of us will not even begin to understand the doctrine.

Consequently, it is not surprising that commentators have had difficulty understanding precisely what Nietzsche's teaching of eternal return amounts to. It may well be that Zarathustra and Nietzsche himself were able to reach no further than an inkling of what the teaching entails. It is not to be expected that the prophet or the great poet should be able to spell out in plain prose what they prophesy or sing. This may be why Nietzsche himself never published the notes in which he sketched out arguments purporting to demonstrate that the doctrine of eternal return holds as a matter of fact. This may be why most commentators on this factual version of the doctrine agree that Nietzsche's arguments for it do not stand up. They are questionable right from the premises or presuppositions that the law of the conservation of energy demands eternal recurrence and that if a state of equilibrium is never reached it follows that such a state is impossible. The arguments and assumptions are so weak that one cannot help wondering whether they are intended as burlesques of the philosophico-scientific style of writers of his day whom he despised. An indication that they are so intended may be the underlining of the word that one published translation renders as "preponderance" when Nietzsche refers to "the recently attained preponderance of the scientific spirit over the religious, God-inventing spirit." Could the italicization of the German "*Überwicht,*" which is not reflected in the typography of the English version cited here, be taken to license the translation of this word as "overemphasis" or "overestimation"? Without forgetting that Nietzsche himself describes his genealogy of morals as a physiology, therefore a sort of "naturalism," and without forgetting that he was a university professor, it should be asked whether the scientific (*wissenschaftliche*) spirit Nietzsche might be mocking could be that which is manifested by the exaggerated claims of scientific reductionism, by a traditional manner of academic philosophizing, and by the kind of scholar we earlier found him teasing when he declined to give his readers the reference for a Latin maxim he had just cited. Such a scholar is (*mea culpa*) "the herd animal in the realm of knowledge."[22] This chastening remark is preceded by the statement: "I have to set up the most difficult ideal of the philosopher. Learning is not enough!" Rather as Kierkegaard is out to make Christianity difficult, and that means laughing at the presumptuousness of traditional philosophy as exemplified by the Hegelians, Nietzsche's new philosophy makes philosophy difficult. And rather as Kierkegaard insists on the necessary inescapability of suffering in the life of the authentic Christian, Nietzsche regards suffering not as what religion and morality require the anti-Christian overman to escape or help others escape ("European" Buddhism or Bodhisattvism), but as what he is required to overcome. Quite literally, suffering means passion or Passion and passion means love. But (to ask it again) whose passion, whose love, and love for whom or what? Christ and Kierkegaard suffered mockery and more. Nietzsche suffered syphilis and migraines. His torment gives a psychological explanation why he should be concerned with the question how pain might be redeemed. But what about a philosophical justification of pain, his pain, the pain of the overman, and the underman's pain? Does Nietzsche care about this last except insofar as it is a condition of the overman's overcoming? Is that his only atheodicy?

## Redemption through Eternal Return

According to Nietzsche's teaching of eternal return, suffering is not redeemed by arrival at a hoped-for goal. That would be to give priority to a state of being. The "same" of the eternal return of the same is not a same *to* which a return is made. It is the same *of* the eternal return itself as such. If there is anything for the sake of which the return is made, it is the circling of the return itself. The only unity affirmed by the Dionysian Amen is the unity of this circling, which is not aimed at unity or community. So, despite what was said above about the conservatism of Nietzsche's doctrine, it must be said now that this is not incompatible with experimentalism, such experimentalism as one expects of the great artist. The doctrine itself is a thought-experiment, an appeal to imagine what will appear unimaginable to the all too human person referred to in *Thus Spoke Zarathustra* as "the last man."

What the last man finds unimaginable is that he should want the eternal repetition not only of his own suffering or that of others, but "all the woe of the world together."[23] He either does not understand or does not accept what Zarathustra says when the latter asks, "Did you ever say Yes to one joy?" and then adds, "O my friends, then you said Yes to all woe as well. All things are chained and entwined together, all things are in love."[24] This is an elaboration of a doctrine espoused by some of the pre-Socratic thinkers of whom Nietzsche writes in his early essay "Philosophy in the Tragic Age of the Greeks," for instance Empedocles, whose antithetical opposition between love and strife is questioned the moment one asks whether the relation between love and strife is one of love or of strife. In Heraclitus, to whom Empedocles may have been indebted, love as harmony enters on the scene as that which gets expressed in the idea of a friendly struggle (*polemos*) that is said to go on among all things. The friendliness of that struggle may appear to get overlooked in those places where Nietzsche's overman is said to be a friend of war and of malice. Zarathustra declares in the section of *Ecce Homo* devoted to *Thus Spoke Zarathustra*: "I should like to rob those to whom I give; thus do I hunger for malice." *Thus Spoke Zarathustra* is a parody of the Bible. The title *Ecce Homo*, "Behold the Man," is an echo of what that book (John 19:5) reports Pilate to have said. Thus spoke Pilate. And when Zarathustra speaks about giving, what he says is meant to bring out the way giving may be a way of achieving mastery over the recipient. Hence instead of holding that it is more blessed to give than to receive, Zarathustra dreams that it is more blessed to steal than to give.

Yet is not mastery over others, in particular those of slavish mentality, the very thing the overman seeks? By no means. The overman's mastery is mastery over himself and over the humanity in himself. It will be recalled that when in the last chapter we touched upon Nietzsche's claim that the new philosopher must do his work with a hammer, it was said that the work must be understood on analogy with the way a physician might tap gently on a part of the body to detect whether there was a weakness hidden beneath, and that if one wished to apply to this work the label "deconstruction," this should not be equated with destruction as ruination. The time has come to add that Nietzsche's new Dionysian philosopher has a second hammer, or uses the first one also in a different way, as a tool with which to destroy. "Among the conditions for a Dionysian task are, in a decisive way, the hardness of the hammer, the *joy even in destroying*."[25] The overman *is* his own hammer. What he destroys is the tablet of the old law. On the new tablet that replaces it is written "Become hard." By the norms of the old regime this will be judged an evil prescription, but that can be an objection to it only if we can make out a case for rejecting Nietzsche's genealogy of morals and the revaluation of all values it entails. Among the laws that the new table of laws replaces is "Love thy neighbor," provided by "neighbor" is meant any other human being whatsoever. For not only, as we have seen, are the duties prescribed by the new table of law not duties for everyone; they are also not duties toward everyone. But Nietzsche writes: "The philosopher as *we* understand him, we free spirits—as the man of the most comprehensive responsibility . . . has the conscience for the collective evolution of mankind."[26] This conscience will require of *us,* us free spirits, the new Dionysian philosophers, "not to want to relinquish or share our own responsibilities; to count our privileges and exercising of them among our *duties.*"[27] Another of our duties will be to love the neighbor so long as by neighbor is meant fellow free spirits and by fellow free spirits is meant those whose ears are fine enough to hear that the return (*Wiederkehr*) of the same (the same *gleich* that returned in the curious passage from Kant cited above in the third section of our first chapter and in the third section of this one?) is at the same time a clean sweep, a *kehren*. If the free spirit philosophizes with a hammer, he also philosophizes with a broom.

Observe that the language of "the most comprehensive responsibility" that is not to be shared or relinquished is the language Levinas uses, but with the quirky difference that whereas Nietzsche claims this responsibility for "*us free spirits*," thereby permitting some degree of sharing after all, Levinas, like Kierkegaard, permits himself to claim this superlative responsibility only for himself. This difference is quirky in the sense of John Galt's quirky Scots explanation of "quirkie" cited in the *Oxford English Dictionary* and included among the epigraphs of this book: "capable o' making Law no Law at a'." Levinas and Kierkegaard do not destroy the law if by that is meant that they deny it. They destroy it in the sense that they destructure it, "erase" it, however not by rubbing it out, but by crossing it out—and Kierkegaard Crosses it out—rather as Heidegger superimposes an X upon "Being" or substitutes for "*sein*" the archaic form "*seyn*." Heidegger's quirk destabilizes a certain conception of Being, conceptual Being, Hegelian Being for example, without simply (to use Hegel's word) canceling it. Levinas and Kierkegaard destabilize the old table of Law by invoking an "experience" (in scare-quotes) from which we learn that the Law is "no Law at a'" and never was. The Law's constated "it was" is re-presented as ethical or ethico-religious performance that resists representation on a public stage. But its secrecy is not that of a private theater of the mind such as that in which, by a method of Platonic anamnesis, one would learn of universal forms that were always already there. The secrecy, as noted earlier, is not that of some thing that could in principle be discovered. If any re-presentation takes place here, it is not that of a presentation that is re-presentable in the way of ideas, whether the ideas be Platonically rational or Lockeanly sensory. Presentation is de-presented. *Shekinah* is shaken. Recall Kant's assertion that if his reader does not see any difference between the prudential and the moral "ought" it were better for him to put the *Fundamental Principles of the Metaphysic of Morals* back on the shelf and return to reading it only when he has done a little more living. Similar advice requires to be offered to those readers of Kierkegaard and Levinas who do not hear that fundamental principles and law impose terroristic power unless their pure legality is lost through their being saved by the violence of an impower which is quirky in the sense given in the *Chamber's Scots Dialect Dictionary* of being a "not positively illegal" stratagem. This hypoCritical impoverishment cannot be learned through the "inwardness" of the soul's dialogue with itself. Kierkegaard says it can be learned only through the inwardness of the soul's decision to hearken to God. One hears it only with what Nietzsche would call the ear behind the ear. A certain hypocrisy is required if the call of the hypoCritical is to be heard by that second ear of responsive obedience (*obaudire*) behind sensory audition (*audire*). Yet what is heard through this hypocrisy is honesty itself, and—to repeat Levinas's deliberate mixing of metaphors—this sincerity is always already staring me in the face, already audible in the eye of the other human being that commands, "Thou shalt not kill." This is not one command among a list of ten or more others. It is the "essence" beyond essence of the ethical according to Levinas, beyond the essentiality of the categorical imperative deemed to be the essence of the ethical according to Kant.

According to Nietzsche the categorical imperative of "old Kant" belongs to the old table. But Nietzsche's eternally-to-be-continued list of new commands bears a parodic relation to the old ones to the extent that the command to love one's neighbor returns in the new table and in the *amor fati* that inspires it, and to the extent that by one's neighbor is meant not only the aristocracy of free spirits but those who come after us. It is primarily for their sake that Zarathustra descends to preach his sermon at the foot of his mount. But does not the doctrine of eternal return imply that future mankind has already existed? If so, the duty of love and love of duty comprised in *amor fati* is directed also to that segment of mankind of which one says "it was" and "it is." Does this mean that it is still only toward the future of the past, present, and future mankind that this love is addressed, rather as if Levinas were to limit the ethical dimension to the dimension of the future, to the dimension "beyond the face," as he puts it, the space and time of generations to come? Not if we take seriously (which with Nietzsche does not mean that we have to keep a straight face) his doctrine that not only is everything connected with everything in our mental life—where, he maintains, willing is a complication of sensing, feeling, and thinking, and thinking is a relatedness of desires—but that everything is connected with everything also in the physical world and between those whom we meet there and ourselves. Given the combination of that doctrine with the doctrine of *amor fati,* and granted our argument that the commandment to love the neighbor appears on the new tablet, does it not follow that the range the concept of neighbor has there is as wide as the range this concept has in the commandment that figures on the old? Even if this inference is denied, there is no denying that the higher man, the highest man, and the overman are moved by love of others. That is to say, even with regard to the relation of the old to the new tablets of law Nietzsche displays his distaste for antithetical opposition. And, as just noted, in line with the unsettling thought that the nature of humanity remains unsettled, the new tablet of laws is fated to remain incomplete. According to the first law that Nietzsche holds to be inscribed on this new tablet, greater love hath no overman than to cry out in face of this incompleteness not "Thy will be done"—for there no longer is nor was there ever a bearer for this personal adjective—but, impersonally and joyfully, "so be it."

But so be *what*? It seems that according to the cosmological interpretation of the doctrine of eternal return Rwanda and the Holocaust will return again and again. But what of the axiological version, assuming that can be disconnected from the cosmological interpretation? The two versions or aspects are referred to together when in the *The Will to Power* it is said: "My doctrine teaches: 'Live in such a way that you should *wish* to relive, that is duty (*Aufgabe*)—for you will relive in any case!'"[28] Plainly a narrational transition to a question of fact from a question of value, but an inferential transition in the opposite direction. The question of value has to do with *how* one lives and relives. The passage continues: "He for whom effort is the supreme joy, let him make an effort! He who loves rest before everything else, let him rest! He who loves above all to submit, obey and follow, let him obey! But let him know well what his preference leads to, and let him not withdraw before any means! What is at stake is *eternity*!" It is not being said here that the repetition of certain events, say the massacres of Rwanda and the Holocaust, is being brought about by those whose preferences are as described here. On the contrary, that is denied. What is repeated will happen again anyway. It is not what happens in the world that is Nietzsche's primary focus here, but the way people do what they do. If they do what they do knowing that these deeds will be repeated over and over again, their state of mind will be quite different from what it would be if they did not know this. They would be on the way to achieving a strength they would not otherwise reach, even if what they want is to submit, follow, and obey. They would at least be obeying with conviction, taking responsibility for their way of life. Desiring the recurrence of the same is not causing the recurrence of the identical. Nietzsche's doctrine of *amor fati* does not put him in the place vacated with his help by the all-powerful God. The effect of saying Yes is an effect on the world only insofar as it has an effect on us. Its effect is not to reduce one's power of choice but to intensify one's choice of power. Further, although Nietzsche speaks of the eternal return as a matter of fact, the knowledge of which changes our lives, might not such a change be accomplished if the cosmological story were false? Would it not be enough if we *imagined* the story to be true? Nietzsche goes on to refer to the story as one in which one might have *faith,* which may not be consistent with his "let him know well." Pierre Klossowski's translation of the words "Live in such a way" ("*so leben*") has us behave "*de telle sorte.*" Do not these German, French, and English expressions approximate "*als ob,*" "*comme si,*" and "as if," phrases that suggest that what is being invoked here is the imagination understood as thinking that is uncommitted as between factuality and counterfactual conditionality, between reality and mere appearance?

Whereas according to Kierkegaard ethics is given back through Abraham's testing by God, according to Nietzsche's doctrine of eternal return the human being becomes revalued by himself and the temporal world is given back to itself. Instead of temporality being redeemed by eternity, eternity is redeemed by temporality.

Nietzsche once wrote, and he was still quite sane when he did so: "A certain emperor always bore in mind the transitoriness of all things so as not to take them too seriously and to live at peace among them. To me, on the contrary, everything seems far too valuable to be fleeting: I seek an eternity for every-thing."[29] Nietzsche's greater love is such that by it after all almost *everything* gets saved, *almost* everything, everything save a certain God and Creation con-ceived as metaphysical things that exist in themselves.

# EIGHT

# God's Ghost

## Trans-ascendence and Transcendental Empiricism

Metaphysics as defined by Deleuze is ontogenetology. Metaphysics as defined by Levinas is the ethicality of the Good beyond being, ethicogenetology. This distinction leaves open the question as to the transcendence or immanence of God. One reason for this is Levinas's temporary readiness on pedagogic grounds to say in *Totality and Infinity*, adapting Heidegger's distinction, that the ethical has ontological and not merely ontic status. As the title *Otherwise than Being or Beyond Essence* suggests, the Heideggerian distinction that Levinas finds initially useful to adopt ceases to be applied in that later work. Even so, it is arguable that the ethical at least has an ontological foundation for Levinas in the more traditional sense of the term according to which the ontic, for instance the empirical, is also ontological because it is a matter of the being or existence of something. It is arguable that for Levinas the ethical has an ontological foundation if we take him to be saying that my responsibility to another human being arises from my existing in my place in the sun, thereby either depriving someone else of the enjoyment of goods that he or she could otherwise have enjoyed, or exposing someone else to an evil from which he or she might have been protected. However, even if this is a valid reading of Levinas (which we shall discover reason to doubt), the founding of my responsibility in this ontic and ontological state of affairs (comparable with the *existenziell* starting point of the existential analysis in *Being and Time*) does not make the responsibility itself ontic or ontological. That responsibility could have two or more equiprimordial foundations. Or it could be an anarchic disruption of any foundation and therefore of a foundation that is ontic or ontological.

There is a third reason why invoking the alleged equivocality of the word "metaphysics" as employed by Levinas and Deleuze does not of itself constitute a ground for questioning the assurance with which one might assert that the metaphysics of Levinas is one of transcendence while the metaphysics of Deleuze is one of immanence. This third reason is that for Deleuze, as for Spinoza and as for Levinas in his early and temporary adaptation to his own purposes of the term "ontology," ethics treats of beings and being, albeit in their prehypostatic becoming, their genetology. For Deleuze the ethical is the genetological. The *phusis* connoted by the "physical" in the expression "meta-physical" is being, but the metaphysical is not for Deleuze otherwise than being or beyond being, *epekeina tēs ousias.* For Deleuze the ethical is metaphysical in so far as it is the *meta* of *phusis,* the productive becoming of *phusis,* its *phuō.* That is to say, for Deleuze the ethical remains metaphysical in a sense other than that which Levinas gives to the word, other than the sense of beyond or otherwise than being. For Deleuze the ethical is what is implied in Proposition VI of Part III of Spinoza's *Ethics,* "Everything, insofar as it is in itself, endeavours to persevere in its being." Except that Deleuze has a very Nietzschean interpretation of this "in itself." And here it becomes relevant to recall Derrida's remark that "Levinas then is very close to and very distant from Nietzsche."[1] From Levinas's and Deleuze's extreme proximity to Nietzsche we cannot infer Levinas's extreme proximity to Deleuze, as the second part of Derrida's remark already indicates. What brings Levinas close to Nietzsche may be different from what brings Deleuze close to Nietzsche. But they both share with Nietzsche a questioning of what it is to be a self. The human being is not in itself. According to Nietzsche and Deleuze at least some human beings desire to be more than merely human, where although the desire is desire for something, it is not the desire for an end, but a human being's desire for its own self-transcendence, the subjectively genitive overcoming of selfhood, and only in that sense the human being's end. It is the death-wish of a supposed substantial self, hence in Nietzschean parlance the death of the transcendent God. This desire would therefore be desire spelled with a lower-case initial. Upper-case Desire would be, as Levinas sometimes puts it, reversely intentional or, as he also says, affective, meaning that what affects comes at what is affected from outside in some way, a way that is inconsistent with my being a substantially independent identical self, because my interiority is inflected, afflicted and, as Kierkegaard would say, offended by an exteriority. Lower-case desire as understood by Deleuze is an impersonal productive flow of life. It is prepersonal and impersonal, implying not even the broken personality implied by Levinas's upper-case Desire.

The genealogy Levinas conducts in *Totality and Infinity* begins with the ego on its own and in its home. However, we have learned that as this analysis is progressively worked out the modality of my selfhood is found not to be that of a nominative I, but of an absolute accusative, an accusative that is not a declension from a nominative.[2] Its grammar is that of an accusative me made to stand out in its selfhood through its being accused by another human being. The ego is transcended both from outside and from within, in that its within, its egological *in se,* is intruded upon from without. So transcendence here is my being transcended rather than my transcending. It is not the fulfillment of my being, but the opening up in it of a space. For this Levinas borrows the name "trans-ascendence" from Jean Wahl (referred to by Deleuze in 1977 as the most important philosopher in France after Sartre).[3] Trans-ascendence is a certain passivity rather than an activity. Hence Levinas's talk of affection. Hence too his talk of "experience." This word usually appears in quotation marks where he uses it of a person's always having heard in advance the other person's command "Thou shalt not kill." Indeed, that command, interpreted minimally as enjoining respect, has been obeyed before it has been heard, rather as a minimum of truthfulness, of undeceit, and of unselfdeception is presupposed by anyone who would universalize the command "Let us all always lie." Ethical obedience precedes phenomenal audience. Hence there is as much to be said for calling Levinas a transcendental empiricist as there is for Deleuze to describe himself thus. Deleuze's transcendental empiricism is no more a sensationalist empiricism than is Levinas's talk of an "experience" of responsibility. The *empeiria* of Deleuze's transcendental empiricism are Ideas in a sense derived through Kant from an esoteric reading of Plato according to which Platonic Ideas are problems. Retained in his transcendental empiricism is the notion of arrival from outside that Levinas indicates by affirming that although responsibility is a priori it is also a posteriori. It is not an innate idea recoverable by anamnesis. Deleuze's term for this arrival from outside is *événement,* event or eventing. It is a term or pseudo-term that is adapted also by Derrida, and it is a revision of what Heidegger calls *Ereignis,* occurrence, which brings with it the idea of gift. For Levinas the gift is not, as it is for Heidegger, the gift of being. It is the backhanded gift of gratitude for being required to give things. Things are not, as Heidegger maintains, gathering-places in the etymological sense of "*Ding*," assembly. For Levinas the thing—and so too the first-person subject—is a *donandum,* something to be given to the other.[4] It and I are gerundive, not gerunds or present participles like Heideggerian "*Sein*" and "*Dasein*." In the words of Rowan Williams, "it is given us to become givers."[5] How can a requirement be at the same time a gift? By being called for without being compelled.

As in the case of Levinas the absolute passivity and passedness of responsibility is responsive, so in the case of Deleuze the experience in transcendental empiricism is experimental. In both cases we have something like what might be expressed in Greek and Sanskrit by the middle voice. Paradoxically, Greek (the language of sunlight and Occidental polytheism) and Sanskrit (the language of what Levinas would deem to be the menace of Oriental polytheism) are better suited than most languages to express a Hebrew moment of language, as Levinas describes it provisionally, rather as Israel provisionally represents, stands, and substitutes for humankind. This "Hebrew" moment would be that of language not as what is said, but of language as the responsive and responsible face-to-face saying encapsulated in phrases such as "After you" at a door and "Yours truthfully" or "Yours sincerely" at the end of a letter. Although Levinas insists on the centrality of a passivity that is more passive than the passivity of sensory data, he also writes—crucially, it seems to me—"The term welcome of the Other expresses a simultaneity of activity and passivity which places the relation with the other outside of the dichotomies valid for things: the a priori and the a posteriori, activity and passivity."[6] We have seen how the opposition of a priori and a posteriori fails to hold for responsibility that welcomes the Other. We must also see how for responsibility the opposition of passivity and activity breaks down. "Yours sincerely" (be-khavod rav) and "see me here, send me" (hineni) may be the expressions of something impressed, expressions of a superimpressionism, as Levinas says. They are expressions as deeds. They are speech acts in which I express myself in relation to another, the relation that makes all other relations possible, according to Levinas, sociality par excellence, a giving of myself in giving my word prior to the giving of any message.[7] Here Levinas could endorse much that is said about state capitalism in Capitalism and Schizophrenia. What he would say about what the authors of that book write about schizophrenia is another question, the question of God's Ghost. We shall be led back to that by the leading question of questioning.

## Questioning Questioning

In the Logic of Sense, which outlines a logic of nonsense, Deleuze adumbrates a sense of sense that is the sense of the question.[8] It is therefore a sense of sense prior to that of affirmation and denial, a sense or meaning anterior in the case of Yes-or-No questions to the disjunction Yes-or-No. Again, in the case of questions beginning with "What?" and "Who?" or "How?," which it is tempting to analyze as open or closed series of Yes-or-No questions ("Is it A or is it B or is it C . . . ?"), there is a sense or meaning (sens, Sinn) that does not yet have the singleness of directionality (sens, Sinn) of the statement as between truth and falsity or as between affirmation and denial.⁹ But the questions whose sense interests Deleuze are ones to which statements are responses. His subject matter here is that of the linguistics fashionable at the time when the book was published (1968), for instance the linguistics of structuralism, Chomsky, Hjelmslev, and the like, the last-named being singled out for particular acclaim by Deleuze because the axis of Hjelmslev's theory is not that of signifier and signified, but that of expression and its form and of content and its form. The form of the expression is the form of the written or spoken mark, what the Saussurian would call the material envelope. When that is taken into account we are presented with the possibility of a nonsense that turns not solely on ambiguity between sound or mark and content of the kind that Lewis Carroll takes to its limits and beyond, through the looking-glass, toward, we might already say, the schizophrenia that will be treated in *Capitalism and Schizophrenia.* This later book will resume and reinforce the qualms regarding the signifier (though not the sign, the signifier taken along with what it signifies) evinced in the *Logic of Sense.* To cite but one case of the "mad" sense of sense whose logic is treated in the *Logic of Sense,* take the word "that" used by the mouse in one of Lewis Carroll's stories. In that story the mouse says "The archbishop found that reasonable." What the archbishop found reasonable was that the lords planned to offer the crown to William the Conqueror. But the duck can understand the word "that" only as the name for a thing, usually a worm or a frog. For him what the mouse says is nonsense. Wittgenstein observes: "When a sentence is called senseless, it is not as it were its sense that is senseless."¹⁰ Deleuze's disagreement with Wittgenstein is an agreement with Husserl, who maintains that sentences which fail to have sense in terms of the principle of formal non-contradiction may have sense in terms of the principles of transcendental logic. It is worth noting too in passing that the Husserlian and Stoic doctrines behind the position adopted by Deleuze is one of Wittgenstein's chief targets in the *Philosophical Investigations,* and that the examples of the sense of nonsense that Deleuze draws from Carroll and elsewhere arise in the field of the semiotics and semantics of the said as this is expressed by signs in sentences. Already the first stage of his passage to a sense of sense and nonsense beyond the judgment is a passage to the question understood as occupying the same logical space as its possible answers, the space for instance of the subject term of the proposition. That the same logical and rhetorical space is occupied by a question and its answer is confirmed if, as we shall find Deleuze may have reason for maintaining, one kind of question at least can be analyzed as a disjunctive proposition plus an imperative of the form "S is P, Yes-or-No. Delete one of the alternatives."¹¹

Despite Deleuze's special interest in the pragmatic dimension of propositions, that is to say the dimension that involves the relation between the proposition and the utterer or hearer, he does not pass on to the sense, Levinas's sense, in which the signifier is the addresser or addressee not of the proposition as what is said, but the addresser or addressee of an appeal for respect dramatically expressed by the imperative "Thou shalt not kill," to which the addresser or the addressee has already responded with an implicit or explicit imperative "see me here." This is not a matter of what is said as propositional content or concept. It is not a question of essence. There is, however, this much agreement here between Levinas and Deleuze: what each of them would wish his reader to attend to is what is beyond essence, what is not a what. At stake for Levinas is not *what* is questioned, but *who* is called into question. At stake too for Deleuze here is the "Who?" assuming, as I shall assume on the basis of what he writes elsewhere, that we can take him to endorse what he finds Nietzsche saying on this question. Who is this who? It is Dionysus, a god. In other words, Deleuze is the one who calls upon God, a god other than that of Judeo-Christianity, while Emmanuel Levinas (notwithstanding the ELohim implicit in his first name) calls upon the human being. So, so far, it is Deleuze who is the theologian and Levinas who is the anthro-apologist.

So far.

## Post-theism and Posthumanity

Although Dionysus is a God through whose drunk divinity the human being's all too human humanity is transcended, in the Nietzschean genealogy this transcendence is a transcendence to a post-humanity, not to a transcendent God. It is a transcendence to a hyper-anthropology rather than to a neo-theology. The human being's way of persisting in its being would be its desiring not to persist as the same being. Its finitude, if not its infinity, would be the eternity of eternal return, a repetition that is literally a re-petition, asking again and again, the incessant renewal of wonder. In Guattari's and Deleuze's repetition of Nietzsche this transition becomes a transition from a sober and sad anthropology, in which the ghost of the God who died lives on in an Oedipal psychoanalysis, to an inebriated and joyful anthropology where the will to power is expressed in the excesses of schizophrenia. Schizophrenia is a name for transcendence, but a transcendence that is immanent in the life of post- or suprahumanity.

What of Levinas's anthro-apology? That is to say, what of the anthropology in which he proposes an *apologia pro vita sua,* a justification for the life that according to Nietzsche and Deleuze seems either to be its own justification or not to need any justification at all? Is Levinas's humanism of the other human being a humanism of the other Other we call or used to call God? If it were, the scope of Levinas's description of the ethical would be both extended and severely restricted. If it were restricted to believers in a religion it would not have the universality he claims for it in calling it a humanism. He denies that he is doing theology in those places where he does write of God. He does not deny that what he calls the ethical is opposed to the religious as defined in terms of historical religions. A person can be religious without being a theologian; one can be Judaically, Christianly, Islamically, Hinduistically, or even Dionysiacly religious without being that. Nonetheless, in explaining his doctrine of ethicality to his reader and to himself Levinas finds it helpful to draw on the Scriptures. This does not limit the range of his account provided these appeals are purely pedagogically illustrative, and not essential to that account. That account, he insists, is as "Greek" in its thinking as are the dialogues of Plato, even if his reading of Plato on the Idea of the Good beyond Being is as unorthodox as Deleuze's Klossowskian reading of Plato's and of Kant's doctrine of Ideas. The reading of Levinas preferred here can be cast in terms of a comparison with a reading of Kierkegaard. Kierkegaard distinguishes two senses of ethicality. There is the ethics that is general and systematic. And there is the ethicality that we are given back after being tested in the heat of religiousness, particularly in the passion and paradox of what Kierkegaard calls Religiousness B, rather as Isaac is given back to Abraham after the test on Mount Moriah. For Kierkegaard Religiousness B is Christianity. For someone else it might be the religiousness of the religion of Judaism. For Levinas ethicality is given back, saved from pure generality and systematicity, without there having to be this passage and passion of a particular confessional religion. Its religiousness, meaning in part at least by that, its non-generality, its secret and singular signification, is due immediately to the "experience" of being face-to-face with another human being. This is not a secular reading of Levinas. It is a religious reading. It is a reading that is religious without being theistic.

This reading will fail if no way can be found to understand non-theistically what Levinas calls "illeity." The difficulty in understanding what he means by "illeity" may perhaps be alleviated by following one or both of the following suggestions. We could try to explain illeity, as mentioned by Levinas in the same breath as that in which he mentions God, in terms of illeity as used without such mention, that is to say, as referring to purely human third-personality. Following this first suggestion would mean accepting that it is possible that no essential reference to God is implied when Levinas distinguishes carefully—perhaps more carefully than Derrida does in *Adieu à Emmanuel Lévinas*[12]—a thirdness of illeity that is other than the third-personality of the "he" or "she" that interrupts the face to face of you and me, thereby raising the questions of justice.[13]

A second way of keeping reference to God at arm's length in interpreting what Levinas calls illeity would be to understand the apparent references to God in those passages in which "illeity" seems to be glossed through references to God or Godhead as really references to the law. But this could be a way out only if in speaking of the law we were not making an essential reference to the Law understood as, say, the Law brought down from Sinai by Moses and inscribed in a God-inspired Torah or the Law dictated to Mohammed.

Whether or not a Godless interpretation of illeity can be achieved by following these suggestions, the interpretation that would not restrict Levinas's notion of the ethical by requiring an essential reference to God could be maintained if the references to God he makes in his exposition of that notion were not essential to it.[14] That no essential reference is implied is supported at least by the following statements in *Totality and Infinity*: "[I]t is only man who could be absolutely foreign to me—refractory to every typology, to every genus, to every characterology, to every classification—and consequently the term of a 'knowledge' finally penetrating beyond the object."[15] "It is our relations with men . . . that give to theological concepts the sole signification they admit of."[16] "The formal structure of language . . . announces the inviolability of the Other and, without any odour of the 'numinous,' his 'holiness.'"[17] The numinous here is the sacred, where the sacred is opposed to the ethical. But not only does Levinas oppose holiness to the numinous and sacred. He equates holiness with divinity when, in a paragraph that keeps both Bergson and Heidegger at a distance, he writes of the trace of the absolutely Other that "this superiority of the superlative, this height, this constant elevation to power, this exaggeration or this infinite overbidding—and, let us say the word, this divinity—are not deducible from the being of beings nor its revelation, even if it is contemporary with a concealment, nor from 'concrete duration.'"[18] Here, writing in the early 1960s, he acknowledges that his reference to divinity will shock some of his readers. A decade later he writes that illeity "makes the word God be pronounced, without letting 'divinity' be said."[19] Note that the word "divinity" is in quotation marks. Are they scare-quotes because now Levinas himself is too shocked to use the word as an equivalent of holiness, which is also referred to along with the trace in the preceding sentence? Or are the quotation marks there because the word is mentioned, not used? They are there for both of these reasons. Divinity as an essence is not permitted to be said, hence neither is the essence of God, for the divinity or holiness that matters here is that of the ethical beyond essence and otherwise than being. This reading of the problem or mystery regarding illeity is non-theistic. To that extent it is neo-Nietzschean. But it is non-Nietzschean in that even if our non-theistic reading respects Levinas's insistence that the ethics of the other human being appeals to the holy, the *heilig,* the *saint,* he also insists on not following Nietzsche when the latter interprets these words in the register in which they mean the wholesome, the hale and the healthy. These words are Janus words that face in one direction toward natural hygiene and medicine, including psychoanalytic therapy of one school or another, and in the other direction toward what Levinas calls the face of the other human being or what others and sometimes Levinas himself call the spiritual. But if the spiritual and the face as intended by Levinas are not to be understood as the physiognomic or the physical, they are not to be understood either as semantic opposites of these. To understand them in this way would be to understand those Janus words as what in chapter 11 will be called Abelian contradictories, whereas it is as at the same time quasi-Abelian contradictories, an appellation to be explained in chapter 12, that these words have to be heard if they are to point in the direction Levinas invites us to go. They must be understood not only through their semantic difference, but through the leap (Kierkegaard's word) from semantic sense to the sense of saying. These Janus words stand at the swing-door between pure formal grammar, logical syntax, and semantic representation on the one side and, on the other, the ethical rhetoric of address. Nay, their quirkiness is such that there are not two opposed sides, but sides that intersect. Here, if anywhere, is it apt to speak with Philo of "the severing word." We shall speak more about this problem or mystery and about the word as a sword before we reach the last page of this book.

## Problem or Mystery

Given that, as was learned earlier in this chapter, the neo-Nietzschean Deleuze has something to say about the question of the question, he can be expected to say something about the problem of the problem, something about problematicity as such. Drawing upon Blanchot, he disagrees with Gabriel Marcel's assertion that a problem is an obstacle. In the spirit of Karl Popper, he prefers to say that a problem is a way through. Drawing also on Pierre Klossowski's interpretation of Platonic Ideas, and helping us to understand why he claims himself to be a transcendental empiricist of Ideas, Deleuze sees Ideas as products of problems, *problemata*, that is to say questions. That is to say imperatives. For, as previously observed, the question, whether of the form "Is it the case that such and such?" or "What (Who, How . . . ) is such and such?," is preceded by an explicit or implicit "Tell me . . . ," and by the demand of the *se demander* of wonder from which, according to Plato and others, all thinking begins. In this imperatival "see me here, send me" Levinas would hear the beginning of ethics. But for Levinas this imperativity would not be that of the categorical imperative any more than it would be that for Deleuze. It would be the beginning of ethics in the sense that it is already an obedience coming from my own saying. Hence its thirdness, its illeity, is that of a trace as opposed to that of a sign, for instance the sign of something said, the sign, for example, of a Kantian or other moral law. Deleuze decries a certain imperialism of language.[20] He means by imperialism of language the way every region of human behavior, especially at the time when he was writing, gets reduced or elevated to a form of language: anthropology for instance with Lévi-Strauss, economics with Althusser, and psychoanalysis with Lacan, all of them following in the wake of Saussure, who, notwithstanding the phonologism to which he subscribes, or into which he slides according to Derrida, takes writing as his model for language generally. But by imperialism of language Deleuze means not only the way language dominates or penetrates all forms of life (compare Wittgenstein on the inseparability of language and forms of life), but also the way our theorizing about language elevates the signifier to a commanding position. However, imperialism in either of these senses is not to be confused with the imperativism of Deleuze's theory of the question. One might expect that this emphasis upon the imperative would go along with a need to emphasize a certain impower or weakness on the part of someone who obeys out of cowardice or laziness. And Deleuze admits that the imperativity he locates in interrogativity may indeed be contemporary with this weak impower. But it is also contemporary, he insists, with the productive impower described by Blanchot as "the impossibility of thinking that is thinking," an original, aleatory blind spot, a moment when we can at most only stutter even when it is in our mother tongue that we attempt to utter something. For those whose mother tongue is French, stuttering is *bégaiement*. Strong advocate of taking chances as Deleuze, following Nietzsche, is, one could imagine him taking the chance to play on the particle *gai* of *bégaiement,* glossing it as the gladness of Nietzsche's *Gaya Scienza*. This moment of the impossibility of utterance is the moment of the greatest power, the moment of the throw of the die, of "the chaosmos from which the cosmos comes,"[21] where the stutterance of "and, and, and, . . ." ("*et, et, et,* . . .") is the nearest one gets to the utterance of a sentence saying what is (*est*). It is not you nor I that casts the die. Nor is the die cast by the gods. They too are subject to the necessity of chance, which is the chance to affirm chance, thereby turning impower into power. Affirming Nietzsche's affirmation, saying Yes to the question that is not yet decided as between Yes and No, Deleuze affirms an obedience to the imperative implicit in every question or problem. Whether this obedience is the obedience Levinas says is implicit in the hearing of the imperative "see me here, send me," which responds to the imperative "Thou shalt not kill," there is an obedience that leads both Deleuze and Levinas to hold that the sameness of the I is split, schizzed by alterity, even if the accounts they give of this alterity are prima facie not the same. And they are not the same precisely because while Deleuze sees difference as an anarchic, that is to say unfounded, immanence of surfaces contrasted with transcendence, Levinas sees difference as the ethically metaphysical anarchy of an illeity that is the profile of a third personal indirectness from which comes the face that faces me directly.[22]

I interrupt these words of Levinas's description of the inseparability of the face to face of the you-me from the profile of the he to cite Deleuze's description of access to a profile view from what he refers to as

> the despotic face seen head-on . . . the authoritarian face which turns away and puts itself in profile. This is even a double turning away, as Hölderlin said concerning Oedipus: God, become Point of subjectivisation, does not cease to turn away from its subject, which in its turn never ceases to turn away from its God. . . . [I]t is in turning away from God who turns away from me that I accomplish the subjective mission of God, as the divine mission of my subjectivity. The prophet, the man of the double turning away, has replaced the priest, the interpreter, the seer.[23]

My divine mission (*mission divine*) succeeds the labor of the neutered hermeneut and seer (*devin*). That is a progress *from* a signifying regime in which the signified continuously makes way for a signifier exercising authoritative control over a realm of ideas in which signs have the negative force of the cheat and the scapegoat. Progress is made from this legislative God as *Point,* point and nullity—null point—and prohibition *to* a positive subjective regime of signs in which sly cunning such as that attributed to reason by Hegel, following Adam Smith, is replaced by a frank betrayal and in which the subjectivity of an allegedly substantial subject subjected to a transcendent despot or God becomes the becoming of a demonic Dionysiac, hence passionate God expressing a subjectivity that is purely immanent flux as portrayed by, for instance, Bergson and Hume.

Here Deleuze is confirming his fidelity to Jean Wahl, for it is Wahl who describes as "the greatest transcendence" "that which consists in transcending transcendence, that is, relapsing into immanence."[24] Levinas's admiration for Wahl is warm enough to lead him to dedicate *Totality and Infinity* to him. Nevertheless, going back now to the point at which we interrupted what Levinas was saying about the profile of the *il* (or *Il*) of *illéité* (or *Illéité*), we discover that he goes on to say of this that it "escapes the bipolar play of immanence and transcendence proper to being, where immanence always wins against transcendence." Herein lies the difference between Deleuze's and Levinas's doctrines of difference and alterity. Herein lies Levinas's strongest challenge both to Wahl's transcendent immanence and to Deleuze's transcendental immanence. Here, in the way in which the problem of the polarity of immanence and transcendence opens a way to a passage beyond this polarity, Levinas provides an exemplification of Deleuze's statement that a problem is not an obstacle. Marcel defines a problem as follows: "A problem is something I meet, which I find complete before me, but which I can lay siege to and reduce."[25] We saw in our second chapter that he contrasts the problem with the mystery. "A mystery is something in which I am myself involved, and it can therefore only be thought of as a sphere where the distinction between what is in me and what is before me loses its meaning and its initial validity."[26] (We shall see in chapter 14 that Derrida takes up and complicates this contrast.) Has Deleuze something more like a mystery in mind when he makes the statement that a problem is not an obstacle but an opportunity for creativity, a necessarily unclosable opening?

If Deleuze's thinking of the problem as otherwise than an obstacle owes much to Nietzsche's teaching of joyful science, it owes something too to Bachelard's concept of science as the approach of knowledge by continuous rectification, and to Bergson's teaching of continuous creation in which what is obstacular is compared with the expended dead matter that falls down as the lively sparks of the *élan vital* fly up. Levinas too subscribes to a doctrine of continuous creation, but for him it is with ethical creativity that creativity starts. It starts or has always already started with the face of the other human being, that is to say, with the Good beyond Being that—one violence in polemic with another—continuously calls into question the ethicality of purely general law of Kantian or Rousseauistic *Moralität* and Hegelian *Sittlichkeit*. It is exterior to and quasi-contradicts the realm of consistency and contradiction carved out by the Kantian moral law. It is other than Hegelian negation or limitation. The Good beyond Being that speaks in the face of the other human being creates a surplus of multiplicity over the One without being an emanation of the One.[27]

# NINE

## Innocent Guilt

### Dionysus versus Oedipus

Dionysus, Nietzsche, Deleuze, and the Hasid invite us to dance. Oedipus is lame and does not. What about Levinas, who is not a Hasid? Would Deleuze and Guattari lump Levinas with the thinkers in whose works they find too much repression and gloom? Did we begin to learn that laughter and joy are not absent from his pages when it was noted in the last chapter that creativity is no less vital a component of his teaching than it is of what is affirmed in *Capitalism and Schizophrenia*? We may not have begun to learn this if, as was also noted in the last chapter, the creativity emphasized by Levinas is not the creativity affirmed in *Capitalism and Schizophrenia*. Schizophrenic creativity is the light creativity of Nietzsche's song and dance. Schizo-analysis is that book's updating of Nietzsche's *Die Fröhliche Wissenschaft ("la gaya scienza")*, which will be referred to here sometimes as *The Gay Science* and sometimes as *The Joyful Science*. *Capitalism and Schizophrenia* cites from *The Joyful Science* the following sentences, noting their similarity to what can be found in the works of Engels and Marx: "We burst out laughing as soon as we encounter the juxtaposition of 'man *and* world,' separated by the sublime presumption of the little word 'and.'"[1] Imagine how much louder the laughter would be when Engels and Marx encounter the juxtaposition "man and world *and* God" or, come to that, its phantom "man and world *and* father." "The question of the father," we are told in *Anti-Oedipus,* "is like that of God: born of abstraction, it supposes that the connection between man and nature or man and world is broken, so that man has to be produced as man by something exterior to nature and man."[2] Such a conception of production or creation fails to recognize that the only "effective" production or creation is that of what Guattari and Deleuze call desire and what Nietzsche calls will. What Nietzsche means, as do Guattari and Deleuze after him, is that the news Zarathustra brings down from the mountain is not simply that God or the father is dead, but that this news is of no consequence, for he never existed, or the God we have killed was already long ago dead. "The announcement of the death of the father embodies one final belief, namely 'belief in the virtue of unbelief,' of which Nietzsche says: 'This violence still manifests the need for belief, for a support, for a structure,'" that is to say, Guattari and Deleuze add, the Oedipal structure.[3] This is the structure that supports guilt, guilt over the infringement of law, in particular the law prohibiting incest, but also more generally the ten laws that Moses brought down from his mountain and the six hundred and thirteen listed in Leviticus and elsewhere.

If Levinas defined responsibility and culpability simply in terms of such laws, what chance would remain of finding in his teachings room for such joy as is radiated by the writings of Nietzsche, Deleuze, and Guattari? On the other hand, if Emmanuel Levinas would then appear to be so enthused by the God of Sinai and Leviticus that joy would be suffocated under an incubus of melancholia, Deleuze and Guattari would appear to be so enthused by Dionysus, so swept away by the gales of Nietzschean laughter, so full of joy (*Freude*) and so afraid (afreudened?) of the fear they see dramatized in the Oedipal, Christian, and Hegelian triangulations, that they are ashamed to shed a compassionate tear over the injustices done to the millions who are not obsessed by those triangulations, to ordinary people, neither masters nor slaves, for whom the ethical is not, as it is for Deleuze and Guattari and Spinoza, a taking of power to the extreme where sadness (*tristitia*) is swallowed up in a bliss (*laetitia*) that is forgetful of others, and where *agapē* is crowded out by erotic love or erotic hate. *Anti-Oedipus* is a repetition of Nietzsche's *The Anti-Christ.* Yet the authors of the former book are reluctant to make anything of the admiration the author of the latter book, laughing till he cries, expresses in it for a certain unresentful Jesus who, as distinguished from the crucified Christ, is not antithetically opposed to twice-born and now maybe thrice-born Dionysus. Of this Dionysus Nietzsche goes as far as to say that after being cut into fragments he comes home (*sic*; Nietzsche's word is *heimkommen*)[4] to his rightful place at the right hand of Zeus. If Deleuze and Guattari fear that Nietzsche's hyphenation of Dionysus and Jesus risks becoming another triangulation, they could easily multiply the sides of the diagram into what Klossowski would categorize as a passively synthetic disjunctive hyphenation of Dionysus-Christ-Buddha-Allah-Levinas-Feurbach-Marx, EngEL(s), et al., so that religion could, if you wish, escape the bad name some lament it gets (*ja, weh*) from being associated with religion, with rELigion, associated, that is to say, with ELohim, that singularly plural name of God, and with the name or proname of the name YHWH.

However, the hypotheses entertained in the first sentence of the last paragraph must be denied. Like Deleuze, Levinas emphasizes creativity. But the creativity that Levinas wishes to bring to our attention is that which modifies the generality of the law, keeps it in touch with the singularity of the first person singular, though with the first person singular not as an I but as me, hence in relation with the other human being, you who in saying "Thou shalt not kill" speak not only on behalf of yourself but also on behalf of third and fourth persons. In so commanding me you produce and create me in my unique singularity. The Latin verb *creo* means to produce, but it can also mean to elect or select. More or less ominous echoes reverberate through these words "elect" and "select." Election and selection are key notions in the Nietzschean resources of Deleuze, where they refer to the joyful choice of the affirmative as that which is to return eternally. They stand for the exclusion of Hegelian negativity from difference.[5] Now Levinas is as unwilling as Deleuze to grant ultimacy to negativity, Hegelian dialectical negativity in particular. Despite this, election as described by Levinas might seem to re-import the negativity that Nietzsche says is illustrated by the biblical history of the Jews, who, after losing their freedom, regarded their exile as a punishment for sin under the eye of God or of the priest who comes to be internalized as the eye or voice of conscience according to a morality of life-denying resentment.

## Absolute Responsibility

How well or ill does Levinas's teaching of creation as election or selection mirror this history of the Jews? Is there not at least one point at which his story and that history are incongruent? If sin is understood as a criminal contravention of divine law, no sin is presupposed in Levinas's notion of my being more responsible than anyone else. What distinguishes this absolute responsibility is that absolute responsibility distinguishes me. It is the responsibility of somebody that I cannot distinguish from somebody else. I am in no position to make comparisons. Comparison is possible only where there is objective representation of the items to be compared, but where there is absolute responsibility there is no room for representation except in the sense that I stand for another as a representative, as Israel stood for the Gentiles.

Absolute responsibility is the responsibility of the somebody that is not the *corps propre*, but, adapting an expression used by Deleuze, following Nietzsche,[6] the body without organs or, more accurately, the body without organism or substance, which according to the Levinasian doctrine is without any right to possession or self-possession other than one conferred by others. This *corps pour autrui* owes its uniqueness to its being the cynosure of everybody's ethical attention except mine, in that I am the somebody I always fail to point to when I point in the direction of my heart and say *me, here, now, hineni,* or when I sign my name, when I, as we say, sign myself, that is to say, make my mark, "make a mark of attention given to someone."[7] And perhaps this is why, contrary to another hypothesis entertained in the immediately preceding chapter, my absolute responsibility does not have an ontological foundation in the fact of my existing at a certain place and time. For the time and space of such existing is either the time and place of the physical body or the time and place of the *corps propre,* the body lived as self-possessedly mine. The body in question, called into question, is that of the I who is another, a *Je* that is an *autre.* Both Levinas and Deleuze quote Rimbaud's words *"Je est un autre."* The meaning Deleuze gives to this is that the other thinks in me. The other, *l'Autre,* gets spelled by Deleuze sometimes with a capital initial Alpha, as when, after saying "such is the education of the senses," where their education is their deregulation (*le dérèglement de tous les sens,* to cite Rimbaud again), he goes on to say: "And from one faculty to the other, violence is communicated, but where the Other is always comprehended in the incompatibility of each."[8] The other or Other who thinks in me is for Deleuze not the other human being, but a changing untotalized whole of interrelated assemblings (*agencements*) in every field of life. The Other, *l'Autre,* is not necessarily *Autrui.* Hence Deleuze's fascination by Michel Tournier's *Man Friday and the Limbos of the Pacific,*[9] which he reads as a demonstration that the only realization of the desert-island dream would be perversion itself, a strange Spinozism in which the oxygen of possibility would be lacking because the human other, who is the condition of possibility, is the victim not of some person's murderous act but of a perverse structure of *autruicide* that leaves a more rarified air, the air of necessity, to be breathed by the survivor. The survivor is not constitutionally perverse, but has been introduced by a neurosis bordering on psychosis to this atmosphere that is so rarified that he feels like an angel as light as helium, as radiant as fire. He hates the earth. He despises fecundation and the objects of desire in a manner that has been systematized by Sade.[10]

Fecundity and psychosis. These are important notions also in Levinas's teaching. Fecundity is treated by him chiefly in the context of his description of human posterity. Psychosis is mentioned by him in the contextless context of being faced, accused, even persecuted. For Levinas it is *Autrui,* the other human being, who persecutes, accuses, and even possesses me, subjects my psyche to "psychosis." Because in psychoanalysis the delusion of persecution is a form of psychosis, Levinas might seem to expose himself to the criticism Deleuze and Guattari direct at Freud. However, Levinas is not vulnerable to this criticism, for the following reason (another reason will be given further on). Levinas is obviously using the language of psychoanalysis in order to show that quasi-phenomenological analysis is as comprehensive as psychoanalysis. There is something to be said for seeing his quasi-phenomenological analysis as closer to schizoanalysis than to Freud, namely the admittedly rather isolated sentence cited in the first section of chapter 8, in which Levinas's stress on the absolute passivity of absolute responsibility goes along with a readiness to say that this passivity is simultaneous with activity. Here again is that sentence: "The term welcome of the Other expresses a simultaneity of activity and passivity which places the relation with the other outside of the dichotomies valid for things: the a priori and the a posteriori, activity and passivity." Is the activity intended here only the activity of a particular act in which absolute responsibility is expressed, corresponding in Kantian ethics to a particular act purporting to be a case of action performed out of respect for the moral law? I think not. As the sentence in question is about welcoming the other, Levinas's reference in it to an activity must be to an activity that is as absolute as is absolute passivity, the passivity that is more passive than the non-absolute passivity we oppose to the non-absolute activity of a particular deed. Hence the appeal in the preceding chapter also to "something like the middle voice" in our reading of the sentence in question. This active aspect of the middle voice of the welcome of the other is the affirmative, outward-goingness regarded as a basis for seeing in Levinas's phenomenological or quasi-phenomenological analysis at least a parallel with schizo-analysis. "The schizo knows how to depart," "*Le schizo sait partir,*" write Deleuze and Guattari.[11] Ethicality, Levinas writes, does not stay at home. Levinas is against the kinds of rootedness favored by Heidegger and Simone Weil. But if the atmosphere of Levinas's thinking is extremely different from that of Heidegger and Weil, it is different too from that of Guattari and Deleuze. For although, like the climate of the island in Michel Tournier's *Man Friday,* the climate of Levinas's thinking is one in which impossibility primes possibility, this is only because for Levinas *Autrui,* the Other, is still on the scene. In the light of the importance Deleuze gives to stuttering in our own language (*et, et, et . . .* ), as though it were the language of another, for him Rimbaud's "*Je est un autre*" might have to be rewritten as "*Je et un autre.*" For both Deleuze and Levinas the *je* is split, *fêlé,* schizzed. But for Levinas the other of "*Je est un autre*" is the other human being. However, this other human being is not one who thinks in me. It is one who, by commanding me, turns the I into a me and so creates me, turns the interiority of the immanent *Je* inside out into the exteriority of a me facing a you, but a you already announcing a he, as signaled by the third person singular "*est*" of Rimbaud's dictum. Taking the "*suis*" not as a part of the verb "*suivre*," "to follow," but as a part of the verb "*être*," "to be," what Rimbaud says is not "*Je suis un autre*," a formulation that would be more conducive to the Heideggerian analysis of human being as suggested by "*ich bin*," with its connotations of dwelling, as in the suffixes *bu, by* and *burgh*. The monadism of the *Je* who is at home, *bei sich, chez soi,* is converted into the nomadism of the wanderer in Georg Büchner's *Lenz* or of the Jew or other human being he represents. This difference between Deleuze and Levinas might well set one wondering whether an ethicality to come, a more "democratic" ethicality, would be one in which their interpretations of Rimbaud intersect.

How "democratic" could this be? We have seen that absolute responsibility is not defined by any historical law. It is outwith every historical law. It is singular. And because it is not defined by any legal, moral, or other principle, it itself cannot give rise to bad conscience over infringement. It is what takes away "the too moral after-taste" that turns Guattari and Deleuze off the royal *logos* and law.[12] Relative responsibility admits of plurality. Relative responsibilities are, roughly speaking, the responsibilities of my station and its perfect or imperfect duties, one of the distinctions treated above in chapter 2. These duties or responsibilities I can fail to live up to, so in relation to them I can experience guilt. Any guilt I may experience with regard to them, however, is fully ethical in Levinas's sense only because it is a culpability with regard to a face. Even my wrongdoing as a fully ethical wrongdoing is possible only because, without being conscious of it, I so to speak "experience" whosoever suffers from my wrongdoing as a face, as exceeding the purely moral law, as defying any law by which the wrongdoing is defined, as defying even any law by which one human being is distinguished from another, any law except the law of such laws that defines only the space of the face of the other human being, the law (*loi*) of loyalty (*loyauté*), the law of fidelity (*fides, foi,* faithfulness) to the singular human face. Guattari and Deleuze redefine "democracy" so that it extends beyond humanism, as, we shall find, does Derrida, who not only will return to "democracy" the repute it lost in the hands of Nietzsche, but will edify (*demo* is not to demolish but to construct!) the paleonym "*dēmos*" beyond limitation to people.

## Absolute Joy

When the meaning of "democracy" gets extended by Deleuze and Guattari humanism gets redefined by them as pantheism, for God gets called by them the All, the Omnitude of reality, *Omnitudo realitatis*. This is the name that

Kant gives to God in the section of the Dialectic of the *Critique of Pure Reason* entitled the Ideal of Pure Reason. This is the Idea of a subject of which we affirm a priori one member of each possible pair of contradictory transcendental predicates, the other being denied. "Such a being is a mere fiction in which we combine and realize the manifold of our ideas in an ideal, as an individual (*besonderen*) being. But we have no right" (B608). We are illegitimately, though by a natural transcendental illusion, attempting to apply constitutively conditions that can be employed here only regulatively, as though the Totality we call God were a real personal intelligence. *Capitalism and Schizophrenia* is a Fourth Critique, a Critique of Psychoanalytic Reason in which the hypostatization to be criticized is this theological one as manifested in the Oedipal theory of Freud. The *Dieu* of Deleuze's transcendental empiricist critique is the non-noumenal and non-numinal energy of a Dionysiac, inclusive, but rhizomatic disjunction in which any paternality or for that matter maternality that might be represented by the syllable EL, rhyming with "*elle*," of the word "religion" is displaced by the eternality of the return that is indicated by the syllable RE. This syllable returns us to the topics of return, joy, and absolute responsibility treated in earlier sections of this chapter. How according to Levinas are they connected to each other?

What could be called the agony of proliferating shortcoming arises out of my absolute responsibility. It arises out of my absolute responsibility faced with the multiplication of the others by whom I am faced here and now or quasi-faced from beyond the face, from across the grave that at my death becomes my new *oikos,* my second home, my dwelling in earth rather than my dwelling on earth. The agony, what I have to contend with, is the arithmetic of the incalculable number of others, contemporary and to come, on whom I turn my back when I face someone to whom I respond. My absolute responsibility is implicated in the joy of intensifying responsibility, but this latter arises directly out of my being faced with a singular other human being or with a plurality of other human beings taken distributively rather than collectively or in competition or contention. When you claim to be responsible I claim to be responsible even for your claim. This is what Levinas means by "*surenchère,*" overbidding. What is meant by this is not quite what is meant in the song that says "Anything you can do, I can do better." For the excession of the bidding of which Levinas writes exceeds the realm of the "I can." We are not speaking of *pouvoir*. Rather are we speaking of an *impouvoir,* which is not to be confused with weakness. It was seen in the second section of the present chapter that Levinas speaks of a *puissance,* a power. He speaks even of an elevation of power. In so doing he offers us the chance to find in his teaching a moment where, as we saw, he follows Deleuze and Blanchot in stressing a certain impossibility that is prior to possibility, and follows Deleuze and Nietzsche and Spinoza in emphasizing a certain continually increasing power. Because Levinas is describing absolute responsibility that injects singularity into the Kantian moral law, he is, as much as Kant, gesturing toward what is outside the sphere of maxims when he gestures toward what we have just called the joy of intensifying responsibility. Levinas's provocative reference to increasing intensity is the mark of a proximity between him and Nietzsche and Deleuze. But what justification can there be for this provocative reference to joy? It is designed to raise the question of a further proximity with Guattari and Deleuze based on the important place given to joy in the metaphysics of all three, notwithstanding that for Guattari and Deleuze metaphysics is, as noted at the beginning of the last chapter, ontogenetic, whereas for Levinas it is ethicogenetic, a genealogy of ethics.[13]

Levinas makes plenty of room for joy in his descriptions of the ego's dwelling on earth. But, perhaps because these descriptions are led or misled by the phrase "*joie de vivre*," they do not distinguish joy from the enjoyment of that from which we live. However, the more important question is whether felicity, joy, gaiety, or gladness are to be found in the sphere of ethical life as described by Levinas. Only if this is so will the stress he lays on bad conscience, reinforced by what we have called the agony of proliferating shortcoming, escape the dolefulness and spiteful resentment Deleuze and Guattari, following Nietzsche and Spinoza, condemn in the Oedipal moralities of good and evil. It is this gladness that is expressed when Levinas speaks of *glory*, sometimes reminding his reader that the Hebrew word for this (*kavod*) is used in the expression "Yours sincerely," which we mentioned in the last chapter in the same breath as *hineni*. Both of these are expressions in which what is signified is not the semantic correlative of a semantic signifier. Rather do they signify the speaker face to face with a You. But You announce an excluded third, a He or a She and a They (and an It?). So the moment of glory is liable to be overtaken by the moment of guilt. Still, the latter moment is the moment of another You. Hence, as the agony proliferates so does the joy become more intense. The moment of glory is a moment of joy, and because joy, unlike enjoyment, surprises and possesses me, its increasing intensity cannot be the increasing intensity of the will to power.

Although the increasing intensity is associated with repetition by Levinas, for whom repetition is the alternation of saying and the said (an alternation reflected in the fact that "representation" may be either semantic signification or pragmatic rhetorico-political standing-for), and although increasing intensity is associated with repetition also by the neo-Nietzscheans Guattari and Deleuze, it is these latter who write that this repetition is eternal. We have observed more than once that Levinas declines to pursue the question of eternity in *Totality and Infinity*.[14] He is keen not to abandon the language of "Greece," the language of philosophy, in that book. Hence when he does have recourse to Hebrew words in that book or in *Otherwise than Being* they are, insofar as the distinction holds, mentioned rather than used. To pursue in these texts the problem or mystery of eternity would be to go back upon the distinction he makes between his philosophical writings and his confessional ones—a distinction similar to the one Heidegger makes between the "edifying" and the theoretical writings of Kierkegaard[15] ("edification" being a word favored by the Jesuits to describe an important constituent of their mission). To pursue that problem or mystery would be to introduce into the philosophical writings questions that, Levinas says, should be confined to the confessional writings, for example the question of messianism. From the standpoint of confession, it may well be that the infinite time of which philosophy can speak is interrupted by messianic eternity. But that is not for philosophy to say, at least philosophy as understood "Greekly" by Levinas and the Hegelian philosophy the sanity of whose borderlines he and Kierkegaard test, borderlines we shall find tested again by what will be said concerning messianicity and democracy by Derrida. On this Levinas is in agreement with Kierkegaard. And even the eternity of the Nietzschean eternal return must wait for the leap into the love that Nietzsche calls *amor fati.*

## Territory

At the end of chapter 7 it looked as though Nietzschean *amor fati* would save everything, or almost everything, in the name of Dionysus. In the present chapter the same saving would appear to be made in the name of *Omnitudo realitas,* the name that for Deleuze is synonymous with God. For Nietzschean Deleuze the Dionysian Totality of Reality would be a god of events, *événements* that keep on coming. It would be a god of becoming in which no substantial being becomes, a becoming in which becoming is all that becomes. Now ethical responsibility on Levinas's account is not a property possessed by a substantive subject. It is the unselfpossession of a me "psychotically" possessed by the other human being for whom I substitute and go bail. How can we make sense of the notion of responsibility that is not the responsibility of a self, however much interrupted? How can we make sense of the notion of responsibility, whether absolute or relative, where what we call the self is a continuously creative happening?

The route to answers to these questions passes through the recognition that although Deleuze's metaphysics of becoming is a metaphysics of deterritorialization, he acknowledges that there is no deterritorialization without reterritorialization. The movement of machination, that is to say passive synthesis—middle-voiced *mechanaomai*—becomes temporary fixation in the mechanical classifications of ordinary language and daily life. These are aspects of what, in the wake of Zarathustra's injunction to "remain true to the earth,"[16] he goes so far as to call *la terre*. But *la terre* is not *terra firma*. It is earthing on analogy with such expressions as "*es blaut*," a verbal way of saying that the sky is blue where the "*es*" does not denote a substantive and where the intransitivity of "*blaut*" is that of the so-called subjective aspect of a double genitive, as in "the blueing of the sky," "the earthing of the earth." Any appearance of substantivity and of inherence of predicates in earthing as analyzed by Deleuze is only appearance. It is a superficial grammatical effect. The self and the object are grammatical epiphenomena. Our Greek grammatical categories lead us to think that the *élan vital* is a productive power hidden behind and by our linguistic categories, whereas deterritorialization and reterritorialization are all there is to the All of reality. Territorialization, deterritorialization, and reterritorialization are three degrees of what Husserl calls passive synthesis, which too is an intransitivity of temporal transition, an ancestor of Bergsonian *durée* and Heideggerian *Sein*.

Territorialization, Deleuze and Guattari tell us, is connective synthesis such as is effected by circumcision, tattooing, or other marks which are inscribed on the body and which constitute the belonging to a tribe or race. This is a process of coding of interacting desires that does not, however, yield personal subjects.

Deterritorialization is not just transition to another territory, as it were, horizontally or horizonally. It is a vertical movement in which there is a separation from the earth on the part of the chieftain or despot who transcends the collectivity, enjoys the spectacle of the pain experienced by the members of the tribe in their being coded, and overcodes the collective by reading the wounds as a punishment for wrongdoing. He sees himself as judge. The chieftain, despot, or king on Deleuze's revision of Marx is non-productive, in contrast to the collective now regarded as subordinate. This account of the emergence of disjunction and classification in society is non-Oedipal because the Oedipal story gives primacy to desire as lack defined in terms of the triangulation of father, mother, and child. On Deleuze's account law does not emerge from this triangulation and is preceded by a stage in which desire is the positive creative production of life itself, not the negative desire of something lacking.

Reterritorialization is a re-earthing in which the disjunction of the despot from the collective is superseded by a conjunctive stage in which the law is internalized, made again immanent when it is sunk into the general ideas of humanity or mankind and the person, where the person is equated economically with the exchangeable value of labor and where humanity is deemed to be the source of law and of the opposition of good and evil.

These three stages correspond roughly to the "primitive" stage, the feudal stage, and the stage of Enlightenment. Here Oedipal psychoanalysis may arise presenting the choice between the father and the mother. How that choice is offered may be illustrated by the pun suggested by the amplification of an analogy Saussure uses in the course of his account of such oppositional structures as those that enframe psychoanalytic theories that analyze desire as lack, theories like that of Lacan,[17] from whom Deleuze and Guattari borrow the term "territorialization." Adapting Saussure's analogy, signification may be conceived as the ripples produced on the surface of the sea by the interaction of currents in the air and currents in the water. The ripples correspond to the structures produced by the materiality of the signifier and the signified meanings. But the sign now stands between us and what we imagine as an original maternal origin, the sea as mother, *la mer* as *la mère*. The sign itself prohibits access to that maternal source, substituting for it the mother defined only by opposition to the father within the field of signification, and defended by the paternal and priestly law against incest.

Schizoanalysis would show how arbitrary and dogmatic psychoanalysis is, and how the hypostatization of the person, man, and humanity is a forgetting of the interplay among pre-personal desiring singular multiplicities. Now although Levinas's notion of the ethical face-to-face self may seem to be that of a person, the person is pre-personal in the sense in which the personal is understood abstractly at the third stage just described as the stage of Enlightenment. The Levinasian face to face may therefore seem to be closer to Deleuze's second stage, in which disjunction, hierarchy, and transcendence or exteriority have been introduced. This comparison has to be rejected. The other human being as you is said to be separated from me and to regard me from a height, in what could be described paradoxically as the absolute relation of the face to face which Levinas sometimes describes as the relation of relations and other times denies is a relation at all, since a relation is between terms and there are no terms in the face to face. *A fortiori,* the other facing me is not in a relation of power over me. Furthermore, while the despot on Deleuze's account embodies law, the face to face is precisely a non-legal moment of ethicality that is separate from universal law. The nearest Deleuzian analogy for Levinas's face to face would be the first of the three stages, the stage of territorialization insofar as this is neither the relation of slave to master as individual despot or authority as State nor abstract personality or universal humanity, but what Deleuze calls haecceity, borrowing the term from Duns Scotus, whose doctrine of the univocality of being he also adapts. What Deleuze calls haecceity corresponds to what Levinas calls uniqueness. However, where the latter belongs to a *socius* involving a human you and human shes and hes, the political and collective character of Deleuze's notion of haecceity covers also the inhuman. Furthermore, his notion of haecceity does not correspond to the thisness of the individual argued for by Scotus; allowing for the fact that Deleuze is thinking of what is beyond essence, Deleuze's notion of haecceity corresponds more closely to the thisness Scotus assigns to the essence.

Because according to Deleuze perceiving extends to the inhuman, there would seem to be no reason why he should not allow a similar extension to the notion of response, for to perceive is to respond, and perceptivity is a responsiveness. Deleuze may be more reluctant to apply the notion of responsibility to inhuman passive synthesis as independent self-connectedness, for responsibility would seem to require a move to the plane of disjunction (deterritorialization) or conjunction (reterritorialization). These planes involve institutions. Now Levinas too would maintain that absolute responsibility works through the relative responsibilities of stations, duties, and laws. Absolute responsibility is interruptive, so it must have something to interrupt. Absolute responsibility "is" interruption. Absolute responsibility is not an abstraction, not a transcendental condition of possibility opposed to concrete situations as Kantian transcendental conditions of possibility are usually taken to be opposed to the empirical. Absolute responsibility is always "earthed" in institutions, not least the institution of language. Although absolute responsibility is traced in the Platonic Idea of the Good beyond being, and although absolute responsibility is exteriority, this exteriority is no less concrete and *engagé* than what Kierkegaard calls inwardness.

Levinas writes that the responsive human being is a Signifier. But the way the Signifier represents is other than the way a signifier stands for what it signifies either on a *nomen-nominatum* account of signification, in which the sign posits what it signifies, or on a structuralist account of signification, in which the sign is constituted by the negative and oppositive relationships it has with other signs. The Signifier "represents" without either the "horizontal" intra-systematicity or the "vertical" intentionality of a relation to an object or objective. It expresses the aspect of ethicality that animates and disturbs the law as criterion of what is good and what is evil. The face to face is beyond good and evil. Here Levinas and Deleuze share a proximity to Nietzsche. Here too they share a proximity to Spinoza as construed by Deleuze. As construed by Deleuze both Spinoza and Nietzsche seek to sidestep morality conceived as juridical control. The very title of Spinoza's book *Ethics* would lead us to expect him not to be, as the title of a book by Jack Caputo declares, "against ethics."[18] Nor is Deleuze "against ethics." For him, as for his Nietzsche and Spinoza, the ethical is creative affirmation. On Deleuze's repetition of Nietzsche and Spinoza, however, the ethics is not centered, as it is according to Levinas, on the human. Nor, as against Levinas, does ethics as conceived by Deleuze and his Spinoza have the other as center of gravity. Yet, no less than with Deleuze and Kierkegaard, with what Levinas calls an ethics of the other human being the ethical is a "resingularization." It is a recreation and a refreshment of the abstract idea of humanity through a concretization of the abstract rationality in terms of which humanity has been defined, for instance by Kant. This concretization is effected by the "experience" of being faced by another human being. Because Levinas says that in the primary social relation of being faced the other pursues and persecutes me (before *je suis* in either senses of the verb, before I am and before I follow), it is tempting to infer that the relation is one of paranoia, and therefore that it is a case of Oedipal repression. This inference is invalid if the face to face is not a relationship between dominant and dominated centers of power. Even the concept of centrality according to which the center is opposed to the periphery is no longer tenable once the center of gravity is displaced from me to you—and to a you whose centrality is challenged by third parties.

Hence the face to face is less like the Oedipal relationship of psychoanalysis than it is like the non-Oedipal relationship of schizoanalysis. In the face to face the self is schizzed. Now insofar as the face to face is the only aperture through which one may pass, if one wishes, to God, the traditional idea of God as Creator, Legislator, and Judge also undergoes a re-creative refreshment. So too does what Levinas calls the judgment of God, distinguishing this from the judgment of history pronounced according to Hegel by reason. The phrase "judgment of God" cannot mean what it means for Deleuze. For him this expression stands for everything about capitalism and psychoanalysis that schizoanalysis would dethrone, namely judgment as Police or Priest or Principle or Law, or as founded on Law. In place of this, schizoanalysis would put anarchy, the divinity of which would be demonic, drunken Dionysiac desire. We know that Deleuzian desire is not desire to fill a lack. We know too that Levinasian ethical Desire is not a desire to fill a lack. My upper-case ethical Desire, although a response to the needs of others, is not a drive to satisfy my need or to achieve any other satisfaction. This does not make it incompatible with joy, at the very least the joy in other people's enjoyment, which would not be possible unless I know what it is to experience my own immediate enjoyments. But, to repeat, joy is not the same as that form of complacency we call contentment. Nor are joy, enjoyment, and contentment the same as the happiness or the felicity about whose presence in Levinas's doctrine of ethicality we have been asking in this chapter. Where the difference lies is not made any easier to decide by the fact that English translations of Nietzsche's works use the word "joy" for his word "*Lust*." Although this practice is supported by dictionaries, dictionaries also support the idea that *Lust* is a *Neigung*, that is to say an inclination. However, joy is a condition, a state, like happiness, but a sudden and intense state that supervenes. As happiness cannot be separated from its happenedness, so a state of joy is the result of an event. One is overcome by it. One is, to use Nietzsche's word, *überwunden* by it. It overpowers us, he and Deleuze would say, by subjugating and "subjecting" us in a way that increases our power. To use Levinas's word, it "produces" our subjectivity, though according to him the increase of our power is effected ultimately by an impower that subordinates the power of free will to responsibility toward others: their calling is what constitutes me as subject by impressing upon me that the freedom of my will is its being called to the service of others.

Joy is not an intense inclination like lust. Although English "lust" is not a good translation of German "*Lust*" (as distinguished from "*Gelüste*"), both are forms of desire, *Begierde*. "*Begierde*" translates Levinas's lower-case "*désir*," denoting the intentionality of an inclination (*Neigung*). If Levinas's upper-case *Désir* can be said to express an intentionality, it is a reversed intentionality coming in from outside, as does joy, which is therefore better translated by "*Freude*" in the context of Nietzsche and Guattari and Deleuze.

## Austere Happiness

Although we have found that there is room for joy in Levinas's humanism of the other human being, it cannot be denied that in his presentation of that teaching the Dionysiac inebriation of the joyful science of Nietzsche, Guattari, and Deleuze gets as sobered up as Kierkegaard's passion. Passion may be love, but passion is a suffering, whether the suffering of increasing superlative passivity or the doubly genitive suffering of joy. These sufferings of the *outrance* of *autrui* come together in what Levinas refers to as austere happiness, *bonheur austère*. If Deleuze and Guattari say that Levinas's word "austere" is an euphemism for "guilty," they should nonetheless acknowledge that the guilt is not guilt over contravening a law. Would it be guilt at spending time enjoying oneself when the time could have been spent relieving the sufferings of others? That construal of guilt would be based on a contrast between happiness and goodness, and that does seem to be assumed as a basis of Levinas's contrast between egological enjoyment and ethical goodness as response to the face of the other human being. But he writes of the austere happiness *of goodness*.[19] It is as though he is making a distinction something like that made by Kierkegaard and Saint Paul between worldly happiness and non-worldly bliss, except that this "higher" happiness would not imply any positive religion, but would be a modality of human goodness, that is to say, of responsibility that is welcomed even if it is also imposed. One must of course take care not to suppose that the austere happiness of goodness means that goodness is its own reward. Responsibility is, Levinas insists, for nothing. He would have reduced the risk of our failing to grasp this if in marking his divergence from Heidegger he had not written "The love of life does not love Being, but loves the happiness of being."[20] Is not what we call love of life love of the things life brings, not being nor the happiness of being, but beings, things, people, or events?

The distinction just drawn between beings and events opens a way forward. On the one hand is Levinas's notion of goodness as responsibility. On the other hand, Deleuze writes, speaking also on behalf of Guattari: "[W]e do not know these notions; they are notions of police or tribunal psychiatry."[21] From what has been said in this chapter it should be plain that these words do not give a just description of Levinas's notion of absolute responsibility. It should also be plain from what has been said in this and the preceding chapters that if the only happiness consistent with absolute responsibility is one that is austere, the price of austerity may be a price worth paying in order that, as an alternative to both personal egoism and to the erotic ethics of the depersonalized will to power of the God Dionysus, room may be made for an ethics of the wisdom of agapeistic (or ahavatic or chesedic?)[22] love of the other human being and—beyond the other human being but this side of any transcendent God—of the non-human beings that come within the scope of Nietzsche's *amor fati* and the ethics of Guattari and Deleuze. But here I am speaking of an ethical regard for beings, whereas the ethics of Guattari and Deleuze is an ethics of events, occurring, and recurrence. No wonder such a concept of ethics does not know the notions of responsibility or irresponsibility defined in terms of the tribunal—or of the Oedipal triad. If the absence from their conception of ethics of responsibility thus defined is an absence from it of any notion of responsibility, and if an appeal is made to Levinas to point a way beyond that seeming complacency, it becomes relevant to note now some remarks in *Totality and Infinity* that may make it less difficult to get the writer of that book and the writers of *Anti-Oedipus* on speaking terms with one another.

## Save Sublimation Itself

Consider first the statement "Metaphysics, the relation with exteriority, that is, with superiority, indicates . . . that the relation between the finite and the infinite does not consist in the finite being absorbed in what faces him, but in remaining in his own being, maintaining himself there, acting here below."[23] The first part of this statement was explained by Levinas's statement that the Good beyond Being—that is to say the Good beyond both the antithesis of good and evil and the antithesis of good and bad—is not negation. Alongside this we should now put his statement that this movement of going beyond being, "the rectilinear movement of a work which goes infinitely to the other," is an abnegation.[24] It is a sort of self-denial then, but the word "denial" or "negation" (*nier*) has to be put in quotation marks in order to distinguish this abnegation or self-denial from any operation of self-reflection. A transcendental methodology may track down subjective, subconscious, psychological, social, or linguistic sources of our direct transcendence toward the other in sincerity, but they themselves presuppose this transcendence "with respect to which immanence is situated." "Nothing of what is sublime does without psychological, social, or verbal sources, save sublimation itself."[25] That, in a nutshell, is the challenge Levinas's *Humanism of the Other Human Being* makes to Deleuze and Guattari. But in support of an attempt to bring these two and Levinas face to face at, so to speak, the heart of a chiasmus, attention should be given to the assertion cited most recently from *Totality and Infinity* that metaphysics, the movement beyond being, consists in acting here below, that is to say, in not going beyond the sublunar and the subsolar sphere. This is not surprising, since we are talking about ethics, practice, works. But because we are troubled by the tension between ethics treating of beings, including at least human beings, and ethics treating of events, it is relevant to remind ourselves that the ethics of beings is also an ethics of actions, and, to put it crudely, actions are less different than beings from events—unless, still speaking crudely, we say that an event is a kind of being or entity, as do even Deleuze and Guattari in the following sentence, one that could have been written by Levinas, given the importance he ascribes to the part played by the concept as a vehicle of criticism, and given the importance criticism has in his analysis of ethicality: "The concept speaks the event, not the essence of the thing—pure Event, a haecceity, an entity, the event of the Other or of the face."[26]

Levinas's metaphysics of ethics, like that of Deleuze and Guattari, may be a metaphysics of events. In the preface of *Totality and Infinity,* questioning Heidegger's notion of the event (*Ereignis*), he asks: "Do the particular beings yield truth in a Whole in which their exteriority vanishes? Or, on the contrary, is the ultimate event of being played out in this exteriority's explosure (*éclat*)?"[27] A few paragraphs later, questioning, like Deleuze and Guattari do, the primacy of objectivating representation, he observes: "Consciousness then does not consist in equaling being with representation, in tending to the full light in which this adequation is to be sought, but rather in overflowing this play of lights—this phenomenology—and in accomplishing *events* whose ultimate signification (contrary to the Heideggerian conception) does not lie in *disclosing*." The italics in which the word "events" (*événements*) is printed are his.

There remains to be considered briefly one further problem, that is to say, in Deleuze's conception of what a problem is, one further chance to move ahead. Where the singularities in the metaphysics of Deleuze and Guattari are collectivities, in the metaphysics of Levinas they are you and me. This would not be a stumbling block to Levinas. For, let us remind ourselves yet again, according to his doctrine my ego, my subjectivity, and my personality are disturbed by you, and in your face speak also the second, the third, and the nth other. Further, this multiplicity of the face proliferates beyond the face into a future that is always acoming, *avenir, événement, avènement,* advent. But this advent is an advent that does not lean on any hope for a Messiah or a messianic ghost. Levinas writes: "The discontinuity of generation, that is, death and fecundity, releases Desire from the prison of its own subjectivity and puts an end to the monotony of its identity."[28] This sentence outlines a desubstantiating but transcendent genetology whose lineage is very different from the desubstantiating but immanent genetology projected by Deleuze and Guattari. Yet this chapter may have removed some of the difficulties that would prevent their welcoming Levinas's outline as what they would call a line of flight *(fuite)* that goes not to a theology, but in the direction of religiousness without any particular religion and without the God or the ghost of the God that haunts Oedipal psychoanalysis. Here we return to that idea of return for which we earlier took the first syllable of the word "religion" to stand. If the rest of this word conveys the idea of being tied or bound *(ligatus),* the boundness is a boundness to a modicum of doubt, to the unboundness of a "maybe." If, in line with the hypothesis that the rest of the word derives not from *ligo,* but from *lego,* as in *relego,* and *lectus,* the idea conveyed would be that of collectivity or assemblage, what Deleuze and Guattari call *agencement.* Levinas would be tempted to call this *ageancement,* as he confesses he was once tempted to write *essance,* rather than *essence,* because what he needed was a verbal noun to mark "the process or event of being,"[29] the doubly genitive processive eventing of being, strung between the poles of activity and passivity. But the notion of collectivity *(colligere)* contains the notion of ligament, string *(fides),* and fidelity, where fidelity or faith must leave room for doubt if it is not to become sealed knowledge and seeing, the answer to a question conceived as a problem and not the response to a question construed as a mystery—or aporia (see below).

If philosophy used to be the handmaiden of theology, perhaps religion is the handmaiden of philosophy now; as it always was if religion is another name for the astonished open-mouthed wonder which the Greeks called *thaumazein,* and which Levinas calls *merveille* when, over and over again, like Descartes interrupted in mid-argument by the urge to praise God and like Kierkegaard unable to suppress the exclamation "Wonderful. Wonderful," he finds himself, without any necessary invocation of God, invoking "the marvel of the family," "the marvel of language," "the marvel of the idea of Infinity," and the marvel of Exteriority.[30] These invocations are tracings of the religious dimension of ethics and therefore of philosophy insofar as ethics is *protē-philosophia.* In saving ethics from the exclusion from religiousness, the exclusion to which he considers ethics is condemned by Kierkegaard, Levinas saves philosophy from the same fate. This is a fate to which traditional philosophy is condemned also by the new philosopher whose Zarathustra proclaims that God is dead. That philosopher's writings are living proof that religiousness is not dead.

One can imagine that that same philosopher and philologist, the lover of words whose *amor fati* is a love of what has been or will have been said, would find evidence for adopting the standpoint from the perspective of which the genealogical *ageancement* of what we call religion is *religāre*. One can imagine him drawing our attention[31] to Horace, Odes, I, 5, 4, where *religāre* means to bind, and to Catullus, *Carmina,* 63, 84, where *religāre* means to unbind. Other such antagonyms will be encountered in our chapter 11, after, in our next chapter, a close look has been taken at negation, a notion that comes into play in the notion of antagonymity, not to mention negative theology. This present chapter closes, however, with the provisional thought that perhaps religiousness and the spirit of religion happen at the threshold between the apparently opposed forces of the word *religāre,* at the crack *(fêlure)* through which there could be an escape *(fuite)* of a ghost, *Geist,* or a gas the smell of which will be detected again before this book is closed.

# TEN

## Origins of Negation

### Criticism and Hypocriticism

If criticism is regress upon the conditions of knowledge as exemplified in the Critical philosophy of Kant, hypocriticism (or hypoCriticism) will be regress beyond those conditions. Strictly speaking, therefore, it is about hypocriticism that Levinas is writing when he refers to criticism as re-ascent (*remontée*) or regress (*régression*) beyond, below, or this side of (*en deçà de*) the condition of knowledge.[1] One of his section headings announces that what is to be treated in that section is "*L'investiture de la liberté ou la critique.*" But what is argued in that section is that the investiture of freedom, whatever that may turn out to be, is called for by freedom, freedom being referred to as the condition of knowledge. Therefore the investiture is beyond that condition. Hence the investiture of freedom should be referred to either in scare-quotes as a "condition" or as a quasi-condition. That is why, strictly speaking, we should distinguish criticism from hypocriticism.

Because the "structures" Levinas says he is examining are very complex (*fort complexes*) his term "criticism" will be retained in what follows in order to avoid multiplying complexities beyond necessity, but what his term hides should not be forgotten. It could be said that his choice of term itself exemplifies a tendency to forget that is one of the topics of the section in question. It indicates a tendency among philosophers to speak of "conditions of possibility" as though they were all presuppositions logically deducible by classical, transcendental, or dialectical logic from what they condition.

Philosophers since Plato have considered it their task to seek knowledge of knowledge by tracing the conceptual or categorical conditions of knowledge. Thus Levinas couples philosophy with criticism. Critique or philosophy, he writes, equating them, "is the essence of knowledge."[2] This is a way of saying that philosophy is knowledge of knowledge. Philosophy is this thanks to such retrocession to the conditions of knowledge as takes place when Plato argues from the untutored slave-boy Meno's learning how to solve a particular problem in geometry to the conclusion that learning is recollection, when Descartes argues from experimental doubting to the indubitability of *sum,* when Kant argues from the admitted experience of temporal succession to the apriority of the forms of sensibility and the principles of the understanding, and when Hegel purports to demonstrate how from the illusion of sense-certainty one is compelled toward the thinking that thinks itself which he calls absolute wisdom.

Levinas argues that philosophy thus conceived as looking for knowledge or philosophy as love of wisdom overlooks philosophy as wisdom of love. The latter is a wisdom where looking arises not simply from being looked at, in the ways described for instance by Sartre; in what could be called sophophily it is learned that looking and being looked at have their "origin" in being looked to, in the ways described by Levinas. Love that has knowledge or wisdom as its object hides love as Desire that is not desire for compresence with an intentional accusative. In love as Desire the lover is accused. Whereas philosophy as love of wisdom is the essence of knowledge, the purpose announced in the title of one of Levinas's later books is to remind us of what is beyond essence. The word "beyond" in that title, *Otherwise than Being or Beyond Essence,* translates not *"en deçà de,"* but *"au-delà de."* Whatever significance, if any, hangs on the choice of the phrase, *"au-delà de"* may be used in the title because this book declares itself to be a book of philosophy in the Greek tradition handed down from Plato. That tradition is occupied with questions as to what makes things what they are, that is to say, with the essence of what is. Therefore if, as in Plato, philosophy finds itself having to press on beyond questions concerning being and what is to questions concerning the good, these last questions will come after the others in the order of inquiry (*ordo cognoscendi*). At the same time, the questions that come later in the order of inquiry can be earlier in what would traditionally be called the order of logic or ontology (*ordo essendi*). In the latter order they will be this side of, *en-deçà de,* the questions of being and essence. But this side of both the ontological order and the epistemological order is the order of what requires to be done. To demonstrate this is the aim of *Otherwise than Being or Beyond Essence* and *Totality and Infinity.* However, one outcome of the demonstration is the putting into question of the idea of a line between an alleged this side and an alleged that side. Consequently, it will make some sort of sense for Levinas to speak of the posteriority of the anterior and to set limits to the traditional opposition between the a priori and the a posteriori.

Note that in the book titles just cited occur so-called logical connectives. The "or" is not the exclusive "or." It is not the equivalent of the Latin *"aut."* It is the equivalent of the Latin *"vel."* That is to say, it does not exclude the sense expressed by "and." Does that mean that it can include the sense that the logical connective "and" has in the title of the earlier book? What sort of conjunction is marked by the logical connective "and" in the title of that book? It is one that requires us to admit an alternative logical or quasi-logical space. It yields an alternative geometry, Levinas suggests, when he writes that what we might call the proto-geometry of proto-ethics is the source of our idea of a geometrical straight line, and that in this proto-geometry beyond mensuration there happens a hollowing out that is the origin of our idea of curvature. How can these thoughts regarding "The Origin of Geometry" (to borrow a title from Husserl) not be challenges to the superficially similar thought Sartre expresses when in the chapter of *Being and Nothingness* on "The Origin of Negation," to which our remarks here will be confined, he writes of holes of nothingness in being?

The "and" of the title of *Totality and Infinity* is a logical connective which demands that conjunction be at the same time disjunction. Like the "and" of Heidegger's title *Being and Time,* a book in which time is discovered to be the meaning of being, the "and" of Levinas's title would have to allow at least for the non-exclusively disjunctive force of *"vel"* as illustrated by the "or" in the title of *Otherwise than Being or Beyond Essence.* Is it conceivable that this "and" might allow space both for the non-exclusive and for the exclusive "or"? This is not conceivable in the terms of the classical logic of contradiction. But Levinas aims to demonstrate the limitedness of that logic, a logic of what he considers to be totalitarian reason, a reason which, he maintains, calls to be supplemented by a reason that is not totalitarian. On this account of the logic of this reason *vel* and *aut* may be compatible. It might be asked whether such a compatibility is what is marked by the slash of the title of Kierkegaard's book *Either/Or,* or whether that stroke marks there only an exclusive either-or-and-not-both, as is commonly supposed. What is clear regarding Kierkegaard is that his teaching is a teaching of passion. But so too, if affect is passion, is the doctrine of Levinas, notwithstanding his teaching of a reason beyond totalitarian rationalism. Here once more, as in our opening chapter we found Hegel arguing against Kant, what seem to be located on opposite sides of a line are not thus simply opposed. Such simple opposition is superseded once there is a complication of interiority and exteriority.

This is why Levinas has to move out of the context of inquiry to which philosophy has traditionally thought it was confined. He turns to what Kierkegaard calls a *confinium* that is not the border or line where parts of space and time meet, but the between of an encounter where there is an ordering of space and time that disorders ordering as formation, for instance formation as form of sensibility in the account of the conditions of experience in general put forward by Kant, and form as harmony in his account of the beautiful[3] and in Nietzsche's account of the Apollonian in art.[4] The very sameness of the notion of simultaneity (*hama*), which for Aristotle is a precondition of the principle of non-contradiction, is discovered to be crossed, though not crossed out, by difference. Classical logic is a logic of contradiction, *Widerspruch.* Levinas's logic is a logic of contra-diction, *contre-dire, wider-sprechen.* What could this mean? It means at least that philosophers must learn that philosophy as the quest for knowledge of what makes knowledge possible must, in paying attention to this what, concern itself more with the who regarded otherwise than in its whatness. This is acknowledged not only by Levinas. It is acknowledged also by Heidegger and Sartre.

## Sartre's Criticism of Hegel and Heidegger

In "What Is Metaphysics?" and in the analysis of the components of questioning carried out in §2 of *Being and Time* reference is made to the alternatives of affirmation and denial as these alternatives relate to questions about the existence, qualities, and relations of things that scientists claim to be the only questions that concern them. Heidegger shows that such questions and the alternatives of affirmation and denial they presuppose are superseded by the question "Why is there something rather than nothing?" because this question is implicit in the very claim made by scientists that they are concerned with nothing other than beings. This concern appears not to be with nothingness as opposed to being but with nothingness as belonging to the being of beings, in particular to the human being that Heidegger calls Dasein in order to emphasize that for this being (*Seiendes*) its being-there-or-here, its where (its *da sein*—though in the German of Bach's *Weihnachtsoratorio* "*da*" also means when) is for it a matter that is in question: *es geht um das Sein* (that *Sein* of which the meaning is time and *Zeit-raum*). Hegel speaks correctly when he writes: "Pure being and pure nothing are therefore the same," "*Das reine Sein und das reine Nichts ist also dasselbe.*"[5] In Hegelian logic this is correct, Heidegger says, because pure being and pure nothing are both indeterminate immediacy, the *unbestimmte Unmittelbare.* Both pure being and pure nothing are without quality or relation. They are empty of any *Bestimmung,* where a *Bestimmung* is a predicated property and the forms of predication are a subject-matter of logic. Now logic and correctness according to its norms treat of propositions about beings in the world. They do not treat of metaphysical truth if the metaphysical transcends particular things in order to embrace their totality. And it is the totality of things that reveals itself as the concern of natural scientists, for instance the physicists in the audience at Freiburg when the inaugural lecture "What Is Metaphysics?" was delivered on July 24, 1929. These physicists discover themselves to be concerned with a meta-physical question the moment that in response to Heidegger's question "What are you studying?" they reply "Nothing other than particular things." In making this reply, Heidegger observes, echoing words that Hegel uses at certain transitional moments in the *Phenomenology* (words echoed too, we shall see in the next chapter, in Freud's paper "*Die Verneinung*"), the physicist is saying something different, saying the opposite of what he means. The physicist is on the road to metaphysical questioning. He is on the way to "an enquiry over and above beings, with a view to getting hold of them again as such and in their totality." Such questions about totalities cannot be handled by the logic of the understanding designed to deal with parts of wholes, members of classes, and the relations between classes other than the class of all classes.

Kant had already warned readers of the Dialectic of the *Critique of Pure Reason* of the contradictions one gets into in attempting to apply either formal analytic logic or transcendental logic to statements about totalities. But why does Heidegger question "the legitimacy of the rule of 'logic' in metaphysics"? Why does he thereby question the legitimacy of the Hegelian logic of dialectical negation, the logic of reason to which Hegel has recourse precisely because of what he regarded as the limitation of the logic of the understanding? Heidegger's judgment is that any logic of negation will be inadequate to metaphysics because metaphysics as defined by Aristotle is the study of being as such, and therefore of its correlative nothingness. But nothingness, Heidegger maintains, and Sartre agrees with him on this, cannot have its origin in negation.

What then is the origin of negation? The origin of negation is not a what. It is a who, the who that Heidegger calls Dasein and Sartre *la réalité humaine* or the for-itself, the *pour-soi*. However, from this much agreement with Heidegger and from Sartre's agreement with Heidegger that nothingness cannot have its origin in negation, no general agreement with him can be inferred. To infer this would be as unsafe as to assume a general agreement on Sartre's part with Hegel because the former's term "*pour-soi*" translates the latter's "*Für-sich*." How could Sartre be in general agreement with both Hegel and Heidegger if Heidegger disagrees with Hegel, as it has just been learned that he does? In any case, Sartre has his own reason for disagreeing with Hegel. Like Heidegger's reason for doing so, it relates to Hegel's statement that both being and nothingness are indeterminate and therefore the same and indistinguishable. Hegel, Sartre maintains, confuses contrariety and contradiction. Only because he plays on the ambiguity of the word "contradiction" can Hegel derive becoming from the opposition of being and nothingness. But, Sartre insists, what Hegel calls pure being and pure nothingness are contradictory opposites as opposed to contrary opposites. However empty of determination or definition being and nothingness may be, it remains that being *is*. The very denial that being is determined implies this. However much we deny of being any determination, we cannot deny without strict contradiction that pure being itself is a plenitude of being. On the other hand nothingness or non-being is a denial of this very plenitude. It is in the very *heart* of being that non-being's denial lurks, like a worm, "*c'est au sein même de l'être, en son cœur, comme un ver.*"[6]

This statement is Sartre's alternative to what he understands to be Heidegger's doctrine that nothingness is outside being. The upshot is that a distinction must be made between pure being *in itself,* which is an enigma for human consciousness, and the being *for itself* of the human being, which founds the human being in that it is what, in being nihilated, enables the human being to be itself. Against Heidegger as read by him, Sartre is questioning the simple opposition of pure being and pure non-being. When Sartre writes that "[b]eing has not been given its due (*sa part*),"[7] he means, however surprising this may seem, that among those who have not given being its due is Heidegger. Heidegger writes: "[S]ince Dasein in its essence adopts a stance toward (*sich verhält zu*) beings—those which it is not and that which it is—Dasein as such emerges in each case from Nothing as already manifest."[8] Then comes a sentence that has given translators of Heidegger a lot of trouble: "*Da-sein heisst: Hineingehaltenheit in das Nichts.*" Since Heidegger writes the first word here with a hyphen, not without a hyphen as in the preceding sentence, the sentence of which it is a part must be telling us something about what is meant when it is said that Dasein or the human being is there or is the-there. Repeating the verb "*verhalten*" used in the previous sentence, Heidegger now says infinitively that for Dasein to be (the) there is for it to hold itself into nothingness. Not just to be held, but to hold itself into nothingness, for the following sentence says present participially that being-there is "*sich hineinhaltend in das Nichts,*" holding itself into nothingness. The argument is that Dasein can inhabit a world with regard to the contents of which it behaves (*sich verhält*) in one way or another only insofar as it holds itself into nothingness. Holding into may bring with it the sense of holding to, *einhalten,* the verb that is used to express the idea that a rule or arrangement or plan is adhered to or respected. Heidegger is saying that Dasein's *da-sein* is its comporting itself toward beings through its comporting itself—indeed transporting and transcending itself—toward nothingness. Sartre thinks that Heidegger does not give being its due because Heidegger separates being from nothingness and gives priority to the latter.

Sartre writes: "Nothingness can be nihilated only on the foundation of being," "*Le néant ne peut se néantiser que sur fond d'être.*" Within a page he warns that "*se néantiser*" is not to be read either as a reflexive or as an active verb. It is to be glossed by "*est néantisé.*" And this in turn is glossed by "*est été,*" "is be-ed" or "made to be." Sartre employs this last formula to convey the idea that nothingness or nothing (*le néant*) has only a borrowed existence. The noun "*emprunt*" can mean either something borrowed or a loan. The verb "*emprunter*" does not as readily allow this much flexibility, and the context makes plain that Sartre uses it with the sense of "to borrow." Of the existence and efficacy of nothingness Sartre says that they are borrowed, rather as a ghost or specter borrows what existence and efficacy it may have. A ghost is an apparition or appearance, and Sartre says of nothingness that it possesses only the appearance of being.[9] So we may also say with Sartre that nothingness, like a specter, haunts being. "A very controversial origin," says the Littré dictionary of the verb "*hanter.*" Littré goes on to speculate that "*hanter*" may go back to the Germanic "*Hant*" and "*Hand,*" or to a frequentative form of "*habiter,*" meaning to dwell or to be in the habit of frequenting, as expressed by the Latin "*verso*" and "*versari.*" This frequentative Latin verb can mean to disturb. So these etymological experiments, for what they are worth, could be taken as an invitation to open a passage from Sartre via Heidegger to Levinas. For Sartre's departure from Heidegger is part of the story that must be told in telling the story of Levinas's departure from Sartre. Further, Sartre's statement that nothingness haunts being opens up also a passage from ontology to what Derrida will call hauntology or revenance, a topic that will frequent later pages of this book.

Sartre departs from Heidegger in both senses of the word. He applauds his insistence on concreteness. Hegel had been too abstract. Recall Sartre's reference to the concreteness that nothingness derives from being, a concreteness different from the concreteness of a synthesis in relation to the abstract theses and antitheses of Hegelian logic. But Sartre also departs from Heidegger in the sense of diverging from him. As well as criticizing Heidegger for not giving being its due he criticizes him, as he criticizes Hegel, for neglecting a vital question. His criticism of Heidegger has the same structure as a criticism he makes of Hegel in the same paragraph. And it is with a matter of structure that his objection is concerned. Although Hegel is commended for saying that the activity of mind or spirit (*esprit*) is to mediate by negation, he does not ask what mind or spirit must be in order for it to be able to perform this negative function. And although, Sartre says, Heidegger holds that negation is the primary structure of Dasein's transcendence of the world, he does not ask what the structure of Dasein must be for it to be able to transcend the world. We could say that where Heidegger criticizes his predecessors for failing to be critical enough in their accounts of subjectivity, that is to say, for not regressing far enough upon the conditions of the possibility of subjectivity, for not making the ascent to Dasein, Sartre criticizes Heidegger in turn for not regressing to the foundation of Dasein. Nothingness may be the foundation of negation, but what is the foundation of nothingness?

## Investiture

Nothingness according to Sartre is obsessed by the being of the external world and by beings within it. So the human being is obsessed by its own being insofar as the human being is a part of the world. It nihilates its own being also. In nihilating the being of the world it nihilates its own being. But it nihilates its own being only insofar as that is the being of itself as part of the world, for instance its essence understood as its past, what it has made of itself, its having been, its *gewesen,* as Hegel would say. Sartre says that I am "older than" my past, hence, in a certain sense of the phrase used in one of Levinas's titles, I am beyond essence. Heidegger too says this. His reason for saying this may be gathered from the following outline of his conception of being-in-the-world.

On the one hand is the non-being from which Dasein finds itself thrown into the world, the non-being toward which Dasein looks back. This finding itself (*Befindlichkeit*) is always determined (*bestimmt*) by a *Stimmung,* that is to say a mood or tonality or affect of one kind or another, for instance boredom or anguish or joy. On the other hand is the non-being of the death toward which Dasein is projected, the finitude of Dasein's being, its being endingly. This is Dasein's comprehension or understanding (*Verstehen*) interpreted as its way of existing the world, which will not be initially the way of epistemic understanding. This "on the one hand" and this "on the other hand" are linked. Although Dasein's arising is experienced by it as contingent, its existential-ontological facticity is its being condemned to respond freely to the particular ontic facticities for which it is not responsible, condemned to decide its future in their terms. Its presence in a world is the where-and-when (*da*) in which it transitively exists in terms of each other what is to come and how it finds itself, thereby making itself responsible for that for which it is not responsible, its facticity. Heidegger is disposed to give more weight to the futural aspect over the past and the passed and the present. While his construal of being-in-the-world pays little attention to Dasein's having been born and emphasizes instead Dasein's being toward its death (an order of importance Hannah Arendt will call into question), Sartre gives priority to the present. This is consistent with the attention he gives to *négatités.* These are states or experiences or ways of behaving described by him as little lakes of nothingness.[10] But these lakes of nothingness are not lacks, for they carry a positive charge. On one page Sartre's text has it that they are ultra- or extra-worldly. A page later they are said to be intra-worldly.[11] Two pages earlier they are said to be "in the depths of being," and with reference to them Sartre asks: "How can we hold that these are at once partly within the universe and partly outside in extra-mundane nothingness?" Here the implication is that they cannot be both of these at once, but that they would have to be both at once according to Heidegger's account. Heidegger fails to appreciate the significance of these negative-positive realities for ontology, notwithstanding that under the description "possible modes of nihilating comportment," "*Möglichkeiten des nichtenden Verhalten,*" they would seem to be acknowledged also by Heidegger himself.[12] Sartre's view is that Heidegger acknowledges them but cannot make sense of them because he has too oppositional a view of being and nothingness. Heidegger's list comprises unyielding antagonism, stinging rebuke, galling failure, merciless prohibition, and bitter privation. He observes that these "have a more abysmal source than measured negation of thought." But they testify to "the saturation of Dasein by nihilative comportment," that is to say to a more profound disposition of Dasein than purely rational and logical negation.

One of Sartre's lists of *négatités* includes distance, absence, regret, traversing or crossing, and otherness. With regard to crossing, he complains that Heidegger fails to recognize that this implies a space crossed. The space or distance crossed will be that of Dasein's entire world when the crossing of that distance is what Heidegger understands by Dasein's transcendence. Failing to acknowledge explicitly Heidegger's reference to "the saturation of Dasein by nihilative comportment," Sartre implies that Heidegger's failure to acknowledge explicitly that there is a nothingness at the heart of Dasein is a case of the form of self-deceit Sartre calls bad faith, *mauvaise foi*. Heidegger's tendency to resort to seemingly positive expressions to describe Dasein—for example to say that Dasein is care (*Sorge*), a being of distances, its own possibilities and outside itself in the world, and his description of Dasein as transcendence as though this were a purely positive way of being—is an illustration of Dasein's desire to become a plenitude in itself despite its half-awareness that this would not satisfy its desire unless it could be conscious of its being this plenitude. This precondition immediately renders the desire futile because consciousness negates and is therefore an unfilling, an unfulfilling, a dis-satisfaction. Here is another irony. What Sartre calls bad faith is a way of being that Heidegger himself diagnoses in his own description of the propensities of Dasein. Dasein's lapsing (into the world among other beings), its *Verfallen*, manifests itself as an inclination to try to escape the consequences of its own freedom and the anguish it suffers when it faces up to its being the sole bearer of responsibility (*Anwortlichkeit*) for how it assumes the fact of its not being responsible for how and where it finds itself thrown into the world. This much agreement between Heidegger and Sartre is agreement between them and Kierkegaard when he insinuates the thought that human beings hide from themselves their disposition to invent a ground where there is no ground to (be) found. As the author of *Being and Time* leads his readers to suspect, perhaps the fundamental ontology outlined in that book is less fundamental than it promised to be. On its penultimate page he puts as a "problem of principle" the question "can one provide *ontological* grounds for ontology, or does it also require an *ontical* foundation?"[13] In the third and ultimate part of the present book will resound what in the style of Husserl we could call a continuity of moments of reverberation of this problem, if indeed it is a problem and not an aporia.[14]

The last of the negativities mentioned in Sartre's list is otherness. This brings Sartre face to face with Levinas. Summarizing the teaching of the early Heidegger, Sartre writes: "For 'Dasein' there is even a permanent possibility of finding oneself 'face to face' ('*en face*') with nothingness and discovering it as a phenomenon: this possibility is anguish."[15]

Using a verb cognate with a noun used by Levinas in a phrase cited in the first paragraph of this chapter, Sartre says that according to Heidegger Dasein is *invested* by being.[16] It is not obvious to me what word of Heidegger's, if any, this italicized word translates. When it occurs a second time in Sartre's chapter it appears between quotation marks.[17] Is he quoting himself? Or are the quotation marks scare-quotes, quotation marks that express the fear and trembling one would experience in the circumstance of being beset by an army at one's walls? However the quotation marks around the word are interpreted, it may be suspected that in taking the word to mean "obsession" Sartre's text is being violently forced in the interest of purporting to discover a similarity of structure between it and Levinas's, a parallelism between my being obsessed by being and my being obsessed and, as Levinas also says, psychotically possessed by the Other. The fact remains that to invest can mean to obsess or besiege, and that these ideas play a prominent part in the arguments of both philosophers. Levinas sometimes writes, we have seen, of being persecuted or pursued, as someone might be pursued by the law and summoned to appear before a tribunal. When he himself writes of investiture it may seem that it is not at all the idea of being obsessed or threatened that he has in mind. Thus it may seem that the idea of investiture intended in the section of *Totality and Infinity* entitled "The Investiture of Freedom, or Critique" is not that of laying siege, but is more like that of being put in a position to lay siege. It was recorded at the outset of this chapter that Levinas adopts Kant's idea of philosophical critique, distinguished by Levinas from criticism in the field of fine arts, as regress upon conditions. In the case of Kant's first *Critique* the conditions in question are those of knowledge. The function of critique according to the second *Critique* is to give "an account of the principles of the possibility of duty, its extent and limits."[18] Levinas writes that to practice critical philosophy is "to trace freedom back to what lies before it, to disclose the investiture that liberates freedom from the arbitrary."[19] Because this process of retracing comes up against what is not strictly a principle but something pre-principial and an-archic, we said that what he calls critique is, in comparison with Kant's account of it, hypoCritique.

There is a non-vicious circularity in Levinas's account of investiture. We are informed that what is uncovered is "the investiture that liberates freedom from the arbitrary." Freedom is set free. In Kant's account freedom is set free by being tied to the moral law. Freedom as understood by Kant is set free by binding. Sartre rejects this grounding of freedom in the moral law, that is to say in pure reason. His and Heidegger's quarrel with Hegel's appeal to reason and logic as described above is of a piece with their criticism of the disclosures claimed by Kantian critique. Levinas criticizes all three, Kant, Heidegger, and Sartre. It is plainly the last-named that he has in mind when he begins the section on the investiture of freedom by proclaiming: "Existence is not in reality condemned to freedom." Adriaan Peperzak brings out graphically the intention of this remark in an image that reminds us of Kierkegaard's phrase "knight of faith" and of the dissimilar similarities and similar dissimilarities among the doctrines of Kierkegaard and Levinas and Sartre. He writes: "As for the medieval knight whose fighting force is justified by making him a defender of powerless innocents, ego's freedom is 'invested' by the demands implied in the Other's proximity."[20] He adds: "I am saved by the acceptance of the critique that comes from the Other's face." Here we meet a further sense of critique, a third sense if we take account of critique as practiced by, for example, literary critics. This third sense is of critique neither as criticism in the humanities nor as philosophical regress upon conditions of possibility. It is critique as a tracing back to one of the hypoCritical conditions of the conditions of possibility disclosed by philosophical critique in the Kantian sense. It is hypoCritical judgment—Levinas will go as far as to say that it is "the judgment of God"[21]—as "pre-ontologically," that is to say pre-analytically, experienced by the human being. What would acceptance of this critique be?

Peperzak observes that when Levinas speaks of accepting (*accueillir*) this critique or judgment, accepting must not be equated with assuming, assimilating, or integrating into myself, my self, or my soul. That would be to absorb the other's alterity, to digest it, as alterities are subsumed and reduced to the same in the conceptual system of Hegel. It would be as though the ego were *nourished* by the acceptance of the Other. This is why it is risky to translate Levinas's "*accueillir*" as "welcome," although in other respects "welcome" is here precisely the right word. It is the right word insofar as the paradigm case of accepting the judgment of the other is welcoming the stranger into my home. But what if I welcome the stranger not only lest he or she suffer hunger or cold? What if

I get enjoyment from doing this? What if I find his or her presence pleasant, desirable? What if I find welcome my welcoming the stranger? Of course, although I may invite the stranger in on account of the agreeableness of his or her company, my welcoming may produce a feeling of agreeableness without this agreeableness being that on account of which I extend the welcome.

To mention one more complication appertaining to the notion of welcome (others will be mentioned in chapter 14), what if the pleasurable feeling that accompanies my welcoming or my thought of welcoming is not solely mine but is shared with the stranger? On Levinas's account my acceptance of the critical judgment coming to me from the face of the Other is the acceptance within an asymmetrical relationship to the Other that is not a simple condition of such sympathy. It is what had better be called a quasi-condition because it renders mutual sym-pathy or com-passion not only possible but impossible as a founding condition. The acceptance of the Other's judgment must be the acceptance of something unacceptable. At the very least I respond to the Other by inviting him or her into my house not because of something I get out of being his or her host. I must do it "for nothing," as Levinas writes. Somewhat in the style of Kierkegaard's mockery of Luther for holding that, since salvation is by grace alone, suffering such as that implied in doing good works is not necessary in order for one to be a Christian, Levinas (more Calvinistic than Lutheran!) goes as far as to say that the host must find the stranger hostile. The Other, as already noted, is experienced as my persecutor.

That my ethical Desire regarding the Other must be found psychologically undesirable by my ego must be taken into account if we are to say with Peperzak, "I am saved by the acceptance of the critique that comes from the Other's face." However pleasurably "welcoming" I may find it to welcome the other, the pleasure is saturated with an irreducible pain. In other words, there persists in Levinas's understanding of investiture, as in Sartre's understanding of investiture, a sense of being besieged. I am as threatened by the other human being as I am by the impersonal being Levinas refers to as the *il y a*. This is why the anonymous being he calls the *il y a*, the there-is, can be confused with what he calls *illéité*, the third personality to which he sometimes gives the name or pro-name "God."

All this illustrates both how Sartre and Heidegger go a step beyond Kant and how Levinas points beyond the Kantian categorical imperative where the imperativity arises from the tension in the human being between the natural law relating to happiness and the moral law relating to what we experience as duty through the "intellectual feeling" of moral respect. The latter experience is painful. However, Levinas says late in his career that he realized he had been concerned throughout that career with holiness, *sainteté*. Could he be meaning holiness in the sense the word "*Heiligkeit*" has for Kant but construed in relation to the face to face rather than only the moral law? If so, would he not be thinking of the possibility of responsibility that is free from the painfulness of the constraint of the categorical imperative? To touch again on a question treated in the chapter immediately preceding this one, could Levinas envisage a responsibility that is the expression of pure joy? Would that not be to admit what he finds objectionable in Hegelianism as he sees it, an indifference to the griefs expressed in the appeal that comes to me from this and that other person's face?

When Levinas writes that deeds exemplifying an ethical response to the face of the other are done "for nothing," he is proposing a conception of nothingness as a hypoCritical "condition of possibility" of nothingness as nothingness is construed by Hegel, Heidegger, and Sartre. By "for nothing" is meant that I respond to the other human being not in exchange for something I get out of responding. It does not mean that the responsible deed is unmotivated. It is motivated by Desire to assist another human being. The response is to the other's behest "Thou shalt not kill," where the "not," Levinas maintains, is "older than" non-being and being. Correspondingly, his notion of investiture is older than Sartre's and than the notion of investiture Sartre finds in Heidegger. Sartre and Heidegger call into question the principle of reason in order that human freedom may be freed. The freedom Sartre thereby saves, no less than the freedom Heidegger rescues, is the freedom of a first-person singular self. The for-itself's or Dasein's world, although shared with others, even others toward whom one behaves non-egoistically, remains egological. Hence Heideggerian and Sartrian investiture is reinvested by Levinas. Like Sartre, Levinas could say that investiture is shame, but it would not be shame of the kind of which one of Sartre's examples is shame at the thought of the ugliness of one's face. The face thus understood is the cosmetic countenance. This is not the face of the face to face as interpreted by Levinas, for whom the shame is a moral culpability that is ineradicable. It is ineradicable because the removal of the arbitrariness of freedom does not remove the relative arbitrariness of endeavors to act justly, as demonstrated by the fact that when I invite a stranger into the house I have turned my back on someone who is in equal or greater need. And the thought of this must surely be a hurt that is ineliminable even in holiness.

If the human being is not condemned to be free in the way Sartre says it is, that is to say, if the human being is not condemned to "naked" freedom,[22] nevertheless "clothed" freedom, freedom that in this third sense of the term is "invested," is condemned to be unjust. Levinas, though for different reasons, can agree with Sartre when the latter says that the human being is "unjustifiable and without excuse."[23] Sartre says this because human beings alone decide on how they will live their lives, even if they choose to go along unquestioningly with the values taken for granted in their community. Levinas says this not on account of one's being condemned to choose. Prior to choice, for instance the choice to enter into a contract, the human being, whatever its particular concrete choices may be, can never produce an *apologia pro vita sua* that will get it off the ethical hook. Indeed, the more "good works" it performs, the more it performs acts that ignore the needs of those who have not been chosen to be the targets of those good deeds. This is what investiture means. It does not mean being dressed up in my Sunday (or Friday or Saturday) best, let alone in clerical vestments. The vestments of what Levinas understands by investiture are not ones I can put off. These vestments are closer to me than my skin. What's more, as thus invested I am vulnerable to the naked vulnerability of others. Their look is not a threat to my freedom as is the look of the other that according to Sartre threatens to turn me into stone. Rather is it an animating challenge to my freedom to respond to the single other by responding to a call not to kill or otherwise harm it. Not only, however, to the single other. For, as we have already learned, when from the eyes of that single other comes the command "Thou shalt not kill," the other is not speaking only on behalf of itself. My inability to catch up with responsibilities that get further and further away from my ability to meet them—responsibilities therefore where the "I ought" does not imply "I can"—is my inescapable culpability. This cutting "experience" of being *coupable* is rather different from the anguish the Sartrian *pour-soi* or *pour-moi* suffers at not being able to satisfy itself because satisfaction would demand nothing less than the self-contradictory being-in-itself-for-itself of absolute wisdom or God. Such unsatisfiable desires may not be egoistic, but even when they are altruistic they are still, as already observed, egological, and they are still in search of satisfaction. The Desire that Levinas spells with a capital initial is outside the sphere of satisfaction. It is heteronomous, not in the sense that it is necessarily altruistic, but in the sense that its "origin" is exterior to the agent and this is an exteriority that is not the contrary or contradictory opposite of interiority. It is an exteriority that resists being absorbed into a total interiority. Nevertheless, this Desire's having its center of gravity exterior to the agent is not inconsistent with its being an ingredient in the agent's psyche, the Other under my so tightly fitting skin.

## Reflexivity

We have seen that Sartre resists the importation of reflexivity into the verbs "*se nier*" and "*se néantiser*" when these are used of *le néant,* nothingness or nihilation. The verbs are passive. They state that nothingness is nihilated or nihiled. But reflexivity is acknowledged in the case of certain verbs when they are used not of nothingness but of the nihilating self, *pour-soi* or human being. Speaking of temporality, for example, and refashioning the Hegelian dialectic of being and nothingness, Sartre says that "the human being reposes first in the depths of being and then detaches itself from it by a nihilating withdrawal."[24] He is not merely detached. He detaches himself. The next sentence underlines this reflexivity when it refers to "the condition of the nihilation as a relation to the self (*rapport à soi*)." But what about the following statement made in the context of a discussion of questioning: "Man presents himself at least in this instance as a being who causes Nothingness to arise in the world, inasmuch as he himself is affected (*s'affecte*) with non-being to this end"?[25] Could we, without betraying Sartre's intention, say "affects himself" instead of "is affected"? Sartre warns his reader explicitly not to translate his statement that nothingness "*se néantise*" as a reflexive. It is equivalent to the unambiguously passive "*est néantisé*." Nothingness cannot actively do anything until it has borrowed efficacy from being. But the nihilative human being has already borrowed that being, so there is no need in this case for Sartre to warn his reader against putting an active and reflexive gloss on the verb. How could he not know that his reader would recognize immediately that he is writing here of a structure analogous to that of which Kant writes when he speaks of self-affection, *Selbstaffektion*? Kant says of this that it is *innerlich, von innen*.[26] The entry under "affect" in Runes's *Dictionary of Philosophy* says: "(Lat. Ad + facere) The inner motive as distinguished from the intention or end of action. Cf. Spinoza, *Ethics*. Bk. III)."[27] This defines what in Sartre's French is called a *mobile*. What he calls a *motif* is what in English would be called a reason. But consciousness, on Sartre's account of it, is, as Husserl maintains, always intentional in the sense that it is always *of* something. It is always noetic-noematic. To this Husserlian analysis Sartre adds that consciousness is always nihilative. Consciousness "refuses" its intentional accusative. This holds therefore for the affects that in French are called *mobiles*. Sartre rejects the analysis and psychoanalysis according to which these are contents of consciousness. From this follows the anguish of the human condition in which, notwithstanding the efficacy nihilation borrows from being or, better, is loaned to it by being, motives are inefficacious in the sense that they are distanced from the agent by a nothingness that gets its efficacy from being.[28] In this inefficacious efficacy my affects are inevitably exterior to me despite their immanence. They are immanent, but transcendently immanent, interiorly exterior.

Levinas maintains that responsibility is an affect.[29] This affect too is both interior and exterior, both immanent and transcendent. How in that case can he still speak of the radical exteriority of the other from whose "nihilative" command "Thou shalt not kill" arises the affect he calls responsibility? Well, the source of an affect is not the same as the affect. Even so, rather as Sartre writes that the exteriority of the motive is different from the exteriority of a spatio-temporal thing,[30] the exteriority which according to the subtitle of *Totality and Infinity* is the topic of that book is not the exteriority of another human being, you or another "first other" who happens to confront me at a particular place and time. I have always already responded to the Other, *Autrui*. So the first incarnation of *Autrui* is not the person empirically over against me in space and time. Levinas is speaking of such empirically present persons as embodying an alterity that is exterior to the exteriority of space and the reach of memory. The Other never was present in such a way that he or she could be re-presented later in recollection. The Other never was and never can be, as Hegel's German so neatly puts it, *erinnert,* that is to say remembered-interiorized. And the "alteration" of the identity of the self is otherwise than the alteration of Hegelian dialectical growth. It is also other than the self-alteration of the being by which nothingness comes into the world "in connection with its own being," as Sartre says, though not loudly enough to prevent Hazel Barnes translating his "*s'altère*" by "is itself changed" even though Sartre is referring at this precise point not simply to nihilation but to the being that nihilates being.[31]

On these questions of immanence, transcendence, auto-affection, and hetero-affection Heidegger is a bridge from Sartre to Levinas. Of the call of conscience he writes: "When the call is understood with an existentiell kind of hearing, such understanding is the more authentic the more unrelationally Dasein hears and understands its own Being-appealed-to."[32] Would it be fanciful to hear "unrelationally" ("*unbezüglicher*") as a forerunner of Levinas's idea that the so-called relation of being face to face with another human being is not really a relation, but the condition of all relationality? Heidegger's "*hört und versteht*" echoes the double sense of the Latin "*obaudire*" and pre-echoes the double sense of Levinas's "*entendre.*" Heidegger goes on to say that the whence of the call is co-called, and that is to say co-disclosed, with the call. He says of the whence that it is the uncanniness of thrown singularization. Uncanniness is *Unheimlichkeit.* Is it possible to hear among the resonances of this word the voice of the unhomed stranger? Singularization is *Vereinzelung.* It corresponds in Levinas's vocabulary to the French *accusation* in the sense that I am made to stand out in my uniqueness by the other's accusing me of failing in my responsibility. What may be another, if tenuous, prefiguring of Levinas is announced when in the same paragraph Heidegger writes that the whence of the calling is the whither to which we are called back. Levinas writes that my understanding of the call "Thou shalt not kill" (which is perhaps interpretable broadly as approximately equivalent to "Love your neighbor and your enemy") is in my response to the other before I have heard the call. This is why the Other as *Autrui* means primarily no particular empirical human being. And this is why Levinas may seem in danger of lapsing into an account of personal identity that is as first-personally projective and monadic as the accounts unrolled by Heidegger and Sartre.

However, Levinas has a recourse available to him that the other two do not. Heidegger's ontology is "older than" theology. He says that being, the matter with which ontology as the thinking of being is concerned, is more divine than God. The very idea of God according to Sartre is the idea of an in-itself that is at the same time a for-itself. But according to him, as already mentioned, this is a nonsensical idea, because the for-itself is a consciousness and consciousness is nihilating, that is to say it would disrupt the density of being-in-itself. Disruption is crucial too in Levinas's doctrine of personal identity. But in that doctrine it does not entail the nonsensicality of the idea of God or, as it had better be said, it does not disrupt God. For God overflows any consciousness and any idea we can have of him. This is what Levinas has read in Descartes's Third Meditation. From that Meditation too there survives the ghost of Descartes's argument that egology is haunted by God. Levinas describes *protē philosophia* as a humanism of the other human being. Moreover, he maintains that it is only through the human being that one can reach God. But once it is realized that the Other that is said to obsess and possess the psyche is not another human being over there facing me at a particular place and time, radical exteriority is no longer guaranteed by the other human being. One begins then to wonder whether that radical exteriority can be rescued only thanks to God. However, as Heidegger's poet Hölderlin did not say, and as Derrida more or less does, "Where rescue is, waxes also danger."

# ELEVEN

# Negation of Origins

## The Interpretation of Nightmares

I had a dream. Or a nightmare. That is to say, according to the *Concise Oxford Dictionary,* I had a visitation by "a female monster sitting upon & seeming to suffocate sleeper, incubus, oppressive or paralysing or terrifying or fantastically horrible dream . . . also haunting fear or thing vaguely dreaded." The female monster had four wheels. She was an automobile vehicle of meanings. Not just of meaning, but of potentially infinite meanings. A concept, but an unbounded one, one that bounded ahead. Or rather, not one, not a unit. Not a *Ding.* Not a gathering. A concept that was not a concept. Not a parked vehicle. But a mobilized vehicle, a vehicle in motion, and at moments in motion not on *terra firma* but, now without legs and with idling wheels, in sickening motion at sea, like an amphibious Volkswagen. At sea, what is more, not on a *mare clausum,* a "sea under jurisdiction of particular country" (ibid.), but at sea on a *mare liberum,* "sea open to all nations [L]" (ibid.). Except that this metamorphic and metaphoric conveyance of more than one meaning reverted to the adjacent unfirm land of the *maremma,* the "low marshy unhealthy country by seashore [It.]" (ibid.). Unhealthy country because the country of marsh gas. Therefore "seeming to suffocate sleeper," enveloping him in the claustrophobic dread from which he would not be saved by returning to the *mare, mer, mère,* for that would only expose him to the nightmare of drowning, perhaps in his own maternal, that is to say internal-external, amniotic fluid.

This dreadful dream could be interpreted as a metaphor for the indefiniteness of the concept, for the concept's recalcitrance to being defined, for its admittance of de-finition. Or in-finition. Would this in-finition be an unfinishedness, a privation of closure (*clausum*)? If so, one might say with Deleuze and Guattari that "The concept speaks the event, not the essence or the thing— pure Event, a haecceity, an entity: the event of the Other or of the face (when, in turn, the face is taken as a concept). . . . In this sense the concept is act of thought, it is thought operating at infinite (although greater or lesser) speed."[1] If, on the other hand, the in-finition is a positive perfected infinity, the concept would perhaps have taken on the form of the Concept or the Notion, the Big *Begriff* conceived as the *telos* in which culminates the dialectical progression from one concept to another by the process in which the higher concepts in a hierarchy repeatedly say No to their predecessors. In this latter case, which would not be merely a case, a *casus,* a falling, but also a rising, the "low marshy unhealthy country by seashore" would have been left well behind. The lethal marsh gas would have metamorphosed into living spirit, reflecting the narrative recounted in the *Oxford English Dictionary,* which says that the word "gas" was invented by someone from a low country. This word, we are told, is

> [a] word invented by the Dutch chemist, J. B. Van Helmont (1577–1644), avowedly suggested by the Gr. χάος ("halitum illum *Gas* vocavi, non longe a Chao veterum secretum." *Ortus Medicinae,* ed. 1632, p. 39a); the Dutch pronunciation of *g* as a spirant accounts for its being employed to represent Gr. χ.
>
> Van Helmont's statement having been overlooked, it has been very commonly supposed that he modelled his word on Du. *geest,* spirit, an idea found at least as early as 1775 (Priestley *On Air* Introd. 3). . . .
>
> An occult principle supposed by Van Helmont to be contained in all bodies and regarded by him as an ultra-rarified condition of water.

Van Helmont says (in Latin in the text) that he has called this vapor or breath *Gas,* in a sense not far removed from that of the ancient Chaos. How far removed from ancient chaos was the horrible dream just recounted? Not far, one might suppose, if its movement was "suggested by" nothing more rationally principled than the alphabetical order of a dictionary and if Hesiod's word "χάος" is taken to mean disorder, rather than a yawning gap, in particular the gap between earth and sky filled with air.[2] This dream was far removed from ancient chaos, one might say, if, in keeping with the supposition that "*gas*" was based on "*geest,*" and if, passing from the jurisdiction of one language to that of a neighboring one, we interpret that dream along the lines of the progress of the Hegelian *Geist* toward absolute wisdom. Then, contradictions that would otherwise be deemed oppressive and paralyzing would be progressive and life-enhancing—unless the absolute wisdom which is the destination of that progress is at least as suffocating, oppressive, paralyzing, and life-diminishing as the nightmarish dream.

Not that the dreamer is oppressed by contradictions if Freud is right when he observes that what in waking life appears as a contradiction may not appear so in a dream. Moreover, contradiction is the motor of the Hegelian dialectic. There formal contradiction in understanding that is oppressive and paralyzing is itself superseded by dialectical contradiction that is benign, the very voice of reason expressing a goodness bigger and better than that of the Kantian good will. It may be said, linking Hegel with Freud, that the end to which the dialectic is on its way is already its beginning and that this philosophical doctrine has a philological parallel in the thought that semantic contradictions may stem from contradictions inherent in the meaning of certain etymologically primal words. These contradictory words that occur in waking life may not be primal in the sense of first. They may arrive in the wake of a series of signifiers of signifieds that become new signifiers of new signifieds that become new new signifiers of new new signifieds, and so on, in the way described by Peirce and Derrida in the wake of Nietzsche's metaphorology.[3]

These antagonyms could be called Musilian, after Freud's compatriot Robert Musil who, in *The Man without Qualities,* writes that one can imagine a ramified "chain of comparisons" in which the uses of a word, for instance "justice" (an instance to which we shall return in this book), extended over time and across semantic space to the point where in two widely separated contexts it comes to have opposite meanings.[4] These antagonyms could be called Abelian in recognition of the reference made to them by Karl Abel in a paper entitled "The Antithetical Meaning of Primal Words," published in 1884. They could be called Hegelian, given the advantage Hegel takes of the anomaly that the word *"Aufhebung"* seems to carry the antithetical senses of a movement up and a movement down. In a moment it will be asked whether they could be called Derridian. But let it be asked first whether they could be called Freudian.

A basis for calling such antagonyms Freudian is the basis for calling them Hegelian, for there are Hegelian resonances in Freud's statement that "[i]t is plausible to suppose, too, that the original antithetical meaning of words exhibits the ready-made mechanism which is exploited for various purposes by slips of the tongue that result in the opposite being said [of what was consciously intended]."[5] Listen to the resonances of this in the words Kierkegaard puts into the mouth of Johannes Climacus when he is made to say that "the immediate is reality, language is ideality, since by speaking I produce the contradiction. When I seek to express some perception in this way, the contradiction is present, for what I say is something different from what I want to say. I cannot express reality in language, because I use ideality to characterize it, which is a contradiction, an untruth."[6]

In his review of Abel's article Freud does little more than paraphrase the original piece. Toward the end of his exposition he turns to a later piece by Abel, "On the Origin of Language" (1885), where the author notes that ancient Egyptian shows evidence not only of reversals of sense, but also of reversals of sound. While welcoming such researches as Abel's and of other philologists into the history of the development of language as confirmation of the regressive and archaic nature of the expression of thoughts in dreams and as confirmation of his own work *The Interpretation of Dreams* published a decade earlier than his review, Freud records that he has problems with Abel's attempt to explain reversal of sound as a reduplication of a word's root. "We," he writes, "should . . . be more inclined to derive reversal of sound from a factor of deeper origin." The factor he considers to be deeper than the doubling of the root is hinted at when he reminds us of the way children take delight in reversing the sound of words and how for various purposes the dream-work performs reversals on the representational material, the latter being now not letters but images.

Whatever this representational material may be, whether images, letters, ideas, or thoughts, Freud's account of the reversal is one in which contradiction is neutralized. It is almost as though *The Interpretation of Dreams* is itself a dream-work in which there takes place a reversal such as is said to take place in some dreams. For toward the end of the first volume it famously declares: "The way in which dreams treat the category of contraries and contradictories is highly remarkable. It is simply disregarded. 'No' seems not to exist so far as dreams are concerned."[7] But already before we turn to the second volume and at several places throughout that second volume he admits cases that contradict this assertion. The first countercase is what, as though with Hegelian *Aufhebung* in mind, he terms the "Up and Down" dream. One of Freud's patients reports a dream that has to do with climbing. The patient's account reminds Freud of the story told by Alphonse Daudet in *Sappho* of a young man who carries his mistress upstairs and discovers that the higher he climbs the heavier she gets. This anticipates the difficulties on which the love-affair will founder, and Daudet sees the moral of his story to be that young gentlemen should not allow themselves to become attracted to girls of inferior status and dubious past. To Freud's surprise, his patient accepts Daudet's story as one that fits his own dream, even though in that dream the climbing had become easier rather than more difficult. What's more, the dream treats of the dreamer's relation to his brother in which the relations of up and down are the opposite of the relation that features in Daudet's story.

Incidentally casting some light on his theory of jokes, Freud recounts the following case.

> So too in my dream of Goethe's attack on Herr M. (see below, p. 439 ff.) there is a similar "just the reverse" which has to be put straight before the dream can be successfully interpreted. In the dream Goethe made an attack on a young man, Herr M.; in the real situation contained in the dream-thoughts a man of importance, my friend [Fliess], had been attacked by an unknown writer. In the dream I based a calculation on the date of Goethe's death; in reality the calculation had been made from the year of the paralytic patient's birth. The thought which turned out to be the decisive one in the dream-thoughts was a contradiction of the idea that Goethe should be treated as though he were a lunatic. "Just the reverse," said [the underlying meaning of] the dream, "if you don't understand the book, it's *you* [the critic] that are feeble-minded, and not the author." I think, moreover, that all these dreams of turning things round the other way include a reference to the contemptuous implications of the idea of "turning one's back on something." [Editor's note: The German "*Kehrseite*" can mean both "reverse" and "backside." Cf. the vulgar English phrase "arse upwards" for "upside down," "the wrong way round."] (E.g., the dreamer's turning round in relation to his brother in the *Sappho* dream.) It is remarkable to observe, moreover, how frequently reversal is employed precisely in dreams arising from repressed homosexual impulses.[8]

In order for the dream to be successfully interpreted, the dreamer must somehow register that a relation must be taken in a sense opposite to that presented in the dream. That means that despite his original statement that "'No' seems not to exist as far as dreams are concerned," it is operative in the not-this-way-but-that-way of the reversal. This contradiction—or rather, in terms of the traditional square of opposition, contrariety—must be acknowledged if the dream is to make sense, if it is, as Freud says, to achieve its purpose. His terminology is highly teleological. For it is part of his program to defend the doctrine that the dream-work, not only the work of recording a dream, is somehow critical, "in marked opposition to the view that dreams are the product of a dissociated and uncritical mental activity."[9] There is a certain method in the apparent madness of the nonsense of the dream according to Freud, a certain method that anticipates Sartre's uncovering of a certain responsibility where others see irresponsibility, for instance in such expressions of emotion as weeping.

Hence, notwithstanding Freud's statements that "[t]he alternative 'either-or' cannot be expressed in dreams in any way whatever" and that "[b]oth of the alternatives are usually inserted in the text of the dream as though they were equally valid,"[10] so that an "either-or" used in recording a dream is to be interpreted as the equivalent of "and," he goes on to allow that in some sense after all the "No" of opposition must be at work in the dream. "I have asserted above that dreams have no means of expressing the relation of contradiction, a contrary or a 'no.' I shall now proceed to give a first denial of this assertion."[11] It is as though in his own dreamlike account of the logic of dreams in the work entitled *The Interpretation of Dreams* an "and" links, on the one hand, the original assertion that dreams know nothing of "No" and, on the other hand, the interpretations of the cases presented after this assertion which demonstrate that the original assertion cannot be maintained without qualification, without the assertion of its apparent contradictory or contrary opposite. Although in the record of a dream there figures an "either-or," this expresses what in the dream is expressed by an "and." In the logic of the theoretical account of what goes on between the work of the dream and the record of the dream the connective is an "and" that conjoins the "either-or" of the record of the dream and the "and" of the dream itself.

This connection of the logical connectives "either-or" and "and" is the equivalent of the non-exclusive connective represented in the Latin of logic by the symbol *v* for *vel*. We could liken it to the double *u* or, as French has it, the *double v* of the first letter of the word "with" to which Abel refers in the second of the articles in Freud's report, of which we read:

> Even today the Englishman in order to express *"ohne"* says "without" (*"mi-tohne"* ["with-without"] in German), and the East Prussian does the same. The word "with" itself, which today corresponds to the German *"mit,"* originally meant "without" as well as "with," as can be recognized from "withdraw" and "withhold." The same transformation can be seen in the German *"wider"* ("against") and *"wieder"* ("together with").

Here the "together with" of Freud's translator conveys the minimal force of the expressions "again," "afresh," and "once more" and of the prefix "re," which are among the English equivalents of *"wieder."* Lexicographers inform us that this and *"wider"* are the equivalents of Old English *"wither"* and its Modern English abbreviation "with." So the senses of against and together, against and again, are both denoted together and against each other in one four-lettered word. Both denoted? It would be better to say that all are denoted if account is to be taken of the duality of "against" as cooperatively in competition with and as in the neighborhood of. So that, however earnestly some may long for an ethics in which cooperation is given its due, we may have to acknowledge not only that competition and cooperation are not mutually exclusive alternatives, but even that each cannot do without the other. Cooperation cooperates with competition, albeit while competing. With "with" we may be touching on the deep grammar of the bewildering construals of what Derrida calls *"aimance"* in the course of what he calls the politics of friendship, a politics that embraces and is disturbed by an ethics of amity and enmity to the point that "the border between the ethical and the political is no longer insured."[12] I say amity and enmity in order not to say love and hate. For two reasons. Derrida is not unfriendly to the thought he comes across in Carl Schmitt's *The Concept of the Political* that there may be enmity and hostility without hate. And although it will be impossible to carry on in English a discussion of amity without using the word "love" as a cognate equivalent, the word "amity" has traveled a long way, an even longer way than French *"amitié,"* and a still longer way than *"amicitia,"* from its presumed source in the Latin *"amor"* (for example *amor fati*) or its cognate verb *"amo."*

Presumed source. Before proceeding something must be said parenthetically now about Derrida's difficulties with presumed sources. Already in *Speech and Phenomena* reservations regarding the idea of source-points are implicit in his reservations regarding the less restricted notion of presence. Even the stirring paragraphs on the nameless source-point of time in Husserl's *Lectures on the Phenomenology of Internal Time Consciousness* lead Derrida to propose that the namelessness of this has not a little to do with the fact that what we have is, instead of a point, a verbal surging forth, a third-personal *sourdre* or a verbal-nominal *soudrance*. What we have is not a what. The so-called source-point, the *pointe de la source*, is not a source, *point de source*. The *Quellpunkt* is quelled. The *Punkt* is punctured and punctuated, as it is, let us not forget, by Nietzsche, though by Nietzsche in a cosmological perspective rather than in the phenomenological perspective taken by Husserl when, distancing himself from naturalistic, cosmological "objectivity," and incidentally reminding us of what Nietzsche says about the flux of metaphors, he writes of the constitutive flux of temporality:

> We can only say that this flux is something we name in conformity with what is constituted, but it is nothing temporally "Objective." It is absolute subjectivity and has the absolute properties of something to be denoted metaphorically as "flux," as point of actuality, primal source-point, that from which springs the "now," and so on. In the lived experience of actuality, we have the primal source-point and a continuity of moments of reverberation (*Nachhallmomenten*). For all this, names are lacking.[13]

With the calling into question of this notion of a once-upon-a-time one-time-present origin goes the falling of the idea of a derivation from such an origin. Discontent over such an idea of derivation is evinced frequently in *La contre-allée*, a sort of travelogue put together by Derrida and Catherine Malabou, where what kind of journeys the book is to deal with is indicated by a citation from Derrida's treatment of Nietzsche and other philologists in *Éperons: Les Styles de Nietzsche*.[14] The citation is of words reproduced, with some deviation, as what would be commonly called an exergue, opposite a prefatory page on which is inscribed the title *L'ECARTEMENT DES VOIES* and the subtitle *DERIVE, ARRIVEE, CATASTROPHE*: "( . . . ) *la marge dans laquelle, à quelque dérive près, je me tiendrai* ( . . . )," "( . . . ) the margin to which, with some deviation, I shall hold ( . . . )." The word "deviation" in this translation deviates somewhat from one sense of "*dérive*," as indeed the exergue as reproduced in *La contre-allée* deviates from its putative source. For in the derivative the word "*dérive*" is surrounded by a continuous line like a nimbus or a television screen, and "*telle*," "such" or "somesuch," is substituted for the "*quelque*" that appears in at least three of the published versions of Derrida's text, including the (ahem) original.[15] Is this second departure meant to signal self-referentially that going on here is such a deviation as is meant by "*dérive*"? What is signaled at least is that if there is going to be any derivation it is going to be a derivation that comes not from a source or a center but from a margin. So much then for the primality of primal words, whether we call them Abelian, Hegelian, or Freudian.

## Outwith

In an article entitled "*Dérive à partir de Marx et Freud*," published in 1972, the year in which, under the umbrella of the title *Nietzsche Aujourd'hui,* he and Derrida participated in discussions at Cerisy, Lyotard charts the distance between driftwork and the "fertile negativity" of dialectical labor. He is skeptical about the view of *Aufhebung* as an experience in which a position transcresces into another that preserves while suppressing it. "There is a forgotten Freud in such an outlook. . . . What is forgotten in dialectic is that one forgets and that forgetting implies the saving of everything, memory being but a selection."[16] Like the selection memory works in a dream. Which returns us to the question as to whether dream-work is underway well out at sea (a sea at least 17, 000 fathoms deep), tied up to *terra firma* or in the intermediate condition of anchorage offshore. It returns us to the question of return, the choice between Odysseus and Abraham—unless that choice is not a straight choice between polar opposites, but the cooperation-competition of the with with-and-against a without. For this cooperation let us appropriate the Scots preposition "outwith." This preposition is all the more appropriate because Lyotard reminds us of the likeness of Hegel's description of the dialectic of spirit to the description of the capitalistic accumulative saving of wealth by the Scot Adam Smith. Lyotard reminds us too of Freud's teaching that one investment, that is to say saving, is not abandoned for another by the psyche. Rather, although (like *p* and not-*p*) the investments are not simultaneously thinkable, they are (unlike *p* and not-*p*) compossible and cooperative in different regions of the psyche, where they produce different effects. The regional difference is not a difference of level, for instance the semiological and the epistemological levels. Levels as degrees of libidinal intensity there may be here, but not levels as parallel strata. So too with the pre-positional and ad-verbial outwith.

The logic of this connective may be characterized with the help of a footnote from Smith's compatriot Hume, a footnote in which, incidentally, the word "design" is Abelian, being ambiguous as between honest purpose and what, following Smith followed by Hegel, might be dubbed a ruse of reason. In that footnote, in appendix 3 of *An Enquiry Concerning the Principles of Morals*, Hume writes: "Natural may be opposed, either to what is *unusual, miraculous,* or *artificial*. In the two former senses, justice and property are undoubtedly natural. But as they suppose reason, forethought, design, and a social union and confederacy among men, perhaps that epithet cannot, strictly, in the last sense, be applied to them." The reason why we both have and do not have an opposition here is that the term in question is equivocal. Justice and property would be both natural and not natural because of an ambiguity. The equivocality or ambiguity is semantic. Semantic too are the contradictions that are tolerated or ignored in dreams, according to Freud, and in the contradictions that maintain the dynamic of dialectic, according to Hegel. And, both in the dream-work and in the toil of the negative, memory is in play, as we have been reminded by Lyotard. Memory, *Erinnerung,* is the field of Freudian psychopathology, the field of Hegelian phenomenology, and, indeed, the field of Husserlian phenomenology, even if, after becoming acquainted with Derrida's plotting of these fields we may wish to borrow his qualificatory clause "*à quelque dérive près,*" "with some deviation." For we may come to wonder whether the interiority of memory even as treated in those Hegelian, Husserlian, and Freudian contexts is entirely without an anomalous and anonymous, nameless outwithness that is more or-and less than semantic. We may come to be overcome by the wonder of this impossible possibility of outwithness that appears to come from outside and to resist interiorization, that is to say *Erinnerung,* that is to say memory.

How does the quirky outwithness of this immemorial remainder escape being semantic? How does what Derrida refers to as *reste* escape semantic being, *estence* or *estance*? How does it escape the meaning of being and the being of meaning? Outwithness cannot escape this in non-being because this is the other that belongs to being, *being's* other. It cannot escape it in the guise of contradiction as defined by the traditional principle of non-contradiction, the contradiction of the understanding. Nor can outwithness escape ontology and semantics if it is construed as reason's dialectical negation, for this is a process that digests and sublimates difference in the sameness of being. Suppose we try to answer these questions departing from what Derrida writes concerning points or non-points of departure, derivation, *dérive*. Derivation corresponds with maternity as this was once understood. You could in theory always trace an offspring to its maternal source. With paternity, at least before genetic coding, matters were different. There, there was the *Spielraum* that would make us want to think of derivation as *dérive*, as drift not entirely free of artificiality, rather than as a natural genetic descendance of the kind that obtained in the maternal line, the kind of a kind, that is to say of a kinship, of a genus, of such a kind that a return could be made without deviation along the line toward the point of origin. Artificiality with naturality then, for what could be more natural than paternity and maternity? Here, however, the simultaneity of the natural and the artificial is not made possible by the ambiguity of the natural pointed out by Hume. It is made possible not by a difference in the meaning of terms, but by what Lyotard in his remarks on Freud calls a difference of region. Such a difference is an instance of a difference in respect, a difference such as must not obtain if there is to be a formal contradiction. If there is to be a formal contradiction between $p$ and not-$p$, one of these two tokens of $p$ cannot be $q$ in disguise.

Not only can the "condensation" of withness and againstness that we are calling outwithness not be a contradiction in the sense of the formal logic of the understanding. It cannot be either a contrariety as defined in traditional Aristotelian logic. This was ruled out when we said that outwithness is more or-and less than semantic. Outwithness is neither purely semantic nor purely syntactic or, in Husserl's or the early Wittgenstein's sense, purely grammatical. To suppose that it is, is as mistaken as to assimilate to formal contradiction either the *Widersprechen* of Hegelian dialectic or what Derrida sometimes refers to as *contra-Diction* or what Freud understands by *Verneinung*. Let us not close the door opened when it was hinted earlier that on reading Derrida on Hegel, Freud, and Husserl (and Heidegger, as we were on the brink of adding), we may be persuaded that in declaring them to be logocentric thinkers we should have recourse to the phrase "with some deviation" that Derrida uses of himself. But let us try to get clearer why we are inclined to declare them to be logocentric thinkers who therefore for the most part fall short of the eccentricity we are marking with "outwith." The attempt to do this for the case of Freud offers opportunities to expose more evidence for the validity of a certain statement made about him earlier only in passing, and to acknowledge a certain complexity in the relation of Freud to Hegel. It also offers a chance to amplify but complicate Lyotard's comments on the conjunction of compossibility with uncothinkability in a way that will show how the little word "not" speaks of the large questions of ethics, life and death, love of death, and love of life.

## *Verneinung*

The title of Freud's paper *"Die Verneinung"* is translated as "Negation" in the standard translation of his works. Despite this practice, it is preferable to translate it into English as "Denial" or into Anglo-French as denegation. Negation is logical, whereas denial is rhetorical. Negation appertains to pure logical grammar, syntax, and language as *langue*. Denial is an operation of pragmatics, that is to say, of acts of speech, of *parole*. It connects system with saying and connects sign with signature, subscription, underwriting, the apposing of one's *firma*. It claims authorship and responsibility. Denial is a response. So the denial of a statement presupposes a question, hence it presupposes also the distinction between saying No and saying Yes. Indeed *Verneinung* is saying No as opposed to *Bejahung,* saying Yes. But whichever of those responses is made, whether the response be affirmative or disconfirmative, and whether what is affirmed or disconfirmed is the truth of a sentence containing the word "not," the response is a claim to responsibility that has always already been made, since it is presupposed by any attempt to affirm or deny.

Freud describes an interplay between *Verneinung* and *Vereinigung. Vereinigung* is union. Note yet again, however, that the prefix *Ver-* invites the thought that in this union there is something amiss, something of which one might not feel proud, something one might wish to repress. To develop the implications of this thought would be to make a detour, a *dérive,* from Freud's theory where union is with what is affectively "good" or "useful," what would be expressed in the language of instinctual orality by a desire to put something in one's mouth, to eat it, to introject it. Opposed to this would be the wish to spit out something associated with what is felt to be "bad" or "harmful." These are both expressions of the pleasure principle, the original pleasure-ego (*ursprüngliche Lust-Ich*). "From its point of view what is bad, what is alien to the ego, and what is external are, to begin with, identical."[17] This opposition of inside and outside is itself inside the original unconscious. Both this opposition and the unconscious have to do with representations (*Vorstellungen*) that are prior to intellectual judgment.

Intellectual judgment is an operation of the reality ego (*Real-Ich*), which is concerned not with whether a representation should be introjected or rejected by the pleasure-ego, but with whether the representation is a representation of something that can be perceived in reality. But the representation is already a re-presentation of what was once perceived. What judgment does in the first place, therefore, is not to discover the object corresponding to the representation but to *re*-discover it. A representation may be repressed, that is to say prevented from entering consciousness. That repression is lifted (*aufgehoben*) by the negative judgment, for example, "I did not think that," "The person in my dream was *not* my mother." While affirmation is the intellectual derivative of affective unifying *erōs*, denial is the intellectual derivative of affective *thanatos,* the instinct of death and destruction. Denial or negation recognizes or acknowledges repression, brings it into consciousness, but without removing the repression. The repression persists even when the labor of analysis makes the further step of overcoming (*besiegen*) the negation in the denial or counter-diction, when, somewhat as the unconscious disregards negation, the analyst considers he is entitled "to take the liberty of disregarding the negation." So that when the patient says, "It was *not* my mother," "we emend this: so it *was* his mother." Somewhat after the manner of the unconscious, the analyst effects a reversal, but now a conscious reversal, consciously contradicting the patient's claim that no significance was to be given to any thought of his mother that may have entered his head.

The allusions just made to the labor of analysis of negation, of recognition, of *Aufhebung* and of *Destruktion* reopen the question of the feasibility of a Freudian reading of Hegel and a deconstructive reading of Hegel or Freud. With this question in mind it has to be noted provisionally that Freud's use of the word *Destruktion* in the paragraph cited *seems* to be one-sidedly negative, lacking the affirmative aspect marked by the second syllable of the word "de-construction." Again, although what is sometimes meant by deconstruction is an operation that someone might perform on a text, as an analyst might treat a patient—a writing-cure instead of a talking-cure—such an operation presupposes deconstruction understood as a happening, a self-destruction of a text that, like Penelope's weaving unweaving itself, *se déconstruit* reflexively or passively or in something like the middle voice. Compare the way in which, *mutatis mutandis,* the phenomenology of spirit described by Hegel as the science of the experience of consciousness—where the "of" of the science of the experience and of the experience of consciousness are both double genitives—presupposes this experience, this *Erfahrung,* that is to say the going-on that the philosopher simply describes. There is a parallel to this in Freud if the unconscious can be regarded as a process proceeding according to laws that the psychoanalyst seeks to describe. The reading we give of Hegel and Freud and Derrida will depend on the extent to which we think of reading as an attempt at secure derivation or rather as experimental *dérive*. These are not mutually exclusive. However anxiously we may seek security, we shall not be able to escape all risk, and however ready we may be to take risks, that we are taking risks presupposes that we have provisionally made some relatively stable distinctions, for instance that between an "economics" and a "dialectic" made in the following judicious remarks on Freud's paper "*Die Verneinung*" by Ricœur in *Freud and Philosophy,* which is subtitled *An Essay on Interpretation* and which follows Ricœur's express preference for translating "*Verneinung*" as "negation" rather than, following our preference, denial or denegation.

> Freud does not say that negation is another representative of the death instinct; he only says that negation is genetically derived from it by "substitution," as in general the reality principle is substituted for the pleasure principle (or as a character trait, avarice, for example, is substituted for an archaic

libidinal constitution, such as anality). We have no right, then, to draw out of this text more than is warranted and to give it a direct Hegelian translation. We may do this on our own account, at our own risk, but not as interpreters of Freud. Freud develops an "economics" of negation and not a "dialectic" of truth and certainty, as in the first chapter of *The Phenomenology of Spirit*. Nonetheless, even within these strict limits this short article makes an important contribution: consciousness implies negation—both in the process of "achieving insight" into its own hidden richness and in the "recognition" of what is real.[18]

Do the quotation marks in this passage signal a readiness on Ricœur's part to go back on his statement "We have no right, then, to draw out of this text more than is warranted" (which in any case sounds like a tautology) in the spirit of the thought that perhaps there are silent or invisible quotation marks, scare-quotes, around Freud's word *"Destruktion"*? That thought, contrary to the thought we expressed provisionally earlier, would be in the spirit of Ricœur's next paragraph:

> It is not surprising that negation is derived from the death instinct by way of substitution. On the contrary, what is surprising is that the death instinct is represented by such an important function which has nothing to do with destructiveness, but with the symbolization of play, aesthetic creation, and with reality testing itself. This discovery is enough to throw into flux the whole analysis of the representatives of instincts. The death instinct is not closed in upon destructiveness, which is . . . its clamour; perhaps it opens out into other aspects of the "work of the negative," which remains "silent" like itself.

Perhaps it opens out into the outwith. We have seen how this opening out is effected in reality testing. It is effected also in the game of *fort-da,* in which, repeating in waking life the repetition that occurs compulsively in its dream, the child symbolizes its mother's disappearance and return. It is effected creatively in the work of art, which is a particular case of the without-and-with of the *fort-da* in which a hidden object of affective fantasy is made public rather as the demiurge of the *Timaeus* creates a world from the elements contained in the receptacle. All of these exercises of outing endow thought, as Freud writes, with a first degree of independence from the results of repression. Ricœur writes, "To play with absence is already to dominate it and to engage in active behaviour toward the lost object as lost," and "the lost archaic object has been 'denied' and 'triumphed over' by the work of art which recreates the object or rather creates it for the first time by offering it to all men as an object of contemplation."[19] So Ricœur's interpretation of Freud, proceeding in the direction of Freud's own earlier-noted reference to the way children take delight in the playful work of reversing the sounds of words, turns on an opposition between, on the one hand, mastery in the field of intellectual judgment and in subsequent practical or productive behavior and, on the other hand, being mastered by the compulsion (*Zwang*) of the pleasure principle in the sphere of the unconscious.

In Ricœur's reading of Freud there is a resonance of the treatment of the conflict of master and slave in the dialectic of Hegel. And the conflict is a conflict of forces. From the struggle between master and slave via speculations on the scene of the family which "is immediately determined as an ethical being" the Hegelian dialectic derives the ethical.[20] But the ethical, whether understood as the done thing, *Sittlichkeit,* or as what ought to be done, *Moralität,* remains polemical in the sense of a negotiation among powers, ultimately one "I can" pitted against another "I can," where the againstness of competition does not, however, exclude but even requires the withness and witness of social cooperation.

Lyotard, it will be recalled, speaks in his *Dérives* of a conjuncture of the uncothinkable with the compossible. But this and the Hegelian or Freudian conjunctures to which it might be applied fall short of the logical (dis)connective that would be marked by our neograffitic prepositional or adverbial "outwith." This is because "outwith" indicates what exceeds both possibility and thinking. It signals an unthinkable impossibility. What is so special about an unthinkable impossibility that it should call for such an outlandish marker? Is not the perfectly ordinary logically contradictory co-impossibility of propositions of the form *p* and not-*p* something unthinkable? It is, provided allowance is made for the fact stressed by Husserl that one must be able to think at least the propositions and the thought of their joint affirmation in order to know that their joint affirmation is impossible. But such an unthinkability rests on semantico-syntactic foundations, whereas what is being hailed as outwithness is not founded in the semantico-syntactic. It is more accurate to say (as we have seen it is to say this also of *Verneinung*) that the uncothinkability signaled by "outwith" is founded in the pragmatic, understanding by this the relation a linguistic unit has to its user, except that outwithness is not founded and is not a foundation. And its impossibility is better called un-possibility, for it is otherwise than both the kind of possibility and the kind of impossibility that are modalities of propositions. Its pre-positionality is a pre-propositionality. And it is pre-propositional not only in the way that a question may be said to be prior to the proposition that answers it. It is even more a priori than a posed question. How is this pre- to be construed?

What—or the unwhat—we are dubbing outwithness is something like what Derrida and Blanchot are getting at when they write of the *sans sans sans,* the without without without which is *sans sens,* without semantic or syntactic significance or direction. Without this outwithness there can be no semantic or syntactic sense. This contradictory French *sans* and the Scottish "outwith" bear witness to the binding of an "auld alliaunce." But the oldness of this alliance is the oldness not just of the archaic. It is the oldness of the anarchic. It is the pre-historic precedence that is immemorial in that it is not within the stream of what may be remembered either in a dream or in the temporality of our phenomenal experience in waking life. Paradoxically like the inwardness of which Kierkegaard writes, the exteriority indicated by the "out" of the outwith cannot be interiorized, *erinnert,* within the flow of consciousness.

## Across the Threshold

Between the unconsciousness of the dream and the consciousness of waking life in which dreams are recounted and interpreted is what Levinas refers to as insomnia. Freud mentions a classification of dreams that equates *enuptia,* dreams of the kind "which gave a direct representation of a given idea or of its opposite—e.g. of hunger or of its satiation—"[21] with insomnia. Insomnia as referred to by Levinas is neither a part of ordinary waking life nor a part of waking life as contrasted with dream. It is not an episode of our empirical psychological existence such as might owe its order to the conceptual categories of the understanding. By insomnia he means the extraordinary meta-categorical wakefulness on the borderline of ordinary waking life and being asleep which is so other than the ontic as to be anonymous and impersonal and therefore easily confused with the insistence of existence, undisturbed by the voice of another, which he refers to as the *il y a,* the there-is. Meta-categorial insomnia is disturbance as such to the point of disturbing the ontological as such, to the point of disturbing the as such. It is where—or, better, the where (the *Da,* the *là*)—to which the absolutely immemorial past belongs, but disrupting belonging: *unheimlich,* disrupting the home to the point that it is not any more only the place where only I enjoy living, but the place where the stranger is to be welcomed as a guest even though he is unwelcome in that he may be an enemy and indeed is always an enemy in that he competes for my place in the sun. This insomniac ex-perience outwith *empeiria* and the truths of logic putatively reachable by analysis or anamnesis is pre-historic, but not in the manner of an alliance covenanted at the beginning of an ancient or modern chronology. How can it be said of it, as we find ourselves wanting to say, that it is pre-supposed by propositions in which empirical and rational truths are affirmed or denied? How can what is supposed before what is posed be anything else than another propositional *Satz* or a principial *Grundsatz* of which one could in principle become mindful? Or does what we read in Derrida, Blanchot, Levinas, Rosenzweig, and Kierkegaard lead us to infer that the immemorial calls for an *Ursatz* or *Grundsatz,* where by *"Satz"* is meant not a proposition but a leap from any ground, a leap from groundedness into anarchy?

Does the answer to these questions lie in the recognition that the anarchic can, at a price, be conceptualized and made the topic of a proposition? Is this not what happens when one says of something non-propositional that it is presupposed by or is a necessary condition of something that is propositional? The non-propositional might be the addressing of a statement to someone which would not be part of what is stated. But is it not transformed into part of what is stated by what we might call a metastatement, a metastatement like those that seem to fill the books of Freud, Hegel, Ricœur, Levinas, Derrida (despite his doubt that there are ultimately any metastatements)? The trouble is that even such so-called metastatements do not include as part of what they state their own being addressed to a listener or reader, who might be oneself or no one in particular, as when Nietzsche affirms his love of fate and seems thereby to will the eternal repetition of the pleasures and harsh realities of life like the innocent child staging the repetition of the appearance and disappearance of the bobbin. The relation of what is stated to its being stated here gives us an inkling of an exteriority. A step in the direction of a further exteriority is anticipated, the exteriority of an act of speech (*parole*) to the linguistic system (*langue*) in the terms of which it is enacted. *Parole* and *langue* together yield *langage,* language in use. It is of this that Levinas says that it is already hospitality, as Derrida reminds the reader of his *"Pas d'hospitalité."*[22] The *pas* is a step, the step one might make across a threshold. But it is also the *pas* of negation, a negation that has at least this much similarity to denial as analyzed by Freud in his paper *"Die Verneinung,"* that the denial may be reversed and taken as an affirmation. However, one cannot say of the *pas d'hospitalité* what Freud says in the case of the dream about Goethe, that it is "just the reverse." A certain outwithness occurs whereby there both is and is not hospitality. Hospitality is not reversed into inhospitality. Hospitality is its own inhospitality. This is why when Derrida mentions hospitality he sometimes adds the clause *"s'il y en a,"* "if there is any such thing." Like the absolute immemorial past, and like the ghost of Hamlet (or of God), hospitality as such is such that we cannot say for sure that it exists. It is such that if it exists it exists only iffily. It is such that it has no as such, so that whatever anyone claims to know about it must be qualified by a non-cognitive "perhaps" reminiscent of Kant's affirmations that knowledge must be denied in order to make room for faith and that no human being can know whether any human being has ever performed a good deed.

Now, following the logic of nominalizing metastatements as characterized so far, the example of outwithness that Derrida calls "hostipitality" is *prima facie* indeed an example, and an example in the sense of an instance or a case falling under a concept, albeit the curious Abelian concept of a word with antithetical senses. It may even become a title, as it does with seminars included in *Acts of Religion*. "Hostipitality" would be a word that gives shelter, as it were under the roof of a circumflex accent (the circumflex accent is called in Welsh a *to bach,* a little roof), to the apparently opposed concepts of hospitality and hostility combined in the word "*hôte,*" which means either host or guest, either the one who offers hospitality or the one who receives it. Whether or not, like Derrida, we have reservations about accepting Benveniste's proposal that "*hôte*" has an etymological connection with the Latin "*hostis,*" meaning enemy, Derrida is ready to follow Levinas's move from ambiguous "*hôte*" in *Totality and Infinity* to "*otage,*" meaning hostage or victim, in *Otherwise than Being or Beyond Essence.*[23] As host I welcome the stranger into my house. Now if one room in my house, the place I inhabit, my *ēthos,* is my language, and if hospitality is coextensive with ethics,[24] whether *an* ethics or that outwith which there is no particular ethics, then language will already be ethics. This will have the consequence of calling into question the familiar concepts of conceptuality, propositionality, and presuppositionality, of which much use has been made in this chapter so far. We shall learn that the question and the answer as we conceive them are called into question through our being called into question ourselves, called to be answerable in a manner that affects the correlation of answers with questions, even the correlation of things stated with their being stated. For the co- of correlation will turn out to be too comfortably cooperative, too cozily with.

If Kierkegaard shows that religion, specifically the religion of Judeo-Christianity, is more difficult than is commonly supposed, Derrida and Levinas show that ethics is more difficult than is commonly supposed. They do it by showing that ethics is religion, though not a religion. The difficulty they detect in ethics is the difficulty adverted to in the title of Levinas's book *Difficult Freedom*. What makes freedom difficult is what is other than freedom of the will, therefore other than a difficulty that could be overcome by trying harder and training oneself into virtuous habits. The difficulty is not even that posed by the impossibility of completing a task such as a Kantian regulative idea might prescribe. It is a "structural" difficulty, Derrida writes.[25] It is structural because the structure in question de-structs itself and its self. This destruction, however, is no more to be taken purely negatively than is the *Destruktion* referred to by Freud in Ricœur's interpretation of him, or *Destruktion* as understood by Heidegger, or *Destruktion* as understood by Nietzsche in his philosophizing with a hammer. In this last case the will of the will to power, the *Wille zur Macht,* is not a faculty contrasted with other faculties as understood in German Idealism, but an indissoluble complication of thought, sensation, feeling, and emotion to which one might consider giving the name "imagination," theoretical and aesthetic and practical and ethical *Einbildungskraft* and *Einbildungsmacht* which is at the same time *Einbildungsohnmacht,* imagination *ohne Macht,* imagination *mitohne Macht,* imagination of which the power comes from being outwith power.

Usually, perhaps always, when Derrida writes of structure it is an oppositional constructure of which he is speaking, usually one we have inherited from the linguistico-conceptual framework of the world in which we dwell. Our very concepts of dwelling, world, constitution, linguistic system, and conceptual frame and of conceptuality itself quiver when their seism or ipseity, that is to say, their selfhood or identity, undergoes the seismic shock of de-con-struction. That happens when the other that is opposed to a concept is found to be not just its other, not just the other that belongs to it as a concept in opposition to which the identity of the first concept is defined. The otherness that belongs to the concept to which it is opposed may be the otherness of the square of opposition and the traditional logic associated with it, or it may be the otherness of the dialectical negation, where the antithetical concepts are brought together in a concept under which they are subsumed. If there should intervene an alterity that is not the alterity of "its" other, conceptuality and subsumption and belonging and hospitality would never be the same again. The logic of sameness would be too weak to cope with it, too weak, too *ohnmächtig,* because too strong, too control-freakish, because the logic of sameness is a logic of deductive or dialectical derivation, whereas the best one can hope for is a logic of *dé-rive* by which even the concept of logic, without of course being simply negated, is dislodged. This dislodgment is an effect of what we could call anarchigraphy or, following Derrida, archi-writing, so long as we remember that this archi- is anarchic, an unfirst first (*archi*), and that its power and authority (*archē*) is its unpower.

We have noted then that what we think we understand by hospitality in the familiar circumstances of everyday life is undermined and underwritten by an absolute hospitality called by Derrida hostipitality. We have also noted that as well as taking his cue here from an etymological point about the Latin "*hostis*" made by Benveniste, Derrida takes as a cue Levinas's *dé-rive,* whereby the notion of hostage, *otage,* arrives on the scene to supplement an account of responsibility that had turned on the notion of *hôte* meaning either guest or host, either visitor or inviter. Would then the notion of hostage, *otage,* be the "common root" of the opposed senses of "*hôte,*" as though (since the word "hostage" derives from the Latin "*obses*") one could be obsessed by, that is to say, a hostage to one's guest under one's own roof? If so, this would not be on account of a Hobbesian competitive hostility among human beings. To say that I am the hostage of my guest, as Levinas says when he makes the step from the *hôte* to the *otage,* is not to say only that my guest and I are in competitive conflict under one roof. It is to say that the other is already under my skin and that I am subcutaneously irritated by a bad conscience.

Levinas's step from *hôte* to *otage* is treated by Derrida in *Adieu à Emmanuel Levinas* (1997). In the seminar entitled "Hostipitality" published in English in the same year, there are paragraphs in which the *Adieu* of Derrida's graveside farewell to his friend takes on a hint of departure in the sense of a philosophical demurrant, itself a way of remaining loyal to Levinas, as we are reminded by Derrida himself or one of the *dramatis personae* in "*En ce moment même . . .*"[26] who observes that simply to return to Levinas what he has given you is to remain locked within the claustrophobic system and symmetricality from which Levinas maintains there is an escape. In these paragraphs of the seminar on "Hostipitality" it appears that it is not only Hegel that Derrida has in mind in writing of an otherness that is properly "its" or "our" or "my" other. In these paragraphs Levinas is associated with Hegel in this regard, and in a way that tells us that Levinas continues to be in Derrida's thoughts (along with his thoughts of Carl Schmitt!) throughout those pages of *Politiques de l'amitié* where it gradually emerges that its author has difficulties with projects that would see fraternity as the key to the family of notions in terms of which politics and ethics are to be interpreted: the notions of the friend, the enemy, the neighbor, and indeed the family. Derrida concedes that when Levinas speaks of the neighbor the nearness or nextness that this implies is tied to a separateness and distancing. So that when the other whom Levinas addresses as "my" neighbor is also addressed as "my" brother, there is still a fission between my brother and me, the fission that may be as wide as the wound Cain inflicted on Abel ("my" brother can be "my" enemy), but also the fission without which there can be no respect. Even so, not only does Levinas's emphasis upon fraternity raise the question how sorority would enter into ethico-political relations; it creates the impression that these relations are originally family relations, so genetic derivations, as does the genealogy of ethics of Genesis on which Levinas's genealogy of ethics is modeled. Although Genesis includes the story of Noah, the use Levinas makes of fraternity as a key to our understanding of whom or what might be an *hôte* in the sense of a visitor or a guest leads him away from the thought that the circumflex accent might represent the roof of the ark, and that to the ark of ethics might be welcomed the animal, not only Noah and his sons and his wife (in that order in Genesis 5:7) and his son's wives, what we so confidently call the family of man.

Furthermore, although Derrida writes that "Levinas always says that the other, the other man, man as the other is *my* neighbour, my universal brother, in humanity,"[27] he is not unaware that this "my" is formed not on the first person singular nominative "I," but on the accusative "me." For when the housed ego enjoying life hears the call of the needy other human being, it experiences itself as accused, traumatically shaken awake from its dream, its *Traum*. The reality principle that accrues to the life the ego lives according to the pleasure principle is an ethical principle, though at first not even a principle, since what converts the I into me is your singular face, an ethical reality prior to the reality of worldhood. Even so, we know that Levinas insists that in the "you" that transforms the "I" into the "me" there waits the "he" and the "she" of universal humanity where the political is implicit in the ethical. This moment of ethico-political representation can but should not be confused with epistemo-semantic representation. The moment of address in which the other's cry for help has always already received the response "*Hineni*," "Here I am," the moment in which I cannot turn a deaf ear, whether or not I go to the other's assistance, is an uncomfortable moment. It is uncomfortable because it is one in which I experience shame at my self-centeredness. It is uncomfortable also because the singular other who affects me with this shame speaks to and on behalf of other others, third parties each of whom is nevertheless unique. And their distress is distressing. Despite the third-personality of ethical principles entailed by the fact that, as we have heard Levinas say, the principle of justice arrives already with language, we find it in principle impossible to live up to that principle. For in coming to the assistance of someone we fail to come to the assistance of someone else. So that although I may manage not to be unjust through violating an instituted law or expectation and although I may not infringe anyone's deducible rights, the instituted law itself falls short of an absolute justice. It falls short of an absolute hospitality, and with it so do I.

It is to this absolute hospitality that Derrida is referring when he writes: "Hospitality, therefore—if there is any—must, would have to, open itself to an other that is not mine, my *hôte,* my other, not even my neighbour or my brother."[28] What is mine is already too late to receive what hospitality through its very concept demands. The guest is to be received unconditionally and un-announced, not with a niche prepared for it in advance in the way a category of the understanding or a temporal or spatial form of intuition according to Kant caters in advance for the immediate data of consciousness. Hospitality that is hospitality only to what is welcome is inhospitality, since it is unjust to the guest who would descend upon us as an absolute surprise, like a Messiah, like an enemy or a thief in the night, as Levinas says, echoing Joel 2:9 and 2 Peter 3:10. As Levinas also says, ethical responsibility is Desire for the undesirable, where lower-case desire as want and will is overcome by upper-case Desire that is not an act of will or an expression of want, but absolute and absolutely passive affect. So surprised must the host be that we can have no conception of that by which it is surprised. It will be as incomprehensible as the God of which Descartes writes that it overflows any idea we may have of it. Therefore if this hospitality is a messianism, it is a messianism without a Messiah, hence at least as mad as that which is madness to the Greeks and a stumbling-block to the Jews, that which Kierkegaard does not allow us to forget.

But where Kierkegaard sees this absurdity as the only route to eternal salvation and perpetual peace, despite the suffering in this world that grace inevitably entails according to him (another "contradiction"), Derrida and Levinas leave us only with Salutation: "Good Day," "Permit me to present myself," "Yours sincerely," "Goodbye"—the always already absolutely past and passive performance of a speech-act prior to formality in face of the unpossibility of hospitality, justice, and ethics, hence too of politics, given that the political has come on the scene with the third party that is in distanced proximity as soon as I am addressed by you. Now if there is anything in the thesis of Carl Schmitt's *Political Theology* that politics is a derivation or *dé-rive* from theology, and if there is anything in the doctrine that there is not anything in the Holy of Holies, that the Presence of the *Shekinah* is an Absence, then the thought of justice and hospitality upon which theories of politics and ethics are based will have to be the unthinkable thought of the impossibility of the possibility of justice and hospitality. However, this thought is not one that may strike only the believer in a particular religion or the theologian, to whom the aporia to which one is led in speaking about God has long been known. Whether he knows it or not, the non-believer is held hostage to this contradiction of being bound to do the impossible.[29] Once a case "is" a face and vice-versa, once the me-you "is" a me-(s)he and vice-versa, as it is from before the beginning of the world, "I ought" no longer implies "I can" as it continues to do in the realm of commissions and omissions judged, for example, according to maxims that pass the test of universalizability set by the moral law. Further, from its being impossible for me, except within these limits, to be just and hospitable, my absolute culpability ensues. Whereas it is usually said that "ought" implies "can," that I cannot be held responsible for failing to do what it was impossible for me to do, we are being told by Levinas and Derrida, as has been already observed, that I am responsible for what it was impossible for me to do.

To say that I cannot be absolutely just or hospitable is not to say that I am prevented by a physical, psychological, or other natural lack. It would be nearer the mark to say that I am prevented by logic, except that, because logic covers only cases and concepts, to say that I am prevented by logic is to say too little and too much. Should it be said therefore that I am prevented by ontology or by the way the world is? That Derrida would be willing to say this might be inferred from his willingness to cite in the exergue of the first chapter of *Specters of Marx* as an expression of this impossibility Hamlet's words "The time is out of joint."[30] The validity of this inference is put into doubt by the fact that Derrida mentions immediately after citing these words that they are cited in *The Oxford English Dictionary* as an illustration of the ethico-political force of the phrase "out of joint," an illustration of, to repeat a word used also by Guattari and Deleuze, a "perversion." He and the dictionary go on to quote Hamlet's next words, "Oh cursed spight, That ever I was born to set it right." These words may suggest that Hamlet believes he can set the time right. Shakespeare casts doubt on that belief. So too does Derrida. Time, the world, ontology are out of joint from before their beginning, from a beginning of which the anteriority is pre-originary, a quasi-original perversion before original sin, at a location where ontology and cosmology are dislocated by the ethico-political, at the crossing of junction and disjunction through injunction, the chiasmus of ontology and the Good outwith Being. Here, where my right to a place in the sun is challenged by the first other and the third party and where the time of my being toward my own death is interrupted by the time of their being toward theirs, I remain unforgivable for failing to do the justice it is impossible for me to do because justice is congenitally unjust and hospitality congenitally inhospitable.[31] Someone or something—who knows?—is always left out in the cold. Human justice is never impartial. But before we say that this is why, and not only for Kierkegaard, from the ethical a leap must be made to the religious, and before we leap from saying this to saying that an ethical humanism of the other human being must finally or initially have recourse to the word "God," let it be noted that this would be another way of saying that the ethical is in the last resort impossible.

If it may be said that with this impossibility the religious or mystical or secret or sacred force of the ethical is touched on,[32] this happens without an appeal to God, without an appeal at any rate to a God of whom we say that it is possible for him or her or it to be absolutely just, absolutely hospitable and absolutely forgiving. For if the impossibility of absolute justice, absolute hospitality, and absolute forgiveness is, in Van Helmont's neologism, the *gas* from which the ethical derives or de-rives its life, then, when we try to imagine a being for whom absolute justice, absolute hospitality, and absolute forgiveness are possible, we have left the ethical behind. Gas, like *chaos*, as Van Helmont says, and as Derrida says, justice, hospitality, forgiveness, ethics, supposing there is any, happen only "in the abyssal and *chaotic* desert, if chaos describes first the immensity, the unmeasurable, the disproportion in the gaping of an open mouth—in the waiting or in the appeal of what we know here without knowledge as the messianic: the coming of the other, the absolute and unanticipatable singularity of the arriving *as justice*."[33] Of course, I can open my mouth and say "Welcome" or "I forgive you," and these are acts of speech in the mode, as has just been said, of the "I can." They are speech acts whereby I perform deeds of welcoming and forgiving. But such acts, derived, so to speak, from my good intentions, are not unconditioned. They presume a context of circumstances, some of which John Austin lists in *How To Do Things with Words*.[34] One of these circumstances, one that is implicit among those that Austin lists, is a certain presumptuousness on the part of the one who welcomes or forgives, a presumption of authority over the one who is welcomed and the one who is forgiven, a presumptuousness Kierkegaard seeks to avoid when he says that he speaks "without authority." If such presumptuousness is unbecoming in our welcoming or forgiving of a human being, it would be even more so in our welcoming or forgiving of God. Such presumptuousness in our welcoming or forgiving a God would fall away only in our welcoming or forgiving a God whose power was limited, yet limited not by an act of its free will. For such an act would only reinforce its power, as it is reinforced by that act by which, according to the Kabbalah, God surrenders part of his power to his creation, by the act that is performed by the Son when He says to his Father, "Thy will be done," and by the deed done by Zarathustra's overman when he affirms, "I will that all pleasures and pains that have been be repeated eternally over and over again." Are all three of these cases of the self-denial of power cases of the exercise of what Nietzsche calls the will to power? Whether or not they are exercises of the will to power, they exercise power over the same realm of possibility as that to which saying "I forgive you" belongs. That is the realm of the physically, psychologically, and ethically possible, where by the ethical is understood, as Kierkegaard understands it, a space governed by a law that requires debts to be repaid and where justice demands an eye for an eye and an I for an I. In such a conception of ethics, justice is done to the case only at the expense of violence being done to the face. The accursed spite of the human condition is that for justice to be done to the face violence has to be done to the case and therefore to the face veiled within or inwith it.

Continuing to use the language of ethics construed as economics, but in order to watch it deconstruct itself, it can be said that justice is done to the face only at the price of doing what is wrong not just relative to a system, but wrong absolutely, in the face of undeconstructible justice, in the space of impower, the ethically impossible, the ethically unforgivable. For however forgivable within the economy of cases relative to stations and places and degrees of proximity, outside that economy, in the absolute, non-relative exteriority of faces where proximity has no degrees, it is unforgivable to respond to someone's cry for help when doing so means that the cries of so many others must go unheeded. But since only by responding ethically to the cry "save me" can I respond to the other as to a face rather than solely as a case, and since only by doing so can one escape the system of exchange within or inwith which what is to be exacted of another or forgiven is calculable, there can be real forgiveness only of what is outwith the system—which does not mean without it. There can be real forgiveness only of the absolutely unforgivable.

The accursed spite of Hamlet's plight, and ours, is not that of the Greek tragedy admired by Nietzsche but scorned by Kierkegaard if the plight of Greek tragedy is construed as a contradiction that admits of resolution in the long run of a Kantian Idea of Reason or the wider view promised by the Hegelian sublimation of an allegedly self-certain I Here and Now. There can be no resolution of ethical conflicts if the axis of the ethical is the relation of relations in which you address to me on behalf of yourself and others the command "Thou shalt not kill" or the cry "Help" and I have responded not *Ego sum* but *Hineni,* "Count on me."

# TWELVE

## Love of Wisdom and Wisdom of Love

### Discounting the Cost

In saying "Count on me" I give you my word. But in saying that I thereby give you my word do I not do the opposite of what I say? For in saying something about giving my word, have I not turned from using that word to mentioning it? This being so, it would seem that instead of giving you my word I do not give you my word. The same would seem to be the case if I say that in saying "I give you my word" I give you my word. Instead of giving it, I apparently save it for myself, save myself from giving it: I keep it. And indeed I do, in deed. I keep it because even in only mentioning certain words I have already kept my word. And that holds if I break my word. I cannot break my word unless I have given it. And if breaking my word takes the form of telling a lie, I am in telling the lie still giving someone my word. This holds even if while telling someone a lie I tell myself that I am, or make what we call "mental reservations." It holds even if, raising a Book aloft in the right hand, I swear "I promise" but cross the fingers of the left hand behind my back. Such clandestine gestures, because they are not clandestine enough, simply do not count.

    The same holds if I say that the word "count" is quasi-Abelian. In mentioning the word in order to say of it that it is quasi-Abelian the word becomes

Abelian, a word in which the opposite senses (here on the one hand the calculative keeping of accounts and on the other hand incalculable accountability) are purely semantic. That is to say, it ceases to count as a word by which I give you my word. But I give you my word nonetheless. I cannot save myself from my responsibility that easily. I do not have that easy a freedom to opt out. Abelian words are words in which opposite senses cooperate or compete. It has been said that when the Chinese conception of *yin/yang* is taken up by "the West" the cooperative nature which the correlation has in *The Book of Changes* changes to one that is competitive.[1] But competitors must cooperate insofar as they have to agree on the rules of the competition and on what counts as winning. Conversely, cooperators are in competition with their own egoistic inclinations to seek a short cut to what they want that does not incur the compromise that cooperation entails. Perhaps one should ask, as has been asked once before in the present book, though without explicit mention of the expression "*yin/yang*," whether this very correlation between cooperation and competition is itself cooperative or competitive. This would be important for our understanding of a correlation of which there has been many an explicit mention in this book, namely that between the active and the passive. For *yang*, one reads, is associated with the active and masculine, whereas *yin*, one gathers, corresponds to the passive and the feminine.[2] Following a traditional concept of conception and of the other concepts involved here, most evidently those of erotic and agapeistic love, competition would be associated with masculinely marked *yang* and cooperation with femininely marked *yin*. Therefore the above-mentioned difference between an Oriental and an Occidental interpretation of the *yin/yang* would be already construed within the *yin/yang*. Have we a firm enough hold on a notion of deconstruction to know whether we have here a self-deconstruction of the oppositions East/West, masculine/feminine, competitive/cooperative, *yin/yang*? We can know this with regard to *yin/yang* only if we are in a position to know what is meant when it is said that the restless changes indicated by the oblique stroke between the *yin* and the *yang* derive from the unity called *tao*, "way," or the breath called *ch'i* of which the *yin* and the *yang* might be, respectively, inspiration and expiration. Gas or *Geist* or *ruah*? The problem exceeds the bounds of this book, as Levinas would say, at least in as far as the problem, as explained by Derrida, is exceeded by mystery.

This book's quirky problem or mystery, quirky because not wholly contained within its binding but "not positively illegal," comes to the surface again with that just-mentioned quasi-Abelian word "counts." This word is one that straddles the semantic-epistemic space of calculation and the space of ethicality. It stands, if it stands at all, at the point where what was referred to in the last sentence of the last chapter as the axis of the ethical crosses the axis of calculation, arithmetic, and the science of accounting. There is nothing new in saying this—unless in saying this everything is new. Kierkegaard, Nietzsche, Heidegger, Sartre, Levinas, Derrida, Deleuze, and Guattari know that the conceptual framework of ethics, with its languages of saving (credit, debit, and debt) and banking ("You can bank on me"), is superimposed upon the framework of economics like a right-hand glove on its incongruent left-hand counterpart. And it is a short step or no step at all (*pas de pas*) from these languages to the idea that these frameworks are also the frameworks of Judaism, Christianity and Islam and of some of their conceptions of how we might come to understand or fail to understand the distribution of God's love.

There is not one of the writers just named who argues for the existence of God. If any of them argues, he argues for the madness of arguing for what an all-but-question-begging genitive calls God's existence. But none of those writers nor the writer of this book argues against the other madness exemplified equally well or ill in both the faith in God and in the faith outwith Him or Her or It. This faith is the fidelity or loyality (*loyauté*), quirkily making the law (*loi*) and breaking it, that throughout this book has been called the "religious," taking this word in the etymological senses of both to bind and unbind, to be bound by the law but at the same time to be unbound from it by being bound to the singular other. "Religious" is a quasi-Abelian word which, like all quasi-Abelian words, becomes Abelian as soon as you say something about it. For a word's quasi-Abelian rhetoric is indeed rhetorical and pragmatic as the rhetorical and pragmatic are non-exclusively opposed to the logical and semantic. Its opposite senses are in the first place or anarchically—outwith place—at the conjuncture-disjuncture where what is said is interrupted by the moment of address when epistemic representation such as is manifested in the accounts of the language of the representation of facts proposed by Husserl's pure grammar and Wittgenstein's *Tractatus Logico-Philosophicus* becomes representation in an ethico-political sense. Whereas in the latter book formal reasons are given for concluding that it is impossible to represent how language represents, in the present book it has been learned that it is for non-formal reasons impossible to represent how ethico-religious and broadly "political" representation works. This is because of the quirk by which the formal moment of language that appeals to me as a moment of safety is disturbed by the non-formal moment of being appealed to by someone else. You, the other, may appeal to and be appealed to by another other and by what Levinas calls illeity or Illeity and Derrida refers to as "God, if you wish." Nietzsche and Deleuze and Guattari might be willing to say "God, if you will," but they would not be willing to say this of a God conceived as transcendent. The unconceived God for whom Kierkegaard decides (God not only incomprehensible like Descartes's God but also inconceivable) is absolutely transcendent, and his God either would be an unconditional God that is absolutely without ifs and buts or it would be a God that is absolutely nothing.

What of the God of Levinas? On that question, it seems to me, the jury is still out. And maybe that is how it seems to him too. Maybe that is what is signified by the word "maybe" (*"peut-être"*) which from time to time he, like Derrida, judiciously inserts into his text. While acknowledging that to make God an essential point of reference for ethics—even an ontologically *point zéro*—would be to extend in one direction the relevance of his doctrine of the ethical for some of his readers, it must be acknowledged too that it would be drastically to reduce its relevance for many other readers in this post-Nietzschean post-thanatheological era. It is not as obvious to me as it is to Alain Badiou that Levinas's "'Altogether-Other' (*Tout Autrement*) . . . is quite obviously the ethical name for God."[3] If it is the ethical name for God, it is not obvious that ethics cannot get by without it. And one could say that ethics could get by without it without being unfaithful to Levinas. For although to be faithful to Levinas we must not merely return to him what he has given to us, what we do not return can lie elsewhere than in the space of the question of the names of God. Badiou is not unfaithful to Levinas in saying that philosophy as the *ancilla* of theology is "philosophy (in the Greek sense of the word) *annulled* by theology, itself no longer a theology (the terminology is still too Greek, and presumes proximity to the divine via the identity and predicates of God) but, precisely, ethics."[4] This is faithful to Levinas in that it gives back something Levinas gives us. But it is faithful too in that it does not give back something Levinas gives us. For only to return to him what he has given would be, he gives us to understand, lacking in generosity. Generosity does not merely give back. (Hence more is given back than was previously given when Isaac and ethics are given back.)

Levinas proclaims that in his major "non-confessional" writings he is speaking "Greek." The word is in scare-quotes because notwithstanding that Levinas sometimes formulates what he is doing in his "philosophical" works in terms of the opposition between the "Greek" and the "Hebrew," he sometimes formulates or deformalizes what he is doing by drawing our attention to what he is *doing,* by reminding us of the spoken or written "speech act" that is performed as he or someone else addresses us. He reminds us further of the superlatively passive (and, we have maintained, superlatively active) *undoing* without which we could not make the distinction between the passive and the active and between the performance of saying and that which is said in the representations of states of affairs.

Badiou is correct again when he writes that

> [t]he ethical primacy of the Other over the Same requires that the experience of alterity be ontologically "guaranteed" as the experience of a distance, or of an essential non-identity, the *traversal* of which is the ethical experience itself. But nothing in the simple phenomenon of the other contains such a guarantee. And this simply because the finitude of the other's appearing certainly

*can* be conceived as resemblance, or as imitation, and thus lead back to the logic of the Same. The other always resembles me too much for the hypothesis of an originary exposure to his alterity to be *necessarily* true.

But this last sentence is not necessarily true either. It is true to what Levinas writes. It explains why Levinas writes that over what he is trying to *say* (compare and contrast Nietzsche's repeated willing of the eternal return of "the same") and trying not to *have said* (compare and contrast Nietzsche's "it was") there presides an unavoidable "maybe." A sociological, psychological, or psycho-analytic interpretation or phenomenological "reduction" of what Levinas says is always possible. And Levinas agrees. But because "ontology" is Greek Levinas would not agree with what Badiou says in his first sentence, not even if we put the word "experience" in quotation marks, as Levinas often does when he is writing of the ethical in language borrowed from Husserl and Hegel. Badiou seems to want to draw a borderline between the Greek and the Hebrew and to say that Levinas wants to do the same but in attempting to do so Levinas prevents himself from ontologically guaranteeing or even, keeping Badiou's quotation marks, "guaranteeing" difference. It seems to me—and it is too late to make this clear now if it has not already been made clear in what has been said in several of the chapters of this book—that we should be attempting, like Nietzschean "attempters," to show that we do not have a simple relation of opposition between the Greek, the philosophical, and perhaps also the theological on the one hand and, on the other hand, the Hebrew and the "non-philosophical" moment of intrusive address, and perhaps also the religious. If there are here two hands, they are not simply opposed. They cross neither in simple competitiveness like two shining swords, nor as hands grasping each other in mutual assistance.

I say that this is what we should be attempting to show. I would say that it is what Levinas is trying to show. But I agree with Badiou that Levinas and anyone else will have much difficultly showing this if showing is understood as a presentation of pure phenomena. Here phenomenology, whose Greek name, whether used by Husserl, by Hegel, or by anyone else, is arguably synonymous with the name of philosophy, either reaches its limit or experiences a change of voice. The breaking of this voice may be already audible in that quirk of the Greek (but also Sanskrit) language that grammarians call the middle voice or the medial diathesis, the powers and impowers of which are to some degree saved in the grammatically passive but semantically active deponent verbs of Latin.[5] Something like this middle voice may be heard in the doubly genitive "of" to which appeal has been made so frequently in these chapters.

What if how language represents cannot be represented by being said? What if the form of semantic representation can only show itself, and that which shows itself passively is something whereof one should remain silent? Then we may have to deny experience in order to make room for faith. Not necessarily faith in a god, nor necessarily faith in the death of God or his ghost, but at least a-theistic faith, or the faith of an ethical responsibility that re-presents, that is to say stands up in deed for the stranger in need and makes representations on his or her behalf. If actions speak louder than words, it may be through that quirk of language we call silence that what cannot be said may show itself. But although showing how something may be shown is of significance for philosophy, what is shown is what is of paramount significance when what is shown is justice and love. Yet love already speaks itself in philosophy's name, as too in the name of philology, the love that Nietzsche embraced and was embraced by.

## Philology

Recalling again Derrida's remark that Levinas is very distant from Nietzsche but also very close, it is noteworthy that although Levinas attaches to the phrase "phenomenology of the face" the phrase "necessary ascent back to God," placing a colon between them, he follows Nietzsche in refusing to the theology of this God "all speculation on a hinter-world" and "all knowledge transcending knowledge." What is more, he says of this "absolute interruption of onto-logy"—where for once the genitive is *not* subjective!—that this interruption happens where "utopian sociality . . . nonetheless commands the whole of humanity in us and where the Greeks perceived the ethical." Who are the "us"? Who are the "ourselves" of the title *Between Ourselves* (or *Between You and Me, Entre nous*) of the collection in one of the essays of which the above-cited words occur?[6] The essay in question formed the preface to the translation of his book *Totality and Infinity* into the language of a people on whose land the memory of his lost family would not let him set foot. It is a book about an alternative to totalitarianism. On the page of that prefatory essay following the page on which the above-cited words occur, Levinas returns to words he had used later in *Otherwise than Being or Beyond Essence,* dedicated to the memory of members of his own family and other victims of National Socialism and anti-Semitism.

Referring to philosophy as the love of wisdom, Levinas maintains that more important than that philosophy is the wisdom of love, *la sagesse de l'amour.* Philosophy is the wisdom of love or wisdom in the guise of love. That the guise is not a disguise is made plain when he goes as far as to speak of philosophy as love of love. Love's love, if you like; and if God is love, God's love of God. Whether or not he would wish to go as far as to say that that love is God, he does go as far as to say that love is the Good. It is the Good announced when Plato speaks in his work on political theory called the *Republic* of the Good beyond being. How much more Greek than Plato can one get? How much more

Greek than Socrates, of whom Levinas is thinking when he reminds us that first philosophy is face-to-face address and therefore ethics, even if ethics turns to politics afterward? Yet how much less Greek can one get if to be Greek is to represent everything and everyone as phenomenon? How much less Greek can one get than Plato and Socrates if, as Levinas here proposes, through what these philosophers say we hear that phenomenal representation calls to be depresented? In the words he recalls from *Otherwise than Being,* his work of love dedicated to the victims of anti-Semitism, "Philosophy is the wisdom of love in the service of love."[7]

Philosophy is *logos,* which is to say language. Philosophy is philology, and philology, for instance the philology invoked in Nietzsche's genealogy of morals, is love of language or of *logos,* for instance the *logos* love of which is understood by Hegel through a speculative genitivity denoting *logos* as the urge (*Trieb*) of and to rationality or wisdom, wisdom's self-affective affection for itself. Here, remembering that wisdom is in different traditions feminine, for instance in the Book of Wisdom and in Tibetan Buddhist iconography, a masculine marking may characterize the search for wisdom, making it a groping that hopes to find the path to *Wissenschaft.* However, this is not a clear-cut opposition, as we learned Nietzsche is at pains to show when in chapter 7 we noted the emphasis he lays on woman's Herr-*schaft* . There is therefore a striking difference between Nietzsche's and Hegel's philology. Where what Hegelian philology loves is reason, that love being itself reason, Nietzschean philology as declared in *amor fati* loves everything, including what remains undigested by organs of the Hegelian system, provided only that what Nietzsche loves is *fatum,* that is to say, *said.* But on Nietzsche's own saying, echoed by Levinas, the said is destined to suffer and already to have suffered a quirk of destiny that binds it to a *saying.* Levinas hears in this saying a rationality that is a hyper-rationality relative to the universal rationality of the philosophical system of Hegel. That system culminates in the concretely universal individuality—that is to say singularity!—of absolute wisdom whose priority is challenged by the individuality of the first person singular that Kierkegaard calls the *Enkelte* and of the second and third person singular that Levinas calls *Autrui.* Nietzsche's autobiographical style of writing, for instance in *Ecce Homo,* might lead us to place him in the lineage of Kierkegaard. His affirmation of *amor fati* might appear to confirm his place in this lineage. Three facts complicate the matter. The first fact that does this is the fact that he and his Zarathustra address themselves to the agenda of promoting not simply their own salvation but the arrival on the scene of noble human beings. The second is the fact that, as argued in chapter 7, Nietzsche's affirmation of himself in *amor fati* is at the same time an affirmation by which the world, this world, is saved. The third complication is that *amor fati* saves the world by making it more beautiful. In the words of his Zarathustra,

"I want to learn more and more to see as beautiful what is necessary in things; then I shall be one of those who make things beautiful. *Amor fati:* let that be my love henceforth!"[8] *Amor fati* would be an aesthetics. Hence it would be at odds with Kierkegaard's love of God and with the ethics that is saved from Hegel and Hegelian ethics, according to him, by the love of God, by the ethics tested as Abraham was tested on Moriah.

One could say that for Nietzsche ethics is saved, given back, when it has survived the test of aesthetics and returns as aesthethics. "I do not want to wage war against what is ugly. I do not want to accuse; I do not even want to accuse those that accuse. *Looking away* shall be my only negation. And all in all and on the whole: some day I wish to be only a Yes-sayer." This affirmation is not merely toleration of or resignation to fate. It sees fate as beautiful and therefore desirable. But, following Rosenzweig, Levinas would maintain that if there is such a thing as aesthethics, its ethicality is that of Desire that inspires desire, and Derrida would maintain, also acknowledging Rosenzweig, that Nietzsche's Yes is accompanied by another Yes, a Yes to the Other, *Autrui,* that accompanies every other Yes as necessarily as according to Kant every idea or representation is accompanied by an "I think." Levinas is keen to speak "Greek" with Plato, Aristotle, and Hegel. So the question arises as to what Greek word he might take himself to be translating when he writes of Desire. The question also arises as to whether, despite his wish to speak the language of Plato, Aristotle, and the German Greek Hegel, Levinas's Greek understanding of Desire is infused with senses conveyed by its nearest Hebrew equivalent, which in the section of chapter 2 entitled "Loves" we took to be "*ahavah.*" If Levinas's teaching can be encapsulated in one word, this is the word. And this word is Abelian, therefore open to a quasi-Abelian application to the singular moment of love expressed in addressing a person or being addressed. Gesenius's lexicon tells us that it may carry the sense of breathing after, hence to be inclined, willing, prone, to wish and to desire. We are told also that with a dative of person it can mean to be willing toward anyone, to be willing in mind, to obey or to hearken. That is to say, the word lends itself to interpretation on lines similar to those suggested by the overlap of hearing (*audire*) and obedience (*obaudire*), implying an incoming such as breathing also implies, the directionality that Levinas provisionally calls reversed intentionality and that Derrida refers to as an arriving and advening (*avenir*) from or of the future (*l'avenir*). In contexts like that of Leviticus 19:18, "Thou shalt love thy neighbor as thyself," "*ahavah*" is translated by "*agapē,*" and "*agapaō*" can mean to welcome and be welcome (*bienvenu*). We are going to rediscover later in this chapter how much stress both Levinas and Derrida place on the enmity (but not necessarily hate) that comes with the welcomed other because the other persecutes me. Some philological— and therefore not entirely safe—grounding for this contrariety is forthcoming from Gesenius. Referring still to *"ahavah"* and its meaning of desire, he writes: "In Arabic it has a power altogether the reverse—to be unwilling, to refuse." So Levinas is speaking Arabic when he tries to speak Greek? When he speaks Hebrew, we have now learned, he is able to furnish us with a clue as to how intentional desire might turn into "reversed intentional" Desire. And by keeping the same French and English words here, acknowledgment is made of the fact that if *"agapē"* would seem to resist replacement by *"erōs"* in contexts like Leviticus 19:18, where it connotes regard or cool rather than hot passion, it, like *"ahavah,"* is occasionally used of sexual love.

Hence to the question whether Levinas's *"Désir"* is a translation of *"erōs"* or *"agapē"* no simple answer can be given. Even Levinas's conception of *erōs* is different from the common notion of desire as teleological. He finds in it what he might provisionally call a reversed teleologicality. In his early work *Existence and Existents* the word *"erōs"* is used for a love that maintains distance and dissymmetry between the lover and the loved.[9] This love is the condition of possibility of symmetrically intersubjective love as communion such as is postulated by Christianity, the Kantian realm of ends and the adaptation of these notions of being-together made by Hegel and Heidegger. It should not be forgotten that when Levinas uses the word *"agapē,"* as he often does when addressing Christian audiences, such love continues to connote the absence of the other in the presence of the other. This dissymmetry, fission, and absence are what make the difference between *Autrui,* the Other in its dimension of height, and *autre,* the other with whom I may be in communion and compassion. That is to say, Levinas shares with Nietzsche a refusal to consider sympathy as a foundation of human relations. It is not surprising therefore that Nietzsche should take a low view of fraternity understood as the belonging to the same genus of all humankind, and that Levinas should seek to preserve the dissymmetry of the rapport of fraternity. In *The Politics of Friendship* Derrida voices reservations not only over the way the use of the notion of fraternity diverts our attention from the sister; he is also not happy with the word because it derives from the notion of family and genealogical derivation which has had such an unhappy history when applied to the field of the political. Derrida has these reservations because this idea of fraternity, *Brüderschaft,* lends itself to the idea of belonging to the land in a way that gave rise to the very creed by which Levinas's own family was destroyed.

## Affirmations

As just indicated, Derrida agrees with Levinas in acknowledging the importance of what Rosenzweig says about the primordial Yes. He cites a paragraph in which Rosenzweig makes it clear that what he calls the primordial Yes is the silent accompaniment not of propositions, but of elements of the proposition, words. The Yes itself is not itself necessarily a word. It can be expressed in gesture or a look. It is the Amen that was, is, and will be in the beginning. The paragraph is cited in a footnote in *Ulysse gramophone,* a volume comprising two lectures that treat of the occurrences of Yes in Joyce, most frequently from the mouth of Molly Bloom. Derrida draws up an incomplete table of the varieties of Yes, but construes Molly's Yeses as encyclopedic. Molly is in the habit of sending notes to herself. Her yeses are self-addressed. Like Ulysses, they come back home. Even if, as Hegel and T. S. Eliot say, home-coming is conceived as a return from the end of absolute wisdom to the beginning that is now known for the first time, this recollective Yes, the Yes of memory and anamnetic recuperation, presupposes a second (or first) Yes. This is the Yes of Rosenzweig, and it may be given a theological turn, as it comes close to being given when Levinas leans on Descartes's third Meditation in the course of his attempt to dislodge the ego from the position of priority it at first appears to be given by Descartes. The argument is that the idea I have of my own finitude implies that I have an idea of the opposite of finitude. This idea must be put in my mind by God, since all my other ideas are of finite entities or are ideas, mathematical ones for instance, that are of infinity only in a negative or, as Hegel would say, "bad" sense, that of what has not yet been reached. In other words, the theory of so-called innate ideas assumes that at least one idea comes in additionally from outside, as Aristotle says of divine *psuchē,* breath, spirit, intellect, at a moment when it is as though into his text from outside come Plato and the Idea of the Good.[10] Except that *psuchē* is not an Idea, but mind itself—the "except for the intellect itself," *excipe intellectus ipse,* Leibniz would say—that you can call God if you will. Except, again, that Arisotle's divinity is not properly nominal, but predicative. So we could call this exceptional *psuchē* (or *ruah*) the Other, *Autrui.* Another name for it, or rather a non-name, might be Yes. Not, however, the Yes of encyclopedic self-possession, but the Yes of a *paideia,* a learning. Not the learning of facts, but the learning of learning as such. Not learning as the acquisition of answers to questions, but learning in the sense of the ambiguity that the expression *oui-dire* has for Derrida's ear: Yes-saying, but also hear-say, strictly speaking (strictly writing) *ouï-dire.* The Yes-saying in question, in any question, presupposed by it, understood, silently *entendu* as standing under any question, is the response given in advance to my addressee. It is the giving of my word, but not necessarily in a spoken or written word, indeed necessarily not in a word functioning as a semantically representative sign. It is an earnest of my attention before any intention to speak, prior to the performing of any speech-act. Not then any ordinary performative such as might be signaled by "hereby," but a quasi-transcendental performative such as might be signaled by the "thereby" used in the second sentence of this chapter, a performative that is per-formative in the sense that it deforms form and breaks rules of formation and transformation, hence "not positively illegal," yet "capable of making Law no Law at all" or, to use once again that word that the dictionary says is "of obscure origin and history," a quirk.

This quirk performs a work. It performs a work of love. At one moment in the film *D'ailleurs Derrida* Derrida says, if I can believe my ears, that before there is any linguistic communication there is already reconciliation. What? Is he saying that for reconciliation we do not need to wait until we have battled passionately through the stages of life's way or run the obstacle course of the negation of negation to absolutely absolute wisdom? But by reconciliation he does not mean a pact or treaty signed after a war, any more than the peace that preoccupies Levinas means the intermission of hostilities. The peace and reconciliation of which they write is not a state of rest. To describe them they have recourse to the metaphors of hostility and war rather than of pacification. Levinas proclaims that the Other persecutes me and makes me hostage. Derrida has me *invited* to the condition of hostage, conjuring up the image of a spider or a bird of prey. When I say Yes to the Other, "Here I am," "*Hineni,*" I am inviting the Other into my home. How can it be that at the same time I am invited by the Other? How can it be that "[i]n a certain manner I am the hostage of the other, and this situation of hostage in which I am invited by the other in wel-coming the other to my house, in which in my home I am there by invitation of the other, this situation of being hostage defines my own responsibility."[11] I am invited because the other speaks not only on behalf of her- or himself. The other commands me to respond not only to her or to him, but also to other others. And even though I may command the other to do likewise, the relation between me and each singular other remains dissymmetrical. This is what makes the difference between this situation and that of the Hobbesian war of each against all. It is also what marks it off from the Sartrian for-itself that says No to the other whose look would subjugate me. The Sartrian other may look down on me from a height, but that height is one of might, like that of the master vis-à-vis the slave in Hegel's *Phenomenology of Spirit.* At the "origin" of the Sartrian and Hegelian negation of the other is the Yes, like the "AA" or "DE" that the signaler sends before he sends a message, like the "Hello" over the telephone before there is signification, like the tapping on the wall of the prison cell of which Levinas sometimes speaks. From the claustrophobia of that cell, although one remains chained to its wall, tapping on it in order to speak with someone on the other side is already an escape.

The *ouï-dire,* hear-yes-say before hearing or seeing, responsibility already made in addressing myself to another, has the ambiguity that belongs to the word "learning" in some languages, where the word for "to learn" is Abelian, meaning either to learn or to teach. Desdemona says to her father, "My life and education both do learn me to respect you." "That'll larn 'im" is still said, though usually in parody, and in all innocence "learn" is often used for "teach" by young learners of the language. *Paideia,* learning-teaching, has to do with the education of the child. The learning-teaching of the innocent child is not yet encyclopedic. The Yes of the child is not that of Zarathustra's donkey carrying a load of knowledge like a Himalayan beast of burden with a filing-cabinet on its back,[12] or bearing the sufferings of the world like Christ on Golgotha or anyone who would imitate Christ, like Kierkegaard. That heavy Yes is to be distinguished from the Yes that dances light-footedly and laughs, the *oui-dire* that Derrida calls a *oui-rire*. The difference between these Yeses is the difference between mechanical repetition and the re-petition that is a re-seeking and a taking of risks. Availing oneself of the ambiguity of the title of Michael Naas's admirable *Taking on the Tradition,*[13] it can be said that on the one hand is the repetition that dolefully takes on what has happened, the "it was" or the "he war" (German *er war*) in the wake of *Finnegans Wake,*[14] and that on the other hand is the wakeful welcoming of the to-come which takes on the tradition in the sense of being prepared to re-evaluate it in the light of categories and laws that are not yet in place but that are "capable of making Law no Law at all." The difference is a difference of tonality, *Stimmung,* a *Wechsel der Töne,* the difference between saving as the economical safe-keeping of the slothful servant, and saving from such saving by the taking of chances, taking joy (rejoycing!) in the thought that if the chance may be a threat it may also be an opportunity. (A week or so before he died my good friend Timothy Sprigge managed to tell me over the telephone that he was taking the opportunity [his word] to prepare a phenomenology of dying.) But what is the relationship of these two Yeses to the Yes Derrida says is anachronistic because it is outwith the temporality of the time of the clock and is also outside the ecstatic time of *Being and Time,* the time of Dasein's being toward its own death? Are we not being told by Levinas and Derrida that this last affirmation is pre-supposed, that is to say already "there" before the *Da* of Dasein and position, *Setzung* and *Gesetz* (law)? Is this primary Yes different from the Nietzschean Yes, or is it a condition both of that Yes and of the conservative "Christian" Yes of Zarathustra's donkey and Molly Bloom? In the latter case, as a condition apparently of all language, it will be a condition no less of the language and logic of the dialectic of negation educated to absolute wisdom. Yet Derrida writes of the Nietzschean affirmation as though it were none other than this absolute affirmation that is the *sine qua non* of all language. But if the absolute Yes is indeed the Nietzschean or Rosenzweigian Amen, is not the encyclopedic Yes of Molly Bloom and of the Hegelian synthesis of negated negation saved: saved from its encyclo-tauto-pediatricity? In that case, what is there to choose between Hegel and Nietzsche in this respect? The only difference would seem to be the difference between groaning and laughing, where the groaning would be converted into laughter as soon as it dawned on us philosophers and theologians that Dionysus haunts the monotheisms of Judaism, Christianity, Islam, and Absolute Religion conceived as the narthex of Absolute Wisdom. Our questions cannot be answered as simply as this. There is groaning and groaning, for instance the groaning of the donkey under the weight of his wisdom and the groaning provoked by an excruciating pun or an Irish joke. And there is more than one sort of laughter. There is the laughter that accompanies Zarathustra's light-footed dance and there is the mocking laughter of Joyce bequeathing to his readers a load of learning they will never be able finally to digest. These two sorts of laughter (a third sort will be distinguished below in a footnote to chapter 13)[15] correspond to two sorts of Yes, or rather to two repetitions of the word "Yes," re-petitions that seek each other out or rather have already discovered each other in that each contaminates the other and each is a parasite upon the other. This parasitism is paradoxical. How can there be such an interparasitism? For there to be a parasite, must not there be a host? Is not the notion of parasite parasitic on the notion of host? This is true. Which of two organisms or organons we call the parasite and which the host, which primary and which not, will be decided partly by historical circumstances, for example the circumstance whether at a point in the history of thinking priority has been given to speech over writing, to spirit over matter, to the signified over the signifier, to the universal, whether abstract or concrete, over the singular. At that point it could be valuable to ask the question whether the order of priority should be reversed or, in case a simple reversal only confirms the structure of dialectical negation, it should be asked at least whether the hitherto underprivileged partner of each of these pairs might be accorded hitherto denied recognition. The answer to this latter question would have consequences for our understanding of such apparently hierarchic relations as that between master and slave in the writings of Hegel and that between the values of the nobles and the values of the slave morality as described by Nietzsche. One of the values of asking this question might be that it would lead to a revaluation of the notion of value itself. What is at stake is the very idea of values as polar opposites. Yet is not Derrida himself consolidating this axiology of polar opposition when in *Ulysse gramophone* he apparently contrasts two Yeses and two kinds of laughter?

Then there are his two Elie's. There is Elie as master of ceremonies, the Elie who supervises the rite of circumcision that confers membership of a community under the law, what Deleuze calls territorialization.[16] But, Derrida reminds us, observing also that he himself was given this name Elie on the seventh day of his life, the name Elie is used of the unexpected stranger for whom a place at the table is required to be laid. The name stands for the master who controls the name of the father, but it represents also the other. So does what was referred to earlier as the primary Yes have to be one of a pair, either, in the case of our earlier example, Molly's memorial Yes with its restrictive retrospective Odysseic economy, or Zarathustra's prospective Yes whose fidelity to what was is manifested in a certain active forgetfulness of it that makes room for what is to come: either the travail of Hegel's speculative *Summa* or the travel of Nietzsche's itinerant Abrahamic eternal iteration where the very word "eternal" gets brought down to earth and, as we have heard Deleuze saying, territorialized, but without any implication of rootedness in a land (*eretz*)? If this is an exclusive either-or, it repeats the patterns of classical metaphysical binary oppositions. And if the exclusiveness is overtaken by a synthesis of the contrasted terms, then Hegel will have won, because we shall have lost the singularities Kierkegaard, Nietzsche, Sartre, Levinas, Deleuze, Guattari, and Derrida, each in his own way, seek to save from being asphyxiated in the Supersingularity of the Big *Begriff.* "Hegel . . . is always right, as soon as one opens one's mouth in order to articulate meaning."[17]

We are pointed in the direction of an exit from this dilemma if we recollect that the Nietzschean-Zarathustran Yes is not one. It is already a Yes Yes, on the way to being the "Yes, yes, yes, yes, yes, yes, yes" with which Mrs. Breen responds to Bloom's story of Marcus Tertius Moses, as cited on page 437 of *Ulysses* and on the last page of *Ulysse gramophone: ouï-dire de Joyce.* Joyce says "we," but care must be taken lest this plurality become an indifferent collective and recollective first-person plural French *nous* or the Greek *nous* understood as reason in general, as it seems to become in the thinking of Hegel. Derrida observes that Hegel "presents himself"—something an individual does when one appends one's signature—as a philosopher whose empirical signature and individuality is of secondary importance and fated to be lost along with all other individuality except the concrete individual known as Absolute Wisdom. "Apparently, Hegel did not sign. Inversely, Nietzsche apparently signs, and signs more than once."[18] Now signing, even if performed when one is alone, is a public event. It calls to be witnessed, if not formally, at least by others to whom I would be ready to authenticate my signature, if necessary by signing again, and if my signature is to function as a signature, others must be ready to countersign it. But when Nietzsche signs up to the doctrine of eternal return of the same he thereby makes it difficult for himself to sign. For since subscribing to the eternal return means selecting whatever intensifies power and what does this is not predictable scientifically but is open to chance, Nietzsche will never be able to sign once and for all. His signatures will be more numerous than the Yeses of Mrs. Breen.

However, it is not just the number of Yeses ("*Nombre de oui,*" says the title of an essay by Derrida) that is our problem here. It is with the kinds of Yeses that our problem is concerned. So far there seem to be only two kinds at stake, the Yes of Nietzsche-Zarathustra and the Yes of Molly-Hegel (or, come to that, Vico, another proponent of cycloid metaphysics). This dualism, if dualism it is, is not the dualism of speaking and writing. This latter is a dualism at the level of speaking and writing in the ordinary acceptations of the terms as understood by Saussure, Husserl, Hegel, and a tradition of thinkers going back at least to Plato, according to which writing is subordinated to speaking and less suited as a medium through which to arrive at and communicate truth, because the author can be separated from what he has said, hence disabled from responding to any call for assistance that a reader might need. In his earliest writings Derrida brings out how speaking in the ordinary sense shares many of the characteristics of writing. For example, just as there have to be spaces between written letters and words, there has to be a temporal spread of phonemes. In both cases meaning is constituted not by the presence of a signified to a signifier that represents it as the name "Fido" stands for a certain dog, but, as Saussure himself argues, by the differences between marks and sounds determined by what sounds or marks can and cannot be substituted for a given sound or mark, as illustrated by the difference in English between "top," "tap," and "tgp" and between "The tap is shut off" and "Off shut tap the is." Sometimes a difference is not registered phonologically, for example the difference between the French words *différence* and *différance* (with an *a*), a neologism or, better, neographism introduced to mark the way an alleged immediate presence to consciousness loses immediacy because its meaning depends on conditional statements about the future and the past. So *différance* (with an *a*) is well suited to pick out a nonordinary sense of writing, which Derrida calls archi-writing, of which both writing in the ordinary sense and speaking are embodiments. But this gives us not a dualism. It gives a trinity in which the dualism of writing as opposed to speaking is now supplemented by the archi-writing that makes the usual opposition possible. It makes it possible, but also impossible in the familiar opposed senses of the words "possible" and "impossible," hence archi-writing is better described not as a transcendental but as a quasi-transcendental condition. If there is a pattern to Derridian deconstructions, this is it.

## Addressings

Our question has been whether this pattern holds for the opposition between Nietzsche-Zarathustra's Dionysiac *ouï-dire* or *oui-rire* and the Yes of Hegelian recollective interiorization which begins as a Dionysiac revel but eventually sobers up. The answer has to be Yes. For Derrida licenses his reader to take Joycean recollective interiorization as a literary analogue of Hegel's philosophical version of this *Erinnerung* and queries the opposition of philosophy to literature in *Glas,* where the left column on the page stands chiefly for the philosophy of Hegel and the right column stands for literature as emblemized by Jean Genet and his bouquets of flowers. In *Ulysse gramophone,* the title of which indicates that among the issues at stake in the book is still the connection of speaking and writing, *ouï-écrire,* and where Molly Bloom's name indicates that at stake too is a particular flower, Derrida writes that although Molly Bloom's letters are addressed to herself, they are inevitably addressed also to others. The particular flower at stake is again the narcissus, which turns out to be a daffodil, none other than the *narcissus pseudo-narcissus* that was discovered in one of our earlier chapters to be the emblem of Søren Kierkegaard. The much talked-of "secret of Hegel" may be none other than the secret of Kierkegaard, namely that the secrecy of his singularizing inwardness, no less than the publicity of Hegel's generalizing recollection-interiorization (*Erinnerung*), is that my singular I, no less than the impersonal It that thinks in me, has always already responded to a singular other. "Affirmation demands *a priori* the confirmation, repetition, minding (*garde*) and memory of the Yes."[19] We are reminded that this holds of Nietzsche when we encounter Derrida's reference to "the minimal *proposition,* equivalent anyway to *I will,* that manifests the hetero-tautology of the *yes* implied in every *cogito* as thought, self-position and will to self-position, equivalent anyway to the *I will.*"[20] Willy-nilly, whatever anyone wants to say, whatever one may mean or intend, one is bound to begin by responding to another. "Notwithstanding . . . the archi-narcissistic and self-affective appearance of this "yes-I," the "yes" is addressed to another and can only call upon the "yes" of the other. It begins by responding."[21]

What is "the minimal *proposition,* equivalent anyway to *I will*"? The italicized expressions go together. The minimal proposition is not a proposition in the sense of a proposition or statement that might be a premise or conclusion of an argument. The word has here its more common meaning of pro-posal, relating to what is pro-, before, any position or positing. That is why it is minimal. And it is here equated with the "I will," prior to my asserting what it is that I will. This "I will" is the *je veux dire,* where *vouloir dire* is to mean or is what is meant by a word or sentence. This being so, we have to return, as promised, to Derrida's statement "Hegel . . . is always right, as soon as one opens one's mouth in order to articulate meaning (*pour articuler le sens*)."

Crucial here is the final clause of this statement, the syntactically final clause "in order to articulate meaning." The open mouth is what Derrida would save from being saved by the Hegelian system. An analogue of it, we have already heard, is the "Hello" that prefaces a telephone conversation. Can this distinction be made? Is not the point of saying "Hello," like the point of signaling "AA" before going on to transmit the message, precisely that of indicating that one wishes to go on to articulate a meaning or message? Perhaps we should not be looking for a distinction here in the sense of a cut. Derrida's point may be that wherever there is such meaning or intending, a *vouloir dire* or *sagen wollen,* the intentionality of the intending is always accompanied by a non-intentional partner. This would be what Levinas sometimes and provisionally refers to as reversed intentionality. Derrida says that the non-intentional partner that always accompanies the meaning or intending that always accompanies every representation is the other whose countersignature is implied by my signature. On one occasion he says that there is a parallelism in this relation. But he reminds us that parallels meet. This is a meeting at infinity. The meeting-place is a long way off. But so too is every other. The infinity and its unfinishedness are "in" the meeting, but the other remains separate. The alternative geometry of the meeting of parallel lines in ethical space is one in which the lines cross chiasmically, each line proceeding in its own direction without there having been a full presence of the one to the other even at the point of intersection. This is the ghost of a meeting, like that between the ghosts in Wifred Owen's poem "Strange Meeting," where the scenario has the drama Levinas ascribes to the face-to-face encounter, for the one who is met tells me, "I am the enemy you killed, my friend." The meeting takes place in Hell, but according to Levinas and Derrida I kill my friend every day. For them too therefore, it could be said, though for a reason different from Sartre's, Hell is other people. What's more, since with Levinas the other persecutes me, since with Derrida the friend is not the direct opposite of the enemy, and since with both Levinas and Derrida the guest/host—*hôte* in its Abelian ambiguity—is a hostage, *otage,* they would be able to say not only with Sartre, *l'enfer c'est les autres,* but *l'enfer c'est autrui.* The Other's "Hello" spells hell.

As Derrida says so often, it is very complicated. And the word "complicated" is to be understood literally as referring to an overlapping of folds (*plis*), here the two Yeses that multiply into a manifold. In the above-mentioned essay entitled "*Nombres de oui*" he investigates the complications of the double Yes by way of comments on some paragraphs of Michel de Certeau's *La fable mystique.*[22] What is discovered in this investigation is that the overlap of Yeses is such that although de Certeau begins by distinguishing two Yeses, and thereby raises the question as to whether they have a single common root, the root is, to use Deleuze's metaphor, a proliferating rhizome. To use Derrida's own metaphor, the so-called original Yes disseminates itself. Origin or center becomes indistinguishable from periphery, to the point that counting becomes impossible. Whereas Hegel denies that calculation can play more than a minor role in philosophy because the logical system of No-saying is a system of inwardizing memory, Derrida says that the arithmetic of memory is dizzied by what exceeds memory.[23] What exceeds memory, and therefore exceeds countability, is accountability. What exceeds memory, he demonstrates in *Of Spirit,* is what exceeds the question, what Heidegger calls *Zu-sage* or *Zuspruch,* address, and what Derrida calls *engagement,* but in a sense more specific than the sense this word has for Sartre. For Derrida engagement is *l'en-gage* of *langage,* but of "*langage sans langage,*" he writes, because "it belongs without belonging to the ensemble that it institutes and at the same time opens."[24] "*Gage*" is quasi-Abelian. It connotes what is given as a security (*en gage*) in a wager, but the security is always at risk. The *en-gage* "exceeds and punctures (*troue*) the discourse (*langage*) to which it nevertheless remains immanent." By *langage* is meant the juncture of *langue* and *parole,* that is to say, the act of using the instituted system of a language.

But how, it is often asked, can a linguistic system ever get instituted in the first place if it is instituted by signing up to a contract? Does that not assume the existence of an already instituted language, and, if so, do we not have an infinite regress? The regress is not avoided by producing a psychological or otherwise naturalistic story to the effect that a linguistic system is generated by at first accidental repetitions of sounds or marks in certain contexts until a community finds itself with a common understanding. This story assumes that we already have the idea of resemblance among sounds, marks, and contexts. It also assumes that the scientific attitude is self-authenticating, that it does not feed on and arise out of the concrete pre-scientific ways of involvement described by phenomenology. But, of necessity and essentially, a certain Husserlian conception of phenomenology and essentiality has to be complicated with a non-phenomenology or redescribed phenomenology that queries the simple oppositions of necessity and contingency and essence and accident. For if these oppositions are not challenged nothing can be said about the complication of outwithness and inwithness where the engagement in a language engages with the engagement of address to a singular interlocutor or intersignatory. Picture a chain of propositions, for instance a syllogism. Now attempt to picture a chain not of propositions, things said, but of the addressings of each of these propositions and each of the words in them to a hearer. One can picture perhaps the facial expressions and bodily gestures that might indicate to which person the message is being addressed, but the addressing itself is unrepresentable. It is necessarily secret, not a secret that might be made public. What might be made public is what might belong to such a chain of forms or figures (*Gestalten*) as are unfolded in Hegel's *Phenomenology of Spirit.* What is necessarily secret— and, inspired by Kierkegaard, Derrida would say also sacred and religious—is the addressings that would be deemed contingent by the standard of Hegelian phenomenology and logic. These addressings continually interrupt the continuity of form and formality, binding what is said to a series of sayings now, past, and future through which the speakers make themselves responsible for what they say, not in the sense that they stand for ever by what they say, but in the sense that they stand by this or that hearer and are always ready to respond to criticism or the request for clarification. This is how Levinas understands coming to one's hearer's assistance as described by Plato in the dialogue *Phaedrus* (276–277), which, as a dialogue, itself performs what it describes. Levinas adds that what is being described there is what is implied in the "Yours sincerely" (*be-khavod*) at the end of a letter.

Derrida introduces the expression "*sériature*" to stand for the series of secret interruptions as contrasted with the series of public things said, where the latter may be what is said in an imperative, interrogative, or optative sentence no less than what is said in the indicative. *Sériature* or *séri-rature* or seri-erasure is the specter of Heideggerian erasure, the operation of superimposing a cross on the metaphysical term "being" in order to revive for it a non-metaphysical application. Also inherited from Heidegger here is the notion of what he calls *Verfallen,* the having fallen. This echoes the idea of original sin, but according to Heidegger it is more original than original sin. In Derrida's reworking of Heidegger it is taken over as the propensity of responsible saying to become institutionalized. This is why Nietzsche's Yes has to return eternally, lest repetition become calculably predictable. And this is why it would be salutary if the expression "deconstruction" were replaced. Derrida confesses that he first used it only in passing. He was taken by surprise at the way it caught on. He cannot simply turn his back on the ghost that has come back to haunt him. However, as new vehicles appear on the scene it is destined to be but one in a trail of discarded husks—differance, supplement, archi-writing, trace, *pharmakon,* hymen . . . deconstruction—like the trail of abandoned metaphors to which Nietzsche likened truth, like the transmogrifications of the vehicle in the dream or nightmare reported at the beginning of the last chapter.

To the vehicles reported at the end of the last paragraph have accrued the words "politics" and "democracy." To these we must finally turn if we are to explain why it can be said that what is being studied in this work at this moment is the trajectory from representation in a semantic or epistemic sense to representation in a sense that is religious or political. We have already explained in what senses the word "religious" is being used here. The religious is the secret hidden in the face-to-face relation between you and me as this is described by Levinas. We have learned with his assistance to begin there, rather than with Kierkegaard's relation with his God. No capital letters are called for, not even that of the name Messiah. It is this idea of a messianism without Messiah, Christ, or other Anointed that is the key to the notions of politics and democracy that recent events have led Derrida to want to save from Hegel. As so often, he is guided by Levinas, that other critic of Hegel. Before we learn how he is guided by Levinas in this matter, something more must be said about Hegel himself and his relationship to Nietzsche, keeping in mind

Derrida's remark that Levinas and Nietzsche are very close to and very distant from each other.

## Keeping the Secret of Hegel

Derrida gives us more than a summary of how things stand between Hegel and Nietzsche when he writes:

> Now, yes, Nietzsche, reader of Hegel, fine, and this is a classical title. Nietzsche is a reader of Hegel and a great critic of Hegel; all of Nietzsche's affirmations can be interpreted as anti-Hegelian affirmations. Now evidently, as always, it will be agreed, when one has an adversary who is great, and Hegel is the great adversary of Nietzsche, there are times when there is a high degree of resemblance between the adversaries. It can be shown easily. There is a dialectic in Nietzsche, a Hegelianism.[25]

Is there also in Hegel a certain Nietzscheanism, and, if so, what name could be put to it? "Dialectic" again? This word occurs frequently in the pages of Derrida's first work, the dissertation of 1953–1954 on *The Problem of Genesis in the Philosophy of Husserl*, which was not published until 1990, and then only under pressure from his colleagues.[26] In the apology for publishing it Derrida apologizes in particular for overusing the term "dialectic" in discussing the effect of contamination he holds is produced with such pairs as transcendental/worldly, eidetic/empirical, intentional/non-intentional, active/passive, present/non-present, punctual/non-punctual, original/derived, pure/impure. He notes that in his introduction to Husserl's *The Origin of Geometry* of 1962 and in *Speech and Phenomena* of 1967 the word is not used except of that without which he wishes us to try to interpret *différance*, "supplement of origin" and "trace." And in the essay entitled *"Différance"* delivered as a lecture in 1968 he writes in paragraphs alluding to Nietzsche's Yes: "From the vantage of this laughter and this dance, from the vantage of this affirmation foreign to all dialectics, the other side of nostalgia, what I shall call Heideggerian *hope* comes into question."[27] What he calls Heideggerian hope is the hope for the finally proper name or name of the name, albeit Being or God. "Differance" is the unname for the disappointment of this hope—unless we want to say that what it re-presents or de-presents is God, whose power, anyway, was always in his apartness, as Levinas insists and as is emphasized by Luther, the theologian from whose writings savings are made in the writings of several of the thinkers—Hegel, Kierkegaard, Nietzsche, Heidegger—that have been reread in the chapters of this book.

Into "differance" is woven a thread that can be traced back to Nietzsche and Freud, and it can be used as a guide to how Derrida sees the relation between Nietzsche and Hegel. Derrida writes, with reference to what Freud says about trace (*Spur*) and inscription (or subscription, *Niederschrift*), "all the oppositions that furrow Freudian thought relate each of his concepts one to another as moments of a detour in the economy of *différance*."[28] What he goes on to say about these Freudian oppositions may be said about the opposition between Nietzsche and Hegel: "One is but the other different and deferred, one differing and deferring the other. One is the other in *différance*, one is the *différance* of the other," where the genitive is once again double. This means that in one sense there is nothing to choose between Hegel and Nietzsche. In another sense, historically and politically, which of them we choose is far from indifferent. There is nothing to choose between them in the sense that singularities are not denied in the system of Hegel. They in their plurality are only said to be outside the system and unessential for philosophy and its singular totality. This is almost precisely what Levinas says. The Other is outside the system ethically speaking according to him, as, according to one mainstream theological tradition, God transcends His cosmos. Hegel does not deny the immediate data of consciousness. He simply maintains that the contingent singulars given to consciousness and taken by the proponent of sense-certainty to be the stuff of reality are not of concern to philosophy. Philosophy purports to offer an account of reality under which all accounts offered by the empirical and mathematical sciences may be subsumed. If the proponent of sense-certainty purports to be offering such an account, he or she must argue the case orally or in writing. But as soon as one accepts Hegel's invitation to write down the word "This" that is supposed to name the essence of reality one will find that generality is on the scene, since this demonstrative pronoun is a "shifter"; it is essential to its logic that it can be used of different things. The same holds for the first personal pronoun "I," in case it be said that it denotes the essence of reality. Once any mark or sound denotes an essence immediacy is lost. So a philosophy of sense- or self-certainty is a contradiction in terms. This is what Hegel means when he says "What is rational is actual and what is actual is rational."[29] If this principle is confirmed by "This" and "I" it is confirmed also by the pronouns "other," "*autre*," and "Other," "*Autrui*," however much one may hope to save the status of a proper name for the latter by writing it with a capital initial. One has written it down, and thereby admitted it to the system of language and *logos*.

In the preface to the *Philosophy of Right* Hegel charges Fichte with "meddling with things to which philosophy is unsuited" when he "carried what has been called the 'construction' (*konstruiren*) of his passport regulations to such a pitch of perfection as to require suspects not merely to sign their passports but to have their likenesses painted on them. Along such tracks all trace (*Spur*) of philosophy is lost."[30] Does this mean that he would say the same to Levinas and Derrida? If so, would they reply that in Hegel's philosophy all trace of the trace is lost, all trace of the trace that is not a sign but the trace of such a face as

Fichte wanted to have represented on the passport? The face is unrepresentable, so unrepresentable in Hegel's philosophy. On this Hegel and Levinas agree. So what is the difference between them? Despite Levinas's wish to speak "Greek" in *Totality and Infinity* and in *Otherwise than Being or Beyond Essence,* the second of these titles makes it plain that he thinks that something important is lost in the essentialism of Hegelianism. Hegel can agree that there is something beyond essence that is important. What he cannot agree is that because something is beyond essence or otherwise than being it is entirely lost. It is saved by being made essential, by being elevated into essence and being thereby brought into the reach of philosophy. When this happens it becomes important for philosophy. Therefore what Levinas and Derrida must be understood to be saying is that Hegelian philosophy overlooks something that is important even though it is otherwise than being (the topic of the first subdivision of Hegel's logic), and beyond essence (the topic of the second subdivision of Hegel's logic) and conceptuality and philosophy defined as love of wisdom (the third subdivision of Hegel's logic). This, which Levinas calls wisdom of love, is important, whether or not it is part of philosophy. Whether it is also important as a part of philosophy is for Levinas and Derrida not the most important question. But by questioning an over-simple understanding of the distinction between inside and outside and the relation of parts to wholes they open the question whether philosophy as defined by Hegel is as purely rational in his sense of rationality as Hegel supposes. It may be "contaminated" (Derrida) and "disturbed" (Levinas) by something otherwise than being or ontology and beyond essence and the concept (Hegel and Heidegger). Levinas, who says that the whole of philosophy may be regarded as a meditation on Shakespeare,[31] might have said also that this something is something that is more than is dreamt of in the philosophy of Hegel and Heidegger. It would be a mistake to suppose that the difference is a purely semantic one about the definition of philosophy. The "more" (*plus*) which is also a less (*plus de*) than philosophy as conceived by Hegel is non-semantic. And it is not purely semantic considerations that lead Derrida and Levinas to question the idea of philosophy as concerned purely with semantic representation. Hegel himself questions this when he demonstrates that when philosophy fulfils itself it transcends representation, including the residual representations embodied in the imagery and metaphors that cling to revealed religion.

## Politics, Singularity, and Singularities

Levinas maintains that philosophy is first of all ethics. Aristotle sees the ethical as a part of the political. But even if Levinas agreed with Aristotle about this, it would not follow that he would agree that politics includes the ethical in the sense that goes back and reaches forward to the singular event of one human being faced with another. Politics, as commonly understood, has to do not with faces but with cases. As such, it could include ethics, but only the ethics of generality, the ethics of Hegel as Kierkegaard for example understands it, and perhaps as Nietzsche understands it when he refers to the ethics of the herd, the ethics of democracy. How we interpret Levinas's thoughts on the relation of the ethical to the political will turn on how we understand the title of his essay *"Politique après."* After what? And what does he mean by "politics" and "the political"? Of Sadat's journey to Jerusalem in 1977, which led to peace between Israel and Egypt, Levinas says that although it may have seemed weak "politically" (his quotation marks), it may have been a manifestation of strength in that it expressed the priority of an ethical peace over "purely political thought."[32] Purely political thought is bracketed with "Hegelian totality," and both are condemned for the undiluted respect they manifest for a universalism of neuter impersonal principles. For the purpose of understanding how Levinas's conception of the political relates to Derrida's it is noteworthy that it is in an essay entitled *"Signatures"* that Levinas pronounces this double condemnation and that it is in what he calls "Messianic texts" that the total universality he refers to as universality in the logical sense of the term is contrasted with a "universalist particularism." The universality of universalist particularism is contrasted with the "catholic" universality of Aristotelian logic and the concrete universality of Hegel. The particularism of universalist particularism consists in its being an ethics in the first place for a particular people, Israel, elected to be of service to the universe.[33] But this messianism of a people is exemplary for the ethicality of people. That is why it is exemplary for the universe, why it is both universalist and particularist, or perhaps one should say singularist, since the term "particular" is used in classical logic for a case falling under an abstract universal.

What Derrida calls messianism without Messiah would be a democracy of the future and a new cosmopolitics. It would be a politics that breaches the limits of any particular instituted city (*polis*), country, or continent. It would breach even the limits of instituted international law. It would breach these by keeping the institution in touch with instituting, that is to say with the performance of inauguration where there is as yet no instituted law and where pragmatic politics of the nation or state becomes ethical by remembering that *tout autre est tout autre*, every other is totally other. That is to say, cosmopolitics detotalizes totality by keeping itself open to whatsoever and whomsoever may arrive. It affirms the necessity of unfinishedness, the *infini*. Messianic cosmopolitics welcomes the unpredictable. Its citizens represent strangers ethico-politically in that they find themselves held responsible toward them without having reduced their strangeness by capturing them inside categories. This is another way of saying that the strangers' secrecy is respected, and this is another way of saying that the ethico-political is religious.

Although as a citizen of a democracy I elect representatives to their political stations and duties, I do not thereby shuffle off the direct and absolute responsibility to which I am elected, albeit by no institution and according to no constitutional law. The unimaginable democracy that Derrida tries to imagine is a democracy of subjects subjected to two laws that are in contradiction with each other, but not a contradiction that can be overcome dialectically by negation. Remembering the distinctions made in chapter 1 between the Kantian and Hegelian conceptions of border, we may say that the border between the two laws distinguished by Derrida is both one that cannot be crossed and one that has to be crossed. We may say that the law of the border between these laws is mad: it is a law we can at best imadgine. And yet it is as familiar as anything could be. Tragically familiar, unless the tragic is conceived as it is conceived by Kierkegaard, as a situation in which a conflict of principles is resoluble by giving priority to one of them or by mediating them in a third. The familiarity is that with which we have already become familiar in reflecting on Levinas's reminder that looking at me in your eyes are the other others to whose assistance I am prevented from coming by my coming to yours. Otherwise said, each he and she is at the same time a you. As Derrida says, every other is completely other, *tout autre est tout autre.*

How does this tragic or worse-than-tragic familiar dilemma get us further than the ethical? How does it get us to the political? It gets us to the political via the concept of democracy. And, paradoxically, it gets us there on Derrida's concept of democracy via the concept of friendship. In French, the intimate friend is he or she to whom we say *Toi.* But an admired and respected friend may be addressed as *Vous,* You. Now it may well be, as Aristotle maintains, that such friends cannot be numerous. He gives no number. And it would be disrespectful to count one's friends.

I am myself a representative, but not in a kingdom of ends defined solely by the moral law which effaces the face in representing it as a case. The representation of my still being a representative is ethico-political—and, we have been arguing, it is religious in a sense that is not defined in terms of religions. But representation understood ethico-politico-religiously suffers the same dissolution as does representation founded on semantic presence. Representation understood as my being responsible for another is inevitably irresponsible. For, as has been repeated many times in the pages of this book, following Levinas and Derrida, my responding to one person means a failure to respond to many others to whom I am equally responsible in advance of specific moral laws. And I must be in advance of any specific moral laws, that is to say, I must be irresponsible, if I am responsible absolutely, that is to say, responsible in a sense not defined in relation to "my station and its duties."

What has been going on in this work and in the works that have been reread throughout it is an ethical rethinking of the epistemological difficulty Husserl failed to resolve in the fifth Cartesian Meditation or elsewhere over how I can come to know that another human being experiences consciousness of presence to himself or herself as I myself seem to experience presence to myself. Already in his earliest publications Derrida calls into question the idea of pure presence in Husserl's own terms. Presence is destabilized when its simple opposition to absence is called into question as the simple opposition of speaking to writing is called into question and shown to be quasi-conditioned by archi-writing.

Similarly, the Hegelian idea of the presence of thinking to itself in absolute wisdom dissolves once that idea is addressed to someone, as certainly as the validity of the claim made by the proponent of sense-certainty dissolves precisely because it is a claim. This becomes evident once he or she accepts Hegel's invitation to write down the word "this" or "now" or "here" or "I." The demonstration that claiming and thinking, even the thinking to oneself expressed as "me-thinks," brings in mediation is contemporaneous with the demonstration that mediation is interrupted by address. This law of law-breaking is the law that makes law. And, in its double genitivity, it holds for the claims and the thinking of thinking put into words by the proponent of absolute wisdom addressed in the first section of the first chapter of this book.

# PART THREE

# THIRTEEN

Oversights

## Helping Hands

It was at the meeting of the Collegium Phaenomenologicum at Città di Castello in the summer of 2003 that some of us learned that Derrida was seriously ill. In the Museo del Duomo in that town hangs Pinturicchio's "Madonna with Child and Saint John." On a card reproducing a photograph of this painting which I sent to Derrida I drew his attention to "the unbelievable play of their hands":[1] the way the positions of the fingers and thumb of the Virgin's left hand, with the thumb and the little finger stretched out from the other three fingers like the arms of a crucifix, match those of the fingers of the crossed hands of Saint John clasping the Bible to his chest. Her first three fingers are grouped together in order to symbolize the Holy Trinity. The Son holds up only the first and second finger, He Himself being the Signifier and Signified of the third member of the Trinity. I also pointed to the way she, handmaiden, *doulē, ancilla, Magd, servante* of him who "hath holpen his servant Israel: as he promised to our forefathers, Abraham and his seed, for ever," is helping her son to hold up his right hand as with it he makes the sign of blessing over the head of Saint John, toward which his gaze is directed. Her gaze too is directed toward the saint's head, but by way of the hand that she, *main tenant*, is assisting her son to hold up. A mutual aid society? At least a family scene in which each member helps each other directly or indirectly. But can this aid be mutual, given that the family has a head? Hierarchy need not mean that the father can receive no help from those under his direction. Even a father can cry, "Help." Help might be forthcoming even from the direction of the so far unmentioned Gentiles. And it is to questions of direction, directness, indirection, and drawing attention that are directed the words I am directing to you now, *maintenant.*

The names of two of the Gentiles just mentioned are also mentioned in the picture of a scene that the scene in Pinturicchio's picture calls up. Another Pinturicchio Mother and Child hangs in the Ashmolean Museum in Oxford. Walking east from that building, along the frontages of Balliol and Trinity colleges, you pass the spot where an archbishop of Canterbury who had a hand in composing the Book of Common Prayer held that hand out into the flames that were about to consume him. You come then to the Bodleian Library. One of the manuscripts in that library is Matthew Paris's *The Prognostics of Socrates the King.* This is the fortune-telling book the frontispiece of which is reproduced on the cover of Derrida's *The Post Card* and on postcards sold at the Library shop. We read in the latter book that at least one correspondent who contributes to it purchased a pile of those cards.[2] One of these cards, its picture facing us, can be seen in the photograph on page 15 of *Jacques Derrida,* comprising *Derridabase* and *Circonfessions,* attributed respectively to Geoffrey Bennington and Jacques Derrida.[3] In the photograph Derrida is shown seated at the computer in his study at his home at Ris-Orangis with Geoff Bennington standing behind him and pointing toward the screen. In the picture reproducing Matthew Paris's illustration Plato stands behind a seated Socrates who writes, contrary to the legend subscribed to by Nietzsche that Socrates never wrote a word. Socrates writes apparently according to the directions of Plato, whose left hand is stretched out so that Socrates can see it with its pointer-finger raised in *hodegetria:* "He is showing the direction."[4] With the pointer-finger of his right hand Plato seems to be prodding Socrates in the back as though he wishes either to add emphasis to what he wants Socrates to write down or to get him to turn around and look him in the face. Plato is alarmed. His eyes bulge and his brow is wrinkled. Socrates' eyes are fully concentrated on the task of charging his stylus with ink. His lips are sealed. Plato's mouth is open, as though he is struck by wonder at what he is saying—that wonder, *thaumazein,* with which he says philosophy begins—or else simply wondering what he should say. Socrates' left foot is supported by the step that forms part of the chair. His other foot rests on a protruding boss that forms part of the leg of the writing-table, his *secrétaire.* Plato is represented as considerably shorter than Socrates. The two of them are designated in some of the missives of *The Post Card* by P or p and S, the symbols used in the predicative proposition in traditional formal logic: S is p. S has his left foot on the back of the chair's platform. So neither Plato nor Socrates has both his feet firmly planted on the ground.

## Secrecies

Leaving open the question of the identity of a scabbard-shaped object that cuts across Socrates' right leg, there can be no doubt that the two personages represented in this philosophical scene set by Matthew Paris are as rapt as are those in the holy scene represented by Pinturicchio. This may be because Plato is transmitting to Socrates an esoteric doctrine, something intended for the eyes and ears only of the initiated, something relatively secret. But it is absolute secrecy that is the topic of the missives in *The Post Card*, the "a-b-s-o-l-u-t-e secrecy"[5] of the *topos* and of *chōra* that are topics also of the *Timaeus,* which may be the work Matthew Paris's picture shows Plato dictating. In the *envoi* to *Envois* that is distinguished from all the other *envois* in *The Post Card* by being signed by Derrida, Derrida says "it is always bad to foretell."[6] "It is bad, reader, no longer to like retracing one's steps." This is bad, reader, not because to retrace one's steps is to go back to a program. It is bad because it supposes that there is a program from which one wishes not to diverge: "[T]his program is indirectly in question throughout this work."[7] The program of the program as such is in question, the program according to which a rule lays down in advance as rigidly as a piston-rod what counts as following it, a question on which Wittgenstein has much to say.[8] One thing I take him to say is that we are not riveted to one way of continuing a series of numerals when we apply a rule, for example the rule "+ 1." If this rule is applied to the series 1, 2, 3, 4 . . . we would expect the next unit to be 5. But the rule "+ 1" would not prohibit a continuation in which the units we are required to add are, say, the squares of each of these numbers, then the squares of these squares, then the squares of those, etcetera. What counts as applying the rule correctly and what counts as a correct interpretation of "etcetera" will turn on actual practice and the pragmatic point of that practice. But the possibility of alternative practices cannot be ruled out. So we shall have to revise our picture of the rigidity of the piston-rod and of the mustness of the logical "must." This will not abolish the distinction between calculation and thinking, but it will prevent our exaggerating, as perhaps Derrida does, the degree of determinacy we attribute to calculation and the way in which what is calculated is pre-programmed.

Derrida says that he can foretell the reactions there will be to his saying that he had ("I swear") forgotten a certain rule he had proposed to follow for the layout of the fragments and the spaces between them. Does his saying that he can foretell this, prognosticate it, that he knows it in advance, make Derrida a bad reader of himself? It tells us that more than one reading can be given of reading and that more than one story can be told about foretelling. What it does not tell us is that dispensing with the rigid piston-rod interpretation means dispensing with all rational control. Dispensing with the piston-rod interpretation does not mean dispensing with the dispensation of law. What it means is that the rule of law is not the rule of calculation, and that there is an undecidability beyond the undecidabilities that may arise in the field of arithmetic, such as those brought to our attention by Gödel referred to in the paper by Quine on the limits of logical theory that Derrida had a hand in translating for the 1964 number of *Les Études Philosophiques*. We could think of this undecidability beyond the limits of logical theory as the undecidability faced by Kierkegaard faced by his Maker, the undecidability not of Gödel, but the undecidability of God. Now not even the so-called subjective thinking of Kierkegaard was withdrawn into a secrecy safe from the law. Without the law, the commandments, there would be no paradox, and without paradox there would be no so-called mad subjectivity, no subjectivity called upon as Abraham was called upon by God.

What is the secrecy that interests Derrida? In seeking an answer to this question it needs to be remembered that his use of this word "interests" goes along with an interest in the fact that old words, paleonyms, do not remain old and that their paleonymity is not simply opposed to neonymity. The secrecy that interests Derrida beyond the scope of benefit, beyond good and evil, is not the secrecy of the esoteric as opposed to the exoteric. One could risk saying that it is the secrecy of the anateric, with ana- having the sense of retro- and re-. Another Abraham, Nicolas Abraham, posits various "anasemic" notions, for instance Pleasure as probably intended by Freud, in contrast to "pleasure" as described noetico-noematically in phenomenology, and to pleasure as experienced in everyday life. Another example of anasemia would be Sex as distinguished from "sex" as described by phenomenology and from sex as understood commonly without the distinction of a capital letter or the protection of scare-quotes. On analogy with these examples one might posit an anasemic notion of the Secret. This would be prior to phenomenological "secrecy." One might think of it as corresponding with the concealment without which there is of necessity no unconcealment according to the phenomenological ontology of Heidegger. The third notion of secrecy would be secrecy as exemplified by the contingent secrecy of an esoteric Platonic doctrine such as may be on the lips of Plato in the Matthew Paris picture, and perhaps by the esoteric doctrine of the Christian Trinity such as Pinturicchio depicts. However, if the capitalized Secrecy that interests Derrida is anasemic, it is not this in the way in which Nicolas Abraham uses the word in *L'écorce et le noyau* to designate a nucleus for which there is no sign (*sēma*) that is neutral as between simple opposites.[9] To use the word in that way is to go back to something like the etymal root for which Heidegger sometimes expresses a love, but of which Derrida expresses suspicion, a suspicion he acknowledges Heidegger himself betrays in some places. Derrida expresses suspicion of this because he is aware of the risk threatened by a certain conception of a ground on which one supposes one can have a firm foothold, a *terra firma* that saves one from the risk of falling, albeit also from the chance of rising up. So the secrecy that moves Derrida to write *Envois* is not the secrecy of "a clever cryptogram" whose code could with ingenuity be cracked. Nor is it the secrecy of the secret the readers of *Envois* might wish to be let into as to who are the senders and intended recipients of the missives. What interests Derrida is the missability of these missives. Not just that they may miss their mark, but that the mark is marked by missability. And the missability is marked also by femininity at least as regards *la destinataire,* though the femininity invoked when this is said is not the femininity that is simply opposed to masculinity. The contexts implicit in this cartography of destinations are those of the question "What if truth were a woman?" posed by Nietzsche in *Beyond Good and Evil,* and the remarks he makes about woman in *The Will to Power* cited above in chapter 7.

At the end of the colloquium that took place at Cerisy in 1972, after the delivery of the talk to be published under the titles *Éperons* and *Spurs* and in response to a (female) questioner who had asked him whether one of the suggestions made in his talk was that philosophy might be done in a feminine way, Derrida responded as follows: "I said 'the woman [wife] (of) Nietzsche' ['*la femme (de) Nietzsche*'], 'Nietzsche's woman' [*la 'femme Nietzsche*']: at the point where he affirms, at the instant where he finds himself loving the affirmative woman, he writes, if one may so put it, 'with the hand of a woman.'"[10] Then, in case the question had been intended as a personal one, he adds: "I should like to write, also, like (a) woman." That is followed by "I try . . . ," but the record of the discussion stops there. I do not recall if the oral discussion continued beyond that ellipsis. It was, however, resumed seven years later at Montreal, when after giving his talk "*Otobiographie de Nietzsche*" he spoke of the importance of the affirmation that is ceaselessly reaffirmed, "yes, yes," in the eternal return, in the covenant or (double) binding (*alliance*), in the hymen.[11] Referring to the question at the end of the report of the meeting at Cerisy in 1972, he reaffirms, "[Y]es, I should like to write, I don't say I shall write, but that I should like to write with the hand of a woman."[12] How could he do that? He could do that if when he writes autobiographically he writes heterobiographically somewhat in the sense of "heterosexually": in the sense that although woman is the addressee, *la destinataire,* she is not necessarily the recipient as construed in the familiar story of woman's receptivity contrasted simply with the activity and mastery of man. In writing his autobiography it is the male JD who is the *destinateur* and may be the signer, but the woman countersigns. The familiar story should be corrected, Derrida observes, "*il faudrait corriger la chose.*"[13] In response to Heidegger's description of Dasein as sexually neutral, Derrida resexualizes philosophical discourse,[14] rewriting in the lower case the capital initial of the feminine word "*Chose*" that nevertheless with an upper-case initial could stand for the phallogocentric Thing of psychoanalysis of which Derrida is provoked to write by Lacan, or for the transcendent Thing-in-itself behind the scenes from belief in which Nietzsche wishes to seduce us.

Such a correction by substitution of the minuscule letter for the majuscule is anticipated when Nietzsche says in *The Will to Power* that woman rules or masters, *herrscht*. We saw that he emphasizes this masculine verb.[15] But he does not do this in order to arrive at a unisexual onefoldness. Derrida elaborates on the twofoldness in Nietzsche's writing of woman by interlacing mastery with a listening out for the other in which power is the power of hearing. So that autobiography is otobiography and autobiography of (the) woman, in the sense of writing about her own life, of her writing the life about which she writes, and of writing's auto-archi-writing. In the polygraphy of *Envois* what is sent is sent to (a) you, (a) *toi*, who is a she, *elle*, a she who provokes, not to say persecutes, the sender. It is as though Derrida is here thinking of Levinas's description of the feminine as the first manifestation of the other.[16] Autoaffection is affected by heteroaffection. This is because she who is called the addressee and *destinataire* in the traditional postal opposition of *destinataire-destinateur* and in the over-simple conception of the structure sending-receiving-directing writes at the same time as what is traditionally called the author. She "lends me a hand." She is my hand-maiden, my *ancilla,* but the hands are so crossed that there is no straightforward answer to the question "Who is writing?" Nor is there a determinable answer to the question "What is the gender of this 'who'?" This is because when Derrida writes, "I should like to write, also, like (a) woman," "*J'aimerais bien écrire, aussi, comme (une) femme,*" he is not imagining a change of biological sex. He is imagining rather a change in our concept of sexuality, a change from the concept to what is not strictly a concept or a word but is that without which there can be no concept or word. This alteration would be a shift like that from the conception of writing as the opposite of speech to writing as archi-writing operative in both. In this shift it is discovered that while writing has been considered since Plato/Socrates to be the inferior partner, it is writing that wears the trousers. Similarly, woman is discovered to wear the trousers once she is rethought as the archi-femininity without which the usual opposition of the feminine and the masculine could not be made. Derrida would like to write also like a woman, where the "also" has the force of "like Nietzsche," but may also have the force of "without ceasing to write like a man." However, if archi-femininity is related to femininity as archi-writing is related to writing, is he not already writing like a woman? He is and he is not. Once the conceit of archi-femininity has struck us, we, whether man or woman, can say in the indicative mood that we are writing like a woman. But if one is addressing someone who may not yet have been struck by this conceit, one for whom the feminine and the masculine are still understood as simple opposites, as they are of course for Derrida in his everyday use of these terms, one has to speak in the subjunctive or optative mood.

When in his reading of the writings of the "misogynist" Nietzsche Derrida emphasizes that affirmation is the appending of one's signature, *firma,* and when he brings out the complexity of the affirmation of fate made in *amor fati,* that is to say the love of the said (recall again that "*fatum*" comes from "*fari,*" to speak), it is not easy to answer the questions "Who is writing and to whom?" For example, in the light of Matthew Paris's reversal of the familiar story, it is not easy to answer these questions when they are asked about the pair Plato and Socrates, the second of whom, it will have been noted, writes in Paris's picture with two hands: writes and unwrites and writes again, for while in his right hand he holds a stylus, in his left hand he holds a scraper with which to efface what he has just written.

> Who is writing? To whom? And to send, to destine, to despatch what? To what address? Without any desire to surprise, and thereby to grab attention by means of obscurity, I owe it to whatever remains of my honesty to say finally that I do not know. Above all I would not have had the slightest interest in this correspondence and this cutting out (*découpage*), I mean in their publication, if some certainty on this matter had satisfied me.[17]

Here—where, as with Socrates, there is obliteration, deletion, cutting out, un-publication, secretarial secrecy—we cannot be satisfied by the discourse of knowledge, certainty, and satisfaction. Something more and less than knowl-edge, certainty, and satisfaction cuts across this discourse where the non-formal form of address is *toi.* It is as though the *elle* addressed in this *toi* corresponds with and to the *il* who takes the responsibility of writing, but in such a way that she shares that responsibility. Her participation is logically constitutive of the responsibility, not merely chronologically prior; but not without reference to time, and logically constitutive in a way that interrupts logic and constitution as understood in formal or transcendental or dialectical logic. The reference to time was made when it was observed that the addressee writes at the same time as the writer. The logic of this simultaneity is represented graphically in the spaces between the missives published in *The Post Card.* These gaps mark what is unpublished, cut out, and burned. But they may be regarded as graphic representations too not only of parts of what might have been a longer message. They may be seen as representations of the unrepresentable event of addressing any message. In the layout of *The Post Card* Derrida is attempting to picture the complex logic of what he calls *sériature* in "*En ce moment même dans cet ouvrage me voici...,*" "At this very moment in this work here I am...," an essay on Levinas from one of whose works the words of the title of Derrida's essay are taken.[18] In *The Post Card* the blanks assume the importance of things left unsaid that might have been said. And they stand for bits that are cut out, excised, circumcised. We saw that the word Derrida uses for this operation is *découpage*. This could be translated as dis-cutting, a setting aside of what in "*En ce moment même...*" is called the *logique de la coupure*.[19] The kind of interruption effected by that logic of classificatory inclusion and exclusion is not the interruption that interests him in the texts of Levinas. The interruption that interests him there is that for which appeal has to be made to a logic of ab-solute de-stricturation. This phrase (*dé-stricturation ab-solue*) is almost pleonastic, for ab-solution is already untying. But of what and from what is it an untying? It is an untying from obligation defined in terms of a particular law, for instance a law marked by circumcision or a cross or a crescent. It unbinds the bonds of a particular dogmatic creed in response to the obligation of religion without dogma. The religiousness of *religio* thus understood is a religiousness of credence as such, credit due to whosoever is addressed: faith, fidelity, in addressing the other, *toi*. If this faith is called faithfulness, it is important to observe that the fullness of faithfulness is qualified by the risk implied in faith, which, like decision, falls short of plenitude of presence. The logic of this addressing is not the logic of safe presence. And it is not simply the logic of what is said (*fatum*). It is the logic or "logic" of the performance of saying. Likewise, the secrecy that interests Derrida is not that of information kept, but the absolute secret that maybe there is no such secret at issue. The secrecy in question, before the question that might have an answer, is the absolute secrecy of correspondence as such, of co-respondence, response and responsibility.

The response and responsibility is not limited to the *dramatis personae* of this correspondence. We, the readers, are told that the signers and addressees may not be the same from one message to another—any more than from one work to another attributed to Kierkegaard—and that the signers are not necessarily the senders, and the addressees are not necessarily the receivers. The secretarial secret of this "private" exchange is an open secret, a very open secret, openness itself. It is openness especially to a future and to a past that are ab-solved from all presence but inscribed in each other in this very same moment, *ce moment même,* which therefore can itself never be pure presence, never an itself at one with itself at one and the very same time, *hama*. Yet this open secret keeps its secrecy. Have we not learned from Poe the secret that the best way to keep a secret is to post it on the mantelpiece or somewhere else in public view?[20]

## *Prego*

Such are Derrida's prolegomena for any religiousness of the future that would not be the religiousness of a particular dogmatic religion. Such was the subject of my talk at Città. My handwriting is small enough for me to have been able to add to what I had said on the card mailed from there to Ris-Orangis that I was embarrassed to think that this attempt to find room for a religiousness without the God of any dogmatic religion appeared to deprive me of an addressee for a petitionary prayer I should like to have been able to make on behalf of the card's addressee, about whose illness I had just been informed.

I mentioned my predicament, when I was back in Edinburgh, to the retired bishop of this diocese, Richard Holloway. My predicament turns on diversion, as what I wrote on my card and what is written in *The Post Card* turn on direction and indirection of address, on the way in which missives are marked by the possibility of missing the mark, and on how the forwarding of epistles—whether to Hebrews, Romans, Corinthians, Galatians, or other foreigners (Gauls, Gaels, or Welsh)—cannot be comprehensively overseen even by persons within the scope of whose duties falls overseeing, *episkopē*. Furthermore, this bishop had been caught up in an intrigue of forwardings occasioned by his citing as an epigraph of one of his books, one dedicated to Archbishop Desmond Tutu, Derrida's words "There is only forgiveness, if there is any, where there is the unforgivable."[21] My sending a copy of this book to Derrida led to a more or less indirect correspondence between its author, his publisher, Derrida, and myself. Whether the Panoptical Author was involved remains to be seen, or not. And precisely this "or not" is what gave rise to the predicament that led me to ask Richard Holloway to amplify a passing remark about godless prayer that he had once made to me after a meal at which one topic that had come up in our conversation was a certain meal with Derrida that had not taken place.[22] He responded:

> I think prayer . . . does not have to be directed at a real god whose aid one is soliciting, though that is usually what intercessory prayer is held to be. Godless prayer would be a sort of directed intentionality of love and regard towards the person prayed for. . . . Kathleen Jamie in her wonderful book, *Findings,* talks about paying attention, often minute attention, to what's going on around us in the natural world, and I like that, and I try to do it. But you can also be paying attention to people, by listening deeply, having regard to them, and not just skiting off the surface. Attention and regard, these are the key words.[23]

I like that. And I do not want to skite off its surface. I shall return to some of the words it contains. For instance to "attention," a word highly prized by Simone Weil, whose works Derrida and my classmates in the 1950s were reading. Levinas too, despite the severity of the reservations he has with respect to some of the things Weil says, must have welcomed her love of the word "attention" as it is overheard in one of her titles, *L'attente de Dieu,* with the bidirectionality and "reversed intentionality" (Levinas) or in-vention (Derrida) of the waiting referred to. And to link attention with regard is to link it to the moral sense of regard, the sense regard has as moral sense, *sens,* direction, listening and looking, looking out for.[24] To regard regarding thus is to take a leaf out of Plato's book at least insofar as to read a book or an icon is both to wait for assistance from the writer or artist and to expose oneself to the risk of being moved by what painters and sculptors say they are moved by when they call that their motif.

Allow me now to look for assistance to another archbishop of Canterbury, holder of an office than which in the hierarchy of the Anglican church you cannot look very much higher. Let us consider another *objet d'art* or, rather, a work of art that resists being turned into an object, one of the icons studied by Rowan Williams in his book *Ponder These Things.*[25] The icon in question is one of the family called the Hodegetria, "the one that points the way." One reason why this icon is the one in question is that it seems not to illustrate what the archbishop says about what he refers to as "most versions" of the Hodegetria. He says that in most versions of this directive icon the son's eyes are on the mother and that the son sometimes has a hand raised in blessing. The son has his hand raised in blessing in the Russian icon Rowan Williams selects to represent the direction-pointing family, but in this icon the son's eyes are not on the mother. It is as though Rowan Williams chooses this one in order to draw out the point that the representatives of each of the three "families" to which he confines his comments have "countless variants." The chosen example of the directive family is the seventeenth-century Russian Tichvine Mother of God in the icon museum at Recklinghausen. In this icon the child's eyes are directed not to anything pictured but to something outside the icon's frame, something parergonal, albeit in the same direction as the direction of his blessing. The child's eyes and his blessing have no single object. They are directed to nothing that could be an object, nothing that could figure as an object in an *objet d'art.* It would be nearer to the truth told to us in this painting to say that the eyes and the gesture are directed at a singular subject or a manifold of such subjects, each one each time unique, *chaque fois unique.* Now the mother in this painting is in pain. She is looking ahead to the child's death. Her eyes are not on us who are looking at her, any more than are the eyes of the child. But they could be on those who are other than us, those who are out of the frame, out of the picture, and because the child is frowning we could say that he is pondering their and his own and your and my rapidly oncoming death.

However, as Bishop Kallistos Ware writes in his foreword to *Ponder These Things,* "We do more than just look at icons or talk about them; we *pray* with them." Now there are as many varieties of prayer as there are varieties of icon. But would an icon have helped me through the seeming impasse I found myself in when in my talk at Città I tried to keep God out of the picture and seemed thereby to prevent myself sending that intercessory-petitionary prayer into the air asking (asking of whom or of what?) that Derrida be returned to good health? Might the Pinturicchio painting have helped in this way? God's ways of working are mysterious, we are told. That does not mean that they are magical. And it may have been as work of magic that I was conceiving petitionary praying. I must have been conceiving it in terms of the possibly unique bearer of a capitalized proper name, for it was precisely my seeking to be rid of such a bearer that seemed to me to conflict with my seeking to lodge a petitionary prayer. It would have been, it seemed to me, a *petitio principii*. One might suppose that I was wanting to take sides with those Gentiles in the picture by Matthew Paris, where Plato's name is spelled with a lower-case p.

One might wonder whether Derrida himself could have come to my aid in my attempt to come to his. Was it not part of his life's work to chart the no-man's land or every-woman's land between proper names or proper pronouns such as figure in dogmatic religions and the common names they cannot avoid becoming, but to insist that this generalizing postal effect of demajusculation does not conflict with each finite or infinite bearer of a name being *chaque fois singulier, chaque foi(s) unique*? For that singularity comes when, as we expressed it earlier (thinking of the poet who wrote a series of poems he called *Tombeaux*, but who failed to write one for his son),[26] the blanks or white spaces take on importance. They take on importance in *The Post Card* when we imagine their asymptotic convergence upon what cannot be said, and not simply on what was not said but could have been. Derrida tells us that, whatever the length of the material omitted, he adopted the arbitrary convention that the space would be that of 52 signs, 52 mute spaces. This was to have been the "clever cryptogram" which he says he himself soon forgot anyway, the cipher whose secrecy was contingent. What we must imagine is the asymptotic convergence of those measured spaces upon a secrecy that is absolute and immeasurable. This would be to imagine the gaze of the child and the blessing in the Hodegetria icon and the Città "Mother with Child and Saint John" directed not beyond the frame laterally or toward Saint John, but vertically at us, making the depth of vision invisible and impredicable. No "S is p": no predication. No "S is P": no identification. That is why Derrida says in "At this very same moment . . ." that what seriature or serirature relates is not moments of the message but the moments, that is to say movements, of their interruption; it is these interruptions that gain importance when I or my eyes say to another, usually but perhaps not necessarily another human being, a being who necessarily can always do with help, "Here I am, at your service. What can I do to help you?" although my absolute responsibility necessarily exceeds what I can. "There is only forgiveness, if there is any, where there is the unforgivable." So there is only responsibility, if there is any, if there is the impossible.

And in *The Post Card* Derrida is doing the impossible. He is addressing himself to what he knows he cannot address himself to: the necessarily secret which he also calls the sacred, and for which as good a word as any (*pace* Levinas) is the word "religious": the *en-gage* of *langage.* This can be the language of pictures or other forms of art, perhaps the tragic art in which the young Nietzsche sought redemption from suffering. Maybe no small part of that suffering was that of not having a god to pray to. The counterpart of that was the suffering of having one to pray to and suffer for, for which Kierkegaard gave thanks, giving thanks thereby that he was spared the need to redeem that suffering in art.

It seemed to me that a work of art would have helped some of us in our work of mourning on the afternoon of October 12 at the cemetery at Ris-Orangis. Derrida died on October 8. Therefore his inhumation took place too soon for many of his overseas friends to witness it, and too soon to arrange more than the most basic ceremonial. (Derrida, we noted earlier, is not one for programs.) The little greenery that there was in the cemetery along the way to his grave was losing the battle against the prevailing ashen grayness adverted to several times in *Feu la cendre,* "this old gray word," "the gray dust of words," "the gray form of these letters," "the gray of mourning,"[27] the gray of the gravestones packed as closely together as our gray vehicles in the municipal carpark, the gray of the dust we let fall upon the coffin, some among us taking care to sprinkle it grain by gray grain for ourselves and for absent friends, others among us not taking care enough to prevent the handful of dust thudding as it struck upon the lid. But some had brought flowers, like those that adorn the right-hand column in *Glas,* flowers of the literature of which Derrida says, "[M]y most constant interest, coming even before my philosophical interest I should say, if this is possible, has been directed towards literature, towards that writing which is called literature."[28] Where was the literature, where were such words as he himself had so often put together to tell and toll the passing of colleagues and friends, among them Roland Barthes, Paul de Man, Michael Foucault, Max Loreau, Jean-Marie Benoist, Louis Althusser, Edmond Jabès, Joseph Riddel, Michel Servière, Louis Marin, Sarah Kofman, Gilles Deleuze, Emmanuel Levinas, Jean-François Lyotard, Gérard Granel, Maurice Blanchot, several of whom had been at the meetings at Cerisy in 1972 where we first met?[29] Among the mourners at Ris-Orangis were Ursula Sarrazin, whose brilliance as an organist he admired, and the distinguished composer and pianist Michael Levinas, son of Emmanuel. I found myself thinking how much Derrida would have enjoyed the thought that nearby after the interment one of these musicians and friends would be playing perhaps a sonata by Praetorius or an invention by Bach. But with the playing of music, as with the writing and reading of words, "such is the absolute risk that is taken here without any strategic assurance for their being put into play" that it "*can always not happen,*" as he underlines in "*Ce qui reste à force de musique.*"[30] Augustine: "What tears I shed on hearing in deep trouble your hymns and canticles. . . . Flowing from my eyes they distilled the truth into my heart . . . The tears ran down, and it did me good to cry."[31]

## The Disseminative Letter of a Smile

Derrida spoke at his burial. As though to confirm his statement "The statement 'I am alive' is accompanied by my being dead, and its possibility requires the possibility that I be dead; and conversely,"[32] he spoke through the voice of his son Pierre, who read from a piece of paper words his father had either written or dictated. I could catch only that these words had to do with smiling. It was several days later that in an e-mail sent to me from America by David Wood and thanks to the Internet (how Derrida would have smiled[33]) I learned the full text of the message—except that the text was still incomplete. It read:

> Mes amis, je vous remercie d'être venus. Je vous remercie pour la chance de votre amitié. Ne pleurez pas: souriez comme je vous aurai(s) souri. Je vous bénis. Je vous aime. Je vous souris, où que je sois.

Should we keep or should we omit from the end of the auxiliary verb the here unsibilant but according to Mallarmé most disseminative letter *s*? There is a difference in pronunciation according as to whether or not that letter is retained, the difference that rhymes with the difference between, say, "*Mai,*" the French name of a month, and "*mais,*" meaning "but." But was whoever put the text on the web unsure? Did Derrida intend the conditional, "as I would have smiled," or did he intend the future perfect, "as I shall have smiled"? Or did he intend to leave it undecided? For all I know, the parenthesis might have been in the "original." In that case the tense of the verb could be described in the words of a section of a piece by Derrida on Lacan as the future anterior in the conditional.[34] At all events, no one was obeying his command. Just about everyone was disobeying his command not to shed tears. Whether they knew it or not, they were responding to something more like Augustine's commands: *flete mecum, et pro me flete,* "Weep with me, and weep for me."[35] Or were these not commands but prayers? Not, no doubt, prayers like those in the *Book of Common Prayer.* But prayers none the less. Or all the more. Common prayers, like "I beg" or "*je vous en prie*" or "*bitte*" or "*prego,*" of which one may wonder whether, notwithstanding or because of their ordinariness, they are the origin or older than the origin of the prayers raised in particular religions; at least as profound as those prayers, despite being borne on the surface of the words we have with one another; and at least as public, while still secret, as that purloined letter placed on the mantelpiece in the story by Poe. This question will revisit us.

Let us allow ourselves to be revisited first by the words Derrida was having with us. The temporality of what was happening that afternoon, of what had happened and of what was about to happen, was complex, however we read the auxiliary verb with its parenthesized letter *s,* supposing that that ancillary verb can be read. Ponder the final subjunctive. That would be most naturally translated into English as the indicative "wherever I am." However, "wherever I may be," "wherever I might be," and "wherever I should be" cannot be ruled out. Some of us may, might, and should go on wondering about this. Derrida's name survives after the death of its bearer. It survives here—"Where?" you hear him ask—in the miniature work of art of his pre-post-humous words. As professors of rhetoric and literature will enjoin their students to do at Irvine, for instance, if no longer at Yale, hear the rhythm of the repetition of "*remercie,*" a word that is already a re-petition in itself, that is to say, not in itself. This is a petitionary prayer. Listen, pray, to the resonance of "*amis*" in "*amitié*" and "*aime.*" There is also a trilogy of smiles. The word "*vous*" occurs six times, and is picked up in "*votre.*" The one word "*chance*" sums up and refuses to sum up a project we inherit from him. "*Mes amis . . .*" revives an agenda that goes back from Derrida through Nietzsche to Aristotle and beyond. Of course, when he says "*Je vous bénis*" he is not speaking *de haut en bas.* On the contrary. These are the words not of an episcopal or archi-episcopal supervisory blessing or a blessing such as is vouchsafed for our salvation by the child in two of the pictures earlier described. He is saying for a third time (a trinity of trinities) that he gives thanks. Like a reader who has come across a favorable prognostication in a fortune-telling book, he is thanking his lucky stars for the good fortune of having had such friends, whoever they may be. He is counting his blessings—or, rather, *not* counting them, for blessings are beyond calculation. You could say that he is saying that he is eternally grateful. He could say that for the chance of having received those blessings his gratitude is directed to God or, as he sometimes says, "God, if you wish," that is to say, directed in no single specific direction. "Where can I go beyond heaven and earth, so that there you may come to me, my God, who have said, 'I fill heaven and earth?'"[36]

For Derrida is not in the business of bidding good riddance to all Capital Letters here or in *The Post Card* or anywhere else. His desire is to show that the upper-case initial of proper names is destined to become the lower-case initial of common ones, but that this does not render impossible the impossibility of what is neither a lower nor an upper case, but, as Levinas might say, a signifying face that is singular but never single, unique but not numerically one. Singleness is marked by a proper name, by what someone is called. Singularity is not marked by what someone is called. It is marked or traced by the call. And it takes at least two to make a call, even if the other is oneself or is in oneself, as the addressee of the missives in *The Post Card,* even when she is time-zones away, seems to be intimate with what we must call their co-writer rather than simply their writer or author. And it is thanks to the call from and to the other and the other others and through the Great Telematic Network in which *thou* and *you* are in indirect contact with *him* and *her* and *it* that there is what Levinas would call the holy (*saint*) but is scared of calling the sacred (*sacré*). Sacred is exactly what this call would be called by Derrida, not least because the fact that "sacred" is an anagram of "scared" may be taken to mark the fact that the sacred is that at which we are right to take fright.[37] But both Derrida and Levinas would be willing to say that what they are speaking of is the religious. In doing so, however, both would be using the word "religious" with a different bias from that which it is usually given by Kierkegaard, whether he intends Religiousness A or Religiousness B. Whereas we could say that Kierkegaard spells it with a capital letter, they write it in the lower case, as in Paris's picture the name "plato" is written and as is written the Quinean predicate "socratises." Derrida does the same with the word "sacred." In the wake of Nietzsche he brings the word down to earth. Levinas would say that if everything is sacred nothing is sacred. Derrida begs to differ. The sacred is something that happens every day. It comes wherever is kept the secret of address, namely in the respect in which naming is also calling to another: most dramatically when the call is the call for help. This would be the call that, as claimed in what is written by Plato's Socrates or Socrates' Plato in the *Phaedrus,* pertains only to speaking, where the "father" of the word is present to be called on to take responsibility for what he has said. The grounds for this claim begin to tremble once Derrida has brought out the ways in which speaking is a kind or quasi-kind of writing, and once it strikes us that all archi-writing and all archi-reading are *sotto voce* calls for help.

Socrates states in the *Phaedrus* (275) also "that writing is unfortunately like painting; for the creations of the painter stand like living beings, but if one asks them a question they observe a solemn silence." Socrates is thinking here only of questions and answers. He is thinking of knowledge, certainty, and truth. In the above meditations on creations of a painter an attempt was being made to think of what is more archaic than questions and answers, to ask whether in the writing of a painting one can read what with Derrida we are calling calling or address, and the absolute response *of* language without which there can be no answer *in* language. For there can be no language, no *langage,* unless there is *l'en-gage,* where the French word "*langage*" means language generally, though not only general language. Linguisticality in this sense belongs to any semiotic system. In this sense it belongs to the language of flowers, those flowers that accompanied Derrida on his last journey from the rue d'Ulm to Ris-Orangis. In this sense a painting may be an act of speech and writing, as iconographers recognize when they speak of *reading* an icon, as one reads Holy Script.

Where are the limits of the holy? In reflecting on this question it is not enough to read the lesson solely from an icon or other painting pertaining to the context of a particular religion. This is why one of the pictures selected for consideration earlier was one that could pass as secular. Another reason for choosing that particular picture was that it comes to our assistance in our attempt to understand what is going on in some of the writings of Derrida. *The Post Card* draws our attention to the fact that Matthew Paris turns the proper name Plato into a common noun, an operation that makes it capable of functioning like the Quinean predicate "platonises," which enables us to say "The author of the *Phaedrus* platonises." It draws our attention also to the possibility that Socrates and Plato are each carrying the name of the other above his head.[38] In both of these circumstances there is predication. But, the author of one of the letters adds (sounding like Levinas sounding like Derrida to the point that one pictures the two of them in the bodies of Socrates and Plato in the Bodleian drawing), the logic of predication is supplemented by a logical operator other than that of the *symplokē* of the copula of "S is p." The supplementary logical operator belongs to the *plokē*, plait, plaid, *plethyn* that binds not the subject of a proposition to its predicate, but the propounder to the propoundee in the logic of promissory address, the logic of the yes, yes.[39]

The double bind of these two logics is tragic.[40] It is normal tragedy,[41] but not normal tragedy construed as a conflict between norms, for instance the law of the state and the law of the family or the divine law as in the *Antigone* of Sophocles. The tragicness of the chiasmus of which the distinction between the constative and the performative is an effect is not the tragicness of tragedy in the Tragic Age of the Greeks or for that matter in the Romantic Age of Wagner, in which the young Nietzsche sought the redemption of suffering. Tragedy was called tragedy because in the first Attic tragedies a goat (*tragos*) was exchanged as payment for a chorus. The tragicness of the chiasmic double bind does not turn on exchange. It turns on a combination of, on the one hand, the non-rigidity of my addressing a promise to (a) *you* who are (is) at the same time a *him, her, it,* or *they* unable, as thus detached from the second personality of *you,* to provide the uptake on which a promise usually depends, and, on the other hand, the possibility of each *him, her,* or *it* being for me (a) *you.* The consequence of the combination of these two factors is that where responsibility is responsibility to a second-person other, I always fall short. For although every other is a possible second-person other to me, the second-personality of most others is diverted into third-personality by the second-personality of those others who happen to be in my thoughts, especially the "first" other, the one with whom I am face to face. And that is a shortcoming of imadgination, where the abnormal, quirky, spelling of this name signals a suspension of law. The question at stake in *Antigone* is whether the public law of the state should be suspended in favor of the law of the family regarding burial of the dead, or vice versa. As analyzed by Hegel the conflict is one between man and woman. Derrida wonders whether the man-woman couple might be reconstrued in a way that does not merely transfer to woman the priority traditionally assumed for man but displaces this idea of one sex counting for more than the other into a thinking in which counting no longer counts, not even counting to two. Think or dream instead of "a chorus, . . . a choreographic text with polysexual signatures," such polyvocal texts as "*Pas,*" "*En ce moment même . . . ,*" and "*Restitutions*" that apply to the concept of binary sexuality the proposal Derrida finds suggested by Nietzsche and Freud which he expresses as early as the "*Différance*" essay as follows: "One is but the other different and deferred, one differing and deferring the other. One is but the other in *différance,* one is the *différance* of the other."[42] This last sentence, reproduced more than once elsewhere in this book, offers a key that opens on to a way of thinking further than binarily opposed criteria. But this would not be with the aim of arriving at some sexual or other neutrality. It is significant that as early as the interview "Choreographies" (1982) Derrida's reservations about such a neutrality are cast in the form of reservations about a concept of democracy that leaves no room for the dissymmetry of one's relation to the other in general and in its singularity. This looks back to Nietzsche's scathing remarks about the democracy of his day and forward to Derrida's new international democracy that, unlike the selective "new international" and Francis Fukuyama's teleo-eschatological ideal of a liberal democratic Promised Land criticized in *Specters of Marx,* would be maximally democratic through being maximally welcoming to the invention of as yet unimaginable political, social, religious, ethical, and cultural experiments.[43] In line with Nietzsche's emphasis on artistic creativity, the work of art would be capable of bringing to expression an imadgination which is "mad" precisely because it imagines the irregular, thereby giving a voice to the singularity of the other. However, the madness of imadgination should not be underestimated. Or, rather, it breaks the bounds of estimation interpreted as the determination of a quantitative or qualitative value, as marking a difference of degree or a difference of kind. *A fortiori,* it cannot be measured by degree of creative novelty or distance of departure from regularity. If we can speak here of distance of departure, the distance is absolute. It is an untying from ties and an untying that I am bound to perform. It is a double-binding and unbinding in that while archi-writing, for example that traced in the Pinturicchio painting, the Matthew Paris drawing, or the sentences blown on the wind at Derrida's grave, is rule-bound, as addressed to an addressee it is unbound from rule at the same time. Its madness is normal, "*cela se produit toujours et 'normalement.'*"[44] It happens normally. But it happens tragically. But, to repeat, it happens tragically not in the manner of tragedy in which there is a conflict between universal or circumscribed universals and-or particulars. It happens tragically rather as the tragedy of the conflict between universality and absolute singularity. The tragedy here is the form of tragedy of the universality *of* absolute singularity which disrupts form.

> What is tragically and happily universal is absolute singularity. How could one speak or write, otherwise? What would one have to say, otherwise? [What, one might also ask, would one have to paint or draw? JL] And all to say nothing, in fact? Nothing which absolutely touches on absolute singularity without straightaway missing it, while also never missing it? . . . This tragedy, I mean this destiny without a strictly assignable destination, is also the tragedy of competence, relevance, truth, etc. There are many, but there has to be this play of iterability in the singularity of the idiom. And this play threatens what it makes possible. The play cannot be separated from the chance, or the condition of possibility from what limits possibility. There is no pure singularity which affirms itself as such without instantly dividing itself, and so exiling itself.[45]

That of which one may be scared, that which presents us with a threat, is also that which one may be happy to welcome, that which holds out a promise. Holds out without holding out anything specific, anything determinate. Holds out without specifying in advance, so without determining that one cannot address also with the words "*Mes ennemis*" those to whom one addresses the words "*Mes amis*"—for do not the neighbors we are commanded to love include our enemies? If the membership of the class of those we call enemies may be called a *société à responsabilité limitée* or "Limited Inc.," recall that it includes Derrida himself in virtue of the fact that S(e)arle appears to have learned something from him.[46] It is possible that Derrida may in turn have learned a thing or two indirectly from Quine; a French translation of one of Quine's papers is, as already noted, one of Derrida's earliest publications, the English version having been delivered by Quine (at Yale) in the same year as saw the publication of Derrida's introduction to Husserl's *The Question of the Origin of Geometry.*[47] That paper lists a series of topics that are to become ones to which Derrida devotes much of his intellectual life. Among these are the topics of metalanguage, the purity of logic, essentialism, incompleteness and inconsistency, excluded middle, exclusion as such, and the as such as such. Quine's paper opens with a complaint about Hegel's and Husserl's "excessive" extension of the term "logic." The title of its French version is "*Les Frontières de la Théorie Logique.*" Derrida's lifework is, as the title of a collection of papers on it says, *Le passage des frontières.* I say his lifework *is* this. Is that because my mourning is incorporative, unsuccessful, and melancholic, as Freud would say, and destined to be always incomplete? Or is it because it is introjective? Or is it because it is something third, something heterocryptic?[48] Not being in a position to answer these questions, I bring this chapter toward its end by confessing that I have been concealing what may be a resolution to the dilemma I reported on my card to Derrida and described above under the subheading "*Prego.*" This avowal will prepare the way for me to report at the beginning of the next chapter a dilemma that Derrida avows (*avoue, à vous*) he is in and to ask whether a resolution can be discovered for that.

I said on that card to Derrida that in projecting a notion of the religious outside specific dogma I appeared to be making it impossible for myself to make a petitionary prayer of intercession on his behalf. That this was perhaps no more than appearance can be shown by making a few distinctions. Atheism is a matter of faith in the truth of an uncircumscribed negative existential proposition, the sort of proposition that cannot be proved. It is therefore a dogmatic religion. Atheism must be distinguished from a-theism. A-theism makes no pronouncement either way upon the existence of God. It may suspend judgment out of indecisiveness regarding a matter of fact. But it may suspend judgment also because it makes a claim that is transcendental or quasi-transcendental. As such it transcends and so leaves aside the question of God's existence at least as this question has been understood traditionally, including in the tradition of negative theology. It follows that if what I was arguing for in my talk at Città was religiousness as a quasi-transcendental condition of religions without itself being a religion, it did not deprive me of an addressee for any intercessory prayer I may have wanted to make. Not unless the quasi-transcendental and what it conditions are necessarily confused with each other in such a way that the former can no more stand on its own than can survive apart from the face the smile of the Cheshire—or Persian or Siamese or Marmalade—cat. Before returning to this question in the next chapter I return to the question of the other smile, the smile addressed to the other of which Derrida spoke in those few sentences he asked one of his sons to read out from the edge of his father's grave.

## *Deuil du Deuil, Deuil du Dieu*

I have another confession to make. The card reporting my supposed dilemma to Derrida was not what would normally be called a postcard. It was not a PC like the one depicting PS, Plato-Socrates, or, if we can stretch the imadgination that far, PC, Plato-Christ, SC, Socrates-Christ, or P-SC. It was more like a birthday card (it was Derrida's birthday that very week, as it was when champagne was drunk at the meeting at Cerisy where he delivered *Aporias*). It was a letter-card, a card you insert into an envelope. So it was the sort of dispatch into which you could insert a *prière d'insérer*, like those Derrida inserted into some of his later publications. An envelope does not need to be sealed like the lips of Socrates or Plato in Matthew Paris's picture. But even if it is, there is every chance of its being intercepted, steamed open en route to its addressee or slit by anyone with a paper-knife like that which may be what is sheathed in the scabbard-like thing across Socrates' right leg. Willy Nilly the Post in Dylan Thomas's *Under Milk Wood* reads everyone's mail before he hands it to the addressee. But he is a personification of the necessary eventuality of being hacked to which all messages are exposed beforehand, a priori, whether they be conveyed electronically or in the more traditional way by letters, by postcards, or by letter-cards into the fold of which can be slipped a *prière d'insérer*.

Such an insertion is neither simply inside nor simply outside the text into which it is inserted. It haunts the margin between. A preposition that marks this unposition is "*sans*" in Blanchot's sense, taken over by Derrida, of the "*sans et le pas sans pas, sans la négativité du pas,*"[49] the "not-with-and-without-a-step," for which we could adopt the Scots idiom "outwith" that was introduced into chapter 11. This quirky "*sans*" and this *pas de pas* or *re-pas* take us back to the edge of the grave, to the subject of (our) mourning.[50]

In his lifelong engagement with the topic of mourning Derrida seeks to *faire son deuil du deuil,* to bid farewell to mourning understood, following Freud, either as "incorporation," which attempts to keep the other safe from the reality of death by making an object out of it and enclosing it in a mental crypt, or as "introjection," which is the so-called successful mourning of digestive appropriation that interiorizes-remembers (*erinnert*) in order to forget. He would like to say farewell to a saying farewell that would be merely a consolatory double blind (*sic*, Hillis Miller, to whom thanks). So would it have been out of place on that day in the gray cemetery at Ris-Orangis to raise a conventional chorus of lamentation, a customary antiphonal dirge? Not, it has been maintained earlier, if the song or the dirge or other work of art were a work of address. The work of art can be an *objet d'art,* the aesthetic object that was a stumbling-block for Kierkegaard and Levinas, and would have been a stumbling block for Nietzsche had the Apollonian not been crossed with the Dionysian and the beautiful with the sublime in his conception of the work of art. All three of these thinkers are conscious that behind them is Hegel with an ultimately too consolatory conception of the work of art as analogous to the work of embalming a body that "in shrouding it, in enclosing it in bands of material, of language, and of writing, in putting up the stele, . . . raises the corpse to the universality of spirit."[51] But a work of art can also be an ethical or religious *working,* even a liturgy in the sense of service without compensation, as Levinas came gradually to acknowledge and as Kierkegaard too should have acknowledged. It can be that because it can be directed by and to another human being or to a divine being, however indirectly.

A dirge is so called after the first word of the eighth verse of the fifth Psalm chanted in the Office of the Dead, *Dirige, Domine Deus meus, in conspectu tuo viam meam,* "Direct my way in Your oversight, O Lord, my God." Even if I had had the capacity to repeat this ancient prayer, and even if an imagined stumbling-block (*problēma*) preventing the acquisition of that capacity may have been cleared away in the work of mourning for Derrida going on in this text at this very moment, I could remain faithful to him only by understanding that that prayer's not being out of place at his graveside would be due in part to the out-of-placeness parergonally intrinsic to this and any other prayer, however determined one might be to secure that it and its addressee are determinate.[52] To remain faithful to Derrida, which means recognizing that there is no way of staying dogmatically on his path, a path which anyway does not stay with itself, it must be remembered that in default of a *tombeau* by Mallarmé, a *reliquat* by Baudelaire, something like Shelley's "A dirge," or something in the ancient Welsh tradition of the elegy, the *marwnad,* he had asked his son Pierre to re-address on that day to his friends there and wherever else they might be a *prière d'insérer* asking them to smile, *comme je vous aurai(s) souri.*

This leads me to raise the following interconnected questions with a view not to concluding this insertion into the loose-leaf binder of responses to the *Veni* of Derrida's inexhaustible writings,[53] but to offering, in the light of his renewed reference to his friends, a reason for and a reason for not removing the parenthesis shielding the letter *s* of that auxiliary verb.

Suppose you do not subscribe to belief in a divine being who might be the Addressee of a prayer made on behalf of a friend. And suppose you conceive of prayer as a sort of Abbacadabra (*sic,* SEC)[54] that might influence that Addressee, if there is one, *s'il y en a.* Would you make that prayer, in the spirit of Pascal's wager, just in case? Would that, the calculated hope, not be precisely what Derrida does not mean by the religious? Or might that be precisely what he does mean by it, for how can it be better to stand on my dignity as a mouthpiece of rational Enlightenment if to do that I must not breathe a possibly magic word to reduce the suffering of a friend? For guidance on what Derrida does mean, think of what his compatriot the bishop of Hippo says, echoing Romans 10:14: "But how does one who does not know you call upon you? For one who does not know you might call upon another instead of you. Or must you rather be called upon so that you may be known?"[55] Is the bishop behind his compatriot, prompting him, or is it the other way around? Does an absolutely past fabulous quasi-performative lie (reside or fib) behind the bishop's performative call? And suppose, like another of our bishops, we can think of even petitionary prayer as a holding in regard and attention: is that possible only because we are ourselves already regarded by someone or something other, if not by God, as was his handmaiden? Kierkegaard: "[T]he true prayer does not exist when God hears what is being prayed about but when the *pray-er* continues to pray until he is the *one who hears*."[56] Karl Barth: "Prayer is a grace, an offer of God."[57] But is it not odd that if grace is a gift of God he should want to be thanked in exchange? Derrida is not scared of capital letters. What scares him but what he would like to like or love to love is the passage between the upper and lower case.

> That is why the man who addressed the Messiah said, "When will you come?" That is to say, well as long as I speak to you, as long as I ask you the question, "When will you come?," at least you are not coming. And that is the condition for me to go on asking questions and living. So there is some ambiguity in the messianic structure. We wait for something we would not like to wait for. That is another name for death.[58]

Whose death? Since the tie between the words "death" and "God" is "probably not fortuitous,"[59] perhaps the death of God? Not if "God" is the name of one with whom one may be fully present. That would be to equate God with one kind of death, but not with death or God as the other. Can this other be overheard in my next and last citation from someone whose job description announces responsibility for oversight, this last time the archbishop of Tours, the name of whose diocese also suggests that he is in a particularly commanding position to carry that responsibility out: "God is over all things, under all things; outside us; within but not enclosed; without but not excluded."[60] So, like a threshold, outwith, a step (*pas*) that is not the *pas* (not) even of negative theology? Is God now the hound of heaven who has seen off the God both of absolute presence and of absolute absence? The Great Telematic Network? A Quasi-Transcendental Upper Case WWW . . . ? And should we be prepared to hear one or other adherent to the doctrines of a particular religion say, like the theologians Derrida imagines in conversation with Heidegger in *Of Spirit,* "Yes, precisely, that's just what we're saying. . . . That's the truth of what we have always said, heard, tried to make heard"?[61] Is not the particularist going to claim that he is a universalist, even when the universality is not the universality that is opposed to particularity, not the universality of "the universalization that hides the ruse of all dogmatisms,"[62] but the universality that, "within but not enclosed; without but not excluded," is crossed by singularity?

When Derrida says that it is of death that "I am scared" he does not mean death as simply opposed to life. He does not mean, with Heidegger, being toward one's own death. He does not mean, with Levinas, being toward the death of the other. He means the other's mortality in me and mine in yours, a simultaneity of myself with you that is destined to become an anachronism when you or I (neither of us in this obsequence knows which will follow which) arrive at an a-destined rendezvous, like the graveside at Ris-Orangis, too early now to mourn the other we have mourned during our lives and too late to know that we may expect to meet one another or oneself. *S'attendre, attendre,* wait for, wait upon, tend, give attention to, regard.[63] Pray for? Smile for, as I would have smiled were I in your place, *comme je vous aurais souri*? Yet, although there is reason for Derrida to say with the lips of his son conditionally, "as I would have smiled," if we mourn the friend in the imadgination of our hearts already during our lives, Derrida has reason to say also future anteriorly (future "perfectly"?), "as I will have smiled." Therefore he has reason to say both, to say both by saying, without being able to pronounce it, *comme je vous aurai(s) souri*. The hardly if at all audible but hereby depicted simultaneity of these two tenses is called for by the singular time and place of our regard toward those who survive us and those we survive. With or without gods, in this time and place survive the sacred and the holy. There, with or without religion, the religious lives on.

# FOURTEEN

# Oasis

## Problem or Aporia

Derrida's dilemma mentioned at the end of the penultimate section of the last chapter is similar in structure to mine mentioned earlier in the same chapter concerning intercessory prayer. Mine, I learned, was the consequence of a confusion. Is his? Is also Derrida's dilemma due to an oversight?

In *Specters of Marx* and elsewhere he distinguishes what he calls messianicity from the messianism of the religions of the Book. He says that messianicity is a-theological and quasi-atheistic, meaning by this what I mean by a-theistic, but meaning also maybe to hint by that "quasi-" at the complication I touched on at the end of the penultimate section of chapter 13. Even more deserted than the religions of the desert, messianicity is apparently deserted by God. But in that case why call it messianicity? Like someone denying the God of Christianity while crossing his fingers behind his back, is that not to trade on powers of the old regime from which one is purporting to make a revolutionary break—"and the messianic is always revolutionary, it has to be"?[1] Is it not to forsake revolutionism for revisionism? Derrida would say rather that it is to revise the idea of revolution and to recognize that the part that history plays in the passing of frontiers is neither as described in the Bachelardian or Kuhnian doctrine of epistemological breaks nor as described in the dialectic of Hegelian elevation. Like the former doctrine, Derrida's proposal would retain an element of unpredictability, but like the latter it would save a certain one-eyed retrospectivism. Messianicity is respect beyond the limits of reason alone as reason is defined by Kant or Hegel. It is absolute justice that respects not only universal law but also absolute singularity. Absolute justice is done to absolute singularity when alteration, although responding to the past, is maximally open to what is to come. To what-or-whomsoever, whotsoever (*sic*), is coming to it from the future it responds Come. To its Yes it says Yes. It is a fidelity or faith that therefore cannot bind itself exclusively to any one particular faith. As the name—or rather the adjective—that Derrida gives to it suggests, the messianic without messianism borrows a certain force from messianism. But does this not compromise the purity of the messianic? Suppose then that the purity of the messianic is protected by its being conceived, if not as a transcendental condition of possibility of historical religions in the style of Kant, as an ontological condition of ontic religions in the style of Heidegger. Why does Derrida say he oscillates between the latter kind of account and one that gives priority to the revelations of historic messianisms as routes through which messianicity is revealed? Why does he confess that he oscillates and hesitates between these two schemes, confessing "this is really a problem for me, an enigma," as though it is a matter of choice between one and the other and as though one cannot affirm both alternatives by saying simply, as Jack Caputo says Derrida should, that the specific messianisms have priority in the order of discovery, whereas the structure of messianicity has transcendental or ontological priority or, if that sounds too Kantian or too Heideggerian, quasi-transcendental priority?[2] Unless the terms "problem" and "enigma" are to be taken strictly in senses that Derrida does not bring out in this context, he seems to be seeing a problem where there is no problem to be seen. He appears to be guilty of an oversight, one of which he is innocent, however, when at the end of the earlier book *Aporias* he says that the Heideggerian existential analysis of death that gives priority to transcendental presuppositions and the approach that gives priority to the historical are equally legitimate and necessary because inseparable.[3]

Despite the appearance that in the later text Derrida is constructing a dilemma and looking for a solution which he has not yet found, might he be expressing the experience of an aporia through which he does not expect to find an exit? There is no reason why he could not be doing both. His use of the term "antinomy" suggests that he is limiting himself at least provisionally to the logic of the antitheses of Kantian or Hegelian dialectic or of the opposition of the ontic and the ontological in what he refers to here explicitly as a gesture of the Heideggerian style. Limiting himself temporarily to that style of thinking, he tells us that for him "The problem remains." But perhaps the problem remains because, although it is not only legitimate but necessary to go over again slowly the ground of the metaphysical tradition that has always been partitioned into opposites, that ground leaves a remainder, a *reste,* a rest beyond *"estance,"* beyond the *est,* the stance, the essence and the ontological difference, a residuum that is otherwise than being. Derrida repeats, "[T]his is really a problem for me, an enigma."

What is an enigma? *"Ainigma"* is Greek for a dark saying. But perhaps its darkness is not that of a glass that may become so clear that we see face to face as foreseen in 1 Corinthians 13:12. Perhaps more relevant here is the face to face as described by Levinas, for whom the enigmaticness of saying is its liability to a confusion of the sign and the trace. Perhaps the enigma is not that of the *ainigmati* of Saint Paul's darkling glass from which we may progress to twenty-twenty vision beyond the grave or outside Plato-Socrates' cave. Perhaps the enigma is that of Derrida's *glas,* one of the manifold meanings of which is voice. Perhaps the enigma is in the modality of the "perhaps," in the trace of the illeity of the absolutely past that is beyond being and all, not only finite, cognition.[4]

What is a problem? Surely not oblivious to the references to the problematic made by Marcel, by Deleuze, and in *Fear and Trembling* by Johannes de silentio, Derrida writes in *Aporias* that a *problēma* can be a project setting a task to be accomplished. But it can be at the same time "the protection created by a substitute, a prosthesis that we put forth in order to represent, replace, shelter, or dissimulate ourselves, or so as to hide something unavowable."[5] It will be said that Derrida does avow; he says, twice, "I confess." Let us not forget that he also says that I can welcome only the unwelcome, give only what it is impossible to give, and that forgiveness forgives only the unforgivable: the only event and the only invention is the one that is impossible. So maybe it is only the unavowable that I can really avow, only the unconfessable that I can truly confess, making a confession like that made by Augustine to God, which is not a possible confession if a confession is the divulgence of a secret, for God already knows all my secrets. So a true confession would not be a confession of a truth, but a confession of faith or love by which I bring about a new relation between myself and the one to whom the confession is made. However, if the one to whom the confession is made is God, we seem to be begging the question in favor of a solution to Derrida's problem that gives priority to the religiousness of a particular religion or family of religions rather than to the religious in general. And if confession is to be an expression of the latter, it must include confession to other others than God, for instance the listeners and readers to whom Derrida says, "I confess this is really a problem for me."[6] I cannot confess a problem without first of all confessing myself. Rather as there are always two prayers, one of them being the prayer that the other prayer be heard ("Lord, hear our prayer, and let our cry come unto Thee"), so that all apparently non-intercessory prayers are after all or before all prayers of intercession, there are always at least two confessions. "Yes, yes," "I confess, I confess." Hence the confessional writings of Derrida or "Derrida" like *Circonfessions* and *The Post Card* are in correspondence, which does not mean communion, with his more recognizably philosophical ones (and this may hold too for the so-called confessional or "Hebraic" and the so-called "Greek" and philosophical writings of Levinas).

Now when we asked whether in making his confession Derrida might be putting into words the experience of an aporia, this question cannot be answered in the affirmative on the basis of equating a problem with an aporia. For he carefully distinguishes the two (unlike Heidegger when he says that "[t]he confusion comes to its highest point when the 'theory of knowledge' in turn is passed off as 'metaphysics of knowledge' and when calculating on the slide-rule of 'aporetic' and 'aporetic' discussion of the very extant 'directions' and 'problem-areas' becomes rightfully *the* method of the most erudite philosophy").[7] The problem is like a shield behind which one protects oneself as behind a border or *Grenze* as defined by Kant in sentences cited in the third section of our first chapter. I can in principle move beyond a border, look at the situation from the other side, and hope thereby to solve the problem retrospectively. This being so, it is difficult to see how Derrida can be treating an aporia as a kind of problem.

There is more than one way in which one may encounter an aporia, that is to say a threshold you cannot simply step across. There may be a border that one cannot cross because one cannot put one's finger on the secret shibboleth that would open a path through—one's indexical finger or one's tongue or one's foot (recollect the "unbelievable play" of Plato's and Socrates' feet in the drawing by Matthew Paris). Or there may be no border, so no this side as opposed to that. Or the conditions of *kinēsis* may be lacking, so that it is impossible to make a step: there would be no topography, so, without *topos* (or without *chōra*), nothing could take place, nothing could come to pass. There would be at best coming to pass with nothing that comes to pass. This is what Derrida calls messianicity. But messianicity and therefore aporia is the unpossible quasi-transcendental condition of the possibility of problems. So that when Derrida says, "I confess this is really a problem for me," by the definition he gives us of "*problēma*" he is confessing that he is having recourse to, to repeat, a protective prosthesis in order to hide something unconfessable. But he says, twice (yes, yes), "I confess." And that is to invoke what exceeds the problem, here the problem of the relation between the transcendental and the historically empirical. It is to call upon the quasi-transcendental, the very name of which declares an inheritance from the transcendental with which it is chiasmically crossed, just as the adjective "messianicity" declares as though to a customs officer at a frontier that it owes something to historical messianisms. It is common knowledge that illegal substances may be hidden in the lining of a suitcase. Derrida himself was once charged in Czechoslovakia with attempting to put such knowledge to profitable use. Of that charge he was innocent. But when he says, "I confess this is really a problem for me," he is guilty of concealing with malice aforethought that behind the problem in question and behind the question and the question of the question raised by Heidegger lies an aporia where the transcendental and the quasi-transcendental collide, making it impossible to disentangle the transcendental condition of possibility from the conditioned historical particulars.[8]

"Quasi-transcendental" is only one of a long series of waymarks ("differance," "*pharmakon,*" "supplement," "archi-writing," "dissemination," "trace," "graft," "*reste,*" "hymen," "cinder," "haunting," "destinerrance," "*demourance,*" "obsequence," . . . ) with which the history of deconstruction can be traced, "deconstruction" being but another "member" of this "class" that defies membership. Because and although "messianicity" stands for the undogmatic, it would be surprising to find Derrida clinging dogmatically to this further expression in the series. He is bound not to bind himself to his currently historically helpful way of construing the relation between, on the one hand, the universality and singularity of what he sometimes describes as maximally democratic hospitality and, on the other hand, the particular historical religions with their dogmatic demands. One corollary of this is that he has to reserve the right to read the texts of these religions "in a way that has to be constantly reinvented,"[9] in a way that allows for strange neographisms traceable to Buddhism, Vedanta, Taoism . . .[10] Nearer home, nearer one of Derrida's homes, in the sands of Egypt justice was signified by *Maat.* It became especially relevant at moments of transition such as the passage from one season to another, from life to death, and at anniversaries. *Maat,* though personified as a goddess, was not a being. So it was not a Messiah. Yet it has been called "the first hint in history of *messianism*":[11] the messianism of the messianicity that Derrida could have called maaticity?

Somewhat as close inspection discovers that Platonism and Hegelianism and Nietzscheanism and Marxism are only in part what goes by those names, so "Within what one calls religions—Judaism, Christianity, Islam, or other religions—there are again tensions, heterogeneity, disruptive volcanos."[12] "Tension" is the term Derrida uses for the relation between a problem and an aporia, such tension as that of the "practical contradiction" between identifying something as a constated problem and making it the subject of the performance of a confession.[13] How a problem relates to a border and how an aporia relates to one do not relate to each other as do two sides of a border. They are related in a way more like that in which reason and sensibility or right and responsibility are related in imagination or imadgination, in a way that may be exemplified in at least some works of art, perhaps at least some of those described in the preceding chapter. This is the way to which we were on the way in our first chapter, "On the Borderline of Madness."

Imagination is related to imadgination as the problematic is related to the aporetic. Both imagination and imadgination have to do with the as, the *comme,* the as-if, the *comme si,* or the quasi—as in the commandment to love your neighbor as (ōs) yourself, as if, as in the Buber-Rosenzweig translation of Leviticus 19:18, you *are* your love of or responsibility to your neighbor. Derrida writes: "[I]n the degree to which responsibility not only fails to weaken but on the contrary arises in a structure which is itself supplementary . . . [i]t is always exercised in my name *as* the name of the other, and that in no way affects its singularity. This singularity is posited and must quake in the exemplary equivocality and insecurity of the 'as.'"[14]

Imagination and imadgination therefore do not necessarily work through images, but they may do so, as they do in the works of art mentioned a paragraph ago. Two of these are works of religious art, works of a particular religion. Derrida writes, it has been noted, that the religious in general is quasi-atheistic. This means that it involves ima(d)gination. It is fictive in a sense that is not the simple opposite of factual. It neither affirms nor denies facts. This is why it is not plainly atheistic. It is not even agnostic. With regard to knowledge and belief and any particular religious faith it is neutral, but its *ne-uter,* its being neither just this nor either just that, is not neutrality. The religious in general, however impossible and impassible and impassable the possibility of it might be, is not incompatible with a particular religion. This, it will be recalled, is why, I confess, I was seriously confused when I thought and said half-jokingly on my card to Derrida that in arguing for a religiousness without the God of any dogmatic religion I was arguing myself out of the ability to make the petitionary prayer of intercession I should like to have been able to make on his behalf. I was guilty of an oversight. Between an affirmative and negative answer to the question whether on a difficulty related to mine Derrida is responsible for an oversight, in the light of what has been said in this section about the paragraphs that puzzle Caputo, I confess that I oscillate. This is because in the passages that puzzle Caputo the problem Derrida confesses he has may be a problem he has specifically with Heidegger's transcendental ontology, namely a problem about the relation of the transcendental-ontological to the ontic. This problem turns into an aporia once the connection between the transcendental and the ontic that Caputo sorts out is discovered to be tied to the quasi-transcendental. Indeed the problematic as what is above board in front of us waiting to be solved is as such a screen hiding its "own" disowning supplement of aporetic insolubility. "By metonymy, if you will, *problema* can come to designate that which, as we say in French, serves as a 'cover' when assuming responsibility for another or passing oneself off as the other, or while speaking in the name of the other, that which one places before one or behind which one hides."[15] What is in front of us can be a front, as the approach of my own death can divert my attention from the mortality of others, which is not to say that the death of friends cannot be the most noticeable reminder of one's own mortality. In *Aporias,* writing of the more familiar (though already *unheimlich*) tie to death analyzed by Heidegger, and distinguishing the transcendental ontological discourse of *Being and Time* from the discourse on death of ontic, historical anthropologies and practices of mourning mentioned only in passing in the latter book, Derrida writes: "Each of these two discourses on death is much more comprehensive than the other, bigger and smaller than what it tends to include or exclude, more and less originary, more and less ancient, young or old."[16] This is the "other scheme," other than the one that is "Heideggerian . . . in style." Not vacillation, more like the pendulatory pending of my time in the time of the other which is in the first place a dissymmetrical depending, this schematism outwith the temporality both of the Kantian and of the Heideggerian schematism, is "really" a problem out of which comes an aporia for Derrida and for us, one that is impossibly and unsurpassably oscillographic between the impossibility that is opposed to possibility in the imagination and the im-possibility with which the imagination is affected and afflicted—offended, Kierkegaard would say between breathless punctuating dashes—by the imadgination that patrols on the borderline of madness not in order to keep the strange and the stranger out, but rather to invite them, please, *prego,* to come in.

Strange gods these strangers may be. Would a god that was not strange be worth its salt?[17] Or a goddess? Or the Mother of God? Let us turn to her before returning to Caputo in order to pursue the path his reference to a certain "formal indication" invites us to follow back from Derrida through Heidegger and Husserl to Kierkegaard.

## More Metaphors

Readers of Isaiah Berlin's *The Hedgehog and the Fox* will recall his citation of the saying attributed to the Greek poet Archilochus "The fox knows many things, but the hedgehog knows one big thing." Readers of Charles Bigger's *Participation* (1968) and *Kant's Methodology* (1996) will come to his more recent book, *Between* Chora *and the Good,*[18] knowing that he knows many things on topics ranging from the exegesis of Plato, the subtleties of the Greek and Latin Fathers, and the sublimities of mathematics to the ingenuities of *E. coli,* the intricacies of the complexity theory of Ilya Prigogine, and the mysteries of the *il y a* of Emmanuel Levinas, via the overarching question whether philosophy is the handmaiden of theology or theology the handmaiden or handyman of philosophy. *Between* Chora *and the Good* maintains that affirmative answers to both of these last questions hold good (but without closing off the possibility that theology and philosophy are the handmaidens of faith). Both answers hold good because of the way in which *chōra* and the Good participate in each other, because of the participation between the Good and God, and because of the participation between participation and a certain parturition. The "between" of participation is Bigger's "one big thing." But this between is the doubly genitive between of metaphor, where metaphor is construed not as one-way transport or transference but as a chiasmus construed as a middle-voiced interference. "In metaphor each term interprets the other, the wolf the man and the man the wolf."[19]

Returning to our other animal metaphors, it can be said that Bigger is both a hedgehog and a fox. The one big thing reconnoitered in *Between* Chora *and the Good* is at the same time many things, the one participating in the many and the many in the one. In what way many? In a way that turns on the analysis of metaphor just sketched. Consider the classic illustration of this analysis applied by Bruno Snell to the metaphor in the *Iliad* where Homer writes that Hector failed to breach the enemy line because it endured just as a rock in the sea endures despite wind and waves. This is what some would prefer to call a simile rather than a metaphor, because in it not only is a comparison being made, but that it is being made is also made explicit. On Snell's broader conception of metaphor (and Bigger treats all tropes as metaphors), this is a genuine metaphor which, following the pattern of all genuine metaphor according to him, illumines human behavior by invoking something else that is itself illumined by analogy with human behavior. In the case of this Homeric metaphor, something inanimate, the rock, throws light on the conduct of animate human beings only because the resistance of the rock is already seen in terms of human endurance.[20] Now to see the rock in anthropomorphic terms and then to see the human behavior in petrine terms is to do more than discover a common factor. It is to move inventively beyond any such shared nucleus. It is upon this interactive creativity of at least genuine metaphor that Bigger and Snell insist. No doubt the degree of creativity will vary historically according to whether or not one's view of the world is more or less animistic. But whatever the degree of creativity the metaphor may manifest, the trope will turn on there being at least in retrospect an untroped core of similarity of greater or lesser degree, either actual or imagined. That is to say, we are dealing here with predication, the sharing of one property by the many, even if in the case in point the plurality is no more than a duality, that of the rock and the enemy line. One of the aims of *Between* Chora *and the Good* is to show that participation as just encountered in the field of predication must be bent, folded, led back, re-duced to participation as communion. Snell's account of metaphor may be interpreted in a manner that commits him to the thesis that the point of at least Homer's metaphors is to reveal to his hearers something about themselves and the forces manifested through them and through the natural world. So it is arguable that we have already passed beyond the sphere of participation understood predicatively to participation understood as communion within the context of an *ēthos*. That this is how Bigger would wish us to interpret his account is confirmed by his frequent allusions to *Befindlichkeit,* which, as introduced in *Being and Time,* has the sense both of where we find ourselves and of how we find ourselves, that is to say in what mode or mood, what frame of mind, what *Stimmung.* How we find ourselves already disposed, attuned or—as is said of a musical instrument, for instance a pipe organ—voiced, *bestimmt,* is not only a matter of *Bestimmungen,* of determinations understood as properties that may be predicated in propositions. It is a matter of how we find ourselves predetermined affectively. For Heidegger this is a matter of how we are co-predetermined. These ambiguities of the term "*Bestimmung*" enable him to convey the notion that its predicative and propositional force is infused with an affective force. Bigger draws also on Bradley and Whitehead when he stresses the primordiality of affectivity. Another author cited in this context is Michel Henry, but Bigger wishes to distance himself from what he considers to be Henry's still too Cartesian doctrine of auto-reflection and auto-affection.

A sense of the richness of Bigger's proposals can be gathered by noting that to say that a *Bestimmung* is voiced is to say what that word itself says. In it we hear "*Stimme.*" Bigger hears in it, with Rilke's help, "*Gesang,*" and the motif that *Gesang ist Dasein,* "Song is existence," where song includes poetry and, more widely, the poietic or productive. He hears in it music and harmony, but not without running the risk of making it difficult for us to understand how he can hear in it what Levinas calls saying or Saying as distinguished from what is said, for although productivity is a key to understanding Levinas, music seems not to be a key to understanding what he means by productivity.[21] The said is the propositional or proponible. Saying is the proposing, not least proposing in the sense of the proposal of a betrothal, of troth as distinguished from factual truth. The pre-predicativity of Levinasian saying or Saying is that of a responsibility that precedes questioning. It precedes in particular the question "What is x?" in particular as that question is asked by the philosopher in the hope of acquiring knowledge of an essence. Responsibility has to do with the Who? It is the responsibility of responding "Yes" to the surprised "Who, *me*?" provoked by the question "Who is responsible?" And this me, insofar as I am concerned, is always out of symmetry, out of synchrony, out of "sync," with every other, yet in syncopation, out of time, out of joint, with the other because I am always already called to serve her or him no matter what I have or have not done. I am the other's obedient servant. This dissymmetry is the mark of distinction that sets off saying from the said. It is not obviously a mark of what Bigger means by saying. As is suggested by the crucial use he makes of a notion of communion, for him saying is communication, a way of reciprocal being-with. It is at least a communion between human beings in the space between *chōra* and the good, where the good is beyond being and beyond ideas, including the idea of the good, but where the relation between and among these human beings is that of a choral togetherness, *choros.* That is to say, it is a being in step. But it is a being in step which allows a degree of being out of step. It is a being together that allows a being apart, a *choros* that does not exclude *chōrismos.* This last word is employed by Plato in the course of his exposition in the middle dialogues of his doctrine of the separatedness of Ideas from that in which they are instantiated. That separatedness must not be confused with the separatedness or beyond-ness (*epekeina*) of the (Idea of the) Good from (other) Ideas. Without simply endorsing the Aristotelian doctrine that universals are *in re,* Bigger turns his back on the separationism of Plato's middle dialogues. But he follows Levinas in embracing Plato's doctrine on the beyondness of the (Idea of the) Good. How closely he follows Levinas here depends on whether we leave in or omit the references to the Idea of the Good just made in parentheses. For Levinas the Good beyond being is a good beyond all Ideas. It overflows all ideas, as does God, so that Good itself will not be an Idea. In Plato (or Socrates) the good is often referred to as an Idea or as that of which there is an Idea. It is therefore not surprising that where Bigger is discussing Plato, he refers to the Good as an Idea. But we have already seen that he wants to go beyond the Idealist intellectualism that might be implied in such talk of Ideas and participation to what he, like Levinas, considers to be a prior concern, where participation and the interrelatedness of ideas is superseded by communion, and this communion is either that among human beings or that between human beings and God—and, in his final chapters, that among the persons of the Trinity. This last step is made via what is said in the *Timaeus* about *chōra,* and via a "tweaking" of this in the direction of choral communion.

That Bigger's tweaking is going to require some violence is clear from the account we have given of his book so far. We have learned that he is on the way to a notion of communion that brings with it the ethical relevance implied by his references to what Plato and Levinas say about the Good. We are going to find that that notion of communion is also theological. How is the way to communion prepared by his account of metaphor, given that metaphor is usually taken to belong to the field of rhetoric and poetics? The answer to this question is that the "Between" mentioned in the title of his book, the relationship to be worked out between the ethico-theological Good and *chōra* interpreted along lines suggested in the *Timaeus,* is itself metaphorical. That is why it makes sense to look first at how metaphors work in the rhetorico-poetic field to which we customarily take them to belong. We can therefore expect that this Between signaled in the title will be bidirectionally creative somewhat after the manner of the example of the metaphor analyzed by Snell.[22]

## Incarnation

The notion of communion developed in *Between* Chora *and the Good* is illustrated in paragraphs devoted to the beauty peculiar to music. This appeal to music seems only to deepen the gulf between what is said about metaphor and what we are beginning to hear said about communion. It augments what would be regarded as a danger by Levinas, who writes in "Reality and Its Shadow" that the arts are essentially musical.[23] That means for him, at least at the time of that essay, that the arts are essentially non-ethical. The arts may even be a threat to the ethical in that they are liable to become the medium in which the "there-is," the *il y a,* is expressed—or rather remains unexpressed, for the *il y a* is inarticulable *apeiron.* It is not as forthcoming as the *es gibt,* which according to Heidegger is a generosity and to that extent may be deemed to participate in what he, but not Levinas, might be willing to call ethicality or proto-ethicality.

That Bigger, despite his avowed debt to and admiration for Levinas, is unable to endorse some tenets that are central to the latter's teaching is indicated by the selection of tenets from Plato which he develops in his own doctrine, not least the high valuation of the beautiful just mentioned. According to Bigger, Beauty and the Good are mutually convertible.[24] The force of the Greek *to kalon* can accommodate this claim, but this claim would not be obviously consistent with Plato's reservations over the place to be given or rather not given in his vision of the ideal republic to poetry and certain sorts of music. Bigger embraces the thought expressed when Pseudo-Dionysus writes that the Good is "celebrated as beautiful and beauty, as *agapē* and beloved. That beautiful beyond being is said to be beauty . . . [and in a play on *Cratylus* (416C)] it calls (*kaloun*) all to itself, whence it is called Beauty (*kallos*)."[25]

The modern reader may well have difficulty understanding how there can be a connection between the ethical and a concept of the beautiful interpreted as aesthetic. The difficulty is alleviated if aesthetic beauty is taken as beauty of form. At a high level of abstractness formal beauty will be that of mathematical shapes or orders. And it is in this realm of geometrical shapes that beauty is treated in the *Timaeus,* the order that is the order of the mathematicals in the *Republic.* At least the notion of order is common to the spheres of the beautiful and the ethical as understood generally. And however far from the Greek context Levinas and Kant (according to Hegel another "Jew") may at first seem to be removed by the fact that they give priority to order as command over order as arrangement, it should not be forgotten that in the *Timaeus* the *demiurgos* exerts a pressure upon the natural and human, even if this is the pressure of persuasion by the allure of the Good rather than an imperative. Perhaps one could go as far as to say that the *demiurgos* imposes a hypothetical imperative, since he appeals to what humans desire to do and what, at the cosmological level, necessity is inclined toward. From this it might seem that the good and the beautiful are instrumental and technical only. However, that this is not so is supposed to be guaranteed by Plato's doctrine that the formation of solids is based on two privileged types of triangles. *Between* Chora *and the Good* too invokes a theological principle that connects the cosmological and the ethical good and the beautiful, but whereas the Platonic *demiurgos* works upon something always already given, Bigger's principle is a Christian Platonist principle that creates *ex nihilo,* where creation *ex nihilo* is given an ethical twist, if not in the same direction as the ethical twist it is given by Levinas.[26] Cosmologically, God would be the only always-already. The phenomenological counterpart of this always-already would be what we have seen that Bigger follows Heidegger in calling *Befindlichkeit,* which is not a purely rational a priori, but affect. It therefore presupposes incarnatedness.

Whether incarnatedness presupposes a becoming carnate will depend on which aspect of Bigger's account one is considering. Presumably a becoming carnate is affirmed in what he will say about the Trinity. On the other hand, the Good is from the beginning incarnate or otherwise *in re.* As already noted, this is not an Aristotelian doctrine of *universalia in re,* since the center of gravity of participation is not something said, hence not a universal. It is the saying, in a sense that owes something to Levinas insofar as saying is addressing rather than message. Incarnation *ab initio* of the Good does not entail that saying loses the sayer's separatedness (Greek and Platonic *chōrismos* glossed through Hebrew *kadosh,* holiness) without which according to Levinas saying would lack ethicality. Ethical responsibility turns on my responding to the saying of another who is vulnerable and therefore, like the respondent, incarnate.

There is another separatedness posited in the doctrine expounded in *Totality and Infinity.* This is the separatedness that is antecedent to the separatedness of the me vis-à-vis the other and the Good, antecedent to the separatedness of the me in the accusative and accused by the other. It is the separatedness either of the ego on its own, in separation from others and therefore from God, hence a-theistic, or of the ego enjoying life from within the security of its home. Levinas will say that when the ego is awakened from this "atheistic" state of nature by the call of another it becomes *dis*incarnate. This does not mean that it is separated ontologically from its flesh. It means that its egological interiority is affected by ethical exteriority in responding to the voice of the vulnerable and therefore incarnate other human being. It is affected by this immemorially, as the affect of *Bestimmung* according to Heidegger is immemorial. This affect is, in Nietzsche's phrase, an "it was." It is older than Dasein can recall. It is Dasein's past that was never present. It is Dasein's finding itself already with that passed past thrown toward the future future when it will no longer be there, finding itself to be a being of two thresholds that, in terms of the Kantian distinction distinguished from Hegel's in chapter 1, are uncrossable positive borderlines (*Grenze*) rather than negative limitations (*Schranke*) that Dasein can in principle cross and look at from either side. In Levinas's version of this apriority the ego discovers that its proper place is the improper inside-out place of the threshold of the home that the ego is always already called to step over or straddle in order to welcome the foreigner in.

The home and dwelling remain pivotal in Bigger's conception of the human condition. It seems to remain from beginning to end of his articulation of that conception. It sometimes seems that Bigger never leaves home. But this is because his conception of home has the breadth of Heidegger's conception of dwelling. Being home is being-in-the-world. The world is our *oikos*. However, as for Heidegger, being home for Bigger does not mean being at home. The home is *heimlich* in the sense of that word that includes its apparent Abelian opposite, the *unheimlich*, the "uncanny." The house is haunted. The home is also the basis from which there is generated a family scene. And, on Bigger's account, it is this that safeguards the home against the menace that haunts it. The key to an understanding of the homeliness of the home is a Holy Family, but one that is more like a Holy Quaternity or Fourfold than it is like the Holy Trinity in terms of which Hegel invites us to construe being-in-the-world.

## Tweaking Plato's Tale

Here is encountered again the aforementioned question as to which of the two, philosophy and theology, is the handmaid of the other. But this is a question whose credentials become dubious if we follow Bigger in taking the *Timaeus* as the point of departure of our enquiry, for gods already visit that work's scenario. The Creator and Divine Director of that scenario so arranges it that while men who achieve the power to control their passions achieve happiness thereby, men who do not are reborn as women. On Bigger's rearrangement woman would not have this inferior status. Not because woman's place is in the home. Woman would *be* the home, in a sense Bigger develops by, as he puts it, tweaking what Plato says about *chōra*, place. His methodology of tweaking is patterned on what we have understood him to say about metaphor. This is how in his own text he puts to work the "suasion" exercised by the Good or the god with regard to *chōra* and to the receptacle, the *hypodochē*. Not all of his readers will be persuaded that *chōra* can be retroread as the Virgin Mary. But that is Bigger's one big idea: to elicit a Christian Platonism from the clues he reads from or into the *chōra* of the *Timaeus* taken together with a multitude of other sources, not least the icon known as the Font of Life, *Zōodochus Pēgē*. With special reference to the fourteenth-century example of this once to be seen in the Church of Saint Savior in Chora in Istanbul, Bigger wrote in *Kant's Methodology:*

> In this little-known icon, the Virgin Mary is represented as sitting in a recep-
> tacle that gives off of itself healing waters and holding the infant Christ. *Chora*
> gives a place from which to gather and channel elemental nature into the life
> she nurtures and shelters as Mary gathered the dynamics of nature to nurture
> and shelter the infant Jesus. She is thus transformed into the originary *archē,*
> "the place of the placeless" (*Logos*).[27]

Earlier sentences make it clear that "*Logos*" is in apposition to "the placeless." In this iconographic "deepening of Plato's insights" Christ is in apposition to Mary.

> Through the merit of her Son, we have been told, she is with Him co-Redeemer
> and, in some Franciscan traditions, co-creator; and while such appellations
> are questionable if not idolatrous, doubtless something important is being
> said. Be that as it may, the gazes that cross our gaze can make us prisoners of
> Grace. Now we know: the darkness is creative, the desert will flower.[28]

Whether or not such appellations are questionable will turn on whether the "co-" in "co-Redeemer" and "co-creator" allows for her co-creativity to be consistent with the Franciscan and Scotist belief that her power of redemptive grace is the result of God's grace. However this Theo-Christo-Mariological matter may be resolved (we shall find Bigger saying that it is a matter of faith), on the logical, metaphorological, and metaphysical matter that concerns him he writes that the *Zōodochus Pēgē* is a metaphor of how the *Logos* incarnate "was given place by the Virgin seated above the receptacle-font-chalice as *chōra*."[29] That this metaphor bears the chiasmic structure that according to Bigger and Snell belongs to all genuine metaphor is suggested by Bigger's state-ment that "this icon is a metaphor about the Good and thus about what it is to be a hypostasis, divine or human, that reconciles differences in the love expressed by the Mother for the child and for us by Christ."[30] In one of the versions of the *Zōodochus Pēgē* this two-in-one love is represented by two receptacles, a scallop-shaped basin in which the mother sits with the son sit-ting in her lap, and a rectangular container, pointing to the four corners of the world, fed by water flowing through holes pierced in the side of the vessel placed in the rectangular container. At one side of the lower basin a blind person holds his wetted fingers to his eyes. At the other side a lame man reaches out to touch the water.[31]

In the example of the metaphor from Homer the rock as which the enemy line is seen is quasi-humanized in anticipation, and the resistance of the enemy phalanx assumes some of the character of the rock. (The rock would be what Max Black calls the focus; the enemy line would be what he calls the frame.)[32] Similarly, in the relationship between the icon and what the icon illumines there is an exchange of humanity or at least quasi-humanity and divinity or at least quasi-divinity. In this context the prefix "quasi-" is necessary in order not to beg any questions as to whether divinity is endued, assumed, imputed, attributed, combined, and so on , and as to how these expressions are to be interpreted. More generally, that prefix is unavoidable insofar as what is at stake is the working of metaphor. Metaphor works through the "as" or "as if" or "quasi-" of seeing-as, hearing-as, and so on, so that the copula of the predicative proposition would be a limiting case of metaphor and the proposition would convey a metaphor that has been made moribund through its isolation from propositioning. For although suasion by the Good turns on the appeal of reason, that appeal is the attractive call of *erōs* that is neither causal nor ratiocinatively logical necessitation. "Since the Good cannot act under compulsion or from the necessity of its nature, it must proposition us in our vulnerability in the guise of *Erōs* and Beauty."[33] This holds whether *erōs* be construed as a desire for possession, or whether it is not thus construed, as with Levinas, who tweaks Heidegger's thesis that all understanding is impassioned toward his own thesis that affect as ethical Desire is high rationality, *ratio* as sober *D(es)ire*.

To repeat, in the operation of metaphor, there is a chiasmic co-operation of receiving and giving, the sort of chiasmus that is expressed in the middle voice. "In kissing do you render or receive?" (*Troilus and Cressida*). Shakespeare has Polonius say, "Neither a borrower nor a lender be," but in some languages one and the same verb does service for both borrowing and lending, for instance the French *emprunter* and the Welsh *benthyca*. However, what call for special attention at this quite literally crucial stage of our reflections on Bigger's provocative text are the Greek words "*zōodochus*" and "*hypodochē*."

This last word is commonly translated as "receptacle." I believe Bigger would agree that it would be a good word to use of the imagination as the receptacle of metaphor, the imagination understood as where the "as" gives and takes place (*chōra*), whether with or without pictures.[34] This is not inconsistent with Bigger's reference in *Kant's Methodology* to "Kant's imagination, a variant of the Platonic matrix,"[35] provided we think of the imagination as kinetically verbal imagining, not as a static hypostasis in the general sense of the term or in the specific sense of person (*persona, prosopon*) that "hypostasis" has in

*Between* Chora *and the Good.* In this text we are told that the matrix appears under such names as *hypodochē/chōra.*[36] This is a name of that for which, as Husserl says, names in a strict sense are lacking. Here nominality has to be parsed as verbality, for it is also said in this text that in the matrix "activity and passivity are completely one," a phrase applied by Levinas to precisely that for which Husserl says names are lacking,[37] to wit the spontaneity of the living present that is origin and creation.[38] Is it this to which Bigger wishes to give the non-name *hypodochē/chōra*? How can the nostalgia he seems to experience for this be reconciled with his admiration for Levinas? In the section of *Otherwise than Being* from which Bigger cites the statement "activity and passivity are completely one," Levinas's aim is to remind us that whereas the Husserlian origin is the origin of the temporality of consciousness and the consciousness of temporality construed with retentions and protentions, there is an "origin" older than this and a creation other than this which is not recuperable in the time of memory and which is non-conscious. Hence, if we are going to be able to say that this pre-historic pre-origin belongs to imagining, this imagining must be the imagining of the unimaginable and unimageable, not the imagination of Kantian recognition in imagination or its Husserlian phenomenological revision. This does not mean that we have to become iconoclasts. But it does mean that the iconography of *chōra* and the imagination that is her *hypodochē* must be not or not only the locus of self-affection; it must be the locus of an affectedness by the Good or by the other or Other or, in the words of the title of Jean-Luc Marion's book, by the *Dieu sans l'être,* that is to say *God without Being,* or, as the French also entitles us to translate Marion's title, *God without Being Him or Her or It.* For all we know, each "or" in the sentence preceding this one may be the "or" that can include an "and"; that is to say, each of them may be a case of the non-exclusive *vel.* The doctrine of the Trinity entitles us to make the long version of Marion's title still longer by inserting another "*or Him*" to cover the persons of the Father and the Son. Further, if the "or Her" already included in the long version of the title is taken as a concession to those who wish to allow for the femininity of God, then another "or Her" may need to be inserted to allow for the place Bigger wishes to allow to the Virgin Mary, who in his construal of the Trinity corresponds to place itself, that is to say the receptacle or nurse or mother called in the *Timaeus* by the non-name *chōra.* Plato tells us that *chōra* can be spoken of only in a "bastard" language. It is only to be expected that in reading *chōra* through the dark glass of the Trinity we are unclear as to the number and gender of the persons hypostatized in it. Is the Trinity a quasi-Quaternity? And if *chōra,* as Bigger suggests, corresponds to Trinitarian Spirit, is the pronoun that corresponds to it "she," "he," or "it"? In his Christianization of Plato the World Soul of the *Timaeus* would be the Mother as soul who would participate in both Being and Becoming and would give life to all that therein comes to be. This Spirit could also give the "saying" through which, according to our creeds, the prophets spoke. If the Holy Spirit is to be effeminated, then She may even be said to occasion Mary's response to the "persuasions" that opened her to the Father and left her with child (Luke 1:35).[39]

The word "therein" in this passage is an allusion to the role of Mary as *chōra*, place, room, womb, and to her part in the participation that is the communion, *koinōnia*, as which we are being invited to rethink Being. *Being as Communion* is the title of a book by John Zizioulas. Bigger acknowledges indebtedness to this book. But he takes exception to his mentor's subordination of love to being in his identification of this love as *agapē* with the Father as hypostatizer of God. He concedes that *agapē* is not a nominal common nature, but, he observes, "as we discovered in Scotus, this nature is common as a medial *essance* (Levinas) or verbal *wesen* (Heidegger)."[40] This is a hard saying, and, as we shall see in a moment, it is a hard saying for the same reason as what he says about "saying" is hard. When Levinas entertains (but resists) the temptation to spell *essence* with an *a* as *essance,* he is thinking the verbality of *Sein,* Be-ing, as underlined by Heidegger—hence *wesen*—and marking out the field of what he, Levinas, calls *existence* and *il y a,* as the impersonal field against which existents are made to stand out by being arraigned by the Good that is voiced by the Other.

Note too that in the quotation from Bigger reproduced a paragraph ago the word "saying" is placed between quotation marks. I suspect that these are meant as reminders of the linkages made earlier in the book to Heideggerian *Sagen,* the saying that is also a showing, hence a clue to what Bigger means in his frequent references to metaphor as deictic showing. This *deixis* is the showing of a singularity, where the "of" may be construed as a double genitive, letting something be seen from itself, middle-voiced *phainesthai,* as when a metaphor lets us see something as though for the first time, always first, however iterated, every time singular, *chaque fois singulier,* as Derrida iterates, "ever Virgin,"[41] "in that first flash," *in ipso primo ictu,* as Augustine says (*De trinitate,* VIII, 2). In Levinas this would be the first-timeness of my being addressed by you, the first other, that opens up to sociality my first-personal hypostasis as existent. This Levinasian hypostasis itself is not yet explicitly third-personally social. But in Bigger's use of the term, "A hypostasis is always social." If we are to avoid confusion, we need to be clear whether the sociality intended here is reciprocal communality, and whether it can allow that, as Levinas holds, the ethically first sociality is the asymmetrical relation of relations (or, because there are no terms in it, the non-relation) of the face to face. We need to be clear too that, as noted above, Bigger is not using the word "hypostasis" in Levinas's sense. But Bigger's appeal to the deictic facilitates the construction of the bridge or, better, stepping-stones across which he daringly picks his way from Levinas via Heidegger to a Christian Platonism in which patriarchism is corrected by attention to the "therein" of the Mother. For although he applies the term "deictic" to the motion accomplished in the *Timaeus* from the greatest kinds (many, same and other, rest and motion) down to mathematics and physics, by a stretch of the etymological imagination *deixis* and *deiknumi* can mean not only showing but also offering or proffering, and both of these (according to Buttmann as reported by Liddell and Scott) stem from a root, *dek,* that either means to stretch out the finger of the right hand to point or means to extend the right hand and take hold of another's in welcome. It is important to observe that this and other etymological displacements are themselves metaphors with the chiasmic structure that all "genuine" metaphors have according to Snell. It is also important to observe that this chiasmic structure is not one of simple synthesis understood as con-struction. It is de-constructive at the same time, hence in a time whose unfolding assumes a folding and vice-versa, like the folding and unfolding of hands—or like the opening between the hands held together in prayer in the *mudra* pictured on the cover of *Between* Chora *and the Good:* opening *between,* offering and proffering a place, *chōra,* and opening *of,* indicating perhaps a relationship between petition and work to be done.

Petition for whom? Work on whose behalf? In the context of the Christian family scene that Bigger describes according to his reading of the *Timaeus,* the work to be done is to be done on behalf of one's neighbor or neighborhood, whether widely or narrowly conceived, and at least some of one's praying will be on their behalf too, a praying for help in helping them. But, paradoxically, these prayers must leave room for prayer for oneself *tout court* as the acknowledgment Christianity requires that one is not self-sufficient. Here one's neighbor *is* oneself. Here one's neighborhood is the here not of the French "*me voici,*" the Hebrew "*hineni,*" or the English "Here I am at your service." Is then the Here of this neighborhood the Here of the ego enjoying life on its own or in its home? And is that Here the neighborhood that is called *chōra*?

The majority of entries in the Lexicon under the term *chōra* identify it as the proper place, a thing's place or one's place or post, where one is at home. *Chōra* is the spatial equivalent of *kairos,* the proper time. It is chiefly under the entry for "*chōros*" that one finds references made to place in a less intimate sense, the sense of land or property. Still, as John Sallis points out, "*chōra*" too is used to cover these senses, often in contrast to "*polis,*" in the not especially philosophical context of the *Laws.*[42] So let us go back to the common root of the first-declension noun "*chōra*" and the second-declension noun "*chōros*" as it is expressed in the verb "*chōreō.*" This last can mean to make room for. It can also mean to go forward. Neither of these meanings conveys the idea of a place at which one stays. So, on reflection, *chōra* may be one's proper place, but it will mean one's proper place as that from which one goes out to invite another in. And, on reflection, we see that this notion of a relation to another was already more than implicit in the idea of a prayer, even when that is a petition on behalf of oneself. We see too that it is suited to the Christian application Bigger wishes to make of Plato's chorology. Insofar as *chōreō* means to make room for another by withdrawing, one could go a step further with the Christianizing of the Greek by hearing in this Greek word the notion of self-sacrifice, human, divine, human-divine, or divine-human. The word could also be heard as the Greek for what Levinas calls substitution. Hebrew may have a better word for what Levinas means: perhaps *lehakreev,* which means to sacrifice, perhaps the sacrifice God makes of himself when, according to the Kabbalistic doctrine of *tsimtsum* that resounds in the Christian theology of *kenōsis,* he withdraws himself in order to leave room for humankind to come to his assistance. However, this is a question that would lead us away from Bigger's central preoccupation.[43]

Staying with that preoccupation, let us take note now that what he says about *chōra* belongs, if it belongs anywhere, to the same semantic field as the *deixis* to which he frequently appeals. *Deixis,* we have learned, is reception, welcome. And so too is *dochē,* as this is uttered in Bigger's iconic *Zōodochus Pēgē,* and in the *hypodochē* of Plato's *Timaeus.* Bigger's and Plato's topic, if there is room to speak here of a *topos,* is how becoming, being, and the good participate in each other. So let us focus on the cognate verb, "*dechomai.*" This means to accept or receive something or someone, for instance to accept someone as an ally or to receive and entertain someone as a guest, hence to give hospitality, which supports Bigger's translation of *Zōodochus Pēgē* as "life-giving source." *Dechomai* can also mean to receive hospitality, that is to say, to receive reception, to be a host to a host. It can also mean to give ear to. All of these meanings accommodate the idea of welcome. But, as underlined above in chapter 10, a distinction must be made between, on the one hand, welcoming as doing something which is pleasant to do because it is accepting something acceptable or receiving someone we find it agreeable to receive, and, on the other hand, welcoming as the performance of welcoming someone even if we do not find agreeable the prospect of his or her accepting our welcome, of his or her accepting our acceptance. The latter circumstance would be exemplified by a further sense given in the Lexicon according to which *dechomai* may mean receiving as an enemy or awaiting the enemy's attack. The distinction is more difficult to make in German than it is in English, because, whereas English has the verb "to welcome," "*willkommen*" is not standardly used as a verb in modern German (and even its use as a noun is comparatively rare). One has to say either "*willkommen heissen*" or, most commonly, "*empfangen.*"[44] Note too that "*fangen*" can denote an aggressive act of capture, raption, or rape, a force remembered in the English noun "fang." True, this force is neutralized when "*fangen*" is put in the context of the prefix "*emp*." Similarly, the variations in meaning of "*dechomai*" and its suggested translations are variations within the meaning of those words taken not in isolation but in a variety of contexts. Running through these different contexts serves only to confirm that what one welcomes need not be something that one likes or loves. When someone says "You are hereby welcomed to . . . ," or "Welcome to . . . ," or when on a doormat is written "Welcome," the affect that may accompany the speaking of these words may be one of hostility rather than friendship, or there may be no accompanying affect at all, unless with Heidegger we count among affects indifference.

## Desert and Garden

The above review of contexts one might imagine in the course of attempting to answer the question "What does *dechomai* mean?" shows too that there is some ground for affirming that Plato's *chōra* receives all things. *Chōra, chōra-hypodochē*, as Bigger writes, is *pandechēs* (*Timaeus* 51a). But, it was noted, he would have us interpret as in the first place a personal relationship whatever belonging there is in the relational property indicated by these Greek expressions. Now Derrida at one point invites such an interpretation. Our English and Greek question "What does *dechomai* mean?" gets asked in his French as "*Que veut dire dechomai?*" Meaning as wanting to say, *vouloir dire,* raises the possibility that *dechomai* is a person of some kind, or of no kind. The same words are put in quotation marks when he writes "*Khōra* 'veut dire': . . ."[45] And *Khōra* is explicitly personalized when he goes on to ask "*Qui es-tu, Khōra?*," "Khōra, who art thou?" where the initial is capitalized as though we were dealing with a proper name.[46] But if, as by this time we have learned, *chōra* cannot be determined as belonging to a class or genus, then she/he/it can have no one gender. Nor can *chōra* bear a proper name. Any more than can God.

Yet both Bigger and Derrida say that *chōra*, for whom or for which names are lacking, bears a similarity to someone who bears a proper name: respectively, Mary and Socrates. In saying this both are following Plato more or less. Bigger is following Plato insofar as *chōra* is linked in the *Timaeus* with Gaia, and is also referred to as mother or nurse. Bigger underlines those feminine principles touched on in the *Timaeus* that would facilitate a metaphorical exchange with the Mother of God. Derrida does not ignore the feminine connections that are made in the story Plato tells and that are enshrined in the fact that this story is told using the femininely gendered word "*chōra*," not the masculinely gendered word "*chōrus*"; and although the likeness he considers at greatest length is Socrates, we remember that Socrates is compared with a midwife. Thus, rather as *chōra,* although compared to a mother, is not a fully maternal origin because she is also compared to a nurse, so Socrates, as midwife, is not a father. He is therefore not the legitimate father to whom, according to the *Phaedrus,* one can turn for assistance in distinguishing mere semblance from truth, *veritas.* He is not the paternal (or ex cathedrally papal) paradigm.

Socrates is not a legitimate father because he cannot legitimate himself. Derrida demonstrates this by distinguishing in the story he tells about Socrates' story-telling in the *Timaeus* seven layers of fiction, seven levels of hearsay, seven levels that become eight when Derrida's own account is counted in, nine, ten, eleven . . . , when we, Derrida's other readers, read him. The seemingly first of these layers—seemingly because it is not bedrock—is that to which the story of the founding of Athens is traced via Critias Junior, who heard it from Critias Senior, who in turn is said to have heard it told by the Greek poet Solon, who is said to have received it from a certain Egyptian priest, who relates that what he tells us was recorded in an archive in his land. The story goes that this priest stresses how indebted his own people are to the traditions of the Athenians recorded in this archive and on the walls of Egyptian temples, whereas the Athenians themselves, lacking the art of writing, have no way of maintaining a hold on their own tradition but have to begin from the beginning again every time they have been destroyed by natural disasters or conquest. The only media that give the Athenians some semblance of continuity are genealogies conveyed by word of mouth, so they are no more trustworthy than nursery tales. Touched on here are two matters treated at length in other writings of Derrida: his questioning of the fundamentality of the distinction between writing and speaking, and his endorsement of the Peircean thesis that the meaning signified is always already in the position of the signifier. The implication of this assertion is that there is in principle no end to interpretation. Bigger believes it implies an entrapment in language, a circumstance he judges to be sterile. Does he believe there is an entrapment in language because he believes that when Derrida writes "*il n'y a pas de hors-texte*" he means that there is nothing outside language? Would believing that not be tantamount to finding Derrida guilty of the "logocentrism" he deconstructs? A viable translation of the French would be "There is no textlessness," meaning only that nothing is without text or context. This does not mean that there is nothing non-linguistic, that there are no non-linguistic referents or subjects or institutions, or that all texts are linguistic.[47] The text referred to in his slogan is what he elsewhere calls the general text, what he also calls archi-text and archi-writing, where the prefix signals that the various sorts of spaced-outness and separation that are alleged to mark writing as opposed to speaking are no less to be found in speaking and are enabling-disabling conditions of this opposition.

Provisionally, we could think of archi-writing as occupying a different level from that occupied by writing and speaking as these are ordinarily opposed. This way of thinking of archi-writing might seem to be a way to reconcile Bigger and Derrida. Wittingly and wittily Bigger does violence to Timaean *chōra* in order to keep a place for a fecundity he fails to find in deconstruction, which he declares barren. Is it too far-fetched to suppose that Abraham stands for Derrida when we read:

> Abraham and his progeny are desert dwellers and our matrix is barren, a wasteland or desert where one seeks God in the place . . . He chose for his revelations. No doubt the creature holds itself up, but its "I can" is bleak. We propose to think metaphor as bounded by a fecund and intricately ordered *chōra* from which the creature can stand upright, and the Good, which can also transform barren places into gardens.[48]

It is a matter of faith with Bigger that the garden par excellence that was called Eden is the one that will come to be called Mary. Referring to her he says: "Her way led to the cross. How that is to mean is a matter of faith."[49] It is a matter of his faith, and it is this, he confesses, that is the absolute presupposition or article of faith taken for granted in the quest undertaken in *Between* Chora *and the Good*. This being so, can we not say that the flowers that Mary enables to bloom in the desert belong to the level of faith and that this level must be distinguished from the quasi-transcendental level at which deconstruction does and undoes its work? Would this not enable Bigger to find an oasis in Derrida's desert? The answer must be No. For talk of levels is here out of place, as Bigger's own reliance on the structure of chiasmus already indicates. Only that structure gets anywhere near reflecting the relation between deconstructive quasi-transcendentality and its various apparent and only apparently simple opposites. Perhaps a symptom of this aporia is the curious fact that the very word *oasis* appears to be an attempt to put into Greek the Arabic word *vah* as if (and "as if" is the phrase used by Liddell and Scott) it had as an analogue *auainō*. This does not mean a place flowing with water. It means being dry, *sec*—or, as Derrida would have taken the chance to say, SEC, "Signature Event Context"![50] This curiosity aside, Derrida's writings are engaged passim in destabilizing the notions of level and parallelism. A monumental example of this is *Glas*, where the alleged parallelism between philosophy and literature is shaken. Deconstruction does not take sides. Quasi-transcendentality is not a level to be opposed to another level as the transcendental is taken to be simply opposed to the empirical, the signifier to the signified, the intelligible to the sensible, life to death, the literal to the metaphorical, and so on. Quasi- (or As-if-) transcendentality is indeed the "name" for this breakdown of opposition, another "name" Derrida borrows for it being *chōra.* Consider the distinction between the transcendental and the empirical as treated by Kant. The transcendental is a condition of the possibility of the empirical. It is what remains constant through the variation of empirical hypotheses. In the religious context it would be what remains constant through the variation of concrete positive religious faiths, the *sine qua non* even of negative theology. Hence, if archi-writing, archi-metaphor, archi-signifier, archi-text, and so on were transcendental conditions of possibility of, respectively, the writing, metaphor, sign, context, and so on to which, respectively, speaking, the literal, the signified, the text, and so on are opposed, then Christian, Judaic, and Islamic faith would be severally compatible with these archi-structures. But these archi-structures are archi-de-con-structive and quasi-transcendental. That is to say, for example, that the metaphoricity ordinarily opposed to literality and assumed to be exterior to it is discovered to be already in place in literality and the signifier is discovered to be already in the place of the signified, with the consequence that literality and metaphoricity conceived as metaphysical opposites are discovered to be effects without firm foundation, *effets,* as Derrida says, something somewhat like but also unlike what Hegel calls *Resultaten,* more like what the opposition between reality and appearance turns out to be when Nietzsche says that when you question the in-itself status of reality you question too the mereness of appearance (or the mereness of the imagined). The resultant oppositions are made possible by a principle or law as traditionally understood throughout the history of metaphysics, but they are made impossible by a "law" of law, by an *archē* that is an-archic. They are made both possible and, as traditionally conceived, impossible at the same time. So that our notions of the same time, Greek *hama,* and of the proper time, *kairos,* are disturbed along with our notion of the proper place, also *kairos,* which gets contaminated by the conceit of an improper time-place. Here (Where? Derrida would ask, in the trace of Hegel's remarks on sense certainty and Heidegger's remarking of human being as Da-sein) is a proper-improper place, a place where properness, property, belonging, and ownership are crossed by impropriety and dispossession. This (Which? Derrida, again in the trace of Hegel, would ask) is the place, neither here nor there and both here and there, *fort-da,* that is marked by the unterminating term "*chōra.*"

That is to say, *chōra* is an ethico-political marker. It marks boundaries and bindings. And it is thanks to this ethico-politicality that Bigger's interpretation of *chōra* need not be inconsistent with Derrida's, provided our conception of consistency is unbound sufficiently from the principle of contradiction appropriate to propositional logic so as not only to allow but also to demand a certain practical contra-diction. This contra-diction is what is announced when Derrida, meditating on Levinas, says "*tout autre est tout autre,*" "every other is totally other," an ethico-political declaration that must be heard in Derrida's announcements of a religiousness without particular positive religion. The religiousness is the *religio* that binds the person who believes in a particular positive religion to a responsibility toward all who do not subscribe to that religion or to any other particular religion, whether extant or to come. This is what he refers to in religious terms as a messianism without Messiah, a messianicity without messianism, and in political terms as a new international democracy and a democracy to come. The question as to which, philosophy or theology, is the ancilla of the other is superseded by the question whether a particular religious faith can have priority over a religiousness that is absolute in the sense that it is attentive, listening and waiting, unconditionally. It welcomes with no strings attached. So that although a particular faith may be where I begin, it cannot be an origin without at the same time being an effect. Not even the Virgin Mary, the second Eve, can be an origin except relative to her relations in the Christian Family Scene and the family of humankind generally. She is an origin only within the sphere of the operations of traditional metaphysics. This metaphysics has not been rendered inoperative. Rather has it been placed in the context—in, to repeat a word from Bigger's subtitle, the neighborhood—of indefinitely producible contexts. Metaphysics is no longer its old self. Nor is metaphor, now that the literal has been so metamorphosed.

Is this metaphormorphosis sterility or fecundity? Does there have to be a *telos* to this process if it is to be fecund? Would not destinerrance without end be more fertile than teleology? One recalls that according to Levinas *erōs* is not teleological and that the direction of the intentionality of consciousness is reversed by the Good, which does not belong to the field of consciousness.[51] Derrida may be remembering this when he exposes egocentrifugal teleology to absolutely centripetal coming in, with no one at the gate holding in his or her hand a checklist of requirements by which it will be decided who or what may come in across the threshold: *tabula rasa,* aneconomic income without preordained criteria, ethico-religious revenue as such. This sheer coming-again would be both a ghost of Nietzschean eternal return and a ghost of presence that haunts distance. If the each time singular event—*événement*—of iterative, that is to say alterative, metaphormorphosis, is to take place, and if it is to have the bidirectionality that Bigger ascribes to the metaphor and the chiasmic structure that Derrida inscribes in deconstruction, then archi-writing, architext cannot be cut off, excised, circumcised from presence. Presence must be promised, *pro-mise, pro-mise en abîme,* that is to say wagered on (*mise*), sent ahead or dreamed of in the guise of an ever future present-ly that would perhaps be the return of a never present past. If this sounds like a denial of knowledge and replacement of it by faith, this is a faith that is general yet singular. It is singular as distinguished from particular. Particularity implies properties, the qualities or relations to which no attention is paid by justice according to the dictum that justice is blind. But whereas this dictum restricts itself to human beings and perhaps to any divine beings there may be, the attentiveness of general and singular *religio* without particular religion is generous and cruel enough not to limit itself to the human, nor indeed even to the living. It embraces at least the earth in its entirety, if the earth has an entirety. This religiousness on the borderline of madness is even more mad than the religiousness of Christianity as distinguished from Christendom by Kierkegaard, more mad than the madness of what is folly to the Greeks and a stumbling-block to the Jews. Indeed, a *problēma* is a stumbling-block, and we have seen that according to Derrida a problem can conceal an aporia that would drive us to the brink of madness. The empirical and historical drive us to the transcendental, and the transcendental drives us to the quasi-transcendental, which can drive us mad. Absolute aneconomic income, revenue at the threshold of the venue, is absolutely mad, that which makes possible and impossible the all too familiar oppositions between madness and sanity and rationality and passion. It is the passionality that gives life to rationality, the heart that has its reasons of which reason does not know. Hence it is not the enemy of reason, a role in which Derrida has sometimes been cast, for example by certain Cantabrigian dons. It is the patience that precedes the judgment that sensibility and understanding are fundamentally opposed to each other. It is the blind justice of blind fidelity, the blind faith that leads the justice within the law which is what we usually have in mind when we say that justice is blind. This passionality is the affectivity *of* rationality, rationality's affectivity. Derrida's *Passions* could have been called *Affections*.[52] About this rational affectivity, which we could also call imadgination, my very good friend Charles Bigger, tweaking the tails of Plato, Heidegger, Levinas, and Derrida, proposes a multiplicity of fecund, alluring, and persuasive suggestions.

## Betwixt and Between

In response to those suggestions and by way of résumé, let us consider whether *Between* Chora *and the Good* locates fecundity in pages of the *Timaeus* but only sterility in Derrida's reading of them because between Bigger's and Derrida's readings different betweens are being emphasized.

In addition to the between of Bigger's title, the between between the Good and *chōra*, is *chōra*'s own between—or her or his or its "own" between, as we should have to say bastardly, since according both to Plato and Derrida *chōra*

has no legitimate ownness and possesses no possessions, property, or properness. Now if the proper means the clean, as it does when one speaks in French
of clean hands, *mains propres,* we have a problem on our hands. For *chōra* is
supposed to be virgin. Derrida writes that *chōra* "appears so virginal that she
no longer has any more the figure of a virgin."[53] It is these words that provoke
Bigger into trying to make us see in *chōra* the figure or face (*figure*) and icon of
the Virgin. His way of doing this is to show that the "between" of his title does
not indicate a separation between two terms. It indicates rather an already given
proximity and communion where the motherhood Plato invokes in speaking of
*chōra* always already participates in the Goodness of the Father, the Christian
God who is Love—as if the hands cupped in prayer pictured on the jacket of
Bigger's book are holding water, the baptismal gift of eternal life and forgiveness, the "gracious gift" of a forgiveness that is forgiveness according to Derrida
only if no strings are attached, only if its unconditionality is so unconditional
that it no longer has any more the figure of a virgin, only if it is mad forgiveness
of the unforgivable.[54]

Derrida's reading of the *Timaeus* mentions parts of Plato's story that facilitate Bigger's Christo-Marian version. For instance, Derrida notes that the
receptacle is compared to a mother, the paradigm to a father, while the child
stands for what is between these. The betweenness of the intermediacy of the
child as a third nature vis-à-vis the father on the one hand and the mother on
the other has as one of its terms the maternal *chōra* that is a between. These
betweens, the between of the relationship between the good and *chōra* and the
between that *chōra* "is," are the two betweens distinguished in the preceding
paragraph. They are not at odds with each other. The second of them affirms
the togetherness of the poles which the first of them distinguishes. For Bigger's
application of Plato's story it is important that *chōra* be feminine and maternal.
This, as he well knows, is at odds with some of the things that Plato says in the
course of demonstrating that one cannot avoid speaking a hybrid language, a
mixed and betwixt language, if one is not to avoid speaking of the family scene
at all.

Where Derrida takes care not to use the definite article with *chōra* (or
*khōra* or *Khôra*) in order to avoid any implication of determinacy as to number
or gender, Bigger's emphasis on the femininity and maternity of *chōra* allows
him to say that both the child and the mother could belong to the third genus,
except that the third genus is not a genus to which anything can belong, because it turns out not to be a genus. Therefore there is no generation. And this is
why the metaphor for *chōra* of the nurse serves Plato's and Derrida's purposes,
though not Bigger's, as well as does the metaphor of the mother. Plato's purpose
here is to tell stories that convey, however inadequately, the conceit of what is
prior to participation—of what is therefore not a what. For that purpose the

nurse, the mother, the receptacle, and the wax-like recipient of impressions can all be no more than as-ifs: *oion tithēnēn,* Plato writes, as-if-a-nurse, an ancilla-so-to-say, *qua si.* For likening *chōra* to a nurse, even a wet nurse, does not suit Bigger. His *chōra* must be likened to a mother, none other than the Mother of God. But common to both his and Derrida's reading of Plato is a certain uncommonness, that of the two-wayness of the *dochē,* its being both receiving or taking and giving, as exemplified in the icon of the *Zoodochus Pēgē* referred to above, in which her reception of the child held in her arms and her and the child's giving his life are supplements of each other. As Derrida observes, in French one can simultaneously give (*donner*) and take (*prendre*) something or someone as an example—for example the Madonna, *Ma-done.*

As Derrida also observes, examples as instances or cases are indecidably examples as exemplars, models, paradigms, Paradigms. The direction of exemplarity is bi-directional. As is metaphorization according to Bigger. This is the "oscillating logic" of metaphor's fertilization. Now some seed may fall on stony or sandy desert ground, but the seed does not die. And when Derrida himself speaks of his religion without dogmatic religion as a religion of the desert, it is the desert in the desert of which he writes, the archi-desert. It is that desert which enables the desert to bloom (and joy(ce)fully to Bloom), whether with the flowers that are the topic of the right column in *Glas,* the flowers of Genesis and Genet's *Our Lady of the Flowers,* or the flowers watered by the *Zōodochus Pēgē.*

Further, bearing in mind the importance given to the experience of the beautiful in Bigger's account, and in anticipation of what will be said in later chapters of this book, here is a good place to plant the thought that the boundlessness of the desert exposes it to the sublime. That thought will lead to a rethinking of justice. Although it may sometimes seem, as it does to Bigger, that while Derrida treats of *chōra* he turns his back upon the Good, the place of the Good is preoccupied by Justice. This undeconstructible justice may not be the justice of total peace, but its violence is less violent than the violence of the justice of rights defined solely in the terms of determinate laws. Without its archi-faithful opening even the opening given and received by Mary *plena gratia* could be the shutting out of other determinate faiths, a consequence Bigger is no less anxious to avoid than is Derrida.

## Formal Indications

My rereadings, backward and forward, of Charles Bigger's fecund book have not yet persuaded me that that quality of fecundity has to be denied to the writings of our late mutual friend. I am grateful that the latter writings have been at least fecund enough to figure among the forces that motivated the writing of *Between* Chora *and the Good*. Because Derrida's, if not Bigger's, considerations of *chōra* and metaphormorphosis prevent our being satisfied with a free-standing polar opposition of verisimilitude and truth, I propose that the Latin dictum "*amicus Plato magis amica veritas*" be translated "Friendship with Plato is important but more important is friendship with faithfulness." I mean faithfulness in a sense that allows something that Derrida says to keep a door ajar for Bigger and me to pass through. At the beginning of this chapter it was seen that in *Deconstruction in a Nutshell* Derrida confesses that it is a problem and an enigma for him whether historical faiths are prior to transcendental conditions or whether the priority goes in the opposite direction.[55] It was also seen there that Caputo wonders why this problem cannot be dissolved by distinguishing priority in the *ordo cognoscendi* from priority in the *ordo essendi*, so that both priorities could be affirmed. Perhaps that is what Derrida himself is affirming when he says that he oscillates between the one and the other. But if this is so, he is granting a large part of what Bigger wants to affirm. Although he is not going so far as to give priority to the particular faith in the Virgin Mary that matters deeply to Bigger, he is at least granting that ontological conditions and our understanding of them are empty until animated by a particular faith of some kind. This faith need not be that of a historical religion, and having it will not necessarily be belief in a formal dogmatic doctrine or principle. It may be belief as that to which one gives one's heart at the level of an unformalized comportment toward the fundamental facts of life of birth, and copulation, and death to which I shall come in the next chapter: one's *credo* in the sense of *cor-dare*, to give one's heart.[56] It may be the faith of a historical religion, but in order to have such a faith we must know what it is like to have the faith that manifests itself in the faithfulness of the friendship or love of another human being. That condition is already enough, in the words of Rowan Williams's meditation on David Jones and Flannery O'Connor, for the world to be more than it is.[57] And, wonder of wonders, the world does not become less than it is when transcendental ontological conditions of the faith in messianism are supplemented by the quasi-transcendental condition that Derrida calls messianicity without messianism. Although a quasi-transcendental condition says *plus de . . .* , that is to say "no more," and *sans,* that is to say "without," for instance without messianism or without Mary, it says simultaneously "plus." That is to say, what is said through the saying of a quasi-transcendental condition is what is said in the saying of the pre-preposition "outwith" as parsed quasi-Abelianly earlier in this book.[58] This quasi-Abelian "outwith" is a preposition that poses opposite senses, but it is a pre-position in the sense that it is also prior to position. That is to say, again, that although the path of the particular faith to which Bigger is committed is not the only path by which one can approach or be approached by quasi-transcendental religiosity, a factical or fictive faith is a *sine qua non*. As Hent de Vries has strikingly said, "the conditioned conditions the condition."[59] Because the condition is a condition of possibility and of impossibility, it would be misleading to say, adapting Kant, that if the religious imadgination is not to be empty it must be called upon by a singular faith. For filling and fulfillment are what quasi-transcendentality excludes. And it excludes exclusion thanks to the non-exclusivity of its exposure to whatever approaches. Its messianicity is openness as such, *archikenōsis*. This exclusion of exclusion on the part of quasi-transcendental messianicity without Messiah cannot not welcome a particular or singular Messiah—which, as Caputo has argued, may bear the name Deconstruction.[60] This "without" must allow the outwith. And it must allow that the place of the Messiah may be occupied by Mary. But other occupants cannot be ruled out, other commitments, for instance to Judaism, Islamism, Anti-Christianity, Darwinism, Dawkinsism, Anti-Islamism, Atheism, Quasi-atheism, Marxism, Scientism, Ecologism, Vegetarianism,[61] and an indefinitely protractable series of more or less indefinitely formalized responses to the practical facticities of birth, engagement—for instance that of Søren and Regine—marriage, copulation, and death.

These -isms stand for what we stand for. They are the "here" of "Here I stand." They name what may be for us articles of faith, absolute presuppositions (Collingwood), prejudices as prejudgments prior to and enabling judgments as propositions (Gadamer), fundamental projects (Sartre), ultimate concerns (Tillich), passions (Kierkegaard, Heidegger, Derrida), commitments to which we stick more or less religiously. Maybe "I can no other" (Luther), but there is more than one way in which the other may be impossible. Whether or not these ways name formal religions, they have to some extent the formality of what in some of his early works Heidegger calls formal indications, *formale Anzeige,* as, we noted above, Caputo brings to our attention.[62] Heidegger's perhaps willfully enigmatic technical term is explained by him in more than one way in different contexts, but in none of them should his word "formal" be taken to exclude the informality of a rough sketch or outline. Indeed, in explaining what he means by a formal indication he sometimes uses the word *"Entwurf,"* which can mean sketch or project. It is itself an anticipatory sketch of the use to which Heidegger will put Kant's notion of a schematism, a function of the transcendental imagination. It is an ancestor of the thisness, *haecceitas,* that he encountered in his study of Duns Scotus and Thomas of Erfurt, and that, in another guise, we ourselves encountered, it will be recalled, in our study of Deleuze and Guattari. It goes back to Husserl's remarks about *Anzeige* and *Anzeichen* in the *Logical Investigations,* remarks that provoked Derrida in essays in *Speech and Phenomena* to give more weight than Husserl was ready to do to indexical expressions, so-called token-reflexives or shifters, such as "this," and "here," "you," "mine." Heidegger had already moved in that direction, seeing such indicators as keys to what he called "*Jemeinigkeit*," Dasein's being in each case mine for that Dasein, *chaque fois unique,* as Derrida says but with more attention to the other than is given by Heidegger. Heidegger and Derrida are drawing also on what Kierkegaard writes concerning the singular individual and the passion that can be communicated to others only indirectly. As noticed earlier in this paragraph, Kierkegaard's word "passion" is repeated by Derrida and Heidegger. "*Passions*" is a title of an essay by Derrida.[63] And Heidegger, breaking with the conception of philosophy as Olympian survey, the view from everywhere or the view from nowhere, writes: "This 'passion' (real [*wirkliche*]) as the only way of philosophizing is something that for a long time has no longer been recognized."[64] To show, indirectly with irony and humor, that it can be communicated only indirectly is to show that there is no direct route from it to such conceptuality as that of the Hegelian dialectic of negation. What in Heidegger eventually gets called another thinking is a thinking of alterity in which the other is not an object about which one thinks. It is in order to forge another way of thinking philosophically that he emphasizes that the guide to it may be the formal indications offered by each singular Dasein's existential inhabiting of passionately held commitments, or, better, commitments that hold Dasein. This being already possessed (*Vorhabe*) is the religiousness that, whatever particular religion or other faith in which it may be invested, saves philosophical understanding from being a *Weltanschauung,* a *view* of the world. And this religiousness in which insistence upon truth takes second place to the persistence of truthfulness that keeps listening is what may save religion from fundamentalism. It is formally indicative of how one is had by a creed, but its passion is a middle-voiced letting-be. "The indication stresses precisely that it should remain open for other contexts of life to be able to temporalize their approach to philosophy and enactment of philosophizing."[65] What holds for philosophy holds also for religions and other creeds insofar as they are the soil from which philosophy grows or grows away. It holds for the faith that would house the other of the other in the place of the mother and discover an oasis in the heart of the desert. And it holds for that faith's counterfaith provided that its "counter" is not the "not" of Hegelian dialectical negation or of any of the other antithetical negativities treated in the chapters of this book that have been concerned with the origins of negation and the negation of origins, and in the chapters describing how Nietzsche traces a genealogy of antithemes that revalues genealogy itself. In the place of the simple safe and sound, *sain et sauf* borderline that would be signified by "not" and "*pas,*" de-con-struction (minus and plus) traces the formally indicative filigree of the Scots "outwith" that re-pledges an "auld alliaunce" with the French "*avec*"-"*sans*"/"*sans*"-"*avec*" committed to paper in Derrida's *Sauf le nom*.[66] *Sauf le nom*, which sounds like *Sauf le non*, is a conversation concerning negative theology in which the historical connection that that apophatic tradition has had with the desert is emphasized, but also de-emphasized to the point where the borderline between apophatic theology and deconstruction threatens to become as unsafe and unsound as in our opening chapter we watched the borderline between the borderlines named "*Grenze*" and "*Schranke*" become in the analyses of madness conducted by Kant and Hegel and Kierkegaard.

It will be recalled that Bigger confesses that his faith in the mother standing at the Cross is what stands behind his attempt to give an account of *chōra* in terms of her. But if that account is to be a preferred alternative to the account he finds given by Derrida, it must be an account of the transcendental, if not also of the quasi-transcendental, unless it is precisely the latter, the "Dionysian" interruption of an "Apollonian" transcendentality that is what is being objected to by Bigger. I suspect that this is not what he is objecting to, for he wishes to acknowledge the violence that is consistent with his Marian revision of the Platonic and Derridian (de)construals. Now it may well be that the (quasi-)transcendental and the historical and biographical are somehow conditions of each other, as we learned from Derrida's avowal of a problem that concealed an aporia and led him to experience an oscillation. Somehow. How? One way, one way that Derrida himself refers to, could be the way in which a logically necessary condition of something would at a particular historical time be understandable only in the language in terms of which what it conditions is inscribed. The mutuality of the conditioning would not be that of a logical if and only if. For history or the education of the imagination might in due course enable the condition to be understood in language other than that through which we understand what it conditions. One illustration of this might be the relation of supposedly secular, allegedly purely philosophical conditions of certain Christian concepts which the former are said to condition, yet which, it might be maintained, we cannot describe without calling explicitly or implicitly upon the language of Christianity. Another illustration might be the conditioning by a Platonic notion, for example *chōra*, of a Christian notion, for example virgin birth, which, it might be maintained, is the only frame currently available through which we can make the Platonic notion to some degree understandable. Both are analogous to the structure of metaphorical analogy as analyzed by Bruno Snell, where the metaphor-metaphored relation is two-way but at the same time dissymmetrical. The "we" involved in both illustrations would have to be historically and biographically determined. The wider its geographical spread and the deeper its historical scope the more difficult would it be to envisage what historical evolution or personal re-imagining would free the logical condition from the particular cultural and cultic conceptuality in terms of which that condition and what it conditions are interpreted over a certain period. On a strictly holistic account which reduces to a minimum the difference between the historico-empirical and the logico-conceptual, such independent variation of the empirical and the conceptual would be impossible. On such an account the empirical is reduced to the logical. Independent variation of the empirical and the conceptual would be impossible also on a strictly atomistic account, where the reduction goes in the other direction.

The situation in the real world falls somewhere between these extremes. Only there can it hold that the logical conditioning at issue is "contaminated" by historico-linguistico-cultural conditioning. Only there can the distinction between the (quasi-)transcendental and the historical and biographical be made in order to allow that the (quasi-)transcendental can condition a particular historical or biographical faith without that faith, as against another faith, being a purely logical necessary condition of it. The parenthetical prefix that features in the last sentence should help us not to forget that the contaminated conditioning of which we have just given two illustrations is itself contaminated by address. It is thus contaminated in both directions of conditioning. This is why Derrida's dilemma examined at the beginning of this chapter oscillates between a genuine problem and an aporia. As the end of this chapter is upon us we may well wonder whether the same oscillation prevents our giving a simple answer to the question whether Bigger assimilates to each other a personal faith, his faith, with its transcendental (or quasi-transcendental) condition? If he is doing that, it may be only at the risk of oversimplification that it can be said that he is doing, though in reverse, what I confessed in chapter 13 that I was doing when, without clearly realizing what I was doing, I assimilated the transcendental (or quasi-transcendental) religiousness I was arguing for in Città to a particular instituted religion, one without which I could not make the intercessory prayer I wanted to make on behalf of a mutual friend of whose illness I had just learned. Transcendentality and quasi-transcendentality neither rule in nor rule out this or that religion. Nor do they rule in or rule out this or that God, for example or Example a God such as might be the addressee of an intercessory or otherwise petitionary prayer.

But what about gratitude, for instance my gratitude that Derrida among others provoked Bigger to write *Between* Chora *and the Good*? Like the prayer of intercession, gratitude appears to suppose a determinate addressee. One of the things to be shown in the next chapter is that that appearance is misleading and, what's more, misleading with regard to the religious understood not as a determinate religion but as a *religio perennis:* it is misleading with regard to the what's more. An aim of subsequent pages will be to demonstrate that from the fact that what we have been calling quasi-transcendental conditions are necessary conditions of the religious it cannot be inferred that they will be necessary conditions of a religion. This is because a religion will be an exemplification of religiousness in general only if it exemplifies one or other of the various forms of religious life that include birth, and copulation, and death, and these forms can be concretely realized while remaining outside the frame of an organized religion.

# FIFTEEN

# Between the Quasi-transcendental and the Instituted

### Birth, and Copulation, and Death

The religious does not have to bypass theistic or atheistic religion, but up to a certain point it can. It can refuse to affirm a particular historical creed, but it cannot refuse to be historical. This is why in "Faith and Knowledge: The Two 'Sources' of Religion at the Limits of Reason Alone" Derrida emphasizes that his topic is religion *today*. Although what the word "religion" means depends in part on how the word "*religio*" was used by Cicero, Catullus, and other Classical Latin authors writing before the birth of Christ, what the word means today for what we have to call "the global West" is massively determined by the climate of Christendom. Therefore the historical context in which a refusal to affirm Christianity is made is a context the language of which is shaped by the global Latinity of Christianity. The values of the Enlightenment, the *Aufklärung,* the *Siècle des Lumières,* and Secularism are deeply Christian. That this is so is an illustration, we could say an *Aufklärung,* of the paradox that transcendental or quasi-transcendental conditions are conditioned by what they condition. This entwining of historical with "logical" conditions of possibility and unpossibility is what made possible up to a certain point a relaxation of a prima facie tension between chapters 13 and 14 of this book. I say, twice, "up to a certain point" because in the remainder of this book flesh, I repeat, flesh will be put on the idea that the crossing of the historical and the quasi-logical conditions is not bound to be a crossing between the latter and belief in an instituted religion. Although the quasi-logical conditions may be themselves conditioned by what they condition, the latter need not be and need not have been an instituted corpus of belief. It may be something that is not socially organized and entrenched. It may be the dispositions and experiences for which I borrow from T. S. Eliot's Sweeney Agonistes the words used as the heading of this section. These dispositions and experiences, I maintain, may embody the quasi-transcendental conditions of the religious as these are spelled out by Derrida, whether or not these conditions are embodied in a religion.

I doubt that in maintaining this I am saying much that is not said by Derrida. I shall be doing little more than applying what he says to what was said by him and one of his sons on 8 October 2004 at the cemetery at Ris-Orangis. I shall be attempting to make it imaginable that although the historical conditions that condition the transcendental and quasi-transcendental ones may be those of an instituted religion, they need not be. Although in doing this I may be using the language of a particular historical religion, I shall be doing so only in the way in which secularism may inevitably be doing this when it affirms itself. But I shall be questioning universal secularism and the scope with which it is commonly credited.

The religious can bypass the religions by going directly to the almost naked elements of human life which the narratives and symbolisms of religions clothe. The almost naked elements of human life are not so naked that they are stripped of language. But the language need not be as developed as, say, that which gives a special status, as special a status as Bigger wishes to give, to the Mary who stood weeping by the cross. It can be as rudimentary as the language spoken by those who surround the bed of an unvirgin mother at childbirth, or as the language spoken or left unspoken by her and the members of the family circle who, with or without the consolations of a religion, sit near her when she is near to her death. The nakedness of the body at birth, in copulation and stripped by death of its belongings, its nakedness exaggerated by its shroud, expresses the very same sacredness as is expressed by non-expression where, in the whispered sweet nothings of sexual intimacy or the mute contact of a kiss, in the child's first cry at birth and in the inarticulacy of the moribund and of the mourned and the mourner, language respectively *is, will be,* and *was* the open mouth of the sharp intake of breath and of address, direction, where hardly a word is emitted. This is the sacredness of the religious as secret and silent binding and at the same time unbinding, ab-solution, release. This is "absolute religion" in a non-Hegelian sense, a sense closer to that of Kierkegaardian religiousness in

that its sociality, although potentially collective (*relegere*), is primarily a binding (*religāre*) and unbinding (*religāre* again) to singularity. That is to say, the
*relegere,* the bringing together or re-reading or repeating, and *religāre,* bonding,
are not without a *relēgāre,* a holding back (Heidegger would say *Verhaltenheit*)
that respects separation. The ab-soluteness of this *religio* is its unbinding from
the bindings of instituted law combined with its binding to responsibility toward singularities: moral conscience become religious. The religiousness of
this absolution and the absolution of this religiousness are not a logical relation that holds in such critical times as those of birth, coupling, and death unless by the logical is understood the towardness of face-to-face address and by
relation is understood the face-to-face relationship before another that is the
pre-condition of the relationality of terms. The "logic" is that of engagement,
as when someone gives a ring to another person or says, "I love you." To say
this is not in the first place to report a state of affairs. It is to bring one about by
performing what is already an act of love.

It is as acts of love that the dispositions and experiences named in the title
of this section are realized as acts of religion, whether or not they are realized
in the context of a religion. In the following pages the open-texturedness of
the concept of the religious will be underlined. The concept of the religious
is open-textured because of the open-texturedness of the concept of love. But
among the features that one would expect to find most commonly instantiated
by what would be counted as acts of religious love would be, to speak with
deliberate vagueness, a desire to save the loved person (or nonperson), to the
point of sacrificing oneself for him or her, perhaps to the point of giving one's
own life. Birth, and copulation, and death, and what in what follows will be
added to that list, can be matters of religion because they are matters of life and
death; and they can be that without being matters of an organized religion. I
say that they can be matters of religion. They can be secular matters. But they
are not bound to be that. After saying that any or all of them can be a matter of
religion without being a matter of a religion I should add that I am aware that in
connecting their being matters of religion with their being matters of sacrificial
love I am inviting the comment that I am thereby reading into the religious the
character of at least one historical religion, for example that according to which
love is *imitatio Christi.* This is an issue that was touched on in passing in the
course of the discussion of what was at stake in the two chapters immediately
preceding this one. It was mentioned in the first paragraph of this one. It is an
issue which, before the end of this book, will have to be tackled head-on. This
will be done in the epilogue.

At the end of *Sauf le nom,* which approaches the topic of negative theology
through the verses of *The Cherubinic Wanderer* of Angelus Silesius, Derrida refers to something that had happened earlier in the year during which, partly in

Nice, he was writing that book. He prefaces his telling of the story of this event with the remark: "—One must here believe in the accident or contingency of a story: an autobiographical alea," "*Il faut croire ici à l'accident ou à la contingence d'une histoire: un aléa autobiographique.*" It is necessary to note that he has reminded us earlier that although "*il faut*" means "it is necessary," etymologically it can mean also that something (or someone) is missing or missed.[1] It is necessary to note too that what we are being told about here is the necessity of a belief or faith ("Here you have to believe in the accident or in the contingency of a (his)story [*une histoire*]"), but that the belief or faith adverted to here is not the theism whose possible missingness from among the beliefs subscribed to by young Jacques so disturbed his young mother that she was afraid to question him on the matter.[2] It is belief in the contingency that

> I chose to bring here with me this given book, *The Cherubinic Wanderer* (and only extracts at that), to bring it to this family place, in order to watch over the mother (*la mère*) who is slowly leaving us and no longer knows how to name. As unknown as he remains to me, Silesius begins to be more familiar and more friendly to me. I have been coming back to him recently, almost secretly, because of sentences that I have not cited today. And furthermore, it takes up little room when one is traveling (seventy pages). Isn't negative theology—we have said this often enough—also the most economical formalization? The greatest power of the possible? A reserve of language. Almost inexhaustible in so few words? This literature forever elliptical, taciturn, cryptic, obstinately withdrawing, however, from all literature, inaccessible there even where it seems to offer itself up (*se rendre*), the exasperation of a jealousy that passion carries beyond itself; this would seem to be a literature for the desert or for exile. It holds desire in suspense, and always saying too much or too little, each time it leaves you without ever leaving you alone (*elle vous laisse chaque fois sans vous quitter jamais*).[3]

There is an almost inexhaustible reserve of things to be said about this concluding paragraph of *Sauf le nom*. To start with, why does its author write "almost," "*presque*"? Why does he not think that negative theology is an inexhaustible, fully inexhaustible, fully unemptiable reserve of language? Does he think then that the reserve is exhaustible? But, thinking of the contingency of his mother and her dying, how can he think that? Given death, how could anyone exhaust that reserve? Indeed, his mother (G., Georgette) is no longer able even to name her son. And the son is unable to respond.

> Alea or arbitrariness of the point of (no) departure (*point de départ*), even irresponsibility you will say, my enduring inability to answer for my name, to give it back to my mother, notwithstanding that I am here, now (*maintenant*), let us suppose, for I shall never be able to demonstrate it, the serial counterexample of what I have never been able to write or of what G. is able to know of it, and the fear that has always claimed me, since at least I am faithful to that,

> which makes me out of tune with myself, menacing me with two apparently contradictory threats, that of the writer who is scared of dying before reaching the end of a long sentence, a full stop that's all, without signing the counter-example, and that of the son who, afraid of seeing her die before the end of the avowal, for this confession promised to death, trembles also at parting before his mother, this figure of absolute survival . . . [4]

I interrupt this Proustianly long sentence and its interminable reaching out in search of lost time. It goes on for the best part of three more pages, telling next of the death of Jacques's elder brother Paul at the age of one and of his younger brother Norbert at the age of two, when Jacques was ten.

> . . . so I see the first mourning as the mourning of my mother, who would not therefore be able exactly to shed tears over me, me merely a replacement, to shed tears over me as should my sons . . .

We have been here before, there where the sons who should shed tears are asked through one of the sons not to shed tears, but to smile. Yet the "should" may not imply a request on the part of the father. It may signal no more than the normal expectation that the father will die before the son. We shall be here again. We are there already, in the frame of our own birth and death, a frame that is broken by the birth and death of others. The frame of life and death *passe partout,* passes us all wherever we may be, whether or not it is in its turn passed by us, and whether we go along with what Kant says about the borderline or with what Hegel says about it or describe the line otherwise than either of those philosophers,[5] for instance as the divided line as constructed by Plato or the divided line as deconstructed by Derrida. In any event, the line marks the mortality of each and every one of us and how each of us regards and is regarded by others in that eventuality of death. Further, as is indicated by Derrida's "as should my sons," *"comme le devront mes fils"*—where *"devront"* speaks, on the one hand, of the future toward which we are bound or (see below) which is bound toward us and, on the other hand, of binding—mortality means moral-ity or ethics, and religion or the religious, which is not the same as a religion. A religion is cooked, whereas, insofar as any aspect of being human can be raw, the religious can be raw. Relatively raw, relationshiply raw, as explained in the second paragraph of this chapter. Through religions that are ecclesial and codi-fied in books we attempt to comprehend the incomprehensibility of death by taking part in the retelling of a story and the performance of cultic practices, not least the funeral rites referred to in passing in *Being and Time* and at length in the works by Philippe Ariès and others mentioned by Derrida in *Aporias.*[6] More often than not, the attempt to comprehend the incomprehensible we call death invokes the incomprehensible we call God, which, unlike religions and religiousness, may be one and the same, namely the absolute other, an idea Hegel toys with when he calls death the Absolute Lord.

These incomprehensibilities of your and my death comprehend each other insofar as the coming of your death, even if I die before you, comes across the coming of mine, cuts across it chiasmically. This is the inconvenient invenience of which Derrida writes in the wake of his friend Levinas who, as we have written so many times, writes provisionally of the "reversed intentionality" of ethico-religious regard or attention which is not a negative reversal but rather a waiting upon the other who looks toward me in the distance.[7] In the wake also of Austin, read by Derrida through the lens of Augustine, this comprehension of one incomprehensibility by another becomes the subsumption of the "hereby" of "*me voici*" or "*hineni*," "I hereby put myself at your disposal," under the understood but incomprehensible and unheard "thereby" of an a priori engagement; so that in truth it is the straightforward intentionality of the constative or the hereby-ish performative that is reversed if there is reversal here, a reversal of and response to the other's address to me even before I can say in so many or so few words "*Me voici*," "See me here." Before, *devant,* owing. This backward dependency is tied to a forward dependency. Without this double bind others could neither rely on what was said by me nor be skeptical about my reliability. The "hereby" appears to require a ghastly, guestly, ghost-written "thereby-hereby" that is never present to consciousness and therefore in principle beyond the reach of memory if not of remembrance. Presence is haunted by absence. The concept, the *Begriff,* holding in one's hand, comprehension of something said, is visited by the religious as saying that ultimately goes without saying and that is in that sense "understood," yet is incomprehensible, like water that at a baptismal font, or sand in a hand held over a grave, seeps between one's fingers.

The hand, the hand that holds another's hand, *maintenant,* not holding it *in* one's hand, shakes. The voice breaks. Between the said and the saying, between the words on the page and the signature, the borderline and the very idea of a borderline tremble. "Wheretofore, my beloved, as ye have always obeyed, not as in my presence only, but how much more in my absence, work out your own salvation with fear and trembling" (Philippians 2:12). The presence and absence referred to in this verse are the presence and absence of the writer of the epistle. But transposed to the context of Kierkegaard's life and works they could be the presence and absence, *fort-da,* of Regine, allowance made for the fact that breaking off his engagement with her did not mean breaking off all communication whatsoever with her, even after she had married someone else. The absence that survives this remainder of communication is her absence from Søren's bed.

> Yet the relationship had to be broken, and I had to be cruel in order to help her—this is "fear and trembling." So frightful did the relationship become that finally the erotic aspect seemed to be absent because the nightmare shifted the

relationship into other categories. I was so much an old man that she became like a beloved child whose sex was more or less of no importance. This is "fear and trembling." And I dare maintain that I wanted the marriage more fervently than she; in the purely human sense it signified for me (like those demoniacs in the fairy tale) my salvation. But I could not enter that harbor; I was to be used in another way. . . . This, you see, is fear and trembling.[8]

That Kierkegaard was religiously scrupulous in matters of punctuation, but perhaps also that sometimes (trembling for fear of becoming the victim of pride?) he relaxed his rigor, is demonstrated here by his referring on the one hand without quotation marks to the fear and trembling of "another way," the way to eternal salvation, but on the other hand with quotation marks to the "fear and trembling" of the temporal salvation (which might be a slip of the pen for "salvation" guarded by scare-quotes), salvation that might happen in a fairy tale like the one told in *Fear and Trembling* to which allusion is here made.[9] But it is the relationship between these two salvations, eternal salvation and temporal "salvation," or eternal "happiness" and temporal happiness, that rouses the fear and trembling experienced and treated by the writers whose works we have been studying.

Mention of "the erotic aspect" in the sentences just cited from Kierkegaard brings us to an aspect of the temporal that is also an aspect of the religious. The temporal and with it the erotic extends into the eternal at least as metaphor or metonymy. Testimony to this are the lines in the Revelation of Saint John the Divine 21:2 that say: "And I John saw the holy city, new Jerusalem, coming down from God out of heaven, prepared as a bride adorned for her husband." Putting flesh on the "as thyself" of "thou shalt love thy neighbor as thyself" of Leviticus 19:18, specifying a neighbor, and perhaps hinting at a condition when that neighbor was man's rib, Saint Paul writes in Ephesians 5:28–30:

> So ought men to love their wives as their own bodies. He that loveth his wife loveth himself.
>     For no man ever yet hated his own flesh; but nourisheth it, even as the Lord the church:
>     For we are members of his body, of his flesh, and of his bones.

There exists an opulent treasury of erotico-religious poetry and prayers from which here are but two examples:

> Yet dearly I love you, and would be loved faine,
> But am betroth'd unto your enemie:
> Divorce mee, untie, or breake that knot againe,
> Take mee to you, imprison mee, for I
> Except you enthrall mee, never shall be free,
> Nor ever chast, except you ravish me.

Thus John Donne, as bent on breaking one engagement in order to keep another as Kierkegaard was bent on (God save the mark) "re-partnering."

> Rowing in Eden!
> Ah! The sea!
> Might I but moor
> To-night in thee!

Thus Emily Dickinson, where the metaphorical exchange between sexuality and spirituality goes together with an exchange of her gender for that of the opposite sex so that it is a man she imagines is speaking. And note that the harbor trope ("Might I but moor") that that imagined man applies to the spiritual side is applied to the sexual and marital side by Kierkegaard ("I could not enter that harbor"). Or is this talk of "sides" misleading, granted the ancientness of the idea that a priest is married to the church?

Not a few of the Welsh hymns of William Williams, Pantycelyn, are expressions of the same tradition of randy religiosity that runs deep in the West but is perhaps most abundantly articulated in Eastern thought and art, most spectacularly in Hindu temple carvings and Tibetan Buddhist tankas. Think of some of the poems of Rumi. Think of the scene of the *Song of Songs*.

> As a man loves a woman, so God loves them both. As a man loves a woman, so Christ loves the Church. As each transparency is lifted there is always the *Song of Songs,* but as one drops them back into place, the scene in this garden of lovers' delights begins to fill with all the combinations and possibilities of love.[10]

Once the spiritual is seen through sexual metaphors and vice-versa, the conventional borderline between the temporal and the spiritual can no longer be drawn. And insofar as the sexual is considered to be a paradigm of the secular, locating the relation of the religious to the secular will call for an alternative topography.

As for the relation between institutional religions and religiousness and God, it is a mistake to suppose that the death of God as proclaimed by Nietzsche entails the death of religion. That this supposition is mistaken follows immediately from the fact that there is a godless version of Buddhism. It is widely supposed also that the death of God entails the death of religiousness. This supposition too is mistaken. The religious defined in terms of religion and God is only the canonic cultic expression of a religious response to birth, and copulation, and death and—since these are not quite "all the facts" as claimed by T. S. Eliot's Sweeney Agonistes—by other critical moments of life ceremonialized in various books of common prayer—and treated in psycho- and schizoanalysis.

Such prayer books (and such therapies) are composed for common use to help us find words where we might otherwise be at a loss for them, either struck dumb by grief or, as at the birth of a child or beside a baptismal font, surprised by wordless joy, when what is said is at most a spellbound stutterance (Deleuze) but when therefore saying as address is most intense and attentive. Consider what one of those handbooks says in connection with marriage. The Anglican manual known as the Book of Common Prayer uses in this context the words "with my body I thee worship." These words lend support to the claim that the liturgical forms of service included in that book are conventional expressions of what might be called a natural religiousness, provided the naturality of this religiousness is not taken to exclude the minimal conventionality of such performative gestures as are put into the words "I will" in the service of marriage. Such words as "I will" change the world by effecting an act accomplished in the utterance of them. What act the utterance of them effects can be made explicit by the use of the operative term "hereby," as in "I hereby promise" or "I hereby pledge," as in the pledge "to hold from this day forward . . . in sickness and in health, to love and to cherish, till death us do part," words which confirm that at least symbolically the hymeneal estate links birth and death. Indeed the ambiguity of the hymeneal estate as both conjugation and a membrane that is a barrier to conjugation, both *Grenze* and *Schranke* (in one word: an *aporia*), reflects the ambiguity of the circumstances that copulation leading to a new life entails cellular death, that—sting of life—as soon as we are born we are borne toward death, and death, our own and that of others, bears down upon us, that sexual conjugation leads to "the little death," and that death, big death as well as this little one, is primitively conceived as leading peradventure to a second birth:

> Ancient *tristesse, La petite mort.*
> So must we die? Must we part?
> Native of Eden, I ache for resurrection.[11]

In other words, not only do the vocabularies of eternal salvation or eternal "happiness" and temporal happiness or temporal "salvation" feed on each other, exchanging their quotation marks, crossing over the line between them,[12] but, further, each member of the trinity of birth, copulation, and death reaches out to the others prospectively and retrospectively (birth perchance "trailing clouds of glory"), each borderline being a vector and a threshold or a hymen, for instance the hymen between copulation and generation. Even if we think of death as a *Grenze* in Kant's sense, as a borderline beyond which there is no passing and through which there is no seeing, copulation and birth are reflected in its glossy black surface. And they, copulation and birth, are as preoccupied by death as is the face of the mother in so many paintings of the Madonna and

Child, not least those described in chapter 13, in which physiognomic expression and fingers play a part in pointing a way and pointing away outside the frame.

It is the meeting of extremes that is our topic, in order above all to demonstrate that what I am calling religiousness is embedded in the connections among the most rudimentary facts of life, whether or not this religiousness becomes articulated in an established mythology or organized religion. I occasionally speak alternatively of the sacred or the holy and the spiritual. But I persist in speaking of the religious because I want to be understood to be saying something that is manifested in the religions, although it does not need to be, not even in a religion in its early stages of systematization. Further, I want to keep hold of the minimal sense of binding carried by "*religio*" in order to retain the ethical force spelled out in the expression "ethico-religious" used by Kierkegaard and Levinas, some of whose thoughts I see myself to be rethinking.[13]

I see myself to be rethinking too the thought David Wood expresses when he writes that

> "God" may be understood as a disposition to open the space of one's ethical complacencies to being challenged, and that it is always a sign of the waning of insight to start up the engines of projection once again. There never was any other realm, but there certainly are radically different ways of inhabiting this one.[14]

The trick is to use "God" without succumbing to the temptation to let it start up once again the engines of projection and protection. Although I do use and abuse "God," I prefer to speak as far as possible of a religious disposition that is not dependent upon God or "God," and that is less disposed than they are to restart those engines. So I see myself to be rewriting some of the things Derrida writes of "religion in general." I am probably less worried than he is (but we shall return to the question of how worried he is) about admitting that the ethicality of the religious is at the beginning an ethicality of the family circle or ellipse. While not denying the dependence of the notion of the family upon the artifice, for instance the artifice of the law, I want to retain the possibility of a relative naturalness and unsophisticatedness for the religious, however codified and institutionalized as a religion it may in due course become.

Nevertheless, I insist on the validity of taking as clues to the substructure of relatively undeveloped religious experience what I find in the superstructure of religions, for instance in those words from Cranmer's Book of Common Prayer, "With my body I thee worship." "With my body I thee worship." How do I do that? "O worship the King" we are bidden in the first line of Robert Grant's great hymn. How do we do that? Some churchgoers, like the Puritans at the Hampton Court Conference of 1604, have difficulty following this bidding because they have reservations over what they hear as a hint of idolatry in the word "worship." The difficulty is compounded especially for Protestants if this suggestion is accompanied by or interpreted as the suggestion that one is being requested to hand over, albeit freely, one's freedom of choice. The difficulty may be deepened especially for women by the masculinity of the addressee of the worship, notwithstanding that the male worshipped at Christmas is a child. The same problem is presented by the fact that in the Form of Solemnization of Matrimony in the Anglican Book of Common Prayer the woman is asked to say "I will" to the invitation to obey the man. Observe too that it is the man, but not the woman, who is asked there to say "with my body I thee worship." This is worth noting not only on account of the onesidedness, a onesidedness reflected in the description of this ceremony as matrimony rather than patrimony or marriage.

While it is solely the man who is asked to say "with my body I thee worship," solely the woman is asked to say that she will obey. She is asked to say also that she will honor her houseband. But to worship is to honor—and indeed in the Alternative Service "honor" is substituted for "worship" in the just-cited phrase. To worship is to acknowledge worth (Old English *weorth,* German *Wert*). So here at least and at last there is some acknowledgment of mutuality. And since to worship is glossed in dictionaries by "adore," to worship each other would seem to be to pray (*oro*) to each other. Not idolatrously, for to pray is primitively and most rudimentarily to ask (*Prego*), and in asking one waits for a response. Praying, my episcopal and other friends have taught me,[15] is attention and *attente,* and this is deferral to whomever the prayer is addressed to, if it is addressed to anyone rather than, say, to one's "lucky stars," the *fatum* that Nietzsche learned to love.

In the prayer book used by William Williams the equivalent of the English "to worship" is *anrhydeddu.* In his time that verb would have brought with it still the idea of contemplating with wonder and astonishment or (see below) being overcome by them, which is very much not to contemplate, but to be gobsmacked, whether or not it is also to be godsmacked. One route through which this sense of wonder is made manifest is the body. It is manifested in regard to the body of the beloved. Earlier in the order of service it is stated that one of the reasons why matrimony was ordained was so that "such persons as have not the gift of contingency might marry and keep themselves undefiled members of Christ's body." Nothing less than the "mystical union that is betwixt Christ and his Church" is signified by the "honorable estate" of hymeneal conjugation that consummates the conjugation of hands. This becoming "coupled together" is to be undertaken "reverently." Venus is to be venerated. As indeed she was, and before Christianity, if the etymology of the verb "venerate" counts for anything.

Not that etymology may generally count for much. But it can count for something sometimes. It is in the faith that this is so that I make such appeals to roots. I do so not as a substitute for argument, but in the hope that the reader will occasionally be as surprised as I am by what these appeals suggest. I make these appeals in readiness to discover with Deleuze that roots may be unexpectedly unsimple rhizomes. And that is the attraction of the project to trace the formality of religions back to the informal and comparatively natural religiousness of the events of birth, and copulation, and death. To these must be added such basic events as eating and drinking and, more significantly, giving to eat and to drink, before the latter become the giving to eat announced by "This is my body" and the giving to drink announced by "This is my blood." The "common meal," already before it becomes Mass, is a communion, but one where what Luther would have called table-talk is minimal, and not only because you do not talk with your mouth full. Such events are the elements at least of human being because they are where the human being is closest to the earth and its nourishments, where the physical and the spiritual are closest to each other because they intersect in a carnation that may be, but does not have to be interpreted as the Incarnation of Christ. It may be interpreted more inclusively along the lines of imadgination construed as imagination as the common root or rhizome of, on the one hand, theoretical and practical reason and, on the other hand, sensory and affective sensibility. Except that affectivity is not restricted to self-affection or socially plural balanced inter-affection as it seems to be in Maurice Merleau-Ponty's notion of flesh (*chair*).[16] It extends to my being affected by the singular other calling for justice, the calling that is marked by the letter "d" that marks that imagination is always already imadgination. Some commentators on Merleau-Ponty's conception of flesh seek to show how justice would fit into it, but the justice they are concerned with is not justice to the singular other. David Levin's important essay "Justice in the Flesh" concludes: "[T]hanks to Merleau-Ponty's work, it is now possible for us to see, in the reversibilities of the flesh, in the mediations of justice already schematized and enacted by our intercorporeality, that the strong human bond required for the institutions of a just society is already being formed and tried." Derrida and Levinas would say that the strong human bond is both not strong enough and too strong unless the reversibility of the flesh is crossed with an irreversibility, an irreversibility that may be hinted at when Merleau-Ponty himself writes: "To begin with, we spoke summarily of reversibility, of the seeing and the visible, of the touching and the touched. It is time to emphasize that this reversibility is always imminent and never realized in fact." It is time to re-emphasize also that, as asserted earlier in this chapter, it is only "to begin with" that Levinas speaks of reversed or inverse intentionality. Levinas's provisional phrase looks forward to what Derrida calls *revenance,* a word that is haunted also by Levinas's statement that "[t]he illeity in the beyond being is the fact that its coming toward me (*venue vers moi*) is a departure which lets me accomplish a movement towards a neighbour."[17] In this in-coming the phenomenological character of consciousness as consciousness of something is replaced by an advention that is not simply adventitious, but is both a posteriori and at the same time a priori. It can be called an "experience" only if by this something ethico-religious is meant, on analogy or "analogy" with the "experience" of moral respect as described by Kant. Except that this "experience" of what Kant calls an intellectual object, meaning the moral law, demands, as though by a second categorical imperative over and above the Kantian one, to be supplemented by the "experience" of the unique other that in the French of Levinas and Derrida goes by the pronoun "*autrui.*" This is a pro-pronoun in that it stands for You and for She and He and They for whom You stand in your turn. *Autrui* may not be an empirical person. *Autrui* is any imaginable human (or divine) being and, as far as religionless and godless religiousness is concerned, at least any other being on the borderline of life and death marked by the very elementary forms of religious life denoted by the phrase "birth, and copulation, and death." I refer to these as the *very* elementary forms because their social structure may be that of a singular You and a singular Me, not yet articulated politically and not necessarily ever articulated empirically as a historical religion. The empirical realization of this social structure need stretch no further than to cases falling under these very elementary forms, provided the formality of these forms and the structure they realize are deformed and destructured by the address between oneself and another that converts imagination, that is to say the power of the if, the as if, and the quasi-, into the impower of the religious imadgination from which the quasi-transcendental on the one hand and the historical event on the other are abstractions. Where the Kantian transcendental and empirical are schematized in the imagination at the intersection of determinative and reflective judgment and where the Kantian Typik occupies an analogous place between practical principles and moral judgments, the religious imadgination is the place of intersection between the quasi-transcendental and the event of hearing a call for justice exceeding the justice of law. For the event to be religious it need not be an event as historically significant as those that are said to have occurred on Sinai or Moriah or Golgotha or in Bethlehem or at Mecca or, for that matter, Lumbini. It may be any of the happenings mentioned and not mentioned in my borrowed shorthand phrase "birth, and copulation, and death."

I do not expect that all of the happenings alluded to by that phrase will be regarded as potentially religious by all of my readers. I expect that many of my readers will regard none of them as that. The best I can do is argue that these are candidates for the epithet "religious," hoping that by the time as yet unper-

suaded readers reach the end of this book some of them will regard as sacred
and sacramental some of those elementary events and eventual elements, at
the very least the passage from life to death of a loved one or friend—although
the vulnerability of the newborn is already a reminder that the passage into
life heralds a passage from it. These "elementary forms of religious life," unlike those studied by Durkheim in the book that uses those words in its title,
are not religions, and more significant than their forms is their disruption of
formality. Indirect evidence for the thesis I may be overlaboring here is the
historical prevalence of ancestor worship. Less indirect evidence can be our
witnessing of these events, where witnessing or testifying retains a reserve of
indirectness. To anyone whose imagination is dead to the religiousness of the
experience of the tying of a bond at the dying and death of a close relation or
friend I can only repeat that this very deadness can be a part of the experience
of the religiousness of mourning. It is as though the apathy of the mourners'
imagination is their way of still being with the dead and of sympathizing with
other members of the community of comatose mourners standing around them
in the cemetery, the *koimeterion,* the place of sleep.[18] And it is because one's
imagination is sleepy that not even that benumbedness may be experienced at
the thought of the death of a stranger. "This is, perhaps, what thinking gives us
to think about, what gives us to think about thinking," *was heisst denken.*[19] This,
perhaps, that when Derrida writes, "These questions can be posed only after
the death of a friend, and they are not limited to the question of mourning,"
the questions that can be asked only then include "What is love, friendship,
memory, from the moment two impossible promises are involved with them,
sublimely, without any possible exchange, in difference and dissymmetry, in the
incommensurable?"[20] And the promise one makes is a promise the "hereby" of
which migrates beyond the living present of memory, beyond the memory of a
living present, and beyond one's own death and the death of the other, whoever
may be the other addressed in the imadgination of one's heart. The passion of
this address is more passive than the passivity metaphysics contrasts with activity. Its act of speech is an act of a *religio* older than dogmatic religion.

Of all religious occasions at the border between another's life and death,
between another's to be and not to be, a friend's crossing the last borderline is
the one of which it is most difficult to deny that it is sacramental in a sense that
does not necessitate that there be gods on the scene or in the wings. Indeed the
passing away of gods from the scene may be one of the eventualties that require
to be added to the list of elementary religious occasions. This would be said by
Hölderlin and Nietzsche. It would be said also by Derrida. For him the secret of
the sacred is the astonishing incomprehensibility of the impossible, inaudible,
immemorial "Thereby-Hereby" that is called for by the operations articulated
in the utterance of such words as "I name," "I will," "We commit": the divided

and unoriginal root of religion more ancient than any instituted religion, god, or pantheon—unless you can say to that fork-rooted Thereby-Hereby "I hereby name Thee God," perhaps even "I hereby name thee Dionysus."

Will it be objected that if such everyday remarks as "I will" and "I promise" and "I name" and "Your health!" ("*Salute!*") carry or are carried by a religious force, the specialness of the religious is lost? Is not the sacred sacrificed for the profane? Worse, since the profane at least implies a temple (*fanum*) or other sacred place outside which it stands and is no less a religious category than is atheism, are we not after all reducing the religious to the secular? The answer to this last question is that there is a reduction to secularity when these inaugural utterances get mistaken for pure statements of fact, mistaken for what for the sake of convenience and only provisionally could be called the prose of the world. That is the charge Kierkegaard makes against Hegel and the Hegelians as he understands them. However, it is a mistake to take a statement as a state-ment of pure fact or pure prose. To see secularity as pure is to be culpable of an oversight. That is deconstruction in a nutshell, a shell (*écorce*)[21] that decon-struction breaks. With the assistance of Kierkegaard and Nietzsche one learns that the prose of this world is broken by its poetry. By *its* poetry, the poetry and productive *poiēsis* of *this* world, which is at the same time the poetry of another world too, only provided we are willing to say of it that there is another world, but it is (in) this one.

## There Is Another World, but It's This One

The words "There is another world, but it's this one" are attributed to Paul Éluard without specific reference among epigraphs of Patrick White's *The Solid Mandala* and of Morris Berman's *The Reenchantment of the World*.[22] The spe-cific source has so far escaped my trawls through Éluard's works. I am inclined to discontinue my search, if only on the excuse that I have already fallen—nay, thrown myself—into a trap set for scholarly curiosity by Nietzsche.[23] Neverthe-less, I shall minister at least to any scholarly curiosity that may assail any of my readers by reporting that in the *Dictionnaire abrégé du surréalisme* reproduced in the Pléiade editions of the complete works both of Éluard and of André Breton the latter's entry under "*Philosophie*" contains the following sentence: "Everything I love, everything I think and feel, inclines me toward a particular philosophy of immanence according to which surreality would be contained in reality itself, and would be neither superior nor exterior to it." The sentence to which the name of Éluard is attached appears to be an endorsement of this one. Éluard gives no sign that he would not endorse the remaining sentences in Breton's entry: "And vice-versa, for the container would also be the content. It is almost as though there were a communicating vessel connecting the content and the container." *"Il s'agirait presque d'un vase communicant entre le contenant et le contenu."*[24] These latter sentences distort the thought for the expression of which I believed I might borrow one version or other of the sentence attributed to Éluard. They do this by implying a too straightforward synthesis and symmetry. They also exclude exteriority, as, it so happens, does the epigraph that follows the one Patrick White cites from Éluard, namely Eckhart's words "It is not outside, it is inside: wholly within," *"Es ist ganz und gar drinnen, nicht draussen; sondern durchaus drinnen!"*: *"es ist zemâle inne, niht ûze, sunder allez inne."*[25] The thought for the expression of which I borrowed and bent the Scots word "outwith" is not the thought of a wholly within, unless the wholly within is also wholly without, both *zemâle inne* and *allez ûze*. If there is an immanence, as Breton contends, it must not be an immanence that is antithetically opposed to a certain too naively figured transcendence. If, as Jean Wahl maintains, the most significant transcendence is the one that becomes an immanence, that can be so only if a traditional idea of metaphysical transcendence is transcended toward a transcendence whose exteriority is not simply opposed to interiority. And it is to mark this complex "transascendence" (Wahl's word) that I use the word "outwith," which can be either a preposition that is prior to positionality and to propositionality, or a conjunction that is at the same time a disjunction, or an adverb of a verb that is passive in the sense of a passedness that is older then the passivity that is classically opposed to activity. To borrow again from Rowan Williams the words that a title of his borrows from R. S. Thomas, in this outwith "the wound of knowledge" is still bleeding, and the wound is knowledge's wound. The wound is in knowledge in the way that the saying of address traumatically interrupts the said not only of reality or the world, but also of what Breton calls surreality or super-reality, "another world." The otherness of the religious imadgination is not the otherness of a second realm, and if this otherness is referred to as the otherness of God, the royalty of the sovereign of His kingdom of ends is still misconceived even if it is insisted, as it is by Kant, that in this kingdom God is also a citizen subject to law.

The otherness of the other world in this one is announced aesthetically in the aura with which things of this world are clothed in certain paintings of, for example, Tintoretto, Rembrandt, Samuel Palmer, Graham Sutherland, and Paul Nash, an aura that according to the gospel of a certain flat-earthism—the doctrine of earthness and world without otherness—would be no more than the representation of a pathetic fallacy. The otherness of the other world is proclaimed also in the way that things of this world described by Wordsworth (of whom more anon) strike us with awe. The world that is more and other than it is, is nothing other than this one. However "aesthetic" the signs or traces of this otherness may be, they call us to action. Their import is ethico-religious and political, as is the import of the following words, ones that, I promise, can be attributed with assurance to Rilke, though they echo those in which we found Nietzsche dismissing the "impudent doctrine of personal immortality":[26]

> What insanity to side-track us toward a Beyond, when we are here sur-rounded by tasks and expectations and futures! What treachery to purloin the images of actual delight so as to sell them behind our backs to Heaven! O it is high time the impoverished earth collected all those loans we have raised on its splendour, in order to furnish something "beyond the future" with them. Does Death really grow any more transparent because of these fountains of light we have slipped behind them? And is not everything that has been taken away from here, since a void cannot maintain itself, replaced by a deception,—is that why the cities are so full of ugly artificial light and noise, because we have handed the true radiance of the song over to another, later enterable, Jerusalem?[27]

To cultivate a responsiveness to the poetry of the world, as Rilke's agenda urges us to do, is to cultivate attention and regard also to the word. A responsive-ness to the world is a responsiveness to the word and a responsibility to name things as though for the first time. It is also responsiveness and responsibility to those to whom such everyday remarks as "I will," "I name," and "I promise" are addressed, for these remarks are precisely those by which responsibility is engaged and recognized in the performative sense of the words "engaged" and "recognized." It is chiefly of the force of these words in relation to the religious that we are speaking, not directly of particular religions. The latter, in their Sunday best clothes or otherwise Sabbatical sartorial formality, maintain their distinctness from the everyday. True, the forms of everyday engagement and initiation hold in reserve opportunities for the extension into weekday life of at least some of the Sabbatical formalities of religions, and the formalities of religions are not strictly entailed by the thought that, to use Philo's words, "each day is a feast day."[28]

Here a clarification is due with regard to what earlier paragraphs have described as the rudimentarity and relative crudeness of these forms of unin-stitutionalized religious life. In *The Idea of the Holy* Rudolf Otto refers to the "'crude,' and rudimentary emotions of 'daemonic dread' which . . . stand at the threshold of religious evolution. *Religion is itself present at its commencement:* religion, nothing else, is at work in these early stages of mythic and daemonic experience."[29] He goes on to list "factors contributing to the crudity of primi-tive 'religion.'" He includes among these "the uncontrolled, enthusiastic form, making for wild fanaticism, in which the numinous feeling storms the savage mind, appearing as religious mania, possession by the numen, intoxication, and frenzy."[30] Although the rudimentary and crude occasions and experiences abbreviated in the title of this chapter's first section may never be far from mania, they can be quite sober and controlled. And they are not limited to primitive and savage mentalities. They may be earlier than and independent of the rituals of more or less sophisticatedly organized religions, but they may also be contemporary with them. The reader should not be surprised therefore if from time to time our argument follows cues given by the more articulated superstructures of religions, for instance the orders of service of the Anglican Book of Common Prayer plundered earlier in this chapter. The validity and necessity of this procedure is a corollary of the quirky circumstance that the condition is conditioned by what it conditions.[31] That is why the same procedure is followed by Derrida, as we are about to be reminded. Before we are so reminded, however, and before this section of this chapter is closed, I must guard against an inference that, as Basil O'Neill has pointed out to me, I may seem in the above to be encouraging my reader to make.

A clarification is called for also of the remark made a few paragraphs ago that the profane is a religious category. So too is the blasphemous. That is to say, the topic of the religious as distinguished from religions is analogous to the moral not as distinguished from the immoral, but as distinguished from the pair moral-immoral. It is, as Nietzsche would put it, beyond good and evil. That is one reason why he is a religious thinker. That is also why, to mention a writer mentioned by Basil O'Neill in his comment, Bataille is in my sense a religious thinker too.[32] Another analogy would be that of Heidegger's existentials, which range over both their effective and their defective modes. Therefore, instead of drawing upon the, to me, relatively familiar universe of discourse of the Book of Common Prayer for clues as to the religious in general, I could have appealed to the material of the, to me, less familiar and more outlandish religions. Or I could have constructed imaginary examples. Indeed it must be evident by now and will become even more so by the end of this study that the stretching of the imagination to the aesthetico-ethical imadgination is what the religious as I construe it is expected to encourage. My dilemma is that, while far from wanting to play safe, I must, if it is to assist me in my agenda, invoke a sphere of discourse in which I and some of my readers feel relatively at home or can remember feeling relatively at home or can imagine themselves feeling relatively at home. For my purposes it is enough if my readers, granting a *mutatis mutandis,* can bring themselves to grant also that people in whose universe of discourse they cannot find their feet may nevertheless find their feet there with themselves. For an implication of my view of the relation of the anthropological to the logical and conceptual I refer to the later sections of my essay "Representation in Language."[33] Suffice it to say here that the view there expressed is precisely to do with the view of worldview, *Weltanschauung,* interpreted not as looking at the world but as being looked at by the world, a conceit that I see as leading naturally to what will be said in my next chapter about quasi- or archi-sublimity, which in turn I see as a way of reading what is said in some of the later writings of Derrida.

It must be stressed too that in the references in these paragraphs to natural religiousness, the natural is not opposed to the conventional. It is not entirely stripped of what Husserl refers to as the garb of language. Husserl's trope is misleading for the same reason that my talk even of relative nakedness can mislead. Language is more like what he and Merleau-Ponty call the body, bones and flesh. The body in its nudity is expressive of vulnerability. Vulnerability is maximal in the undress of address. That is why we put pennies on the eyelids of the dead. When Levinas writes of "responsibility for the other, for the first-come in the nudity of his face," the face is a synecdoche for the body, and so are the eyes.[34] As for the natural, I have just been treating of this as what feels natural, where we feel up to a point at home, in order now to stress that this inhabitedness of a religious form of life is essential to its religiousness in the sense in which I am using this word. This sense will escape us if we limit ourselves to the external point of view of a certain kind of documentary anthropology, what, adapting Husserl's phrase, we could call the "naturalistic attitude," what was referred to provisionally above as the prose of the world. The natural or relatively natural has another meaning, however, which is also vital for the understanding of religiousness in general as distinct from the religiousness specifically of historical religions. In this other sense the natural or relatively natural is defined in terms of the rudimentary events of life: birth, drinking, eating, copulation, aging, illness, death . . . , all candidates for elevation into sacraments of historical religions. Note too that these rudimentary events are only relatively elemental, for their momentaneity and momentousness are that of the crossing of thresholds that lend themselves to being understood neither as Kant nor as Hegel understand the borderlines charted in our first chapter. To the extent that they are understandable, they are best understood by following the construal of *séri(r)ature* and seriousness that in "At this Very Moment in this Work Here I am . . ." Derrida, binding *serō* (to bind) and *sēriō* (seriously, in all sincerity), puts at our disposal to help us not to understand too quickly how Levinas construes what he calls the *"choses sérieuses"* addressed in saying *"hineni."*[35]

## Faith and Knowledge

Although in the foregoing and forthcoming the focus of concern is the religious rather than religions, and although it is to Derrida's reaction to Austin that is owed the description of the quasi-grammatical chiasmus offered in these pages

as a key to an understanding of the religious or at least as a key to an explanation why it surpasses understanding, Derrida's essay "Faith and Knowledge"
makes room for the subject of religions in the plurality of their historical occurrences. One of the inferences he draws from his reflections on this plurality
is that plurality is a feature of the very idea of religion. Is it because he questions
whether we have a clear understanding of the concept of family (and sex, and
race, and gender, and genre: in a word *Geschlecht*) that he does not argue that
the concept of religion is one of family resemblance, that is to say a concept that
can be analyzed in terms of a modifiable cluster of criteria a varying selection,
but no fixed one or more, of which determines what falls under the concept?
The main difficulties he has with ideas pertaining to the family are ones that
arise when those ideas are applied in the field of politics, for instance to shape
a suspect notion of nationality predicated upon fraternity.[36] He would not be
averse, I suspect, to the suggestion that the concept of the family is itself one
of family resemblance. Nor, I suspect, would he quarrel with the author of an
article in the *Encyclopaedia of Religion and Ethics,* who writes:

> The term "religion," whatever its best definition, clearly refers to certain char-
> acteristic types of data (beliefs, practices, feelings, moods, attitudes, etc.). Its
> use presupposes criteria, and therefore some preliminary conception of what
> does and what does not come under the category. But it soon appears that
> there is no absolute gulf between religion and what, in some one respect or
> other, closely approximates it (e.g., art, morality). Different people draw the
> line differently.[37]

The line referred to in the last sentence of this entry is the line between different groupings of criteria in terms of which people define the word "religion."
The lines that are of particular interest to Derrida and us are those that cross
each other, defying attempts to give a simple definition of the term "religious,"
because criteria and characteristics are exceeded at the heart of a chiasmus
by what is other than criteria and characteristics, namely the address of the
other or the other other whom many would like to call God, if only to say that
we address no more than his "back parts" (Exodus 33:23), or (at the cost of the
sacrifice of the chance of making an intercessory prayer for a friend) not even
them. So, picking up the parenthetical reference to morality in the encyclope-
dia entry, the religiousness of what Derrida calls "religion in general," what we
might call the archi-religious as distinct from particular historical religions,
not only approximates to morality but is "constitutive" of morality or ethics;
so that the ethical is spelled out as the ethico-religious, as we find it spelled out
in, for example, the works of Kierkegaard and Levinas. The relation between
religion and ethics and art may be what the paragraph from the *Encyclopaedia
of Religion and Ethics* refers to as approximation. But the relation that enables
the approximation of the ethical and the aesthetic to religion is the "relation"

or relationship of address which is either not a relation or is the relation that makes relationality possible, not least the relationality of the family relation. This relation par excellence is less approximation than proximity, but proximity that retains the distance of holiness, *kadosh,* between me and the neighbor and, maybe but maybe not, between me and God.

Reference has just been made to Derrida's qualms over the security we ascribe to our understanding of the notion of the family and all the other notions included within or associated with it, notions of class, race, sex, genesis, and generation. It is just worth noticing that these qualms extend to the notion of secularity if, as dictionaries tell us, the history of that notion is the history of the stem, *stat-,* of "*serere,*" to sow. The security of secularism will be exposed to the fortunes and misfortunes of dissemination. The line between the secular and the sacred or the religious will be more difficult to draw than religious and scientistic fundamentalisms allow, for instance the fundamentalism, at once scientific and, I would say, religious, presupposed by Richard Dawkins in *The God Delusion.*[38] Dawkins keeps religiously to the dogma that religiousness can be properly defined only in terms of religions and belief in God. It is no part of my agenda to argue for or against the proposition that God is a delusion. It is part of my agenda to argue that it is a delusion to think that if God or a given religion is a delusion there is no room for religious experience or dispositions. Dawkins knows full well that this agenda may be taken up. His very first chapter sets out to clear it off the deck. That chapter attempts to do this via the citation of remarks made by respected scientists who ascribe to themselves a religious attitude, meaning an attitude of awe and wonder before the natural world and the laws that describe the behavior of things within it. He cites the following words of Einstein: "To sense that beyond anything that can be experienced there is something that our mind cannot grasp and whose beauty and sublimity reaches us only indirectly and as a feeble reflection, this is religiousness. In this sense I am religious."[39] On this Dawkins comments: "In this sense I too am religious, with the reservation that 'cannot grasp' does not have to mean 'forever ungraspable.' But I prefer not to call myself religious because it is misleading. It is destructively misleading because, for the vast majority of people, 'religion' implies 'supernatural.'" He goes on to say that where this implication is dropped physicists and others are using the word God in a special metaphorical sense. But in saying this he has switched from saying something about religiousness to saying something about God. He adds: "The metaphorical or pantheistic God of the physicists is light years away from the interventionist, miracle-working, thought-reading, sin-punishing, prayer-answering God of the Bible, of priests, mullahs and rabbis, and of ordinary language. Deliberately to confuse the two is, in my opinion, an act of intellectual high treason." In my opinion, deliberately to confuse God and religiousness is something like that. As for ordinary language, the science of physics would be hard pushed to get by without departing from ordinary language in both senses of "departing from," namely starting out from and leaving behind. And do we understand the distinction between ordinary language and the metaphorical? Ordinary language is replete with metaphors, as is the language of science, and not only the language of the science or *logos* of God, theology.

Dawkins runs together not only God and religiousness. He runs together also God and religion. And these two assimilations get assimilated each to the other so that religiousness is assumed to be indistinguishable from religions. The assumption is encouraged by the fact that although "religion" can be used in a way in which it allows a plural, as in "Islam and Judaism are different religions," it can be used also in a way in which it does not allow a plural, for example when somebody who may just have been converted to one of the religions is said to have "got religion," meaning been got by religion. In this latter context the word "religion" has no plural form. Although this slide to "religion" as a count noun from "religion" as a mass noun may tempt us to make the former the necessary basis of our understanding of the words "religious" and "religiousness," to show that this temptation must be resisted is one of the aims of this book.

There are other equivocations in *The God Delusion* that could hinder the achieving of that aim. In one sentence Dawkins writes that "'religion' implies 'supernatural.'" In the next, by way of support for this, he quotes Carl Sagan's statement that "if by 'God' one means the set of physical laws that govern the universe, then clearly there is such a God." No wonder Dawkins disclaims concern with "other religions such as Buddhism or Confucionism," then goes back on this form of words, for which there is a lot to be said, in order to propose that "there is something to be said for treating these not as religions at all but as ethical systems or philosophies of life,"[40] so that a Buddhist would not be a religious person. There is something to be said for treating as Confusionism the assumption underlying all this, the assumption that either God or religion or both are not natural but something supernatural pictured as analogous to the natural, except that it is something above the natural world that is the subject matter of the natural sciences. Dominican Master Eckhart devoted much of his life to preaching against this analogy, though, admittedly, for doing so he got into trouble with the cardinals. It is usual to classify Eckhart as a mystic, and in fairness to Dawkins it should be said that his book is not directed against mysticism, not at least unless the mysticism in question is one that posits God as a hypothesis and by doing so invites testing in the same way as any scientific hypothesis. Creationist theism does extend this invitation, but there are brands of theism that are a little more subtle than them. A refutation of scientistic theism will not suffice to show that God is a delusion. Theists sympathetic to

Wittgenstein's philosophy of religion, for instance Dewi Z. Phillips,[41] would be as critical of "the God hypothesis" as are atheists like Dawkins.

Dawkins cites Einstein's conjunction of beauty and sublimity. The importance of distinguishing these will emerge in the next section. It will be important to distinguish also there and in later sections religious belief from holiness, a distinction that is needed if one is to avoid confusing religiousness with religions and God. It will be important to distinguish further the religious with regard to our experience of the wondrousness of how things are—which Einstein and Dawkins applaud (as I do too), though Dawkins objects to the use of the word "religious" to describe such experience (as I do not)—from the religious with regard to the sheer existence of singular things, their that as distinguished from their what and their how.

Still picking up references made in the passage cited from the *Encyclopaedia of Religion and Ethics,* let us return now to the question of belief. Belief is one of "The Two Sources of 'Religion' at the Limits of Reason Alone" announced in this subtitle of Derrida's essay "Faith and Knowledge." (The other source is the holiness just mentioned.) Among theologians who take religious belief to be belief in certain propositions it would be uncontroversial and possibly tautologous to say that in monotheistic religions the primary object of belief would be the proposition "God exists." Affirmation of this proposition has led non-theists to ask "How do you know?" It has led theists of a theological or philosophical turn of mind to respond with a plethora of proofs. More circumspect thinkers, Kierkegaard for example, and Kant and perhaps Anselm, have held that these arguments presuppose either the truth of or belief in what they are aiming to prove. Kierkegaard adds the comment that "the best proof for the immortality of the soul, that there is a God, and the like, is the impression of it one has of this from one's childhood, and therefore this proof, unlike those numerous scholarly and high-sounding proofs, could be stated thus: It is absolutely certain, for my father told me."[42] Kierkegaard's Danish requires him to write "father" with an upper-case initial letter, so we must decide for ourselves whether the reference is to his earthly or to his heavenly father, as we must decide for ourselves whether what our father told us is true. But saying this may suggest that our decision is a decision as to the truth of a proposition, a proposition of which we are prone to say, as we have just said, that it is presupposed by the traditional arguments. What we say is said in terms of the relations of logical implication among propositions and concepts. How could it not be if we are talking of truth and of proof? How in these circumstances can we not talk in that way? We may not be able to avoid talking thus. But there is another way that is, as we inevitably say, presupposed by the way of logic. This presupposed way is a way that Kierkegaard calls the way of passion—where his Danish orthography gives this word too an ambiguous upper-case initial. A pointer to his other way is the way the word "truth" might be translated into the Hebrew "*amen*," which connotes constancy understood not solely as the constancy of a proposition that may be relied on, but also as the constancy of the one who affirms: his or her reliability, fidelity, faithfulness. Here truth is trust and troth. Here the Hebrew helps to explain why for Kierkegaard "Christianity is not a doctrine."[43] Not a doctrine, it is not knowledge (*Videns*) that may be learned and taught. It is, Kierkegaard says, a capability (*Kunnens*). A capability is communicated indirectly. Such communication requires "reduplication." That is to say, I do not merely talk about what is said. "I am existentially that which is spoken." I execute or, as Austin will say, I perform it.[44] Kierkegaard divides capability into the aesthetic, the ethical or "oughtness-capability (where there is unconditionally no object)," and religious capability or "oughtness-capability (where there is an object insofar as there is first a communication of knowledge)."[45] The dialectic and therewith the reason for saying that the religious is strictly ethical-religious, perhaps even aesthetical-ethical-religious (see below), are explained as follows:

> The difference between upbringing in the ethical and upbringing in the ethical-religious is simply this—that the ethical is the universally human itself, but religious (Christian) upbringing must first of all communicate a knowledge. Ethically man as such knows about the ethical, but man as such does not know about the religious in the Christian sense. Here there must be the communication of a little knowledge first of all—but then the same relationship as in the ethical enters in. The instruction, the communication, must not be as of a knowledge, but upbringing, practising, art-instruction (*Opdragelse, Indøvelse, Kunst-Undervisning*).[46]

The second of these three Danish words in the parenthesis is the one used in the title of one of Kierkegaard's books that is translated as *Training in Christianity* or *Practice in Christianity*. The "little knowledge" first of all is such knowledge as was communicated, but not as theoretical knowledge, to little Søren by his God or-and his Dad.

When the child is told something by its father—or mother (though Kierkegaard is as silent about his mother as Derrida and Augustine are unsilent about theirs)—the child has implicit faith in him. But when the child is approaching the estate of man or woman, there may come a moment when taking for granted has to be converted into commitment. The commitment becomes comic if construed simply as the commitment to belief in the proposition that God exists. This is why Kierkegaard says that the commitment is not to belief that God exists ("God does not exist [*existere*], he is eternal"[47]), but rather to the paradox that God became man. Once that paradox is what is faced in the moment of decision, belief must be belief as trust in a person regarded as you regard face to face, body to body, *corps à corps,* eye to eye, someone you love, as, before he turned his back on Moses, "the Lord spake unto Moses face to face, as a man speaketh unto his friend" (Exodus 33:11).

Would it not be comic to postpone commitment to a person until you had checked and rechecked not only his or her credit and credibility but whether he or she exists? Yet if this is taken as an analogy of one's relationship with the second person of the Trinity, where would decision fit in on the side of your relationship with persons in a wider community? For Kierkegaard himself a decision was called for as to whether his engagement with Christ would allow him to continue his engagement with Regine. That decision was not a decision as to whether he could place his trust in her. He did that and continued to do it even after the engagement was broken off and after she had become married to Schlegel. To the extent to which an analogy can be expected to hold between the relationship to the Person and a relationship to a person, decision in the latter relationship would be necessary only where one had undergone an experience so disturbing that it led you to wonder whether the other person could be trusted. To suppose that such an experience would be possible in the relationship with the Person would be to fail to understand the difference between a person and the Person. The latter, Kierkegaard would say, is to be trusted whatever happens. A failure of trust with regard to Him is a failure on your part, not His.

## Two Sources of "Religion"

In the paragraph most recently cited from Kierkegaard "(Christian)" is specificatory, not appositional. That is to say, the dialectic of communication sketched in that paragraph and its neighbors in the *Journals and Papers* is geared to a dialectic of religions. That this is so is confirmed by what Kierkegaard says elsewhere about Religiousness A. Notwithstanding the religious primacy Kierkegaard gives to Christianity, religiousness is not confined by him to that religion.

However, there is a religiousness that is neither the worship of a god or gods nor a determinate religion. Although such a religiousness may predispose one toward such worship of a god or gods and therefore to a determinate religion, it need not go that far. It may seem that this scarcely needs arguing. Yet it is not uncommon to find it being said or assumed by apologists of religious or scientistic fundamentalism that the field of human experience is divided up without remainder into religion in the determinate sense on the one hand and secularity on the other. In view of the reactive impetus Hegelianism gives to the works of Kierkegaard which are the point of departure of this book, it will be useful to examine how this assumption of a dichotomy between religion and secularity is made in R. G. Collingwood's neo-Hegelian conception of a dialectical progression from art and aesthetic religion to religion in which according to him the nature of religion is most fully expressed. What Collingwood writes will oblige us to return to the writings of Derrida. That return will oblige us to turn to the thought that not only need the religious disposition not go as far as a determinate religion; it may dispose us not to go that far or, if we do go that far, it may dispose us not to go as far as to indulge in mutual persecution over determinate religious differences.

In the part of Collingwood's *Speculum Mentis* devoted to religion the topic is precisely religion, not the religious. Although he occasionally uses the phrases "religious consciousness" and "religious experience," it is from the notion of religion that these phrases get the only sense Collingwood allows them. Furthermore, to speak of religion for him is to speak of God. On the first of those pages that treat of religion in the book *Speculum Mentis* he refers to his book *Religion and Philosophy* in order to agree with those critics of it who deemed it too intellectualistic.[48] It was too intellectualistic, he concedes, because it failed to acknowledge that the religious symbol is an end, not the means to the expression of an abstract concept. But *Speculum Mentis,* published eight years later, remains highly intellectualistic insofar as it argues that religion is essentially assertive.

> Just as art solidifies out of the chaos of infantile imaginings into the order and clarity of developed aesthetic form, so out of the primitive welter of gods the religious mind by its own inner dialectic rises to the higher religion. The mainspring of this dialectic is the recognition of the true nature of assertion.[49]

In brief, "religion is essentially assertion, belief." This holds, he says, even of what he refers to as religion in its most primitive phase. It is only because religions are assertive that they may contradict one another and occasion mutual persecution. Granted this, one wonders whether, as suggested a moment ago, a certain religiousness might be precisely what might forestall such persecution among adherents to different religions. This religiousness would not be the assertion of belief. It would not propound a creed. It would not be propositional. In his *Essay on Metaphysics* Collingwood distinguishes propositions from presuppositions, and distinguishes absolute presuppositions from relative ones.[50] "Every event has a cause" is one of the examples that book gives of what was at a particular epoch of scientific thought an absolute presupposition. One of the logical features that marked it out as an absolute presupposition was that at that point in history it formed part of the framework of thinking within which one asked about the truth and falsity of propositions, but it was not itself something of which it made sense to ask after its own truth. When this "article of faith," as Collingwood calls the absolute presupposition, was superseded, it became a relative presupposition, that is to say a proposition about which it now made sense to ask whether it was true or false. But absolute presuppositions can appear to have propositional form, otherwise they could not become demoted or promoted to the condition in which they can lose their absoluteness and be asserted and denied. It is significant that one of Collingwood's other examples of an absolute presupposition is "God exists." When that becomes a relative presupposition we are well on the way to discovering that we have killed God. Our question is whether that death might be survived by a religiousness that is not analyzable primarily in terms of the assertion, the proposition, or the proponible. Collingwood tells us—and with this we touch again on Derrida's second source of "religion," holiness—that the explicit differentia of religious experience is the holiness of God, and he describes this as "the necessity of falling down before him in adoration."[51] "This sense of holiness or attitude of worship is the centre and nucleus of religion, and any account of the religious consciousness depends for its success on the way in which it deals with this feature."[52]

The attitude of worship may be the center and nucleus of religion, but is it the center and nucleus of the religious consciousness or religious conscience? Further, since Collingwood has told us that religion is essentially assertive, he will have to say that religion has two centers or nuclei. Religion will be an ellipse. This is what is said also in Derrida's account of the "two sources." Hence, one way of making the distinction between religion and the religious is to take these so-called two sources of religion, namely belief and holiness, assign holiness to religiousness and assign belief (perhaps in conjunction with holiness) to religion. Here belief will be in what is asserted by the assertions that Collingwood considers essential to religion, but religious experience will not necessarily entail assertion. Belief will be expressive of the holiness which may be a necessary aspect of religions, but which may be detached from the assertedness of belief Collingwood holds to be also necessary to them. Holiness would be a necessary but not sufficient condition for being a religion. It can be a condition of a religiousness that is not necessarily that of a religion. Religion, whether theist or otherwise, does not exercise a monopoly over the religious. There is a religious margin between religion and secularity not dreamed of in the philosophy of those who assume that religion and secularity are separated by an exhaustive and exclusive either-or. The religious is too important to be left to the rabbis, bishops, and imams. It follows that the secular is too important to be left to the high priests of a certain scientism. While on the one hand the faith of religions and the religious, the faith that Heidegger would like to have kept at a distance from thinking,[53] is unavoidably distanced from itself by the archiscripturality of modern and postmodern tele-technologies, on the other hand "[n]othing seems therefore more uncertain, more difficult to sustain, nothing seems here or there more imprudent than a self-assured discourse on the age of disenchantment, the era of secularization, the time of laicization, etc."[54]

The "two sources" distinguished by Derrida are not holiness and assertion, but holiness and belief. And we have distinguished between belief in what may be asserted and belief in someone to whom or by whom an assertion or other speech act is addressed. Belief in both senses is distinguished by Derrida as one of the two sources, but it is perhaps when belief is taken as trust and faith that it can be understood to be, as Derrida says it is, mingled with the other source of religion, namely holiness, respect, the sacred, or (questioning the sharpness of Levinas's distinction between the *sacré* and the *saint,* which, we shall find in the next chapter, enables him to make disenchantment a necessary condition of the holy) the sacrosanct. It will be as assertable opinion or creed that belief will be most readily associable with a religion according to the Collingwoodian conception. This is not to say that belief as faith or trust may not be a component of a religion at the same time.

It is of belief as faith that Bonhoeffer writes when he tells the story of an occasion on which a French pastor and he were asking each other how they saw the purpose of their lives.[55] The German said it was to learn to have faith. The Frenchman said his was to become a saint. The French pastor, Bonhoeffer suspects, would be in danger of directing his attention too closely on his inner self and its suffering, the danger, we have seen, that Kierkegaard courts, the danger invited by the practice of some oriental spiritual exercises for which the good is feeling good, the danger of which Levinas would steer his readers clear in his polemic against "interiorization," which is comparable with what is called "the beautiful soul" by Hegel, but which is not to be confused with what is called inwardness (*Inderlighed*) by Kierkegaard. The life of faith chosen by Bonhoeffer would be a life directed to the tele-technological world and the sufferings of others in it as represented by the suffering of Christ. His idea of Judeo-Christianity is very Judaically this-worldly without being preciously interiorizing. For him, we might say, the other world is this one. Yet, we might say too, the life of faith as self-forgetfulness is a life of saintliness or holiness, although Bonhoeffer himself, again like Kierkegaard, would consider that focusing one's life on becoming a saint would be too self-centered. That is to say, as Derrida would, in that life the "two sources" of religion are mingled. Of the two sources or roots (*souches*) that are said to "overlap, mingle," he writes that they *se croisent, se greffent.*[56] They do not remain side-by-side. They cross each other. They are in chiasmus. They hybridize each other. The one is grafted on to the other. And each is already a family. The "deux *sources*" are "*deux* familles." The two sources are a double source, a resource, and then a multiple source. They contaminate each other. They contaminate each other to the point that even the notion of the family lacks the purity that would enable us to answer the question "What is a family?" by describing a self-contained essence. Insofar as essence implies presence, albeit presence in the past, *Wesen*, no such essence can be identified in answer to those "What is . . . ?" questions posed in *Memoires for Paul de Man*, "What is love, friendship, memory?" What is mourning? This holds too for my question "What is the religious as distinct from the religion?" So one had better not say as blithely as I said in reference to Collingwood that one can distinguish these by "assigning" propositional belief to the religion and the holy to the religious. For assigning is always traceable to signing or signifying in Levinas's sense of *"signifiance,"* where the signifier is the one who addresses himself or herself to the other in response to the other, that is to say where the Signified, the accused and assigned me, is always in the place of the Signifier who says "See me here, send me," (*hineni*), that is to say where, in the words of Derrida again, "two impossible promises are involved . . . , sublimely, without any possible exchange, in difference and dissymmetry, in the incommensurable." Such unpossible promises, speech acts outwith the logic of "I can," are presupposed by assertions of matters of fact or matters of essence such as are raised by questions of the form "What is . . . ?" They are presupposed also by other performative utterances in the way that saying, for example, "I promise" engages me to another person only if we can bank on what could be called, mimicking Derrida again, "promise in general," which has already commanded our attention in the past and at the same time regards the future because the yes of the making of a promise implies a yes by which the promise is remade anew. The presentness of its "hereby" is divided. These promissory repetitions in turn presuppose certain matters of fact as conditions of what Austin calls the "felicity" of a speech act, conditions the defeasibility of which Derrida believes Austin treats too lightly. For as soon as the yes commits us to another yes the stability of the factual and conceptual context can no longer be taken for granted. Contamination of concepts, for instance the concepts of holiness and belief or faith, is a corollary of the necessary iterability of the promise. This is why the signifiance of address can be only comparatively naked of predicative signification. This is why in order to get an inkling of the religious we may have to borrow from the religions in one or more of their historical varieties, and why today the concept of the secular is not as securely untrammeled by the religious as is widely assumed. This is why, apropos of our invocation of Caputo and de Vries, the borderlines between a problem and an aporia and between the comparative and the incomparable or sublime are each both a *Grenze* and a *Schranke*. And perhaps it is in the light of these reciprocal but dissymmetric crossings that we should read Collingwood's claim that absolute presuppositions are articles of *faith*. We described him as a neo-Hegelian. The maturing thought of Hegel moves from giving priority to religion over philosophy to giving priority to philosophy over religion. Compare the development in Collingwood's coming to understand in his later years that in his earlier account of religion he had been too intellectualistic. Although that development may appear to be a reversal of Hegel's, it is its duplication.

Derrida is chary of the logic of presupposition, in particular as this is exemplified by Heideggerian *Voraussetzung*. This is because the "*vor*" and the "*aus*" and the "pre" and the "sup" or "sub" tempt one to suppose that the presupposed is a layer below another layer, like a layer of gneiss below a layer of sandstone, these layers being related to each other by the classical logic of the *Satz* or by the modern logic of the sentential calculus. This is why, impressed by the analogy of James Hutton's substitution of a Plutonian interruptive theory of geology for the Neptunian parallelist theory, I have sometimes been tempted to put the offending word in scare-quotes. It is difficult to avoid this word altogether. There is no need to avoid it if we are aware of the danger we run in using it in expounding or expanding the writings of Derrida. The danger goes all the way back to his rumination of what Husserl took to be a crisis in European sciences and learning and of Husserl's faith that indexical expressions could be dispensed with, in principle if not in practice, in favor of pure non-indexical expression. There is no purity either of propositional-predicative meaning or of performative acts of speech. What each is said to presuppose is more internal to them than is allowed for by the prepositional "pre" and "*voraus*." Even Levinas, who sometimes seems to flirt with the hope of a pure here and hereby (recall Wittgenstein on the vanity of raising one's voice to draw attention to *this*, and recall Hegel's treatment of sense-certainty),[57] grants that where there is saying there is something said, hence putative factuality and historicality that contaminates the putative purity of address. And vice-versa. Derrida's qualms about a certain "empiricism" in Levinas, meaning an "experience" of the ethical demand put on one, on me, by the other, by you (recall Kant on the *Faktum* of the ought), are matched by qualms about a sensory empiricism that pretends to be free from any intrusion of ethical engagement.

It was in order to recognize the dependence of performatives on constatable conditions that a couple of paragraphs ago I wrote of a religiousness that is not analyzable *primarily* in terms of the assertion. Many more paragraphs ago was invoked the specter of a monstrous but indemonstrable demon or god who pronounces what Derrida would call a perverformative Hereby that would seem to be the utterance of an utterly absolute presupposition of every human "hereby" and "*hineni*," but one that is outwith human memory and expectation and quotation.[58] Suppose we apply to that the comment Kierkegaard makes about the certainty that the soul is immortal and that there is a God, namely that "[i]t is absolutely certain, for my father told me." That is to say (and perhaps this was missed in the account of learning to speak given by Augustine that triggered the remarks about learning a language made in the *Philosophical*

*Investigations* by Wittgenstein),[59] engagement in language, *l'en-gage du langage,* which means engagement in forms of life often wrongly taken to be disengaged from language, never was originally an act, never was a leap of faith. It always was originally unoriginal. It always was where we find ourselves always already thanks to what my father, or my mother, told me. Or, rather, thanks not quite to what they told me, to the message or information they communicated, but rather to their telling. For, to revert to our by now rather Aristotelian and Pascalian Kierkegaard, "The instruction, the communication, must not be as of a knowledge, but upbringing, practising, art-instruction." This Kierkegaard is the one read by the Wittgenstein for whom questions about God's identity and existence are questions about the language learned by people who participate in the forms of life we call religion.[60] To make this point more generally, not only do we obey rules blindly, as Wittgenstein says.[61] We acquire them blindly as well. This is no less astonishing than the story of "the miraculous birth of language," according to which language begins with a big bang. There never was a big bang at the beginning of language, never an "original contract" or covenant sworn with one's hand held solemnly in the air or holding a book. The covenant (Hebrew *breet*) that began it was always already in the air. It was, is and will be the air, the atmosphere and breath (OE *bræth*) in which the alliance (Latin *religio*) will always have been agreed immemorially, a spirit and ghost (Du *geest*) of nothing but itself.

In the beginning was the word, the giving and granting of a promise, but there never was a beginning. This would be no less astonishing than are those Abelian words alleged to convey antithetical meanings and imagined to be "the origin of language."[62] Discovery that they are not primal or that primality is dual or manifold is discovery that wordhood and the worldhood from which it cannot be detached is unprosaic, that the world of the languages we inhabit and the languages of the world are each an inexhaustible poem where words are spoken or written or sung as though for the very first time. They are each a work of morality engaging people, but they are each also a work of art engaging these worlds in the margin denied by those who hold that there is an exhaustive and exclusive dichotomous division between religions and secularity. Unlike Monsieur Jourdain, we discover that what we have been speaking all of our life is poetry as well as prose. If I am bound ethico-religiously to my neighbor, my friend, and my enemy, the moment I open my mouth to address them I am bound to be scrupulous with regard to how I say what I say, however sloppily I may in fact speak.

The aesthetic (for example the poetic), the ethical, and the religious so-called "stages" on life's way nourish each other. To split them off from each other—and it is not Kierkegaard's purpose to do this—is to invite forms of idolatry at any of the three so-called levels. Derrida, Levinas, and Kierkegaard are among those who have underlined how susceptible to idolatry can be the sphere of the ethical. But the sphere that has seemed most susceptible to idolatry is the sphere of the aesthetic. This is in part because in treatises on aesthetics that sphere has so often been largely if not entirely limited to the sphere of art and artifacts, and these have been regarded as *objets d'art,* mostly as objects over against the spectators or other appreciators of these objects. This point of view gets transferred to the natural world when that is viewed aesthetically. Nature gets viewed as the image of its images. Further, more often than not, nature gets viewed under the category of the beautiful. That is how the Creator must have seen his creation when he stood back, compared his plan with the world he had just made in its image, and found this world good, *kala.* If that was an aesthetic judgment, its aesthetics was an aesthetics of beauty, *to kalon*—even if of what is called "God's better beauty, grace" by Gerard Manley Hopkins when he asks "To What Serves Mortal Beauty?" God's aesthetics would be an aesthetics of satisfaction, like that which seems to satisfy Collingwood, who writes "Holiness is to religion what beauty is to art."[63] Or can the good that God and Collingwood see in the beautiful be at the same time painful, like the painfully beautiful fuchsia hedge across the way from me as I write, so that the beautiful might have the complexity Kant attributes to the sublime?

Nowhere in *Speculum Mentis,* or in *Religion and Philosophy,* or, incredibly, in *Principles of Art,* does Collingwood make mention of that aesthetic category, the sublime, the category of what refuses to be categorized. One imagines that it may have been with a sigh that the Creator said of what he had created, "It is good." One imagines that he was relieved when between Adam and Eve and Himself there loomed up original sin. How claustrophobically fully rounded creation threatened to be for him without that modicum of madness, that modicum of the unmodicum and immodest that turns imagination into the human imadgination and twists the intentionality of the consciousness of the beautiful back on itself through a hundred and eighty-one degrees to make way for the sublime to storm in as though from outside like the god Dionysus in a hurry to keep a rendezvous with Apollo. Or like Christ, or Dionysus-Christ, so that the world could be a place of sublime beauty. Perhaps one reason why the God of the Kabbalah sacrificed some of his power to the human beings he created was that he saw that he was in danger of sacrificing the experience of sublimity because he himself would be its realization and therefore its loss.

"Sublime beauty" is a phrase I came across in a program-note on Louis Vierne's Adagio for Organ op. 28. I think that I understand what the author of the note was wanting to say. I also think that I would have been puzzled if he had written "beautiful sublimity." That combination of words would have failed to express the maximum degree of praise I assume it was his intention to evince. Although the noun "sublimity" might do this, qualifying it with the adjective "beautiful" would defeat his purpose by conceding a retreat from that presumably intended maximum. Read Kantianly, the combination of words actually used in the program-note suggests a combination of the aesthetic and the moral, with the adjective marking a primarily aesthetic quality as does also the adverb, except that the latter carries a moral loading too. It does that according to Kant because the experience of the sublime is a by-product of one's self-flattering consciousness of the ability to determine one's actions out of respect for the universal moral law rather than out of desire for pleasure. Without canceling the reference to law, without suspending it, as Kierkegaard would say, might not sublimity be at the same time a by-product of one's respect for singularity, the singularity, say, of another human being, but without flattering consciousness? Without consciousness at all, if that is understood as the intentional consciousness of an object or objective of consciousness. For sublimity would be an "experience" analogous to that of suffering a wound: not the wound of knowledge of which the saint John of the Cross and the poet R. S. Thomas write, but a wound of non-knowledge, a wound to my pride, rather than something of which to be proud, if that by which I am affected from outside is the call of someone to whom I have omitted to give shelter or to invite to my table.

# SIXTEEN

## Eucharistics

### Specters of Feuerbach

To mention shelter and food and drink, as was done at the end of the last chapter, is to approach another dimension of religiousness that is not necessarily the religiousness of a religion or of the worship of a god. Rather as one may be tempted to postulate a God to whom to direct an intercessory prayer, one may postulate a god in order to meet a felt need for someone to whom to direct the gratitude we wish to express for earthly nourishments and for the raw materials from which our dwellings are made. But it is not irrational to be grateful for these even when one does not believe that they had a divine creator and when it is not only for the work of farmers, carpenters, brick manufacturers, masons, electronics engineers, and the like that one is grateful. We may not thank them in so many words, but we think of them now and again, for instance when we realize how much attention and care has been put into the pointing of the brickwork or the fitting of the joints. This is one reason for linking thinking with thanking, as Heidegger does.[1] If such thinking is prayer or is likened to prayer, let us not call it a secular prayer unless we do not simply oppose the secular to the religious. And let us not say that such prayer is religious because it is prescribed by an organized religion or performed in memory of a religion a pillar of whose architecture is prayer. Spontaneous religious gratitude and praise is rather the forerunner of designed religions, as eating at table to maintain one's strength or simply out of enjoyment usually precedes eating or drinking at an altar. Think of those times when, dying for a sip of water, you were able at last to quench your thirst. Did you not experience an almost visceral gratitude? If not, I suspect you were in a position similar to that of the reader of *The Fundamental Principles of the Metaphysic of Morals* who, its author imagines, cannot distinguish a prudential "ought" from a moral one and is therefore expected by the author to postpone his reading of that book until he has discovered that he can make this distinction between a fact (for a prudential imperative is ultimately a hypothetical indicative) and a categorical ethical *Faktum* (which would be a fact only for a wholly holy will). Or you have never known what it is to be really thirsty. Insofar as you experience such a gut-feeling of gratitude the experience is religious, whether or not you think there is somebody or somespirit to thank. Feuerbach writes:

> [F]or the sake of comprehending the religious significance of bread and wine, place thyself in a position where the daily act is unnaturally, violently interrupted. Hunger and thirst destroy not only the physical but also the mental and moral powers of man; they rob him of his humanity—of understanding, of consciousness. Oh! if thou shouldst ever experience such want, how wouldst thou bless and praise the natural qualities of bread and wine, which restore to thee thy humanity, thy intellect! It needs only that the ordinary course of things be interrupted in order to vindicate (*uberzugewinnen*) to common things an uncommon significance, *to life, as such, a religious import.* Therefore let bread be sacred for us, let wine be sacred, and also let water be sacred! Amen.[2]

To the behest to let bread and wine and water be sacred to us I too say Amen. However, I do not say Amen without qualification to the thesis Feuerbach would have these sentences support. He bids us deem wine and water sacred because they are necessary conditions of the sustenance of the humanity of the human being. Bread is the staff of life. It is something for which the human being should be grateful to other human beings, for instance the baker, and grateful to nature for the water on which the growth of the grain depends. The service these elements do for humankind is enough to consecrate them. For consecration they do not have to await the administration of a priestly ritual. This illustrates the general humanism of Feuerbach's conception of religion and of the Christian religion in particular. His conception is general in that the religious according to him operates at the level of the human species and its laws: "[T]here is no other essence which man can think, dream of, imagine, feel, believe in, wish for, love and adore as the *absolute,* than the essence of human nature itself."[3] How remote this is from the Levinasian notion of the religious is underlined by Feuerbach's insistence that "the consciousness of God is nothing else than the consciousness of the species; that man can and should raise himself only above the limits of his individuality, and not above the laws." Not above the laws that are the laws of religion, because for Feuerbach they are the laws of morality understood as generalized prudence. For Levinas man's individuality is that to which the ethico-religious raises man, or, rather, raises me: I am raised to singularity by the singularity of the other human being. Feuerbach advocates a humanism that retains not a little from Hegel, despite his break with the Hegelianism to which he adhered in his early writings. Feuerbach's humanism is a humanism of humanity in general, a humanism of the essence of the us. Levinas's humanism, not a little of which is retained by Derrida, is a humanism of the singular other human being.

However, it would be misleading to say that Derrida is a humanist or that he advocates a humanism of the other human being. This would be misleading because Derrida does not retain from Levinas the latter's shyness about allowing that an ethico-religious claim is made upon us by non-human things independently of how they sustain and promote human life. Feuerbach only appears to grant this when, having referred in his text to "human nature itself," he amplifies in a footnote: "Including external nature; for a man belongs to the essence of Nature,—in opposition to common materialism; so Nature belongs to the essence of man,—in opposition to subjective idealism. . . . Only by uniting man with Nature can we conquer the supernaturalistic egoism of Christianity." Elsewhere Feuerbach characterizes and caricatures his naturalism by affirming that essence or nature or substance is sustenance. Essence, we may risk saying, is *essen*. As he himself notoriously risks saying, overawed by Jakob Moleschott's *Science of Foodstuffs, "Man ist was er isst,"* "One is what one eats," and "Sustenance is the . . . essence of essence. Everything depends upon what we eat and drink. Difference in essence is but difference in food."[4] Easy to ridicule though these assertions are, they are the biological beginning of a road that leads, via the *Theses on Feuerbach,* in which Marx criticizes the abstractness of Feuerbach's notion of nature, to the former's sociological analysis of the nature of man. The road runs parallel to one *from* Feuerbach's defense of contemplative sensory intuition (*Anschauung*) against Hegel's critique of sensory certainty *via* the interpretation of sensibility as interaction among individuals in civic society *to* a socialized humanity in which the atomism of individuals has been superseded by a recognition of the ways in which the individual is shaped through and through by concrete institutional, cultural, and historical factors whose changes and differences must be brought to attention, not concealed under the epithet "natural" as they tend to be by Feuerbach.

Despite Marx's counter-theses, and notwithstanding Feuerbach's Moleschottian excesses, the philosopher whom Marx nicknames the "Stream of Fire" establishes a bridgehead for the thought that things of the natural world have a religious significance. In so doing he establishes a bridgehead against the Dawkinsian thought that "religion" implies "supernatural."

What Feuerbach may fall short of establishing is that the religious significance of things of the natural world is something that belongs to them independently of any service they perform for human beings. We are agreed that where such a service is performed the religious significance may imply gratitude. I am arguing that gratitude is implied by many forms of religiousness but that this is so when the gratitude is not for a benefit received by me, nor even for a benefit received by another. The gratitude may be gratitude for the sheer existence of a gift, the gift of another human being or of a non-human being, not for any utility or for any pleasure that derives from it. The gratitude may be gratitude for the thing's own sake, which, according to Aristotle at *Nicomachean Ethics* 1156b, is the best kind of sake for which one can ever love a friend: "[T]hose who wish well to their friends for their sake are most truly friends." The gift, whether given or ungiven, may not be one that meets a need. It may not be the object of desire. It may or may not be an occasion for joy. It certainly does not have to be something enjoyed, as Feuerbach implies that it has to be when he writes the following sentences, many of which I nevertheless endorse:

> Bread and wine typify to us the truth that Man is the true God and Saviour of man.
>
> Eating and drinking is the mystery of the Lord's Supper;—eating and drinking is, in fact, in itself a religious act; at least, ought to be so. Think, therefore, with every morsel of bread which relieves thee from the pain of hunger, with every draught of wine which cheers thy heart, of the God who confers these beneficent gifts upon thee,—think of man! But in thy gratitude towards man forget not gratitude to holy Nature! Forget not that wine is the blood of plants, and flour the flesh of plants, which are sacrificed for thy well-being! Forget not that the plant typifies to thee the essence of Nature, which lovingly surrenders itself for thy enjoyment! Therefore forget not the gratitude which thou owest to the natural qualities of bread and wine.

We can say Hear Hear to this without understanding as other than hyperbolic personification the reference to nature lovingly surrendering itself. But how are we to understand the reference to "holy Nature"?

## The Sacred and the Holy

Feuerbach's word for "holy" in the phrase "holy Nature" is "*heilig*," but this is also the word the translator of *The Essence of Christianity*, George Eliot, renders by "*sacred*" in, for example, the already cited sentence "Therefore let bread be sacred for us, let wine be sacred, and also let water be sacred!" Let us look more closely at the distinction between the sacred and the holy.

Levinas would say that the phrase "holy Nature" is a contradiction in terms if "holy" is given the sense he gives to the Hebrew word "*kadosh*," which he translates as "*saint*." Nature or *phusis* or being is sameness. The holy as the *saint* and the *kadosh* is difference, the difference of the good beyond being. It "is" other than what is because it is saying as address as distinguished from what is said. This distinction corresponds with a distinction between the concept of the holy and the concept of the sacred, but we are liable to find ourselves going around in circles unless we keep on reminding ourselves that this distinction between concepts turns on a distinction between the conceptual and the non-conceptual. However, our failure to maintain our bearings can be excused, for if we accept Benveniste's account of the history of the *sacré*, the sacred, and the *saint*, the holy, we must accept that these concepts are inextricably entangled with each other. He writes:

> The adjective *sacer* goes back to an ancient *\*sakros*, which has a variant form in the Italic *sakri-*, which recurs in Old Latin in the plural form *sacros*. This form *\*sakros* is a derivative in *-ro-* from a root *\*sak-*. Now *sanctus* is properly the participle of the verb *sancio*, which is derived from the same root *\*sak-* by means of a nasal infix.[5]

Benveniste goes on to say, "This Latin present tense in *-io-* with a nasal infix stands to *\*sak-* as *jungiu* 'to join' in Lithuanian does to *jug-*." But it is the Latin rather than the Lithuanian connection that is relevant to the difficulty one experiences in attempting to explain the accidental or unaccidental confusions encountered in certain of Levinas's pages in which the distinction or otherwise between the sacred and the holy is treated.

The need to get a grip on how Levinas understands this distinction is particularly urgent if we are to understand how his attitude to art and the aesthetic more generally relates to his doctrine of the ethical and the ethico-religious. For Levinas music is the essence of art, including plastic art such as the paintings treated in chapter 13. In art, he maintains, the concept is replaced by the image, and every image is musical. Levinas holds that the essence of the musical is rhythm. Music is in movement. It does not stand still. "To insist on the musicality of every image is to see in an image its detachment from an object, [ . . . ] independence from the category of substance."[6] Levinas could allow that the musical in this broad sense overlaps the religious only if by the religious were meant the sacred, the *sacré*, as contrasted with the holy, the *saint*, only if the religious were of the kind that is closer to what he calls the *il y a*, the there-is, what we might call ilyaity, than of the kind that is closer to what he calls *illéité*, illeity. What does he mean by these expressions? It so happens that the distinction between them has to do with that *jungiu* mentioned by Benveniste, the distinction between conjunction and disjunction.

> Illeity lies outside the "thou" and the thematization of objects. A neologism formed with *il* (he) or *ille,* it indicates a way of concerning me without entering into *conjunction* with me. To be sure, we have to indicate the element in which this *concerning* occurs. If the relationship with illeity were a relationship of consciousness, "he" would designate a theme. . . . The illeity in the beyond being is the fact that its coming toward me is a departure which lets me accomplish a movement toward a neighbour. The positive element of this departure, that which makes this departure, this diachrony, be more than a term of negative theology, is my responsibility for the others.[7]

That is to say, if this "he" is a pronoun for which could be substituted the word "God," this latter word would not be the name of any present or absent phenomenal or noumenal being. The "he" of illeity is the pro-noun of the coming toward me, the *venue vers moi,* the invenience, of the absolute past without which I could not be for, pro-, another. But in the "there is," the *il y a,* on the other hand, there is neither he nor thou nor any other existent.

> The impersonality of the sacred in primitive religions, which for Durkheim is the "still" ("*encore*") impersonal God from which will issue one day the God of advanced religions, describes on the other hand a world where nothing prepares for the apparition of a God. Rather than to a God, the notion of the *there is* leads us to the absence of God, the absence of any being.[8]

It leads us away from God conceived as a being. No wonder then that Levinas tells us that ilyaity can be confused with illeity, which is "in the beyond being."[9] So too the sacred can be confused with the holy. This liability to confusion is demonstrated in Levinas's rhetoric in the essay entitled "Desacralization and Disenchantment" published in a collection whose original title is *Du sacré au saint.* The first word of this title should be interpreted as an indication that the essays published under this title are going to be concerned with a movement, not with a static contrast. Although a section of the essay bears the subtitle "The Sacred and the Holy," as though a clear distinction between two concepts were at stake, the section is about the dynamics of desacralization, as the essay's main title proclaims. The essay is an exegesis of the *Tractate Sanhedrin,* pp. 67a–68a, in which, Levinas observes, there is no mention of the sacred. The hermeneusis he performs on that text picks out the places in it where the holy is an issue in order to show that holiness is possible only in a world that has been desacralized. The sacred masquerades as the holy. Hence the ambiguities in the language Levinas uses in treating of the relation between the holy and the sacred, which latter is the realm of ambiguity and deception that Nietzsche, Derrida, and Levinas himself elsewhere associate, we have seen, with a certain femininity. Because the sacred is image, it can be spoken of only in terms of that of which it is the image. So we find Levinas employing a vocabulary of degrees of illusoriness, as when he compares the most coarse Sacredness (*le Sacré le plus grossier*) with the really sacred—holiness (*le sacré véritable—la sainteté*).[10] The most coarse Sacredness is the sacredness of sorcery, superstition, and the spiritualism (*spiritualisme spirite*) of horoscopy, table turning, and the foretelling of the future by communication with the dead. So when Levinas asks, "How is degradation possible?" and "How can holiness be confused with the sacred and turn into sorcery?" the question would be how the really sacred can degenerate. But does the "really sacred" here stand for the holy, or does it stand for the Sacred with an upper-case sibilant, that is to say, for the really unreal, the Sibylline (feminine?) image? Levinas declares that the question "How is degradation possible?" is a mad one. For if the really sacred is the holy, that is to say the Absolute, that is to say the separate and pure (*kadosh*), no explanation can be given why it separates itself from its separation, why it becomes confused with appearance, how "holiness, that is, separation or purity, the essence without admixture that can be called Spirit and which animates the Jewish tradition—or to which the Jewish tradition aspires—can dwell in a world that has not been desacralized." How can that pure Spirit degenerate into the techniques of impure spiritualism by which the human being is bewitched?

Levinas notes in passing that these questions are versions of a question that Spinoza failed to answer when he failed to explain how God can separate himself from himself in order to allow for the possibility of mere opinion, which Spinoza called the first way of knowledge. Levinas could have added that these questions are versions of a question that it would be difficult also for Plato and for us to answer if we started with the unadulterated Platonic Idea of the Good. Levinas could have added too that a solution to this Platonico-Spinozan problem might be offered by the Kabbalistic doctrine of *tsimtsum,* according to which God, the One, contracts his own power, perhaps in more than one sense of the word "contracts," in order to allow the cooperation of human beings. We know that Levinas does not regard this aspect of Kabbalism as a stumbling block.[11] For, read as ontology, the end-point of this contraction, God's contraction to nothingness, would make way for the post-ontological and post-ontic God of ethical responsibility by which—up to a point like Heidegger but also going beyond Heidegger's thinking of Being—Levinas would have onto-theology overtaken. Levinas's compunction with regard to the sacred is a compunction not only with regard to the impersonal god of primitive religion. It is also a residue of his diffidence with regard to the multiplicity of gods of paganism. And it is true that pagan piety found it difficult to find room for veneration of the cosmos unless that was mediated by worship of gods. But the starry sky above does not have to be transfigured into a constellation of gods in order for it to make a call upon religious veneration. Why cannot our relation with the non-human being be construed along lines analogous to those along which Levinas construes our relation to the other human being? When we give voice to that sentence in the marriage service of the Book of Common Prayer about worshipping one's partner with one's body, we are not being required, are we, to make her or him into a goddess or god?

The difficulty in determining how Levinas draws the line between the holy and the sacred is a difficulty arising from the Abelian or quasi-Abelian nature of the word "sacred." As it will become important to recognize below, the sacred can be the holy. But it can also be the unholy, the accursed. Both words belong to the vocabulary of religion in the wide sense in which the word has been used in this book to include the blasphemous and other deficient modes of the religious. The sacred can be what should not be touched because, for example, it is polluted, where the pollution may be the pollution that is often associated with the corpse. But this *noli me tangere* can retain at the same time the purity of the holy. In Daniel Owen's novel *Gwen Tomos* we read: "on visiting these cemeteries I somehow feel that it is the cemetery that bestows sacredness on the church, not the church that confers it on the cemetery," "*teimlaf rywfodd wrth ymweliad â'r mynwentydd hyn mai y fynwent sydd yn rhoi cysegredigwydd ar yr eglwys, ac nid yr eglwys ar y fynwent.*" If by "church" were meant not the building but the institution, the cited sentence would be halfway to affirming that the religious is prior to the religions. Halfway only, not all the way, if we agree with Derrida that the religious has two sources, the holy or perhaps sacred, and belief or faith. It is, however, not the institution but the building that is meant in Owen's sentence by "the church." But what is meant by "sacredness" ("*cyseg-redigwydd*")? Although it may be slightly more natural to think of sacredness as something that is conferred, for example by an event that occurred at a place now regarded as sacred, whereas holiness is an original condition, and although it may be that "sacredness" is more commonly used of places and buildings than "holiness" or "sanctity" ("*sancteiddrwydd*"), which are more commonly used of persons, the latter words, "holiness" and "sanctity," are applicable also to buildings and places (for instance to the "holy places" of Jerusalem, Rome, and Mecca). The word "sacrosanct" articulates the ambiguity. But "sacro-" is already ambiguous, and its ambiguity seems to be Abelian, for it holds between opposite senses, pure and impure, clean and dirty (for instance, fecal). That the word "sacred" is ambiguous in this way has been asserted by Abel himself, by Freud in *Totem and Taboo,* by Warde Fowler in "The Original Meaning of the Word *Sacer,*"[12] by Émile Durkheim in *The Elementary Forms of Religious Life,* and by Rudolf Otto, the title of whose best-known book, *Das Heilige,* is sometimes translated as *The Idea of the Holy* and sometimes as *The Idea of the Sacred*. A more accurate title for this would be *The Idea of the Numinous*. This is the word Otto uses in the body of the book to pick out an aspect of the notion of the holy that remains after its ethical force has been abstracted. It is the latter force that, against Otto, Levinas aims to re-emphasize, the force he marks by the Hebrew word "*kadosh*." He does this by interpreting the Hebrew word as address, saying as distinguished from what is said. Once this is done, any surviving opposition of forces will be not Abelian but quasi-Abelian. A borderline between meanings placed each side of a line will have been replaced by a chiasmic crossing in which something said is interrupted by a saying. This is why the adjective "religious" is quasi-Abelian and quasi-ambiguous in the use to which it has been put in this book, where its sense is not limited to that of the religions. An account of the religious or ethico-religious and its sacred and holy aspects will be misleading unless it exceeds the space of conceptual ambiguity. Any borderline or threshold invoked in an unmisleading account will be a borderline or threshold that is tainted with madness, tainted and cleansed. The distinction between interiority and exteriority, between inclusion and exclusion, will have become undecidable, and with them the distinction between life and death, the distinction not only upon which turn such social concepts as that of the scapegoat, but on which pivot also the singular elements of religious life referred to throughout this work as birth, and copulation, and death. If there is confusion at this borderline it is not that of fusion as opposed to fission, but that of an inability to separate fusion and fission from each other. Perhaps this holds for the line between what in the heading of a section of *Totality and Infinity* is called interiority and what in that book's subtitle is called exteriority. Perhaps this is how things stand at the threshold of what Derrida calls democracy to come, where the to come, as Levinas has already advised us, is not what is yet to come (*à venir*) chronologically, but what comes to pass, happens, or advenes (*advient*),[13] and where advention has the direction that is the reverse of the intentionality of consciousness, converting the *destinateur* into a *destinataire*. Remembering the undecidability as between directionality and undirectionality on which turn the to-ings and fro-ings of the missives collected in Derrida's *The Post Card*, this conversion of addresser into addressee might be dubbed Levinas's postal principle. According to this principle, which is a principle of unprincipiality, unfirstness, addressing is always already preceded by being addressed, so that addressing is always already a response. This principle explains why the religiousness of gratitude for benefits received, for instance the bounties of nature as exemplified by the passages cited above from Feuerbach and by the section of *Totality and Infinity* that treats of the economics of enjoyment, is subsumed under religiousness defined in terms of the claim of the other, provided we do not insist that a claim must be put into words, provided by the other we mean any other existent, whether human or not, and provided we grant that for a claim to be put into words the advocacy of a human being may be called for.

I would remind any readers who cannot bring themselves to grant any or all of these provisos that it is not an aim of this book to furnish sufficient and necessary conditions for a disposition or experience or sentiment or situation to count as religious independently of any connection with an established religion. Here are a few that could qualify. My aim will have been achieved if at least one of them touches my readers' religious imadgination: (a) At a bend of the Water of Leith in Edinburgh, near the Scottish Gallery of Modern Art, and at this time of the year surrounded by drifts of rose bay willow herb, a seat has recently been set in place. Its metalwork includes representations of those red ribbons that invite us to think of people who have died of AIDS. Water of Leith, Water of Lethe. (b) In an Edinburgh cemetery, a municipal cemetery that is not attached to a church either architecturally or institutionally, is the tiny grave of Paul. Cards tied to the wreathes and toys on that grave record that Paul was less than one year old when he died. Shortly after his birthday one could read on one of the cards the following words, though some words had been obliterated by the rain: "The blue sky is filled with fluffy clouds . . . the soft wind blowing . . . the sound of the birds in the morning, and the smile on Emma's face . . . flowers growing in the bright green grass . . . the sweet smell of Spring in the air . . . many memories of when u were here. I miss u so much. My pain for u is so sore. I spend my time thinking how I can fix this all. I realize I can't. No words or action can explain the way I feel. All I know is that ure gone. I panic when I realize its real. I'll never hold you, kiss you or cuddle you again. My real sadness is for all the things u never got to do. I'll never forget . . . u are always on my mind and in my heart. Never apart. x Mummy x." (c) Should I have refrained from copying these words down? Is copying always a copying *down*? Yet should I even have read those words? (d) A climber spends six hours ascending a pinnacle above a churning sea. As she finally arrives at the summit there are tears in her eyes. (e) Picasso's weeping woman. (f) Coleridge's Ancient Mariner freed at last from the albatross hanging around his neck. (g) D. H. Lawrence's snake-watcher who missed his chance with one of the lords of life and has a pettiness to expiate. (h) A high skein of scarcely audible geese changing course. (i) An orgasm of gratitude as the final chords of Buxtehude's Prelude and Fugue in D Major die away. To what is this Prelude a prelude? From what is this Fugue a flight? (j) It is reported that in Dafur women who leave the refugee camps for fuel are in danger of being gang-raped. A mother is so undernourished that she cannot produce milk for her child. While being nursed on its mother's lap a child is beheaded. (k) Not being able to pray.

You cannot help feeling the need for help: help to help, help to endure the grief, help to bear the joy. You feel bound to ask for help. You feel bound to ask, *pregare*. You feel bound.

## The Sacro-Sarcous and the Sacro-Sanct

One of Levinas's boldest strokes is to construe the Idea of the Good as the non-idea of a human being faced by another human being in need of food and drink and shelter, that is to say, I would say, in need understood in terms of the parameters of birth, and copulation, and death. The ethical or the ethico-religious is from the beginning carnate. There is no need for it to be mediated by incarnation. So the idea of the Platonic Good beyond Being will mislead when appealed to as a clue to the Levinasian ethico-religious unless we keep our feet planted firmly on the temporal earth. Recall Levinas's refusal toward the end of *Totality and Infinity* to pursue questions regarding eternity. Recall too his admission "I wonder whether time, in its very diachrony, is not *better* than eternity" and whether time is not "the very order of the Good."[14] It is always already too late for the ethico-religious to inhabit the dimension of a "Platonic heaven" of spirit exterior to this world or interior to sentimentality or other mentality. What saves the holy from the sacred according to Levinas—and Nietzsche is not far away—is the sarcous materiality of the holy.

The use of the phrase "orgasm of gratitude" in speaking a paragraph ago of the experience of hearing the final notes of Buxtehude's fugue die away was intended to emphasize that gratitude, which, I have maintained, is one thread that runs through much of the length of the rope of the religious, may not be as remote as we may think from the cluster of forms of religious life that are elementary in the sense that they are indeed forms of *life* in its embodiment. Orgasm suggests copulation. Gratitude might be gratitude for gratification. Therefore we may be inclined to infer that if this gratitude is a thread in the fabric of the religious, it is the religious as sacred rather than the religious as holy that we are here considering. Yet this inference is not one that even Levinas would make. For him holiness is a practice conducted through the material carnateness of the human being. Levinas too would say that birth, and copulation, and death are the elementary forms of the religious provided these forms are acknowledged to be ways in which one's self is traumatized by the other.

Does the fact that we can also speak of being traumatized by the hearing of a musical cadence mean that when we do speak of this we have stepped from the world of the ethico-religious of everyday life into a special world of the aesthetic, the world of the "*petite phrase*" in the sonata of Vinteuil that Proust's Swann found "superior to everyday life" with its banal Hellos and Goodbyes?[15]

Levinas would have us go back from the musical phrases to the phrases in which human beings address one another, not least in those Hellos and Goodbyes. The route he maps out passes through the predicativity of the conceptual and critical exegesis of the music. Only by translating the poietic, plastic, and musical prepredicativity into the predicative prose of the everyday world do we attain to a new prepredicativity, this time the ethico-religious prepredicativity of address. What is lost in that transition from the prepredicativity of singing, for instance the singing of a paean of thanksgiving or the chanting of a hymn of praise, via the predicativity of the said, to the prepredicativity of saying are the modalities of the verb as distinguished from the substantive or the adjectival. In order to save the saying Levinas is ready to let being, which Heidegger is so keen to save, be hypostatized as beings that are said and that therefore make room not only for a correlative saying but for the anarchi-saying or anarchi-scripture that I suspect is part of what he means by "illeity" and that is the epilogical condition of the possibility of the contrast we ordinarily make between what is said and the saying of what is said.

Can we not save both the holy in Levinas's sense and the sacred in the sense it has, according to Levinas, for Heidegger and Hölderlin? A few paragraphs ago it was repeated that, just as in his Gifford Lectures William James is willing to allow that there is a variety of phenomena to which the name religion is given, the religious as distinguished from religions comes—and coming is of its essence beyond essence—in a multiplicity of forms. No thread in the rope of the religious may run through it from end to end. So the religiosity of the religious may be the religiosity of the sacred as well as of the holy. Even so, it will not have passed unnoticed that I have tried hard to describe the religious in such a way as to keep open in it the dimension of address. The concept of address in its turn is not one for which there are necessary and sufficient defining characteristics. But it is less the concept of address that we are invoking here than addressing, and addressing neither is nor is made up of threads that run continuously or discontinuously through the rope of the religious. It is what or, rather, the unwhat that interrupts sequence, that cuts across seriality at every point.

Nor will it have passed unnoticed that the musical example mentioned above keeps the unmeasurable dimension of address open in that it is human beings, the composer and the performer, who launched the musical masterpiece in question upon our astonished ears. Therefore, in order to get across an ampler and, as Derrida would say, more democratic sense of address, a step back must be made beyond the necessity for the possession of human or divine agency on the part of that by which we are addressed.

Address, we are bound to say, is a claim on our attention. If we agree with an opinion shared by certain friends cited in chapter 13 of this book, address would therefore be a call to prayer, albeit not necessarily a summons by bells in the tower of a church or by the voice of a muezzin. However, we have maintained, no more than does a claim to our gratitude need such address be put into words, except insofar as it may be incumbent on those to whom the claim is addressed to voice the claim on behalf of the claimant, to act as advocate for the latter. In taking this step beyond the necessity of human and divine intervention we do not exclude the eventuality of such intervention, though we leave somewhat open what we might wish to call God. This step is one that goes some way toward saving for the religious the forces Heidegger and Levinas give to the words of their languages that are translated into English by the word "holy." This step enables us to have the best of both of their worlds without sacri-ficing the Good. It is arguable that this compromise is prepared for by Levinas's concession, made, however, by him without taking the step beyond human address, that there can occur a reversal of the progress from the sacred to the holy, *du sacré au saint,* from ilyaity to illeity, from emphasis on an aesthetics of verbal and adverbial modalities, hence being and essence, to the nominal and predicative prose of the world and thence to ethics. The aesthetics to which this reversal would take us back would be an aesthetics of the beautiful. "Through art essence and temporality begin to resound with poetry or song. And the search for new forms, from which all art lives, keeps awake everywhere the verbs that are on the verge of lapsing into substances."[16] Paradoxically, this lapsing would be the reduction via names and predicates in the direction of the prepredicativity of the ethical. In the lapsing of this lapse, in the relapse (*Verfallen*) from ethics to aesthetics, "The said is reduced to the Beautiful, which supports Western Ontology." Is it then to the beautiful (*to kalon*) that is reduced also the sublime (*to hupsos?*)? And is this because Western Ontology is Greek, while, as Coleridge and others have held, sublimity has a Hebrew origin, in the Book of Job and on Mount Moriah?

Remaining up to a point faithful to Kierkegaard, Nietzsche, Heidegger, and indeed Levinas, Derrida ventures nevertheless where Levinas fears to tread. In the name of justice he affirms the imadginability of human beings addressed by the non-human and non-divine. If we take this step with Derrida, we shall have to put in a wider context everything that has been said in this book about the minimal predicativity that remains in chiasmus with the therefore not quite stark nakedness of address implicit or explicit in the expression of the loosely knit family of elementary forms of religious life assembled under Sweeney Agonistes's words "birth, and copulation, and death." We shall have to put in a wider context, it would seem, Levinas's and Kierkegaard's limitation of ethico-religious address to the bilaterally human and-or godly. Levinas would say that we would not be widening the context but narrowing it to "Western Ontology" understood in abstraction from the concrete contribution he considers was made by historical Israel and has been inherited by every human being in the line of Abraham, that is to say, he maintains, by every truly human being.[17] This is an inheritance from the Torah whose teaching leads beyond the rhetoric of philosophy toward personal responsibility that, Levinas maintains, "cannot appear perhaps in its originary purity except through this text."[18] Different readers will give different weights to Levinas's "perhaps," as they will to the same word when it occurs in the last of the following sentences:

> I am not saying that the human being is a saint, I am saying that he or she is the one who has understood that holiness is indisputable. This is the beginning of philosophy, this is the rational, the intelligible. In saying that it sounds as if we are getting away from reality. But we forget our relation to *books*—that is, to inspired language, which speaks of nothing else. The book of books, and all literature, which is perhaps only a premonition or recollection of the Bible.[19]

Levinas's thus qualified contentions raise again that dilemma Derrida declared himself to be in over the conditioning force of the historical conditions conditioned by the quasi-transcendental. The only point I wish to make at this late stage about Levinas's contention is that he makes it because he sees the embeddedness in law (*torah, mitzvot*) to be what alone enables humanism of the other human being to hold off the threat of the "cunning" or "ruse" (he would say "sorcery") of reason construed solely in terms of the universality of "Greek" predication and the humanism of Enlightenment perceived as the humanism only of human beings in general. If this is a way of saying that truth is not to be isolated from troth to the singular beings that address us, it is a truth that this book has endorsed.

The point that calls to be made now is one that abstracts from predication. It abstracts from predication in the way that address does. However, by now it should be clear that address is to be understood, following Derrida, as a claim that can be made upon me by something solely on the strength of its existence, and whether or not the existent in question can articulate an act of speech. Levinas himself sometimes offers leverage to this reading when he writes that "Thou shalt not murder" or "Thou shalt not kill" (he seems to be untroubled by this distinction) is spoken in the eyes of another, in the other's face. Or, as Levinas also offers leverage for us to say, in the other's muzzle!

## Return of Bobby

The religious character I attribute to the varieties of what I call elementary forms of religious life, for instance mourning the death of a friend, can characterize the mourning of what we call man's best friend, his dog. If Levinas wishes to reserve the word "*saint*," "holy," for the meaning he hears in the Hebrew word "*kadosh*," who am I to gainsay him? I too would want no one to be deaf to the call Levinas would have us hear in that Hebrew word, the call another addresses to me in the words "Thou shalt not kill." This call announces to me the other's mortality. It inflicts an opening wound upon my self-contained selfhood, not merely turning love of self into love of another, but traumatizing the complacent identity of that self, compelling an alteration of the identity of identity. If indeed Levinas wishes to reserve the word "*saint*," "holy," for the meaning he hears in that Hebrew word "*kadosh*," so be it, even if (but is he so sure?) the meaning of that Hebrew word prevents his using it of a dog, be that dog named Orloff or Jacky or Bobby, names that stand for a continuation—(l), (m), (n)—of the list begun earlier in this chapter.[20]

Orloff, a black greyhound cross, was one of the family dogs of whom Raimond Gaita writes in *The Philosopher's Dog* that when he died, "We gave him 'a burial,' and by standing at the graveside we observed a simple ritual of mourning. But no words were said over his grave."[21]

Standing at another graveside, my wife and I shared the silence with each other and with Jacky, the German Shepherd dog to whom I dedicated my first book.[22] A chapter of that book treats of Derrida. I did not know then that when Derrida was a boy he was known in his family as Jackie. Nor did I know then that when he was a man he would write somewhere that he did not believe in coincidences.

Bobby was the dog who made himself at home in a German camp for Jewish prisoners of war who included Levinas. Bobby greeted prisoners and guards each morning and evening with equal glee. Levinas says of him that he was "the last Kantian in Nazi Germany." He does not inform us of the dog's breed, though he does suggest that "his friendly growling, his animal faith, was born from the silence of his forefathers on the banks of the Nile." There is an allusion here to the dogs of Exodus 11:7 and 22:31, who refrain from growling during the night of the "death of the first-born of Egypt" when the Israelites are about to be released from captivity. "At the supreme hour of his instauration, with neither ethics nor *logos*, the dog will attest to the dignity of the person. This is what the friend of man means. There is a transcendence in the animal!" "Wonderful, wonderful," as Kierkegaard would say. Here is a concession that a being without *logos* may not be without at least the dignity of being able to attest to the dignity of the human being. It will not be a dignity sufficient to make him an ethical being, but his apparently being unable to have ethical regard for others should not prevent human beings, beings with *logos*, making a subject of ethical regard out of him, and if there is no ethics without *logos*, why is not the *logos* of human beings sufficient to meet that condition? Kant thinks that we can be in an ethical relationship only with something that can be in an ethical relationship with us, hence, according to him, only with a being that can act on principles, that can possesses universal *logos*. Levinas's conception of the ethical is no less centered on language, notwithstanding that it is language as singular address that he emphasizes.

While Levinas's endorsement of the dog's attestation to the dignity of the person is to be applauded, is not the dignity of the dog in its own right to be endorsed also? While no one should be deaf to the call of the holy that Levinas would have us hear in the Hebrew word "*kadosh,*" no one should be deaf either to the unarticulated call implicit in the vulnerability and fragility of the non-human. When Levinas writes of dying for the other, he calls this both *sacrifice* and "holiness (*sainteté*) in charity and mercy."[23] And have we not seen both from his own rhetoric and from the historical observations of Benveniste that the notions of the holy and the sacred as they figure in ordinary discourse are not clearly and distinctly different. Under "sacred" we find in the Concise Oxford Dictionary "made holy," "hallowed," "sacrosanct." Can one not accept these glosses of the word "sacred" and use that word in any of those senses of an animal, and of an animal in its own sake, not because it is being sacrificed for the sake of the safety of human animals. Can one not accept these glosses of the word "sacred" and use that word in any of those senses of the non-sentient, of the inorganic, of any other existent as such, or, rather, independently of its such?

## Return of Gratitude

Thanking, giving thanks, giving, forgiving, hospitality, responsibility fall short of themselves, Levinas and Derrida maintain, if they are no more than sorts of exchange, a return of gratitude. Kierkegaard says something close to this about good will, but in the context of Christianity. What he says anticipates what Derrida says about calculation. Kierkegaard makes a distinction between two kinds of gratitude. There is a gratitude that belongs to the realm of the temporal world, and, he says, there is a gratitude that belongs to eternity. The latter, Christian gratitude, is gratitude for the suffering entailed by the imitation of Christ that does not count the cost. The former kind of gratitude, which he says is "pagan or Jewish," is gratitude for the goods of the world, where the good will expressed in our gratitude is a return for what we think of as the good will of God or, as Feuerbach would prefer that we say, for gifts of the natural world and of our human contemporaries and forebears. But only when we can show gratitude for what by the world's standards are its bads do we learn that "in this gratitude and by this gratitude he [God] has overcome the world."[24] That is how he shows truly good will. That is benevolence that does not fall short of benevolence. That is how we learn that Christ came into the world to save us from statistics. To learn this is to learn that our world in the chiasmus of time and eternity is analogous to a penal colony.

> Think of a penal institution where to a certain degree prisoners have the power to plan their lives the way they want to—but they recognize that the authority's idea is that their life should be the suffering of punishment: if then they do everything to make life for themselves very enjoyable, cozy, and pleasant—and then are ready to thank the authority for the good days they have—this would be making a fool of the authority, for it would be just the opposite of his intention.[25]

This would be making a fool of God. Christianity is foolish, but not in this way. That it is a folly to the Greeks and a stumbling-block to the Jews does not mean that it does not make sense from the point of view of eternity.

However, here looms a problem or aporia. For from the point of view of eternity, suffering has become bliss. Does this not mean that for the world of calculated exchanges of enjoyments dependent upon our being carnate has been exchanged a heaven of exchanges of spiritual bliss, whether or not the exchanges are calculated and whether or not the bliss includes bliss dependent upon the resurrection of the body? Furthermore, although we are used to the idea that Kierkegaard is for making Christianity more difficult than Christendom is inclined to make it, one does not have to be an aspiring *imitator Christi* to find too difficult to swallow the idea of a Divine Authority that intends the infliction of suffering. Isn't that Authority or at least that Authority's Son authorized to forgive with a forgiveness that exceeds exchange, so exceeds exchange of punishment for crime and for sin, a forgiveness that, as we put it with reference to Derrida, would not fall short of itself because it does not fall short of giving one's life or (and here's the rub) of giving, sacrificing, what one values more than one's life, for example one's son Isaac or for Example one's Only-begotten Son Jesus Christ?

Derrida, like Levinas, points in the direction of a way that exceeds exchange and is to that extent a repetition of Heidegger's thought of a thinking that "is true thanks, does not need to repay, nor be deserved, in order to give thanks . . . but . . . remains an offering (*Entgegentragen*)."[26] Derrida, Levinas, and Heidegger are here remembering also Kierkegaard, but their way of repeating him does not incur the embarrassments that ensue from conjoining his salutary clue with the superstructure of a religion of salvation. Although God, religions, and belief in another world may be invoked to make sense of the thought that the world is sublimely and incomprehensibly more than it is, religiousness without them is also capable of making sense of that thought and of the thought that, yes, there is indeed another world, but it is this one. Without that superstructure a gratitude can be imadgined that is not owed to a being that gives that for which we are grateful, where the givenness of that for which we are grateful extends no further than the gratuity of the *es gibt.* There is room for gratitude toward those whom, if they were contemporaries, we could have thanked to their face, those masons mentioned earlier, the carpenter, the baker, and the candlestick-maker, Pinturicchio and Piero della Francesca, mighty Bach, *Bach mawr,* and after Bach Palestrina and Praetorius and Beethoven and Buxtehude, the Psalmists whose songs Bonhoeffer read every day, and Homer and Shakespeare, the authors of the great texts of Oriental and Western religion, the authors of the great texts of science like Richard Dawkins's Bible *The Origin of Species,* the authors of the great texts of philosophy, including those written in the margin of religion between Kierkegaard and Derrida that have been invoked in this book. There is room both for gratitude and for saying thanks when the one to whom one says thanks is beside you but in his or her grave. This is the closeness of a specter, a closeness that is between the closeness of one with whom you are speaking *viva voce* and the distance of one to whom you are writing, except that this latter distance can sometimes be closer than the closeness of an interlocutor.

The gratitude in which I am most interested here is the gratitude that is not necessarily addressed to anybody one could thank, least of all a deity. Call it a secular prayer of thanksgiving, a secular eucharist, if you wish, but if you do, and if you oppose the secular to the religious, do not, I pray, think that the religious is always clothed in the surplices, cassocks, miters, and suchlike raiment of organized religions. Do not think either that in stressing the part played by gratitude in some forms of religious experience I am insensitive to the circumstance that a life may be so fraught with pain that to the one who lives it there may seem to be nothing for which to be grateful—not even the consolation of a religion. This circumstance would be another explanation of the fact, acknowledged in earlier chapters, that what this book has been calling forms of religious experience are no part of the experience of some people. I hesitate to say that instead of feeling gratitude some people feel cursed, for, although this is true, the idea of being cursed (but not, I maintain, or not so irresistibly, the idea of grace) tends to bring with it the idea of a supernatural agency responsible for inflicting the curse, and this latter idea would return us to the stories of gods and religious mythologies our religious suspension of begodded religions attempts to hold in suspense.

One challenge offered to readers of Nietzsche's account of *amor fati* and eternal return is the challenge to interpret these teachings in a manner that does not return them and us to one form or another of the old, old story. That return would be effected once again if I attempted to render the acknowledged fact of non-gratitude or ingratitude consistent with my emphasis upon gratitude by saying with Kierkegaard and a multitude of other religious thinkers that suffering can be seen or experienced as a good and thus redeemed. Perhaps Nietzsche can say that in his passage to redemption through love of fate (his love of fate presumably without fate's love of him) the opposition of curse and blessing upon him is unmade. Perhaps I can say at least that while a realistic admission must be made of the horrors suffered by millions of our fellow human (and non-human) beings, some, maybe many, of these latter would ask you not to forget those others for whose lives gratitude is possible and due. The gratitude would be apt either because of the joys experienced in those lives or because of the courage with which those who lived them faced their sufferings. These possibilities are relevant to the question raised earlier in this book as to the connection between Nietzsche's teaching on *amor fati* and eternal return and the horrors of the Holocaust. The horrors of the Holocaust were all too well known to Levinas. I suspect that the difficult gratitude on which our paragraphs here have touched may have been in his thoughts when he expressed astonishment at and gratitude for the possibility that one can be grateful for the possibility of being grateful. "Men have been able to be thankful for the very fact of finding themselves able to thank; the present gratitude is grafted on to itself as onto an already antecedent gratitude."[27] The antecedence of this gratitude would be the antecedence of the Yes as variously parsed by Nietzsche, Rosenzweig, Heidegger, and Derrida. And if this gratitude is part of what we are calling the religious beyond the religions, the religious has this antecedence too. It would be an antecedence that antecedes even the antecedence of morality as the condition of the opposition between the moral and the immoral. So a correction must be made to the sentences of the second section of the last chapter in which an analogy was drawn between the moral as a category "beyond good and evil" and the religious as contrasted with the religions. The opposition between the morally good and the morally evil is an opposition along the lines of that between the accursed and the blessed, which is an opposition dependent on the idea of an authority that separates the sheep that go to the right and the goats that go to the left. If it is a religious opposition, its religiosity is that of a special religion, not of the religious in Derrida's understanding of the words "religion in general." It is not even an opposition operative at the transcendental level. The religious affirmation and the religious gratitude on to which a present gratitude is grafted is quasi-transcendental, that is to say, as Levinas would say, an immemorial saying, *Dire,* signifiance and assignative addressance of oneself that is what makes possible the common distinction between the saying (*dire*) of something and what is said (*dit*).

Now immediately following the words about this quasi-transcendental gratitude, Levinas writes: "In a prayer in which the believer asks that the prayer be heard, the prayer as it were precedes or follows itself." Depending on how we analyze the "or" in the words "precedes or follows itself" and depending on how we construe the phrase "as it were" that indicates perhaps that the imadgination is here being brought into play, might it be possible that a non-believer who was prevented from making an intercessory prayer by his non-belief had nevertheless made a quasi-transcendental prayer to someone, himself or someone other, albeit other than God, the God in which he does not believe?

As to non-belief in "another world," if you are tempted to think, for your own sake or for that of some god, that this world is to be sacrificed for the sake of another world, give thought to the possibility that the otherness is in this world, staring you in the face from the eyes of fellow human beings and in the eyes of Piero's resurrected Christ, by whom this world is said to have been overcome.

The overcoming of the world is its sublimity understood not as that which exceeds our understanding because we cannot reach far enough forward, but as its over-reaching us and our power to contain it. If God overbrims every idea of God, so does the world, this world, overbrim every idea of the world. This is what one can learn from reading what Derrida writes in *The Truth in Painting* about sublimity that exceeds the frame of the idea, of the book, and of the picture (for instance the frame of the Recklinghausen icon invoked in chapter 13) alongside what he writes about messianicity without messianism. Remember, however, that this "without" (*sans*) stands neither for the without of simple negation nor for the simple negation to which apophatic theology restricts its statements about God nor for the double negation (*re-pas*) of Hegelian dialectical digestion. The practical and political lesson that those who have an ear to hear can learn from that and the other texts reread in this book is that religions, whether theistic or atheistic, require to be somehow kept in touch with the religious disposition that does justice to and is grateful for the singularities and thisnesses of this world while experiencing this world's archi-sublimity.

Why *archi*-sublimity? The place to answer this question might be an appendix, if, as Kant tells us, the place to discourse on the sublime is an appendix, the part that is only partly a proper part of a book. Derrida (who called the attic library in his house his *sublime*) summarizes as follows Kant's comment on the appendicity of the sublime: "Because the sublime is not in nature but only in ourselves, because the *colossal* which derives from it proceeds only from us, the analytic of the sublime is only an appendix (*einen blossen Anhang*) to the aesthetic of natural finality."[28] Derrida writes this in *The Truth in Painting*. He does not write this in an appendix added at the end of that book, but his not doing this does not mean that he is being unfaithful to Kant. His comments are made under the heading "Parergon," and "appendix" is not a bad translation of that Greek word. Kierkegaard's Johannes Climacus does add an appendix to what he calls a Concluding Postscript. His Appendix includes a revocation (*Tilbagekaldelse*) advising that the author of the Concluding Postscript has been writing "without authority" and that it must be left to each reader of his book to decide the issue at stake. Readers of my book will decide whether what will be added in its forthcoming final chapter is a revocation of what has been said in its predecessors regarding the word "God."

# SEVENTEEN

## The World Is More Than It Is

### Sublimities

Under "sublime" the Concise Oxford Dictionary says: "of the most exalted kind, so distinguished by elevation or size or nobility or grandeur or other impressive quality as to inspire awe or wonder . . . reaching up to the lintel," from Latin "*limen*," which may also mean threshold. But what would be the *archi*-sublime? Insofar as this question makes contact with what Derrida says about what Kant and Hegel say about the sublime, it reintroduces the question, broached in chapter 1, of their disagreement over borderlines and limits, and of Kierkegaard's thoughts on where the line of madness is crossed. Kant conceives the boundary, *Grenze*, as a positive borderline. One of his examples is precisely a drawn line. A line is divided from a surface in one direction and from a point in another. Its geometry would be different from theirs, one that is intermediate in complexity. Yet all three are geometries. All fall within space. Despite the positive divisions between them, progress from the simpler to the more complex geometry is progress within one and the same mathematical continuum. But Kant denies that a progression in a shared continuum is possible in the step from understanding to reason. Between understanding and reason the *Grenze* is fixed. This is what Hegel challenges. There is no such *Grenze* there. Instead there is a *Schranke*, a limit understood as only a negative restriction to the progressive extension of the constitutive rationality of knowledge. As it is with the line in Kant's conception of geometrical *Grenze*, so is it, Hegel maintains, with the limit between understanding and reason. It is a confinium in a continuum. Hegel argues that Kant fails to acknowledge the continuum of reason within which the negativity of a *Schranke* does not hinder the forward movement of thought but rather facilitates it.

Consistent with what he says about the *Grenze* in mathematics, movement forward is retained in Kant's account of the mathematical sublime. There is an advance in apprehension as the imagination progressively synthesizes under numerical concepts (foot, perch, mile, etc.) the magnitude of the natural world. This advance is infinite insofar as the mathematical imagination is concerned. But, Kant argues, the imagination must listen to reason, and reason demands that even the infinite be comprehended as a single given totality. However, no such comprehension of a totality is possible. There corresponds to it no object of either sensible or intellectual intuition. This failure of comprehension is felt as the distance between imagination's sphere of mathematical comparison and the idea of nonintuitable unity and totality postulated by practical reason. This idea is not a concept that subsumes under itself a phenomenal object. Therefore the sublimity of the magnitude of nature is an aesthetic modification of the mind, a *Gemütsstimmung,* in which the place of moral law as proper object of respect gets to be occupied by an object of nature functioning in lieu of that law.

In the *Critique of Pure Reason* Kant divides the categories and principles of the understanding into two groups which he calls the mathematical and the dynamic. The former apply to the purely spatio-temporal forms of intuition, the latter to concepts and modalities employed in the investigation of the material world. Out of a possibly misplaced desire to maintain some architectonic uniformity, parallel distinctions are made in the *Critique of Judgment.* Nevertheless, it is with reference to the mathematical sublime that he says that the mind feels itself moved in the representation of the sublime in nature. So, despite his devoting separate sections to the mathematical and the dynamic sublime strictly so called, the mathematical sublime is dynamic, if not in his technical meaning of the term. Therefore I do not here charge Kant with inconsistency. But I anticipate a turn, a *Kehre,* toward an archi-sublimity that is the condition or quasi-condition of Kant's distinction between the mathematical and the dynamic sublimes, and between the sublime and the beautiful.

While, according to Kant, the beautiful is an object of restful contemplation, the feeling of sublimity moves to and fro between the uneasiness (*Unlust*) associated with the imagination's failing to form a representation of the unity and totality demanded by reason and, on the other hand, pleasure (*Lust*) at the thought that it is our human rationality that sets the standard that our imagination cannot meet. The restfulness of the aesthetic judgment of the beautiful is the harmony between imagination and understanding working in concord. In the judgment of sublimity the harmony is less serene. It is that of the cooperation of faculties in conflict. This conflict between the faculties is especially evident with the dynamic sublime. The latter is distinguished from the mathematical sublime by the part played in it by fear, but fear filtered by the "as if" of the imagination. Just as an appetite or other personal interest in something interferes with the free play of the imagination necessary for judging the thing beautiful, so fear of a thing prevents our judging it sublime. In the feeling of the sublime we resist a threat from a safe distance. The terror is not "seriously entertained."[1] Children are adept at inventing games in which fear is imagined in this way. But if as an analogue of this we cite Wordsworth's account in Book 1 of *The Prelude* of his childhood escapade on Ullswater we should not forget that it was he who wrote too that the child is father of the man.

> I fixed my view
> Upon the summit of a craggy ridge,
> The horizon's utmost boundary; far above
> Was nothing but the stars and the grey sky.
> She was an elfin pinnace; lustily
> I dipped my oars into the silent lake.
> And, as I rose upon the stroke, my boat
> Went heaving through the water like a swan;
> When, from behind the craggy steep till then
> The horizon's bound, a huge peak, black and huge,
> As if with voluntary power instinct
> Upreared its head. I struck and struck again,
> And growing still in stature and grim shape
> Towered up between me and the stars, and still,
> For so it seemed, with purpose of its own
> And measured motion like a living thing,
> Strode after me. With trembling oars I turned,
> And through the silent water stole my way
> Back to the covert of the willow tree;
> There in her mooring place I left my bark,—
> And through the meadows homeward went, in grave
> And serious mood;

The grave and serious mood lasted several days during which the sense of being as if pursued gave way to

> a dim and undetermined sense
> Of unknown modes of being; o'er my thoughts
> There hung a darkness, call it solitude

Or blank desertion. No familiar shapes
Remained, no pleasant images of trees,
Of sea or sky, no colours of green fields;
But huge and mighty forms, that do not live
Like living men, moved slowly through the mind
By day, and were a trouble to my dreams.

If this is still a sense of the sublime in nature, the powers implicated in it and
the relations between them are different from those at work in Kant's analysis.
In Kant's analysis the feeling of the sublime in nature combines the sense of the
limitation of the imagination with a release from that sense of limitation thanks
to the implication of the thought of our

> pre-eminence (*Überlegenheit*) above nature that is the foundation of a self-
> preservation of quite another kind from that which may be assailed and
> brought into danger by external nature. This saves humanity in our person
> from humiliation, even though as mortal men we have to submit to external
> violence.[2]

What according to Kant humanity is ultimately saved from is humiliation
thanks to its being saved from what he and Kierkegaard and Luther and Paul
call "the world," and our worldliness, meaning by that preoccupation with
secular happiness, with, in Kant's words, "worldly goods, health, and life." The
feeling of the sublime in nature, thanks to its reliance upon the idea of unity
and totality borrowed from reason, therefore not after all simply in nature, gives
us a hint of "forces of the soul above the height of vulgar commonplace," forces
Kant locates in reason by comparison with which even immeasurable nature is
small. Contrast this with Wordsworth. Although "the mean and vulgar works
of man" to which he refers may be among those carried out in pursuit of the
worldly goods to which Kant refers, Wordsworth does not judge them mean in
comparison with the superiority of human practical reason or with the human
being's respect for the moral law. He judges them mean in comparison rather
with nature, life, passion, and the grandeur of the heart:

> thus from my first dawn of childhood
> Didst thou intertwine for me
> The passions that build up our human soul;
> Not with the mean and vulgar works of man,
> But with high objects, with enduring things—
> With life and nature—purifying thus
> The elements of feeling and of thought,
> And sanctifying, by such discipline,
> Both pain and fear, until we recognise
> A grandeur in the beatings of the heart.

Addressed here with gratitude is the

> Wisdom and Spirit of the universe!
> Thou Soul that art the eternity of thought,
> That givest to forms and images a breath
> And everlasting motion. . . .

*The Prelude* is subtitled "Growth of a Poet's Mind." That growth is acknowledged again when in the *Lines Written a Few Miles above Tintern Abbey* the poet writes:

>                     I have learned
> To look on nature, not as in the hour
> Of thoughtless youth; but hearing oftentimes
> The still, sad music of humanity. . . .
>                     And I have felt
> A presence that disturbs me with the joy
> Of elevated thoughts; a sense sublime
> Of something far more deeply interfused,
> Whose dwelling is the light of setting suns,
> And the blue sky, and in the mind of man,
> A Motion and a spirit, that impels
> All thinking things, all objects of all thought,
> And rolls through all things.

As though to subsume Wordsworth under Hegel's understanding of pantheism, the Knox translation of Hegel's *Aesthetics* adopts this last phrase to get Hegel to say that "the One is this thing and another and another again and rolls through all things (*sich in allem herumwirft*)."[3] This is only one side of pantheism as properly understood. As properly understood, as understood by Hegel in a way that smooths the path to the inclusion of pantheism within the teleology of universal reason "in which the substance is purified from everything apparent and particular and therefore from what fades away in it and is inadequate to it," the "pan" of "pantheism" denotes not this, that and the other individual thing, but All in the sense of the one substance or universal soul in its unity. Hegel maintains that pantheism so defined "belongs primarily to the East," in contrast to the Christian mysticism of, for example (his example) Angelus Silesius "who, with the greatest audacity and depth of intuition and feeling, has expressed in a wonderfully mystical power of representation the substantial existence of God in things and the unification of the self with God and of God with human subjectivity."[4] Against this, strictly Eastern pantheism "emphasizes rather the contemplation of the *one* substance in all phenomena and their sacrifice by the subject who thereby acquires the supreme enlargement of consciousness as well as, through the entire liberation from the finite, the bliss of absorption into everything that is best and most splendid."[5]

Although Wordsworth prefers the words "Spirit" and "Soul" over "God," he is closer to Christian mysticism than to the Eastern pantheism thus described by Hegel. He is not for sacrificing the phenomena. So he is not for subordinating sensibility as it is subordinated in both Kant's and Hegel's analyses of the sublime. Hegel does not follow Kant in reducing the sublime to no more than a subjective power of the mind. It is for Hegel a moment in what we might call the growth of the philosopher's mind toward the light of absolute knowledge or wisdom. It is therefore no less objective than subjective. Nevertheless, Hegel says, Kant's reduction "must be recognized as correct to this extent, that sublimity—as Kant says himself—is not contained in anything in nature but only in our minds, in so far as we become conscious of our superiority to the nature within us and therefore to nature without."[6] This superiority resides in our idea of universality, concrete universality Hegel would say, universality that has "concresced," grown under the guidance of the methodology of dialectical negation.

Here then are what might be called two sources of sublimity, a Kantian-Hegelian one and a Wordsworthian. They are also two sources of religious experience insofar as what Derrida calls religion in general as distinguished from religions in particular may be regarded as archi- or quasi-sublime. Archi-sublimity would be what makes possible sublimity as analysed by Kant and Hegel with emphasis upon universality. It is what makes possible sublimity as analysed by Wordsworth, who baulks at sacrificing singular sensible things to the concept or idea; as too does Kierkegaard at least where the singularity is that of the human individual. The Kantian-Hegelian source stresses (emphasizes and strains) reason while the Wordsworthian source stresses (again in both senses) sensibility. Reason and sensibility participate in each other primitively in imagination. Imagination has its source in what we could call archi-imagination or imadgination which is the locus of archi- or quasi-sublimity. Since this locus is as unstable as *chōra,* the imagination as source of the distinction between reason and sensibility and the archi-imagination or imadgination as the source of imagination would be more accurately described as quasi-sources or "sources," where the scare-quotes make the word tremble as violently as did the young Wordsworth's oars. This trembling is of a piece with the fear and trembling of and with which Paul and Kierkegaard speak when, in the passage cited in the first section of our chapter 15, Kierkegaard slides from citing Paul to making Paul's words his own: "This is 'fear and trembling'. . . . This, you see, is fear and trembling." For the two sources of sublimity, the Kantian and the Wordsworthian, are the two sources of the religiousness of what Derrida calls religion in general. This explains why among the exergues of this book is the statement made by Karen Armstrong, but ever so slightly modified, "The imadgination is the chief religious faculty."

## The Chief Religious Faculty

Archi- or quasi-sublimity is related to the beautiful somewhat as archi-writing is related to speech. There is a philosophical tradition according to which speech is understood to be present to itself and to the thoughts of the speaker and, provided those thoughts are successfully communicated, to the hearer. Derrida has demonstrated that speech is punctuated by the blank spaces that are supposed by philosophers and others to pit the surface of writing—holes mimicked by the gaps on the pages of *Glas, The Post Card,* and *The Truth in Painting.*[7] So the author of these works introduces the conceit of archi-writing to denote the distantiation and deferment that is shared by writing and speech and that makes the usual polarity impossible except as surface effect. Similarly, quasi-sublimity is that power of the imadgination (which is the seat, albeit shaky, trembling—Kant uses the word "*Erschütterung*"—of the quasi-) that makes it possible at the level of surface grammar but impossible at the level of depth grammar to draw a sharp borderline between the beautiful and the sublime—and between surface and depth. So the phrase "sublimely beautiful" reproduced from that program-note adverted to in chapter 15 is both contradictory and pleonastic, depending on whether we focus on the ordinary sense or the archi-sense of the adverb "sublimely." Recall too Wordsworth's phrase "blank desertion," Derrida's references to blank spaces and his production of them *à la* Mallarmé in the pages of books mentions of which in this book range from *Glas,* the topic of chapter 3, through *The Post Card* attended to especially in chapter 13, to *The Truth in Painting* mentioned several times in the present chapter and its immediate predecessor. Then again, Wordsworth's "desertion" calls to mind Derrida's desert in the desert and his citation of Angelus Silesius reproduced as one of the exergues of this book: "I must, transcending God, into a desert flee." The nomad passes through the desert as Kierkegaard passes through despair and Levinas through godlessness. These passages are "formal indications" of the restlessness of the absolute archi-sublime that (to use again Wordsworth's word, and Levinas's) disturbs the good conscience of our enjoyment of the beautiful and our confidence in happy endings. This is a restlessness we suffer (Kierkegaard's word, and Nietzsche's) even if, "transcending God," God is subtracted by us from Søren's story of salvation.

In allowing imagination to mutate into imadgination we are playing on words, as imagination is wont to do. This does not mean that there is not something serious at stake, something that is important ethically, politically, and religiously. To demonstrate this let us go back for a moment from the sublime to the beautiful. Kant tells us that the beautiful can exist in nature. But he tells us that in judging something to be beautiful, as against in judging something to be good, no interest in the existence of the thing moves us. Speaking generally of matters of taste, he says "One must not be in the least prepossessed in favour of the real existence of the thing, but must preserve complete indifference in this respect. . . ."[8] One must not be prepossessed (*eingenommen*) in favor of it, but must one not be postpossessed in favor of it? For beauty inspires love and therefore a concern for the continuing existence and integrity of the beautiful thing. And possession is the point on which archi-sublimity turns. It is the point at which possession defined in terms of the law of property turns into being possessed as this term is used in psychopathology. How often, when people exclaim how beautiful they found something, perhaps something in a shop window or at an auction sale, we hear them say "I simply had to have it." But with sublimity as described by Kant and Hegel there is a reaching out as if to possess even the unpossessible. For them the sublime is what exceeds our reach. In the case of the mathematical sublime the imagination aspires toward a completed infinity which it fails to comprehend. As remarked above, the movement is one of progressive teleological synthesis. It is in terms of this that Kant and Hegel define the setback suffered by the imagination. If one is, so to speak, thrown back on one's heels, that is because the initial movement is directed forward ec-statically.

But the incomprehensibility intrinsic to the feeling of the sublime is amenable to a different construal. Instead of being a frustrated attempt to take possession, it may be a being possessed. And here the possession and obsession may be described as psychotic. Leading us to consider that there may be not only a "neurosis of health" (of the *heil*), as Nietzsche suggests,[9] but also a psychosis of the holy (the *heilig*), it is precisely as psychosis that Levinas describes inverted intentionality. However, we have insisted that if intentionality is taken to imply the consciousness of an object or objective, it is misleading to describe as intentionality the other's looking at me face to face in Levinas's ethical sense of this last phrase. Although the other's look is responsible for my being a me in the accusative, not firstly a first-person singular I, the look accuses me and alerts me to my responsibility. The "experience" in question, the "experience" that puts me in question (and Levinas himself uses scare-quotes here), can be conveyed only in our being face to face with someone or with something that regards us, even to the point of putting us on the spot, challenging us to justify our occupancy of a place in the sun between the event of our birth and the event of our death in the presence of other fragile beings which is also the presence of the thought of their absence. Think again of Piero's painting of the resurrected Christ or a reproduction of it on a card. I choose advisedly an example from the iconography of a religion other than Levinas's because in doing so I come back to the ethico-politico-religious point which is the serious issue at stake in this chapter. I chose advisedly also and for the same serious reason the example given us by Wordsworth when, however much safeguarded by the phrase "as if" that is the hallmark of the imagination, he records that it was as if he were being pursued by the "huge peak, black and huge," as the poet says stutteringly, reminding us of other poets, George, Hölderlin, Eliot, Rimbaud, who speak of the significance of the insignificance that happens when words break.[10] One is tempted to say that it was as if Wordsworth were being not only pursued by the monstrous, *ungeheuer,* promontory, but prosecuted or persecuted; and not because the boat had been stolen, for nowhere does he give us reason to suppose that he had qualms about that: the law of the ethics of possessions is suspended by the unlaw of being possessed. The moral imagination is at work when we are struck by the thought that also a she and he, other others, are looking at me through your eyes. The moral imagination or imadgination is at work when we are struck by the thought that through your eyes I may be regarded too by an it. Imagination or imadgination is the zone of the quasi-. Hence the term "quasi-sublime" as an alternative to "archi-sublime," where the prefix of the former expression avoids the implication of firstness and of authority normally carried by "*archi*" and "*archē,*" so as to register that in the beginning was the unbeginning of the imadgination. We are on the borderline of madness here, wherever here may be. This is the invisible borderline between the desire to overcome something out there and being overcome by something out there. Except that the out there, the other, is at the same time in here. The other and the other others by which we are obsessed are not in pure reason as the Kantian faculty of practical law, but in the imagination or imadgination of our hearts, "the chief religious faculty," where reason and sensibility engage each other in concord and discord.

To say heart is to say love, as to say beauty is to say love. So it is almost to say sublime, as we should expect to be able to say if we say that the archi-quasi-sublime stands to the contrast between the sublime and the beautiful as Derrida says archi-writing stands to the contrast between writing and speaking. Kant holds that the contemplation of a beautiful object is restful, as contrasted with the restlessness of the feeling of the sublime. But he holds also that beauty inspires love. However restful the contemplation of the beautiful may be, love is not true love unless it is motivated to take care of what it judges to be beautiful, even if taking care means taking care to leave it alone. To find a thing appealing is to feel as though one were being appealed to by it. Here then is a power of magnetic attraction, *aimance,* that is a power both of the beautiful and of the sublime, even if some of the power of the sublime is the power of a threat. The power of the beautiful and of the sublime is a power that disturbs the opposition between contemplation and practice, discourages the baleful connection between the aesthetic and the idea of the aesthete, and overcomes the separation of the aesthetic from the ethical, translating aesthetic distantiation from the *objet d'art* into the ethico-religious distance in proximity of the other. So that there is room not only for a *Critique of Practical Reason* and a *Critique of Aesthetic Judgment*, but also, in view of the fact that in the index of my edition of Kant's *Religion within the Boundaries of Reason Alone* no mention is made of the imagination, for a Critique of Practical Imagination, one that would be at the same time a Hypocritique of the Religious within the Boundaries of Imagination. Further, somewhat as there is in the feeling of the sublime according to Kant the tension between attraction and repulsion to which we have just referred,[11] so in the agapeistic love inspired by loveliness there is an impulse to avoid favoritism in the directing of one's favor and, moved by the generosity inherent in agapeistic love, but also by the sense of justice inherent in it but often absent from *erōs*, a Desire to attend to what has so far escaped one's attention, in case we are being blinded by our first love to the attractions of what through prejudice we have hitherto judged ugly or indifferent. Following Kant, we may say that there would be an archi-sublimity of the ugly. But what Gerard Manley Hopkins might have called the overwhelm of archi-sublimity is already implied by the circumstance that just as the he and the she and the distributive they address me in your face, I am addressed by other its through this it.

At this point we do well to recall Nietzsche's confession: "A certain emperor always bore in mind the transitoriness of all things so as not to take them too seriously and to live at peace among them. To me, on the contrary, everything seems far too valuable to be fleeting: I seek an eternity for everything."[12] It is of fleetingness that Nietzsche speaks, not of beauty. But the beauty of a thing gives rise to the poignant sense of its fleetingness.

> Fair daffodils, we weep to see
> You haste away so soon.

Fleetingness, fragility and mortality are not, however, confined to the beautiful. They are also the fate of the ugly, the dumpy, and the plain. We may even feel that this fate is more unfair to the ugly and plain (to the un-fair, the unlovely) than it is to the lovely, for while the lovely lasts it enjoys so to speak the privilege of being patently lovely and lovable. We weep for the passing of the unlovely too and can wish that it too could be saved. Sometimes we can bring ourselves to imagine, if only for a passing while, that we would die for someone or some thing, for, say, the handsome blackbird that returned every spring for seven years to sing its heart out at the top of the holly tree in your garden, or the ugly duckling that, unlike the one in the story told by Kierkegaard's contemporary and compatriot Hans Christian Andersen (both of whom, like Sartre, deemed themselves ugly), does not turn out to be a swan. Perhaps, despite Kant's characterization of the beautiful as restful (though note that it is in the context of the *contemplation* of the beautiful that his characterization is made), the attractiveness of the beautiful is attracted toward the sublime. Maybe a suggestion of this is the fact that if you look up in a German dictionary "*erhaben*," Kant's word for "sublime," you will find that it can in some circumstances mean beautiful; again, one Welsh word for "sublime," "*arddunol*," is based on "*ardd*," "high," which is cognate with "*hardd*," "beautiful." And, by the way, this last word is based on "*bellus*," which is based on "*bonulus*," which is a diminitive form of "*bonus*," which means good. There are, however, manifold forms of goodness, so that this etymological complication need not require further distinctions to be made than are made explicitly or implicitly by Kant when he says that in judging something to be beautiful as against in judging something to be good no interest in the existence of the thing moves us. In any case, appeals to etymology should not be based on too reverential an attitude to bases. How a word is used at a particular time is not umbilicaly tied to how it was used by our great, great, great grandmother, or by Eve.

Understanding the sublime as the artistic conquest of ugliness and horror, Nietzsche writes in *The Birth of Tragedy* that "our sense of beauty . . . craves great and sublime forms."[13] Nietzsche is writing at this point about art, whereas Kant, in the statements most recently cited from him above, is writing about nature. But Kant himself insists that judgments of the sublime are dependent upon a high degree of culture,[14] and it is through art that in *The Birth of Tragedy* Nietzsche seeks redemption of the sufferings of life; again, if, as Kierkegaard insists, redemption of suffering is not the same as escape from it, art that secures such redemption cannot be so illusory as not to draw on life for the forms and metaphors it employs. On the other hand, the informal interpretations and reinterpretations that form, inform and unform our everyday world have something in common with the organized forms of artistic artefacts. We are touching here upon the chiasmic structure of the relation between nature and art. We are touching here also on the thought that the nature of nature in the widest possible sense of the word is not exclusive of artefactuality, convention and culture. "Nature" is a word, so it is exposed to the slow mobilities of culture. To this degree, the difference between not quite naked because not entirely unlinguistic religiousness in general and organized religions will be one of degree. To this degree we agree with Nietzsche. And with Derrida, as we see when we recall the following statement in *Margins of Philosophy* of what we may regard as a complication of the procedure of imagination that Kant calls schematism. Recall too that this statement of Derrida's, part of which was reproduced in chapter 13, is a key to what was said in chapter 11 about the working of negativity in Abelian words and in dreams as analysed by Freud:

one could reconsider all the pairs of opposites on which philosophy is constructed and on which our discourse lives, not in order to see opposition erase
itself but to see what indicates that each of the terms must appear in the *différance* of the other, as the other different and deferred in the economy of the
same (the intelligible as differing-deferring the sensible, as the sensible differing and deferred; the concept as different and deferred, differing-deferring
intuition; culture as nature different and deferred, differing-deferring. . . .[15]

That is to say, a difference can be seen as both a difference in degree and a difference in kind provided we can bring ourselves to recognize the historical and
cultural contingency to which the necessity of what constitutes a kind or an
essence is exposed. That is how I propose we regard the difference between the
natural religiosity of the intimacies of birth, and copulation, and death and the
religiosity of the more organized religions. As the latter have been occasions for
bigotry, intolerance and persecution, so too our unsystematized religious behavior in the face of birth, death and sexuality bears witness to the aptitude of our
will for perversion, whether or not that be attributed to, in the words of the title
of a section of Kant's *Religion within the Boundaries of Reason Alone,* a radical
evil in human nature, a topic to which a return will be made in the Epilogue.
But, to repeat, by the religious in general is meant a sphere of human response
that may be benign or malignly violent as judged in terms of the opposition of
good and evil. In Levinas's words, it is possible to be violent only to a face, only
to a singularity. And it is this reference to singularity that marks off the religious
or the ethico-religious *in general* from the ethical *as general.* It was precisely in
order to put the emphasis on singularity that we began this book with chapters
treating some of the writings of Kierkegaard and his pseudonymous authors, in
order then to follow the subsequent history of the thinking of singularity in the
writings of Nietzsche, Deleuze and Guattari, Levinas and Derrida. The field of
what Derrida calls the religious in general is the field of the singular as defined,
as we have been defining the field of the religious, by the interconnected parameters of birth, and copulation and death, and as distinguished from the fields
of the religions in which putatively universal tables of laws are laid down and
justice is understood in their terms. The field of the rudimentarily religious, as
the field of the singular and unique, is the field of the archi-sublime. However,
the archi- or quasi-sublime is vacuous except insofar as it interrupts with its own
singular justice universal justice as demarcated by determinate and determining
laws. This is the law of the chiasmus of such laws and the archi-quasi-sublime.

This law is the law of the relation of chiasmus between these two sorts of
justice or, we should say (since it is the fate of the sortal to be exceeded) of these
"two sources of justice" or, we should say (since it is the fate of sources to become unoriginal) of these two "'sources' of justice": justice as right defined by
law, and justice as responsibility to singularities not so defined but as the "mys-

tical" source of justice, the "mystical" force of the law.[16] Kant and Hegel—not to mention Luther, Paul and a Judaism often caricatured by Kant and Hegel and Kierkegaard—have made us familiar with the idea of sacrificing the singular sensations in order to save the law. Derrida and again Kierkegaard have made us familiar with the idea of sacrificing the law in order that the singular be saved—if only momentarily, for law reinscribes itself the moment we speak, the moment we think. This theme, which is also the Kierkegaardian theme of the secrecy that escapes thematization, is enlarged upon in all those places where Derrida writes of the democracy to come, the to-come, the *à venir,* the New International, messianicity without messianism, the *à dieu* and the *adieu* that is between the salutations Hello and Goodbye. For the to-come of democracy is not to be confused with democracy in the chronologically future, any more than the philosophy of the future announced in the subtitle of *Beyond God and Evil* is only philosophy in the chronologically future. This to-come of democracy is not to be confused with democracy in that future any more than *Die Zukünftigen,* the ones to come of Heidegger's *Contributions to Philosophy,* are beings considered only historically (*historisch*). Among the ones "to come" according to Heidegger are Hölderlin, who, regarded chronologically, belongs to the past. The futurality of democracy to come is not, to use words used by Rilke in the citation reproduced in chapter 15, "beyond the future." It is, to paraphrase the words used in a citation attributed to Éluard in that chapter, another world, but another world that is or is in this one.

A propos of the Hello just mentioned, democracy and philosophy of the future are at the same time democracy and philosophy of the past in that they do not turn their backs on the religious astonishment in which philosophy was found by Plato and Aristotle to have already begun. The Hello is a priori. A propos of the Goodbye, even if the Messiah has already come, we cannot know that another Messiah won't succeed him, her or it. Messiahship is a priori a posteriori. And the messianicity of messianicity without messianism would be unjust and prejudiced if its "without" was a simple No to any Messiah—unless we define the word "Messiah" in such a way that one Messiah cannot be succeeded by another, which would be to define away the absoluteness of the openness of the future. The "without" of messianicity without Messiah, the "*sans sans sans,*" the "*pas sans pas,*" is not a logical connective confined to the space of empirical or other factuality. Its space is the between at the heart of the chiasmus of the factual and the quasi-transcendental, at what Levinas would call its *cœur* and Derrida its *chōra* or *khôra.*[17] As Derrida's new New International is haunted by the ghost of the historical New International and hence by Marx and historical materialism, so his messiancity retains a trace of historical messianism. In a similar manner, the old word "democracy" with its implications of institutional obligation fixed by law is adopted to stand for a sociality in which singular responsibility will be given room to breathe through law: given through law room to breathe, and given room to enliven the letter of the law with breath. This is why when Derrida writes of the democracy to come and of the new International, the "religion in general" that they exemplify is none other than the religiousness we earlier described in terms of the moments of birth, and copulation, and death, for it is in these terms that are addressed the singularity of the democracy of responsibility to the in-coming that gets neglected in the democracy that is restricted to equality and rights. These terms and the *religio* they define in turn define the "political" terms Derrida uses. The latter, as used by him, mark the minimum of predicativity, the maximally unconditional openness of welcome for whatever is to come and therefore the nearest approach to pure address: the maximally unconditional *ouvrance* and *öffnen* or *Offen* that conditions the opposition between the *Offenbarung,* revelation, of historical religions and the *Offenbarkeit,* manifestation, of being and beings.[18] Whatever, whoever, whatever is to come in its singularity addresses each one of us, and each one of us has already responded to it in those moments of relatively simple religiousness where the other facing me in its natality and mortality and fleetingness faces me as a you, but as a you in which are implicit the she and the he and the they and therefore the turn of political sociality. The coming of this sociality, insofar as it does not forget the justice of singularity, is what Derrida calls democracy to come and its religiousness is what he calls religion in general.

Religion as religion in general, that is to say in its respect for the singular, disorganizes organized religion, disorders the very generality of its precepts and principles by responding to an archi- that is also an anarchi- where principles are no longer first, but are exposed to unclosure, unconclusivity, postscripture, the appendix which is an appendix included in this world notwithstanding the alterity of its oncoming archi-sublimity. Therefore "archi-sublime" and "archi-writing" are misnomers insofar as they seem to point to a principle of all principles. However, that is precisely why they do the job one wants them to do. No proper name can do that. That task can be performed only by a pro-nominal parody where the "archi-" hides a "quasi-." This, we have seen, is none other than the "as if" of imagdination on which draw both the "as if" of the act of practical faith ("pure reason" according to Kant, the leap according to Kierkegaard, and according to Heidegger *der Satz vom Grund* and *der Sprung*)[19] and the "as-if" of theoretical hypothesis, each of these "as-ifs" conditioning the other and being conditioned by it, but without this resulting in a purely formal biconditionality. For the formality of the laws of logic is here intruded upon by the sublimity of a justice that is not definable solely in terms of law. When we speak directly of "quasi-sublimity" this is not to evoke a non-sublimity or a false sublimity. It is to evoke a reorientation in which, instead of a being launched forward ecstatically, sublimity is instatic, advenient and passive in the sense in which Levinas writes of passivity that is more passive than the passivity that is simply opposed to activity. Like light coming in through a window or an open door, quasi-sublimity is what makes apprehension and comprehension possible as understood in the Age of Enlightenment. But in the New Enlightenment the incomprehensibility of incoming light would be a trope for the unprogrammability of invention. It would be a dangerous trope to use if it blinded us (as does looking the sun in the eye) to the fact that the light of knowledge is being used here as an analogue of a justice that is blind because it is the justice of a singularity. The reason why this singularity is unknowable is different from the reason Aristotle gives for our not being able to gain scientific knowledge of the singular. It is unknowable for another reason given by Aristotle when he says in *de Interpretatione* (17a) that prayer (*euchē*) is beyond the opposition of the true and the false. What we have been calling address could be called prayer. And it is called that by Derrida in the essay "*Comment ne pas parler,*" "How to Avoid Speaking," or "How not to Speak," where one of his aims is to separate deconstruction from so-called negative theology.[20] He seeks to realize that aim by reminding his readers that his title announces a sense of "*pas*" or "not" that is not the sense of simple negation, one that effects a de-negation in a sense that is not that of the Freudian "*Verneinung*" treated in chapter 11. Nor is this the "not" of dialectical negation touched on at the beginning of chapter 1, in chapter 10 and elsewhere. While in "What is Metaphysics?" Heidegger relies on his readers' conception of nothingness to point them in the direction of the thought of being but without reliance on Hegelian dialectic, Derrida attempts to bring his readers from a Pseudo-Dionysian (not pseudo-Dionysian) and Eckhartian understanding of negation that is at the same time an affirmative way of speaking of God, to an understanding of affirmation that is prior to predication and therefore prior to the polar opposition of positive and negative (for example the positivity of a *Grenze* and the negativity of a *Schranke*) and may therefore be likened to prayer. But if we do call this affirmation prayer, it is a prayer that is not limited to our addressing God. It is a prayer without which there is no determinate addressee at all, whether God or any other other. It is a prayer which, if it were pure and direct address, that is to say, direct directedness, would render theology and theology otiose. But, as "contaminated" by the hyperspace and hypermateriality of archi-writing, this prayer, this calling, is called for by theiology and theology and religion.

> If there were a purely pure experience of prayer, would we need religion and affirmative or negative theologies? Would we need a supplement of prayer? But if there were no supplement, if citation did not bend prayer, if prayer did not bend itself, did not bend itself to writing, would a theiology be possible? Would a theology?[21]

This prepredicative address of prayer, whether or not prayer prayed on bended knee, this prayer in general but each time unique would have been prior to the intercessory prayer that was a concern in chapter 13. It is an intercessory prayer that would be prior even to the cry "Lord, hear our prayer and let our cry come unto Thee" mentioned in chapter 14. This *"Prego,"* although singular, would be one that would be directed to any and every other, for example in the case of my plight reported in chapter 13, directed in the direction of, among others, Derrida. In addressing my card to him was I making the intercessory prayer I had difficulty addressing to God? And could he have forwarded it to God or to "God" if he had wished? And, at the side of his mother's deathbed, was he, for once at a loss for words, reduced or raised, reduced and raised, to the nearest possible, nearest impossible, proximity to that purely pure experience of prayer? And, at the side of his grave, was it that proximity that the tears of his family and his friends secretly expressed? This link of the copula of address that is before predication and earlier than or too late for what Kierkegaard would call communication, is this what makes religious the occasions of birth, of copulation prior to the predicational copula, and of death? So many beds. So many *beddau.* ("*Bedd*" is the Welsh word for grave, and "*beten*" is German for to pray.)

## Without Authority

The paleonyms listed in the preceding paragraph and an open series of other related markers stand at the threshold that is crossed in both directions where the giving of an invitation and the giving of the acceptance of an invitation take place in the space of the incomprehensibility of archi- or quasi-sublimity. As, gradually, *pas à pas,* we have been learning since chapter 13, Derrida comes to see that historical or imagined examples are indispensible conditions of their quasi-transcendental conditions. On the interpretation made above of the Wordsworthian notion of the sublime, as with the Kantian and Hegelian notions, the sublime does not belong to things in the manner of primary or secondary qualities—or even in the manner in which on some enumerations beauty is counted to be a tertiary quality, in the eye of the beholder yet according to Kant in nature too; for for him it is to the beholder, albeit transcendental, that external nature owes its constitution. In the Kantian, Hegelian and Wordsworthian notions of it, the feeling of or for the sublime is stirred by what Wordsworth would call an "interfusion" of human nature and outward nature. Further, whereas the emotion appropriate to the beautiful is love, the emotion appropriate to the sublime is *Achtung,* respect or awe, the kind of attention (*achten* is to heed) of which we asked in chapter 13 whether it is a key to our understanding of what it is to pray. The chief difference between the Kantian and

Hegelian accounts of the sublime on the one hand and the Wordsworthian and, according to Hegel's (questionable) suggestion, the Silesian accounts on the other hand, is that whereas the primary focus of respect in the former accounts is law and its universality, the primary focus of respect in the latter accounts is the plurality not merely of particulars—for the particular is a function and case of the universal—but of singulars. The universal and the particular are the classified, the genus, the species or the differentia. The singular is respected and attended to in its singularity, as someone or something that addresses us either itself or through the voice of someone who speaks to us on its behalf, or as one we imagine addressing us, to whom we defer in the name of other others.

We are addressed by the future, by the to-come as such, prior to classification and whatever may or may not come. The to-come, the *avenant,* the inventive and adventive, includes the return of the past, its *revenant,* its ghost, as Derrida comes back to haunt the all too capitular chapters of this book. That is how the being-ahead-of-oneself of Heideggerian hermeneutic ecstasis and hope, the not-yet and the already of Hegelian dialectic and the geneticity of Nietzsche's genealogies are overcome when they deconstruct themselves according to a necessity that is not the polar opposite of chance. Address as such is the incomprehensible that overcomes them, rather as whatever we might wish to follow Descartes in giving the quasi-name "God" to overcomes any concept and overbrims any idea or image, misspells every word, quirkily, so that tears of mourning mix with tears of sublime laughter. Not the Hobbesian laughter in which the "sudden glory" is the triumphalist self-glorification of the laugher, a pre-echo of the self-congratulation of human beings who, according to Kant, in judging something to be sublime preen themselves on being superior to (other) animals by dint of their being able to act out of respect for the moral law.[22]

> Perhaps there is no more sublime passage in the Jewish Law than the commandment: Thou shalt not make unto thee any graven image, or any likeness of any thing that is in heaven or on earth, or under the earth, etc. This commandment can alone explain the enthusiasm which the Jewish people, in their moral period, felt for their religion when comparing themselves with others, or the pride inspired by Mohammedanism.[23]

Yet Kant himself concedes at least by implication that the very lack of a *Vorstellung* can stand for, *darstellen,* sublimity. Compare the way silence speaks volumes, for example the pause that precedes the "*Et Resurrexit*" of the *Credo* of Beethoven's *Missa Solemnis* or the silence that follows the last note of the last song of Mahler's *Song of the Earth* entitled "*Der Abschied,*" "The Farewell," "*L'adieu.*" Visual equivalents of these pregnant silences are the ellipsis or *points de suspension,* the directedness of the Virgin's gaze across the edge of the painting toward the anticipated death of the Son she holds in her arms, and, thirty-three years later, the Son's looking directly at us through Piero's de-piction of

Him. Other visual equivalents are the gaps and transgressed frames in *Glas, The Post Card,* and in the text entitled "Parergon" contained (barely) in *The Truth in Painting* where Derrida notes that, in his sections on the sublime, Kant compares the comparable with the incomparable, and where Derrida compares the logic of this with the logic of Anselm's proof of the existence of God than which nothing greater can be conceived.[24] The incomparability of the archi-sublime turns not on there being nothing greater than it on a continuous or indeed discontinuous scale, for instance on the heavenly ladder of the historical Johannes Climacus or on a continuum such as would admit borderlines in the spatial and temporal continua of mathematics and the mathematical sublime as conceived by Kant. This incomparablity is not that of a "more of," but of a "more than" such as that of which Silesius writes, employing the trope of light the dangers of which were commented upon above:

> *Die über GOttheit ist mein Leben und mein Liecht*
> The more than DeITy is my life and light[25]

where IT iterates the *iter,* the going, of the itness of the God that according to Meister Eckhart must go. Into Silesius's "*über*" may be read an echo of the call of conscience as care that, we are told in *Being and Time,* "comes from (*aus*) me and yet over (*über*) me."[26] I am overcome by it. However, if Heidegger and Silesius are not to mislead us in our reading of Derrida, this echo can be only a very distant echo of "the essential swaying of be-ing," *der Wesung des Seyns,* heard in section 50 of the *Contributions to Philosophy.* In that section Heidegger is trying to point to the way in which the echo (*Anklang*) of *Seyn* is heard in our need to remember that we forget *Seyn.* We forget that it is not *a* being; that it is not an it (though note that although "it" functions as a pronoun standing for something that can be counted, *an* it, it can also stand for a mass or something else that is innumerable, for example the *il y a* as described by Levinas, Heideggerian *Sein* or *Seyn* or the *es* of *es gibt,* and maybe that by which Derrida sometimes says we are haunted). Our need (*Not*) to remember that we forget *Seyn* is a necessary distress and a distressful necessity (*Not*), most distressful when we are most forgetful of it, when we experience *Notlosigkeit,* lack of distress. Wittgenstein once remarked that Bertrand Russell's problem was that he suffered from lack of problems, *Problemslosigkeit,* a certain unseriousness. *Aporialosigkeit,* Derrida might prefer to say. *Besessenheitslosigkeit,* unobsessedness, unpossessedness, we could add, in which the balance of mind is chronicly undisturbed. What Derrida hesitates to repeat is Heidegger's, or, since there is more than one Heidegger, a certain Heidegger's intoning of the themes of the belonging together of *Seyn* and *Da-sein,* and of the owning or enowning of *Ereignis.* The notes struck by Heidegger that provoke Derrida are those that chime with the concepts of propriety and cleanliness.

Cleanliness is the property of which it is said proverbially that it is next to godliness, the property to which we have been forced to return toward the end of a book throughout the length of which we have been attempting to fend off God in favor of a concept of religiousness that does not depend on Him. Buber says in one of the epigraphs of this book, "We cannot clean up the term 'God' and we cannot make it whole, but. . . ."[27] But what? You cannot just drop a word, especially if the word is "God," and, as Edmond Jabès is alleged to have said, "God was, or *was no more than* the only word for grief sufficiently vast, sufficiently empty that all griefs may be contained within it."[28] So to do the work of the word "God" or "G-d" we might borrow the expression "*l'ouvrance*" or the word "*l'ouverture*," "opening," used by Jean-Luc Nancy in the sublimely beautiful talk he addressed to children published under the title *Au ciel et sur la terre*.[29]

Derrida does not simply drop the name Heidegger or abandon out of hand what Heidegger says under the heading "But how about the Gods?": "[Gods] not from within 'religion': *not* as something extant (*Vorhandenes*), nor as an expedient [or makeshift, *Notbehelf*] of man, rather [they come] from out of being [*Seyn*], as its decision, [they are] futural in the uniqueness of the *last one*."[30] They are, we could say, the *religio* of religiousness or, as Derrida says, "religion in general," which is outwith what Heidegger means in this paragraph by, placing the word between inverted commas, "religion." As Heidegger says in this paragraph, the Gods (which have to be written of with a capital initial letter in German, but could be no more than lower-cased gods if you like) have, to speak vaguely and indecisively, something to do with decision. And how about decision? Decision, *Entscheidung,* for Heidegger is not, as it is for Kierkegaard, a choice between an Either and an Or. It is better understood through that reference to the last god. One might be reluctant to allow any decisive force to *a* being in pages where what is getting stressed is our need to remember to think be-ing, to think *Seyn* rememberingly, to think away from being as a being, a highest being or ground, to another thinking of being as abground, no longer in terms of the principle of sufficient reason, the *Satz vom Grund,* but in terms of a leap from ground, a leap not just from the ground, but a leap from groundedness as such. What Heidegger calls the gods or the divinities are not the gods of the Greek pantheon, the philosophers' first cause, or the Christian Creator. They are more like a category under which such and other gods are subsumed, except that they, in co-operation with the other three contributors to the fourfold, namely earth, mortals and sky, are not fundamental forms of representational or conceptual thinking, as categories are, but belong to the other way of thinking to which Heidegger would have us leap forward or step back. The divinity may therefore manifest itself in what the Heidegger of *Being and Time* might call its deficient mode, as absence or default (*Fehl*), which "is not nothing; rather it is precisely the presence, which must first be appropriated, of the hidden fullness and wealth of what has been and what, thus gathered, is presencing, of the divine in the world of the Greeks, in prophetic Judaism, in the preaching of Jesus,"[31] in, he might have added, the prophesying of Mohammed. Moreover, he goes on to say in the same paragraph, this no-longer is at the same time an oncoming (*Ankunft*) of the not-yet, for "In the destiny of Being there is never a mere sequence of things one after another: now frame [*Gestell*, therefore representation], then world and thing; rather, there is always a passing by (*Vorbeigang*) and simultaneity of the early and late. In Hegel's *Phenomenology of Spirit, alētheia* presences (*west*), though transmuted."

These last two citations point to two directions of Heidegger's thinking in which Derrida is not ready to follow him without demur: derivation and gathering. Gathering is none other than what is collected under the Latin "*relegere,*" except insofar as there is always something other in the Latin translation of Greek.[32] Heidegger, like Karl Abel, is tempted to invoke *etyma*, root words such as "*alētheia.*" Derivation is a corollary of the destining or sending of Being, the *Geschick des Seins* understood according to Heidegger's interpretation of truth as unconcealing, *a-lētheia.* The history, *Geschichte,* of Being is a *Geschehen,* a happening of epochs in which the world presents itself in different metaphysical guises (idea for Plato, *energeia* for Aristotle, totality of created beings for Christianity, subjects and objects for most rationalists and empiricists, freedom for German Idealism, power for Nietzsche) in which Being as such withdraws through finding itself cast in the mode of a being. Derrida brings out in *Of Spirit* that these modes are articulations of sameness liable to be confused with the sameness of *Geist* whose history is narrated in the *Phenomenology of Spirit.* Reading the thinking of Heidegger and Hegel via the hypermetaphor of postcards (or e-mails or textings) that have written into them, from the beginning and before, the eventuality of not reaching their destination,[33] Derrida translates mission and envoy (*Geschick*) as *en-voyage,* and this voyage is one from which the voyager does not return home, like Odysseus, but, one in which the traveller, like Abraham, is always on the move. Arrival at a destination is forever deferred. There is no final gathering of Being, least of all if the gathering of Being is gathered under the gathering of God, as toward the end of *Of Spirit* Derrida imagines Being being gathered by "certain Christian theologians" via the elision of Being and Spirit, and as one might be encouraged to let Being be gathered by tracing the word "religion" back to "*relegere,*" to collect together, without retaining a trace of "*religāre,*" in its Abelian ambiguity as between binding and unbinding or separation, *relēgāre.*

In place of arrival at a destination Derrida proposes a futural arriving from, but with nothing that arrives and no despatcher or source, no Messiah sent by God. How does this differ from the giving of the *es gibt* of Being? How does what we have called the quasi-sublime escape collapse into the generosity of the donation of Being? It does so by way of a religion in general where "religion" is glossed both through *relegere* and *religāre* without vexation over whether either or both of these derivations is "authentic." For what is called authentic or the author is always, to use Kierkegaard's phrase, "without authority." Authenticity is always already contaminated by, to use another expression much used by Kierkegaard, pseudonymity. So that a seemingly sincere performance such as saying "I promise" or "I confess" must, if it is to function as a genuine, authentic, commitment or avowal, always be construable as a "performance," as though acted on stage in a theatre, as though the production of theatrical effects. Here production (*poiēsis*) is simultaneously making something appear and making or doing something.[34] This ambiguity is that of the performativity of so-called speech acts. Hence at issue is the "hereby" of the "Here I am, I hereby offer myself" that the speaker of Hebrew performs in saying "*hineni.*" More solemnly, he or she and we say "Here I am in the name of God." And Derrida is not unwelcoming to our saying this. We have recorded earlier that he says "God, if you wish." The "you" includes Hölderlin, the poet of the philosophers and of the passing of the gods in terms of which Heidegger develops his thinking of Being, be-ing or *Seyn* in the 1930s and 1940s, the span of time during which he wrote the Rectoral Address that made painful reading to so many, not least to Derrida.

## The Future of Fecundity

After being concerned in recent paragraphs with some aspects of the connection between Derrida's work and that of Heidegger, and before making one or two clarifications on that subject in paragraphs to come, now is a good time to say that when Derrida writes about precisely the "to come" he is remembering Heidegger's meditations on Hölderlin's mourning of the passing of the ancient gods and on the coming of another god. This god is called the "last" in the sense of the "highest" because this god (who may not be the only god who can "save" us according to what Heidegger says to the interviewer from *Der Spiegel*) will appear in the space of being as such. Using words he uses of the relationship between Levinas and Nietzsche, Derrida comments that his own account of postal sendings is both very close to and very distant from Heidegger's account of the comings and goings of the gods and the epochs of the history of metaphysics. The two accounts are separated by the delicate but decisive difference that whereas the sendings according to Heidegger are ordered periods of an unilinear history of being, the multidirectionality of sendings and relays described by Derrida do not admit of historical periodization and progression.[35] They admit of the historical, but they admit of the historical as conditioned by the "if you wish." And whether or not you wish, whether for example or for Example you wish to call upon God or "God" or "democracy," will depend upon the point there may be in doing this. For what you mean (*voulez dire, sagen wollen*) by these words is inseparable from the point in using them, and the point one may have is unpredictable.

It is usually not noticed that when Wittgenstein is reported as saying that meaning and rules go together with point,[36] this last word translates the German word "*Witz*."[37] He says this in the context of a comparison of language with games, in particular the game of chess where, he says, rules define roles and the meaning of a piece is its role in the game. So that to speak a language is to play a game with words. One may be playing with words when one is telling a joke, a *Witz*. But the point of a joke, the *Witz* of a *Witz*, may be serious. Wit is not antithetically opposed to wisdom and witness. And the quirkiness of language witnessed to in this book is not antithetically opposed to seriousness, any more than the range of forces encompassed by the word "spirit" and its cognates in English and other languages excludes the force that may be conveyed in French by the words "*jeu d'esprit*," which can mean a joke. In chapter 15 attention was drawn to the fact that the word "spiritual" has been used only sparely in this book. It has not been used to do the work the word "religious" has been asked to do. Levinas says about the word "love" ("*amour*") that it has become *usé*, worn out, and *galvaudé*, debased, trite, banal.[38] Alas, the same may be said about the word "spirit." But "spirit" is in danger of contamination by the connotations that "spiritual" and "spirituality" have acquired in the thinking that under the name New Age substitutes for the organization and doctrines of "Old Age" religions a system of dubiously scientific beliefs. Rowan Williams rightly says that the word "spirituality" has become emasculated.[39] He could have said, as Levinas says of the word "*amour*," that the word "spirituality" has become *galvaudé*. I have therefore been abstemious in my use of this word. I haved tried to avoid it, as in *Of Spirit* Derrida notes Heidegger too tries to avoid (*vermeiden*) an unqualified use of the word "spirit." We both fail. Indeed, I confess to a sneaking fondness for that word. It enables us, following Saint Paul, to contrast spirit and law yet to speak too of the spirit of the law and of *l'esprit des lois*. Further, its breath sets atrembling the pretensions to antitheticality of being and nothingness, turns ontology toward hauntology, and raises hope that the monotheisms and the members of the Christian Trinity beside Spirit may be interpreted if not relationally, nonetheless as something like a relationship of address such as Levinas holds to be prior to logical relations.[40]

Therefore the word "spirit," with its spectrum of connotations ranging over and beyond those of Hebrew "*ruah*," Arabic "*rūh*," Greek "*pneuma*," Taoist "*ch'i*,"[41] and Dutch "*geest*"[42] still haunts what I write, as its Hegelian and Christian connotations haunt the pages in which Derrida writes of spectrality. At the same time I persistently employ the word "religious" in order that the connotations of binding and unbinding which I read in or into it may be read back into the word "love," returning to it some of its lost power.[43] The power restored by these connotations is a power that "*agapē*" has more often conveyed than has the word "*erōs*." But love may be understood as the chiasmus of these, where "*agapē*" lends itself to expressing a notion of justice with regard to the beloved and where "*erōs*" expresses not the desire to possess but the for ever not-yet. Levinas describes this power of impower as the non-personal and the feminine beyond the face to face with the other, which latter he describes in masculine terms. These descriptions are to be interpreted not as biological or gender classifications but as "categories," in the broad sense that he, like Kierkegaard, sometimes gives to this word. In this context he uses the word "son" to mark the category of engendering. The father both is and is not the son in engendering. Engendering copulation is a category of transubstantiation that transcends the alternatives of being and nothingness and does not fall under the traditional category of possibility. Power as possibility is subverted by the impower of incoming. Hence the aptness of Derrida's terms "haunting," "*revenance*," and "to-come," and perhaps of "something like the middle voice" used as early as the essay entitled "*Différance*." Hence too the relevance of the sexual metaphors for the religious, and the religious metaphors for sexuality invoked above in the first section of chapter 15, and of the invocation there of copulation in its conjunction with birth and death to articulate the inarticulacy of religiousness without religion.

*Stabat mater. Stabat filius,* namely Pierre (Derrida) Alféri articulating the words given him by the father before him in the grave. That father's philosophical writings articulate what Nietzsche says about woman. They articulate also a political dimension of what Levinas calls voluptuosity. For although the very non-personality and non-sociality of the voluptuosity of erotic intimacy desires to exclude the universality of the third person, the personal is not swallowed up in them. This voluptuosity is precisely the lovers' refusal to surrender themselves in the vertigo of their abandon.[44] This refusal is the equivocal voicing of the narcissism that Derrida insists is not eliminable from selfhood. Voluptuosity, Levinas writes, "does not aim at the other but at its voluptuosity; it is voluptuosity of voluptuosity, love of the love of the other."[45] Therefore "to love is also to love oneself in love, and thus to return to oneself." However, just as erotic love does not possess the other—voluptuosity is not the struggle for mastery or recognition—neither does it possess the future. Its future is the future of fecundity.

Fecundity, it will be recalled, is what my good friend Charles Bigger wishes to safeguard in the *Magnificat* sung by him in the *magnum opus* treated above in chapter 14. Fecundity is what seems to him to be missing from Levinas's *filioque* clause and from the pages of Levinas's reader Derrida. It is through fecundity that Levinas explains voluptuosity. This is to say, in terms of the categories of Levinas adapted in Derrida's construal of the politico-religious, femininity is explained by paternity and sonship. The equivocity and indeterminacy of femininity as glossed in the adjustments Levinas and Derrida make to Nietzsche's thinking of the woman are accomplished in the recommencing and re-coming, *as if* from outside but not from another world, in which the return to oneself is not the recycling of a fully rounded Parmenidean identity in which the self-same self grows old. It is instead the alteration of the self thanks to offspring. It is both sameness and the absolute otherness of infinitely future youth across the discontinuity of generations. Once again, this lexicon of gender and generation is categorial. It is "formally indicative" to the point that it holds for the relationship in which a teacher addresses and is addressed by a pupil and in which an author, say Nietzsche, is interpreted by a reader, say Levinas or Derrida—or, indeed Deleuze, for what we are now exposing through the language of genetic conception cannot but lead to a revision of the concept and of the concept of philosophy whereby these become invention. "Philosophy itself constitutes a moment of this temporal accomplishment, a discourse always addressed to another," Levinas writes, adding, as Derrida and other writers might say, "What we are now exposing is addressed to those who shall wish to read it."[46] This addressing has the indeterminacy of the category of the feminine as described by Nietzsche, Levinas, and Derrida, the category of the uncategorial, insofar as the word "category" is glossed in terms of its Greek etymological sense of accusation. But its femininity puts it in the company of the wisdom literature of the Hebrew Bible, and of what Levinas calls the wisdom of love as distinguished from the Greek love of wisdom named philosophy.

## Archi-sublimity

Among the notions we have touched on in glossing "religion" and the "religious" in the above pages have been those of prayer, address, belief, holiness, sacrifice, singularity, attention, and gratitude. In the last section of chapter 16, the one devoted to the last of these notions, gratitude was distinguished from giving thanks in order to allow that there seeming to be no one to whom to direct one's thanks does not render gratitude impossible or irrational. To thank is to perform a speech act. Gratitude comes over one. It is a passion. But, like other passions, gratitude expresses itself in action. Among the things for which gratitude may be felt mention was made of the natural products and artifacts necessary to life or which make life enjoyable and enrich it. Being grateful for these is a way of holding them attentively in our regard and recollection. We owe gratitude also to the dead for their contribution to that enrichment of our lives through what they have been or done or made. But our grieving and gratitude for dead friends sublimely exceeds the concept of debt. It exceeds exchange. And it exceeds exchange in a way that differs from the way in which exchange might be thought to be exceeded when the gratitude might be considered to be by some measure greater than is called for by that for which the gratitude is felt. It exceeds measure. It exceeds calculation. This is one reason for agreeing with Kant when he says that "[f]riendship has mainly the character of the sublime, but love between the sexes, that of the beautiful."[47] We can express that gratitude in private grief or public mourning without thanking God, and without our mourning ceasing to be religious. Because there is nothing, unless perhaps God, that is as other as death, it would be difficult to imagine a more religious practice or process than mourning, independently of whether or not it is mediated by a rite conducted in the presence of priests. Independently too of whether or not the one mourned is dead. For, as Derrida and Simone Weil have underlined, mourning is multiply tensed. Although in what is usually meant by mourning the presence of a friend in life haunts her or his absence in death, in mourning understood more profoundly, the absence in death of a friend haunts her or his presence in life. Although we may thank friends for particular acts of kindness, we rarely thank them for their friendship. Their friendship is something for which we do not need to thank them. But it remains something for which we are grateful. Although that gratefulness is manifested conventionally in the celebration of the life of someone who has died, it is silently experienced in the experiment performed when, following Weil's suggestion, we imagine that someone who is alive has died. This imagining is the imadgining of *Abgeschiedenheit*. This is Eckhart's word for disinterestedness or detachment,[48] but the detachment he means by it is that which is testified to in the testament of the *Adieu*, albeit the *Adieu* to or of the gods. The complexity of the tenses, of the quasi-factualities, and of the factual and the counterfactual conditionalities implicated in grateful remembrance is further complicated by the knowledge that my death may precede the other's, and we are unable to decide between "as I would have smiled" and "as I shall have smiled" in trying to understand what Derrida may have meant in those words read out for him at his graveside by his son.

Remembrance and commemoration are sacred forms of recollection. They are therefore forms of imagination, the "faculty" of the *quasi-*, of the *if* and of the *if only* to which philosophers, among them Aristotle and Kant, have traditionally assigned memory. Therefore *relegere*. But remembrance in mourning friends is a remembering we owe them. Therefore *religāre*. However, we owe them this remembrance beyond any duty defined by law. We owe it to them in the ethico-religious singularity of the immemorial that interrupts imagination. Therefore *relēgāre*. And therefore imadgination. The madness of this imadgination is that of supererogation, but a supererogation that refuses to oppose "from love" and "from duty," yet without the responsibility voiced by the latter canceling the spontaneous passion voiced by the former.

We also owe our friends gratitude. But we can owe gratitude also even if there is no one to whom we owe it. We are bound. We are doubly bound. For if imadgination is memory (*Gedächtnis* or *Andenken*) fired by the immemorial it is also attention. Attention is also *attente,* waitfulness, but the fullness of this waitfulness echoes in the emptiness of the desert. Gratitude, furthermore, can be gratitude for what has not yet happened. It can require a waiting fired by an absolute future, a future that will never be the happening of something present. Waiting is what we are bound to do in the face of the incomprehensible archi-sublimity of whatever and whosoever is, as Heidegger would say, *immer unterwegs:* always on the way, but not on the way to a destination. Waiting is a response to the archi-sublime, not an anticipation of it. The archi-sublime would not be archi-sublime if it were anticipated. This waiting is a response not to Being but to the call for quirky justice to be done to the singular, justice that is not defined by the law but yet is, as one of the exergues of this book puts it, "not positively illegal."

One of the other exergues of this book refers more exactly to "A quirkie bodie, capable o' making Law no Law at a'." In other words, "quirky" seems to be "itself" a quirky word. It is so quirky that we cannot say that it is autological in the special sense of Grelling's paradox of heterologicality, which asks whether the word "heterological" is heterological or autological and discovers that if it is the one it is also the other. Logicians use the term "autological" of a word that itself possesses the property it denotes. A word is heterological if it does not possess the property it denotes. Unlike "English," which is English, therefore autological, it is not clear that "quirky" has an itself, an *autos.* It is not clear that it is a word, a *logos,* so it is also not heterological, as "*anglais*" is, whether or not "heterological" is heterological. Judging by some of the exergues of this book, it is not clear even whether "quirky" is English or Welsh or Scots. These are reasons why "quirky" lends itself to being used of quasi-Abelian words.

"Justice" is a quasi-Abelian word. It points in two directions at once, toward the universality of the law and toward singularity, just like imadgination. What makes justice mad and what makes the word for it quasi-Abelian is that the contrariety of its senses is not purely semantic. For the singularity is not the particularity of something said. It is the singularity of address understood not as the destination toward which a thought or an act or a speech-act, for instance a prayer, is directed, for Instance God, but as the sending or doing or saying: the performance, the per-form-ance which interrupts formality, for instance the formality of an institutional religion or liturgy. The formality and beauty (*forma*) of rote liturgy is interrupted by the sublimity of liturgy understood as the work I perform for nothing for a singular addressee who is always already an addresser, addressing to me a call for assistance. The assistance that addressance calls for is first and foremost that of undeconstructible justice. The response to the call for undeconstructible justice is responsible only because it is not programmed by instituted law. For if it were so programmed there would be no decision to make. There would be no room for responsibility. There would be room only for calculation. There would be room only for general ethics as contrasted with the religious by Kierkegaard and by Johannes de silentio in their account of what passed between Isaac and Abraham and God on Mount Moriah. In his account of an ethics of the other human being Levinas adjusts the borderline between ethics and religion in the direction of a justice in which the singularity of the betweenness of the hyphen of God-Abraham is translated by the betweenness of the hyphen of Abraham-Isaac, so that the ethicality of the ethical and the religiousness of religion become the hyphen of the ethico-religious. Following Levinas's reminder that the singular other you speaks also on behalf of a him and a her (and an it, Derrida would add), and remembering that each she and he hides a you more primordially than beings hide Being, Derrida emphasizes even more than Levinas that the third-personality or impersonality of deconstructible law cannot be dispensed with if undeconstructible justice is to be dispensed. This is the aporia of justice to the singular other and to the other other that must be endured by everyone who makes a decision that is not either on the one hand an arbitrary decision or on the other hand a programmed calculation.

Justice to alterity is a response to the absolutely incomprehensible and unidentifiable event of a threatening and inconvenient invenience the archi-sublimity of which irrupts into and disrupts the unity and totality that Kant hoped practical reason would guarantee and that Hegel believed would be ultimately saved by the No No of dialectical *Aufhebung*. Some translators have been bold or mad enough to call Hegelian *Aufhebung* sublimation. "Sublimation" is the word whose meaning is subjected to a violent twist when Levinas writes: "Nothing that is sublime can do without verbal, social, or psychological sources save sublimation itself."[49] Yet in this justice sought without being meted or measured out to the singular other does there not survive a moment of negation like that of the Kantian categorical imperative interpreted as a prohibition of acts whose maxim is not universalizable? If Derrida is outlining not an ethics but a metaphysics of ethics or of the ethico-religious in Levinas's sense of "metaphysics," what he says about the aporia of justice does not give us a rule telling us what we should do, any more than does Kant's metaphysics of ethics. Does it, like Kant's metaphysics of ethics, give us guidance at least as to what we should not do, what we should avoid? Kant's metaphysics of ethics tells us that we should prescribe to others the rule to avoid acting according to maxims that are not universalizable. But his metaphysics of ethics prescribes by describing practical reason. The moral law describes how a holy will would act. Kant himself prescribes only insofar as he ventriloquizes the voice of reason, something Hegel will fancy he too can do. As good will incarnate Kant gives voice to the law as categorical imperative, that is to say, as prescription. Addressing itself to the specter of Kant and to what Nietzsche calls the ear behind the ear of each of his readers, Derrida's metaphysics of ethics tells us and prescribes not that we should avoid prescribing fundamental rules to others, but, as Kierkegaard observed before him, that this prescription cannot be direct. It can be heard only when voiced in the voice behind the voice. This is the voice that is ventriloquized by the *dramatis personae* of Derrida's prologues, polylogues, and postcards. Where Wittgenstein invites philosophers to "Think how many different kinds of things are called 'description,'"[50] Derrida and Kierkegaard invite philosophers to think how many different kinds of things are called "prescription." Among these one might consider the prescribing that is implicit in Kierkegaard's or Johannes de silentio's description of what happened on Moriah. But what interests Derrida especially, in the wake of Kierkegaard, Nietzsche, Rosenzweig, and Levinas, is the unfamiliar yet ubiquitous archi-prescription that makes possible the familiar contrast between description and prescription, so that it does not make sense to ask in terms of this contrast whether what makes it possible is itself descriptive or prescriptive. And if we call this archi-scripture affirmation, it is not the affirmation that is opposed to negation, for instance to the negations of negative theology. Archi-affirmation is ad-firmation, adding my *firma*, my signature, though adding it *ante rem* and *ante dictum,* before I have said anything such that I can then add to it my mark. My mark is always a re-mark. It remarks the minimal hospitality of address.

I am hospitable to others only if I ultimately leave the other to decide his or her decidings. In acknowledging this Derrida is being faithful to Kierkegaard, as he acknowledges he is in the words cited as the first of the exergues of this book. But acknowledgment is a performance in a rule-governed language, and, as Levinas observes, in words Derrida endorses, "language is justice."[51] What Derrida underlines is that there is both justice as defined by law and justice I owe to the singular other. This is what Kierkegaard calls the paradox. This is what Derrida calls aporia. It is to this that one says Yes, a Yes that lies beyond the choice between negative and positive prescription. This is the Yes of silent address, as in the sublimely innocent but also sometimes and simultaneously embarrassingly ridiculous moments of naked truthfulness named birth, naming, death, copulation (Molly Bloom's Yes), or fecundity (the Virgin Mary's), but also where these first, last, and interim rites have become canonized, interiorized, or incorporated in the institution of a synagogue, church, or mosque. In these moments on the threshold facing another's natality, fecundity, and mortality, whether these be clothed in the garb of a culture or a cult or, on the other hand, reduced almost to address that is almost naked, rudimentary, and crude in our sense (but not in Rudolf Otto's sense of "crude" distinguished in the second section of chapter 15), I bind myself to another without requiring that the other bind herself to me. Indeed, if the unconditionality is absolute, it must bind itself to the eventuality of others that are incapable of binding themselves to me or to anyone else in so many words. This incapacity is not incompatible with its being *as if* those others spoke to me. They do address me in the silence of my ethico-religious imadgination where I have already made at least a silent response. For, to recite another of the epigraphs of this book (and to echo Husserl's remark that imagination is the essence of phenomenology), the chief religious faculty is the imadgination.

That the imadgination has to be invoked here is witnessed to once one asks who or what or whot are these "others that are incapable of binding themselves to me or to anyone else in so many words." This phrase was used a moment ago in order to meet two circumstances. It provides on the one hand for others who do not "have the word." It is not only that their not having the faculty of speech is consistent with my speaking as their advocates, but that my plain words on their behalf may be uttered in response to the silent clamor of the call they make to my ethico-religious imadgination, for instance the call made through the eyes of a vixen as the hunter levels his rifle at her.[52] The phrase provides also for others who in this categorial sense are possessed of language but whose principles are such that they think that they cannot find words in which to communicate with us. We cannot find our feet with them because one of us and not the other cannot believe, for instance, that it could be in order to bury someone up to the neck and stone her to death. When there is such a "conflict of principles," let us let ourselves be overcome as though by the call that waits to be heard in the eyes of that fox. Let us. That is to say, neither in the active voice of prescription nor in the passive voice of what gets described, let us, in something like the middle voice, allow the sleeping subconscience of our imadgination to be disturbed by the appeal made by the eyes of the victim, whether human or not. For, paradoxical though this will seem to those who insist that where there is the religious there too must be God, and notwithstanding Heideggerian rumors about what it is for a human being to be, there is a chiasmus of the human and the animal such that the nearer the human being approximates to the animal the more brightly glows the human being's religiousness without dogma and divinity. To say this about what cries out in the eyes of the vulpine victim is not to deny what Piero says in paint about the call that is heard in the gaze of the chiasmus of the human and the divine that goes by the name Jesus Christ. Can there be a triple chiasmus, in particular of the animal, the human, and the divine? That there can may be being hinted by Heidegger, despite himself, when he writes of the *Benommenheit,* numbedness, of the animal's way of being in the world, although that word describes well the condition, referred to earlier in this chapter, into which Socrates throws his interlocutors, the condition in which, according to Plato and Aristotle, philosophy begins.[53] This condition before principles would be a condition before being because it would be the alterity Levinas calls the exteriority of the Good beyond being. That is what we called the outwith, the *mitohne,* following Karl Abel and Freud.[54] According to Heidegger, Derrida reminds us, "*ohne*" says something like "*wahn,*" "mad," as in the madness of the imadgination where principles tremble.[55]

Not doing without principles, but daring to imagine that how they are to be interpreted can never be finally imagined, we turn mere toleration of those who hold principles different from ours into respect for the singularity of those who hold them when it strikes us that only if we go back behind principial knowledge, *scientia,* and the love of wisdom, *philosophia,* can we go forward to what overcomes them, the "knowing" that is more like knowing in the biblical sense of bodily acquaintance, copulation (*Paarung,* Husserl might say), and more like *sapientia,* the wisdom of love that is absolutely unconditional. Only if this unconditionality is absolute is there hospitality, so only on that unconditional condition is there love. Only on that condition of unconditionality am I obsessed by the future as such, hostage to it ("hostage," it will be recalled, translates Latin "*obses*"): "for there to be a future (*avenir*) as such—which means surprise, alterity—one must no longer see it coming, *voir venir.*" "And thus the fact that the future comes onto me (*survient*) in a rush, precisely where I don't even expect it, don't anticipate it, don't 'see it coming,' means that the other is there before me, that it comes before (*prévient*)."[56] What Derrida says about the future as such that rushes toward me echoes what Levinas writes about the "infinitely future" where we are faced with "a new category," neither being nor non-being, but, as Derrida says, haunting.[57] However, if the other is always there before me, therefore already mourned, the future that rushes unto me, the absolute future, is at the same time absolutely past. It is more past than any past I can remember, more passed than any time I lived through and am now seeking to refind. *L'absolu arrivant* is more past than any nostalgia and more future than any teleological hope.

Instead of my running on toward my death in the manner described in *Being and Time,* the future, and with it my and your death, rushes on to me, as "The horizon's bound, a huge peak, black and huge" rushed on to the young

Wordsworth—save that the future rushes on to me without even a horizon's bound, without even an "utmost boundary," for, for there to be a future as such, "there must not even be a horizon of anticipation, a horizon of waiting." The deferment that interrupts presence is eschatology, a deal of death, without being teleology, such teleology for example as belongs to the structure of the Kantian Ideas of reason. So that while on the one hand the attention and regard that responsibility requires me to direct to singularities requires me to wait until I have assessed the circumstances, on the other hand responsibility demands that I do not wait. So I am always too late, always overtaken by events. This is the aporia that must be endured by responsibility that merits its name. And the same has to be said of giving, forgiving, and hospitality, assuming there is anything they name.

The ethico-religious urgency of the invasive archi-sublimity of justice leaves no time for the cozily protected enjoyment of horror from a safe distance such as is allowed by the aesthetic experience of the teleological Romantic sublime as described by Kant and Hegel. It is more like the a-teleological and a-theological sublime that overcame that allegedly most typical of Romantic poets, Wordsworth, when, subsequent to his experience on the lake, he was overcome by a sense of what he describes as "blank desertion" followed by a sense of a presence which is that of a "presently" between absence and approach: a haunting haunted perhaps by something like what Derrida describes as the experience of the desert in the desert, the experience whose horror alerts us to the horror of the permanent discrepancy between on the one hand the justice of law and on the other hand the law of justice that demands responsibility to the singular, reminding me that your and my death can come at any time, before I have attempted to help you as I have nevertheless already promised to do in a promise I must repeatedly renew. The dignity (*Würde*), "which Kant sometimes calls 'sublime,'"[58] conferred by the idea of belonging to a kingdom of ends under justice defined by the moral law, is what compensates for the pain of the humiliation involved in the experience of the sublime analyzed by Kant—a pain that may be foreshadowed in the experience of the painfully beautiful.[59] For Kant the experience of the sublime is a tension between sovereign rationality and the imagination that cannot fully comprehend. It is a tension between the humiliation felt over this failure of comprehension and the humility manifested in a person's submission to the moral law. Of humility, as of dignity, Kant says that it is sublime.[60] For him, as observed in the second paragraph of this chapter, the imagination must listen to reason. This holds too for Hegel. For both Kant and Hegel reason would be the rationality of sovereign freedom of will. Speaking at once descriptively and prescriptively or neither, speaking constatively and performatively or neither, speaking doubly (and, to repeat, perhaps speaking doubly, duplicitously and hypoCritically in this way is speaking in something like the middle voice), Derrida would have that rationality and its freedom of active will listen to a reason and freedom whose voice is neither simply active nor simply passive. The former reason is the reason of a juridical rationality that calculates. The latter is the reason of the incalculable. And each must listen to the other. "A reason must let itself be reasoned with," "*Une raison doit se laisser raisonner,*" one reason must let itself re-sound.[61] Reason that claims to be sovereign is subject to the vigilance of reason that calls to inspect, *arraisonne.* Therefore conflicts between one religious dogma and another, between one political principle and another, and between a religious dogma and a political principle will never close off the responsibility to go on listening and responding. Rights and the claim of truth are thus bound to responsibility and the claim of truthfulness of address that implies a capacity to imadgine that what we take to be the truth is capable of being disconfirmed by what the future holds in store. Indeed we owe it to others, as others owe it to us, to expose our beliefs to disconfirmation in the manner Karl Popper and Peter Medawar would have scientists stretch their imaginations and endanger their hypotheses.[62] Taking such risks would be part of what is required by a democratic "open society" according to them, as it would be according to Derrida, for whom, let it not be forgotten, democracy is not a state to come, but eternal coming and deferring and critical deference. Such critical deference, therefore, is not to be contrasted with the scientific imagination. If we call such critical deference *sapientia,* such sapience, as I have argued elsewhere, is not excluded from science, and the critical does not exclude the hypoCritical.[63]

One can imagine hearing Derrida saying that perhaps reason resounds as the hypocritical imadgination understood as the "space of a hypocritical faith, one without dogma and without religion, irreducible to any and all religions or implicitly theocratic institutions."[64] Then, where the Kantian imagination would be the putatively pre-eminent (*überlegen*) power contributing to a teleological sublimity beyond its reach and where this falling short is compensated for by the idea of universal law, the imadgination would be the not simply negative im-possibility of an impower. In this impower the sublime humility of submitting oneself to the law of universal reason would be supplemented by the sublime humility of submitting oneself to a momentary suspension of law lest singularities of which one has no inkling be outlawed. This impower of imagination overwhelmed by imadgination would contribute to an archi-sublimity where the concepts of limit, *Grenze* and *Schranke,* whether interpreted along the lines of Kant or of Hegel, are exceeded by the monstrosity of an archi-exceptional singularity so absolutely unconditioned that one might be tempted, after all, as Derrida is, accepting his own invitational "God, if you wish," to call it God or, since the absolutely unconditioned in question is the absolute condition of theology, "God." God if you wish, but only if we remember that it is thanks to the primary religious liturgy of the word addressed to another human being that meaning accrues to the word "God" in the religions, in language, and in philosophy.[65] "God" seems to be one paleonym that is sufficiently indeterminate and undeterminating to bear the weight of the responsibility of welcoming the acoming of whatever is due (for example, the burden of an intercessory prayer), although whatever is due is independent on any determinant or reflective judgment, and although—shades of Kierkegaard—this responsibility outwith knowledge, inwith imadgination, "can always be judged 'mad.'"[66]

"Democracy to come" is another name sufficiently empty to bear this weight and this wait—a long wait, as it happens, *comme il arrive, en l'occurrence,* for, unlike the summer of "Sumer is icumen in," democracy to come is always acoming, always arriving but never arrived: never something or someone of which one can say that it is; always something or someone that remains, *reste* (*r-est-e*), yet to come—but before the distinction is made between someone and something and even before that distinction is quirkily collapsed into a whatever. "Democracy" or "God" or "god." "The democracy to come, will this be a god to come? Or more than one? Will this be the name to come of a god or of democracy? Utopia? Prayer? Pious wish? Oath? Or something yet other? *Ou autre chose encore?*"[67] Something yet other. Something yet other than God as the absolutely sublime sovereign being. Something yet other than being, *Sein* or *Seyn* than which according to Heidegger God is less divine. Something yet other than justice, *dikē,* conceived in the manner of Plato and Heidegger as principle of order. This is why there is no verb "to be" in Derrida's phrase "democracy to come and justice."[68] For the first to turn up in this democracy is not only not necessarily a bearer of some such metaphysical determination as human person or subject or consciousness or kin or neighbor or fellow religious follower or compatriot; he, she, or it is also not *Da-sein* or *Da-seyn.* He, she, or it. For of democratic equality Derrida asks:

> [M]ust we extend it to the whole world of singularities, to the whole world of humans assumed to be like me, my compeers—or else, even further, to all nonhuman living beings, or again, even beyond that, to all the nonliving, to their memory, spectral or otherwise, to their to-come or to their indifference with regard to what we think we can identify, in an always precipitous, dogmatic, and obscure way, as the life or the living present of living (*la vivance*) in general?[69]

Of the *force* of demo*cracy,* and of its *fors,* the outside that is inside it, Derrida goes on to ask how far it is to be extended: "To the dead, to animals, to trees and rocks?" This question gives rise to two further interconnected questions, both of them somewhat Platonic.

## Faecundity

(a) If the force of democracy is extended thus far, should not the list of the facts of the lives of the human and nonhuman living beings that inhabit that democracy, namely birth, copulation, aging, death, eating, and drinking, be extended to include defecation? Should this question strike us as a surprising one for a philosopher to put, note that surprise is as much the mark of philosophy to come as wonder is the mark of where philosophy begins according to Plato and to the Aristotle who came to be known as the Philosopher. Indeed, philosophy to come and where philosophy comes from are not mutually independent extremes. Note too that this surprising question is one that goes back to Plato's question as to whether there can be Ideas or Forms of hair or mud. Whether the addition of faeces to his list of what have Forms should be made would depend on how close to the limit of predication the faecal is deemed to be, how close to the apeiretic. Whether this addition is to be made to our inevitably and inveniently open list of relevant features relating to the limit of life and death and the limit of existence and non-existence will turn on whether we think that the faecal is beyond the limit of address. For by relevant features we mean religious features in a sense that is defined by the indefinable because non-predicative moment we have been calling address. So it is not irrelevant to our question that, unlike the fundamental facts of life in our list so far, defecation has not, as far as I know, become the focus of an organized religious sacrament, notwithstanding the claim of the poet Islwyn that *"Mae'r oll yn gysegredig,"* "Everything is sacred."[70] Our decision may turn on whether *apeiron* is beyond address, either as our addressing the apeiretic or its addressing us. For, however strange this may seem, however strange this may be, however much the thought may boggle the imadgination, we are invited by Derrida to entertain something close to the aporetic thought of being addressed by the apeiretic. We have to say, as just said, "something close to" because what Derrida would have democracy opened up to is "the whole world [Islwyn's *oll*] of singularities." Can *apeiron* be a singularity? Well, it can be an it, for, as noted earlier, "it" can apply not only to something determinate that can be counted but also to what at least at the molar level is amorphous stuff, for instance dung.

Levinas cites from the Sanhedrin tractate the following anecdote:

> Rab was telling Rabbi Hiyya: I once saw an Arab cut a camel into pieces with his sword. Then he beat the drum before it and the camel came back to life. Rabbi Hiyya responded: Did you find blood and dung [after this performance]? It was only an illusion.[71]

Levinas comments:

> Of course, sorcerers have no power over the living. I recognize a whole litera-
> ture of conflicts and emotional problems here, of paradoxical situations in
> which there is not a single teardrop, not a single drop of warm human blood,
> not a single bit of real human pain. Ah, if at least in the aftermath of all these
> dramas and crises were left a small amount of warm dung!

Philosophers have allowed their attention to kalology to distract their attention from kakology. One suspects that a little more attention to the latter might
reveal that the range of the former, aesthetics of the beautiful, extends more
widely than our prejudices permit, to an aesthetics that is also an aesthethics,
politics, and *religio* of the non-human, such as that to which we are pointed by
Derrida. Derrida lets the scope of democracy be opened up to the point where
questions of justice and responsibility are posed by whatever exists in advance
of how the existent is characterized.[72] As for the question of the recognition
in organized religions of matters faecal as formal sacraments, it is arguable
that such recognition is at least implicit in the ritual of ablution such as is to
be performed before praying in the mosque. And is not Nietzsche expressing
a fact worthy of religious celebration when he writes that "[t]he world . . . lives
on itself: its excrements are its food,"[73] so that in a religious service of harvest
thanksgiving it would be perfectly in order to sing "We plough the fields and
scatter the good dung on the ground"? To sing this would be to celebrate a recycling where, as William James observes in *The Varieties of Religious Experience,*
"dirt" and "excrementitious stuff" would be consecrated after the manner in
which negativity is saved by being *aufgehoben* in the dialectic of Hegel. Defecation would be coupled with fecundity in faecundity. James also observes
that another variety of religious experience would reject this compostmental
optimism, considering the faecal to be unassimilable waste, a marker of radical evil.[74] In the sixth part of *The Unbearable Lightness of Being* Milan Kundera
refers his readers to Scotus Erigena for a prolegomenon of a theodicy of faeces.
Against Saint Jerome, he allows that there was pleasure in Paradise, but not that
there was excitement. There was excrement, but only after God expelled man
from Paradise did it cause a feeling of disgust.

(b) There are Platonic overtones also to the second issue raised by Derrida's
question concerning the expansion of the notion of democracy today. For, as
it is with religion and the religious today that Derrida is concerned,[75] so it is
of democracy today that Derrida is writing, and of how it is in process of de-
constructing itself at this time of global tele-technology. The reinvention of a
notion of democracy that will allow us at least to speak of the injustices of this
internationalization and watch out for them relates to "the supposedly human
order of the ethico-juridico-political" not only as justice "writ large" in the
state, but as justice "writ small" in what Plato calls the soul, what "a bygone

psychoanalysis" calls the ego, the superego, consciousness, the subconscious, or the unconscious. In the analysis of the elementarily religious outlined in the above pages this is called address and comes from a singular other that is other than alter-ego. It comes in the spellbond of birth, death, and their copulation in the promise of a fecundity that may be human, justice writ small, or may be other than human, justice writ very large, larger than in the political state. This fecundity is that of the messianicity that is larger than messianism because it announces responsibility toward whatever one is unpredictably overcome by. The fecundity of this messianicity is what was touched on when in the section entitled "Loves," of the second chapter of this book, was cited Derrida's statement "The messianic can only be caressed."[76] We can barely touch on messianicity in its immeasurable magnitude and on the archi-sublimity of oncoming democracy in general. And they can barely touch on us. They haunt us in those singularizing moments at the thresholds of life and death, the *Grenzmomente* or *Schrankenmomente* of mourning, where we neither welcome nor thank enough and where grief after the death of a loved one or a friend threatens or promises to reduce thinking to the silence of address paralyzed by the aporetic paradox that saying enough is saying too much.

# EPILOGUE

## Again *(iterum)* of God, If You Wish

The topic of William James's *The Varieties of Religious Experience* is not organized religion. Nor has that been the topic of this book. But whereas the descriptions of personal religious experiences he analyzes frequently make references to God or gods from the very first lecture and throughout its successors, I have sought to postpone such references for as long as I can. I have done this in the faith that there is an area of human experience the religious character of which is not dependent on the invocation of God and is not necessarily that of an organized religion. In case it be said that the term "religion" is being used in a metaphorical sense when it is applied to a movement like communism or to a passion for a particular sport or to the life of an artist who lives for his art, and in case these be classed as secular phenomena, I repeat that I want to find space for a space that lies between secularity and organized religion as these are commonly opposed. That marginal space could hardly be secular if it in turn admitted the invocation of a God or of gods, as do many of the cases of unorganized religion described by James.

I have been arguing for acknowledgment of a religiousness that hovers on the border between life and death. I have explained why I generally prefer to say that my topic is religiousness rather than spirituality.[1] But I have emphasized that the meanings of the term "religion" and its cognates cannot be pinned down by the specification of necessary and sufficient conditions.[2] James makes this point when he says that "religion" is a collective noun. And the same can be said of the word "God." When, following Derrida's use of the phrase "'God,' if you wish," I tried to make acceptable a sense of "religious" in which God is an optional extra, I was not unaware of the varieties of things that have been given the name "God" by philosophers, mystics, poets, and others.[3] Nor am I unaware that the "if you wish" is vulnerable to the point Dewi Z. Phillips made when, interrupting a friend who was about to launch into an account of the God he wanted, he exclaimed, "It's not the God you want that matters. What matters is the God you are bloody well going to get."[4]

It may be naive but I hope not unhelpful to say that the use of the word "God" I have been reluctant to make in my account of non-theological religiousness is a use of this word that has been traditionally dominant in the monotheisms of Judaism, Christianity, and Islam, though I have wanted to avoid any essential use of that word as it functions in polytheistic religions too. The solemnity, gladness, and love with which that word is used are prefigured, I have been maintaining, in the religious experience at the borders between life and death without any appeal to deity or divinity, but not without appeal to alterity and to the dissymmetry of the relationship between the other and myself where troth toward whoever addresses or is addressed is compatible with skepticism toward truths. If I owe the truth to people, to you as no more than one among many or to people indifferently as "one" or as Heideggerian *das Man,* I also owe it to *you* in your singularity because I owe you truthfulness. Of course, the concept of truthfulness implies a concern for the truth, but it also implies a concern for others who have a concern for truth. In her lively and life-enhancing *The Trouble with Islam Today* Irshad Manji writes: "Our global responsibility now is not to determine who owns what identity, but to convey to future generations what we owe each other."[5] Among the things we owe each other is acknowledgment of our differences from each other, not least the unforeseen differences of future generations. We owe it to each other and to the truth that concern for the truth should keep open a welcome for these unforeseen differences, however unwelcome they may turn out to be, however difficult they may make it for us to maintain our own position and to pursue what we understand to be our mission, *envoi,* or *Geschick.* Here is how the difficult freedom of this difficult gospel of differences is described from a Christian point of view by one interpreter:

> In the process of encountering those of other faiths, and witnessing to Christ among them, we will find ourselves sent back to see Christ differently, to ask different questions—difficult questions, which shake what we have seen to be the "obvious" ways of interpreting and following him. The process of "mission" will involve *us* being questioned and challenged and shaken and changed—it will involve, we might say, *our* ongoing conversion.[6]

It will involve imadgination.

## Ungodgiven Gifts

Imbalance of imadgination at the chiasmus of universality and singularity, injustice as the disorder outwith which there is no justice, *adikia* paradoxically outwith *dikē* but crying out for justice, this is what preoccupies the religious frame of mind, the frame of mind that says Yes to the breaking of frames: its own, the frame whose most conspicuous components are the borderlines of its natality, fecundity, and mortality interrupted by another's; the frame that would prevent our seeing that there is another world but that it is this one, though not in the reconciliatory way a certain Hegel would have wished; the frame that seems to have directed the attention of Islamic transmitters of Greek philosophy away from the *Politics* of Aristotle (Averroes) and from everything in Plato except the ideal of rulers as philosophers treated in the *Republic* (Al Farabi);[7] the frame of Christendom as criticized by Kierkegaard; the frames of organized religions; the frames, boundaries, and bindings of books and of Books. Kierkegaard breaks such bindings when he writes in the voices of pseudonymous authors. Derrida breaks them when he writes polylogues in the voices of anonymous authors. The bindings they break are sometimes the bindings of books, *reliures.* It is as though they unpick them at the spine where the pages are held together, *reliées,* either, as with Derrida, in order that inserts, *prières d'insérer,* may be slipped between them, or, as with him again and with Kierkegaard, in order that readers be put under pressure to decide in which of the pseudonymous or anonymous voices, if any of them, they themselves will speak. This operation of unbinding and rebinding is a trope of the way in which facing up to one's own singular responsibility is defaced when that singularity becomes, as it unavoidably will become, a particularity subsumed under a law. But insofar as religions are subsumed under the religious, this becoming is liable to become subsumed within the to-come of archi-sublimity.

To repeat, not only are there no necessary and sufficient conditions for counting as a religion; there are no such conditions either that define the religious. Not possessing such conditions is a necessary meta-condition of sublimity. It will be recalled that according to Kant sublimity depends on a tension between the incapacity of the imagination to comprehend something in its totality and the capacity of a person to subject itself to the moral law. He says that that subjection is humility and that humility and dignity are sublime. The archi-sublime does not allow itself to be domesticated by the *limen.* It is outwith the universality of law. Its humility is its subjection to the singular. It inherits the whirlwind. Its norm is the exception. It is an exception, for example, to the norm of exchange. And it exemplifies the putting of exemplarity to the test. It tests Derrida's claim to be following the example of Kierkegaard as made in the confession cited as the first epigraph of this study that "it is Kierkegaard to whom I have been most faithful."

Derrida's fidelity and indebtedness to Kierkegaard is plain from what has been said about justice and debt in the preceding pages. From that too it is plain that Heidegger and also Levinas are indebted to Kierkegaard for the same reasons. Allowing for the difficulties that surround the very idea of influence and origin, difficulties of which Derrida frequently warns, it could be demonstrated that Heidegger, Levinas, and Derrida are indebted for similar reasons to Nietzsche. These reasons connect with the welcome Nietzsche extends to the quirks of fate. They connect with the notion of gratitude. And they connect with a notion of grace. However, the notion of grace in question is that of a gift that is not bound to be or bound to the grace of God, as it is apparently so bound for Kierkegaard. Yet at least something of what Kierkegaard says about grace is a key to a notion of religiousness that is not necessarily tied to the notion of a religion. It is exemplified by what is said in *Fear and Trembling* concerning the test endured on Mount Moriah and the test recorded in the Book of Job. What Kierkegaard says is very simple. Among others who have said it is Simone Weil, some of whose writings Derrida says he had read before he had written much himself. This simple idea is that however concerned you may be that another's rights be respected, whatever rights you may have vis-à-vis your debtors are for others to claim on your behalf. What on Moriah was a teleological or unteleological suspension of the ethical may be interpreted as the suspension of the *lex talionis* of the Old Testament in favor of the New. Yet there are no stronger advocates than the Jews Emmanuel Levinas and Jacques Derrida of the exceptionality of the first person singular to that law of "an eye for an eye" or indeed of "one good turn deserves another." Before Christ Israel was chosen as the exception, exceptional in the suffering and, judged by the standard of the *lex talionis,* the injustice Israel was to bear. "Israel" could be another pseudonym for Kierkegaard, although he would consider acceptance of that analogy blasphemous. However we may determine these questions of comparative religion, and however much guidance we may take from these or other religions, the incomparability of the archi-exceptional first person singular distinguishes religiousness from religions and their God(s). But although one may understand why Eckhart prays to his God to be saved from gods conceived as things, the word "God," as observed earlier, is so acceptive and at the same time so rejective of the meanings history imposes upon it, and therefore so versatile, that although in any one of the senses given to it, for example one of the senses given to it by Eckhart, its employment may be prohibited, it would be irrationally dogmatic to prohibit in advance its use in other senses. It was also observed earlier that Derrida is not against our using the word "God," as he says, "if we wish." We might wish to use it of the coming toward us of the archi-sublime. Nevertheless, its use is not inescapable, any more than the word "democracy" is for the work Derrida asks it to do, work that, if you wish, you might ask to be done by the word "God." In particular the use of the word "God" is not inescapable in the context in which by religiousness without religion is meant that everything I receive is a gift, not mine by right. My thought that what I receive is not mine by right and my thought that what is given has no giver discourage the narcissistic and flattering thought that I have been picked out as worthy of receiving the gift. And the thought of this gratuitousness encourages the thought that what I have received is a *donandum,* something to be shared with or passed on to others. I don't flatter myself that I am the chosen *destinataire* of the cello suites of Bach, but I consider myself lucky to have been born after he composed them, so lucky that I owe it to others not to keep them for myself.

Granted distinctions made by Derrida in *The Post Card,* I can be the recipient of something without my being the one to whom it was directed. What is received need have no director or Director at all. Something or someone can be given, *donné* or *donnée,* without its having been given by someone or something. So, just as there may be no one for me to pray to, there may be no one for me to thank. This does not prevent my being thankful. And such undirected gratitude, like an undirected prayer, could be religious. It would indeed *be* a prayer if as Catherine Chalier writes, paraphrasing Levinas, "the highest prayer is to give thanks, to know how to give thanks even when life becomes painful."[8] Notwithstanding the possible independence from a God or a religion of the gratitude expressed in thanksgiving, it could be a gratitude for what might be called, as Nietzsche might call it, fate. Such free-standing gratitude could be gratitude for what might be called, as Kierkegaard might call it, grace, but in a not necessarily theological sense of that word. As mentioned in an earlier chapter, I once read somewhere that in one of his translations Tyndale uses the pronoun "It" of God, but this claim proved to be unfounded. Emerson sometimes uses the neuter pronoun of God. So too does the text of Bach's *Christmas Oratorio.* This use of "*es*" as a pronoun for God is perhaps a relic of the fact that an early form of the word "*Gott*" was neuter, not, as it is in modern German, masculine.[9] It allows both for a theology that respects sexual difference and for one that is sexually indeterminate. Both of these corollaries would be allowed by the coming of an unprejudiced democracy. The neuter pronoun would also allow "*es gibt,*" "there is," to oscillate between an ontotheological and a non-ontotheological use, an oscillation that reflects the ambiguity of the Greek "*to on*" as between a sense that admits a plural, "beings," and a sense that does not. These equivocations are crucial for the translation of "*Ereignis*" as used by Heidegger in "On Time and Being" and *Contributions to Philosophy,* and for Derrida's turning of the ownness, enowning, or self-possession of *Ereignis* into the otherness or unowning of *événement*, eventuality, and the adventuality of the archi-sublime, in defiance of Heidegger's judgment that the French word "*avènement*," with its memory of Christian Advent, is wholly unsuitable as a translation of "*Ereignis*."[10]

The religious defined as the archi-sublime is not divorced from the religious defined in terms of those "elementary forms of religious life" ranging from the birth to the death of another. The interconnectedness of these forms—forms whose formality is broken by address—is witnessed to by the mourning that begins with the other's birth, as shown in the sadness that accompanies the joy in the eyes of the mother nursing her child figured in some of the paintings referred to earlier in this book. Her being haunted beyond being and nothingness, beyond ontology and meontology, by the child's impending death, is an exemplification in the story of one religion of a haunting from beyond the grave that comes with the religious as the archi-sublime without story, as messianism without Messiah. To repeat the memorandum of Simone Weil, "Never to think of a thing or being we love but have not actually before our eyes without reflecting that perhaps this thing has been destroyed, or this person is dead."[11] Notwithstanding the reservations Levinas entertains regarding Weil and what he regards as her Orientalist flirting or dancing,[12] the thought experiment she bids us perform puts into words the experience of being addressed by another that Levinas puts into the words "Thou shalt not murder" heard as "Thou shalt not harm." These words speak to us not as predication but as address. That is one reason why address, as we have insisted, is not utterly naked. These words express the mortality of the other. They are inscribed on the other's face, as fragility is inscribed also in the look of the non-human. The elementary forms of religious life at the borderline between life and death are haunted by mortality, and the look of the non-human is haunted by the fleetingness that Nietzsche imagines he could redeem and by the fragility, finitude, and indeed mortality to which Derrida refers when he writes, of what could be a church, a synagogue, a mosque, or a religion that

> [o]ne cannot love a monument, a work of architecture, an institution as such except in an experience itself precarious in its fragility: it hasn't always been there, it will not always be there, it is finite. And for this very reason I love it as mortal, through its birth and its death, through the ghost or the silhouette of its ruin, of my own—which it already is or already prefigures. How can we live except in this finitude? Where else would the right to love, indeed the love of right, come from?[13]

The other's finitude is implied too in Derrida's thought that "I promise" and indeed any other words I address to another imply the other's death in the sense that the necessary repeatability of words is testamentary.[14] Their universality survives the death of both the addresser and the addressee. That is the nature of language in the broadest possible sense of the word. Hence the bond between the quasi-transcendental conditions of religiousness—whose "quasi-" signifies the signifiance (*sic*) or addressance that distinguishes quasi-transcendental conditions from ones that are only transcendental—and the very "elementary forms of religious life" whose interconnectedness is effected by their all being forms of life in death and death in life, the religious resonance of the infant's and the mother's screams at birth, of the dying person's stuttered last word—so often the word "Mother"—and, between scream and word, of the copulative groan.

The language of an infant is by definition thin on predication and therefore closer to sheer stark naked address. Its language would therefore meet one of our open list of criteria for being described as religious, the criterion of not being significantly bound by criteria. But a second criterion of the religiousness of language is how it is moved by the thought of another's death. It is that thought that all but silences predication. One might expect by this criterion that a child would be less able to follow Weil's injunction than an adult, for one would usually expect a little child to be too little acquainted with grief. But Weil's injunction is directed to our imagination, and it is arguable that the child's fear of its mother's being gone, her *Fortsein,* is a manifestation of its being acquainted to the point of obsession with grief, notwithstanding that in playing with a bobbin it has some control over turning the *fort* into a *da.* This is one piece of psychoanalytic support for the interconnectedness between birth and death as elementary forms of religious life. There is a mass of such support for the connectedness of those two forms with copulation and sexuality more generally. It would not be an exaggeration to say that that connectedness is a main thesis of most psychoanalysis. Rather than pursue that thesis here, I return to the third in Eliot's trinity of overlapping elements (elements, therefore, that are not atomic) and to Weil's precept regarding it.

Her proposal is a recipe for detachment from the persons and the things of the earth that we love. She appears to be as generous as Derrida is when he seeks to do justice to the non-human by welcoming it into adventitious and adventurous democracy. But she could not endorse the words of Camus when, remaining faithful to Nietzsche, he writes "I . . . chose justice in order to remain faithful to the Earth."[15] She is being faithful rather to a certain Kierkegaard when he says of the double-minded person, the one who does not will one thing, that it is "the reward—earth's reward—that he is looking for."[16] It is as if she and Kierkegaard are unable or unwilling to imagine that things of the earth may be loved not only for the enjoyment they bring or because they cater to our needs and for that reason earn our gratitude. It is as if she and he are unable or unwilling to grant that such things, like persons, may be loved joyfully and with veneration for their own sakes, with a regard that is blind to any idea of reward or other advantage, with an attachment that is a detachment from self-centeredness. It is as if for her such love must be reserved for things of another world, perhaps because she thinks that things of the earth are metaphysically dependent on things that are not of this earth, in virtue perhaps of the conception of them as created by a Creator-God.[17] She is being faithful to Saint John of the Cross when he writes (in the words of one of the epigraphs of T. S. Eliot's *Sweeney Agonistes* based on the fourth chapter of the first book of the *Ascent of Carmel*), "Hence the soul cannot be possessed of the divine union until it has divested itself of the love of created beings," as though such love were necessarily covetous or concupiscent. She is being faithful to Kierkegaard when, as paraphrased by Dewi Z. Phillips, she says that only after dying to particular things of life do we come to see the value of the eternal,[18] and when she puts in the context of the hard saying "Love your enemies" the hard saying of Luke 14:26, "If any man come to me, and hate not his father, and mother, and wife, and children, and brethren, and sisters, yea, and his own life also, he cannot be my disciple."[19] Her way of being faithful to Kierkegaard by conjoining these two hard sayings, as hard as any saying implied by the hard morality of Nietzsche and Zarathustra, is not Derrida's way of being faithful to Kierkegaard. Derrida's way of being faithful to Kierkegaard—and to most of the authors whose writings the former's writings deconstrue—is to exercise that kind of double-mindedness we have learned to call double reading. This exercise entails the discovery that, on the one hand, those authors who seem to belong to the tradition in which metaphysical oppositions are maintained betray that tradition, and that, on the other hand, those authors who take themselves to have broken with the simple polarizations that define the structure of metaphysics have not cut themselves as cleanly from those too simple oppositions as they suppose. Sometimes, in the same place or in different places, these two directions are taken by one author. Often, this is because the conceptual oppositions, for instance the oppositions between sensibility and reason and between theory and practice that are already challenged by the Januarial bidirectionality of Abelian words, are further disturbed by the quasi-Abelian relationship forged in the imadgination that binds conceptuality religiously to address. That is to say, the said cannot be safely sealed off from the saying. The one is outwith the other, with an outwithness of testification and witness. Neither is cut off from the other as parallel lines are by the space between them. The one cuts across the other in a chiasmus. At the heart of that chiasmus, the heart where for a syncopated moment Kierkegaard's and Derrida's paths cross, we cannot tell whether the borderline between them where they are touched or just fail to be touched by each other is a *Grenze* or a *Schranke*. Perhaps this undecidability is the mark of a religiousness that belongs to neither of the kinds Kierkegaard denotes by the first two letters of the alphabet. Perhaps it is the mark of a religiousness that belongs properly to no kind and only quirkily to any alphabet, a religiousness of not belonging, of not belonging of necessity to any religion or God—a not belonging, *nota bene,* that is not to be confused with necessarily not belonging to any religion or God.

Save that the emptiness of the name "God" is so fecund that you can decide to call this religious undecidability God, if you wish. This kenotic and kinetic God would not be the God the non-existence of which would worry the Kierkegaard who says, "God does not exist, He is eternal." This self-disempowering God would not be the God whose non-existence seemed to prevent my making the intercessory prayer referred to half-jokingly on that card sent from Italy to an ill friend in Paris. Imagine I made the prayer just in case there existed a God to receive it. Why, as I have already asked, should I stand on my dignity? Why should I not, in the spirit of Pascal's wager, though for the sake of my friend's health rather than for the sake of my own salvation, see the risk of deceiving myself as worth running in case it was an opportunity to secure some help for him? Because, as the saying goes, it is always preferable to be a friend of the truth than a friend of a friend, be that friend Plato or Derrida or Bigger? I suspect that Derrida would have said that I have to remain faithful to the truth in order for me to remain faithful to Plato or to himself and vice-versa; for economy with constative truth or with performative truthfulness over such questions as, for example, whether God exists is haunted by the absolutely past and absolutely future (Kierkegaard would say eternal) subjectively and objectively genitive affirmation of what we might, if we wished, call God. This would not be a God one could worship, not a God to whom one could pray, not a God that one could thank. It would be that God in the name of which these worshipful, prayerful, and thankful acts of religion could be done. It would be that God in the name of which it could be said that the elementary forms of life, birth, and copulation, and death, are neither exclusively forms of religion nor exclusively forms of secularity, but a quasi-transcendental eschatological condition at the margins where the borderline of the one is interrupted by the borderline of the other. That is to say, this God would be the God outwith a proper name. It would be the nameless prepredicative precondition of our having been called each time uniquely from time immemorial and from time to come to an increasingly difficult responsibility. But increase in the difficulty of that responsibility does not mean decrease in gratitude for the gratuitous gift of human and non-human others, grief over whose passing Derrida, in faithfulness to Kierkegaard, names Passion, without, however, being so faithful as to bind that name to any particular religion or religions.

## Epigraphs

Turning from the first epigraph of this book to the last, to Derrida's remark "These questions can be posed only after the death of a friend," let us take these words, written after the death of one of his friends, as a cue to review swiftly the argument of the last part of this book. That argument was guided by the structure of eventuality laid bare in the course of chapters 13 and 14, where it began to emerge that structure and event are not as simply opposed as some have supposed, and that the "of" of the phrase "structure of eventuality" may be a double genitive. In these chapters an apparent disagreement between two of my friends and myself was explained by my initial failure to grasp that complexity. If we take the referent of the phrase "these questions" in the just cited final epigraph to be questions concerning quasi-transcendental conditions, one of the questions posed will ask what these conditions condition. In the order of the exposition of the overall argument of Kant's Critical project (an order that must be followed but then reversed), transcendental conditions are in the first place conditions of empirical knowledge and in the second place conditions of practical knowledge or reason. With regard to empirical knowledge Kant famously remarks that without a particular sensory given the transcendental conditions are empty (I am tempted to say kenotic, as was said a moment ago of God). He adds that without transcendental conditions what is given is blind. Provided we distinguish theoretical knowledge from practical knowledge and practical thought, something analogous could be said about ethical judgments in relation to the moral law and the "experience" of the latter that Kant calls *Achtung,* moral respect, awe, heed, attention. This is a feeling with regard to an intellectual object or objective, namely the moral law prescribing minimally the avoidance of actions determined by maxims that cannot be universalized or willed to be universalized. Bearing the Kantian structure in mind, it can be said that Derrida, following Kierkegaard and Levinas, complicates the Kantian account by stressing that respect for the law is not enough. It calls for supplementation by what exceeds the enough. Somewhat as for there to be empirical knowledge there must be both a universal transcendental condition and a particular sensory given, the one connected with the other in the mathematical schematism of the imagination, so for there to be ethically just decision the universality of law must be brought into contact with the singularity of the vulnerable other. We could say that this connection, which is both a proximity and a distancing, the distancing implied by respect, is "experienced" as what Kierkegaard and Derrida agree in calling passion. The double binding to and unbinding from the universal and the singular is the work of the hypoCritical imadgination, which is, to cite again one of the epigraphs of this book, "the chief religious faculty." The chief religious faculty is in the first place religious as defined by the elementary forms of religious life exemplified by those mentioned in the subheading of the first section of chapter 15: birth, and copulation, and death. It was conceded in the same section that the lives of some people may not testify to the religiousness of the experience of these forms in their relationship with others, even in their relationship with members of their own family or close friends, even with the form of life that is lived in the experience of another's death or annihilation. Some people's imagination may be so dulled that they cannot rise to the demonstrative passion of tears. However, dullness can be a sign not of the absence of the religious passion of grief, but the manner of its manifestation; that is why mourning is so easily transmuted into melancholia, which is a self-absorbed modality in contrast to the self-detached modality of gratitude. Meditating and mourning Paul de Man, Derrida writes:

> True "mourning" seems to dictate only a tendency: the tendency to accept incomprehension, to leave a place for it, and to enumerate coldly, almost like death itself, those modes of language which, in short, deny the whole rhetoricity of the true (the non-anthropomorphic, the non-elegiac, the non-poetic, etc).[20]

Meditating and mourning in advance Derrida and others, and, in passing, casting light and shadow over Derrida's faithfulness to Kierkegaard, David Krell writes:

> We cannot remain faithful to the departed one, . . . not merely because our attention span is too limited but because, in a sense that is difficult to articulate but hard to deny, these loved others were *never fully there* for us when they were alive, never fully *present* to us when they were alive, never fully present to us, never palpable in the way our dreams promised—if only because *we* were never fully there *for us* while they were alive. Even when *they* were there for us, there never was any *there* there for us. Perhaps the other as other comes to us for the first time, therefore, in the experience of mourning, absence, default.[21]

Perhaps it comes to us for the nearly last time in the experience of what Heidegger refers to as the *Fehl des Gottes,* that is to say in the endurance of the default of God.[22]

## Reversed Intentionality

From the published versions of the discussions that took place between Derrida and Jean-Luc Marion at the conference on Religion and Postmodernism at Villanova University in 1997 it emerges that some of their real or apparent disagreements arise from their different conceptions of phenomenology. Both of them could be said to be seeking to employ the resources of phenomenology in order to transcend phenomenology. This could be said too of Levinas. All three authors take Husserl as their point of departure.

That point of departure for Levinas is what Husserl writes about passive synthesis. Husserl's reference to a synthesis that is passive or suffered is a reference to a temporality that is a phenomenological equivalent of the passivity that belongs to time as a form of sensibility in the account of time given by Kant, who contrasts this (in the broad sense of the word) "aesthetic" passivity with the activity of the syntheses attributed to the understanding. The incoming centripetal character of passive synthesis is also exemplified in those places in Husserl's works where he uses the trope of "rays" projected toward the percipient by what is perceived. This is a manner of speaking that we come across also in Pre-Socratic theorists like Alcmaeon and Empedocles, and possibly in historical remarks in Post-Socratic theorists, including perhaps Plato. Empedocles explains perception in terms of effluences or emanations that are projected from what is seen, heard, touched, and so on, and that are more or less successfully received by pores, pathways, or gates in the organs of sense.

The "reversal" of intentionality to which reference has been made so often in this book is not a simple change of direction. It cannot be that if the intentionality of consciousness is its directedness to an object or objective. Although this so-called reversal turns the ego into an accusative me under the look of the other, that look does not freeze the freely willing subject into a noematic object. Rather does it stir me accusingly into a more stinging sense of responsibility. The reversal is a change from the field of intentional consciousness with the ego at its source to the field of deep conscience, archi-conscience, nay, anarchi-conscience, with the other at its center of gravity. It is an alteration from a phenomenology of perceptual consciousness to a quasi-phenomenology of the ethical, where the "quasi-" denotes address or calling. Derrida in his way repeats this move in what he writes about democracy to come and its justice. The ethico-religious and political implications of what Derrida writes are retained in what we have called the (an)archi-sublime.

## Saturation

What Kant says about the sublime in the *Critique of Judgment* is invoked in what Marion writes about saturated phenomena in §§21 and 22 of *Being Given*.[23] He reminds us of the ethical dimension of sublimity in Kant's analysis. But Marion's appeal to this in the course of his account of saturated phenomena in those sections is part of a phenomenology of perception. The saturated phenomena he treats in those sections belong to the field of how things appear.

It is precisely the how of things that is bracketed off in Derrida's account of the archi-sublimity of the incoming of democracy. If his account can still be described as phenomenology, it is a phenomenology in which the existence of particular things is bracketed off, as in Husserlian phenomenology, but in order that justice be done to whotever exists or is to come into existence, independently of how we should treat it on account of its how. Marion's saturated phenomena are phenomena that resist control by the spatio-temporal forms of sensibility and categories of the understanding as described by Kant and in their phenomenological versions as described in Husserl's accounts of perceptual objectivity.

Saturation is explained through the thought that a concept may be or may fail to be fulfilled by intuition. Intuition may be inadequate. It may be inadequate in the sense that it does not meet the criteria for the application of a particular concept. This inadequacy is not to be confused with a certain incompleteness of experience that holds, Husserl maintains, for cases where intuition supports the application of a concept, for instance an empirical concept, but where it must remain possible in principle for further intuitions to be had, where there is an "and so on" of aspects on, for example, a physical thing, further *Abschattungen.*

While intuition may be inadequate as distinct from extendible, intuition may also be more than adequate. The phenomenon constituted by intuition and concept may be saturated. A sponge is saturated when there is more than enough (*satis*) liquid to fill its every pore. Satisfaction is exceeded in experiences of submergence and inundation. In *Being Given,* following the order of topics treated in the *Critique of Pure Reason,* Marion argues that it is with respect to quantity (unity, plurality, totality) that a saturation by a surplus of intuition takes place in the case of an event, for instance the Battle of Waterloo as described by Stendhal in *La chartreuse de Parme,* where the *Abschattungen* experienced by different participants fail to make up a coherent whole. In the work of art it is with respect to quality (reality, negation, limitation) that saturation by a surplus of intuition takes place, for instance in the flooding in of light in certain paintings of Turner and Claude. Relation (inherence and subsistence, causality and dependence, community or reciprocity between agent and patient) is what is exceeded in the pressure (not limited to the caress) of flesh on flesh. Quantity, quality, relation, and the formal concepts or categories of modality (possibility and impossibility, existence and non-existence, necessity and contingency) are saturated in the experience of the face of the Other. As with the other categories as treated by Kant, guides, *Leitfaden,* to the categories of modality are certain forms of judgment: the problematic, the assertoric, and the apodeictic. Of the modalities of the forms of judgment Kant says that, unlike their quantity, quality, and relationality, they contribute nothing to the judgment's content. The modality of judgments "concerns only the value of the copula in relation to thought in general" (B100). The categories of modality inherit this special meta-status. Marion's fifth class of saturated phenomena are in an analogous manner second-order. These phenomena presuppose the four classes of saturated phenomena so far listed. Their saturation is a saturation of saturation. To their phenomenality he gives the name revelation. This is where it becomes relevant for our study of the relation between Kierkegaard and Derrida to mention that Marion refers to saturated phenomena as paradoxes. They go beyond *doxa*, beyond opinion or judgment. That is not to say that they go beyond faith, but Marion is anxious not to forsake too rapidly the Husserlian phenomenological context in which *doxa* would be one sort of noematic object which in the paradox would be flooded by an abundance of intuitive evidence. So Marion has not yet broken with phenomenology. He is still exploring the conditions of possibility of phenomena. But the phenomena he cites as examples of these quantitative, qualitative, relational, and modal phenomena of revelation are such declarations as, to give a quantitive and eventive illustration, "the lightning comes from the East and shows itself [*phainetai*] as far as the West" (Matthew 24:27); to give a qualitative illustration, "I still have many things to say to you, but you do not yet have the power to bear them" (John 16:12). The unbearability alluded to here echoes the menacing quality of what we have variously called the quasi-sublime, the archi-sublime, and the anarchi-sublime. Recall the circumstances described at the end of the second section of chapter 16 where the burden of pain or joy was more than one person could bear. Recall too that the word "*advient*," (advenes, comes upon) used by Marion in describing how we may be affected by music is the word we have found used by Derrida in describing the oncoming of the future,[24] the future's in-stacy, we might say, though without meaning that the instatic as contrasted with the ecstatic in the etymological and Heideggerian sense of the word rules out ecstasy in this word's untechnical connotation.

With Marion's "phenomena of revelation (*Offenbarung*)" we are at the threshold of the phenomenological and the theological. We step on to that threshold between the possibility of phenomena of revelation and the Actuality, Factuality, and Event of Revelation in a section of *Being Given* entitled, though without explicit mention of Kierkegaard, "Either . . . Or . . ." The crossing of that threshold is anticipated in the final paper of a collection whose English title is *In Excess*.[25] It is anticipated too when in the third of his Meditations Descartes stresses that God overflows every human idea. But in Article 50 of *The Passions of the Soul*, an article cited by Marion, Descartes gives us a non-theological—which is not to say non-religious—version of saturation that forces us to face once more the question of the curious connection between conditions or quasi-conditions of possibility and the actuality of religions that proclaim the glory of God. Descartes writes:

> When the first encounter with some object surprises us, and we judge it to be new or very different from what we formerly knew, or from what we supposed that it ought to be, that causes us to wonder and be surprised; and because that may happen before we in any way know whether this object is agreeable to us or is not so, it appears to me that wonder is the first of all passions; and it has no opposite, because if the object which presents itself has nothing in it that surprises we are in no wise moved regarding it, and we consider it without passion.[26]

Marion and Derrida share a concern with horizonless and unconditioned experience. They share with Descartes—and Kierkegaard—a concern with passion. And Descartes shares with them a concern for the unconditioned, for is it not to this that reference is being made when Descartes says that astonishment happens "before we in any way know whether this object is agreeable to us or is not so," agreeable or disagreeable or, I believe he would allow us to add, useful or unuseful? In this paragraph, Descartes, the philosopher associated with the mission of showing us how to win technological control over the world by capturing things where possible in clear and distinct concepts, is granting that the world, not only God, exceeds our concepts. What is more, Descartes's (and Bacon's) scientific methodologies require moments in which allowance is made for this excess.[27] This is a requirement that is built into Derrida's notion of democracy to come, into Marion's notion of saturated phenomena, and into my notion of archi-sublimity where sublimity understood in the teleological manner of Kant as what we try but always fail to reach is overwhelmed by a counter-teleological sublimity that pursues us like a returning wave or the crag that seemed to pursue the young Wordsworth in the episode of *The Prelude* describing his adventure on the lake.

Both Derrida and Marion (in the wake of Descartes) invoke the word "God" in treating the horizonless and unconditioned zone to which they apply respectively the terms "democracy" and "saturation." This zone corresponds in Kant's thinking to religion within the bounds of reason alone. We have seen that from analyses of phenomena at the sensory extreme of experience Marion endeavors to find a passage through phenomenological manifestation (*Offenbarkeit*) that is consistent with religious revelation. Derrida, who says of himself that he rightly passes for an atheist, endeavors to mark out a space for a religiousness that exceeds the Heideggerian alternative of *Offenbarung* and *Offenbarkeit* and, with the assistance of Levinas, relocates the bounds of reason as defined by Kant, with the result that Kantian rationality of principles is crossed with a passion for the singular. More faithful to Derrida than to Marion, and taking as point of departure the crossing of reason and feeling in the imagination and imadgination, this book has attempted to bracket the existence of God, a bracketing that, after all, is itself a fairly traditional move among religionists, for instance Kierkegaard, not to mention phenomenologists. But whereas in the phenomenological reduction of classical phenomenology questions of existence are suspended in favor of description of meanings and intentions, the reduction to be practiced first according to this book is one that temporarily suspends description of meanings in order that existence be given its due, that is to say, in order that the responsibility due from us to other existents as such be heard.

When that first reduction has done its work, that reduction will be reduced. The suspension of everything other than existence will be suspended. In this second phase the world in its brightness and darkness will be given back. Adapting the trope of a *Weltanschaung* in which the world and the things in it are what are doing the looking (the *anschauen*), but still following clues in remarks made by Derrida, this book has attempted to give religion an ecological turn. We have not been unaware that doing this might well have provoked from Derrida the remark that we are cultivating another religion. If that is what we are doing, it is a religion whose articulation would benefit from closer heed than we have had space to give to Marion's phenomenology of the how of saturated phenomena. That articulation could not be achieved at the expense of neglecting responsibility to existents as such. One way of meeting that responsibility would go via theology and the thought of God as Creator of a world the glory of which would call to be sung and praised because it is His creation. That way is the way followed by Marion, in the wake of a crowd of witnesses that includes Saint Francis, Saint Bonaventura, and Urs von Balthasar, not to mention the Psalmists and the Celtic saints. I have argued that if we cannot follow the way of the religions, the honor done to God through the word "God" and the other names of the Name may be done to the world by calling upon those names to honor the world, even by calling upon the word "God," if you wish. I do not wish this, not unless the quirkinesses of that extraordinary word are laid bare, as some of them are by both Derrida and Marion, both of whom show that some of those quirkinesses were laid bare already by the Greek fathers who, Marion suggests, liberated the Christian theological concepts from the Greek (and perhaps metaphysical) horizon where they first arose: metaphysical concepts like ground, essence, being, presence.[28] This book has attempted to loosen from a Christian but not exclusively Christian theological horizon the concepts of grace and gift and the sacramentality of such sacraments as baptism and burial, rites of passage across or toward borderlines between life and death, eschatological eventualities. The aim of the first part of that attempt, before turning to some all too brief remarks about the how of things, has been to free from the concept of a Creator the notion of a thing in its sheer existence.

# Eternity's Mark

Kierkegaard abstracts from the qualities that make neighbors different from one another in order that he may concentrate on the humanity they have in common. "Dissimilarity," he writes, "is temporality's method of confusing that marks every human being differently, but the neighbour is eternity's mark—on every human being."[29] Might what makes existents neighbors be, we have asked, not their predicated humanity, but their unpredicated existence? Would not existence be eternity's mark? Would not the unconditionally next on the scene be the existent, rather than the existent on condition that it is human? Does not one's thinking of the existence (the that it is, the *hoti estin*) of a singular existent other than oneself independently of its what (its predicates, its essence, its *ti estin*) already expose one to responsibility toward it?[30]

It may seem obvious that these questions regarding the that of existence are matters of ontology, not of what Derrida calls hauntology. It may therefore seem obvious that the attempt to clear a way for the existent to be given its due clashes with what Derrida writes about hauntology as what exceeds not only the "to be or not to be" of ontology and ontotheology but also the Heideggerian thinking of being. However, the thinking that gives the existent its due also exceeds these, for according to that thinking one is already placed under a prima facie responsibility toward a thing other than oneself by its being an existent, whatever its what (or its whot), since its mere existence is a good to that thing, a good that is the good of its being beyond its being, its more than it is. As suggested by the examination of the dilemmas that almost brought us to a standstill in chapters 13 and 14, hauntology and ontology are not strata parallel with each other. Hauntology intrudes archi-sublimely into ontology. Hauntology is none other than the doubly genitive addressing of the other that Derrida calls invention. It is the absolute responsibility that comes with the coming into existence that could be called avenience, advent, or adventure, and that Derrida would have us understand independently of the how of whom or what supervenes. It is in the very absence and defection of advent (*avent, Ankunft*) that Heidegger hears the announcement of the "last God." In the sentence in which Derrida cites Heidegger's remark to this effect he also cites Levinas's words "God is the future," "*Dieu est l'avenir.*"[31]

Of course, the absolute responsibility just adverted to does not absolve us from the responsibilities that depend upon the how of existents, on how they touch, trouble, and, in more than one sense of the word, appeal to us, on how they address us otherwise than in virtue solely of their existence. But it would be over-hasty to attribute these responsibilities beyond existence simply to predicates of things, to what we say about them. That would be to reduce things to cases. If things address us in their singularity, their addressing us is, again in more than one sense of the word, affection. This is a *rapport* in depth, prior to the properties and lateral relations in virtue of which things become objects. It is this sphere of affection, of the love that some say God is, that is the terrain of ethico-religious responsibility on which we must learn to walk once we have been struck by how open that terrain is thanks to the responsibility to which we are bound already by the naked existence of whatever approaches us.

To say that the existence of a thing, whatever the thing, no matter what its predicates, is a good for that thing, is to say with Derrida that the unpredictable is to be welcomed for its own sake. And it is not only the to-be-welcomed yet-to-come existence of the thing that is spelled out as a presently, hence as neither presence nor absence as simple opposites. The presentness of something existent is that of the presently to-come of a future that can never be present and of an absolute past that was always passed. Its presentness "knows no boundaries."[32] Derrida borrows from Plato the expression "*chōra*" to mark the place at the heart of a chiasmus of this syncopated out-of-jointness. This out-of-jointness of place and of time is the out-of-jointness of what Levinas and Pascal call my place in the sun, just as the "to be" of the description "to be welcomed oncoming" is, as the French "*devoir*" may be, not simply descriptive or predicative or predictive, but also prescriptive or obligative or gerundival. It marks my responsibility toward the trans-tensedly existent. If the existence of existents over against me may be said to be revealed in their resistance to me, this resistance is to be accounted for not as negativity but as my ethico-religious responsibility toward them. This account, as just hinted, is a rethinking of the beyondness of the Platonic teaching of the good beyond being, the good in chiasmus with *chōra*. This account is a plea for the extension of ethico-religious honor to every other thing *qua* singular existent, quasily *qua* because the singular existent is prior to the *qua* of quality, prior to zero-level predication, because existence is not a zero-level predicate. The argument for this extension is that a thing's existence is a good for that thing, which therefore addresses to me a demand to address to it ethico-moral consideration.

In his essay "Force of Law" Derrida cites Kurt Hiller's statement that "higher even than the happiness and the justice of existence stands existence itself."[33] He reports Walter Benjamin's reaction to this statement. Interpreting existence as the life of a human being, Benjamin finds unacceptable the idea that mere life is higher than the just life, but he accepts that not living is lower than living a life that is not yet just, for being alive leaves open the possibility of living justly. However, in thus being interpreted as being alive existence is being turned into a predicate, where the higher and lower is a matter of comparison of values. We, on the contrary, are interpreting existence as other than a predicate, or at least other than a predicate of the same level as being alive or being just. On this interpretation existence is not comparable with a just existence on the same scale. This does not prevent our granting that the existence of something is a good for that existent. But to grant that is not to make a judgment about the value of existence in general, as Benjamin is doing, though equating existence with life; and it is not to claim in general that existence is more valuable than another given value. If existence is higher than other values, its being higher means being logically or ontologically prior. Any axiology that may be relevant to our argument is not a matter of value in general. It is restricted to the value of existence and non-existence *for the existent*. That is why "democracy" is an apt term here. Each and every existent has a vote, at least by proxy.

We have remarked that the hallowing that is owed to existents as existents is in danger of being eclipsed by the hallowing of God, somewhat as we are liable to be rendered blind to the holiness of this world and to our responsibilities to our fellows and all other things in it by preoccupation with a future that is, in Rilke's words, "beyond the future." "Talk of heaven! You disgrace earth," writes Thoreau in the same vein.[34] Anyone predisposed to question the point of this aphorism may object that in saying what I have just said about being distracted by God from the honor due to existents I am failing to acknowledge the honor due to God as one among these existents, and that I am therefore contradicting myself. The reply to that objection is that God is not an existent. In the words of Kierkegaard cited earlier,[35] "God does not exist." So God is not a competitor for honor with existents. Not that honor is necessarily thinned when honor is spread. But it is a second-class and derivative honor that we do to the world or things in it if we do it only because we think of the world or things in it as the works of a divine Creator. We are not honoring the world for its own sake.

It may be objected also that the argument I have just put forward is a two-edged sword. I argued that because God is not an existent we cannot be charged with inconsistency and prejudice in maintaining that justice calls to be done to all existents as existents. But if God is not an existent, how can we hold that directing good will toward Him runs the risk of diverting our good will from the world? The response to this must be to point to the fact that many theists who have difficulty thinking of their God otherwise than as an existent still betray no signs of recognizing that an attempt to think otherwise may be called for. The difficulty is one they share with non-theists. It is the counterpart of the difficulty of thinking of the world as other than an existent—of thinking of it as being more than it is. This is so deep a difficulty that Kant calls it a transcendental illusion. It is a pitfall that, I confess, may not have been always avoided when in preceding paragraphs recourse has been had to the hendiadys "the world or things in it," where the "or" has the sense of "or rather." Only if both the theological and the cosmological versions of this transcendental illusion are avoided can we forestall the further objection that our hope of finding a way forward—or backward or both forward and backward—to a hallowing of the world or things in it is destined to end in an idolatry in which the world itself is turned into a god.

As long as the way of thinking of God as an existent prevails there remains room for the a-theodicy outlined in this book. But, yes, that a-theodicy may turn into a theodicy once we are freed from the notion of *theos* as an existent. It may turn into a new theodicy that in some aspects is as old as some of the theologians cited by Derrida in, for example, "How to Avoid Speaking: Denials" and *Sauf le nom* and by Marion in, for example, *Dieu sans l'être, Being Given,* and *In Excess:* Dionysius the Areopagite, Gregory of Nyssa, Maximus the Confessor, and so on. If we still cannot do without that word "God," instead of construing it as the name of a present existent or existent beyond the future, we might wish to construe it as the very incoming of futurity along the lines of Derrida's revaluation of democracy in the name of what in this book has been called the archi-sublime—an archi-sublime which may be at the same time anarchi-sublime, since there is no more guarantee that its sublimity has a ground or a source than there is guarantee that a gift must have a giver. Thus construed, God, too important to be left to what used to be and widely continues to be called by that quirky scare-quoted name or unname, would be this world's being more than it is and the self-excession of language: the religious beyond the conditions imposed by religions, "justice as it promises to be, beyond what it actually is,"[36] outwith but not without law, this world's overcoming of itself from out of its future to which Derrida applies the political name "democracy."

It is the ecological implications of democracy on Derrida's construal of its unconditionality that I have sought to pursue and to mark by (on analogy with "whose" as an alternative to "of which") coining the word "whot." In this pursuit I have been doing little more than spelling out what Derrida writes when, in the names of birth, and copulation, and death, we have said what we have said in Part Three of this essay regarding the most elementary forms of religious life. In the section of chapter 15 which combined these names in its title I wrote:

> I do not expect that all of the happenings alluded to by that [title] will be regarded as potentially religious by all of my readers. I do expect that many of my readers will regard none of them as that. The best I can do is argue that these are candidates for the epithet "religious," hoping that by the time they reach the end of this book some of its as yet unpersuaded readers will regard as sacred and sacramental some of those elementary events and eventual elements, at the very least the passage from life to death of a loved one or friend.

I said that the best I could do would be to *argue* this.

But there may be something better than this best. In the opening paragraph of this epilogue, referring to William James, I wrote:

"whereas the descriptions of personal religious experiences he analyzes frequently make references to God from the very first lecture and throughout its successors, I have sought to postpone such references for as long as I can. I have done this in the faith that there is an area of human experience the religious character of which is not dependent on the invocation of God and is not necessarily that of an organized religion."

I said that I had done this in a certain *faith*. Like all faith, that certain faith is not certain. In writing in that faith I was being faithful to Derrida in his declared faithfulness to Kierkegaard. That is why readers of this book may, like its first reader, have been struck by the thought that the weakest parts of it are those where it argues regarding those very elementary forms of religious life on the borderline of death, say the death of a friend. On this borderline, I have said, what is said gives way to almost naked saying, to address. So, on this borderline, argument, which appeals to public rules of inference and the law of contradiction, ultimately to the sun of Enlightenment, steps aside, though without leaving the scene altogether, in order to make room for faith. In Kierkegaard's translation of the Kantian version of this transition from understanding to reason and of the Hegelian revision of the Kantian version of the transition with which it was compared in the first chapter of this book, this is a transition from the publicity of universality to the privacy of the singular. That is why Kierkegaard teaches that in matters of faith communication can be only indirect, a matter that only our addressee can decide. Perhaps that is why I may have disappointed any addressees of this book who expected me to give more reasons than I have given (if I have given any) in defense of my claim that what I have called the very elementary forms of religious life are not necessarily forms of positive religions. Such readers may be consoled, if consolation is called for, by the reminder that I said of these forms that they are forms of experiences in which the political extreme of what Derrida calls democracy to come comes to a head in the other extreme, the personal extreme. This holds too for what I have called the archi- or anarchi-sublime. Of neither, it will be recalled, can we harbor expectation. Who or what comes must be a surprise. The surprise may be astonishing. Or, as Marion says of saturated phenomena, we may be surprised to discover that the surprise is banal. Whot comes may strike us dumb with wonder or it may strike us dumb with stupor. It strikes us dumb, as one may find oneself struck on learning of the death of a friend or in witnessing his burial. I wrote that to anyone who is dead to the religiousness of the experience of the tying of a bond at the dying and death of a close relation or friend one must say that that very deadness can be an aspect of the religiousness of the experience of mourning.[37] This state of numbness and isolation amounting to epistemological solipsism is supplied with a quasi-transcendental condition when Derrida writes of the proto-narcissistic secret solitude of my unresponsive occupation of my place in the sun: "No responsiveness. Shall we call this death? Death dealt? (*La mort donnée?*) Death undergone? (*La mort reçue?*) I see no reason not to call that life, existence."[38] No responsiveness, he says, putting the noun in English. He does not say, No responsibility.

When John Austin was dying of cancer he attended a lecture on death given by Gabriel Marcel, to whom he is reported to have said after the lecture: "Professor Marcel, we all know we have to die, but why do we have to sing songs about it?"[39] Not knowledge that we have to die, but knowledge that others have to die or have died has been one of the circumstances in which it has been claimed in this book that religion may be encountered which is not necessarily the religion of an organized church, temple, or other institution. But knowledge of the death of someone else is still something about which we may find ourselves experiencing the need to sing lamentations. It is the need to make the unbearable bearable, the need to turn suffering into art that was experienced by the young Nietzsche. The need is experienced more or less urgently under all the circumstances I call, with the assistance of Emile Durkheim's title, elementary forms of religious life. These so-called forms are disruptive of form, deformative: such deformative circumstances as, to abbreviate with T. S. Eliot's Sweeney, birth, and copulation, and—the ultimate abbreviation—death. These and related circumstances relate to the borderline between another's life and death or fragility. They relate to the borderline between the beautiful that may be sung in a song and the archi- or anarchi-sublime that takes our breath away: a borderline, but, as in chapter 7 we learned that Nietzsche learned, one that is neither a *Grenze* nor a *Schranke,* but "is" the crossing at the heart of a chiasmus between two powers of the imadgination, one differing and deferring the other,[40] one, the Apollonian, driving toward integrity, the other, the Dionysian, driving toward disintegration—not to say fragmentation, lest a fragment implies a whole.[41] The anarchi-sublime comes at us, with a violence from which we may endeavor to protect ourselves by making an attempt to convert the sublime into the beautiful, the disorderly into a semblance of order, an attempt such as that which is going on at this very moment in this work. The anarchi-sublime is the drive of the raw and in every sense elementary deforming forms of religious life toward an organized religion of one form or another. But not irresistibly. There are exceptions.

## Exceptions

The quirky quasi-transcendental conditions of our unconcluding list of elementary forms of religious life are also conditions of the open-ended invention of the political and eco-political forms of what Derrida dubs "democracy to come" and that we have heralded under the name of the archi-sublime. Democracy to come, the archi-sublime, the saturative—which ceases to saturate a phenomenon and exceeds the phenomenological once it becomes Revelation—are various ways of indicating a resource that resists the suppression of the exception. Nevertheless, each of these resources may strike us either as excess or as arid banality (*pace* Charles Bigger and Robyn Horner).[42] Without implying a utopic other world, without healing all the wounds of this one, without taking as its paradigm the God who from outside His creation overflows any idea that any of his creatures may have of Him, transcendence becomes the transcendence *of* or outwith this world, the transcendence *of* or outwith immanence, the excess *of* or outwith the banal, the extraordinariness *of* or outwith the ordinary, the exceptionality *of* or outwith the normal.

Of the exceptional, Kierkegaard writes:

> In the course of time one grows weary of the perpetual patter about the universal, always the universal, repeated to the most tedious extreme of insipidity. There are exceptions. If one cannot explain them, neither can one explain the universal. Commonly one does not notice the difficulty because one does not think even the universal with passion but with an easygoing superficiality. On the other hand, the exception thinks the universal with serious (*energisk*) passion.[43]

The exception is what both makes and breaks the law. And the exception, Derrida says, is what is not taken sufficiently seriously by John Austin when he considers the exception to be extrinsic to what he would call the normal case, for instance the exceptional circumstances of words uttered on the stage rather than in "serious" discourse in "real life," or a counterfeit signature on a check—or on the title page of a book published by Kierkegaard. Austin takes the "serious" too seriously and the unserious not seriously enough, Derrida says, burlesquing Austin's and John Searle's use of the word "seriously."

At least as early as his so-called confrontation with Austin and Searle there is an anticipation of the interest Derrida will take in the political theology of Carl Schmitt.[44] That interest is attracted mainly by Schmitt's doctrines that political structures are analogous to theological ones and that the political is defined in terms of public hostility rather than private unfriendliness. But who decides which states will be enemies and which allies? Who decides which to accept and which to except? Who decides where between enemy and ally the borderline is to be drawn? This question raises again the question of the exception.

Paraphrasing Schmitt, and using him to ventriloquize his own suspicion that the distinction between a conceptual or a transcendental possibility and a real possibility or eventuality may be more difficult to make than is widely assumed, Derrida writes:

> The exception is the rule of what takes place. . . . The exception grounds the decision on the subject of the case or the eventuality. . . . An event as such is always exceptional. . . . It is, then, the improbable situation, the exceptional case (*der Ausnahmefall*), the "perhaps," perhaps, . . . which exceptionally, *qua* exception, unveils the essence, the centre and the heart of things. It is that which may not happen, that which happens only in so far as it might just as well not happen, this undecidable eventuality qua real possibility, that makes the decision and makes the truth [*fait la décision et fait la vérité*]. This undecidable decision bestows the force of unveiling. This deciding signification which unveils the kernel of things (*den Kern der Dinge enthüllende Bedeutung*) accrues to the decision.[45]

According to the first words of the first chapter of Schmitt's *Political Theology*, "Sovereign is he who decides on the exception. Only this definition can do justice to a borderline concept."[46] On Giorgio Agamben's gloss of Schmitt, the sovereign is defined as he who has the *legitimate* power to suspend the law.[47] The sovereign is within the law and outside it. So the operation of the law should be understood not simply as application, but as inclusive exclusion or, as we might say alternatively, as an included appendix, as quirky in the sense of what is not positively illegal yet at the same time is not in complete conformity with the law. The normal field of application of the law is best understood, says Agamben, in terms of the law's suspension. This brings us back to the excerpt from Kierkegaard about exception which, it so happens, is cited also by Schmitt at the end of the first chapter of *Political Theology*.

The norm is applied to the exception to the law in being disapplied to the exception. The word "exception" is to be taken here in the etymological sense of *ex-capere* and *aus-nehmen,* to take outside. We could take the verb "to except" in the sense of to take outwith, for Agamben and Schmitt would want us to resist the temptation to regard this taking outside as a taking outside the jurisdiction of one law in order to be taken inside the jurisdiction of another law promulgated in order to accommodate a certain factual state of affairs. To think along these lines would be to think along the lines of, for example, the constitution of the Weimar Republic in which a special law is promulgated to cope with a special extenuating factual circumstance such as that of something's presenting itself as a danger to public safety. Agamben seeks to demonstrate that what he calls the modern condition is one in which a new paradigm operates where the sovereign produces or wills the exception which therefore falls neither purely within the realm of fact nor purely within the realm of law. In both senses of the phrase, the sovereign lays down the law, imposes and deposes it.

How modern is this paradigm of what Agamben calls the modern condition? About as modern as the paradigm of the papal pronouncement *ex cathedra* on questions of faith or morals? Does not the simple opposition of the *quid facti* and the *quid juris* collapse there too? It collapses with any performative pronouncement, for example with the "hereby" implicit in what Derrida called the "archi-exception" he made when he declared himself willing to allow a remark of his to be cited as a blurb promoting someone else's book even though as a matter of principle, a principle to which he still held, he never provided blurbs.[48] The exception is the spirit of the law, as Paul the Apostle and sender of epistles (if not of postcards)[49] maintains when he suspends the letter of the law of the Hebrews in order that from being what according to him does little more than lay down the borderlines of sin and death it becomes the expression of faith and love inspired by what Badiou describes as "the exceptional 'but' of grace, of the event, of life."[50]

Archetypes of the archi-exceptional are the events on Mounts Moriah and Golgotha. But Derrida has told us, it will be recalled, that what happened on Moriah happens every day. We perform a sacrifice whenever we speak performatively, and whenever we speak we do that, if only *sotto voce*. Words are deeds. Suppose then that he had declined to make what he called an archi-exception in the circumstances described in chapter 13 and just recalled. He would still have made an archi-exception, an exception to a principle, albeit not an exception in favor of the author of the book in question. He would have made it in favor of someone else, perhaps in favor of himself. This happens whenever we speak, because whenever we speak the addressee is unique every time, *chaque fois singulier*. We saw that according to Carl Schmitt, "Sovereign is he who decides on the exception." That is a statement about the sovereign head of a state. It is about a sovereignty that is an application of political power. If Schmitt's words were co-opted to say what Derrida wants to say, sovereignty would have to be a disapplication of power, an application of impower, the absolute passivity that echoes the pastness inevitably appealed to in the performative activity engaged in in all acts of speech, albeit through the absolute future of the promise presupposed by them all. It would be the *sous-veraineté,* the subvereignty, of the religious unconditionality without power[51] that subjects to exceptionality the sovereignty of the power of the theology from which according to Schmitt the structures of politics arise.

> A performative produces an event only by securing for itself, in the first-person singular or plural, in the present, and with the guarantee offered by conventions or legitimated fictions, the power that an ipseity gives itself to produce the event of which it speaks—the event that it neutralizes forthwith insofar as it appropriates for itself a calculable mastery over it. If an event worthy of this name is to arrive or happen, it must, beyond all mastery, affect a passivity.[52]

It is to that passivity and to the retrospective aspect of promissory engagement that we now turn.

## Suppositions

Suppose we define a religion as, in Derrida's words, "an instituted apparatus consisting of dogmas or of articles of faith that are both determinate and inseparable from a given historical *socius* (Church, clergy, socially legitimated authority, people, shared idiom, community of the faithful commited to the same faith and sanctioning the same history)."[53] And suppose that it is of religion thus defined that Derrida is thinking when he invites us to "Suppose, *concesso non dato,* that religion has the slightest relation (*la moindre rapport*) to what we thus call God." Suppose (*concesso dato*) he means by "what we thus call God" not the God of theology and the religions but the God that will have preceded the God of theology and the religions, namely the "'nameable-un-nameable,' present-absent witness of every oath or of every possible pledge"[54] Taking not to grant a supposition as neither to deny it nor to affirm it but to leave the question of its truth open, what precisely is the concession that is not granted here by Derrida? Is what he wants to leave open the question whether there is any relation between these two Gods? But if by "what we thus call God" is meant what Derrida calls the "'nameable-unnameable,' present-absent witness of every oath or of every possible pledge," then it is the witness of the pledges made in the context of the historically instituted religions. There *is* a relation, a relation admittedly not of identity but a relation of transcendental or quasi-transcendental conditioning. Hence not to take sides regarding the truth of the supposition "that religion has the slightest relation to what we thus call God" would have to be to entertain reservations as to whether the conditioning works in the other direction, that is to say, as to whether the quasi-transcendental God invoked as a witness is conditioned by the God of historical religions. Not to grant that supposition is not to reject it, in both senses of this "not." It is to allow for an irreducible per-haps, a *peut-être* that cannot be replaced by knowledge because knowledge itself depends upon the perhaps of the faith that is intrinsic to the performativity (per-form-ativity) of promise. It may therefore be necessary to imagine another Latin *"concesso non dato"* clause inserted when later in the same paragraph Derrida invites us to consider the further supposition that we could *understand,* in a sense of understanding (*comprendre*) handed down from the modern age of Enlightenment (not the Enlightenment of the religion of the Reformation), "what-is-going-on-today-in-the-world-with-religion" and what the Modernity or Postmodernity of this today is as contrasted with Religion. To suppose that one could have an understanding of religion in the sense of understanding that sees itself to be simply opposed to the religious is to suppose a supposition that is without legitimation; it is to suppose that we can understand the ununderstandable,

comprehend the incomprehensible. Or, at least, what that modern Enlightenment understands by legitimation must be radically revised to the point where
it is seen that legitimation is without—or outwith—legitimation, because it is
quirkily "not positively illegal," but "capable o' making Law no Law at a'." Our
vision of legitimation and, with that, our understanding of understanding,
must undergo such radical revision that it is no longer totally blind to what
Derrida refers to as radical evil. What he refers to as radical evil is radical in
that it is beyond the evil that is traditionally opposed to the good. The good
beyond being is contaminated by evil the malignity of which is too deep-seated
to be uprooted by having the power of the evil genius overpowered by the
proof of the existence of God. The proof of the existence of God would be *too
good* to banish this evil, since any proof has as its point of departure the point
of reference in the name of which we name things, name or denominate even
God, and that point of reference that we name God can be neither absent nor
present. This is how Derrida endorses Kierkegaard's statement "God does not
exist." The "atheism" one might suppose to be declared in this statement is not
quite the atheism of the Enlightener, the *Aufklärer,* not if the God to which this
statement refers or fails to refer is the one that the Enlightener's light presupposes. But it can only be enlightening to discover that what that light ultimately
presupposes is not more light, not presentness to intuition such as that to which
scientific and philosophical rationality has so often traditionally aspired, but a
performatory deed of engagement. Modernist rationality and science speak the
language of Western religion, the Latin of *religio,* of binding as performed in
making a promise, notwithstanding that as soon as that promise is made it falls
under the retrospective purview of constatable history. But that is not the end
of history. For, as Austin came to see, the constative and the performative are
not mutually exclusive. Not only does a constative perform an act of speech; it
performs a constative act of speech that presupposes the making of a promise,
the entering into an agreement.

This is why the institution called religion that charges itself with the mission of protecting and promoting the holy can do so nowadays by co-opting
the profane powers of the technology of the mass media that are the product of
rationality and science. And this is why Derrida had to confess he was in the
dilemma or aporia treated in the first section of chapter 14 and why, we now see
more clearly, he could not find an exit from this by distinguishing the logical or
ontological order from the historical order of discovery. He does not deny the
usefulness of this distinction between *ordo essendi* and *ordo cognoscendi* as a
preliminary, but he is unsure about the security of the basis on which it is made.
He is unsure about the basicness of the basis and of the groundedness of the
classical notions of logical order and presupposition. This is an unsureness he
shares with Wittgenstein, and it explains why with Wittgenstein (and Nietzsche

and Collingwood) philosophy becomes descriptive or "linguistic phenomenology." It also explains the inconclusiveness of the attempt made in chapter 14 to resolve a certain friendly polemic by distinguishing between historical religions and the religiousness of quasi-transcendental conditions. We now see more clearly why this distinction is not clear. We now see too why it might be said that the confrontation between Derrida and Austin and Searle over the status of the pseudo was a pseudo-confrontation and why from it too we learn that the exceptional is something that happens every day.

Austin focuses less on *langue* than on *parole,* acts of speech, although in doing so he is following the hint Wittgenstein gives when he says that words are deeds. Neither of these philosophers simply opposes the terms of Saussure's distinction between *langue* and *parole.* They both recognize that these are abstractions from *langage,* language in use. So too does Derrida. His attention to the performance of acts of speech discovers that these are acts of religion. They are this not necessarily within the context of instituted religions, but in the institutive acts of binding, the *religāre* that is common to religion and to reason because presupposed by any address, whether from a pulpit or from a professor of philosophy's rostrum or desk (for example the desk represented on the postcard of the picture by Matthew Paris), whether uttered across a laboratory workbench, e-mailed, spoken in direct speech face to face with any interlocutor, or texted or telephoned or telegraphed.

Indeed all address is telephonic or telegraphic in that it is *tele*-communication, communication at a distance. To begin with, address is at the distance by which the implicit or explicit promise to be truthful addressed to whosoever addresses me is separated from the witness called on to guarantee any such promise. That first and last witness before whom I promise has been always already before me like a specter, a ghost, a spirit. This is the ghost that haunts the Holy Ghost, the spirit that haunts the Holy Spirit, but with a holiness that is tainted, a holiness that makes it difficult to keep holiness wholly safe from the sacred as Levinas sometimes wishes to do. Levinas wishes to do this because the sacred has always been prone to pollution, paganization, and profanity. The word given in swearing and swearing in, answearing, answering to the other, responding, is liable to turn into a swear-word and the gift of the word into a poisoned, *vergiftet,* chalice.

The presence of the first and last witness is an infinite absence, always behind us and always to come. Expressed in Levinas's terms, the apriority of this witness is that of the Saying (*Dire*) before and after the saying (*dire*) that is opposed to the said (*dit*). In Derrida's neo-Austinian terms, the distance of this apriority is the immeasurable distance by which my *hereby* is preceded by a *Thereby.* In the terms of the Hebrew Bible, it is my always having been passed by God, the One in whose name one promises. The reported deaths of the Judeo-Christian God are incidental and passing representations of God's absolute pastness and of the absolute pastness invoked in the testimony human beings make to each other every day.[55]

## Testaments

Testimony, *testis,* test, unless it is such an exceptional testimony as was made before God by Abraham on Moriah or in the "Thy will be done" of the *amor fati* of Christ on Golgotha, is testification before a third party, a *tertius,* who is mortal and moribund, a third who is bound to die. It is also a testament, a certification forwarded by a mortal.[56] Without the boundness and boundedness to the boundary line of death there is no binding. In making a promise to you I invoke the witness and withness of a we that calls upon a her or a him who could call on other others. But they, all these others, call upon another that is wholly other, *tout autre.* This is the other or Other that we have learned, perhaps like Kierkegaard from our father or Father, to call God—so that, after all, Moriah and Golgotha are not such exceptions as we supposed, supposing that an exception can have a such. Whether or not this totally Other that we have learned to call God is the God of a particular instituted religion, the religion is the religion of the living: "The religion of the living—is this not a tautology?"[57] The living here are those who address to one another the living word. That livingness depends on the enactment of pledges that we can be relied on to repeat in the future. They are pledges from whose bindingness we are not released even by our death. Our death is intrinsic to their life. So too is the death of God as the absolute other in whose name those pledges are made, the God that is figured in the passed God whose face Moses is prohibited from seeing. As Derrida writes, in the trace of Kierkegaard, if that God were always present, there would be no place for acts of faith.[58] There is a place for the sworn word without which words are dead letters. But there is such a place only in the presence of the absence of God that we may in the trace of Levinas call Illeity and in the trace of Plato *chōra*—the empty place, the vacant holy of holies, the touchstone that cannot be touched, the stone on which one reads the dead letters of the encrypted inscription of life.

Hence the non-existence of God proclaimed by Kierkegaard in good faith. Hence the living death and dying life of this God, a *deus ex machina* the putative purity of whose holiness—*kadosh,* distance—is distanced from itself by the distance of telegraphy. Hence the "quasi-transcendental addressing machine" which, according to Derrida's essay "Faith and Knowledge," injects life into death and vice-versa. This is the engine that takes over the work of motivation that Hegel and Sartre attribute to negation in their conceptions of dialectic.

Dialectic is displaced by destinerrance, the "errant cause" that explains why the missives of *The Post Card* are never quite returned to their sender and why who their readers will be defeats all prediction. In that book, it was noted in chapter 13, Derrida proposed to distance each slab of writing by the "clever cryptogram" of fifty-two mute spaces. It is not evident that that encryption is fully decrypted by taking this number as the number of the weeks to an anniversary, the time it takes for a complete revolution of the sun or the moon. What is evident, nevertheless, is that a seemingly lunatic recourse to calculation is taking place here, one whose madness is made to appear madder when we notice that that number, fifty-two, is also the number of sections into which he decides to divide his paper "Faith and Knowledge," and that halving that number yields the number of the letters of the English alphabet and of the sections in Derrida's commentary on Austin and Searle in *Limited Inc.* Calculation is given low marks by Hegel and Heidegger. Derrida too is alert to its dangers. Perhaps the purpose of his games with numbers is to bring to our attention that, despite these dangers, we sometimes have to say *calculemus,* let us count. Maybe their purpose is to show that although numbers are not obviously vehicles of life, that although they are the shell rather than the nucleus, particularly when they are employed cryptogrammatically or in clear and without guile to formulate a program to be applied mechanically, we cannot avoid doing arithmetic at a certain stage even where what is at stake are decisions regarding matters of morals and faith, least of all where what is at stake is distributive justice. As is maintained by Kierkegaard, to whom Derrida says he has been most faithful, these decisions remain underdetermined. They are always made in faith, in the name of a *deus ex machina:* "*both* calculation *and* the incalculable *are necessary.* . . . I would say that what is 'reasonable' is the reasoned and considered wager of a transaction between these apparently irreconcilable exigencies of reason, between calculation and the incalculable."[59]

Of the essay "Faith and Knowledge" Derrida writes in a note added fifty-two weeks or so after its delivery, "This, perhaps, is what I would have liked to say of a certain Mount Moriah." So what he would have liked to say of that hill would be what he would have liked to say regarding Johannes de Silentio, de Silentio's silence and Abraham's, and regarding the exception. But we have heard him say too that what happened on Mount Moriah happens every day. It happens whenever we are faced by the boundaries of life and death marked throughout the third part of this book on the margins of religion by the words "birth, and copulation, and death" borrowed from the eponymous anti-hero of T. S. Eliot's *Sweeney Agonistes*—who says, "Death is life, life is death." It happens especially whenever we experience what Martin Buber calls "that special intimacy which binds us at times to the dead and to them alone."[60] It happens after the death of a friend. That experience and the experiences on the boundary bound up with it in the family of experiences indicated by Sweeney's words are not necessarily experiences of the religiousness of historically instituted religions which, in order to effect at least a partial rapprochement between friends, we found it important in chapter 14 to distinguish from the religiousness of the quasi-transcendental conditions reviewed in subsequent chapters and in this epilogue. They are experiences of the religious imadgination. If the imagination is the "faculty" of "this little word 'as'" (Derrida),[61] of the "as if," the "quasi," and of the "if . . . then" that haunt "the little word 'is'" (Kant)[62] and make existence iffy (Austin),[63] if it is the place of conditionality and supposition (whether conceded or withheld, *dato* or *non dato*), the imadgination with a letter d is this *dunamis,* this power, as overpowered by whatever addresses it unconditionally. It is the place (perhaps *chōra*) of the "perhaps," the "*peut-être,*" where reason and energetic passion—passion that both comes over one and moves one to act—are not yet opposed to each other, between the religiousness of quasi-transcendental conditions and the religiousness (A or B) of any historically instituted religion, between the Derrida who is said to pass for an atheist and the Kierkegaard who passes for a Christian.

Because the elementary forms of religious life referred to in the abbreviation "birth, and copulation, and death," for instance the death of a friend, are more elementary than the empirically historical religions, would they be safe from the aporetic difficulty of keeping the quasi-transcendental conditions safe from intrusion by the empirico-historical forms of those religions? Or would they be all the more endangered because not protected by the shielding shell of a religion nor mastered within an aesthetics of the beautiful, but exposed to the unconsolatory aesthethics of singular responsibility toward the archi-sublime? They would at least be shielded from the danger of being thus shielded. And salvation from that danger is the effect, the "errant effect," of archi-sublimity. The religiousness of the dispositions and experiences summarized in the words "birth, and copulation, and death" was shown earlier in this book to occupy a margin between the quasi-transcendental conditions of religion and instituted religions.[64] It was argued there that the religiousness of those dispositions and experiences is connected with the possibility of their being matters of life-sacrificing love. It was conceded that in making this connection I am inviting the comment that I am thereby reading into the religious the character of at least one historical religion, for example that according to which love is the imitation of Christ.

Is not this comment one that Derrida has made at least indirectly? Is it not implicit in his contention that what passes for secularist Enlightenment borrows the Latinate language of Christianity? However, that one borrows that language leaves open whether in that language one affirms or denies a creed or at least a fragmentary clause of a creed that is couched in it. Both affirmation and denial of a creed suppose shared concepts. Nevertheless, it is arguable that a secular Enlightenment that denied or ignored the credal clauses that inform, say, Christianity, might at least be in practical contradiction with itself, that is to say, a contradiction not directly between two propositions, but indirectly between something said and a fact implied in the saying of it. Such a contradiction, a practical or pragmatic contradiction, is a step nearer to the affirmation that is neither the affirmation of a belief nor the denial of that belief but is the affirmation that throughout this book has been called, following Derrida and Levinas, address. Derrida refers to address as performative Yes. Levinas refers to it as Saying, *Dire,* with an upper-case initial. This address is presupposed not only by the contrast between a statement and its negation. It is presupposed also by the contrast between lower-case saying, *dire,* the speech act, and a proposition that may be said, the *dit.* It is the absolute presupposition of any position. And it is address that is the strongest candidate for being considered as what is common across the multiplicity of languages, in particular the languages in which the creeds of this or that religion are couched. But its commonness would be its being beyond the common, its being, for example in this very text now, the moment that is unique, singular, and exceptional.

In address I address myself, perhaps in something like the Greek or Sanskrit middle voice, to someone, *je m'adresse à quelqu'un.* Derrida is struck by the fact that in English not only someone but also something, for example a topic, can be addressed transitively.[65] In address I say something concerning something, constatively, imperatively, interrogatively, or in some other mood. In the address effected in this text at this moment an attempt is being made to say something about address. So address, as we have remarked at earlier moments of this text, is never absolutely naked. Address is never entirely without dress, stripped of the guise or disguise of language. It is therefore fitted to conceal as well as to reveal the truth. An attempt to reveal the truth about address will therefore be couched in a language that may well be in some respects the language of Christianity; and, as Derrida insists, for us in the World Wide Web of the West today the language that predominates is the Latinate language of Christianity. That does not mean that its Latin has lost every trace of a Greek accent, the accent in which Levinas endeavors to say something that might seem to be more readily sayable in Hebrew, at the threshold of the home, wherever home is, waiting for the arrival of the complete stranger, the completely strange stranger who may speak a language we do not understand. At the threshold of the *oikos,* which may mean at the edge of a grave, we are at the threshold of the understanding, at the borderline where understanding is infused by passion. The calling is a religious calling, calling typically, we have argued, for the sacrifice of oneself for another that goes under the name of love. Dare one say that it is in the language of Christianity that Emmanuel Levinas hears that calling? What Levinas says about incarnation—and what Adriaan Perperzak writes in his essay "The Significance of Levinas's Work for Christian Thought"[66]—suggests that we should describe this language instead as the language of Judeo-Christianity. Doing that, performing this historical and, some would say, baleful hyphenation, brings forcefully to our attention that some of the presuppositions of this language are mutually inconsistent. Wondering what further tensions may be set up by pressures exerted on that already fissured language by the languages of Islam and other religions or non-religions cannot but teach us that what the understanding is enpassioned and calls to be astonished by is the archi-sublime imadgination which is both the chief faculty of the religious and the chief faculty of change.

Derrida once remarked that Bergson's book on the immediate data of consciousness was perhaps the first book he read in the knowledge that he was reading a philosophical text. Later writings of Bergson develop that work's concern with change and the new. These become concerns of the writings of Derrida. But Bergson's image of change and renovation is the ascending firework, the rocket, and his notion of the *élan vital* is akin to the intentionality that appertains to consciousness according to Husserlian phenomenology and to the ec-sistentiality of Heideggerian ontology. Derrida, adapting Levinas's idea of creation as proto-ethical and reversed or inverted intentionality, equates the new with the approach toward the subject, toward me, of the other, the *alter*. Change is my *alteration,* the arriving, if not the arrival of another from out of the future.[67] To paraphrase a sentence cited at the end of the first section of this epilogue, my being sent is my being converted. As the title, *Time and Freewill,* of the English translation of Bergson's book makes explicit, this is a book that treats temporality. It treats temporality primarily not as *temps,* meaning by that the spatialized time of chronology, but as *durée,* temporality as duration, as lived and endured. Still adapting Levinas, Derrida interprets duration not according to the Bergsonian image of the snowball to which fresh snow adheres as it rolls, or in the manner of Heidegger as primarily my being toward my own death; he interprets it as primarily the temporality of the death of the other. This is a time in which I am required to be just to the other with a justice that is defined by law but not only defined by law, for it is the justice of what is more than a case. And this is an impossible justice in that by being just to someone I am bound to be unjust to others. I am in a double bind. I am bound to do the impossible, bound to fall short of my responsibility. I am therefore bound to ask for forgiveness. But this forgiveness in turn is a forgiveness that cannot be given with a clear conscience. For of the other too is required a justice to other others that is more than the justice that consists in repaying a debt. Furthermore, it is only according to such an economic justice that I can count myself among those other others.

If, as Carl Schmitt says, the sovereign is the one who decides on the exception, and if, as Agamben puts it, that decision is legitimate, the decision is at the same time illegitimate in the sense that the illegitimacy of the exception is legitimized by the authority of the sovereign, who, Schmitt and Agamben agree, is both within and without the law. The sovereign is, as we might say, quirkily outwith the law. But Schmitt and Agamben are analyzing circumstances that relate to exceptions to the laws of nations and states, where the exception is definable by predicates that reflect matters of fact. With their analyses it is the opposition between the *quid juris* and the *quid facti* that is shaken. With the predicament that Derrida would have us face what trembles and causes us to tremble is the opposition between this deconstructed opposition and undeconstructible justice. The sovereign who decides on the exception is faced with an undecidability. To the sovereign's surprise *every* other, without exception, is discovered to be an exception. The sovereign's sovereignty is always already undone. Does this mean that whereas in the Kantian Kingdom of Ends the sovereign God is a citizen, in the Derridian democracy that is acoming every citizen is a sovereign? Only if sovereignty is indeed always already undone.

But a decision still has to be made; and urgently, for the time of the other's death and the time of my own are unforeseeable. I must respond. This is the aporia—Kierkegaard would say paradox—of a duration that has to be endured. This is why decision is mad, folly to the Greeks. If Kierkegaard and his pseudonymous authors invite their readers to imadgine how much more difficult Christianity is than Christendom is inclined to notice, Derrida and his anonymous or polyonymous senders of postcards invite their readers to imadgine the difficulty of a religiousness that comes over us archi-sublimely from out of the future, whether or not Kierkegaard or anyone else learns that there is a God because his father or his Father told him so: whether or not we embrace or are embraced by the difficulty of Christianity or any other institutional religion.

# NOTES

### 1. On the Borderline of Madness

1. Aristotle, *Metaphysics* Book XII, chapter 7, 1072b, trans. W. D. Ross, in *The Basic Works of Aristotle,* ed. Richard McKeon (New York: Random House, 1941), p. 880.

2. G. W. F. Hegel, *Science of Logic,* trans. A. V. Miller (London: Allen and Unwin, 1969), p. 50.

3. Ibid.

4. G. W. F. Hegel, *Logic,* First Part of the *Encyclopaedia of Philosophical Sciences,* trans. William Wallace (Oxford: Oxford University Press, 1975), §25, p. 45.

5. Ibid., §27, p. 46.

6. Ibid., §18, p. 23.

7. G. W. F. Hegel, *Phenomenology of Spirit,* trans. A. V. Miller (Oxford: Clarendon Press, 1979), pp. 126–38.

8. Søren Kierkegaard, *Philosophical Fragments or a Fragment of Philosophy, by Johannes Climacus,* trans. David F. Swenson, revised by Howard V. Hong (Princeton, N.J.: Princeton University Press, 1936), p. 55. Søren Kierkegaard, *Philosophical Fragments: Johannes Climacus,* ed. and trans. Howard V. Hong and Edna H. Hong (Princeton, N.J.: Princeton University Press, 1985), p. 44. I thank Alastair McKinnon and Eileen Dickson of New College Library at Edinburgh for making available to me the former's invaluable Kierkegaard Computer Workshop CD. For helping me with the technological facilities at the Søren Kierkegaard Research Centre at Copenhagen I thank Joakim Garff. I thank James Giles for pointing out to me various oversights in a draft of this chapter.

9. Søren Kierkegaard, *The Corsair Affair and Articles Related to the Writings,* ed. and trans. Howard V. Hong and Edna H. Hong (Princeton, N.J.: Princeton University Press, 1982), pp. 73–75.

10. P. A. Heiberg, V. Kuhr, and E. Torsting, eds., *Søren Kierkegaards Papirer* (Copenhagen: Gyldendal,1968–70), 13 vols.; *Søren Kierkegaard's Journals and Papers,*

ed. and trans. Howard V. Hong and Edna H. Hong, assisted by Gregor Malantschuk (Bloomington: Indiana University Press, 1967–1978), 7 vols. (henceforth *JP*), *JP* 1581, II A 808.

11. Jacques Derrida, *Glas* (Paris: Galilée, 1974); *Glas*, trans. John P. Leavey Jr. and Richard Rand (Lincoln: Nebraska University Press, 1986).

12. Kierkegaard, *JP* 4420, IV C 94.

13. Ibid., 1518, II A 808.

14. Kierkegaard, *Philosophical Fragments: Johannes Climacus,* p. 52. See 1 Cor 1:23.

15. Kierkegaard, *JP* 2236, V III 1 A 358.

16. Kierkegaard, *Philosophical Fragments or a Fragment of Philosophy, by Johannes Climacus,* p. 64.

17. Immanuel Kant, *Critique of Pure Reason,* trans. Norman Kemp Smith (London: Macmillan, 1968), p. 280.

18. Immanuel Kant, *Prolegomena to Any Future Metaphysics That Will Be Able to Present Itself as a Science,* trans. P. G. Lucas (Manchester: Manchester University Press, 1953).

19. Jacques Derrida, "Cogito and the History of Madness," in *Writing and Difference,* trans. Alan Bass (Chicago: University of Chicago Press, 1978). Michel Foucault, *Madness and Civilization: A History of Insanity in the Age of Reason,* trans. Richard Howard (New York: Pantheon, 1965).

20. Claude Lévi-Strauss, *The Savage Mind* (London: Weidenfeld and Nicolson, 1966).

21. See Daniel Berthold-Bond, *Hegel's Theory of Madness* (Albany: State University of New York Press, 1995).

22. G. W. F. Hegel, *Phenomenology of Spirit,* trans. A. V. Miller (Oxford: Clarendon Press, 1977), p. 226.

23. Derrida, *Writing and Difference,* p. 63.

24. Ibid., p. 59.

25. Ibid., p. 62.

26. Ibid., p. 62.

27. Ibid., p. 37.

28. Immanuel Kant, *Anthropology from a Pragmatic Point of View,* trans. Mary J. Gregor (The Hague: Nijhoff, 1974), p. 88. Only the parentheses around the German expressions are added.

29. Kierkegaard, *JP* 1070, IV A 46.

30. Ibid., 3198, X 2 A 441.

31. But on friendliness see Jacques Derrida, *Politiques de l'amitié* (Paris: Galilée, 1994); *Politics of Friendship,* trans. George Collins (London: Verso, 1997).

32. Kierkegaard, *JP* 491, IX A 360.

33. Jacques Derrida, *Spectres de Marx: L'état de la dette, le travail du deuil et la nouvelle Internationale* (Paris: Galilée, 1993), p. 19 and passim; *Specters of Marx: The State of the Debt, the Work of Mourning, and the New International,* trans. Peggy Kamuf (New York: Routledge, 1994), p. 3 and *passim.*

34. Søren Kierkegaard, *The Point of View on My Work as an Author,* ed. and trans. Howard V. Hong and Edna H. Hong (Princeton, N.J.: Princeton University Press, 1998), pp. 129–41.

35. Ibid., pp. 50–56.

36. Kierkegaard, *JP* 1300, X3 A 499. Compare: "If my genius can be said to be connected with anything, it is with being in the minority" (Kierkegaard, *JP* 6260, A 307), and the observation that he would have been "regarded as a genius of the first rank" in any other country, but "by being born in a demoralized provincial town quite logically turned out to be a sort of Mad Meyer" (Kierkegaard, *JP* 6382, X1 A 247). Of Mad Meyer the editors of *JP* note: "Presumably Edvard Meyer (1813–80), journalist, founder of the humor paper *Kjøbenhavns Morskabsblad* (1842), a competitor of Goldschmidt's *Corsaren*. Meyer himself and his activities had something of a comical cast, and he was the object of jokes by students and others. See *Corsaren*, 407, July 7, 1848, col. 11."

37. Søren Kierkegaard *The Concept of Anxiety: A Simple Psychologically Orienting Deliberation on the Dogmatic Issue of Hereditary Sin,* trans. Reidar Thomte in collaboration with Albert B. Anderson (Princeton, N.J.: Princeton University Press, 1980), p. 108; Kierkegaard, *JP* 623, V A 19.

38. Kierkegaard, *JP* 5695, IV A 154.

39. Ibid., 1029, IV A 148.

40. For a discussion of difficulties concerning the connection between what Kierkegaard says about suffering in the context of Christianity and his account of anxiety see James Giles, "Kierkegaard's Leap: Anxiety and Freedom," in *Kierkegaard and Freedom,* ed. James Giles (Basingstoke, England: Palgrave, 2000).

41. Kierkegaard, *JP* 6518, X 5 B 206.

42. Søren Kierkegaard, *Fear and Trembling,* ed. and trans. Howard V. Hong and Edna H. Hong (Princeton, N.J.: Princeton University Press, 1983), pp. 82–83.

43. Kierkegaard, *JP* V B 6: 16, *Philosophical Fragments,* pp. 99ff.

44. Ibid., 3085, X 2 A 389.

45. Ibid., 5981, VIII 1 A 33, *JP* 5983–5986, VIII 1 A 35–38.

46. Søren Kierkegaard, *The Book on Adler,* trans. Howard V. Hong and Edna H. Hong (Princeton, N.J.: Princeton University Press, 1998), p. 107. *The Book on Adler* is also a book on Hegel, whether or not with Derrida we pronounce the German's name as the French do and thereby assimilate it to *"aigle"* or "eagle," that is to say, "Adler."

47. Kierkegaard, *JP* 2236, VIII 1 A 358.

48. As we are reminded by the title of Joakim Garff's monumental *SAK: Søren Aabye Kierkegaard. En Biografi* (Copenhagen: Gads Forlag, 2000).

49. Kierkegaard, *JP* 844, X 2 A 617.

50. Søren Kierkegaard, *Either/Or: A Fragment of Life,* trans. Walter Lowrie, 2 vols. (London: Oxford University Press, 1946), vol. 2, p. 179.

51. I am grateful to Jacques Derrida for drawing my attention to this text.

52. Derrida, "Violence and Metaphysics," in *Writing and Difference,* p. 110.

53. Kierkegaard, *Either/Or,* p. 179.

54. Kierkegaard, *JP* 1070, IV A 46.

55. Ibid., 491, IX A 360.

56. Ibid., 3035, X 2 A 389.

57. Søren Kierkegaard, *Practice in Christianity,* ed. and trans. Howard V. Hong and Edna H. Hong (Princeton, N.J.: Princeton University Press, 1991), p. 81, note.

58. Ibid., p. 139.

59. Kierkegaard, *The Corsair Affair,* p. 74.

60. Kierkegaard, *Practice in Christianity,* pp. 23–68.

61. Ludwig Wittgenstein, "A Lecture on Ethics," *The Philosophical Review* 74, no. 1 (January 1965): 8, cited by D. Z. Phillips, "Self-Deception and Freedom in Kierke-

gaard's *Purity of Heart*," in Giles, *Kierkegaard and Freedom*, p. 168. In this essay Phillips argues that the distinction between morality and immorality does not coincide with the distinction between single-mindedness and double-mindedness. His citation from Wittgenstein is followed by one from Kierkegaard: "How wonderful, here is a border-line (*Grænse*), a borderline that is invisible, like a line that is easy to overlook with the senses, but one that has the strength of eternity in resisting any infringement" (*Purity of Heart Is to Will One Thing*, trans. Douglas Steere [New York: Harper, 1958], p. 97). Refer-ring apparently both to what Kierkegaard says and to what Wittgenstein says, Phillips writes: "All seem to testify to a freedom in the midst of affliction." Need descriptions of moral situations where freedom seems not to survive affliction undermine Wittgen-stein's avowal of a feeling, or Kierkegaard's oblique references to first-personal passion? And, as we have noted, according to Kierkegaard the paradox of the higher freedom that goes with the higher madness is that one reaches it only by being unfree. "In order truly to be a great genius a man must be the exception. But in order that there shall be seriousness in being the exception, he must himself be unfree, forced into it. Herein lies the significance of his dementia" (Kierkegaard, *JP* 1300, X 3 A 499).

## 2. Stay!

1. Immanuel Kant, *Critique of Practical Reason and Other Works on the Theory of Ethics*, trans. Thomas Kingsmill Abbott (London: Longmans, 1909), p. 181.

2. Immanuel Kant, *Fundamental Principles of the Metaphysic of Morals*, in ibid., p. 41.

3. Ibid.

4. Ibid., p. 181.

5. Ibid., p. 38.

6. Ibid., p. 181.

7. Emmanuel Levinas, *Noms propres* (Montpellier: Fata Morgana, 1976), p. 108; *Proper Names*, trans. Michael B. Smith (London: Athlone, 1996), p. 74.

8. Emmanuel Levinas, *Totalité et Infini: Essai sur l'extériorité* (The Hague: Ni-jhoff, 1961), p. 188; *Totality and Infinity: An Essay on Exteriority*, trans. Alphonso Lingis (The Hague: Nijhoff, 1969), p. 213.

9. Levinas, *Noms propres*, p. 109, *Proper Names*, p. 74.

10. Wilfred Owen, "The Parable of the Old Man and the Young," in *The Poems of Wilfred Owen*, Jon Stallworthy, ed. (London: Chatto and Windus, 1990), p. 151.

11. Jacques Derrida, *Donner la mort*, in *L'éthique du don* (Paris: Metalié-Transi-tion, 1992), p. 97; *The Gift of Death*, trans. David Wills (Chicago: University of Chicago Press, 1995), p. 67.

12. Ibid., pp. 118, 85.

13. Jan Patočka, *Essais hérétiques sur la philosophie de l'histoire* (Paris: Verdier, 1981).

14. Derrida, *Donner la mort*, p. 99, *The Gift of Death*, p. 69.

15. Ibid., pp. 101, 71.

16. Jacques Derrida, *Passions* (Paris: Galilée, 1993), p. 81, note 5, "Passions," trans. David Wood, in *Derrida: A Critical Reader*, ed. David Wood (Oxford: Blackwell, 1992), p. 30, note 6, "Passions," trans. David Wood, in *On the Name* (Stanford, Calif.: Stanford University Press, 1995), p. 137, note 5.

17. Gabriel Marcel, *Being and Having*, trans. Katherine Farrer (London: Dacre Press, 1949), p. 171.

18. Derrida, *Donner la mort,* p. 110, *The Gift of Death,* p. 78.

19. Søren Kierkegaard, *Fear and Trembling,* trans. Howard V. Hong and Edna H. Hong (Princeton, N.J.: Princeton University Press, 1983), p. 74; *Upbuilding Discourses in Various Spirits,* trans. Howard V. Hong and Edna H. Hong (Princeton, N.J.: Princeton University Press, 1993), p. 223.

20. John Nolland, *World Biblical Commentary,* vol. 35B, Luke 9:21–18:34 (Dallas, Tex.: World Books, 1993), p. 762.

21. Jacques Derrida, *On Cosmopolitanism and Forgiveness,* trans. Mark Dooley and Michael Hughes (London: Routledge, 2001), p. 55.

22. *Søren Kierkegaards Papirer,* ed. P. A. Heiberg, V. Kuhr, and E. Torsting (Copenhagen: Gyldendal, 1968–70), 13 vols.; *Søren Kierkegaard's Journals and Papers,* ed. and trans. Howard V. Hong and Edna H. Hong, assisted by Gregor Malantschuk (Bloomington: Indiana University Press, 1967–1978), 5981, VIII, I, A, 33. See also Robert Gibbs, "I or You—the Dash of Ethics," in Elsebet Jegstrup, ed., *The New Kierkegaard* (Bloomington: Indiana University Press, 2004).

23. Jacques Derrida, *Politiques de l'amitié* (Paris: Galilée, 1994), especially chapters 6 and 9; *Politics of Friendship,* trans. George Collins (London: Verso, 1997).

24. Anders Nygren, *Agape and Eros,* trans. Philip S. Watson (London: S. P. C. K., 1953), p. 30.

25. K. J. Dover, *Greek Homosexuality* (London: Duckworth, 1978), p. 50. I thank David Robinson for bringing this book to my attention.

26. Gottfried Quell and Ethelbert Stauffer, *Love* (London: Adam and Charles Black, 1949), p. 33.

27. Derrida, *Donner la mort,* p. 107, *The Gift of Death,* p. 75

28. Derrida, *Passions,* p. 31, "Passions," *Derrida: A Critical Reader,* p. 11, *On the Name,* p. 12.

29. Jacques Derrida, *Points de suspension: Entretiens,* chosen and presented by Elisabeth Weber (Paris: Galilée, 1992), p. 209.

30. Ibid., p. 212.

31. Jacques Derrida, *Le toucher: Jean-Luc Nancy* (Paris: Galilée, 2000), p. 94.

32. Levinas, *Totalité et Infini,* p. 232, *Totality and Infinity,* p. 254.

33. Simone Weil, *Gravity and Grace,* trans. Emma Craufurd and Mario von der Ruhr (London: Routledge and Kegan Paul, 2002), p. 15.

34. Cited by Jean-Luc Marion, *Prolégomènes à la charité,* 2nd ed. (Paris: La Différence, 1986), p. 92.

35. Jacques Derrida, *"Foi et savoir: Les deux sources de la 'religion' aux limites de la simple raison,"* in Jacques Derrida and Gianni Vattimo, *La religion* (Paris: Seuil, 1996), pp. 27–28; "Faith and Knowledge: The Two Sources of 'Religion' at the Limits of Reason Alone," trans. Samuel Weber, in *Acts of Religion,* ed. Gil Anidjar (New York: Routledge, 2002), p. 56; *Spectres de Marx* (Paris: Galilée, 1993), p. 56; *Specters of Marx,* trans. Peggy Kamuf (New York: Routledge, 1994), p. 28.

36. Jacques Derrida, "Hostipitality," in *Acts of Religion;* Jacques Derrida, *Cosmopolites de tous les pays, encore un effort!* (Paris: Galilée, 1997); "On Cosmopolitanism," trans. Mark Dooley and Michael Hughes, in *On Cosmopolitanism and Forgiveness, "Le principe de l'hospitalité,"* in *Papier machine* (Paris: Galilée, 2001); *Anne Dufourmantelle invite Jacques Derrida à répondre de l'hospitalité* (Paris: Calmann-Lévy, 1997).

37. See Émile Benveniste, *Indo-European Language and Society,* trans. Elizabeth Palmer (London: Faber and Faber, 1973), chapter 7.

38. Emmanuel Levinas, *Autrement qu'être ou au-delà de l'essence* (The Hague: Nijhoff, 1978), p. 71; *Otherwise than Being or Beyond Essence,* trans. Alphonso Lingis (The Hague: Nijhoff, 1981), p. 55.

39. Martin Heidegger, *Being and Time,* trans. John Macquarrie and Edward Robinson (Oxford: Blackwell, 1967), trans. Joan Stambaugh (Albany: State University of New York Press, 1996), p. 275.

40. Jacques Derrida, *Politiques de l'amitié,* pp. 42, 259, *Politics of Friendship,* pp. 24, 232.

41. Levinas, *Noms propres,* p. 115, *Proper Names,* p. 79.

### 3. Philosophical Fragments

1. Søren Kierkegaard, *Concluding Unscientific Postscript,* trans. David F. Swenson and Walter Lowrie (Princeton, N.J.: Princeton University Press, 1941), p. 314; *Concluding Unscientific Postscript to "Philosophical Fragments,"* trans. Howard V. Hong and Edna H. Hong, 2 vols. (Princeton, N.J.: Princeton University Press, 1992), vol. 1, p. 351. The hungry monster is the big bird, the eagle, that is named when the name of Hegel is pronounced in French, the *aigle* whose eyrie is named in the second syllable of *Glassaire,* the French version of the title of *Glassary* (Lincoln: University of Nebraska Press 1986), to the compiler of which, John P. Leavey Jr., I hereby express my indebtedness. For their comments on this chapter I am grateful to Robert Gibbs, James Giles, Anders Klitgaard, Per Krogh Hansen, Roy Sellars, and other participants in the research seminar and symposium on *Glas* held at Koldinghus, Kolding, on 25–26 May 2001.

2. Jacques Derrida, *Glas,* trans. John P. Leavey Jr. and Richard Rand (Lincoln: Nebraska University Press, 1986), 200ai; *Glas* (Paris: Galilée, 1974), 224ai-25ai.

3. Søren Kierkegaard, *Two Ages,* trans. Howard V. Hong and Edna H. Hong (Princeton, N.J.: Princeton University Press, 1978), p. 99.

4. Jacques Derrida, *Spectres de Marx: l'état de la dette, le travail du deuil et la nouvelle internationale* (Paris: Galilée, 1993); *Specters of Marx: The State of the Debt, the Work of Mourning and the New International,* trans. Peggy Kamuf (London: Routledge, 1994).

5. For sincere hypocrisy, see John Llewelyn, *The HypoCritical Imagination: Between Kant and Levinas* (London: Routledge, 2000). For a remark on Derrida's recognition of this further significance of SA or s.a., see Jacques Derrida, "Limited Inc, a b c . . . ," trans. Samuel Weber, *Glyph* 2 (1977): 254, and note, "Limited Inc, a b c . . . ," Supplement to *Glyph* 2 (1977): 81, in *Limited Inc,* trans. Samuel Weber and Jeffrey Mehlman (Evanston, Ill.: Northwestern University Press, 1988), pp. 109–10. See also *Glassary,* pp. 29–30.

6. Derrida, *Glas,* 119bi (136bi).

7. Søren Kierkegaard, *Stages on Life's Way,* trans. Howard V. Hong and Edna H. Hong (Princeton, N.J.: Princeton University Press, 1983), p. 463.

8. Kierkegaard, *Concluding Unscientific Postscript,* p. 85 (vol. 1, p. 92).

9. Derrida, *Glas,* 233ai (260ai).

10. Ibid., pp. 291–92. I am reminded by this of the way the index of my copy of Burton's *The Anatomy of Melancholy* gives half a dozen references to Tertullian and then contents itself with a weary "etc."

11. Kierkegaard, *Stages on Life's Way,* p. 442.

12. Søren Kierkegaard, *Fear and Trembling: A Dialectical Lyric by Johannes de silentio,* trans. Robert Payne (Oxford: Oxford University Press, 1939), p. 126, trans. How-

ard V. Hong and Edna H. Hong (Princeton, N.J.: Princeton University Press, 1988), p. 86.

13. Kierkegaard, *Stages,* p. 446.

14. Søren Kierkegaard, *The Book on Adler,* trans. Howard V. Hong and Edna H. Hong (Princeton, N.J.: Princeton University Press, 1998), pp. 37, 355.

15. Neil Douglas-Klotz, *The Genesis Meditations: A Shared Practice of Peace for Christians, Jews, and Muslims* (Wheaton, Ill.: Quest, 2003), p. 48.

16. Søren Kierkegaard, *Either/Or: A Fragment of Life,* trans. Walter Lowrie, 2 vols. (London: Oxford University Press, 1946), vol. 2, pp. 216–17.

17. Derrida, *Glas,* 110a (126a).

18. G. W. F. Hegel, *Jenaer Schriften, Werke,* 20 vols. (Frankfurt am Main: Suhrkamp, 1970), vol. 2. p. 522: "*sie (die Philosophie) die Ansicht der Einzelheit und Zufälligkeit so aufhebt, dass sie von ihr zeigt, wie sie das Leben nicht an sich hindert, sondern das dieses, indem es sie bestehen lässt, wie sie nach der Notwendigkeit ist, sie doch zugleich dieser entreisst, sie durchdringt und belebt.*"

19. Derrida, *Glas,* 110b, 121b (127b, 139b).

20. For a transaccidentiation of the wine that leads to an unorthodox doctrine of transubstantiation, see Jean Genet, *Story of the Eye,* trans. Joachim Neugroschel (New York: Urizen, 1977), p. 87, cited on p. 78 of *Glassary*: "And as for the wine they put in the chalice, the ecclesiastics say it is the blood of Christ, but they are obviously mistaken. If they really thought it was blood, they would use *red* wine, but since they employ only *white* wine, they are showing that at the bottom of their hearts they are quite aware that this is urine."

21. Derrida, *Glas,* 162a (183a). For further rumination of the glutinous and the doughy (*dejgagtig*) see, relevantly not only to the White Knight but also to the Knight of Faith, Roy Sellars's sublime *communication* on non-communication "'As If His Mouth Were Full of Dough': Lewis Carroll and the Gagging of Metaphysics," Colloque Lewis Carroll, University of Nancy II, November 1999.

22. G. W. F. Hegel, *Wissenschaft der Logik, Werke,* vol. 5, pp. 113–14; *Science of Logic,* trans. A. V. Miller (London: Allen and Unwin, 1969), p. 107.

23. Derrida, *Glas,* 232ai–33ai (259ai–60ai).

24. Ibid., 54a–55a (65a). See note 1 above.

25. Kierkegaard, *The Book on Adler,* p. 298, citing *Søren Kierkegaards Papirer,* ed. P. A. Heiberg, V. Kuhr, and E. Torsting, 13 vols. (Copenhagen: Gyldendal,1968–1970); *Søren Kierkegaard's Journals and Papers,* ed. and trans. Howard V. Hong and Edna H. Hong, assisted by Gregor Malantschuk, 7 vols. (Bloomington: Indiana University Press, 1967–1978) (henceforth *JP*), VIII 2 B 9:10 2. Kierkegaard's reason for saying that theft in the world of the mind is impossible may be that mind is either ultimately mine, springing from my incommunicable choice of myself, or that when mind is regarded Hegelianly as Concept, the distinction between mine and thine is abolished.

26. G. W. F. Hegel, *Phänomenologie des Geistes, Werke,* vol. 3, pp. 132–34; *Phenomenology of Spirit,* trans. A. V. Miller (Oxford: Oxford University Press, 1970), pp. 100–101.

27. For comments on Tertullian I am indebted to the late John O'Neill.

28. Derrida, *Glas,* 227a–28a (254a).

29. James Hutchison Stirling, *The Secret of Hegel, Being the Hegelian System of Origin, Principle, Form and Matter* (Edinburgh: Oliver and Boyd, 1898).

30. Kierkegaard, *Concluding Unscientific Postscript,* p. 107 (vol. 1, p. 118).

31. Aristotle, *De interpretatione* 17a. For a different interpretation of Aristotle here see Martin Heidegger, *Die Grundbegriffe der Metaphysik—Welt—Endlichkeit—Einsamkeit* (Frankfurt am Main: Klostermann, 1997); *The Fundamental Concepts of Metaphysics: World, Finitude, Solitude,* trans. William McNeill and Nicholas Walker (Bloomington: Indiana University Press, 1995), §73.

32. Kierkegaard, *Concluding Unscientific Postscript,* pp. 383, 385 (vol. 1, pp. 428, 430).

33. Kierkegaard, *Fear and Trembling,* p. 93 (p. 65).

34. It should give one pause that the Greek refers to the offense of this stumbling block in the middle voice: *skandalizesthai.* For the Jew it is not reason that is offended. The offense is rather a matter of passion, but a passion where offense is *taken.* There are passions and passions. See Jacques Derrida, *Passions* (Paris: Galilée, 1993); "Passions," trans. David Wood, in *Jacques Derrida: A Critical Reader,* ed. David Wood (Oxford: Blackwell, 1992), pp. 5–35, trans. David Wood, in *On the Name* (Stanford, Calif.: Stanford University Press, 1995), pp. 3–31; Søren Kierkegaard, *Philosophical Fragments or A Fragment of Philosophy,* trans. David Swenson and Howard V. Hong (Princeton, N.J.: University of Princeton Press, 1967), p. 62, trans. Howard V. Hong and Edna H. Hong (Princeton, N.J.: Princeton University Press, 1955), p. 50, note.

35. Hegel, *Philosophie der Geschichte, Werke,* vol. 12, p. 115.

36. Martin Heidegger "Letter on 'Humanism,'" trans. Frank A. Capuzzi, in *Pathmarks,* ed. William McNeil (Cambridge: Cambridge University Press), pp. 269–70.

37. Derrida, *Glas,* 242a (270a).

38. Kierkegaard, *Concluding Unscientific Postscript,* p. 448 (vol. 1, p. 501).

39. And has been said. See Merold Westphal, "Kierkegaard's Suspension of Religiousness B," in *Foundations of Kierkegaard's Vision of Community: Religion, Ethics, and Politics in Kierkegaard,* ed. George B. Connell and C. Stephen Evans (Atlantic Highlands, N.J.: Humanities Press, 1992), pp. 110–29.

40. Kierkegaard, *JP,* X 3 A 293.

41. Ibid., X 4 A 572.

42. Jacques Derrida, *"Donner la mort,"* in *L'éthique du don* (Paris: Metalié-Transition, 1992), p. 102; *The Gift of Death,* trans. David Wills (Chicago: University of Chicago Press, 1995), p. 109. See in these, respectively, p. 108, note 11, and p. 95, note 35, for cross-references to *Glas.*

43. Derrida, *Glas,* 232ai-33ai (259ai-60ai).

44. Søren Kierkegaard, *Either/Or,* vol. 2, p. 179.

45. Kierkegaard, *JP,* IX A 360.

46. Derrida, *Glas,* 35b (45b). The *Concise Oxford Dictionary* says that a jennet, f. F *genet* f. Sp. *jinete* light horseman, etym. dub., is a small Spanish horse, and that jenneting, prob. f. F name *Jeannet,* is a kind of early apple. As early as Adam's?

47. Jacques Derrida, *De l'esprit* (Paris: Galilée, 1987), p. 184; *Of Spirit: Heidegger and the Question,* trans. Geoffrey Bennington and Rachel Bowlby (Chicago: University of Chicago Press, 1989), p. 113.

48. I am indebted to the late Monica Woolley for her helpful remarks on these texts.

49. Emmanuel Levinas, *Noms propres* (Montpellier: Fata Morgana, 1976), p. 109; *Proper Names,* trans. Michael B. Smith (London: Athlone, 1996), p. 74.

50. Derrida, *Passions,* pp. 57–63, "Passions," in *Jacques Derrida: A Critical Reader,* pp. 20–22, and in *On the Name,* pp. 24–27. See also Jacques Derrida, *"Economimesis,"*

in *Mimesis des articulations* (Paris: Aubier-Flammarion, 1975), pp. 55–93, trans. Richard Klein, *Diacritics* 11, no. 2 (1981): 3–25.

51. Jacques Derrida, *"En ce moment même dans cet ouvrage me voici ,"* in *Psyché: inventions de l'autre* (Paris: Galilée, 1987), pp. 189–192, "At this very moment in this work here I am," trans. Ruben Berezdivin, in *Re-Reading Levinas,* ed. Robert Bernasconi and Simon Critchley (Bloomington: Indiana University Press, 1991), pp. 36–39.

52. See, for instance, Jacques Derrida, *"Foi et savoir. Les deux sources de la 'religion' aux limites de la simple raison,"* in *La religion,* Séminaire de Capri sous la direction de Jacques Derrida et Gianni Vattimo (Paris: Seuil, 1996); "Faith and Knowledge: The Two Sources of 'Religion' at the Limits of Reason Alone," trans. Samuel Weber, in Jacques Derrida, *Acts of Religion,* ed. Gil Anidjar (New York: Routledge, 2002).

53. Jacques Derrida, *"Cogito et histoire de la folie,"* in *L'écriture et la différence* (Paris: Seuil, 1967), pp. 67–68; "Cogito and the History of Madness," trans. Alan Bass, in *Writing and Difference* (London: Routledge and Kegan Paul, 1978), p. 42.

54. Derrida, *Glas,* 72b (24b).

55. Plato (?), *Hippias Major* 304. This fragment (*peritmēma*) from a dialogue attributed (some scholars say pseudonymously) to Plato is put to work as an outwork in Søren Kierkegaard, *Concluding Unscientific Postscript,* which describes itself as "A Mimical-Pathetical-Dialectical Compilation. An Existential Contribution. By Johannes Climacus."

## 4. Standstill

1. *Søren Kierkegaards Papirer,* P. A. Heiberg, V. Kuhr, and E. Torsting, eds., 13 vols. (Copenhagen: Gyldendal, 1968–1970); *Søren Kierkegaard's Journals and Papers,* ed. and trans. Howard V. Hong and Edna H. Hong, assisted by Gregor Malantschuk, 7 vols. (Bloomington: Indiana University Press: 1967–1978), (henceforth *JP*), JP 2140, X 3 A 672.

2. *Luthers Werke, Kritische Gesamtausgabe* (Weimar, Germany: Hermann Böhlau, 1883ff.), vol. 12, p. 99; *Luther's Works,* American ed., ed.Helmut Lehmann and Jaroslov Pelikan (St. Louis: Concordia, 1955ff.), vol. 28, pp. 10–11.

3. Arthur Schopenhauer, *The World as Will and Representation,* trans. E. F. Payne, 2 vols. (New York: Dover, 1966), vol. 2, pp. 625–26.

4. Kierkegaard, *JP* 2622, XI 2 A 150.

5. Ibid., 2619, XI 1 A 254.

6. Ibid., 2548, XI 1 A 108.

7. Ibid., 2546, XI 1 A 61.

8. *Luthers Werke,* vol. 54, pp. 179–87, *Luther's Works,* vol. 34, pp. 327–38.

9. *Luthers Werke,* vol. 1, 525–27, *Luther's Works,* vol. 48, pp. 65–70.

10. Psalm 39. See also Psalms 62 and 77, and Numbers 32:12. Some commentators maintain that in at least some of these places the word is a proper name. In his commentary on Psalm 120 Luther writes of the description "psalm of ascent" applied to this one and fourteen others that on the literal interpretation the reference is to the fifteen steps climbed by the priest, and that the mystical or transferred sense is that he who progresses from virtue to virtue to virtue must be light-hearted and sing for joy. *Martin Luthers Psalmen-Auslegung,* ed. Erwin Mülhaupt (Göttingen, Germany: Vandenhoeck and Ruprecht, 1965), Band 3, p. 447.

11. Kierkegaard, *JP* 983, X 2 A 208.

12. Ibid., 2546, X 1 A 61.

13. Ibid., 2988, XI 2 A 90.

14. Ibid., 2066, X 1 A 384.

15. Ibid., 6837, X 5 A 72.

16. Ibid., 4700, X 5 A 81.

17. Ibid., 6837, X 5 A 72.

18. Ibid., 6783, X 4 A 395.

19. Ibid., 4799, X 3 A 286.

20. Ibid., 6837, X 5 A 72.

21. Ibid., 4688, X 4 A 593.

22. Ibid., 4922, XI 1 A 296.

23. Ibid., 4922, XI 1 A 296.

24. Ibid., 4016, IX A 341.

25. Ibid., 1108, IV A 117.

26. Ibid., 2446, XI 1 A 406.

27. Ibid., 700, III A 112.

28. Ibid., 1536, X 4 641.

29. Ibid., 3096, X 4 A 641.

30. Ibid., 2449, XI 1 A 459.

31. Richard Holloway, *Godless Morality: Keeping Religion out of Morality* (Edinburgh: Canongate, 1999).

32. Søren Kierkegaard, *The Sickness unto Death: A Christian Psychological Exposition for Upbuilding and Awakening,* trans. Howard V. Hong and Edna H. Hong (Princeton, N.J.: Princeton University Press, 1980), pp. 45–46.

33. Søren Kierkegaard, *Concluding Unscientific Postscript,* trans. David F. Swenson and Walter Lowrie (Princeton, N.J.: Princeton University Press, 1941), pp. 144–45; *Concluding Unscientific Postscript to "Philosophical Fragments,"* trans. Howard V. Hong and Edna H. Hong, 2 vols. (Princeton, N.J.: Princeton University Press, 1992), vol. 1, p. 162.

34. Kierkegaard, *JP* 2556, XI 2 266; Søren Kierkegaard, *Works of Love,* trans. Howard V. Hong and Edna H. Hong (Princeton, N.J.: Princeton University Press, 1995), p. 78.

35. Kierkegaard, *JP* 4489, XI 2 A 29.

36. Ibid., 4013, VIII 1 A 497.

37. *Luthers Werke,* vol. 39, part 1, p. 46, *Luther's Works,* vol. 34, p. 111.

38. Kierkegaard, *JP* 6642, X 3 A 168.

39. Ibid., 263, X 2 A 324. Compare Kierkegaard, *Concluding Unscientific Postscript,* pp. 99ff. (vol. 1, pp. 109ff.)

40. Ibid., 831, I C 80.

41. Ibid., 834, II A 5 70.

42. Ibid., 832, II A 100.

43. Ibid., 3772, X 5 A 58.

44. Ibid., 1108, IV A 117.

45. Ibid., 6642, X 3 A 168.

46. Ibid., 6863, XI 1 A 76.

47. Ibid., 3346, X 2 A 202.

48. Ibid., 6837, X 5 A 72.

49. Martin Heidegger, *Being and Time,* trans. John Macquarrie and Edward Robinson (Oxford: Blackwell, 1967), trans. Joan Stambaugh (Albany: State University of New York Press, 1996), p. 178 (marginal).

50. Kierkegaard, *JP* 6863, XI 1 A 76.

51. Søren Kierkegaard, *For Self-Examination: Judge for Yourself,* trans. Howard V. Hong and Edna H. Hong (Princeton, N.J.: Princeton University Press, 1990), p. 83. Compare *The Sickness unto Death,* p. 45.

52. Kierkegaard, *JP* 2388, III A 89.

53. Ibid., 2389, III A 120.

54. Ibid., 1940, XI 2 A 434.

## 5. Works of Love

1. Søren Kierkegaard, *Upbuilding Discourses in Various Spirits,* trans. Howard V. Hong and Edna H. Hong (Princeton, N.J.: Princeton University Press, 1993), p. 162.

2. "Ich selbst betrachte eigentlich die Landschaft gar nie," Martin Heidegger, *"Schöpferische Landschaft: Warum bleiben wir in der Provinz?"* in *Denkerfahrungen* (Frankfurt am Main: Klostermann, 1983), p. 9.

3. Martin Heidegger, *"Der Ursprung des Kunstwerkes,"* in *Holzwege* (Frankfurt am Main: Klostermann, 1972), pp. 22–23; "The Origin of the Work of Art," in *Poetry, Language, Thought,* trans. Albert Hofstadter (New York: Harper and Row, 1971), pp. 33–34.

4. Søren Kierkegaard, *Works of Love,* trans. Howard V. Hong and Edna H. Hong (Princeton, N.J.: Princeton University Press, 1995), p. 56.

5. Kierkegaard, *Works of Love,* p. 152.

6. We shall return in the chapter entitled "Oversights" to the question of directionality and pluridirectionality and undirectionality. Meanwhile we raise in passing the question whether the daffodil raises its face in the direction of God. Daffodils in Welsh are *cennin Pedr,* Peter's leeks. Why the reference to Peter? Not, or not chiefly, I think, because the daffodil is in bloom in the land of which it is the national emblem at roughly the same time as certain feast days of Saint Peter, for these are of far less significance in the church calendar than his main festival, June 29. A more likely explanation is that the daffodil is associated with Peter's hanging his head after denying Christ. In some parts of Wales the daffodil is referred to as *lili bengam,* the head-hanging lily (so that daffodils are among "the lilies of the field"). But these explanations are not mutually exclusive.

7. Kierkegaard, *Works of Love,* p. 85.

8. Søren Kierkegaard, *Practice in Christianity,* trans. Howard V. Hong and Edna V. Hong (Princeton, N.J.: Princeton University Press, 1991), p. 65.

9. Kierkegaard, *Works of Love,* p. 218.

10. Ibid., p. 216.

11. Ibid., p. 215.

12. Martin Heidegger, *Being and Time,* trans. John Macquarrie and Edward Robinson (Oxford: Blackwell, 1967), p. 235, note vi, trans. Joan Stambaugh (Albany: State University of New York Press, 1996), p. 235, note 6.

13. Kierkegaard, *Works of Love,* p. 142.

14. Ibid., p. 153.

15. Ibid., p. 148.

16. Søren Kierkegaard, *The Concept of Anxiety,* trans. Howard V. Hong and Edna H. Hong (Princeton, N.J.: Princeton University Press, 1980), p. 162.

17. Jacques Derrida, *De l'esprit: Heidegger et la question* (Paris: Galilée, 1987), p. 183, *Of Spirit: Heidegger and the Question,* trans. Geoffrey Bennington and Rachel Bowlby (Chicago: University of Chicago Press, 1989), p. 113.

18. Martin Heidegger, *Beiträge zur Philosophie (Vom Ereignis)* (Frankfurt am Main: Klostermann, 1989), *Gesamtausgabe* 65, *Contributions to Philosophy (From Enowning)*, trans. Parvis Emad and Kenneth Maly (Bloomington: Indiana University Press, 1999), §126.

## 6. Between Appearance and Reality

1. Friedrich Nietzsche, "Morality as Anti-Nature," §3, *Twilight of the Idols* and *The Anti-Christ*, trans. R. J. Hollingdale (London: Penguin Books, 1968), p. 43.

2. Friedrich Nietzsche, *The Birth of Tragedy Out of the Spirit of Music*, trans. Shaun Whiteside (London: Penguin Books, 1993), §6, p. 9.

3. Ibid., §21.

4. Nietzsche, *The Anti-Christ*, §41.

5. Friedrich Nietzsche, *Human, All Too Human*, trans. Marion Faber and Stephen Lehmann (London: Penguin Books, 1984), §475.

6. Friedrich Nietzsche, *Beyond Good and Evil: Prelude to a Philosophy of the Future*, trans. R. J. Hollingdale (London: Penguin Books, 1973), §186.

7. Ibid., §42.

8. Ibid., §188.

9. Ibid., §272.

10. Ibid., §54.

11. Ibid., §2.

12. Nietzsche, *Twilight of the Idols*, p. 41.

13. Ibid., §21.

14. Ibid., §42.

15. Ibid., §20.

16. Ibid., §2.

## 7. Love of Fate

1. Friedrich Nietzsche, *Beyond Good and Evil*, trans. R. J. Hollingdale (London: Penguin Books, 1971), §225.

2. Ibid.

3. Friedrich Nietzsche, *The Dawn of Day*, trans. J. M. Kennedy (Edinburgh: Foulis, 1911), §63.

4. Walter Kaufmann, *Nietzsche: Philosopher, Psychologist, Antichrist* (New York: Vintage Books, 1968), p. 84.

5. Friedrich Nietzsche, *The Will to Power*, trans. Walter Kaufmann and R. J. Hollingdale (London: Weidenfeld and Nicolson, 1967), §864.

6. Ibid.

7. Friedrich Nietzsche, *The Gay Science*, trans. Walter Kaufmann (New York: Vintage Books, 1974), §339.

8. Nor will I ever discover where, according to the Tyndale specialist David Daniell, whom I thank for his response to my query.

9. Friedrich Nietzsche, *The Twilight of the Idols*, trans. R. J. Hollingdale (London: Penguin Books, 1968); "The Four Great Errors," §3.

10. Nietzsche, *The Gay Science*, preface, §4.

11. Nietzsche, *The Will to Power*, §864.

12. Ibid., §865.

13. Nietzsche, *The Twilight of the Idols,* "What the Germans Lack," §1, §4.

14. Nietzsche, *The Will to Power,* §894.

15. Ibid., §893.

16. Nietzsche, *Beyond Good and Evil,* §248.

17. Walter Kaufmann, ed., *The Portable Nietzsche* (New York: Viking, 1968), pp. 46–47; Friedrich Nietzsche, *Early Greek Philosophy and Other Essays,* trans. Maximilian A. Mügge (Edinburgh: Foulis, 1911), p. 180.

18. Friedrich Nietzsche, *Ecce Homo,* "Thus Spoke Zarathustra," §1, in *On the Genealogy of Morals* and *Ecce Homo,* trans. Walter Kaufmann and R. G. Hollingdale (New York: Vintage, 1967).

19. Nietzsche, *The Will to Power,* §1066.

20. Ibid., §1062.

21. Nietzsche, *Beyond Good and Evil,* §53.

22. Nietzsche, *The Will to Power,* §421.

23. Nietzsche, *Beyond Good and Evil,* §30.

24. Nietzsche, *Thus Spoke Zarathustra: A Book for Everyone and No One,* trans. R. G. Hollingdale (London: Penguin Books, 1969); "The Intoxicated Song," §10.

25. Nietzsche, *Ecce Homo,* "Thus Spoke Zarathustra," §8.

26. Nietzsche, *Beyond Good and Evil,* §61.

27. Ibid., §272.

28. Friedrich Nietzsche, *Sämtliche Werke, Kritische Studienausgabe,* ed. G. Colli and M. Montinari, 15 vols. (Munich: Deutsche Taschenbuch Verlag, 1980), vol. 9, p. 505.

29. Nietzsche, *The Will to Power,* §1065.

## 8. God's Ghost

1. "Levinas then is very close to and very distant from Nietzsche and Bataille." Jacques Derrida, "Violence et métaphysique," in *L'écriture et la différence* (Paris: Seuil, 1967), p. 151; "Violence and Metaphysics," in *Writing and Difference,* trans. Alan Bass (London: Routledge and Kegan Paul, 1978), p. 102.

2. Emmanuel Levinas, *Autrement qu'être ou au-delà de l'essence* (The Hague: Nijhoff, 1978), pp. 180–81, *Otherwise than Being or Beyond Essence,* trans. Alphonso Lingis (The Hague: Nijhoff, 1981), p. 142.

3. Gilles Deleuze and Claire Parnet, *Dialogues* (Paris: Flammarion, 1977), p. 72, *Dialogues,* trans. Hugh Tomlinson and Barbara Habberjam (London: Athlone, 1987), pp. 57–58.

4. "Men have been able to be thankful for the very fact of finding themselves able to thank; the present gratitude is grafted onto itself as onto an already antecedent gratitude. In a prayer in which the believer asks that his prayer be heard, the prayer as it were follows or precedes itself." Emmanuel Levinas, *Autrement qu'être ou au-delà de l'essence,* p. 12, *Otherwise than Being or Beyond Essence,* p. 10.

5. "To receive something from God is not (despite the crude models that have arisen in both the Catholic and Protestant traditions) to have a possession, Williams insists. 'It is to be caught up in a stream of God's action. . . . And if we begin from . . . the life of God as Trinity, the gift of God as the gift of God's own life, we shall come by a roundabout route to what I always think is one of the basic principles of sensible thinking about stewardship: that it is given to us to become givers.'" Cited from a talk to the 1996 Stewardship Advisers' National Conference. Rupert Shortt, *Rowan Williams: An Introduction* (London: Darton, Longman and Todd, 2003), p. 63.

6. Emmanuel Levinas, *Totalité et Infini: essai sur l'extériorité* (The Hague: Nijhoff, 1980), p. 62, *Totality and Infinity: An Essay on Exteriority*, trans. Alphonso Lingis (The Hague: Nijhoff, 1969), p. 89.

7. Emmanuel Levinas, *De Dieu qui vient à l'idée*, (Paris: Vrin, 1982), p. 122, *Of God Who Comes to Mind*, trans. Bettina Bergo (Stanford, Calif.: Stanford University Press, 1998), pp. 74–75.

8. Gilles Deleuze, *Logique du sens* (Paris: Minuit, 1969), *Logic of Sense*, trans. Mark Lester and Charles Stivale (London: Athlone, 1990), 3rd, 5th, 9th and 11th series.

9. See John Llewelyn, "What Is a Question?" *Australasian Journal of Philosophy* 42 (1964): 69–85.

10. Ludwig Wittgenstein, *Philosophical Investigations*, trans. G. E. M. Anscombe (Oxford: Blackwell, 1967), 500.

11. Compare R. M. Hare, *The Language of Morals* (Oxford: Clarendon Press, 1952).

12. Jacques Derrida, *Adieu à Emmanuel Lévinas* (Paris: Galilée, 1997), pp. 61, 66, 110. Derrida takes Levinas to apply his neologism *illéité* both to the tertiality of the other human being and to a tertiality that is other than this. There are two tertialities. If there are not also two illeities, then it may be my reading of Levinas that lacks care, not Derrida's. Perhaps the full story is that two illeities may be distinguished but not separated from each other.

13. Levinas. *Autrement qu'être*, p. 191, *Otherwise than Being*, p. 150.

14. Emmanuel Levinas, "*Dieu et la philosophie*," in *De Dieu qui vient à l'idée*, p. 125, "God and Philosophy," in *Of God Who Comes to Mind*, p. 77; *Collected Philosophical Papers*, trans. Alphonso Lingis (The Hague: Nijhoff, 1987), p. 172.

15. Levinas, *Totalité et Infini*, p. 46, *Totality and Infinity*, p. 73.

16. Ibid, p. 51, p. 79.

17. Ibid., p. 169, p. 195.

18. Emmanuel Levinas, "*La signification et le sens*," in *L'humanisme de l'autre homme* (Montpellier: Fata Morgana, 1972), p. 61; "Signification and Sense," in *Humanism of the Other*, trans. Nidra Poller (Urbana: University of Illinois Press, 2003), p. 42; "Meaning and Sense," in *Collected Philosophical Papers*, p. 105.

19. Levinas, *Autrement qu'être*, p. 206, *Otherwise than Being*, p. 162.

20. Gilles Deleuze and Félix Guattari, *Capitalisme et schizophrénie 2: Mille plateaux* (Paris: Minuit, 1980), pp. 84, 178, *A Thousand Plateaux : Capitalism and Schizophrenia*, trans. Brian Massumi (Minneapolis: University of Minnesota Press, 1987), pp. 73, 158.

21. Gilles Deleuze, *Différence et répétition* (Paris: Presses Universitaires de France, 1972), p. 257, *Difference and Repetition*, trans. Paul Patton (New York: Columbia University Press, 1994), p. 199.

22. Levinas, "*La signification et le sens*," in *L'humanisme de l'autre homme*, p. 59, "Signification and Sense," in *Humanism of the Other*, p. 41; "Meaning and Sense," in *Collected Philosophical Papers*, pp. 103–104.

23. Deleuze and Parnet, *Dialogues*, p. 129, *Dialogues*, p. 107. "Thus in the chorus scenes of 'Oedipus,' the lamenting, the peaceful and the religious, the pious lie ('If I am an augur,' etc.) and, to the degree of utmost exhaustion, the compassion for a dialogue which will tear apart the soul of just these listeners with its wrathful sensitivity; in the scenes the frightfully festive forms, the drama like an auto-da-fe, as language for a world where under pest and confusion of senses and under universally inspired prophecy in idle time, with the god and man expressing themselves in the all-forgetting form of

infidelity—for divine infidelity is best to retain—so that the course of the world will not show any rupture and the memory of the heavenly ones will not expire.

At such moments man forgets himself and the god and turns around like a traitor, naturally in saintly manner,—In the utmost form of suffering, namely, there exists nothing but the condition of time and place.

Inside it, man forgets himself because he exists entirely for the moment, the god [forgets himself] because it is reversed categorically at such a moment, no longer fitting beginning and end; man, because at this moment of categorical reversal he has to follow and thus can no longer resemble the beginning in what follows.

Thus Haemon stands in 'Antigone.' Thus Oedipus himself in the tragedy of 'Oedipus.'" Friedrich Hölderlin, "Remarks on 'Oedipus,'" in *Essays and Letters on Theory*, trans. Thomas Pfau (Albany: State University of New York Press, 1988), pp. 107–108.

24. Jean Wahl, *Existence humaine et transcendence* (Neuchâtel: Éditions de la Baconnière, 1944), p. 38, cited by Levinas in "*Énigme et phénomène*," in *En découvrant l'existence avec Husserl et Heidegger* (Paris: Vrin, 1982), p. 205, note; "Phenomenon and Enigma," in *Collected Philosophical Papers*, p. 63, note.

25. Gabriel Marcel, *Being and Having*, trans. Katharine Farrer (London: Dacre, 1949), p. 117.

26. Ibid.

27. Levinas, *Totalité et Infini*, pp. 268–69, *Totality and Infinity*, p. 292.

## 9. Innocent Guilt

1. Friedrich Nietzsche, *The Gay Science*, trans. Walter Kaufmann (New York: Vintage Books, 1974), §346, p. 286.

2. Gilles Deleuze and Félix Guattari, *Capitalisme et schizophrénie*, vol. 1: *L'Anti-Œdipe* (Paris: Minuit, 1975), p. 128, *Anti-Oedipus*, trans. Robert Hurley, Mark Seems, and Helen R. Lane (London: Athlone, 1983), p. 107.

3. Ibid., p. 127, p. 107.

4. Friedrich Nietzsche, *The Will to Power*, trans. Walter Kaufmann and R. J. Hollingdale (London: Weidenfeld and Nicolson, 1967), 1052, pp. 542–43.

5. Gilles Deleuze, *Nietzsche et la philosophie* (Paris: Presses universitaires de France, 1962), pp. 217–18, *Nietzsche and Philosophy*, trans. Hugh Tomlinson (London: Athlone, 1986), pp. 189–90.

6. "Belief in unconditional substances and identical things is likewise an old, original error of all that is organic." See Friedrich Nietzsche, *Human, All Too Human*, trans. Marion Faber and Stephen Lehman (London: Penguin Books, 1984), p. 26.

7. Emmanuel Levinas, "*Dieu et la philosophie*," in *De Dieu qui vient à l'idée* (Paris: Vrin, 1982), p. 125, note 24, "God and Philosophy," *Of God Who Comes to Mind*, trans. Bettina Bergo (Stanford, Calif.: Stanford University Press, 1998), p. 201, note 39; *Collected Philosophical Papers*, trans. Alphonso Lingis (The Hague: Nijhoff, 1987), p. 172, note 25.

8. Gilles Deleuze, *Différence et répétition* (Paris: Presses Universitaires de France, 1972), p. 214, *Difference and Repetition*, trans. Paul Patton (New York: Columbia University Press, 1994), p. 131.

9. Michel Tournier, *Vendredi ou les limbes du Pacifique* (Paris: Gallimard, 1967).

10. Gilles Deleuze, *Logique du sens* (Paris: Gallimard, 1969), pp. 370–72, *Logic of Sense*, trans. Mark Lester (London: Continuum, 2001), pp. 318–21.

11. Deleuze and Guattari, *L'Anti-Œdipe*, pp. 155–56, *Anti-Oedipus*, p. 131.

12. Deleuze and Guattari, *Capitalisme et schizophrénie,* vol. 2: *Mille plateaux* (Paris: Minuit, 1980), p. 458, *A Thousand Plateaux,* trans. Brian Massumi (Minneapolis: University of Minnesota Press, 1987), p. 408, citing Nietzsche, *The Will to Power,* 630, p. 336.

13. Citing the subtitle of John Llewelyn, *Emmanuel Levinas: The Genealogy of Ethics* (London: Routledge, 1995).

14. Emmanuel Levinas, *Totalité et Infini: essai sur l'extériorité* (The Hague: Nijhoff, 1980), p. 261, *Totality and Infinity: An Essay on Exteriority,* trans. Alphonso Lingis (The Hague: Nijhoff, 1969), pp. 284–85.

15. Martin Heidegger, *Being and Time,* trans. John Macquarrie and Edward Robinson (Oxford: Blackwell, 1962), p. 235, note vi, trans. Joan Stambaugh (Albany: State University of New York Press, 1996), p. 235, note 6.

16. Friedrich Nietzsche, *Thus Spoke Zarathustra: A Book for Everyone and No One,* trans. R. J. Hollingdale (London: Penguin Books, 1969), p. 42.

17. Ferdinand de Saussure, *Course in General Linguistics,* trans. Wade Baskin (London: Fontana-Collins, 1974) p. 112.

18. John D. Caputo, *Against Ethics: Contributions to a Poetics of Obligation with Constant Reference to Deconstruction* (Bloomington: Indiana University Press, 1993).

19. Levinas, *Totalité et Infini,* p. 268, *Totality and Infinity,* p. 292.

20. Ibid., p. 118, p. 145.

21. Gilles Deleuze, *"Sur Capitalisme et Schizophrénie: Entretien avec Félix Guattari et Gilles Deleuze," Deleuze, L'Arc* 49 (n.d.): p. 55.

22. See the third section of chapter 2 above.

23. Levinas, *Totalité et Infini,* p. 268, *Totality and Infinity,* p. 292.

24. Emmanuel Levinas, *"La signification et le sens,"* in *L'humanisme de l'autre homme* (Montpellier: Fata Morgana, 1972), p. 52, "Signification and Sense," in *Humanism of the Other,* trans. Nidra Poller (Urbana: University of Minnesota Press, 2003), p. 35; "Meaning and Sense," in *Collected Philosophical Papers,* p. 99.

25. Ibid.

26. Gilles Deleuze and Félix Guattari, *What Is Philosophy?* trans. Graham Burchell and Hugh Tomlinson (London: Verso, 1994), p. 21.

27. Levinas, *Totalité et Infini,* p. XIV, *Totality and Infinity,* p. 26.

28. Ibid., p. 281, p. 304.

29. Emmanuel Levinas. *Autrement qu'être ou au-delà de l'essence* (The Hague: Nijhoff, 1978), p. 3, note 1, *Otherwise than Being or Beyond Essence,* trans. Alphonso Lingis (The Hague: Nijhoff, 1981), p. 187, note 1.

30. Levinas, *Totalité et Infini,* pp. XV, 269, 283, *Totality and Infinity,* pp. 27, 292, 306; *L'humanisme de l'autre homme,* pp. 52–53, "Signification and Sense," in *Humanism of the Other,* pp. 35–36; "Meaning and Sense," in *Collected Philosophical Papers,* pp. 99–100.

31. As mine was drawn by my very good friends Percy Jack and Carol Pompa, whom I hereby thank.

## 10. Origins of Negation

1. Emmanuel Levinas, *Totalité et Infini: Essai sur l'extériorité* (The Hague: Nijhoff, 1980), pp. 56–57, *Totality and Infinity: An Essay on Exteriority,* trans. Alphonso Lingis (The Hague: Nijhoff, 1969), pp. 84–85.

2. Ibid., p. 57, p. 85.

3. See chapter 15 below.

4. See chapter 6 above.

5. Georg Wilhelm Friedrich Hegel, *Wissenschaft der Logik* (Frankfurt am Main: Suhrkamp, 1970), p. 83, *Science of Logic,* trans. A. V. Miller (London: Allen and Unwin, 1969), p. 82.

6. Jean-Paul Sartre, *L'être et le néant: essai d'ontologie phénoménologique* (Paris: Gallimard, 1943), p. 57, *Being and Nothingness: An Essay on Phenomenological Ontology,* trans. Hazel E. Barnes (London: Methuen, 1958), p. 21.

7. Ibid., p. 27, p. xxxvi.

8. Martin Heidegger, *Wegmarken* (Frankfurt am Main: Klostermann, 1976), p. 115 (12), "What Is Metaphysics?" in *Pathmarks,* ed. William McNeill (Cambridge: Cambridge University Press, 1998), p. 91.

9. Sartre, *L'être et le néant,* p. 58, *Being and Nothingness,* p. 22.

10. Ibid., p. 55, p. 19.

11. Ibid., pp. 57, 58, pp. 21, 22.

12. Heidegger, *Wegmarken,* p. 117 (14), *Pathmarks,* p. 93.

13. Martin Heidegger, *Being and Time,* trans. John Macquarrie and Edward Robinson (Oxford: Blackwell, 1967), trans. Joan Stambaugh (Albany: State University of New York Press, 1996), p. 436.

14. Edmund Husserl, *The Phenomenology of Internal Time Consciousness,* trans. James S. Churchill (The Hague: Nijhoff, 1964), §36.

15. Sartre, *L'être et le néant,* p. 53, *Being and Nothingness,* p. 17.

16. Ibid.

17. Ibid., p. 60, p. 24.

18. Immanuel Kant, *Critique of Practical Reason,* trans. Lewis White Beck (Indianapolis: Liberal Arts Press, 1956), p. 9.

19. Levinas, *Totalité et Infini,* p. 57, *Totality and Infinity,* pp. 84–85.

20. Adriaan Peperzak, *To the Other: An Introduction to the Philosophy of Emmanuel Levinas* (West Lafayette, Ind.: Purdue University Press, 1993), p. 146.

21. Levinas, *Totalité et Infini,* p. 224, *Totality and Infinity,* pp. 246–47.

22. Ibid., p. 84, p. 57.

23. Ibid. p. 77, p. 39.

24. Sartre, *L'être et le néant,* p. 62, *Being and Nothingness,* p. 25.

25. Ibid., p. 60, p. 24.

26. Immanuel Kant, *Kritik der reinen Vernunft* (Hamburg: Meiner, 1956), B68–69, B153, B156n.

27. Dagobert D. Runes, *Dictionary of Philosophy, Ancient-Medieval-Modern* (Ames, Iowa: Littlefield, Adams, 1958).

28. Sartre, *L'être et le néant,* pp. 71–72, *Being and Nothingness,* p. 34.

29. Emmanuel Levinas, *Hors sujet* (Montpellier: Fata Morgana, 1987), p. 68, *Outside the Subject,* trans. Michael B. Smith (London: Athlone, 1993), p. 47.

30. Sartre, *L'être et le néant,* p. 71, *Being and Nothingness,* p. 34.

31. Ibid., p. 59, p. 22.

32. Heidegger, *Being and Time,* p. 280.

## 11. Negation of Origins

1. Gilles Deleuze and Félix Guattari, *What Is Philosophy?* trans. Graham Burchell and Hugh Tomlinson (London: Verso, 1994), p. 21.

2. G. S. Kirk and J. E. Raven, *The Presocratic Philosophers* (Cambridge: Cambridge University Press, 1960), p. 27. F. M. Cornford, *From Religion to Philosophy, A Study in the Origins of Western Speculation* (Princeton, N.J.: Princeton University Press, 1991), p. 66.

3. C. S. Peirce, *Collected Papers* (Cambridge: Harvard University Press, 1931–1958), 2.303. Jacques Derrida, *De la grammatologie* (Paris: Éditions de Minuit, 1967), pp. 70ff., *Of Grammatology*, trans. Gayatri Chakravorty Spivak (Baltimore, Md.: Johns Hopkins University Press, 1976), pp. 48 ff.

4. Robert Musil, *The Man without Qualities*, trans. Sophie Wilkins and Burton Pike (New York: Knopf, 1995), pp. 1318–19. I am indebted to Percy Jack for bringing this passage to my attention.

5. Sigmund Freud, "The Antithetical Meaning of Primal Words" (1910), *The Standard Edition of the Complete Psychological Works of Sigmund Freud*, trans. James Strachey (London: Hogarth, 1957) , vol. 11, p. 161, note.

6. *Søren Kierkegaards Papirer*, ed. P. A. Heiberg, V. Kuhr and E. Torsting, 13 vols. (Copenhagen: Gyldendal,1968–70), *Søren Kierkegaard's Journals and Papers*, ed. and trans. Howard V. Hong and Edna H. Hong, assisted by Gregor Malantschuk, 7 vols. (Bloomington: Indiana University Press, 1967–1978); *JP* 2320, IV B 14:6.

7. Sigmund Freud, *The Interpretation of Dreams, The Standard Edition* (London: Hogarth, 1953), vol. 4, p. 318.

8. Ibid., pp. 326–27.

9. Freud, *The Interpretation of Dreams, The Standard Edition* (London: Hogarth, 1953), vol. 5, p. 662.

10. Freud, *The Interpretation of Dreams,* The Standard Edition, vol. 4, p. 316.

11. Ibid., p. 328.

12. Jacques Derrida, "Hostipitality," trans. Gil Anidjar, in *Acts of Religion,* ed. Gil Anidjar (New York: Routledge, 2002), p. 364.

13. Edmund Husserl, *The Phenomenology of Internal Time Consciousness,* trans. James S. Churchill (The Hague: Nijhoff, 1964), §36.

14. Catherine Malabou and Jacques Derrida, *Jacques Derrida: La contre-allée* (Paris: La Quinzaine Littéraire, Louis Vuitton, 1999).

15. Jacques Derrida, *Éperons: Les styles de Nietzsche* (Paris: Flammarion, 1978), p. 28, *Spurs: Nietzsche's Styles,* trans. Barbara Harlow (Chicago: Chicago University Press, 1979), p. 36.

16. Jean-François Lyotard, *Driftworks* (New York: Semiotext(e), 1984), p. 12.

17. Sigmund Freud, "Negation" (1925), in *Collected Papers,* vol. 19, p. 237.

18. Paul Ricoeur, *Freud and Philosophy: An Essay on Interpretation,* trans. Denis Savage (New Haven: Yale University Press, 1977), p. 317.

19. Ibid, p. 314.

20. G. W. F. Hegel, *Phenomenology of Spirit,* trans. A. V. Miller (Oxford: Clarendon Press, 1977), p. 268.

21. Freud, *The Interpretation of Dreams,* The Standard Edition, p. 59.

22. *Anne Dufourmantelle invite Jacques Derrida à répondre: De l'hospitalité* (Paris: Calmann-Levy, 1997), p. 119.

23. Ibid., p. 99.

24. Ibid., p. 133.

25. Ibid., p. 131.

26. Jacques Derrida, "*En ce moment même dans cet ouvrage me voici,*" in *Psyché: Inventions de l'autre* (Paris: Galilée, 1987), pp. 161–63, "At This Very Moment in This

Work Here I am," trans. Ruben Berezdivin, in *Re-Reading Levinas,* ed. Robert Bernasconi and Simon Critchley (Bloomington: Indiana University Press, 1991), pp. 13–14.

27. Jacques Derrida, "Hostipitality," in *Acts of Religion,* p. 363.

28. Ibid.

29. Ibid., p. 388.

30. Jacques Derrida, *Spectres de Marx: L'État de la dette, le travail du deuil et la nouvelle Internationale* (Paris: Galilée, 1993), *Specters of Marx: The State of the Debt, the Work of Mourning, and the New International,* trans. Peggy Kamuf (New York: Routledge, 1994).

31. Derrida, "Hostipitality," p. 388.

32. Jacques Derrida, *La force de loi: "Le fondement mystique de l'autorité"* (Paris: Galilée, 1994), "Force of Law: The 'Mystical Foundation of Authority,'" trans. Mary Quaintance, in *Deconstruction and the Possibility of Justice, Cardozo Law Review* 11, nos. 2–5 (July–Aug. 1990): 920–1045; *Acts of Religion,* pp. 228–98.

33. Derrida, *Spectres de Marx,* p. 56, *Specters of Marx,* p. 28.

34. John Austin, *How To Do Things with Words,* ed. J. O. Urmson (Oxford: Clarendon Press, 1962).

## 12. Love of Wisdom and Wisdom of Love

1. A. C. Graham, *Yin-Yang and the Nature of Correlative Thinking* (Singapore: Institute of East Asian Philosophies, 1986), p. 28.

2. One reads this, for example, in the book mentioned in the previous note. But for further guidance on this and other aspects of Oriental thought I thank Alexander Beveridge and James Giles.

3. Alain Badiou, *Ethics: An Essay on the Understanding of Evil,* trans. Peter Hallward (London: Verso, 2001), p. 22. I thank Chris Jupp for bringing Badiou's comments on Levinas to my attention.

4. Ibid., pp. 22–23.

5. See John Llewelyn, *The Middle Voice of Ecological Conscience: A Chiasmic Reading of Responsibility in the Neighbourhood of Levinas, Heidegger and Others* (London: Macmillan, 1991), chapter 10.

6. Emmanuel Levinas, preface to the German edition of *Totality and Infinity,* in *Entre nous: essai sur la pensée à l'autre* (Paris: Grasset, 1991), p. 251, *Entre nous: on thinking-of-the-other,* trans. Michael B. Smith and Barbara Harshav (London: Athlone, 1998), p. 199.

7. Emmanuel Levinas, *Autrement qu'être ou au-delà de l'essence* (The Hague: Nijhoff, 1978), p. 207, *Otherwise than Being or Beyond Essence,* trans. Alphonso Lingis (The Hague: Nijhoff, 1981), p. 162.

8. Friedrich Nietzsche, *The Gay Science,* trans. Walter Kaufmann (New York: Vintage Books, 1974), §276, p. 223.

9. Emmanuel Levinas, *De l'existence à l'existant* (Paris: Vrin, 1981), pp. 161ff, *Existence and Existents,* trans. A. Lingis (The Hague: Nijhoff, 1978), pp. 94ff.

10. Aristotle, *De Generatione Animalium,* 736b 29. I thank Dory Scaltsas.

11. Jacques Derrida, *Sur parole* (Paris: Éditions de l'Aube, 1999), p. 66.

12. Or like the author of this book carrying in his rucksack up the Maritime Alps a copy of Hegel's even heftier *Science of Logic* (it weighs a good kilo)?

13. Michael Naas, *Taking on the Tradition: Jacques Derrida and the Legacies of Deconstruction* (Stanford, Calif.: Stanford University Press, 2003).

14. James Joyce, *Finnegans Wake* (London: Faber and Faber, 1975), p. 258; Jacques Derrida, *Ulysse gramophone: deux mots pour Joyce* (Paris: Galilée, 1987), p. 16.

15. John Llewelyn, "*Le pas du repas*," in *Jacques Derrida* (Paris: L'Herne, 2004), pp. 96–111. See also chapter 13, note 22, of the present book.

16. See the fourth section of chapter 9.

17. Jacques Derrida, "*De l'économie restreinte à l'économie générale: un hégélianisme sans réserve*, in *L'écriture et la différence* (Paris: Seuil, 1967), p. 386, "From Restricted to General Economy: A Hegelianism without Reserve," in *Writing and Difference*, trans. Alan Bass (London: Routledge and Kegan Paul, 1979), p. 263.

18. Jacques Derrida, *L'oreille de l'autre: otobiographies, transferts, traductions, textes et débats avec Jacques Derrida*, ed. Claude Lévesque and Christine V. McDonald (Montreal: VLB, 1982), p. 79.

19. Derrida, *Ulysse gramophone*, p. 110.

20. Ibid., p. 130.

21. Ibid.

22. Michel de Certeau, *La fable mystique*, vol. 1: *XVIᵉ–XVIIᵉ siècle* (Paris: Gallimard, 1982).

23. William Shakespeare, *Hamlet*, Act V, Scene 2.

24. Jacques Derrida, "*Nombre de oui*," in *Psyché: inventions de l'autre* (Paris: Galilée, 1987), p. 644. See also Jacques Derrida, *De l'esprit: Heidegger et la question* (Paris: Galilée, 1987), pp. 147n–154n, *Of Spirit: Heidegger and the Question*, trans. Geoffrey Bennington and Rachel Bowlby (Chicago: University of Chicago Press, 1989), pp. 129n–136n.

25. Derrida, *L'oreille de l'autre*, p. 82.

26. Jacques Derrida, *Le problème de la genèse dans la philosophie de Husserl* (Paris: Épiméthée, 1990).

27. Jacques Derrida, "*La différance*," in *Marges de la philosophie* (Paris: Seuil, 1972), p. 29, "Différance," in *Margins of Philosophy*, trans. Alan Bass (Chicago: University of Chicago Press, 1982), p. 27.

28. Ibid., p. 19, p. 18.

29. G. W. F. Hegel, *Philosophy of Right*, trans. T. M. Knox (Oxford: Oxford University Press, 1967), p. 10.

30. Ibid., p. 11.

31. Emmanuel Levinas, *Le temps et l'autre* (Montpellier: Fata Morgana, 1983), p. 60, *Time and the Other*, trans. R. H. Cohen (Pittsburgh, Penn.: Duquesne University Press, 1987), p. 72.

32. Emmanuel Levinas, "*Politique après!*," in *L'au-delà du verset: lectures et discours talmudiques* (Paris: Minuit, 1982), p. 228, "Politics After!" in *Beyond the Verse: Talmudic Readings and Lectures*, trans. Gary D. Mole (London: Athlone, 1994), p. 195.

33. Emmanuel Levinas, *Difficile liberté: esais sur le judaïsme* (Paris: Albin Michel, 1976), pp. 126, 128, 375, *Difficult Freedom: Essays on Judaism*, trans. Seán Hand (Baltimore: Johns Hopkins University Press, 1990), pp. 95, 96, 293.

## 13. Oversights

1. Jacques Derrida, *La carte postale de Socrate à Freud et au-delà* (Paris: Flammarion, 1980), p. 47, *The Post Card from Socrates to Freud and Beyond*, trans. Alan Bass (Chicago: University of Chicago Press, 1987), p. 41.

2. Ibid.

3. Geoffrey Bennington and Jacques Derrida, *Jacques Derrida* (Paris: Seuil, 1991).

4. Ibid., p. 52, p. 46.

5. Ibid., p. 53, p. 46.

6. Ibid., p. 8, p. 4.

7. Ibid., p. 9, p. 5.

8. Ludwig Wittgenstein, *Philosophical Investigations,* trans. G. E. M. Anscombe (Oxford: Blackwell, 1953), ¶¶ 201ff.

9. Nicolas Abraham and Maria Torok, *L'écorce et le noyau* (Paris: Flammarion, 1987), *The Shell and the Kernel,* trans. Nicholas T. Rand (Chicago: University of Chicago Press, 1994).

10. *Nietzsche aujourd'hui,* Colloque de Cerisy (Paris: Union Générale d'Éditions, 1973), vol. 1, p. 291.

11. Jacques Derrida, *"Otobiographie de Nietzsche,"* in *L'oreille de l'autre,* ed. Claude Lévesque and Christie V. McDonald (Montreal: VLB Éditeur, 1982), p. 64.

12. Ibid., p. 108.

13. Ibid.

14. Jacques Derrida, *"Choréographies,"* in *Points de suspension: entretiens* (Paris: Galilée, 1992), p. 111.

15. Friedrich Nietzsche, *Nachgelassene Fragmente,* ed. Georgio Colli and Mazzino Montinari (Berlin: Walter de Gruyter, 1972), vol. VIII3, p. 158; *The Will to Power,* trans. Walter Kaufmann and R. S. Hollingdale (London: Weidenfeld and Nicolson, 1967), ¶ 864.

16. Emmanuel Levinas *Totalité et Infini: Essai sur l'extériorité* (The Hague: Nijhoff, 1961), pp. 124–25, *Totality and Infinity: An Essay on Exteriority,* trans. Alphonso Lingis (The Hague: Nijhoff, 1969), pp. 150–51.

17. Derrida, *La carte postale,* p. 9, *The Post Card,* p. 5.

18. Jacques Derrida, *Psyché: inventions de l'autre* (Paris: Galilée, 1987), pp. 180ff.

19. Ibid.

20. Derrida, *La carte postale,* p. 30, *The Post Card,* p. 25, and see *"Le facteur de la vérité"* in the same volume.

21. Richard Holloway, *On Forgiveness: How Can we Forgive the Unforgivable?* (Edinburgh: Canongate, 2002).

22. See John Llewelyn, *"Le pas du repas,"* in *Derrida,* ed. Marie-Louise Mallet and Ginette Michaud (Paris: L'Herne, 2004), pp. 96–101, reproduced here with their and the publisher's kind permission. It tells the story of a missed occasion for hospitality that became an occasion for smiling between Derrida and me, but that was, unlike the missed occasion mentioned half-jokingly on my card to him from Città, an occasion the missing of which I cannot attempt to excuse on theological grounds.

## Le Pas du Repas

### Hors d'œuvre

Ce sacré pas du repas! Un motif de sourire entre nous . . . L'occasion en fut donnée par le colloque "Victor Cousin, les Idéologues et leurs rapports avec la philosophie écossaise" qui eut lieu au Centre international d'Études de Sèvres, en 1982, sous la direction de Derrida du côté français, de moi du côté écossais, et de Pierre Alexandre qui, alors directeur-adjoint du Centre et ancien directeur de l'Institut

Français d'Écosse, était bien placé pour coordonner nos efforts. Le professeur Henri Gouhier nous avait honorés de sa présence et de ses commentaires. Au cours du weekend les participants visitèrent la Bibliothèque Victor Cousin à la Sorbonne. Pour terminer le colloque, Derrida nous invita à une réception à l'École Normale Supérieure. Le dernier soir, plusieurs d'entre nous, y compris mon cher collègue George Davie, dînâmes ensemble dans un restaurant de la rue Descartes. Mais sans Derrida. Nous avions omis de l'inviter! Pas tout à fait sans raison. Pour ma part, j'avais pensé qu'il préférerait sans doute retourner aussitôt à son travail d'écrivain. Mais quand même nous aurions dû l'inviter! C'est à dire, j'aurais dû le faire, moi, qui étais trop peu sensible et peut-être à la fois trop sensible.

*Entrée*

Peut-on être trop sensible? Est-on responsable de ne pas être trop sensible? Est-on responsable de ne pas être trop *responsive,* comme on dit en anglais, trop suscep-tible aux susceptibilités d'autrui? Si oui, serait-ce peut-être à cause du mot "trop," parce qu'on ne doit pas être trop quoi que ce soit, même pas trop bon? Selon Ar-istote l'homme de la sagesse pratique, le *phronimos,* doit éviter le trop, soit le trop peu, le trop court, soit le trop tout court. Excès ou défaut, le trop est dans les deux cas et de trop et un défaut: toujours une faute, toujours un manque, toujours un *shortcoming.* Évitons donc pour le moment le mot "trop," non seulement afin de ne pas contrarier Aristote, mais puisque tout énoncé de la forme "il ne faut pas faire trop de *x*" est vraisemblablement tautologique. En tant qu'énoncé tautologique il ne pourrait pas servir de maxime pratique. Une tautologie n'entraîne qu'une autre tautologie. Évitant toujours le mot "trop," dirait-on alors plutôt qu'il faut ménager les susceptibilités d'autrui, qu'il faut y être susceptible? Est-ce que ménager les susceptibilités d'autrui est une façon de se conduire avec modération?

Ménager c'est épargner, ne pas être prodigue, économiser. Et pour qu'il y ait un ménage il faut qu'il y ait un *oikos.* Ménager est une façon de *to manage,* de manier et de manœuvrer. Du *ménage* on passe par le *household* à la *manus* et à la *maintenance* du touchant-touché. Or, si c'est à Merleau-Ponty, parmi d'autres, que Derrida nous renvoie quand il parle du touchant-touché, dans *Le Toucher, Jean-Luc Nancy,* c'est chez Merleau-Ponty aussi qu'on trouve l'idée de la juste distance perceptive. Et celle-ci se trouve elle-même au juste milieu de l'idée aristotélicienne du juste milieu, du *mesotēs.* L'excès, le défaut et le juste milieu appartiennent à l'appartenance et à l'à-part-tenance. Mais il y a deux dimensions d'appartenance. Il y a celle de l'excès ou du défaut par rapport au juste milieu, et il y a celle de l'agent par rapport au *phronimos.* Le premier rapport est porté par l'agent et par le *phroni-mos.* Mais le rapport que porte l'agent ne reproduit pas celui que porte le *phroni-mos.* Il faut que le rapport que porte le *phronimos* soit adapté à l'état psychologique et circonstanciel de l'agent particulier. Comment cette adaptation se fait-elle? Non pas à la lumière d'un deuxième *phronimos,* puis d'un troisième, et ainsi de suite à l'infini. Plutôt au clair-obscur d'un savoir mélangé avec un non-savoir. On juge. Et la justesse du jugement n'égale jamais la justice constituée par rapport à des lois. La justesse comme disposition, comme modalité et comme savoir-faire ne se confond pas avec la justice comme état de choses connaissable. La justesse du savoir-faire peut ne pas atteindre la justice du droit sans pour autant manquer de justesse. Car tandis que la justice ainsi conçue a affaire aux critères universels et publics, la justesse regarde l'occasion particulière et personnelle. C'est pour cette raison que ma responsabilité éthique n'est pas seulement de faire la justice. Faire la justice ne serait que faire l'acte prescrit par la loi. La responsabilité éthique demande que l'acte réponde aux nuances de l'occasion, à son *ēthos*. Elle demande que ce que l'on décide de faire exprime l'esprit de finesse. La responsabilité éthique ne peut pas ne pas s'exercer d'une manière *responsive*.

Selon cette figure aristotélicienne, la responsabilité serait aussi une *ability*. Elle serait un "je peux." La première responsabilité de la responsabilité serait d'apprendre une habileté. Et cette habileté serait une habileté qui comprend une "habilité," en l'occurrence la qualité qui qualifie quelqu'un à servir d'exemple parce qu'il porte en lui l'exemplaire du *phronimos*, exemplaire comme paradigme logique et "pathétique," comme *logos* selon lequel on agit et réagit. Sauf que ni moi ni ce "type" que je porte en moi ne répond à toute question qui se pose. Je ne peux m'en servir pour calculer ce que je dois faire, et personne ne peut se servir de moi comme axiome d'un pareil calcul. Le *phronimos* n'est pas un paradigme dans le sens platonicien. Il est toujours quelqu'un en chair et en os, comme le sculpteur dont la production et le produit incorporent la juste mesure de la beauté ou comme le médecin qui ordonne un traitement qui exprime la juste mesure de la santé. Chez Aristote la vertu s'entend comme état de santé. Cela ne veut pas dire qu'Aristote soit un Nietzsche avant la lettre. Car tandis que chez lui la santé qui définit la vertu s'identifie à la juste mesure par rapport à un milieu, chez Nietzsche la santé n'est pas un état, donc *a fortiori* pas un état moyen; elle est un processus vers un extrême, un excès où ce qui est excédé est l'humain trop humain. Voici un excès tropique, excès qui tourne le dos à un "trop" humain, trop humain, c'est à dire trop humainement moyen, afin de chercher un "trop" humainement super-latif, c'est à dire humain-surhumain, extrême dont la science est un gai savoir qui est en même temps une gaie folie plutôt qu'une sobre sagesse. La "science" de la science morale est folle parce que là où il y a morale il n'y pas de mathématique; il y a la décision pour laquelle il n'existe pas de procédure ou de méthode. En fin de compte, la décision éthique est folle précisément parce qu'elle est la fin du compte, du nombre, du calcul et de la mesure: parce qu'elle est la fin de la précision mathé-matique et le commencement du "précis," du sommaire et de l'enthymème dont les prémisses manquantes sont contingentes. Question encore du *tingere*, du tact, du toucher, du manuel, de la *manus* et de la *rule of thumb*. Question de ce genre de question dont la responsabilité de la réponse n'est jamais sans crise, sans saut, sans irresponsabilité.

C'est Aristote qui insiste sur le fait que prévoir l'exactitude mathématique dans le champ de l'éthique serait aussi inopportun que de se contenter de la rhé-torique persuasive dans le champ de la mathématique. Nonobstant cette déclara-tion d'Aristote, c'est lui aussi qui affirme non seulement qu'il pourrait y avoir une science, une *epistēmē*, de l'éthique, mais que l'éthique est une *epistēmē*, c'est-à-dire le savoir pratique ou la sagesse qu'il appelle la *phronēsis*. Nous savons que la *phronēsis* est la vertu entendue comme la compétence pratique pour se conduire selon la juste mesure, disons la justesse. Mais nous devons ajouter qu'elle est simul-tanément la science théorique de cette pratique. La disposition qui se dit sagesse pratique est en même temps une sagesse théorique.

Pensant peut-être à ce que veut dire la sagesse pour Aristote et pour Hegel, tous deux amis d'une notion de sagesse ultime conçue comme *noēsis noēseōs*, Derrida se sert du mot sagesse avec précaution. Il "ose" s'en servir, a-t-il dit un jour. Mais, sans employer ce mot pour nommer cette sagesse extrême, il s'en est servi en adressant un compliment à un ami. Il est donc ami de ce mot, ou au moins n'en est-il pas ennemi. Mais l'expression dont il ne se servirait jamais, a-t-il dit aussi, c'est la "sagesse post-déconstructive." Que pourait signifier, si elle signifie quelque chose, l'expression "sagesse post-déconstructive"? Recommençons avec la sagesse non de l'homme supérieur ou du dieu mais de l'homme moyen doué de la vertu de trouver le juste milieu tel qu'Aristote le décrit. Le *phronimos* auquel cet homme moyen fait appel ne permet pas d'exception. S'il ne permet pas d'exception, cependant, ce n'est pas à cause de la rigueur d'une loi, mais parce qu'il fonctionne comme guide en fonctionnant comme exemplaire, donc sans qu'il y ait lieu de formuler une loi ou une règle. De ce point de vue l'éthique d'Aristote s'approche plus de la *Critique de la faculté de juger* (ou inversement), qu'elle ne le fait de la *Critique de la raison pratique*. Et lorsque Derrida, contre ceux qui l'accusent d'anarchisme, répète qu'il n'est pas contre la loi, sa réplique emprunte le langage "juif " de cette deuxième *Critique*. Voilà une base sur laquelle se fonde la possibilité de parler d'exception. Sans règle ou maxime ou loi, il ne peut pas y avoir d'exception. Mais ce n'est pas l'exception ainsi conçue qui est l'exception la plus intéressante invoquée dans les écrits de Derrida. Une telle exception fait partie de l'ensemble de concepts qui comprend aussi ceux de l'équité et de la réforme de la loi. Elle fait partie de l'espace de la légalité et de l'égalité. Infiniment plus intéressante que cette exception est celle que Derrida appelle l'archi-exception. L'archi-exceptionalité est infiniment plus intéressante aussi que l'exceptionalité d'une sagesse exceptionnelle. Une telle sagesse est une sagesse d'un degré peu commun. Néanmoins, entendue dans le sens d'Aristote, une telle sagesse resterait une manifestation de la *mesotēs*—de ce que les Romains appelleront la *mediocritas*. Elle resterait critique, jugement et critique de la faculté de juger. D'un infiniment plus grand intérêt que ces deux sortes d'exceptionalité, plus intéressante puisque hors du champ de l'intér-esse-ment, l'archi-exceptionalité manifeste, sans manifester, une essence, une essence sans essence, une essence hypo-critique. Nous avons observé que le jugement entendu comme justesse, comme sensibilité répondant aux nuances de la situation particulière, se distingue de la justice déterminée à la lumière de principes. L'archi-exception est plus principe encore que le principe et encore plus *hypo* que la justesse ainsi comprise. Elle est plus "archi," si bien qu'on ne peut la dénommer "archi" sans une certaine hypocrisie, sans affecter une vertu qui manque. L'exception archi-anarchique est une exception absolue, mais absolue dans un sens tout autre que ne l'est la sagesse absolue.

La sagesse absolue con-struit le savoir et le su. L'archi-exception s'absout du savoir. En elle la construction se déconstruit. Sauf que simultanément se déconstruit le "se." Ce "se" se laisse-t-il comparer à l'"*es*" de l'"*es gibt*" heideggerien, ou au "se" de l'accusatif absolu de Levinas? Pour ne pas chercher plus loin, ce "se" du se déconstruire se trouve et se perd dans l'héritage de l'"*es*" heideggerien et du "se" absolument accusatif de Levinas. Ce "se" a une histoire, comme l'histoire elle-même. Peut-on comparer des choses sans quoi il n'y a pas de *peut* et pas de "je peux"? Est-il possible de comparer les conditions de la possibilité de la possibilité et de la comparaison? Lorsque c'est de l'être de la raison et de la raison d'être qu'il s'agit, lorsque c'est de l'être *um* lequel *es geht,* ou lorsque ce qui est en question dans n'importe quelle question théorique ou pratique est celui ou celle qui pose de telles questions, on ne peut parler que de quasi-conditions, de quasi-possibilités, de quasi-comparaison. Ici le quasi est le *als ob,* le "comme si" d'une prétention à une comme-paraison et comme-par-raison, prétention hypocrite et hypo-critique, donc faute pré-originelle: faute "par défaut," un peu dans le sens du programme d'un ordinateur, mais avant tout calcul, avant toute fondation et avant toute con-struction. Donc indéconstructible.

Derrida dit de la justice qu'elle est indéconstructible. Comment indéconstructible, étant donné qu'il dit aussi que même la déconstruction se déconstruit? Mais dire ceci ne veut pas dire que la déconstruction peut être dépassée. Rappelons ce "se" déjà cité. Dire que la déconstruction se déconstruit c'est dire que la déconstruction n'est jamais dépassée, car se déconstruire veut dire, sans vouloir, se supplémenter toujours du plus de l'en sus et du (ne) plus du moins. Elle est toujours trop et toujours trop peu. Elle est toujours *exotique,* à la différence de la sagesse *mésotique.* Et puisque la justice indéconstructible quasi-conditionne la sagesse, il ne peut pas y avoir de sagesse post-déconstructive.

À partir de la justice indéconstructible l'esprit géométrique de la justice judiciaire et l'esprit de finesse de la justesse s'hybrident. Avant la simple lettre de la loi, avant la simple sensibilité du jugement particulier et avant toute construction, à partir de la justice indéconstructible la particularité du cas et la singularité se croisent l'une l'autre. Et si la justice est aveugle, la justice indéconstructible est aveugle pluriellement. À la cécité de la justice judiciaire du tiers, la justice indéconstructible supplée par la vigilance envers la deuxième personne et le tiers exclu. Cette suppléance a lieu au point aveugle où cette cécité et cette vigilance se provoquent l'une l'autre. Ce point est le *point* de construction, son point zéro, son pas. Il est le "là" où la construction ne peut être comprise, le "là" qui nous oblige à avouer qu'il ne peut pas y avoir de science purement théorique, surtout de science théorique de la pratique telle qu'Aristote l'envisage, qu'il ne peut pas y avoir de philosophie purement spéculative, qu'il ne peut pas y avoir d'amour de la sagesse sans qu'il y ait sagesse de l'amour. Non-lieu au cœur d'un chiasme où "il," "elle" et "vous" se syncopent, où, comme dirait Deleuze, on bégaie même en parlant sa propre langue, comme si celle-ci était une autre langue, la langue de l'autre, et comme si, dirait Derrida, ma langue propre était toujours la langue de l'autre. Non-coïncidence, comme dirait Levinas, du dit et du dire dans le Dire du Désir, c'est-à-dire dans la sophophilie. Non-coïncidence dans l'archi-écrire, comme dirait encore Derrida. Non-contenance du *dans* dont l'intériorité s'extériorise grâce au "me voici" non citable—car les guillemets coupent mon souffle—où je suis cité et incité quand même, assigné par autrui à comparaître, sans comparaison et sans être coupable d'aucune faute par commission ou par omission.

*Plat de résistance*

Faute d'avoir invité Derrida à ce repas dans la rue Descartes il y a plus de vingt ans, je lui ai donné le don d'être donateur, et, comme le dit, entre autres, Aristote, cité par Derrida, il semble que l'amitié consiste moins à être aimé, c'est-à-dire à recevoir, qu'à aimer, c'est à dire à donner. Ferait-on mieux de ni donner ni recevoir? D'une telle abstention même le solitaire n'est pas capable. C'est la condition humaine que de récolter des dilemmes d'échange sans échelle justicière d'après laquelle les mesurer et les résoudre. Voilà pourquoi l'être humain pourrait se définir comme l'animal qui sourit. Et voilà pourquoi ce pas du repas est un motif de sourire entre Derrida et moi. Ce faux pas du repas, *false step* et *full stop,* inertie, point, n'est pas une privation des plus graves. Personne ne court le risque d'en souffrir sérieusement ou d'en mourir. Pas de trépas encouru par ce pas. Mais sous ce sourire, comme l'Écrire sous le Dire, il y a le Sourire qui définit la mortalité de la vie humaine, qui marque la finitude humaine, sa façon d'être finie, *finished, over and done with,* terminée, et d'être en même temps infinie, *unfinished,* inachevée: infinie parce que finie, et finie, définie par la finitude, parce qu'infinie. Il faut avouer que j'écrivis à Derrida que je l'invitais, et je l'aurai(s) invité *hereby,* par la présente, à un repas où il aura(it) mangé de "la miellée" et bu "le lait du Paradis."

*For he on honey-dew hath fed,*
*And drunk the milk of Paradise.*

Ce sont les derniers vers de *Kubla Khan,* poème infini, *unfinished,* parce que pendant sa composition Coleridge fut interrompu par un visiteur, le fameux *"person from Porlock."* Je disais un jour à Derrida que j'avais toujours peur en lui écrivant d'être *"the person from Porlock,"* tant il lui faudrait de temps, à son bureau, pour composer un si grand corpus d'œuvres si scrupuleuses.

Pour plus de précaution et pour le cas où ce que Austin appelle les conditions de justesse ou de bonheur (*felicity*) de mon *speech act* performatif ne seraient pas toutes satisfaites, je lui offre en souriant ce petit écrit trop peu scrupuleux et peut-être trop scrupuleux ou sensible à la fois. La meilleure part de ce que j'écris ici lui redonne ce qu'il a donné, mais suivant ce qu'il disait un jour à propos de Levinas et comme le pas du repas, sans réciprocité totale ni totalisante. Cet écrit, bien qu'il puisse sembler boucler la boucle, n'apporte pas de solution à notre dilemme. Il ne trouve pas de synthèse. Car, s'il y a dilemme ici, ce n'est ni ce que Cicéron appellerait une *complexio* de deux énoncés, ni un équilibre de revenus (un *lemma* est un profit reçu). Appelons ce dont il s'agit ici un "di-lemme," entendu comme complication d'énoncés et de revenus d'un côté et, de l'autre, comme recevoir "de" celui qui donne, dans les deux sens, "objectif" et "subjectif," de ce génitif. Ce serait une complication de la symétrie possible et de l'asymétrie impossible. Donc pas de résolution, pas de réponse à ce sacré problème du pas du repas où peut-être le sacré est plutôt le saint et le problème plutôt un mystère. Et ce "donc" résonne dans une syllogistique où l'intériorité du *dans* s'affecte de l'extériorité d'autrui, et où, donc, l'auto-affection s'affecte de l'affection de l'autre, encore dans les deux sens de ce "de" et dans le sens de ce "se" qui peut donner l'apparence que le se donner est réciproque, mais où cette apparence simultanément cache et exprime, comme fait le sourire, qui est à la fois expression physiognomique et plus que physiognomique. Plus que physiognomique parce que tragique, est-on tenté de dire, pourvu que le tragique ne soit pas pris en termes de contradiction formelle. Autrement tragique, le Sourire sous le sourire physiognomique mais en même temps s'y insinuant, est, comme la tragédie, chose sérieuse. Sérieuse parce que sérielle. Sérielle parce que se rapportant à la série, mais à la série non dans le sens de classe ou de *set* de la théorie des ensembles, mais au sens où Derrida nous la donne à entendre en expliquant la complication du dit, du dire et du Dire dans les écrits de Levinas.

Ouvrons une parenthèse pour parler brièvement de la bouche ouverte du rire et du comique. On rit parfois afin de ne pas pleurer. Mais le rire en tant que tel n'est jamais d'évasion. On rit parfois pour ne pas gêner autrui ou soi-même. Mais comme la rose d'Angelus Silesius, en tant que rire, le rire est sans pourquoi. On ne rit que pour rire. Comme on ne pleure que pour pleurer, quoique souvent en pleurant on pleure une personne ou quelque chose et en pleurant on se soulage. Puisque pleurer c'est *to cry,* on comprend pourquoi le rire s'accompagne souvent de larmes, comme le tragique s'accompagne du comique. Ils ont la même structure, la structure déstructurée, déconstruite, schizo-psychotique. Archi- et anarchi-hypocrite, le rire et le pleurer sont néanmoins la sincérité même. Le rire et le pleurer nous arrivent *sponte sua*. Ils nous surprennent. Ils portent tous deux la trace de la surprise par excellence, de l'excès qui affole le juste milieu. Ce qui rend possible et impossible ce *mesotēs* d'Aristote c'est le *thaumazō*, le (s')être étonné dans lequel, et c'est encore Aristote, entre autres, qui le dit, la philosophie a son commencement, la philosophie—et la sophophilie, qui est peut-être le commencement de la vie, au moins de la vie adulte. (Rit-il ou pleure-t-il, l'enfant qui s'écrie au moment de naître? Et quoi de l'animal nouveau-né, l'animal qui, dit on, reste à jamais *infans*, l'animal, pour ainsi dire anautobiographique?)

C'est Hobbes qui écrit que le rire est une gloire soudaine, *a sudden glory (sudden gl-ory,* suis-je tenté d'écrire). *Exaiphnēs,* le rire est un *glad start (gl-ad start),* un commencement qui nous surprend, nous *startle.* Si Hobbes a raison, on regarde de haut en bas lorsqu'on se couvre de gloire, de *kudos,* comme dit le Grec pensant par exemple à l'honneur gagné dans une guerre. Pensons donc plutôt au mot hébreu *kavod,* dont se sert Levinas quand il glorifie la gloire. Pour lui ce mot veut dire le respect et la révérence sans lesquels il n'y a pas de paix, si ce n'est celle qui signifie la fin d'une guerre. Bien que dans le *kavod* respectueux sonne une note sombre—et en effet le mot hébreu peut signifier la lourdeur dans un sens figuratif—le *kavod* entendu comme condition de la paix reste quelque chose dont on jouit. Et la joie, non moins que la conscience morale selon Heidegger, n'arrive pas simplement du dedans de moi. Elle arrive comme d'en dessus de moi et ainsi sans m'autoriser à me vanter ou à regarder autrui de haut en bas. C'est cette idée de regarder de haut en bas qui est à l'œuvre lorsque Hobbes qualifie le rire de gloire soudaine. Et c'est de la notion grecque de la gloire qu'il se sert quand il estime que le rire exprime un sentiment de supériorité relativement à quelqu'un, quelqu'un par exemple qui n'a pas pu saisir une plaisanterie. L'homme qui rit se réjouit d'une petite victoire soit sur autrui, soit sur le moi lui-même, jugé moins éminent avant qu'il ait joui de cette gloire soudaine. Ce rire hobbesien peut être un rire *avec,* mais il est toujours aussi un rire *de.*

Ce fut un rire purement *avec* qui éclata à l'occasion d'un autre repas, qui cette fois ne manqua pas d'avoir lieu, un repas avec Derrida et d'autres amis. Ce repas eut lieu à l'aéroport de Nashville, après un colloque à Vanderbilt où les discussions ne s'écartèrent guère de la question de la signature. On mangeait. On causait. Puis, soudain, on rit, glorieusement. Parce qu'à mesure que Derrida vidait son assiette, et nous les nôtres, se découvrait, dans le fond, comme émaillé (on aurait dit des pièces de Sèvres) un seul mot: *Signature.* Généralement, donc non sans exception, il faut ouvrir la bouche pour rire, comme pour parler et pour manger, tandis que, tout aussi généralement, on sourit sans ouvrir les lèvres, sans ouvrir la bouche. Sans ouvrir la bouche, je parle ici du sourire qui n'est pas un moindre degré du rire, le degré le plus bas sur l'échelle "gélotique," même pas un rire *avec (syggelaō)* qui est plus près que le rire *de* du sourire, ce sourire sans agitation dont il s'agit en ce moment. Le sourire *(smile)* auquel je pense est un sourire *dé-ri,* sans *ridere* et tout à fait sans dérision, un *subridere* ou *surridere* ou archi-sourire qui est dans un certain sens silencieux, sygétique. Voici un silence qui se communique sans rien dire, silence de l'écrire, silence, dirait Derrida, de l'archi-écrire. Et il faut dire que le sourire du pas du repas qui est un motif de sourire entre nous est un sourire essentiellement épistolaire, entre nous entre les lignes . . . Sourire postal et à-la-carte-postale, sourire de *meal* et de *mail: mailsmile, meidēma.* Nous parlons d'une lettre et du ne pas parler de la lettre *m*, en particulier de l'*m* de *muō*, mot grec qui, sans savoir rien dire, veut dire fermer. On suppose, supposant qu'une chose telle que dérivation existe, que *muō* dérive de *mu'* ou de *mu'*, qu'on prononce en fermant les lèvres, et qui s'associent au sanscrit *mū*. Le dictionnaire se demande si ce dernier se lie au latin *ligāre*, lier, éventualité qui ouvrirait la question de savoir si ce lier n'est pas seulement le *ligāre* de *religāre*, ni seulement le *legere* de *relegere*, rassembler, mais se lie aussi au délier du *lēgāre* de *relēgāre*, renvoyer, éloigner, isoler, de telle sorte que la religion aurait quelque chose à voir avec le mystère et avec la mystique, dont les appellations sont dérivées ou dé-rivées de *muō*. Si bien qu'on pourrait imaginer quelque chose comme un sourire qui renverrait à la force mystique non directement de (la) loi, soit loi éthique soit loi politique, mais à la force mystique de celles-ci par la simple politesse ou décence, telle celle à laquelle renvoyait Derrida, je m'en souviens, au cours d'un colloque sur sa lecture de Husserl, à Memphis dans, le croira qui voudra, une pyramide.

### Des(s)ert

Ne rions pas. S'il ne faut pas exagérer la gravité de la négligence qui avait mené à la place vide à la table dans le restaurant de la rue Descartes, négligence dont le pire aurait été de traiter Derrida en machine à écrire, il ne faut pas négliger non plus ce à quoi je pensais quand, souriant, je me trouvais porté à décrire ce pas du repas comme sacré. Y a-t-il chose plus sacrée qu'un repas? Y a-t-il chose plus sacrée que le re- et le pas d'un repas? Sans parler de la scène de la Cène ou du dire merci Eucharistique, je pense à la collation du colloque de Cerisy sur l'œuvre de Levinas où l'auteur de l'essai "Nom d'un chien et le droit naturel" et moi avons échangé des pensées au sujet de l'animal et, sensibles au fait qu'on passait outre au protocole de l'étiquette, de la viande dans la bonne soupe.

J'ai assisté aux autres décades de Cerisy, y compris celle de 1972 dédiée à Nietzsche au cours de laquelle Derrida a posé "La question du style," la décade de 1980 intitulée "Les Fins de l'homme: à partir du travail de Jacques Derrida," et celle de 1992 intitulée "Le passage des frontières: autour du travail de Jacques Derrida." À chacun de ces colloques et aux autres réunions auxquelles j'ai assisté avec Derrida aux universités d'Édimbourg, d'Alabama, de Chicago, de New York et de Berkeley, nous étions tous les deux convives, hôtes-*guests*, sans occasion d'être hôtes-*hosts*. Ainsi en était-il une fois encore au colloque de Pérouse traitant, entre autres thèmes, de la classification, à la suite duquel je me suis trouvé dans un train qui s'est arrêté dans une gare où j'ai pu lire sur un panneau, juste en face de ma vitre, le nom *Classe*. Malheureusement, je n'ai pas assisté au colloque de Cerisy de 1997 intitulé "L'animal autobiographique: autour de Jacques Derrida." Pourquoi? Parce que bien qu'on mangeât fort bien à Cerisy, et il faut bien manger, je ne pouvais pas me résoudre à manger l'autre animal. Les cuisinières cordon bleu du château de Cerisy avaient du mal à comprendre le concept de végétarisme. Elles étaient du côté d'Abel plutôt que du côté de Caïn. Quelle ironie! Car Derrida trouve ce concept, sinon facile à saisir, au moins suffisamment compréhensible pour pouvoir dire un jour à David Wood et moi-même, autant qu'il m'en souvienne, que nous avions failli le convertir au végétarisme. En tout cas, au cours des dix jours pendant lesquels il a parlé, dix heures durant, du *bios* et de la *zōē*, il disait que la question de l'animal avait toujours été pour lui la question la plus importante et la plus décisive, depuis le temps où il avait commencé à écrire. Pour soutenir cette déclaration il esquissait ce qu'il appelait une zoo-auto-bio-bibliographie qui énumère les bêtes qui ont été invitées à bord de l'archi-arche de ses écrits. Quelle chance a-t-on laissé passer quand on a décidé de ne pas assister à ce colloque où il parlait de "L'animal que donc je suis (à suivre)" et quand on a omis de l'inviter à nous suivre dans la rue Descartes! Quelle chance perdue de causer, face à face, à table avec lui, au sujet de ce mystère du sacré-sacrificiel pas du repas dont le *pas* est déjà le *re-* parce qu'il cache sa dérivation présumée de *paître*, si bien ou si mal que, couteau et fourchette à la main, on se repaît de ce qui quelque temps auparavant paîssait à sa place au soleil!

Derrida aurait été et a été effectivement plus prêt que Levinas à mentionner, d'un même souffle, deux inadvertances, et à se demander s'il se peut que l'une des deux, celle qui pourrait sembler ne soulever que des questions de cuisine apparemment banales, ait affaire à l'autre, celle de l'holocauste, dont personne ne doit nier la monstruosité éthique et politique. On se demande aussi si de telles inadvertances éthiques ou hyper-éthiques pourraient soudre d'une inadvertance d'impolitesse telle que l'omission d'inviter quelqu'un à vous rejoindre à table. Ne rions pas. Avouons au moins entre nous que bien qu'une telle omission soit un motif de sourire entre Derrida et moi, dans la gloire soudaine du coup de glotte du sourire sœur du sanglot, il y va du sous-dire et du souscrire hypogélotique qui témoignent d'un autre juste milieu, juste mi-lieu entre la proximité et la distance où le *kavod* traverse le *kudos* et où, de la réciprocité du sourire entre nous au sujet du pas du repas, sourd sourdement et soudainement la reconnaissance sans connaissance et sans naissance d'Elie ou de l'autre autre qui aura été pour toujours en dehors de la réciprocité, l'étranger qui aura été à jamais le jamais invité.

23. Kathleen Jamie, *Findings* (London: Sort of Books, 2005). A "wonderful book," as Richard Holloway says.

24. See John Llewelyn, *Seeing Through God: A Geophenomenology* (Bloomington: Indiana University Press, 2004), especially chapter 9, entitled "Regarding Regarding."

25. Rowan Williams, *Ponder These Things: Praying with Icons of the Virgin* (Norwich: Canterbury Press, 2002).

26. For thoughts on Mallarmé's mourning for his son that bear on the present meditation (is it a *Tombeau*?) see John Llewelyn, "Derrida, Mallarmé, and Anatole," chapter 2 of John Llewelyn, *Appositions of Jacques Derrida and Emmanuel Levinas* (Bloomington: Indiana University Press, 2002), also in *Philosophers' Poets,* ed. David Wood (London: Routledge, 1990).

27. Jacques Derrida, *Feu la cendre* (Paris: Des Femmes, 1987), pp. 15, 21, 25, 33.

28. Jacques Derrida, "The Time of a Thesis: Punctuations," in *Philosophy in France Today,* ed. Alan Montefiore (Cambridge: Cambridge University Press, 1983), p. 37.

29. Jacques Derrida, *Chaque fois unique, la fin du monde,* ed. Pascale-Anne Brault and Michael Naas (Paris: Galilée, 2003).

30. Derrida, *Psyche,* p. 97.

31. Saint Augustine, *Confessions,* Book 9, chapter 6, translated from the citation by Marie-Louise Mallet, "*La musique et le Nom: 'Comment ne pas parler?'*" in *Le passage des frontières: Autour du travail de Jacques Derrida,* Colloque de Cerisy (Paris: Galilée, 1994), p. 519.

32. Jacques Derrida, *La voix et le phénomène* (Paris: Presses Universitaires de France, 1967), pp. 60–61, 108, *Speech and Phenomena,* trans. David B. Allison and Newton Garver (Evanston, Ill.: Northwestern University Press, 1973), pp. 54, 96–97.

33. As he would have on learning that I had learned also of his death by e-mail (thanks to Elsebet Jegstrup and Marie-Louise Mallet).

34. Jacques Derrida, *Résistances de la psychanalyse* (Paris: Galilée, 1996), p. 57.

35. Saint Augustine, *Confessions,* Book 10, chapter 33. Geoffrey Bennington and Jacques Derrida, *Jacques Derrida* (Paris: Seuil, 1991), pp. 95, 96.

36. Saint Augustine, *Confessions,* Book 1, chapter 2.

37. The anagram is noted by Jack Caputo and Mary Shelley.

38. Derrida, *La carte postale,* p. 133, *The Post Card,* p. 121.

39. Ties, tapes, double binds. "I like your tie," Derrida once remarked. It was one designed by Escher, a cunning mosaic in which the shapes between birds are still more birds. I had bought it at the Scottish Gallery of Modern Art. They had a slightly pinker version, which I sent him. That he liked it is confirmed by photographs that appeared in French newspapers brought to my attention by Ursula Sarrazin and Alain David. *Plethyn* is the title of a Welsh folk-singing group, one of whose tapes I sent Derrida to play in his car as he shuttled between Ris-Orangis and the rue d'Ulm.

40. Derrida, *La carte postale,* p. 9, *The Post Card,* p. 5.

41. Ibid., p. 29, p. 24.

42. Jacques Derrida, *Marges de la philosophie* (Paris: Minuit, 1972), pp. 19-20, *Margins of Philosophy,* trans. Alan Bass (Chicago: University of Chicago Press, 1982), p. 18.

43. Francis Fukuyama, *The End of History and the Last Man* (New York: Free Press, 1992). Jacques Derrida, *Spectres de Marx: L'État de la dette, le travail du deuil et la nouvelle Internationale* (Paris: Galilée, 1993), *Specters of Marx: The State of the Debt, the Work of Mourning, and the New International,* trans. Peggy Kamuf (New York: Routledge, 1994), chapter 2.

44. Jacques Derrida, *"Survivre,"* in *Parages* (Paris: Galilée, 1986), p. 197.

45. Derek Attridge, ed., *Acts of Literature: Jacques Derrida* (London: Routledge, 1992), pp. 65-66.

46. Jacques Derrida, *Limited Inc,* trans. Samuel Weber and Jeffrey Mehlman (Evanston, Ill.: Northwestern University Press), p. 105.

47. Edmund Husserl, *L'origine de la géométrie,* trans. and introduction Jacques Derrida (Paris: Presses Universitaires de France, 1962), *Edmund Husserl's Origin of Geometry: An Introduction,* trans. John P. Leavey, Jr. (New York: Nicolas Hays, 1978).

48. Jacques Derrida, *"Fors,"* introduction to Nicolas Abraham and Maria Torok, *Cryptonymie: le verbier de l'homme aux loups* (Paris: Aubier-Flammarion, 1976), pp. 15ff., 42n.

49. Derrida, *"Survivre,"* in *Parages,* p. 189.

50. They take me back also to the oversight treated in *"Le pas du repas."* See note 22 above.

51. Jacques Derrida, *Glas* (Paris: Galilée, 1974), 163a, *Glas,* trans. John P. Leavey Jr., and Richard Rand (Lincoln: University of Nebraska Press, 1984), 144a.

52. Parergonality, already invoked early in this chapter, is treated in Jacques Derrida, *La vérité en peinture* (Paris: Flammarion, 1978), *The Truth in Painting,* trans. Geoff Bennington and Ian McLeod (Chicago: University of Chicago Press, 1987). Among questions that I have had to neglect is that of the relation of the framed blanks in *The Truth in Painting* to the omissions in *The Post Card.*

53. As I now insert the following final anecdote on behalf of some of those friends. Two of them arrived from outside France too late to be at the interment. So Ursula Sarrazin drove them to the cemetery on the following day. They observed a grave near Der-

rida's that was marked by a very simple wooden cross. They learned from the cemetery attendant that this was the grave, a "pauper's grave," of a member of the community who had died, as one says, "on the parish," too poor to meet the cost of burial. When I heard about this I could not help thinking of the beggar, the pray-er, in Baudelaire's *"La Fausse Monnaie,"* the text that was the subject of the first seminars of Derrida's that I attended, making my way to them by way of another cemetery, passing the tomb of Baudelaire.

54. Jacques Derrida, *"signature événement contexte,"* in *Marges de la philosophie,* pp. 365–93, "Signature Event Context," in *Margins of Philosophy,* pp. 307–30.

55. Saint Augustine, *Confessions,* Book 1, chapter 1. Romans 10:14 was part of the lesson I was once asked to read in the pilgrimage church on Bardsey, Ynys Enlli, the little island off the tip of the Llŷn Peninsula in Wales, site of a Celtic and subsequently Augustinian monastery and, allegedly, burial place of 200,000 Celtic saints.

56. Søren Kierkegaard, *Journals and Papers,* trans. Howard V. Hong and Edna H. Hong (Bloomington: Indiana University Press, 1975), vol. 3, p. 558. In "hearing" (*"høren"*) Kierkegaard wants us to hear being obedient (*hørig*), as in the equivalents in Latin and German and French do Heidegger and Levinas.

57. Karl Barth, *Prayer,* ed. Don E. Saliers, trans. Sara F. Terrien (Philadelphia: Westminster Press, 1985), p. 33.

58. John C. Caputo, ed., *Deconstruction in a Nutshell: A Conversation with Jacques Derrida* (New York: Fordham University Press, 1997), p. 25.

59. Jacques Derrida, *Apories: Mourir—s'attendre aux "limites de la vérité"* (Paris: Galilée, 1996), p. 49, *Aporias: Dying—Awaiting (One Another) at the "Limits of Truth,"* trans. Thomas Dutoit (Stanford, Calif.: Stanford University Press, 1993), p. 22.

60. Hildebert of Lavardin, Archbishop of Tours, *Epistles,* circa 1125.

61. Jacques Derrida, *De l'esprit: Heidegger et la question* (Paris: Galilée, 1987), p. 184, *Of Spirit: Heidegger and the Question,* trans. Geoffrey Bennington and Rachel Bowlby (Chicago: University of Chicago Press), p. 113.

62. Jacques Derrida, *Politiques de l'amitié* (Paris: Galilée, 1994), p. 65, *Politics of Friendship,* trans. George Collins (London: Verso, 1997), p. 44.

63. Derrida, *Apories,* p. 133; *Aporias,* p. 76.

## 14. Oasis

1. Jacques Derrida, *Spectres de Marx: L'État de la dette, le travail du deuil et la nouvelle Internationale* (Paris: Galilée, 1993), p. 267, *Specters of Marx: The State of the Debt, the Work of Mourning, and the New International,* trans. Peggy Kamuf (New York: Routledge, 1994), p. 168.

2. John D. Caputo, ed. *Deconstruction in a Nutshell: A Conversation with Jacques Derrida* (New York: Fordham University Press, 1997), p. 170.

3. Jacques Derrida, *Apories: Mourir—s'attendre aux "limites de la vérité"* (Paris: Galilée, 1996), pp. 139–40, *Aporias: Dying—Awaiting (One Another) at the "Limits of Truth,"* trans. Thomas Dutoit (Stanford, Calif.: Stanford University Press, 1993), pp. 80–81.

4. Emmanuel Levinas, *"Énigme et phénomène,"* in *En découvrant l'existence avec Husserl et Heidegger* (Paris: Vrin, 1982), p. 214, "Phenomenon and Enigma," trans. Alphonso Lingis, in *Collected Philosophical Papers* (The Hague: Nijhoff, 1947), p. 71, "Enigma and Phenomenon," trans. Alphonso Lingis (revised), in *Emmanuel Levinas: Basic Philosophical Writings,* ed. Adriaan T. Peperzak, Simon Critchley, and Robert Bernasconi (Bloomington: Indiana University Press, 1996), p. 75.

5. Ibid., p. 30, p. 11.

6. *Deconstruction in a Nutshell*, p. 23.

7. Martin Heidegger, *Beiträge zur Philosophie (Vom Ereignis)* (Frankfurt am Main: Klostermann, 1989), p. 94, *Contributions to Philosophy (From Enowning)*, trans. Parvis Emad and Kenneth Maly (Bloomington: Indiana University Press, 1999), p. 65.

8. See Hent de Vries, *Philosophy and the Turn to Religion* (Baltimore: Johns Hopkins University Press, 1999), pp. 141ff.

9. *Deconstruction in a Nutshell*, p. 21.

10. See Derrida, "*Survivre*," in *Parages*, p. 209, on *laisser*, which recalls Heidegger's references to *tao* in connection with his *lassen*, and Levinas's references to passivity.

11. E. W. F. Tomlin, *Great Philosophers of the East* (London: Arrow Books, 1959), pp. 51, 65.

12. *Deconstruction in a Nutshell*, p. 21. Jacques Derrida, "The Eyes of Language: The Abyss and the Volcano," trans. Gil Anidjar, in *Acts of Religion*, ed. Gil Anidjar (New York: Routledge, 2002), pp. 191–227.

13. Derrida, *Apories*, p. 30, *Aporias*, p. 12.

14. Jacques Derrida, *Passions* (Paris: Galilée, 1993), pp. 27–28, "Passions," trans. David Wood, in *Derrida; A Critical Reader*, ed. David Wood (Oxford: Blackwell, 1992), pp. 10–11, trans. David Wood, in *On the Name* (Stanford, Calif.: Stanford University Press, 1995), p. 11.

15. Ibid., p. 27, p. 10, p. 10.

16. Derrida, *Apories*, p. 140, *Aporias*, p. 81. The aporia is reminiscent of the predicament that taxed Husserl in his *Crisis* and "The Origin of Geometry." See Edmund Husserl, *The Crisis of European Sciences and Transcendental Phenomenology: An Introduction to Phenomenological Philosophy*, trans. David Carr (Evanston, Ill.: Northwestern University Press, 1970). This aporia is not unrelated to Derrida's paragraphs on Gödel in the introduction to *Husserl's Origin of Geometry*, which bear in turn on what Quine writes about Gödel and the purity of logic in the paper Derrida helped to translate. The difficulties experienced by Husserl concerning what he calls the *Lebenswelt* haunt Derrida from his earliest writings up to "*Survivre*" and beyond. Another way of putting deconstruction in a nutshell, not to bury it nor to praise it, would be to say that it is a meditation on the threshold between the *Lebenswelt* and the *Todeswelt*, a tracing of the moment and the movement between the world and word of life and the world and word of death. When this meditation is also a meditation on the variety of circumstances subsumed in the remainder of this book under T. S. Eliot's phrase "birth, and copulation, and death," it is a meditation on one of the meanings of this book's title. Another margin meant by that title is the margin of the religious between the religions and the secular.

17. On this and related questions I have learned much from Elizabeth Templeton's vibrant *The Strangeness of God* (London: Arthur James, 1993), as too from convivial discussions when Timothy Sprigge, Basil O'Neill, and I have shared the hospitality she and Douglas extended to us at Tenandry manse. I have been surprised too by Richard Holloway's *The Stranger in the Wings: Affirming Faith in a God of Surprises* (London: SPCK, 1994), on page 33 of which are cited lines from Louis MacNeice's poem "Mutation," including the warning:

The stranger in the wings is waiting for his cue
The fuse is always laid to some annunciation.

18. Charles P. Bigger, *Participation: A Platonic Inquiry* (Baton Rouge: Louisiana State University Press, 1968); *Kant's Methodology: An Essay in Philosophical Archeology* (Athens: Ohio University Press, 1996); *Between* Chora *and the Good: Metaphor's Metaphysical Neighbourhood* (New York: Fordham University Press, 2005). Except when citing the title of the last of these books, I add indications of the length of the Greek vowels. My reason for doing this will become clear in due course.

19. Bigger, *Between* Chora *and the Good,* p. 193.

20. Bruno Snell, *The Discovery of the Mind: The Greek Origins of European Thought,* trans. T. G. Rosenmeyer (Oxford: Blackwell, 1953), cited by Karl Löwith, *Gesammelte Abhandlungen: zur Kritik der geschichtlichen Existenz* (Stuttgart: Kohlhammer, 1960), p. 222, and Emmanuel Levinas, "La signification et le sens," in *L'humanisme de l'autre homme* (Montpellier: Fata Morgana, 1972), p. 23; "Signification and Sense," in Emmanuel Levinas, *Humanism of the Other Man,* trans. Nidra Poller (Urbana: University of Illinois Press, 2006), p. 12; *Collected Philosophical Papers,* trans. Alphonso Lingis (The Hague: Nijhoff, 1987), p. 78.

21. Emmanuel Levinas, *Totalité et Infini: essai sur l'extériorité* (The Hague: Nijhoff, 1968), p. XIV, *Totality and Infinity: An Essay on Exteriority,* trans. Alphonso Lingis (The Hague: Nijhoff, 1969), p. 26. Levinas's use of the notion of productivity is discussed in John Llewelyn, *Emmanuel Levinas: The Genealogy of Ethics* (London: Routledge, 1995), pp. 31–32, 67–68, 74–75.

22. Bigger acknowledges a special debt to Eugene Gendlin's work on metaphor.

23. Emmanuel Levinas, "La réalité et son ombre," *Les temps modernes* 38 (1948): 769–89; "Reality and its Shadow," trans. Alphonso Lingis, in *Collected Philosophical Papers,* pp. 1–13.

24. Bigger, *Between* Chora *and the Good,* p. 378.

25. Ibid., p. 238.

26. Levinas, *Totalité et Infini,* pp. 269–70, *Totality and Infinity,* pp. 293–94.

27. Bigger, *Kant's Methodology,* p. xxviii.

28. Bigger, *Between* Chora *and the Good,* p. 379.

29. Ibid., p. 378.

30. Ibid.

31. A reproduction of this icon can be seen in *Kant's Methodology.* See also P. A. Underwood, *The Kariye Djami,* 4 vols. (Princeton, N.J.: Princeton University Press, 1975).

32. Max Black, *Models and Metaphors* (Ithaca, N.Y.: Cornell University Press, 1962). Gennadios Limouris, comp., *Icons: Windows on Eternity: Theology and Spirituality in Colour* (Geneva: World Council of Churches, c1990).

33. Bigger, *Between* Chora *and the Good,* p. 155.

34. John Llewelyn, *The HypoCritical Imagination: Between Kant and Levinas* (London: Routledge, 2000).

35. Bigger, *Kant's Methodology,* p. xxxi.

36. Ibid., p. 321.

37. See the first section of chapter 11.

38. Edmund Husserl, *The Phenomenology of Internal Time Consciousness,* trans. James S. Churchill (The Hague: Nijhoff, 1964), p. 100. Emmanuel Levinas, *Autrement qu'être ou au-delà de l'essence* (The Hague: Nijhoff, 1978), p. 146; *Otherwise than Being or Beyond Essence,* trans. Alphonso Lingis (The Hague: Nijhoff, 1981), p. 113.

39. Bigger, *Between* Chora *and the Good,* pp. 397–98.

40. Ibid., p. 396.

41. Ibid., p. 378.

42. John Sallis, *Chorology: On Beginning in Plato's Timaeus* (Bloomington: Indiana University Press, 1999), pp. 116–17.

43. See Dennis Keenan, *The Question of Sacrifice* (Bloomington: Indiana University Press, 2005).

44. I am grateful for the assistance of Thomas Bedorf in this matter.

45. Jacques Derrida, *Khôra* (Paris: Galilée, 1993), p. 58; "*Khôra*," in Jacques Derrida, *On the Name*, trans. Ian McLeod (Stanford, Calif.: Stanford University Press, 1995), p. 109. In the text I have adopted a different convention for indicating long vowels.

46. Ibid., p. 63, p. 111.

47. Jacques Derrida, *Moscou aller-retour* (Paris: l'Aube, 1995), pp. 108ff.

48. Bigger, *Between* Chora *and the Good*, p. 335.

49. Ibid., p. 378.

50. Jacques Derrida, "*signature événement contexte*," in *Marges de la philosophie* (Paris: Minuit, 1972), pp. 365–93, "Signature Event Context," in *Margins of Philosophy*, trans. Alan Bass (Chicago: University of Chicago Press, 1982), pp. 307–30.

51. Levinas, *Totalité et Infini*, pp. 243–44, *Totality and Infinity*, pp. 265–66.

52. Jacques Derrida, *Passions*, "Passions," in *Derrida: A Critical Reader*, pp. 5–35, and in *On the Name*, pp. 3–31.

53. Derrida, *Khôra*, p. 95, "*Khôra*," in *On the Name*, p. 126.

54. Jacques Derrida, "On Forgiveness," in *Cosmopolitanism and Forgiveness*, trans. Mark Dooley and Michael Hughes (London: Routledge, 2001), pp. 44, 45, 55.

55. *Deconstruction in a Nutshell*, p. 170.

56. Karen Armstrong, *A History of God. From Abraham to the Present: The 4000-Year Quest for God* (London: Heinemann, 1993), p. 111.

57. Rowan Williams, *Grace and Necessity: Reflections on Art and Love* (London: Morehouse, 2005).

58. In chapter 11.

59. De Vries, *Philosophy and the Turn to Religion*, pp. 141ff.

60. John D. Caputo, *The Prayers and Tears of Jacques Derrida: Religion without Religion* (Bloomington: Indiana University Press, 1997), p. 142.

61. Jacques Derrida and Gianni Vattimo, *La religion* (Paris: Seuil, 1996), p. 67, *Acts of Religion*, p. 86.

62. At p. 177 of *Deconstruction in a Nutshell*. But see also Caputo, *The Prayers and Tears of Jacques Derrida*, pp. 139–42.

63. Jacques Derrida, *Passions;* "Passions," in *Derrida: A Critical Reader* and in *On the Name*.

64. Martin Heidegger, *Phänomenologische Interpretationen zu Aristoteles. Einführung in die phänomenologische Forschung* (*Gesamtausgabe* 61), (Frankfurt am Main: Klostermann, 1985), p. 37, cited in John van Buren, *The Young Heidegger: Rumor of the Hidden God* (Bloomington: Indiana University Press, 1994), p. 339. Pp. 324–41 are rich in hints concerning formal indication, as are the pages on that topic referred to in the index of Theodore Kisiel, *The Genesis of Heidegger's Being and Time* (Berkeley: University of California Press, 1993). There is a stimulating treatment of the topic in Hent de Vries, *Philosophy and the Turn to Religion*.

65. Heidegger, *Gesamtausgabe* 61, pp. 66–67, cited in *The Young Heidegger*, p. 338.

66. Jacques Derrida, *Sauf le nom* (Paris: Galilée, 1993), p. 95, "*Sauf le nom*," in *On the Name*, p. 76.

## 15. Between the Quasi-transcendental and the Instituted

1. Jacques Derrida, *Sauf le nom (Post-Scriptum)* (Paris: Seuil, 1993), p. 96, trans. John P. Leavey Jr., in Jacques Derrida, *On the Name,* ed. Thomas Dutoit (Stanford, Calif.: Stanford University Press, 1993), p. 76.

2. Geoffrey Bennington and Jacques Derrida, *Jacques Derrida* (Paris: Seuil, 1991), pp. 146–47.

3. Derrida, *Sauf le nom,* pp. 113–14, *On the Name,* p. 85, translation modified. Only the first and third parentheses are in the original text.

4. Bennington and Derrida, *Jacques Derrida,* pp. 51–52.

5. See the third section of chapter 1.

6. Martin Heidegger, *Being and Time,* trans. John Macquarrie and Edward Robinson (Oxford: Blackwell, 1967), trans. Joan Stambaugh (Albany: State University of New York Press, 1996), pp. 238–39; Jacques Derrida, *Apories: Mourir—s'attendre aux "limites de la vérité"* (Paris: Galilée, 1996), pp. 55ff, 83ff, *Aporias: Dying—Awaiting (One Another) at the "Limits of Truth,"* trans. Thomas Dutoit (Stanford, Calif.: Stanford University Press, 1993), pp. 26ff., 43ff.

7. This is a cue to recommend Richard Holloway's *Looking in the Distance: The Human Search for Meaning* (Edinburgh: Canongate, 2004).

8. *Søren Kierkegaards Papirer,* ed. P. A. Heiberg, V. Kuhr, and E. Torsting, , 13 vols. (Copenhagen: Gyldendal, 1968–1970), *Søren Kierkegaard's Journals and Papers,* ed. and trans. Howard V. Hong and Edna H. Hong, assisted by Gregor Malantschuk, 7 vols. (Bloomington: Indiana University Press: 1967–1978) (henceforth *JP*), *JP* 6473, X 5 A 150.

9. Søren Kierkegaard, *Fear and Trembling,* trans. Howard V. Hong and Edna H. Hong (Princeton, N.J.: Princeton University Press, 1983), pp. 103–108.

10. Kathleen Richards, cited in David M. Carr, *The Erotic Word: Sexuality, Spirituality and the Bible* (Oxford: Oxford University Press, 2003), pp. 148–49.

11. Michael O'Sidhaul "Making Up," in *Love Life* (Tarset, Northumberland: Bloodaxe, 2005), p. 30.

12. I thank Basil O'Neill for alerting me to the relevance of this to Heidegger's "*Über 'die Linie,'*" in *Martin Heidegger zum 60 Gebürtstag* (Frankfurt am Main: Klostermann, 1959), "Concerning 'the Line,'" in Martin Heidegger, *The Question of Being,* trans. Jean T. Wilde and William Kluback (New Haven, Conn.: College and University Press, 1958).

13. See the fourth section of chapter 17.

14. David Wood, *The Step Back: Ethics and Politics after Deconstruction* (Albany: State University of New York Press, 2005), p. 108.

15. See chapter 13.

16. For references to places where Merleau-Ponty treats flesh and reversibility see Jacques Derrida, *Le toucher, Jean-Luc Nancy* (Paris: Galilée, 2000). See also Galen A. Johnson and Michael B. Smith, eds., *Ontology and Alterity in Merleau-Ponty* (Evanston, Ill.: Northwestern University Press, 1990), Part 1; Maurice Merleau-Ponty, *Le visible et l'invisible* (Paris: Gallimard, 1965), p. 194, *The Visible and the Invisible,* trans. Alphonso Lingis (Evanston, Ill.: Northwestern University, 1958), p. 147, cited by Claude Lefort, "Flesh and Otherness," in *Ontology and Alterity in Merleau-Ponty,* p. 7. See p. 44 of that book for the remark cited from David Levin.

17. Emmanuel Levinas, *Autrement qu'être ou au-delà de l'essence* (The Hague: Nijhoff, 1978), p. 15, *Otherwise than Being or Beyond Essence,* trans. Alphonso Lingis (The Hague: Nijhoff, 1981), pp. 12–13.

18. Mark C. Taylor and Dietrich Christian Lammerts, *Grave Matters* (London: Reaktion Books, 2002), p. 13.

19. Jacques Derrida, *Mémoires pour Paul de Man* (Paris: Galilée, 1988), p. 143, *Memoires for Paul de Man*, trans. Cecile Lindsay, Jonathan Culler, and Eduardo Cadava (New York: Columbia University Press, 1986), p. 149.

20. Ibid.

21. Nicolas Abraham, *L'écorce et le noyau* (Paris: Flammarion, 1975).

22. Morris Berman, *The Reenchantment of the World* (London: Bantam, 1984), p. 147. The Rilke scholar Anthony Phelan brought to my attention that the words "*Il y a un autre monde, mais il est dans celui-ci*" are attributed to Éluard. This attribution is confirmed by a website reached by typing in this French sentence plus the French poet's name. On p. 167 of *Grace and Necessity: Reflections on Art and Love* (London: Moorhouse, 2005) Rowan Williams attributes to Rilke the statement "There is another world but it is the same as this one." Elsewhere he gives reason to believe that this attribution is based on a misrecollection (an "oversight," *episkopē*) of the epigraphs of Patrick White's novel *The Solid Mandala*. P.S. The attribution to Éluard seems to be based on the following words from Paul Éluard, *Œuvres complètes* (Paris: Gallimard, 1968), vol. 1, p. 986, which are a citation of a citation: "Il y a assurément un autre monde, mais il est dans celui-ci et, pour atteindre à sa pleine perfection, il faut qu'il soit bien reconnu et qu'on en fasse profession. L'homme doit chercher son état à venir dans le présent, et le ciel, non point au-dessus de la terre, mais en soi. Ignaz-Vitalis Troxler, cité par Albert Béguin dans *L'Âme romantique et le Rêve.*"

23. Toward the end of the first section of chapter 7.

24. Paul Éluard, *œuvres complètes,* vol. 1, p. 766; André Breton, *œuvres complètes* (Paris: Gallimard, 1992), vol. 2, pp. 244, 832.

25. Herman Büttner, ed., *Meister Eckeharts Schriften und Predigten* (Jena: Eugen Diederichs, 1923), Bd. 1, p. 82, *Deutsche Mystiker des vierzehnten Jarhunderts,* ed. Franz Pfeiffer, Bd. 2, Abt. 1; *Meister Eckhart* (Leipzig: G. J. Göschen, 1857), p. 8.

26. In the second section of chapter 6.

27. Rainer Maria Rilke, in the "Worker Letter," in *Selected Letters of Rainer Maria Rilke 1902–1926,* trans. R. F. C. Hull (London: Macmillan, 1946), p. 339.

28. I am glad to have heard perceptive variations on this theme made by Norman Wirzba in a paper entitled "The Ecology of the Sabbath" read at New College, Edinburgh, in March 2006. Philo, *On the Special Laws,* 2.12.42, cited by Jean Pépin, "Cosmic Piety," in *Classical Mediterranean Spirituality: Egyptian, Greek, Roman,* ed. A. H. Armstrong (London: Routledge and Kegan Paul, 1986), p. 430.

29. Rudolf Otto, *The Idea of the Holy,* trans. John W. Harvey (Oxford: Oxford University Press, 1924), p. 136 (italics in the original).

30. Ibid., pp. 137–38.

31. See the seventh section of chapter 14.

32. See, for example, Georges Bataille, *Théorie de la religion* (Paris: Gallimard, 1973), *Theory of Religion,* trans. Robert Hurley (New York: Zone Books, 1989).

33. John Llewelyn, "Representation in Language," in *Art and Representation: Contributions to Contemporary Aesthetics,* ed. Ananta Ch. Sukla (London: Praeger, 2001), pp. 29–58. This overlaps with my "On Not Speaking the Same Language," parts I and II, *Australasian Journal of Philosophy* 40 (1962): pp. 37–48, 127–45.

34. Emmanuel Levinas, "*Notes sur le sens,*" in *De Dieu qui vient à l'idée* (Paris: Vrin, 1982), p. 249; "Notes on Meaning," in *Of God Who Comes to Mind,* trans. Bettina Bergo (Stanford, Calif.: Stanford University Press, 1998), p. 165.

35. Jacques Derrida, "*En ce moment même dans cet ouvrage me voici*," in *Psyché: Inventions de l'autre* (Paris: Galilée, 1987), pp. 159–202; "At this very Moment in this Work Here I Am," trans. Ruben Berezdevin, in *Re-reading Levinas*, ed. Robert Bernasconi and Simon Critchley (Bloomington: Indiana University Press, 1991), pp. 11–48.

36. Jacques Derrida, *Voyous: Deux essais sur la raison* (Paris: Galilée, 2003), p. 92, *Rogues: Two Essays on Reason*, trans. Pascale-Anne Brault and Michael Naas (Stanford, Calif.: Stanford University Press, 2005), p. 61. See also the final pages of Jacques Derrida, *Politiques de l'amitié* (Paris: Galilée, 1994), *Politics of Friendship*, trans. George Collins (London: Verso, 1997).

37. Stanley A. Cook, in the article on Religion in *Encyclopaedia of Religion and Ethics*, ed. James Hastings (Edinburgh: T. & T. Clark, 1908–1926).

38. Richard Dawkins, *The God Delusion* (London: Bantam, 2006).

39. Ibid., p. 19.

40. Ibid., pp. 37–38.

41. See, for example, D. Z. Phillips, *Faith after Foundationalism* (London: Routledge, 1988).

42. Kierkegaard, *JP*, IX A 118.

43. Søren Kierkegaard, *Concluding Unscientific Postscript to "Philosophical Fragments,"* trans. Howard V. Hong and Edna H. Hong, 2 vols. (Princeton, N.J.: Princeton University Press, 1992), vol. 1, p. 379.

44. Kierkegaard, *JP*, VIII 2 B 88.

45. Ibid., 281 VIII 2 B 84.

46. Ibid., 280 VIII 2 B 82.

47. Kierkegaard, *Concluding Unscientific Postscript*, p. 332.

48. R. G. Collingwood, *Religion and Philosophy* (London: Macmillan, 1916).

49. R. G. Collingwood, *Speculum Mentis, or, The Map of Knowledge* (Oxford: Clarendon Press, 1924), p. 114.

50. R. G. Collingwood, *Essay on Metaphysics* (Oxford: Clarendon Press, 1940).

51. Collingwood, *Speculum Mentis*, p. 119.

52. Ibid.

53. Martin Heidegger, *Phänomenologie und Theologie* (Frankfurt am Main: Klostermann, 1970), "Phenomenology and Theology," in *The Piety of Thinking: Essays by Martin Heidegger*, trans. James G. Hart and John Maraldo (Bloomington: Indiana University Press, 1976).

54. Jacques Derrida and Gianni Vattimo, *La religion* (Paris: Seuil, 1996), p. 85; Jacques Derrida, "Faith and Knowledge: The 'Two Sources' of Religion at the Limits of Reason Alone," trans. Samuel Weber, in *Acts of Religion*, ed. Gil Anidjar (New York: Routledge, 2002), p. 100.

55. Dietrich Bonhoeffer, *Letters and Papers from Prison* (London: Fontana, 1959), pp. 124–25. David F. Ford, *Self and Salvation: Being Transformed* (Cambridge: Cambridge University Press, 1999), pp. 259–60.

56. Jacques Derrida and Gianni Vattimo, *La religion*, p. 38; Jacques Derrida, "Faith and Knowledge," in *Acts of Religion*, p. 63.

57. "And also the word 'this' and a name often occupy the same position in a sentence. But it is precisely characteristic of a name that it is defined by means of the demonstrative expression 'That is N' (or 'That is called "N"'). But do we also give the definitions 'That is called "this"' or 'This is called "this"'? . . . And we can also say the word 'this' to the object, as it were *address* (*ansprechen*) the object as 'this'—a queer use of this word, which doubtless only occurs in doing philosophy." Ludwig Wittgenstein,

*Philosophical Investigations*, trans. G. E. M. Anscombe (Oxford: Blackwell, 1953), 38. See also Hegel on sense-certainty in the *Phenomenology of Spirit*.

58. Jacques Derrida, *La Carte Postale de Socrate à Freud et au-delà* (Paris: Flammarion, 1980), p. 148, *The Post Card from Socrates to Freud and Beyond*, trans. Alan Bass (Chicago: University of Chicago Press, 1987), p. 136.

59. Wittgenstein, *Philosophical Investigations*, 1, Saint Augustine, Confessions, Book 1, Section 8.

60. See D. Z. Phillips, *The Concept of Prayer* (Oxford: Blackwell, 1961).

61. Wittgenstein, *Philosophical Investigations*, 219.

62. See chapter 11.

63. Collingwood, *Speculum Mentis*, p. 119.

## 16. Eucharistics

1. Martin Heidegger, *Was Heisst Denken?* (Tübingen: Niemeyer, 1971), pp. 92ff., *What Is Called Thinking?* trans. Fred D. Wieck and J. Glenn Gray (New York: Harper and Row, 1968), pp. 140ff.

2. Ludwig Feuerbach, *Gesammelte Werke*, vol. 5: *Das Wesen des Christentums*, ed. Werner Schuffenhauer (Berlin: Akademie Verlag, 1973), pp. 453–54, *The Essence of Christianity*, trans. George Eliot (New York: Harper and Row, 1957), pp. 277–78.

3. Ibid., p. 444, p. 270.

4. Ludwig Feuerbach, "*Die Naturwissenschaft und die Revolution*" (Review of Jakob Moleschott, *Lehre der Nahrungsmittel. Für das Volk*), in *Gesammelte Werke*, vol. 10: *Kleiner Schriften III*, ed. Werner Schuffenhauer (Berlin: Akademie Verlag, 1971), p. 358.

5. Émile Benveniste, *Indo-European Language and Society*, trans. Elizabeth Palmer (London: Faber and Faber, 1973), p. 453.

6. Emmanuel Levinas, "*La réalité et son ombre*," *Les Temps Modernes* 38 (1948): 776, "Reality and its Shadow," trans. Alphonso Lingis, in Seán Hand, *The Levinas Reader* (Oxford: Blackwell, 1989), p. 134.

7. Emmanuel Levinas, *Autrement qu'être ou au-delà de l'essence* (The Hague: Nijhoff, 1978), p. 15, *Otherwise than Being or Beyond Essence*, trans. Alphonso Lingis (The Hague: Nijhoff, 1981), pp. 12–13.

8. Emmanuel Levinas, *De l'existence à l'existant* (Paris: Vrin, 1981), p. 99, *Existence and Existents*, trans. Alphonso Lingis (The Hague: Nijhoff, 1978), p. 61.

9. Emmanuel Levinas, "*Dieu et la philosophie*," in *De Dieu qui vient à l'idée* (Paris: Vrin, 1982), p. 115, "God and Philosophy," in *Of God Who Comes to Mind*, trans. Bettina Bergo (Stanford, Calif.: Stanford University Press, 1998), p. 69, in Seán Hand, *The Levinas Reader* (Oxford: Blackwell, 1989), p. 179.

10. Emmanuel Levinas, *Du sacré au saint: cinq nouvelles lectures talmudiques* (Paris: Minuit, 1977), pp. 98–100, *Nine Talmudic Readings*, trans. Annette Aronowicz (Bloomington: Indiana University Press, 1990), pp. 146–47.

11. Emmanuel Levinas, "'À l'image de Dieu' d'après Rabbi Haïm de Voloziner," in *L'au-delà du verset: lectures et discours talmudiques* (Paris: Minuit, 1982), pp. 182–200, "'In the image of God,' according to Rabbi Hayyim of Volozhiner," in *Beyond the Verse: Talmudic Readings and Lectures*, trans. Gary D. Mole (London: Athlone, 1994), pp. 151–67. See also Levinas's preface to Rabbi Hayyim de Volozhyn, *L'âme de la vie: Nefesh Hahayyim* (Paris: Verdier, 1986).

12. W. Warde Fowler, "The Original Meaning of the Word *Sacer*," in *Roman Essays and Interpretations* (Oxford: Clarendon Press, 1920).

13. Emmanuel Levinas, "The Proximity of the Other," trans. Bettina Bergo, in *Is It Righteous to Be? Interviews with Emmanuel Levinas,* ed. Jill Robbins (Stanford, Calif.: Stanford University Press, 2001), p. 216.

14. Emmanuel Levinas, "Who Shall Not Prophesy?" in *Is It Righteous To Be? Interviews with Emmanuel Levinas,* p. 221.

15. Marcel Proust, *Remembrance of Things Past,* trans. C. K. Scott Moncrieff and Frederick Blossom (London: Chatto and Windus, 1922–1930), vol. 1 *Swann's Way,* p. 451.

16. Emmanuel Levinas, *Autrement qu'être ou au-delà de l'essence,* p. 52, *Otherwise than Being or Beyond Essence,* p. 40.

17. Levinas, *"Judaïsme et révolution,"* in *Du sacré au saint,* p. 19, "Judaism and Revolution," in *Nine Talmudic Readings,* p. 99.

18. Levinas, *"Modèle de l'occident,"* in *L'au-delà du verset,* pp. 48–49, "Model of the West," in *Beyond the Verse,* p. 32.

19. Emmanuel Levinas, *"Philosophie, Justice et Amour,"* in *Entre nous: Essais sur la pensée-à-l'autre* (Paris: Grasset, 1991), p. 127, "Philosophy, Justice and Love," in *Entre nous: On Thinking-of-the-Other,* trans. Michael B. Smith and Barbara Harshav (London: Athlone, 1998), p. 109.

20. Emmanuel Levinas,*"Nom d'un chien ou le droit naturel,"* in *Difficile liberté: Essais sur le judaïsme* (Paris: Albin Michel, 1976), pp. 199–202, "The Name of a Dog, or Natural Rights," in *Difficult Freedom: Essays on Judaism,* trans. Seán Hand (Baltimore: Johns Hopkins University Press, 1990), pp. 151–153. This essay is discussed in John Llewelyn, "Am I Obsessed by Bobby? (Humanism of the Other Animal)," in *Re-Reading Levinas,* Robert Bernasconi and Simon Critchley (Bloomington: Indiana University Press, 1991), pp. 234–45; *The Middle Voice of Ecological Conscience: A Chiasmic Reading of Responsibility in the Neighbourhood of Levinas, Heidegger and Others* (London: Macmillan, 1991), chapter 3.

21. Raimond Gaita, *The Philosopher's Dog* (New York and London: Routledge, 2002), For persuading me not to postpone any longer my reading of this profoundly humane book I am grateful to David Wood.

22. John Llewelyn, *Beyond Metaphysics?: The Hermeneutic Circle in Contemporary Continental Philosophy* (London: Macmillan; Atlantic Highlands: Humanities Press, 1985).

23. Emmanuel Levinas, *"Mourir pour . . . ,"* in *Entre nous,* p. 230, "Dying for . . . ," in *Entre nous,* p. 217.

24. *Søren Kierkegaards Papirer,* ed. P. A. Heiberg, V. Kuhr, and E. Torsting, 13 vols. (Copenhagen: Gyldendal,1968–1970), *Søren Kierkegaard's Journals and Papers,* ed. and trans. Howard V. Hong and Edna H. Hong, assisted by Gregor Malantschuk, 7 vols. (Bloomington: Indiana University Press: 1967–1978) (henceforth *JP*), *JP* 1507, III A 143. See also *JP* 1516, X 4 A269, 1518, XI 1 A 176.

25. Ibid., 1519, XI 2 A 224.

26. Heidegger, *Was Heisst Denken?* p. 158, *What Is Called Thinking?* p. 146.

27. Emmanuel Levinas, *Autrement qu'être ou au-delà de l'essence* (The Hague: Nijhoff, 1978), p. 12, *Otherwise than Being or Beyond Essence,* trans. Alphonso Lingis (The Hague: Nijhoff, 1981), p. 10.

28. Jacques Derrida, *La vérité en peinture* (Paris: Flammarion, 1978), p. 151, *The Truth in Painting,* trans. Geoff Bennington and Ian McLeod (Chicago: University of Chicago Press, 1987), p. 132.

### 17. The World Is More Than It Is

1. James Creed Meredith, ed., *Kant's Critique of Aesthetic Judgement* (Oxford: Clarendon Press, 1911), §28, p. 110.

2. Ibid., p. 111.

3. G. W. F. Hegel, *Aesthetics: Lectures on Fine Art*, trans. T. M. Knox, 2 vols. (Oxford: Clarendon Press, 1975), vol. 1, p. 362.

4. Ibid., p. 371.

5. Ibid.

6. Ibid., pp. 362–63.

7. Also by the hole that may be imagined passing from the front to the back of the cover of the paperback edition of John Llewelyn, *Seeing Through God: A Geophenomenology* (Bloomington: Indiana University Press, 2004).

8. Meredith, *Kant's Critique of Aesthetic Judgement*, §2, p. 43.

9. Friedrich Nietzsche, *The Birth of Tragedy out of the Spirit of Music*, trans. Shaun Whiteside (London: Penguin Books, 1993), §4, p. 7.

10. On this question see especially Robert Bernasconi, *The Question of Language in Heidegger's History of Being* (New Jersey: Humanities Press, 1985), in particular chapter 4.

11. Meredith, *Kant's Critique of Aesthetic Judgement*, §27, p. 107.

12. Friedrich Nietzsche, *The Will to Power*, trans. Walter Kaufmann and R. J. Hollingdale (London: Weidenfeld and Nicolson, 1967), §1065, already cited above at the end of chapter 7.

13. Nietzsche, *The Birth of Tragedy out of the Spirit of Music*, §21, p. 103.

14. Meredith, *Kant's Critique of Aesthetic Judgement*, §29, p. 113.

15. Jacques Derrida, *"La différance,"* in *Marges de la philosophie* (Paris: Minuit, 1972), p. 18, *"Différance,"* in *Margins of Philosophy*, trans. Alan Bass (Chicago: University of Chicago Press, 1982) p. 17.

16. Jacques Derrida, *Force de loi: Le "Fondement mystique de l'autorité"* (Paris: Galilée, 1994), "Force of Law: The 'Mystical Foundations of Authority,'" trans. Mary Quaintance, in *Deconstruction and the Possibility of Justice, Cardozo Law Review* 11, nos. 5–6 (July–Aug. 1990): 919–1045, and in *Acts of Religion*, ed. Gil Anidjar (New York: Routledge, 2002), pp. 228–98. On law, laws, and the law investigated against a background shared by the work of Kierkegaard and Derrida, see Theodore W. Jennings Jr., *Reading Derrida/Thinking Paul* (Stanford, Calif.: Stanford University Press, 2006). I am grateful to Elsebet Jegstrup for the gift of a copy of this ingenious book.

17. *"En soulignant l'importance des questions posées par Derrida, nous avons voulu dire le plaisir d'un contact au cœur d'un chiasme."* Emmanuel Levinas, *Noms propres* (Montpellier: Fata Morgana, 1976), p. 89.

18. Martin Heidegger, *Sein und Zeit* (*Being and Time*), trans. John Macquarrie and Edward Robinson (Oxford: Blackwell, 1967), trans. Joan Stambaugh (Albany: State University of New York Press, 1996), p. 134.

19. Martin Heidegger, *Der Satz vom Grund* (Pfullingen, Germany: Neske, 1957); *Der Satz vom Grund* (Frankfurt am Main: Klostermann, 1997), *Gesamtausgabe* 10, *The Principle of Reason*, trans. Reginald Lilly (Bloomington: Indiana University Press, 1992); *Beiträge zur Philosophie (Vom Ereignis)* (Frankfurt am Main: Klostermann, 1989), *Gesamtausgabe* 65, pp. 227ff., *Contributions to Philosophy (From Enowning)*, trans. Parvis Emad and Kenneth Maly (Bloomington: Indiana University Press, 1999), pp. 161ff.

20. Jacques Derrida, *"Comment ne pas parler: Dénégations,"* in *Psyche: Inventions de l'autre* (Paris: Galilée, 1987). pp. 535–95.

21. Ibid., p. 595.

22. See chapter 13, note 22, under the sub-heading *"Plat de résistance."*

23. Meredith, *Kant's Critique of Aesthetic Judgement,* §29, p. 127.

24. Jacques Derrida, *La vérité en peinture* (Paris: Flammarion, 1978), p. 157, *The Truth in Painting,* trans. Geoff Bennington and Ian McLeod (Chicago: University of Chicago Press, 1987), p. 137.

25. Cited at Jacques Derrida, *Sauf le nom (Post-Scriptum)* (Paris: Seuil, 1993), p. 75, *"Sauf le nom,"* trans. John P. Leavey Jr., in Jacques Derrida, *On the Name,* ed. Thomas Dutoit (Stanford, Calif.: Stanford University Press, 1993), p. 65.

26. Heidegger, *Being and Time,* p. 275.

27. Martin Buber, *Two Types of Faith,* trans. N. P. Goldhawk (London: Routledge and Kegan Paul, 1951), p. 12.

28. Attributed to Jabès by Elisabeth de Fontanay in her introduction to the symposium *"Le scandale du mal. Catastrophes naturelles et crimes de l'homme,"* *Les Nouveaux Cahiers* 22 (1986): 5.

29. Jean-Luc Nancy, *Au ciel et sur la terre* (Paris: Bayard, 2004).

30. Heidegger, *Beiträge,* p. 508, *Contributions,* p. 357.

31. Martin Heidegger, *"Das Ding,"* in *Vorträge und Aufsätze* (Pfullingen, Germany: Neske, 1967), II, p. 57, *"The Thing,"* in *Poetry, Language, Thought,* trans. Albert Hofstadter (New York: Harper, 1971), p. 184.

32. For a succinct characterization of the convergence and divergence between Heidegger and Derrida see Robert Bernasconi, "Heidegger," in chapter 12 of *Understanding Derrida,* ed. Jack Reynolds and Jonathan Roffe (London: Continuum, 2004), pp. 121–27.

33. See chapter 13.

34. Emmanuel Levinas, *Totalité et Infini: essai sur l'extériorité* (The Hague: Nijhoff, 1980), p. xiv, *Totality and Infinity: An Essay on Exteriority,* trans. Alphonso Lingis (The Hague: Nijhoff, 1969), p. 26.

35. Jacques Derrida, *La Carte Postale de Socrate à Freud et au-delà* (Paris: Flammarion, 1980), pp. 206–207, 74, *The Post Card from Socrates to Freud and Beyond,* trans. Alan Bass (Chicago: University of Chicago Press, 1987), pp. 192, 66–67.

36. See the second section of chapter 13.

37. Ludwig Wittgenstein, *Philosophical Investigations,* trans. G. E. M. Anscombe (Oxford: Blackwell, 1953), 564.

38. Emmanuel Levinas, *"Amitié judéo-chrétienne,"* in *À l'heure des nations* (Paris: Minuit, 1988), p. 185; *Éthique et Infini: Dialogues avec Philippe Nemo* (Paris: Fayard, 1982), p. 51, *Ethics and Infinity: Conversations with Philippe Nemo,* trans. Richard A. Cohen (Pittsburgh: Duquesne University Press, 1985), p. 52.

39. Rowan Williams, *On Christian Theology* (Oxford: Blackwell, 2000), p. 124.

40. See J. Zizioulas, *Being as Communion: Studies in Personhood and the Church* (New York: Crestwood, 1985).

41. See the first section of chapter 12.

42. See the first section of chapter 11.

43. See chapter 15.

44. Levinas, *Totalité et Infini,* p. 242, *Totality and Infinity,* p. 264.

45. Ibid., pp. 243–44, p. 266.

46. Ibid., p. 247, p. 269.

47. Immanuel Kant, *"Beobachten über das Gefühl des Schönen und Erhaben,"* in *Kant's Werke,* II, *Vorkritische Schriften* II (Berlin: Georg Reimer, 1905), p. 211, *Observations on the Feeling of the Beautiful and the Sublime,* trans. John T. Goldthwait (Berkeley: University of California Press, 1965), p. 52.

48. Meister Eckhart, "About Disinterest," in *Meister Eckhart: A Modern Translation,* Raymond B. Blackney (New York: Harper, 1941), pp. 82–91.

49. Emmanuel Levinas, *"La signification et le sens,"* in *L'humanisme de l'autre homme* (Montpellier: Fata Morgana, 1972), p. 52, "Signification and Sense," in *Humanism of the Other,* trans. Nidra Poller (Urbana: University of Illinois Press, 2003), p. 35, "Meaning and Sense," in *Collected Philosophical Papers,* trans. Alphonso Lingis (Dordrecht: Nijhoff, 1987), p. 99.

50. Wittgenstein, *Philosophical Investigations,* 24.

51. Levinas, *Totalité et Infini,* p. 188, *Totality and Infinity,* p. 213.

52. See John Llewelyn, "Ecosophy, Sophophily and Philotheria," in *Consciousness, Reality and Value: Essays in Honour of T. L. S. Sprigge,* ed. Leemon McHenry and Pierrefrancesco Basile (Frankfurt: Ontos Verlag, 2007).

53. See under *"Benommenheit"* in the index of David Farrell Krell, *Daimon Life: Heidegger and Life-Philosophy* (Bloomington: Indiana University Press, 1992), a remarkable book by a remarkable writer to whom I hope this note will convey my thanks.

54. See the first section of chapter 11.

55. Jacques Derrida, *De l'esprit: Heidegger et la question* (Paris: Galilée, 1987), p. 142, *Of Spirit: Heidegger and the Question,* trans. Geoffrey Bennington and Rachel Bowlby (Chicago: University of Chicago Press, 1989), p. 90.

56. Jacques Derrida and Maurizio Ferraris, *A Taste for the Secret,* trans. Giacomo Donis (Cambridge: Polity, 2001), p. 84.

57. Emmanuel Levinas, *Totalité et Infini,* p. 244, *Totality and Infinity,* p. 266.

58. Jacques Derrida, *Voyous: Deux essais sur la raison* (Paris: Galilée, 2003), p. 186, *Rogues: Two Essays on Reason,* trans. Pascale-Anne Brault and Michael Naas (Stanford, Calif.: Stanford University Press, 2005), p. 133. Immanuel Kant, *Fundamental Principles of the Metaphysic of Morals,* in *Critique of Practical Reason and Other Works on the Theory of Ethics,* trans. Thomas Kingsmill Abbott (London: Longmans, 1959), p. 53.

59. See the fourth section of chapter 15.

60. Meredith, *Kant's Critique of Aesthetic Judgement,* §28, p. 114.

61. Derrida, *Voyous,* p. 217, *Rogues,* p. 151.

62. Karl R. Popper, *The Logic of Scientific Discovery* (London: Hutchinson, 1972); *The Open Society and Its Enemies,* vol. 1 (London: Routledge and Kegan Paul, 1945), vol. 2 (London: Routledge and Kegan Paul, 1957). P. B. Medawar, *The Art of the Soluble* (London: Methuen, 1967).

63. John Llewelyn, *Seeing Through God,* chapter 3. John Llewelyn, *The HypoCritical Imagination: Between Kant and Levinas* (London: Routledge, 2000), pp. 230–32.

64. Derrida, *Voyous,* p. 211, *Rogues,* p. 153.

65. Emmanuel Levinas, *"Le dialogue,"* in *De Dieu qui vient à l'idée* (Paris: Vrin, 1982), p. 230, "Dialogue," in *Of God Who Comes to Mind,* trans. Bettina Bergo (Stanford, Calif.: Stanford University Press, 1998), p. 151.

66. Derrida, *Voyous,* p. 199, *Rogues,* p. 145.

67. Ibid., p. 113, p. 77.

68. Jacques Derrida, *Spectres de Marx: L'État de la dette, le travail du deuil et la nouvelle Internationale* (Paris: Galilée, 1993), p. 268, *Specters of Marx: The State of the Debt, the Work of Mourning, and the New International,* trans. Peggy Kamuf (New York: Routledge, 1994), p. 169; Jacques Derrida, *Politiques de l'amitié* (Paris: Galilée, 1994). p. 83, *Politics of Friendship,* trans. George Collins (London: Verso, 1997), p. 64.

69. Derrida, *Voyous,* p. 81, *Rogues,* p. 53.

70. Cited at Cynwil Williams, *Yr Archesgob Rowan Williams* (Caernarvon, Wales: Gwasg Pantycelyn, 2006), p. 91.

71. Emmanuel Levinas, *Du sacré au saint: cinq nouvelles lectures talmudiques* (Paris: Minuit, 1977), p. 106, *Nine Talmudic Readings,* trans. Annette Aronowicz (Bloomington: Indiana University Press, 1990), p. 151.

72. This claim regarding the sheerly existent and the question of the prejudices referred to here are treated in the final pages of my *Seeing Through God* and in the epilogue of my *The HypoCritical Imagination.* (I return to it briefly in the epilogue of the present book.)

73. Friedrich Nietzsche, *The Will to Power,* trans. Walter Kaufmann and R. J. Hollingdale (London: Weidenfeld and Nicolson, 1967), §1066.

74. William James, *The Varieties of Religious Experience* (London: Collins, 1960), p. 142.

75. See the first paragraph of chapter 15.

76. Jacques Derrida, *Le toucher: Jean-Luc Nancy* (Paris: Galilée, 2000), p. 94.

## Epilogue

1. See the fourth section of chapter 17.

2. See the second section of chapter 15.

3. To get an idea of the varieties of things that have been given the name "God" by philosophers one could hardly do better than start with T. L. S. Sprigge's monumental *The God of Metaphysics* (Oxford: Clarendon Press, 2006).

4. For this anecdote I thank Walford Gealy.

5. Irshad Manji, *The Trouble with Islam Today* (London: Mainstream, 2004), p. 226.

6. Mike Higton, *Difficult Gospel: The Theology of Rowan Williams* (London: SCM Press, 2004), p. 121. For a clear-headed and sensitive treatment of humility in the context of pluralism see Margaret Paton, "Coming to Grips with Pluralism," *The Religious Education Journal for Australia* 21, no. 2 (2005): 33–38.

7. Jacques Derrida, *Voyous: Deux essais sur la raison* (Paris: Galilée, 2003), p. 55, *Rogues: Two Essays on Reason,* trans. Pascale-Anne Brault and Michael Naas (Stanford, Calif.: Stanford University Press, 2005), p. 31.

8. Catherine Chalier, "Lévinas maître," in *Emmanuel Lévinas: philosophie et pédagogie* (Paris: Éditions du Nadir, Alliance Israélite Universelle, n.d.), p. 69.

9. For pointing this out to me I am grateful to Barrie Wynn.

10. Martin Heidegger, *Seminare, Gesamtausgabe* 15 (Frankfurt am Main: Klostermann, 1986), "Zeit und Sein," in *Zur Sache des Denkens* (Tübingen: Niemeyer, 1969), *On Time and Being,* trans. Joan Stambaugh (New York: Harper, 1972).

11. Simone Weil, *Gravity and Grace,* trans. Emma Crawford and Mario von der Ruhr (London: Routledge, 2002), p. 15.

12. Emmanuel Levinas, "*Simone Weil contre la Bible,*" in *Difficile liberté: essais sur le judaïsme* (Paris: Albin Michel, 1976), "Simone Weil against the Bible," in *Dif-*

*ficult Freedom: Essays on Judaism,* trans. Seán Hand (Baltimore, Md.: Johns Hopkins University Press, 1990). "I often say, although it's a dangerous thing to say publicly, that humanity consists of the Bible and the Greeks. All the rest can be translated; all the rest—all the exotic—is dance." Raoul Mortley, *French Philosophers in Conversation* (London: Routledge, 1991), p. 18.

13. Jacques Derrida, *Force de loi: Le "Fondement mystique de l'autorité"* (Paris: Galilée, 1994), p. 105, "Force of Law: The 'Mystical Foundations of Authority,'" trans. Mary Quaintance, in *Deconstruction and the Possibility of Justice, Cardozo Law Review* 11, nos. 5–6 (July–Aug. 1990): 1009, and in *Acts of Religion,* ed. Gil Anidjar (New York: Routledge, 2002), p. 278.

14. Jacques Derrida, *La voix et le phénomène* (Paris: Presses Universitaires de France, 1967), pp. 60–61, *Speech and Phenomena and Other Essays on Husserl's Theory of Signs,* trans. David B. Allison (Evanston, Ill.: Northwestern University Press, 1973), pp. 54–55.

15. Albert Camus, *Resistance, Rebellion and Death,* trans. Justin O'Brien (London: Hamish Hamilton, 1961), p. 21.

16. Kierkegaard, *Purity of Heart Is to Will One Thing,* trans. Douglas Steere (New York: Harper, 1938), p. 66.

17. I thank Basil O'Neill for expressing my point thus.

18. Dewi Z. Phillips, "Angau a Thragwyddoldeb," in *Athronyddu am Grefydd: Cyfeiriadau Newydd* (Llandyssul, Wales: Gwasg Gomer, 1974), p. 148.

19. Weil, *Gravity and Grace,* p. 15.

20. Jacques Derrida, *Mémoires pour Paul de Man* (Paris: Galilée, 1988), p. 51, *Memoires for Paul de Man,* trans. Cecile Lindsay, Jonathan Culler, and Eduardo Cadava (New York: Columbia University Press, 1986), p. 31.

21. David Farrell Krell, *The Purest of Bastards: Works of Mourning, Art, and Affirmation in the Thought of Jacques Derrida* (University Park: Pennsylvania State University Press, 2000), p. 18.

22. For a helpful discussion of Heidegger's use of the phrase *"Fehl des Gottes,"* see Robert Bernasconi, *The Question of Language in Heidegger's History of Being* (New Jersey: Humanities Press and Macmillan, 1984), especially pp. 41ff.

23. Jean-Luc Marion, *Étant donné: Essai d'une phénoménologie de la donation* (Paris: Presses Universitaires de France, 1997), *Being Given: Toward a Phenomenology of Givenness,* trans. Jeffrey L. Kosky (Stanford, Calif.: Stanford University Press, 2002).

24. Ibid., p. 302, p. 216.

25. Jean-Luc Marion, *De surcroît: Études sur les phénomènes saturés* (Paris: Presses Universitaires de France, 2001), *In Excess: Studies in Saturated Phenomena,* trans. Robyn Horner and Vincent Berraud (New York: Fordham University Press, 2002). For an earlier version of the last essay in this collection see Jean-Luc Marion, "In the Name: How to Avoid Speaking of 'Negative Theology,'" in *God, The Gift, and Postmodernism,* John D. Caputo and Michael J. Scanlon (Bloomington: Indiana University Press, 1999), pp. 20–53.

26. Elizabeth S. Haldane and G. R. T. Ross, eds., *The Philosophical Works of Descartes,* 2 vols. (Cambridge: Cambridge University Press, 1931), vol. 1, p. 358. See John Llewelyn, *Seeing Through God:* chapter 4. Article 53 of *The Passions of the Soul* is cited on p. 66, where, but for a computer's over-zealous spell-checking mechanism, I would have said that the word "wonder" translates Descartes Latin word *admiratio.*

27. I have argued this in *Seeing Through God*, chapter 3.

28. Marion, *In Excess*, pp. 155–56.

29. Søren Kierkegaard, *Works of Love*, trans. Howard V. Hong and Edna H. Hong (Princeton, N.J.: Princeton University Press, 1995), p. 89.

30. See John Llewelyn, *The Middle Voice of Ecological Conscience: A Chiasmic Reading of Responsibility in the Neighbourhood of Levinas, Heidegger and Others* (London: Macmillan, 1991), preface; *The HypoCritical Imagination: Between Kant and Levinas* (London: Routledge, 2000), pp. 222–25; *Seeing Through God: A Geophenomenology* (Bloomington: Indiana University Press, 2004), pp. 161ff.

31. Jacques Derrida and Gianni Vattimo, *La religion* (Paris: Seuil, 1996), p. 73; Jacques Derrida, "Faith and Knowledge: The 'Two Sources' of Religion at the Limits of Reason Alone," trans. Samuel Weber, in *Acts of Religion*, p. 91.

32. Jacques Derrida, *Force de loi*, p. 109, "Force of Law," in *Deconstruction and the Possibility of Justice*, p. 1011, and in *Acts of Religion*, p. 280.

33. Ibid., p. 125, p. 1029, pp. 288–89.

34. *Walden*, "The Ponds," in *The Portable Thoreau*, ed. Carl Bode (New York: Penguin, 1977), p. 448. My attention was drawn to Thoreau's remark by Steven Winspur, *La poésie du lieu: Segalen, Thoreau, Guillevic, Ponge* (Amsterdam: Rodopi, 2006), p. 167. Winspur and the authors of which his sensitive book treats respond chiefly to the address of things in the natural world.

35. In the third section of chapter 15.

36. Jacques Derrida and Maurizio Ferraris, *A Taste for the Secret*, trans. Giacomo Donis (Cambridge: Polity, 2001), p. 20.

37. In the fourth section of chapter 15.

38. Jacques Derrida, *Passions* (Paris: Galilée, 1993), p. 70, "Passions," trans. David Wood, in *Jacques Derrida: A Critical Reader*, ed. David Wood (Oxford: Blackwell, 1992), p. 24, trans. David Wood, in *On the Name* (Stanford, Calif.: Stanford University Press, 1995), p. 31.

39. Kai Nielsen, "Death and the Meaning of Life," in *The Meaning of Life*, ed. E. D. Klemke (Oxford: Oxford University Press, 2000), p. 154.

40. Jacques Derrida, "*Différence*," in *Marges de la philosophie* (Paris: Minuit, 1972), p. 20, *Margins of Philosophy*, trans. Alan Bass (Chicago: University of Chicago Press, 1982), p. 18. I thank Basil O'Neill for persuading me to emphasize here that Nietzsche's antipathy regarding antithetical oppositions extends to the difference between the Apollonian and the Dionysian.

41. David Tracy, "Fragments: The Spiritual Situation of Our Times," and Response by Jacques Derrida, in *God, the Gift, and Postmodernism*, ed. John Caputo and Michael J. Scanlon (Bloomington: Indiana University Press, 1999), pp. 170–184.

42. On Charles Bigger on the alleged barrenness of Derridian deconstruction, see chapter 14. See also Robyn Horner, *Rethinking God as Gift: Marion, Derrida, and the Limits of Phenomenology* (New York: Fordham University Press, 2001), p. 159, where it is suggested that Marion is to Derrida as excess is to aridity.

43. See Søren Kierkegaard, *Repetition: An Essay in Experimental Psychology*, trans. Walter Lowrie (New York: Harper and Row, 1941), pp. 133–34.

44. Jacques Derrida, *Limited Inc*, trans. Samuel Weber and Jeffrey Mehlman (Evanston, Ill.: Northwestern University Press, 1988).

45. Jacques Derrida, *Politiques de l'amitié* (Paris: Galilée, 1994). p. 151–52, *Politics of Friendship*, trans. George Collins (London: Verso, 1997), pp. 127–28.

46. Carl Schmitt, *Political Theology: Four Chapters on the Concept of Sovereignty,* trans. George Schwab (Cambridge, Mass.: MIT Press, 1985), p. 5.

47. Giorgio Agamben, *Le temps qui reste: un commentaire de l'Épître aux Romains,* trans. from Italian by Judith Revel (Paris: Éditions Payot and Rivages, 2000), pp. 165ff. See also Giorgio Agamben, *State of Exception,* trans. Kevin Attell (Chicago: University of Chicago Press, 2005), and *Homo Sacer: Sovereign Power and Bare Life,* trans. Daniel Heller-Roazen (Stanford, Calif.: Stanford University Press, 1998).

48. See the third section of chapter 13.

49. Douglas Templeton writes to me in e-mails that "John Cochrane O'Neill . . . behaved in such an abbreviatory or ab Brief-iatory fashion with the Epistle to the Romans (much of the text was attributed to a series of unknown authors) that it was re-named by a wit as 'Paul's Postcard to the Romans,'" and that "a New Testament friend in Oxford tells me that an oral tradition attributes the 'Paul's Postcard to the Romans' to (Sir) Henry Chadwick (formerly Regius Professor of Divinity in the University of Oxford and author of *The Early Church* (in The Pelican History of the Church). "

50. Alain Badiou, *Saint Paul: The Foundations of Universalism,* trans. Ray Brassier (Stanford, Calif.: Stanford University Press, 2003), p. 73.

51. Jacques Derrida, *L'université sans condition* (Paris: Galilée, 2001), p. 15, note, "The University without Condition," in *Without Alibi,* trans. Peggy Kamuf (Stanford, Calif.: Stanford University Press, 2002), p. 301, note.

52. Derrida, *Voyous,* p. 209–10, *Rogues,* p. 152.

53. Derrida and Gianni Vattimo, *La religion,* p. 76; Derrida, "Faith and Knowledge," in *Acts of Religion,* p. 93.

54. Ibid., p. 40, p. 65.

55. Ibid., pp. 39–40, p. 67.

56. Ibid., p. 40, p. 65.

57. Ibid., p. 65, p. 85.

58. Ibid.

59. Derrida, *Voyous,* p. 208, *Rogues,* pp. 150–51.

60. Martin Buber, *Pointing the Way: Collected Essays,* trans. Maurice Friedman (London: Routledge and Kegan Paul, 1957), p. 233.

61. Derrida, *L'université sans condition,* p. 74, "The University without Condition," in *Without Alibi,* p. 234.

62. Immanuel Kant, *Critique of Pure Reason,* trans. Norman Kemp Smith (London: Macmillan, 1968), B626.

63. J. L. Austin, "Ifs and Cans," in *Philosophical Papers* (Oxford: Clarendon Press, 1961).

64. See chapter 15.

65. Derrida, *Force de loi,* p. 36, "Force of Law," p. 945; *Acts of Religion,* p. 243.

66. Adriaan T. Peperzak, "The Significance of Levinas's Work for Christian Thought," in *The Face of the Other and the Trace of God: Essays on the Philosophy of Emmanuel Levinas,* ed. Jeffrey Bloechl (New York: Fordham University Press, 2000), pp. 184–199. See also Adriaan T. Peperzak, *To the Other: An Introduction to the Philosophy of Emmanuel Levinas* (West Lafayette: Purdue University Press, 1993) and *Beyond: The Philosophy of Emmanuel Levinas* (Evanston, Ill.: Northwestern University Press, 1997).

67. This arriving without arrival is memorably and memorially evoked by David Farrell Krell in *The Purest of Bastards.*

# INDEX

**John Llewelyn** has been Reader in Philosophy at the University of Edinburgh, Visiting Professor of Philosophy at the University of Memphis, and Arthur J. Schmitt Distinguished Visiting Professor of Philosophy at Loyola University of Chicago. He is the author of several books, including *Appositions of Jacques Derrida and Emmanuel Levinas* (Indiana University Press, 2002) and *Seeing Through God* (Indiana University Press, 2004).